# NEW OXFORD HISTORY OF MUSIC
## VOLUME VI

# THE VOLUMES OF THE
# NEW OXFORD HISTORY OF MUSIC

I. Ancient and Oriental Music

II. Early Medieval Music up to 1300

III. Ars Nova and the Renaissance (1300–1540)

IV. The Age of Humanism (1540–1630)

V. Opera and Church Music (1630–1750)

VI. Concert Music (1630–1750)

VII. The Age of Enlightenment (1745–1790)

VIII. The Age of Beethoven (1790–1830)

IX. Romanticism (1830–1890)

X. The Modern Age (1890–1960)

# CONCERT MUSIC
## (1630–1750)

EDITED BY

GERALD ABRAHAM

OXFORD   NEW YORK
OXFORD UNIVERSITY PRESS
1986

Oxford University Press, Walton Street, Oxford OX2 6DP

Oxford New York Toronto
Delhi Bombay Calcutta Madras Karachi
Kuala Lumpur Singapore Hong Kong Tokyo
Nairobi Dar es Salaam Cape Town
Melbourne Auckland

and associated companies in
Beirut Berlin Ibadan Nicosia

Oxford is a trade mark of Oxford University Press

Published in the United States
by Oxford University Press, New York

British Library Cataloguing in Publication Data
The New Oxford history of music.
Vol. 6 : Concert music 1630–1750
1. Music—History and criticism
I. Abraham, Gerald
780'.9     ML160
ISBN 0–19–316306–3

Library of Congress Cataloging in Publication Data
Main entry under title:
Concert music, 1630–1750
(New Oxford history of music ; v. 6)
Bibliography: p. 695
Includes index.
1. Music—17th century—History and criticism.
2. Music—18th century—History and criticism.
I. Abraham, Gerald, 1904–    . II. Series.
ML160.N44 vol. 6   780'.9 s   85–2950
ISBN 0-19-316306-3  [780'.903'2]

Set by Hope Services
Printed in Great Britain by
Richard Clay (The Chaucer Press) Ltd.
Bungay, Suffolk

# CONTENTS

ILLUSTRATIONS                                                      xii

INTRODUCTION TO VOLUMES V AND VI                                  xiii

EDITOR'S NOTE                                                      xxi

I. ODE AND ORATORIO IN ENGLAND.
    (a) DIALOGUE AND ODE. *By* ROSAMOND MCGUINNESS,
    *Senior Lecturer in Music, Royal Holloway College, University*
    *of London*                                                   1
    The Problem of Nomenclature                                    1
    The Biblical Dialogues                                         2
    Court Odes                                                     7
    Texts of the Odes                                              8
    Literary Origins                                               9
    Charles II as Catalyst                                        10
    The Earlier Restoration Odes                                  11
    The Heyday of Blow and Purcell                                15
    Handel's Birthday Ode                                         21

    (b) ORATORIO AND RELATED FORMS. *By* ANTHONY
    HICKS *and* GERALD ABRAHAM                                     23
    The First English Oratorio                                     25
    Text and Music of *Esther*                                     26
    The Chapel Royal Connection                                   30
    Gates's Performances                                           31
    Oratorio, Ode, and Serenata: 1732–41                          34
    Oratorio at Covent Garden                                     34
    Handel's *Deborah*                                            37
    *Athalia*                                                     40
    *Il Parnasso in Festa*                                        42
    Variety of Forms: 1736–40                                     45
    *Alexander's Feast*                                           47
    *Il Trionfo* Reworked                                         50
    *Saul*                                                        51
    *Israel in Egypt*                                             54
    The Cecilia Ode and *L'Allegro*                               56
    An Alternative Tradition                                      64
    Greene's *Deborah*                                            65
    Boyce's *David's Lamentation*                                 70
    Greene's *Jephtha*                                            74
    Boyce's *Solomon*                                             78
    *Messiah*                                                     82

The Oratorio Concept 84
Handel's Last Decade of Oratorio 88
*Jephtha* 92
Arne's *Judith* 92

II. SOLO SONG AND VOCAL DUET.
(a) ITALY. *By* HANS JOACHIM MARX, *Professor of Musicology, University of Hamburg* 97
The Chamber Cantata 97
The Cantata in Rome 99
Venetian and Bolognese Composers 102
Alessandro Scarlatti 106
Handel's Italian Cantatas 110
Neapolitan Cantatas in the Early Eighteenth Century 114
The Chamber Duet 120

(b) GERMANY. *By* HANS JOACHIM MARX 124
Diffusion of the Italian Cantata 124
German Cantata Texts 126
The German Secular Cantata 127
The German Continuo Song 130

(c) ENGLAND. *By* IAN SPINK, *Professor of Music, Royal Holloway College, University of London* 134
Declamatory and Tuneful Ayres 134
Purcell and his Contemporaries 139
Cantata and Ballad: 1710–50 147

(d) FRANCE. *By* DAVID TUNLEY, *Professor of Music, University of Western Australia* 154
The Seventeenth-Century French *Air* 154
Categories of Seventeenth-Century Song 159
Poetic Texts 160
Serious Songs 161
Dance Songs and Drinking Songs 167
Antecedents of the *Cantate française* 172
New Influences on the Cantata 172
Stylistic Traits of the *Cantate française* 173
Cantata Texts 180
Development of the Cantata 181
The *Cantatille* 183

III. MUSIC FOR INSTRUMENTAL ENSEMBLE: 1630–1700.
*By* WALTER KOLNEDER, *Professor of Musicology, Hochschule für Musik, Karlsruhe* 186
Variety of Instrumental Forms 186
The *Canzon* in Italy 189
The *Canzon* in the German Lands 191

The *Sonata da chiesa* 194
The *Concerto grosso* 206
Corelli's *Concerti* 210
Origins of the Contrast Principle 214
The Opera Overture 217
The French Overture 220
The Three-Movement *Sinfonia* 225
The Suite 227
The Dominance of French Influence 230

IV. ORCHESTRAL MUSIC IN THE EARLY EIGHTEENTH
    CENTURY. *By* WALTER KOLNEDER 233
Conditions and Resources 233
Constitution of Orchestras 236
Output of Works 238
The Suite 239
Telemann's Suites 242
The *Charaktersuite* 247
The Suite in Italy 248
The Suite in England 250
Bach's Orchestral Suites 250
The Opera Overture 256
The Orchestra in French Opera 257
The Non-Operatic Overture 259
The *Concerto grosso* 260
The Handelian 'Grand Concerto' 262
Bach's Brandenburg Concertos 263
Other Masters of the *Concerto grosso* 268
The Concerto in England 272
The Concerto in France 274
The *Concerto ripieno* 276
The Orchestra in Church Music 284
Music of the Lutheran Church 286
From *Sinfonia* to Symphony 290
The *Sinfonia* in Transition 292
The Change in Melodic Style 296
The Merging of Streams 300

V. THE SOLO CONCERTO. *By* WALTER KOLNEDER 302
Solo Concerto Movement and Solo Concerto in Vivaldi 303
Structure of the Ritornello 307
Recurrences of the Ritornello 315
Recapitulation 316
Solo in the Ritornello 318
The Solo Sections 320
Ritornello Motives in the Accompaniment 328

The Solo Cadenza 339
The Middle Movement 341
Early History of the Solo Concerto 342
Torelli's *Concerti Musicali* 344
Torelli in Germany 350
Albinoni 351
Jacchini's Cello Concertos 352
Torelli's Later Works 354
The Solo Concerto in Germany 355
Bach and the Italian Style 356
Bach and the Concerto Form 358
The Keyboard Concerto 362
Other Means of Contrast 363
Quantz on the Concerto 364
The Solo Concerto in France 365
The Keyboard Concerto in England 368
The Italian Solo Concerto after Vivaldi 369
Tartini and his School 372

VI. CONCERTED CHAMBER MUSIC. *By* ERNST H. MEYER,
    *Professor Emeritus, Humboldt University, Berlin* 377
Music for the Individual Listener 377
The Forms and Styles of 'Abstract' Music 378
Methods of Unification 380
The Fugal Element 384
Melodic and Harmonic Style 385
Italy 388
Venice 390
Bologna 393
Modena 395
Corelli's Trio Sonatas 397
Changes in Terminology 399
Austria 400
Bohemia and Moravia 402
Instrumental Music in Poland 408
Germany 412
The North German School 418
Central and South German Composers 420
Switzerland and Scandinavia 424
The Netherlands 425
France 429
England 432
Foreign Influences 437
Purcell and the *Basso continuo* 439
The Climate of the New Century 442
Aesthetic Characteristics 443

New Emotionalism 444
Cosmopolitan Tendencies 444
New National Consciousness 449
Three Stages of Development 450
The New Textures 451
Instruments 453
Varied Combinations 454
The Trio Sonata 454
The String Quartet 456
Classical Sonata Form 458

VII. THE SOLO SONATA. *By* CHARLES W. HUGHES, *Professor Emeritus, Herbert H. Lehman College, University of the City of New York* 462
Variations on a Bass 463
The *Canzon* 465
Elaboration of the Bass 468
The *Sonata da camera* 470
Solo Music for Viols 474
Early Italian Masters of the Violin Sonata 477
Corelli and his Influence 480
Vivaldi 482
Dall'Abaco 483
Veracini 484
Tartini 485
Locatelli 487
The Violin in England 489
Geminiani 490
Other Sonata Composers in England 492
Popular Violin Music 492
Violin Music in France 493
The Situation in Germany 498
French Influence in Germany 499
Biber 499
J. J. Walther 500
Handel and Bach 502
Bach's Contemporaries 503

VIII. KEYBOARD MUSIC: 1630–1700. *By* JOHN CALDWELL, *Lecturer in Music, University of Oxford* 505
Instrumental Idioms 505
Secular Forms and Styles 506
The Liturgical Background 510
Tonality 512
Frescobaldi 514
Frescobaldi's Contemporaries 516

Southern Italians                                                    518
Italian Organ Music                                                  523
Bernardo Pasquini                                                    523
Pasquini's Variations and Toccatas                                   525
Alessandro Scarlatti                                                 526
Spain and Portugal                                                   528
Juan Cabanilles                                                      531
French Keyboard Music                                                536
Chambonnières and Louis Couperin                                     538
Lebègue and D'Anglebert                                              540
French Liturgical Music for Organ                                    544
Austria and Southern Germany                                         551
Froberger's Music                                                    552
Froberger's Contemporaries and Successors                            556
Northern and Central Germany: Treatment of the Chorale               559
Chorale Fantasia and Free Forms                                      563
Secular German Keyboard Music                                        568
The European Periphery                                               570
The Netherlands                                                      573
England                                                              578
The Suite in England                                                 580
Purcell, Blow, and Croft                                             584
English Organ Music                                                  588

IX. HARPSICHORD MUSIC: 1700–1750. By PHILIP
        RADCLIFFE, Fellow of King's College, Cambridge               590
Introductory                                                         590
François Couperin                                                    593
Rameau                                                               602
Italy                                                                604
Scarlatti                                                            608
Handel                                                               616
Handel's Contemporaries                                              620
Suite and Sonata                                                     625
Bach's Variations                                                    626
Bach's Miscellaneous Works                                           631
The Partitas                                                         634
The English Suites                                                   635
The French Suites and Inventions                                     637
Das wohltemperirte Clavier                                           639
Musicalisches Opfer and Die Kunst der Fuge                           646

X. ORGAN MUSIC: 1700–1750. By WALTER EMERY                           650
The Instrument                                                       650
Changes of Style                                                     651
Italy                                                                652

Spain                                                      656
France                                                     657
England                                                    663
Catholic Germany                                           665
Bohemia                                              ·     667
Protestant Germany                                         668
Böhm                                                       668
J. G. Walther                                              672
Bach                                                       675
Chorale Preludes                                           676
Trio Sonatas                                               683
Preludes, Fantasias, and Toccatas                          683
Fugues                                                     685
Types of Prelude                                           687
Bach's Pupils                                              691
Conclusion                                                 693

BIBLIOGRAPHY                                               695

INDEX                                                      763

# ILLUSTRATIONS

I. MUSICK
Frontispiece to John Playford's *Select Ayres and Dialogues* (1659)
*Cambridge University Library*

II. FROM BLOW'S 'DIALOGUE BETWEEN DIVES AND ABRAHAM'
Published in Henry Playford's *Harmonia Sacra* (1688)
*British Library, London*

III. COLLEGIUM MUSICUM
From *Musicalischer Arien Erster Theil* (Stralsund, 1647)
*Landesbibliothek und Murhardsche Bibliothek, Kassel*

IV. VIVALDI: VIOLIN CADENZA
From the Concerto in D (1712) (Dresden, Landesbibliothek Cx. 1043)
*Biblioteca Nazionale, Turin*

V. EARLY 18TH-CENTURY GERMAN VIOLINIST
From Johann Christoph Weigel's *Musicalisches Theatrum*
(Nuremberg, *c*.1722)

VI. PURCELL'S *LESSONS FOR THE HARPSICHORD* (1696)
(i) 'Rules for Graces'; (ii) Saraband from the Second Suite
*British Library, London*

VII. HARPSICHORDIST OF BACH'S TIME
From Johann Christoph Weigel's *Musicalisches Theatrum*
(Nuremberg, *c*.1722)

VIII. ABENDMUSIK
The Jena Collegium Musicum (1744) (watercolour by an unknown artist)
*Museum für Kunst und Gewerke, Hamburg*

# INTRODUCTION TO VOLUMES V AND VI

## By J. A. Westrup

La Fontaine, having related the fable of the frog and the ox, pointed the moral:

> Le monde est plein de gens qui ne sont pas plus sages:
> Tout bourgeois veut bâtir comme les grand seigneurs,
>   Tout petit prince a des ambassadeurs,
>   Tout marquis veut avoir des pages.

Apart from the rhyme he might equally well have written 'musiciens' instead of 'ambassadeurs'. It was an age of 'conspicuous expenditure', restricted only by limited resources, not by any lack of ambition. Patronage was not new, but in the seventeenth century it cost more. The principal reason for this was opera, which involved not only the expense of singers and orchestra but also paying for scenery and costumes. The spectacle was all-important. Except in the relatively few places where commercial opera flourished it was an aristocratic entertainment which enhanced the prestige of the ruler. In France in particular it was a means of glorifying the king, whose praises were sung in a prologue.

Opera and ballet were mainly responsible for establishing the orchestra as a standard ensemble. But their influence on music in general went further. The idioms of the opera aria were transferred to oratorio and in Germany to the church cantata. The dance movements of the ballet found their way into instrumental suites and concertos. Opera also left its mark on instrumental movements in the form of pointed rhythms which recall the feminine endings of Italian verse, of broad and expressive melodies in the style of the slow aria, of dramatic programme music, and poignant slow movements which reflect in their intensity the idioms of accompanied recitative. Instrumental music in turn had its influence on opera, particularly in the lengthy ritornellos which often introduce an aria; and there was much in common between the *da capo* aria and the solo concerto. Instrumental music reached a wider public than opera, since it was performed outside court circles. There were no concert halls until the Holywell Music Room was opened in Oxford in 1748. Concerts were given in any convenient building—in a church, in a theatre, in a coffee house or a tavern, in a private house, and in the open air. There was also a growth of amateur or student activity—in private circles, in universities, in the Italian conservatories.

The sheer mass of music produced during this period is staggering: hundreds of operas, oratorios, cantatas, concertos, and sonatas. Composers were prolific not from a persistent itch to write music but in order to satisfy a demand, even if it meant setting the same libretto more than once. Both the courts and the public, where there was one, wanted a constant supply of new operas, just as the Lutheran church needed an ample repertory of cantatas. The very fact that composition was their daily bread gave composers a reliable technique which enabled them to write quickly, quite apart from the fact that they were ready to adapt earlier works if it would save time and labour. Since they were all practical musicians, active as conductors or performers, they must have led very busy lives; yet many of them were not averse to social intercourse, and some of them wrote books.

Opera and instrumental music, in particular, called for and encouraged virtuosity. Though travel was slow and often un- comfortable, singers and players sought positions anywhere in Europe where their talents could be rewarded. Alternatively impresarios went to find them, as Handel did when he was organizing opera in London. Sometimes the virtuosos were merely birds of passage. At other times they settled in an adopted country, making money not only by performing but by teaching. Kusser (or Cousser), born in Bratislava and trained in Paris, held posts in several German cities before he visited England and finally settled at Dublin, where he died. Geminiani, a pupil of Corelli and one of the most distinguished violinists of his time, also established himself in Dublin after Kusser's death, though without any official appoint- ment. Tartini, equally distinguished, spent a few years in Prague; but for most of his life he stayed in Padua, where his school of violin-playing was famous and attracted pupils from all over the Continent.

In this way Italian music became widely known, though it had little success in France. But familiarity did not depend on personal contacts. Operas and church music more often than not remained in manuscript: the sumptuous editions published in Paris were on the whole an exception. But a considerable quantity of instrumental music was published, frequently in sets of six or twelve works, and composers or their publishers began to adopt the practice of labelling the sets with opus numbers. No doubt many of the concertos and *sinfonie* were bought for performance by court orchestras; but they may also have been played by amateurs, who certainly found plenty of scope for their activity in what is now known as chamber music. Instrumental resources differed widely. Few court orchestras in the eighteenth century had more than thirty players, and many had less. Outside court circles directors of music had to make do with what they could get. Even in a thriving city like Leipzig Bach was seriously embarrassed by the difficulty of finding adequate players and would have been even more embarrassed if he had not been able to call on pupils at the school and university students, with the addition of members of the *Stadtpfeifer*. The *Stadtpfeifer*, or city waits, were members of a professional guild which maintained a traditional standard of wind playing. They taught younger musicians, and their art was often handed down from father to son through several generations.

The 120 years covered by these two volumes form the greater part of what is currently known as the 'Baroque' period. The word, though allegedly derived from the Portuguese *barocco*, a rough or misshapen pearl, is of uncertain origin. In the eighteenth century it was used, like 'Gothic', in a derogatory sense. Hasse, in his old age, told Burney that he found the music of Durante 'not only dry, but *baroque*, that is, coarse and uncouth'. Rousseau defined 'une musique *baroque*' as 'celle dont l'harmonie est confuse, chargée de modulations & de dissonances, le chant dur & peu naturel, l'intonation difficile, & le mouvement contraint'. In the late nineteenth century, largely through the work of Heinrich Wölfflin, who published his *Renaissance und Barock* at the age of 24, it was applied to a particular style of Southern European architecture, which in its addiction to elaboration and ornament was a reaction against the Classical or Palladian style of the sixteenth century. The term was not adopted by historians of music until the early part of the twentieth century, apparently in the belief that there were parallels between the architecture and the music of the same period. As a sort of code name for the period it is harmless enough: as a description of the music it is virtually meaningless. It is true that there are certain features which are common to most of the composers of the time: contrasts of texture and dynamics, vivacious rhythms, the use of a definite key centre, and extended melodies. But there are also many differences. It would be difficult to see anything in common between the recitatives in Handel's operas and Bach's harpsichord suites. The chief impression made by the music of this period is its astonishing diversity.

This is true even of the works of individual composers. The contrapuntal elaborations of *Die Kunst der Fuge* and the cheerful ditties of the *Peasant Cantata* seem to belong to different worlds. Historians often speak of the firm establishment of tonality in 'Baroque' music, but lingering evidence of modality is not hard to find, particularly in the frequent use of the flattened seventh of the key, which is often introduced at the very beginning of a movement, e.g. the Minuet of Bach's First Brandenburg Concerto. In accompanied recitative key is often abandoned in favour of unpredictable modulations, and the same thing may happen in purely instrumental music, e.g. in the second movement of Vivaldi's *L'Autunno* (Op. 8, no. 3), which begins and ends in D minor but migrates through several keys in the course of 45 bars. In movements of a more regular construction modulation was generally more strictly controlled and served in fact as a structural element in a composition.

The music of this period rested on a firm diatonic basis. In the sixteenth century, chromaticism tended to be used as a melodic device which might incidentally result in unusual harmonic progressions. In the seventeenth and early eighteenth centuries it still had melodic significance, notably in the chromatic ground bass; and there are traces of older methods in Purcell's fantasias and even as late as Bach, e.g. in his harmonization of the chorale melody 'Mach's mit mir, Gott, nach deiner Güt'' (to the words 'Durch dein Gefängnis, Gottes Sohn') in the St. John Passion, or the final cadence of the three-part Invention in D minor (BWV 790), where the independent movement of the parts results in an unpredictable harmonic progression. But for the most part chromaticism was treated as a logical harmonic process within a diatonic framework, and some of its procedures, e.g. the Neapolitan sixth (originally a melodic alteration), became regular formulas.

Among the technical features of the period were the regular use of a *basso continuo* and what in Italy was called the concertato style. The *basso continuo* could either serve as a support for the full harmony of voices or instruments or both, or provide the harmonic background for a texture consisting merely of melody and bass. In the former case it was sometimes dispensed with, e.g. in the aria 'Patrii numi' in Alessandro Scarlatti's *Il Mitridate Eupatore*, where its absence is still striking. As a harmonic background it served to supply all that was necessary without distracting attention from the strong melodic character of the two principal parts. So important was the bass line that it was often used to provide the ritornello for an aria. The concertato style was one in which clear contrasts were established between voices and instruments, between groups of instruments, or between one or more solo instruments and the main body of the orchestra. Apart from the trombone, which was reserved for the accompaniment of church music, and the double bass, which did not emerge into the limelight until later in the eighteenth century, there was hardly a single instrument of the period which was not used as a soloist, either in concerted instrumental music or as an obbligato in vocal works. The term concerto, though widely used for instrumental compositions, with or without soloists, was also still used, like symphonia, as the title of a work for voices and instruments, e.g. Bach's cantatas. Though the concertato style invaded church music everywhere, the older contrapuntal forms without independent accompaniment also survived, particularly in Germany, though in a harmonic language firmly founded on the bass.

Ornamentation was an essential element in 'Baroque' music, as it had been in the preceding period. It was sometimes written into the text but more often was left to the performer to improvise. No doubt it was used most lavishly in the theatre, where singers were competing for applause, and by instrumental soloists. It would be a mistake, however, to suppose that it was merely a way of showing off. The English word 'grace' indicates that it was regarded as a refinement. Its execution was a matter of taste, for which there was no universal criterion. An enterprising publisher (Roger of Amsterdam) issued an edition of Corelli's violin sonatas (Op. 5) in which the solo part of six of the slow movements was furnished with an ornamented version, allegedly representing what the composer played. Roger North roundly condemned it: 'Upon the bare view of the print any one would wonder how so much vermin could creep into the works of such a master'. Though much of the ornamentation consists of little more than superficial decoration, there is some justice for North's criticism in those places where there is excessive elaboration. In fact the edition did little service to interpretation since it presented in a stereotyped form what should have been the natural expression of the player's personality. Some writers of the period expressly warn against excessive ornamentation. Where taste was the guide, there were bound to be lapses. The positive value of improvised ornamentation was that it prevented any performance from being hidebound. The same applies to modifications of rhythm, both rubato within the bar and the lengthening or shortening of notes within the beat. When Couperin observed that French composers did not write what was actually played he was affirming the principle that performance must not be rigid and that the niceties of a fluid interpretation cannot be notated.

Purcell, in his contribution to the twelfth edition of Playford's *Introduction to the Skill of Music* (1694), recommended that the two upper parts in simple three-part harmony should run in thirds. He added: 'I'm sure 'tis the constant Practise of the *Italians* in all their Musick, either Vocal or Instrumental, which I presume ought to be a Guide to us'. Mattheson put it more bluntly when he said of the English: 'Itziger Zeit *imitirt* diese *Nation* platterdings den Italiän-ischen *Stylum*'. He was writing in 1713, by which time there were some grounds for his criticism. It would not have been true in Purcell's day, when French music exerted a considerable influence, particularly on instrumental music. In Germany, French and Italian music for long held equal sway: composers like Georg Muffat handled both styles with equal assurance. Italy, on the other hand, was impervious to outside influences: Corelli is reported to have failed to play an overture of Handel's as the composer wanted because it was in the French style. Throughout this period musicians were fully aware of the differences between French and Italian music. A dialogue in Lully's *Ballet de la Raillerie* (1659) is an amusing parody of the two styles. François Raguenet in 1702 published what professed to be a reasoned comparison between the music of the two countries, but after initial praise of Lully it proved to be heavily weighted in favour of the Italians.

Mere imitation cannot reproduce a style. It is hardly surprising that Corelli is said to have expressed a poor opinion of Purcell's sonatas: their English ancestry was too clearly marked. Nor would the so-called 'Italian airs' or *ariettes* in eighteenth-century French opera have deceived anyone who was acquainted with the genuine article. Composers such as Purcell, Bach, and Rameau were not only men with a local tradition behind them: they were individuals, who are now seen to have been among the élite of their time, however little they may have been known when they were alive. But even with individuals there were cross-currents. Domenico Scarlatti might reasonably be claimed as the most original composer of the period; yet he is recognizable as belonging to the same century and the same race as Vivaldi. There were other cross-currents: the same idioms served both the church and the chamber, however different the words might be. Baron Pöllnitz said of the Venetians: 'They spend half of their time in committing Sin, and the other half in begging God's Pardon'. Suitably adapted, it might well do as a motto for the period.

One cannot help admiring the sturdiness of composers who continued their work in spite of the chances and changes of this mortal life. Vivaldi suffered from asthma all his life and never went out of doors on foot. Handel faced bankruptcy. Bach produced thirteen children during his time in Leipzig, in addition to the four who survived from his first marriage.They showed an equal resilience in the face of political changes. Purcell served three very different monarchs with apparent unconcern. Schütz might lament the setback that church music had received from the Thirty Years War, but between 1631, when Saxony was involved, and 1648, when the war ended, he managed to publish five substantial works. In general musicians were too busy to have time for other activities. But Steffani managed to be not only a composer but a bishop *in partibus* and a diplomat as well. In the latter capacity he seems to have shown the courtesy expected from ambassadors. 'He was', says Hawkins, 'perfectly skilled in all the external forms of polite behaviour, and, which is somewhat unusual, continued to observe and practise them at the age of fourscore.'

The musical literature of the time was considerable. Of the books listed by Bukofzer in *Music in the Baroque Era* some 380 were published between 1630 and 1750. They range from polemical pamphlets and elementary instruction books to the voluminous works of Mattheson and Rameau. There was clearly a desire among the educated public to learn about music and musicians. Works like Brossard's *Dictionnaire de musique* (1703), Walther's *Musicalisches Lexicon* (1732), and Mattheson's *Grundlage einer Ehrenpforte* (1740) supplied information in a convenient and accessible form. Many of the books were didactic and therefore have something to offer to the present-day performer, provided he accepts what they have to say as an expression of opinion and not as the voice of God. The tone of these works was not necessarily pedantic. Couperin advised learners not to make faces when playing the harpsichord. Heinichen explained that if the intermediate cadences for the harpsichord in recitative were delayed the singer would be left in the air with nothing to do. Rameau said: 'One can judge music only through the medium of hearing: reason has authority only inasmuch as it agrees with the ear'; and again: 'Fugue is an ornament in music whose only principle is good taste'. Mattheson held that practice was more important than absorbing dusty doctrines from the past.

The division between Vols. V and VI of the *New Oxford History* is purely a matter of practical convenience, designed to ensure that the material is more or less evenly distributed between the two. For that reason Vol. VI, the bulk of which is devoted to instrumental music, begins with chapters on English Ode and Oratorio and Solo Song. These subjects are clearly related both to opera and to church music, but they can hardly be said to fall within either category. No apology is needed for devoting two volumes to a period which was so rich in the production of music and in musical activity and from which so much that is memorable has become a necessary part of our existence today.

# EDITOR'S NOTE

VOLUME VI was entirely planned by Sir Jack Westrup. He edited, or partially edited, Chapters III–V, VII, and IX–X, and was working on VI when he died in 1975. It is clear from the 'Introduction to Volumes V and VI' (reprinted above) that he conceived the two as a single unit, the division between them being purely a matter of practical convenience.

The contents of Volume VI all fall within a category that was originally called *musica da camera*, music for a 'room' that might be in a princely court or in a private house, and came to be applied to all music intended for neither church nor theatre. The title 'Concert Music' has hence been preferred to Sir Jack's provisional title 'The Growth of Instrumental Music'.

GERALD ABRAHAM

# I

# ODE AND ORATORIO IN ENGLAND

## (a) DIALOGUE AND ODE

### By ROSAMOND MCGUINNESS

THE PROBLEM OF NOMENCLATURE

BOTH English and Continental composers of the seventeenth century were preoccupied with the challenges of emerging forms and extensive musical design achieved through principles of organization other than those used in the cyclic Mass. In an era in which new forms were being clarified, complication of nomenclature was particularly prevalent. What composers or publishers chose to call works depended on whim, and indications of the genre were not accorded the importance subsequently given them by historians.

In the seventeenth century, 'the most slippery of the larger musical forms' as Winton Dean aptly expresses it, was the oratorio.[1] Even Hawkins, who was considerably closer to the inception of these works than we are, was aware of the linguistic complications. When he was considering the derivation of the word 'oratorio', he pointed out 'how inadequate the powers of language are to our ideas';[2] yet he too was imprecise in his terminology, referring to the oratorio in one chapter as a *cantata spirituale*,[3] in another as a 'dialogue of the dramatic kind',[4] and in yet another as a *concerto spirituale*.[5] He was not even clear firstly whether he was referring to the early 'cantata' predominantly written in the rather unrelenting monodic recitative style or in the slightly later lyrical monodic style, and secondly whether he was referring to the narrative style or the idiom that began to emerge from about 1630 onwards when aspects of the madrigal style were fused with those of the narrative tendency. Of course, what may seem imprecise to us

[1] *Handel's Dramatic Oratorios and Masques* (London, 1959), p. 3.
[2] *A General History of the Science and Practice of Music* (London, 1776; repr. New York, 1963), reprint, ii, p. 529n.
[3] Idem, p. 529.
[4] Idem, p. 595.
[5] Idem, p. 889.

may simply reflect the looseness of terminology at that time, though we know from other instances that Hawkins was not always as cautious as a present-day historian would have liked him to be. Composers write because they are required to do so by their position or because of some inner compulsion. Certainly in the seventeenth century, though there are instances of similar attitudes in subsequent years, their first consideration was what they wrote and not what they called it.

In his discussion of the terminological difficulties with the word 'oratorio', Dean states that before Handel 'no other species of oratorio had previously crossed the Channel' to England.[6] Hawkins suggests that before Handel the oratorio was 'little known' in this country.[7] Burney indicates that though oratorios were common in Italy, they were 'never attempted in England, either in public or private, till the year 1720 when Handel set *Esther*'.[8] Dean's statement is precise, but it is not clear to what form of pre-Handelian oratorio either Hawkins or Burney was referring. The Handelian oratorio was a unique art form, and earlier works by various composers differed from each other even when they were entitled 'oratorio' by the composer himself.[9] Certainly if one attempts to find English works written before Handel and specially designated 'oratorio', one is disappointed. The question is whether during the seventeenth century there existed in England a form we may consider to be of the same genre.[10]

THE BIBLICAL DIALOGUES

The closest to such a form are the English biblical dialogues written throughout the seventeenth century.[11] Since the Middle Ages England has maintained a strong tradition of religious drama on a variety of subjects. As time went by the sacred drama moved

[6] Op. cit., p. 3.

[7] Ibid., p. 889.

[8] *A General History of Music* (London, 1776–89; repr. New York, 1957), reprint, ii, p. 775.

[9] The historian soon comes to the view that 'oratorio' was simply a convenient term encompassing forms on a spiritual text and called by a variety of names, including sacred opera, dialogue, *cantata spirituale*, *concerto spirituale*, or even oratorio, and that in trying to interpret the composer's outlook when he created such works one must refer, as Dean suggests, to a given composer, period, and country.

[10] Howard E. Smither, 'The Baroque Oratorio', *Acta Musicologica*, xlviii (1976), p. 50, 70–6; also his *A History of the Oratorio* (Chapel Hill, 1977), ii, pp. 175–8.

[11] Basil Smallman, 'Endor Revisited: English Biblical Dialogues of the Seventeenth Century', *Music & Letters*, xlvi (1965), p. 137; Ian Spink, 'English Seventeenth-Century Dialogues', *Music & Letters*, xxxviii (1957), p. 155; H. E. Smither, 'The Latin Dramatic Dialogue and the Nascent Oratorio', *Journal of the American Musicological Society*, xx (1967), p. 403.

from its liturgical beginnings through various phases to a period when there was a strong assimilation of secular and sacred elements. The year 1577 saw the publication in London of Arthur Golding's English translation (1575) of *Abraham sacrifiant* (1550) by the French Protestant theologian, Théodore de Bèze. Golding, a celebrated translator and a man with strong and influential connections, enthusiastically upheld the ideals of the English Puritans and admired the luminaries of the French Huguenots. This work enjoyed greater popularity than many other works of a similar nature and apparently served as a model for subsequent dramas, notably on subjects from the Old Testament. Among the very popular *scenas* were Job, Saul, and Solomon. It is difficult to believe that those developments did not have some bearing upon the inception of the English biblical dialogues, though to what extent remains open to conjecture. What is interesting for us is that Solomon and Job were the subjects for at least two known dialogues and that the most popular was 'Saul and the Witch of Endor'. There were also dialogues upon religious themes though not necessarily from the scriptures: for instance, a 'dialogue between a Dying Man, The Devil, and an Angel' and a dialogue between two penitents.

The composers of the biblical dialogues, which apparently were performed not in church but probably in the home, employed the monodic style,[12] a mode of expression particularly apt for conversation between various characters. It is not unusual for new stylistic developments to take root initially within the theatre or dramatic sphere and in the case of the *stile nuove* England followed the continental example. Shortly after 1600 native English composers employed this style in such secular music as songs either in masques or independent compositions. Only subsequently did they use monody in their liturgical and devotional music and then primarily in the verse anthem, a form which was not dissimilar to the early Italian lyrical cantata, though whether it was directly derived from it or simply a parallel development remains to be seen. Composers of the biblical dialogues varied in their approach to the *seconda prattica*. Earlier examples seem to be more in the recitative monodic style with the emphasis simply upon narrative, while later dialogues show the incorporation of dramatic techniques and are considerably more lyrical. By comparison with contemporary Italian extended works in the monodic style these biblical dialogues were

---

[12] Spink, op. cit., p. 157.

short; Basil Smallman's designation of some of these as 'miniature oratorios'[13] is perhaps misleading. Their scope alone would suggest that 'cantata', in the early seventeenth-century sense, is perhaps more appropriate, or *cantata spirituale*, to use Hawkins's designation, or even simply 'chamber duet'. At most they can be seen simply as a section of an early monodic 'sacred drama', such as Cavalieri's *Rappresentazione di Anima e di Corpo*. A comparison of John Wilson's 'Dialogue between a Dying Man, The Devil and an Angel' (1649)[14] and Blow's 'A Dialogue between Dives and Abraham'[15] will illustrate this change in approach.

Both dialogues follow a similar procedure and one that was used also in the contemporary secular dialogues. They alternate solo sections whose varying lengths depend upon the way in which the text was presented, and conclude the whole with the concerted singing by as many individual characters as were involved in the earlier part of the dialogue.[16] In both examples the key relationships of sections are fairly close, and the sections are so arranged as to create a continuity of narrative. Appropriate voice parts delineate the various characters. Also in each case the texts seem to be the dominating influence as they were in the comparable early Italian dialogues or operas.

The essential difference between Wilson (1595–1674) and Blow (1649–1708) lies in their settings of the texts and their attitudes to the voice, with the consequential differences in the overall dramatic effect of each dialogue as a whole. Wilson seems to be preoccupied solely in ensuring that the text is heard and allows nothing to impede this. The harmonies are not startling and he relies upon a through-composed syllabic setting with little or no repetition. There are some instances of word-painting with clichés from the madrigal technique applied to conventionally evocative words, but these consist of syllabic figures such as a rising interval of a fourth for 'arise' and descending motion for 'night' rather than the highly figurated ornaments which become so characteristic of vocal writing later in the century. Towards the end of the dialogue there is a decided intensification at the words, 'Ther naile thy selfe bee Crucifyed', and a vehement setting at 'I finde my Mallice strucken lame'. The settings of both these lines are made all the more

---

[13] Smallman, op. cit., p. 137.

[14] Brit. Lib. Add. MS. 29396, fo. 86v–89.

[15] Printed in Henry Playford, *Harmonia Sacra* (London, 1688), i, p. 49. Both volumes of *Harmonia Sacra* contain other examples of the biblical dialogue.

[16] The rubric 'chorus' in the final sections does not imply a large number of voices but simply the total number of characters involved in the earlier part of the dialogue.

powerful because of the contrast with the relatively bland setting up to that point:

Ex. 1

Blow's approach differs and here, as we shall see, there is a parallel with the change in melodic style which occurred also in the ode in the last two decades of the century when vocal virtuosity became a considerable factor, possibly because of the growing influence of the later seventeenth-century Italian style of vocal display, the availability of particularly agile vocalists, and an increased taste for this sort of virtuosity. Like Wilson, Blow sets his text on through-composed lines, employing repetition very sparingly and only when he wishes to emphasize quantitative words: 'little, little Dew' or 'far sooner, far sooner'. The vocal melody consists of florid runs on every possible word that will allow it, a more complicated rhythm, and extended range, and a much more disjunct line. The singer must do considerably more than merely expound the text, though clarity is still an important element. Wilson's concluding concerted verse is largely homophonic, as are many in other early dialogues. The texture of Blow's so-called 'chorus' is more complex, with its use of imitation and contrasting ideas:

Ex. 2

It is not simply a question of the two voices singing simultaneously in homophony. Elements of dialogue are carried into the chorus, though presented in the *concertato* style with some overlapping rather than successively with one voice following the other. The whole has greater dramatic intensity than Wilson's works. The contributions of Purcell as well as Humfrey to this genre are, perhaps predictably, more similar to Blow's than to Wilson's. In Purcell's case, in particular, we see the greatest grasp of the dramatic possibilities: 'In guiltie night'[17] is a good illustration of this. It is interesting, though not surprising—for stylistic trends in various different contemporaneous forms often run parallel to each other—that the differences between early and later biblical dialogues mirror the differences between the early and later Court odes.

## COURT ODES

Although our picture of the biblical dialogue is by no means complete, comparison of available music and contemporary accounts enables us to infer how much more significant was the role the ode played in English society at this time and especially after the Restoration. Changing political and religious factors chiefly account for this. The masque tradition had been strengthened by the particular circumstances of the Commonwealth, though these had inhibited the development of an encomiastic artform directed primarily towards the Court. Encomium in general was however becoming more frequent; for instance, after the Court odes had been established, odes were performed on St Cecilia's Day.

The music of the Court tributes written shortly after the Restoration reveals to a great extent the monodic influence that had filtered through the cantata, solo song, dialogue, and verse anthem. In fact, the one extant pre-Restoration tribute which approximates to our notion of an ode—Orlando Gibbons's 'Do not repine, fair sun', a welcome song for James VI/I on his visit to Scotland in 1617[18]—is hardly distinguishable from a verse anthem except in function, title, and subject matter. The ode became an autonomous form, and then but gradually, only when Blow and Purcell were involved with it in the last two decades of the century. This autonomy was encouraged by the need to write consecutive series of odes over an extended period of time, and the composers learned from each other.

---

[17] *Purcell Society Edition*, xxxii (London, rev. ed., 1967), p. 128.
[18] New York, Public Library, Drexel 4180–5, ed. Philip Brett (London, 1961).

Textually the odes reflect indigenous literary influences: the masque and the sort of panegyric verse which was being written with increasing frequency and for almost every conceivable occasion. One of the textual characteristics of the English ode, including the Court odes, is the 'stanza', a word which literary critics question because the divisions of a poem are inconsistent. Stanzas are irregular and vary from ode to ode as do the rhyme patterns, though rhyme itself is very much in evidence. Also prominent is the element of address—a remnant of classical influence—as well as those of supplication and personification, and there is an abundance of words of imagery, particularly those relating to Nature. Ample references to specific political events occur, indicating the date of performance where none has been given.

The texts of many Court odes are anonymous and their style is so generalized that it is difficult to identify the authors. There is at least one case of a composer's providing a text for a colleague to set: the words of Matthew Locke's 'Come Loyall hearts, make no delay' (for 1 January 1666) were written by Nicholas Lanier.[19] Poets definitely known or surmised to have contributed Court odes included Flatman, Shadwell, D'Urfey, Sedley, Tate, Prior, and Motteux, all notable for their writing in other spheres. Very few of their odes deserve a place among the great poetry of the century, but their texts served the purpose for which they were intended, though verses such as

'Tis only for great Caesar's sake
More coming years we long to see.
He each new day does happy make
That else would a new torment be.[20]

must have caused composers some consternation. Nevertheless study of the odes not only indicates the artistic level of Court society, but throws light upon the way in which composers coped with limitations. It is particularly revealing to see how a composer of the stature of Purcell gradually came to terms with them and with his own gifts. It is paradoxical, though an accepted aesthetic principle, that limitations do in fact give the artist considerable freedom and we probably owe Purcell's growing self-awareness as a dramatic composer more to his writing of odes than to anything

[19] Bodl. Ashm. 36–7, fo. 167.
[20] In Blow's ode for 1 January 1688, 'Yee Sons of Phoebus', London, Royal College of Music, MS 1097, fo. 159.

else he composed before 1690. Few English composers either then or at any time have set words to music as sensitively and imaginatively as he when at his best. Writing music annually and sometimes biannually over a period of fifteen years, to texts which frequently were execrable, taught him how to discipline his talents and allow his very special gifts to come through. Blow also had moments of extreme sensitivity, but it was not within his capabilities to maintain a high level throughout his odes.

## LITERARY ORIGINS

It is significant that the early Restoration tributes are directly derived from Ben Jonson whose masques had played such an important role under the early Stuart kings. By the last decades of the century the masque was being supplanted by other forms including the ode. With this, as with the oratorio, there is some confusion of nomenclature which can only be understood if we consider the literary background. In his study of the ode as a literary form G. N. Shuster[21] has indicated that there is no adequate definition of the word, that it has meant a variety of things, and that it has been called by different names. To find 'ode' and 'song' used interchangeably is not unusual, particularly among poems set to music. Shuster contends that the ode entered English literature as one of the 'refined' forms when various writers wished to raise the standard of poetry. What he considers to be the ode proper was influenced by Ronsard and he proposes 1582 as a significant date. In that year Ronsard and his ode made their appearance in England with Thomas Watson's *Passionate Centurie of Love* which was soon followed by others that interpreted Ronsard's style. Soon, however, Ben Jonson's classically inspired ode supplanted Ronsard's and the attitude towards the relationship of poetry and music altered; what Shuster calls 'libretto odes' came into being. The Pindaric ode was 'domesticated' and Jonson himself introduced the 'birthday ode' into English literature. Oxford and Cambridge encouraged encomiastic verse and every conceivable occasion seemed to call for some imitation of an English imitation of a Pindaric or Homeric ode. Encomiastic verses became so prevalent that, as Dryden expressed it in another context in 1668, a person in battle 'could scarce have wished the victory at the price he knew he must pay for it, in being subject to the reading and hearing of so many ill verses as he was sure would be made on that

---

[21] *The English Ode from Milton to Keats* (Gloucester, Mass., 1964).

subject'. Adding, 'that no argument could scape some of those eternal rhymers, who watch a battle with more diligence than the ravens and birds of prey.'[22] It must be said that though Dryden was critical of the frequency and quality of these works, nevertheless he recognized how beneficial such a genre could be at a time when poets were eager to translate the classical imagery then in vogue. The ode afforded greater freedom than most other poetic forms in England.

### CHARLES II AS CATALYST

Fervent encomiastic verse was intense when Charles II returned to England. Jonson had established a precedent for the more regular delivery of odes on royal occasions with his series of works written from 1629 to his death in 1637.[23] Though music for them has not come to light, rubrics suggest that at least some of them were sung. The King's birthday coincided with the actual day of the Restoration and an Act of Parliament made it an occasion for annual remembrance. Charles had witnessed the glorification of the monarch at the French Court which must have impressed him, and his appetite for panegyric would have been whetted by the masques dedicated to him as a child.[24] By 1680 the ode was regarded as a standard part of celebrations at Court, particularly for the royal birthday and New Year. It was not the only celebration but one of many tributes which included elaborate fireworks, dancing, and the like.[25] While Charles II did not 'invent' the Restoration ode or even play the most significant part in its creation, we must not overlook his role as a catalyst in a procedure which remained an integral part of Court life until the early years of the nineteenth century, even though the structure of the texts and music was altered at the beginning of the eighteenth.

We have no balanced or complete picture of the seventeenth-century Court odes nor, for that matter, of the odes for St Cecilia's Day.[26] From the first two decades of the Restoration we have only a handful of works and contemporary documentation is sparse. Apparently sung odes or 'welcome songs' (odes in everything but

---

[22] *An Essay of Dramatic Poesy*, ed. W. T. Arnold (Oxford, 1952) p. 10.

[23] McGuinness, *English Court Odes, 1660–1820* (Oxford, 1971), pp. 1–11.

[24] E.g. one by Thomas Nabbes entitled 'A Presentation Intended for the Prince his Highness on his Birth-day, the 29 of May, 1638. annually celebrated'; *The Works of Thomas Nabbes*, ed. A. H. Bullen (*Old English Plays*, ii) (London, 1887), p. 256.

[25] McGuinness, 'A Fine Song on Occasion of the Day was sung', *Music & Letters*, 1 (1969), p. 290.

[26] W. H. Husk, *An Account of the Musical Celebrations on St Cecilia's Day* (London, 1857).

name) did not appear with any regularity for a particular occasion and the writing of neither texts nor music appears to have been entrusted to any particular Court nominee. The royal birthday and 1 January summoned forth odes most frequently and there was, occasionally an ode on the birth of a member of the royal family, on the odd subsequent birthday, and on royal marriages.

## THE EARLIER RESTORATION ODES

The first work we can consider to be an ode, though only an incipient one, was 'All things their certain periods have' by Matthew Locke (1622–77) probably performed in 1666.[27] Locke's ode recalls the dialogues already discussed, as well as masque and anthem. In other words, his ode is a synthesis of various musical elements. No instruments were used and the ode consists of the alteration of various solos and duets with a 'choral' refrain—probably for solo voices. Although it is a relatively short work, one can appreciate Locke's sensitivity to dramatic shaping and his awareness of the power of the Italian affective style.

Ex. 3

Henry Cooke (c.1616–72) and Pelham Humfrey (1647–74), both musicians of the Chapel Royal, also composed odes at this time. Cooke's three short examples,[28] though slightly more substantial than Locke's, notably because of their instrumental element, stylistically lean heavily upon the verse anthem and are barely distinguishable from it. Verse anthem influence is also to be seen in

[27] London, Brit. Lib. Add. MS. 33234, f. 35. For a discussion of the dating of this and subsequent manuscripts, see McGuinness, *English Court Odes*, chap. 2.
[28] Birmingham, Barber Inst., Barber MS. 5001, fo. 1.

Humfrey's three odes,[29] though in quality they do reveal that he was both sensitive to his text and alive to the exigencies of the occasion. His generous use of the 'step tripla', which the King is known to have favoured, intimates that he was aware of his patron's tastes.[30] Humfrey's different arrangement of solo verses, duets, and choral sections in all three odes shows that he was not writing these works according to a formula, but adjusting the various elements to give the address to the King a special impact on each occasion. He offers ample evidence of a well-developed sense of a total composition by balancing instrumental symphonies with vocal sections and using choruses effectively as recurring refrains, and he introduces chromaticisms in 'When from his throne':

Ex. 4

A few years before 1680 Blow apparently initiated, with 'Dread Sir, the Prince of Light', his long series of odes, a series which continued until the turn of the century. After Purcell's death he was joined by Purcell's brother Daniel (c.1663–1717) and Nicholas Staggins (1645–1700).[31] We have only the texts of Staggins's odes. The music of Daniel Purcell shows that he relied particularly upon the later style of Blow; in fact he even included some of Blow's music in one of his odes, though he was also influenced by his brother's music.

Blow's odes, particularly the two written in 1678 and 1679—'The Birth of Jove' and 'Great Janus, tho' the Festival be thine'—appear to be a bridge between those of Cooke and Humfrey and the later odes. In their structure and in aspects of the musical language we

[29] Brit. Lib. Add. MS. 33287.
[30] *Roger North on Music*, ed. John Wilson (London, 1959), p. 300.
[31] See McGuinness, *English Court Odes*, chap. 2 for the dates and sources of these odes.

see Blow's debt to both Cooke and Humfrey and to the other musical forms such as dialogue, masque, and anthem. This was an era in which sacred and secular elements were amalgamated and the ode continually exemplifies this fusion very clearly. Though Blow, like Purcell, never ventured abroad himself, he absorbed aspects of both the French and Italian styles from music that he would have heard or performed, possibly from his contemporaries such as Humfrey who did travel on the Continent, and from copying continental works. We know that Purcell valued this exercise and gave his own musical language additional vitality by assimilating foreign elements and digesting them thoroughly, producing in the end work which had an English foundation but which in many respects showed a mixture of styles.

Blow's three early odes[32] were conceived on a slightly larger scale than any of the earlier ones by Cooke and Humfrey, a trend common to most forms during the latter part of the century on the Continent as well as in England. It was not necessarily that ode texts generally became longer, though occasionally there were particularly long ones; it was rather that composers began to learn how to exploit the various possibilities of repetition of material. To make a point or conclude a section, they would repeat ends of phrases in a solo song by a chorus, or instrumental ritornello; occasionally they would employ the concertato principle with an echo effect.

In both odes and anthems Cooke had relied upon three string parts for his instrumental sections. Humfrey had enlarged this to four, possibly as a result of his experience abroad, and Blow followed his example. Like Humfrey, also, Blow achieves unity through close key relationships and planned repetition of sections and gives his pieces rhythmic impetus through the recurrence of the popular trochaic pattern and strongly defined beats. There are ample instances of the Anglo-French rhythm which characterized Restoration music in general. Blow tends to restrict himself to tuneful solos which are largely syllabic with only the occasional flourish on an evocative word. Sections in the more intense monodic style as opposed to melodious, rhythmically driving tunes are sparse. All in all, Blow does not make the vocal demands which he and Purcell required later when gifted singers appeared at Court and Blow himself felt sufficiently comfortable to become more adventurous. His forte in later odes lay in beautifully shaped melodies and soaring lines that show an understanding of the voice, but in

[32] All three in Brit. Lib., Add. MS. 33287.

these early odes there is little evidence of what was to come. Pleasant, often patriotic-sounding tunes, reminiscent of the many popular lightweight songs that were published at that time, and ditties dominated by the ♩. ♪ ♩ pattern with little harmonic or rhythmic variety, characterize these early works. Though the ground bass had been a feature of Italian opera for forty years, it played no part as yet in the Court tributes. Like both Cooke and Humfrey, Blow favoured duets which move along blithely in parallel thirds, and thumping choruses which rely heavily upon homophonic texture. The combination of a definite rhythm, uncomplicated texture, and syllabic word-setting made it easy for the King to get the message if he chose to listen. (Accounts of the uproar during performances indicate that the courtiers were not very attentive listeners.)

It would probably be fair to say that at this stage Blow had not yet found how to reconcile the demands of the occasions with the possibilities of well-wrought, aesthetically pleasing works of art, though 'Great Janus' shows some enterprise. Here Blow supplements some of the vocal sections with instrumental obbligatos and the string interludes have a vitality not apparent in the other two odes.

The New Year ode for 1680, 'The New Year is Begun', composed immediately before Purcell began his series, is substantially better. Blow seems to have been inspired here by his earlier commission for the Oxford University Act, 'Awake, awake my Lyre', for the degree ceremony in 1678 (though not performed until 1679). Perhaps the circumstances of the Act Song gave Blow the impetus he needed for his Court works. The plan of the 1680 ode does not differ substantially from those of the earlier or indeed subsequent odes, although the latter are more highly organized as well as more extensive. There is an opening instrumental movement followed by a sequence of solos, duets, choruses, and instrumental interludes, concluded by a chorus; however, the opening solo and ensuing chorus and some of the subsequent instrumental sections have a charm lacking in its predecessors. The use of a minor key for a change, in this case E minor, is most effective.

Purcell is alleged to have written some sort of Birthday ode in 1670 when he was eleven,[33] but this has disappeared; his earliest

[33] William H. Cummings, *Purcell* (London, 1881), p. 20, said that Edward Rimbault's library contained a manuscript in the handwriting of Humfrey entitled *The Address of the Children of the Chapel Royal to the King, and their Master, Captain Cooke, on his Majesties Birthday, A.D. 1670, composed by Master Purcell, one of the children of the said Chapel.*

known ode appears to have been written in 1680 when he initiated a group of 'welcome songs' greeting Charles II and the Duke of York on their returns to Windsor or London. Like Blow, he also wrote a consecutive series of odes, until his death in 1695. Thus with the exception of two odes by William Turner (1651–1740) which appear to date from the reign of Charles II, the music for the royal panegyrics was mainly by these two composers.

On the other hand, for the odes celebrating St Cecilia's Day, which were composed annually with few exceptions after c.1683, a number of poets and composers were enlisted. Texts were provided by Fishburn, Oldham, Tate, Fletcher, Dryden, Shadwell, D'Urfey, Brady, Parsons, Yalden, Bishop, and Addison, music by Purcell, Blow, Turner, Draghi, Robert King, Gottfried Finger, Daniel Purcell, and Jeremiah Clarke. Their stylistic approaches naturally differed slightly though, with few exceptions, the structural framework of the odes is similar to that of the Court works.

## THE HEYDAY OF BLOW AND PURCELL

It has already been suggested that the commission for the Oxford Act Song in 1679 encouraged Blow in his Court odes; one cannot help thinking that an additional spark may have been given when Purcell joined in these tasks. Certainly his odes from 1680 onward show more ability, and in the hands of these two masters the Court ode enjoyed its heyday during the years from 1680 until 1695. Two factors make this period particularly interesting: the survival of so many scores and their consecutive sequence. We can see quite clearly how the ode developed both as changing elements impinged upon it and as the composers came to grips with it. Among the influences must be included the appearance of gifted vocalists and instrumentalists with specific talents, such as the exceptional range of John Gostling's bass voice and the instrumental expertise of the trumpeters John and Matthew Shore. Their talent encouraged other performers to develop similar skills and incited composers to introduce the element of virtuosity. They also had larger forces at their disposal as the Chapel Royal singers developed, as female voices became available, and as the inclusion of oboe, trumpet, recorder, and five string parts became feasible. Another stimulating factor was the increasing influence of the contemporary Italian style with its use of concertato technique, clarification of aria forms, and harmonic organization. By comparison with his last odes, those for Queen Mary's birthday—'Now does the glorious day appear' (1689), 'Arise my Music' (1690), 'Welcome, welcome glorious morn' (1691), 'Love's goddess' (1692), 'Celebrate this festival' (1693), 'Come ye sons of art away' (1694)[34]—Purcell's early welcome songs appear clumsy, though they tower above earlier ones by other composers. Yet, even allowing for their deficiencies, they give us a glimpse of a composer with the potential for a highly sensitive dramatic approach. As we move from the first welcome song 'Welcome, vicegerent of the mighty King'[35] to the last great ode for the Queen, 'Come, ye sons of art', we can see how Purcell gradually began to understand how to translate this potential into a very powerful actuality. Clearly he was fully aware of his compositional strength by the end of the 1680s, when he began his significant works for the theatre and wrote the odes which must be considered as the most masterly of all those written for Court occasions. Purcell's last royal ode, 'Who can from joy refrain?' for the Duke of Gloucester's birthday (1695)[36] is memorable for its final chaconne.

Blow's odes show that he gradually altered his view of them, but they do not give the same sense of steadily increasing self-awareness or the same awareness of dramatic potential. Dramatic sense was not the core of his creative ability; he was at his best in solo songs or duets, and comparison of a contemporary series of his anthems with his odes, shows that he was obviously more inspired by sacred texts. Within an ode he would be fired by one or two sections of the text, but he was not as adept as Purcell in maintaining a high standard throughout a complete ode.

Systematic, comparative study of the odes of Blow and Purcell shows that each influenced the other. There are, for instance, significant similarities between the ode of one year by one of them and that of the same or subsequent year by the other. The striking resemblance of some of the melodies, the overall arrangement of movements in an ode, the instrumental openings and interludes, the choruses, and the ground bass and its treatment—to mention only a few of the more blatant parallels—are evidence of careful study enhanced, most probably, through participation in the actual performance.

Comparison of early and late odes by both men will illustrate not only how they differed but how they altered as they matured. Both wrote works in 1681: Blow, an ode for the New Year, 'Great Sir,

---

[34] The first three are in the *Purcell Society Edition*, xi, the others in xxiv.
[35] Ibid., xv, p. 1.
[36] Ibid., iv.

the joy of all our hearts',[37] and Purcell, a welcome song or ode for
the King's return from Windsor in August, 'Swifter Isis, swifter
flow'.[38] Blow's work is still of moderate length, though it is slightly
more extensive than any earlier odes. He still relies on a limited
tonal palette for individual words and the overall scheme, but he
shows a greater sense of co-ordination of the various components,
and a sense of a larger individual section within the complete ode.
It is not simply a question, as it is with Cooke and Humfrey, of a
solo repeated by a chorus or alternating with it. There are larger
sections which consist of a variety of elements: for instance, a solo
expands into a duet followed by a chorus and then a ritornello. The
four-part string texture is made slightly more interesting than in
earlier works by the mixture of quasi-counterpoint and homophony
and the more complex, syncopated rhythms. The instrumental introduction is more substantial than earlier ones; influence of the
French overture is evident in the dignified opening section which
leads into a longer one, in binary form, and with imitative texture
at the opening. The solos are more complicated and ornamented in
line and at least one, 'The British Legion through the World was
fam'd', foreshadows the kind of rumbustious arioso for the bass
which was very soon to become a regular ingredient, expected,
necessary, and often one of a number of such solos or duets. There
are still plenty of recurring rhythmic patterns in triple metre, repeated somewhat monotonously in some of the solos and choruses:

Ex. 5

Then long may he live and long may he reign By

whom we are blest with so happ-y a chain.

[37] Brit. Lib. Add. MS. 33287, fo. 115.
[38] *Purcell Society Edition*, xv, p. 24.

A new element, and one which like the arioso was to become expected, was the ground bass movement, the counter-tenor's 'Of
you, Great Sir, Our Druids Spake', written above a characteristic
Italianate moving bass:

Ex. 6

and incorporating a variety of elements, vocal and instrumental.

Purcell's ode reveals its indebtedness to Blow's in overall structure and some of its elements. It is slightly longer and shows
greater variety in the combination of forces; the text offers greater
possibilities for musical suggestion, as in the case of music for the
approaching royal barge, with its martial ground bass:

Ex. 7

The tonal scheme is limited and though there is still reliance on
tonic and dominant alternation, the harmony is more colourful.
The various elements are combined in a more imaginative way than
Blow's; short choral interjections are used to make a particular
point. Imitation, though still only rudimentary, plays a more significant role in the second part of the 'French overture' introduction.
Triple rhythm recurs throughout the ode, but Purcell manages to
inject variety into such movements by subtle variants of the
rhythm, usually motivated by his particular sensitivity to the textual
stress, and unexpected harmonies: 'Your Augusta he charms with
no lesser delight, Who tells he the King *keeps his court* here
tonight.' There is the same sort of bass arioso solo as in Blow ('But
with great devotion meet') and a ground bass movement ('The
king, whose presence, like the spring') on an Italianate bass similar
to Ex. 6. Even at this early stage Purcell had a larger conception of
the genre than Blow, revealed in the fuller orchestration and
greater length of the whole and of individual parts. The extension

is both of sonority and duration. His more acute dramatic sense comes through in his imaginative setting of the various verses and their organization, building up progressively to a rousing end as the final cadence is approached.

Adequate, indeed effective, though these works are, there is something tentative about them. The contrast with their more mature works is striking. By the end of their series both Blow and Purcell were manifesting the confident control which comes from experience. Purcell's mature style can be seen in the 1694 ode for Queen Mary, 'Come, ye sons of art away'.[39] The large-scale conception already present in the early works, is here significantly manifested in the enlarged resources rather than in extended length. Trumpets and oboes are added to the strings both in the symphony—later borrowed for *The Indian Queen*—and in the choruses. Although the work is long when compared with the earliest odes, here there is compression; obviously Purcell has recognized the power of economy. In addition, his style is much more interesting. There is much more drive and variety—for example in both the brilliant voice-part of the bass aria 'These are the sacred charms' and the vigorous *basso ostinato*. And there are effective uses of key change, though overall the ode remains firmly in the same key. There are the usual triple rhythms, but the trochaic pattern has given way to other patterns subtly integrated with the text, as in the superb final chorus. Repetition of words as well as of entire sections contributes to the dramatic intensity. Furthermore the text is underlined by the appropriate timbres of accompanying instruments—for example, the recorder with counter-tenor—and by conventional though effectively placed florid ornaments. Power is combined with subtlety, *joie de vivre* with depth. These transcend the spirit of the earlier works and pervade most of the odes for Queen Mary. It is the spirit of the fuller anthem or the 'Te Deum' which prevails here, the sort of large-scale church composition which Purcell had written and which Handel was later to copy in similar works, notably his Coronation anthems. This is no longer the miniature style of the Biblical dialogues or early odes, but one adumbrating the splendour of the mid-eighteenth century.

Though to a lesser degree, Blow's later odes, such as the St Cecilia Ode for 1691,[40] reflect the same trends: consolidation, economy, effective repetition, extended scope, splendour, and clarification of movements. Blow never achieves the acuteness of

---

[39] Ibid., xxiv, p. 87.
[40] Miniature score, ed. Maurice Bevan (London, 1980).

dramatic expression which is the hallmark of a Purcell ode; yet these later odes are not the uneasy, uneven works of the inexperienced composer but those of a confident artist, writing something which by then must have become second nature. Neither he nor Purcell was ever heedless of new stylistic fashions. In the later odes there is a tendency towards clarification of sections as in later Venetian opera. However, there is a fundamental difference in detail; in Italy, recitative and aria were beginning to be clearly demarcated and opera was beginning to consist of a sequence of scenes made up from these two elements: the so-called 'number opera'. In the odes the clarification lay in series of self-contained solos, rather than solo sections, combined with a variety of other musical elements into a larger, more heterogeneous area. As for recitative, the English declamatory style was related to both the French and Italian in its careful declamation, but always retained a distinctive flavour thanks to the fundamental differences in linguistic rhythm and syntax.

Blow's already mentioned skill as a writer of solos, at which he became even more adept, and changing stylistic trends account for the particular arrangement in the ode for 1 January 1700,[41] an arrangement which had gradually emerged as the ode developed, particularly in Blow's hands. This ode 'Appear, appear in all thy pomp' which we may compare with Purcell's 'Come, ye sons of art', consists of four solos of distinctive types, framed by choruses which recur within the ode. They are a gentle, tender, 'indulgent' F major solo for tenor in a gently lilting triple rhythm; a 'summoning' C major solo on 'assemble' for counter-tenor with vigorous, semiquaver movement; a pensive and intense D minor solo for counter-tenor with emotive words 'wailing, groaning, gasping, dying' set to a predictable descending melody in 3/2, notated in semibreves; and a B flat jig with a minimum of text and a maximum of repetitions:

Ex. 8

Here we have a clear division into well-defined aria types, each distinguished by a particular and, by that time, characteristic key, rhythm, melody, harmony, orchestration, and voice part. These are the song types which became the mainstay of eighteenth-century Italian opera which Handel used.

Surveying the ode from its early years to this point one can see how a systematized musical language and structure gradually emerged from a rather amorphous, tentative form which was hardly more than an extended dialogue with choral interjections. The ground was prepared for the eighteenth-century ode composers who relied upon sequences of solos and duets expressing individual, specific affects. They generally restricted choruses to the beginning or the end, and instrumental sections either to the opening or to instrumental ritornellos and accompaniments which asserted the *Affekt*.

### HANDEL'S BIRTHDAY ODE

Unfortunately the later ode-composers—Daniel Purcell, John Eccles (1668–1735), Jeremiah Clarke (*c.*1673–1707), and the rest—were not of Blow's calibre. Early in the eighteenth century the composition of the annual Court odes became one of the duties of the Master of the King's Music, who was then Eccles, and it long remained so. But in 1713 Eccles was temporarily eclipsed by Handel's 'Ode for the Birthday of Queen Anne'[42] which was performed at the Court on 6 February. This was one of Handel's earliest attempts at setting English words and, as in the *Te Deum and Jubilate* for the Peace of Utrecht composed at exactly the same time,[43] he obviously sought a model for an acceptable 'English style' in the work of Purcell. The very first number, 'Eternal source of light divine' for counter-tenor with trumpet obbligato:

Ex. 9

[42] *Georg Friedrich Händels Werke*, ed. Friedrich Chrysander, xlvi.
[43] See Vol. V, pp. 542–4.

the ground-bass-founded tenor and bass duet 'Let rolling streams', the powerful bass solo 'Let envy then conceal her head', all proclaim their Purcellian origins. Each of the seven numbers ends with a choral setting of the couplet:

The day that gave great Anna birth
Who fix'd a lasting peace on earth

but with different music in the five intermediate movements. In the Queen Anne celebration we have a link—admittedly slender—between the Purcellian ode and the Handelian English oratorio.

## (b) ORATORIO AND RELATED FORMS

*By* ANTHONY HICKS *and* GERALD ABRAHAM

FROM 1732 onwards theatrical seasons in London were enlivened by a species of work new to the British public. As a vocal entertainment dominated by self-contained solo arias and recitative and filling a whole evening it was closely related to opera, but it had two distinctive features. In addition to the solo vocal items there were substantial choruses in which a professional ecclesiastical choir reinforced the soloists, and the whole work—though presented in a theatre and often dramatic in nature—was given without action and generally without specialized costumes or décor. The composer responsible for introducing the new form was George Frideric Handel, German-born, but mainly resident in England since 1710 and a naturalized British subject since 1727. Although a few other British composers took an interest in producing comparable works, their contribution during Handel's lifetime remained slight. Not until Handel's death did the new form establish an existence in Britain independent of its inventor, and by then it had become sufficiently restricted in scope to permit accurate use of the usual designation 'English oratorio'.

The question of terminology is unfortunately no mere quibble, because the application of the term 'oratorio' to works not so considered by their composers has led to persistent misunderstanding, the roots of which go back to Handel's own time. At first Handel saw oratorios—works on sacred subjects—simply as a sub-set of a wider genre of theatre works without action, for which no adequate descriptive term has ever existed. Within six weeks of first public presentation of his oratorio *Esther* in 1732 Handel revived his pastoral opera *Acis and Galatea*[44] in a version without action. During the next seven years, while Handel continued to compose and promote normal Italian opera, two other works (*Il Parnasso in Festa* and *Giove in Argo*) were produced in the same way as the 1732 *Acis*, and performances of English oratorios were interspersed with odes, an Italian oratorio and the happily unclassifiable *L'Allegro, Il Penseroso ed il Moderato*. Even after the final abandonment of Italian opera in 1741 and the encouragement of successful oratorio productions in Dublin, Handel still did not devote himself to sacred subjects: *Semele* (1744) and *Hercules* (1745) were both based on classical myth. By this time, however, the London musical public were already associating the new genre with scripture and the Lenten season, and hence with piety and solemnity. Despite their high musical worth, *Semele* and *Hercules* were not appreciated and confusion as to their nature was at least partly to blame. The description of the presentation of *Semele* as 'after the manner of an oratorio' marked the beginning of the end of the

---

[44] See Vol. V, pp. 293–6.

wider possibilities of the new genre: it was becoming defined—and hence limited—by the characteristics of one of its sub-sets. To avoid pedantry and linguistic awkwardness the terms 'oratorio' and 'oratorio form' will appear in the rest of this chapter in reference to both sacred and secular works, but only in contexts where form and manner of presentation rather than subject matter are under consideration. In any case generic classification is not of vital importance.

## THE FIRST ENGLISH ORATORIO

English oratorio came into being quite suddenly with the composition and performance of Handel's *Esther*, probably in 1718. Whereas opera in England had had its own native development from the Stuart masque on the one hand and from continental models on the other, there was no parallel evolution of oratorio. On the face of it, this is surprising. Composers in the Restoration period were equally active in church and theatre, there was great interest in Italian music, and many continental musicians visited England. Some attempt on the lines of Carissimi's oratorios might have been expected, yet no English equivalents in fact appeared. As we have seen above, a repertory of dramatic sacred dialogues came into being—the most striking being Purcell's setting of the anonymous scena 'In guiltie night'[45]—but these seem to have been composed primarily for private delectation; they founded no line of succession and it makes no sense to regard them as embryonic oratorios.

The prime factor inhibiting early interest in English oratorio was surely the Protestant ethic. A work treating a sacred subject and smacking of theatricality was felt to be improper, and not merely because the theatre was associated with lewdness and profanity. There was also the suspicion of propaganda. At a time when religious conflicts were highly political, dramatic paraphrases of Biblical stories could be seen as undermining the Protestant stress on the plain word of God, finally revealed to every Englishman in the Authorized Version of the Bible. The furthest musicians could go was in the florid, French-influenced verse anthems favoured by Charles II, and some even found those irreverent. When Handel's oratorios came before the public in the 1730s the ideas of the early enlightenment had loosened the grip of religious fervour, but even so the relics of Puritanism influenced the manner of the theatrical

[45] See p. 7.

presentation of oratorio and caused open controversy over works setting specifically Biblical texts.

The original production of *Esther* seems to have been a purely private affair and caused no disturbance. Its circumstances are regrettably obscure, both the exact date and the venue being uncertain. According to the first published word-book (printed for a privately arranged revival in 1732) it 'was compos'd originally for the most noble James, Duke of Chandos . . . In the Year 1720' and this has been the accepted date since Burney gave it prominence. However, an important early copy of good provenance has the title 'The Oratorium Composed by George Frederick Handel Esquire in London, 1718'. The earlier date is the more likely, as it falls in the period from 1717 to early 1719 when Handel was certainly working at Cannons, the seat of James Brydges, Earl of Edgeware and (from April, 1719) Duke of Chandos. For Brydges Handel wrote eleven substantial anthems and a *Te Deum* as well as *Acis and Galatea*, all scored for a chorus without normal alto parts and a small orchestra without violas. (*Acis* was composed in May 1718, but the other works cannot be precisely dated.) *Esther* is similarly scored, though on a larger scale with the addition of a solo trumpet (a feature shared with the *Te Deum*), two horns, two bassoons (probably played by the oboists), a harp, and, in the last three choruses, a viola. The enlarged orchestra and the statement on the manuscript that London was the place of composition raises the possibility that London may also have been the place of the first performance. The Duke had a residence in Cavendish Square and could easily have arranged the première there or in private rooms. Until some clear evidence comes to hand, the time and place of the first hearing of an English oratorio must remain conjectural.

### TEXT AND MUSIC OF *ESTHER*

What motivated the creation of *Esther* is also unclear. The music itself provides some clues. Out of twenty numbers (excluding plain recitatives) ten are based substantially on items in Handel's setting of the Passion text by Barthold Brockes.[46] This appears to have been composed around 1716 and perhaps was performed under Handel's direction at Hamburg that year. As is clear from his work of the previous decade, Handel greatly disliked music being 'wasted' on single performances. His opera *Agrippina*, produced at Venice early in 1710, virtually anthologizes the compositions per-

[46] See Vol. V, pp. 660–2.

formed in other Italian centres during the previous three years, and the early London operas likewise plunder the same store. On the other hand the Passion setting has very few borrowings from earlier work (Handel may have thought his German colleagues would be familiar with his Italian compositions) and the existence of such a large body of new music must have given Handel an incentive to find a new context for it in England. The subject of the oratorio was undoubtedly suggested by the recent (1715) publication of a translation of Racine's sacred drama *Esther* made by Thomas Brereton. The play was well suited to oratorio adaptation as it included a number of choral interludes sung by a group of Israelite women (the play was written for a girls' college). They comment on the action in the manner of a Greek chorus but, being attendant upon Esther, are also involved in her fate and that of the Jewish people as a whole. The prayerful phraseology draws its inspiration from the Psalms, forming a fundamental model for the English oratorio chorus.

The anonymous author or authors of *Esther* (the libretto was attributed both to Pope and John Arbuthnot in Handel's lifetime but firm evidence for either is hard to come by) took over much of Brereton's language but hopelessly obscured the motivation that prompts the action. The various scenes are ill-balanced and the major solo numbers distributed with little regard to the comfort of the singers: in the central throne-room scene Ahasuerus has a duet and two substantial airs in immediate succession. The versification is often bizarre, particularly in the recitatives which are rhymed throughout in curiously irregular metrical patterns hard to parallel elsewhere in English verse; possibly they are an attempt to imitate the Italian *verso sciolto*. In short, the libretto shows every sign of having been thrown together without the authors having any clear idea of what sort of piece they were producing.

The music, too, displays considerable uncertainty of aim, though much of it is of high quality. In its original version *Esther* is divided into six scenes and plays for about two hours. After an overture (based on a trio sonata, not the usual Lullian model) the action begins abruptly: in an air without *da capo* Haman orders the persecution of the Jews captive in Persia and a chorus of bloodthirsty soldiers echo his commands. The *turba* choruses of the Passion are recalled, though in fact this particular chorus is not derived from them. By contrast, most of the remaining scenes seem rambling and over-extended. The airs generally have full *da capo* and are variable in interest, the best being those employing some special touch of orchestral colour, such as the exquisite 'Tune your harps' in which a serene oboe melody unfolds over plucked strings. The dramatic aptness of Haman's opening air is not resumed until the final scene, where his belated attempt at repentance (the fine arioso 'Turn not, O queen') is decisively rejected by Esther in the air 'Flatt'ring tongue, no more I hear thee', begun without preliminary ritornello. Finest of the choruses (which increase in weight as the oratorio proceeds) are 'Ye sons of Israel, mourn':

Ex. 10

a grief-laden siciliana foreshadowing many another of comparable intensity in later oratorios, and the powerful 'He comes to end our woes', enriched by the horns. (Perhaps these were the same instruments that rang out over the Thames during the water procession of 1717: there are many affinities between the chorus and the first Allegro of the Water Music.) The final chorus, 'The Lord our enemy has slain' is an amazing but somewhat regrettable example of Handel's occasional tendency to overwork his material (the conclusion of the Chandos *Te Deum* is another instance from this period). Fairly fast tempos are relentlessly maintained for nearly a quarter of an hour, and there are at least two false endings. It epitomizes the prodigal invention and structural ungainliness of the oratorio as a whole.

### THE CHAPEL ROYAL CONNECTION

In 1719 Handel was appointed as the leading composer and musical director of the Royal Academy of Music, founded to provide fashionable London with regular performances of Italian opera of the finest quality. There was no incentive, indeed hardly any opportunity, to repeat the experiment of *Esther*. The seed of English oratorio, though planted, remained dormant. Meanwhile, however, Handel was careful to maintain an interest in choral music through a connection with the choir of the Chapel Royal, an association of great importance for the later development of English oratorio. His first contact with members of the choir had come in 1713 with the composition and performance of the Utrecht *Te Deum and Jubilate*, but the connection seems to have lapsed with the death of Queen Anne the following year. It was resumed in 1723 when Handel was formally appointed 'Composer to His Majesty's Chapel Royal', apparently to allow him to supplement the work of the leading Chapel Royal composer William Croft with the writing of occasional anthems, mainly connected with the returns of George I from his visits to Hanover. In 1727 a number of significant events followed in quick succession. Handel became a naturalized British subject in February; George I died abroad in June; Croft fell ill and died taking the waters at Bath in August; King George II was crowned in October. Handel was perhaps in hope of succeeding Croft, who also held the posts of Chapel Royal organist and Master of the Children, and may even obtained his naturalization in anticipation. If so, he was disappointed, for Maurice Greene became first organist and composer while Bernard Gates became Master of the Children. Nevertheless Handel was allowed to compose all the new music for the Coronation and justified himself in four masterly anthems, perfectly proportioned and their sonorities exactly calculated for maximum impact in a large building. Unfortunately the performances at the Westminster Abbey ceremony were a shambles, with the result that, as with the Brockes Passion, music of great worth passed into limbo. Once again Handel had an incentive to seek a new context for it.

GATES'S PERFORMANCES

The chain of events which finally brought English oratorio before the public at large was begun by Bernard Gates. He had known Handel since 1713 (when he sang a solo in the Utrecht *Jubilate*) and the two men must have co-operated closely during the preparations for the 1727 Coronation. Early in 1732 Gates took the remarkable step of presenting three staged performances of *Esther*, using the children of the Chapel Royal for both soloists and chorus. (John Randall, later Professor of Music at Cambridge, sang Esther, while John Beard, Handel's future leading tenor, was

Priest of the Israelites.) These were given privately at the Crown and Anchor Tavern in the Strand, the first two for the Philharmonic Society on 23 February and 1 March, the third for the Academy of Ancient Music on 3 March. The date of the first performance—Handel's forty-seventh birthday—strongly suggests a deliberate tribute to the composer, as does the lack of any post-Restoration precedent for the use of the Chapel Royal choir in this way. What prompted Gates's gesture at this particular moment is not certain, but the performance for the Academy of Ancient Music is significant: it was the first time they had promoted any music by Handel. Founded in 1726 'chiefly for grave ancient vocal music' (but also performing new music written in older forms) the Academy had been largely dominated by a pro-Bononcini faction and Handel had avoided it. However in 1731 came the famous affair in which a madrigal supposedly written for the Academy by Bononcini was exposed as a composition of Antonio Lotti. Gates was one of the judges in the matter and one of the signatories to the letter in which the Academy found against Bononcini. Maurice Greene, who had championed the other side, was obliged to resign and, taking the choir of St Paul's Cathedral with him, founded a rival academy at the Devil Tavern, soon to be the venue for the first attempts at English oratorio by native composers. From then on, Handel's music was regularly included in the Academy's programmes.

The manner of Gates's production is of considerable interest. The original word-book explains that 'Mr Bernard Gates . . . together with a number of Voices from the Choirs of St James's, and Westminster, join'd in the Chorus's after the Manner of the Ancients, being placed between the Stage and the Orchestra'. This avoided the difficulty of an acting chorus without detriment to music or drama. Viscount Perceval confided to his diary after the first performance: 'This oratoria or religious opera is exceeding fine, and the company were highly pleased, some of the parts being well performed.' Burney, relaying information given to him by Randall and Barrow, two of the boy singers, says: 'Mr Handel himself was present at one of these representations, and having mentioned it to the Princess Royal [Princess Anne, one of Handel's pupils] Her Royal Highness was pleased to express a desire to see it exhibited in action at the Opera House in the Hay-Market, by the same young performers; but Dr. Gibson, then bishop of London, would not grant permission for its being represented on that stage, even with books in the children's hands.' Nevertheless *Esther* duly appeared at the King's Theatre, though in an extensively revised version. The advertisement for the performance read as follows:

The Sacred Story of ESTHER: an Oratorio in English. Formerly compos'd by Mr Handel, and now revised by him, with several Additions, and to be performed by a great number of the best voices and Instruments. N.B. There will be no Action on the Stage, but the House will be fitted up in a decent Manner, for the Audience. The Musick to be disposed after the Manner of the Coronation Service.

Thus began the series of Handel's theatre productions without action that were later to settle into 'English oratorio'. Burney's account has sometimes been interpreted as indicating that the manner of the presentation was entirely due to the Bishop's ban, but this is to stretch the evidence too far. A plain reading of Burney suggests he is merely speaking of a repetition of the Gates production on a public stage, and he makes no mention of one other significant event. In mid-April another performance of *Esther* was advertised for the 20th of that month at York Buildings, Villiers Street, stress being laid on the fact that the work was 'Never Perform'd in Publick before'. The unknown promoters of this production were clearly acting without Handel's authority (having presumably acquired a pirated copy of the score) and were effectively denying him the public première of his own work.

The new version of *Esther*, first given on 2 May, was Handel's reply. While the Bishop's predilections may well have been a factor in the avoidance of an acted version, a number of other considerations must also have played a part, notably the need to mount the production quickly near the end of the theatrical season and, above all, to make use of the Coronation anthems, which would have been hard to accommodate in meaningful action. Whatever the motivation, the result proved very successful, the new *Esther* being repeated five times on consecutive opera nights (Tuesdays and Saturdays). The new music was partly based on earlier material, including the Coronation anthems 'My heart is inditing' (complete) and 'Zadok the priest' (with a new text, the second section being cut). Dramatically the main addition was a new scene at the start, explaining a little of the background to the story, though by no means enough for full understanding. The final chorus was re-written to accommodate a six-part chorus and extended solo Alleluias for the alto castrato Senesino (who sang Ahasuerus); it still seems over-long, but has more sense of direction than the original. Overall, the 1732 *Esther* is better balanced in its mixture of solo arias and choruses, but at the expense of greater dramatic diffuseness and an even more disconcerting medley of musical styles. Its prime importance is historical, in that it established the viability of a new genre.

## ORATORIO, ODE, AND SERENATA: 1732–1741

Within a month Handel was faced with a second act of piracy. *Acis and Galatea* was announced for performance at the New Theatre in the Haymarket 'with all the Grand Chorus's . . . being the first Time it ever was performed in a Theatrical Way'.[47] Handel's response could only be as before: a new version of *Acis* to render the original out of date. Again the advertisements for Handel's revival specified 'no action on the Stage', but a standing set was promised of 'Rocks, Groves, Fountains and Grotto's; amongst which will be disposed a Chorus of Nymphs and Shepherds, Habits, and every other Decoration suited to the Subject'. As the chorus in this case consisted merely of the soloists reinforced by an ensemble drawn from the actor-singers who regularly performed in the London theatres, the decision to give the performance without action had nothing to do with episcopal decree. The new *Acis*, described as a Serenata, was an extraordinary conflation of the large cantata *Aci, Galatea e Polifemo* (written in Naples in 1708) and the Cannons pastoral; other Italian cantatas, the Brockes Passion, and the Birthday Ode for Queen Anne also provided material. Mostly the language was Italian, many numbers from the Cannons version being sung in translation. This was a concession to the Italian opera singers, especially Senesino and Bertolli, whose treatment of the English language in *Esther* had come in for ribald criticism.[48] Indefensible by any artistic standards, the 1732 *Acis* was nevertheless enjoyed by the public. It was thus an important influence on Handel's decision in subsequent seasons to allow a mixture of languages whenever it seemed advantageous, and to promote comparatively undemanding non-acted Italian works alongside the more solemn delights of English oratorio.

## ORATORIO AT COVENT GARDEN

The next season saw various developments. A new theatre opened at Covent Garden on 7 December 1732. Other composers started to take an interest in oratorio. In September or October Maurice Greene wrote for his new-founded Apollo Society a choral

---

[47] See Vol. V, p. 296.
[48] See Winton Dean, *Handel's Dramatic Oratorios and Masques* (London, 1959), p. 207.

work simply described as a setting of 'Part of the Song of Deborah and Barak paraphras'd', which could easily be thought of as a short oratorio.[49] Though it was hardly an attempt to rival Handel's large-scale public productions, the fact that Handel produced a *Deborah* of his own within six months suggests he was moved to put Greene in his place. More ostensible rivalry came from the Flemish composer William Defesch, or de Fesch, (1687–1761), recently arrived in London from Antwerp. His *Judith* (to a libretto by William Huggins) was given at Lincoln's Inn Fields in February 1733 after some difficulties involving the singer Cecilia Young, who (according to newspaper announcements by Defesch) feigned sickness to avoid fulfilling an undertaking to sing. The music is mostly lost, the only sections extant being Judith's air 'Gayly smiling' in Act II:

Ex. 11

---

[49] See below, p. 65.

and two and half bars of a chorus of Assyrians in Act I visible in Hogarth's famous engraving of one of the rehearsals. The libretto is conceived quite operatically, but it is not clear to what extent it was given with action, if at all. Act I deals with Holofernes' decision to take Bethulia and his punishment of the Ammonite captain Achior for predicting the ultimate victory of the God of Israel. In Act II Judith rebukes the despondent Bethulians and resolves to deal with Holofernes herself. Her plan is carried out in Act III: Holofernes is beheaded while asleep and the oratorio ends quickly with a Grand Chorus and March as his head is paraded on a spear. Though the libretto is well-shaped and keeps the story moving, it illustrates one of the dangers inherent in oratorio, that of over-literal dramatization. Holofernes' decapitation is presented directly. According to the stage directions, Judith 'cuts off his head . . . pulls down the canopy of his bed . . . comes forward . . . puts the head into her basket'. Whether an audience witnesses a simulation of this scene or is merely required to imagine it while the singer declaims, the result is equally embarrassing. Defesch's *Judith*, for whatever reason, had no success and except for a solitary revival for the composer's benefit at the Crown and Anchor on 29 February 1740, was not heard again.

## HANDEL'S *DEBORAH*

The advertisement for Handel's response to Greene and Defesch, *Deborah*, affirmed it would be 'the last Dramatick Performance that will be exhibited at the King's Theatre till after Easter', showing that oratorio was still regarded as a slightly aberrant feature of the opera season. In fact only the first performance (17 March 1733) came before Easter, five others and a short revival of *Esther* afterwards; but this was the start of an association of oratorio with the season of Lent which became firmer in subsequent years. The music of *Deborah* shows that Handel was still thinking of oratorio as a display case for the fruits of past labours rather than an art form in its own right: eight items from the Brockes Passion not used in *Esther* or the 1732 *Acis* were pressed into service, as were the two Coronation anthems not used in *Esther*, and additional material came from the Birthday Ode, the 1707 *Il Trionfo del Tempo* and the big choruses of 'Dixit Dominus'. (As Handel went through the score of *Il Trionfo* he would have been reminded of the curious sonata for organ and orchestra and the following aria with organ obbligato. The latter inspired the similarly accompanied *Deborah* air 'In the battle' while the former sowed the seed of the

genre that was shortly to become a special feature of oratorio performances—the organ concerto.) In the newly composed numbers
for *Deborah* Handel moves a little way from *da capo* form: two
virtuoso airs for Barak (sung by Senesino) retain it as does Jael's
last air (her only original music, apart from recitative), but the
other new numbers for solo voices, all of which are of high quality,
are through-composed. The opening chorus—newly composed out
of old materials—deploys the trumpets and drums and eight-part
chorus much in the manner of the Coronation anthems, but there is
a fresh note in the minor-key choruses, especially 'O hear thy lowly
servant's prayer', where the overlapping phrases passing from one
to another of the eight voices build to a powerful and moving
climax:

Ex. 12

No overture seems to have been used at the early performances of *Deborah*, although at least two were used during later revivals.

### *ATHALIA*

With *Athalia*, first performed as part of the Oxford degree ceremonies in the Sheldonian Theatre on 11 July 1733, Handelian oratorio took a major step forward in terms of musical integrity and dramatic consistency. Samuel Humphreys, who had supplied the words for the additions to *Esther* and written the libretto for *Deborah*, was again required to exercise his slender talents. His source was Racine's second Biblical play *Athalie*, a natural choice and one that could provide strong meat for a composer with a notable dramatic flair. His stock of earlier choral music largely used up, Handel was compelled to originality (the few borrowings from the Brockes Passion are trivial and fully absorbed) but Humphreys had preserved enough of Racine to ensure that not much coercion was needed. *Athalia* begins with a sparkling overture in the Italian fast-slow-fast form. (During this period Handel avoided the standard French form for oratorio, while rigorously maintaining it for operas). The first scene finds the Israelites celebrating the giving of the law. After Josabeth's opening air—*da capo*, and somewhat undistinguished for its position—a new flexibility in the use of the chorus is immediately apparent. Four numbers follow in which solo and chorus combine in different ways. The second, 'Tyrants would in impious throngs' is the most striking: it begins as a virtuoso soprano air but the chorus suddenly interrupts with the cry 'Tyrants! ye in vain conspire' and the exchange continues until all voices unite for the conclusion. Joad's lament 'O Lord whom we adore' consists of the first and second sections of a *da capo* air, but instead of the return to the start the chorus take over, raising the music to greater intensity. All these devices, as well as delighting the ear by their variety, make a dramatic point in expressing the unity of the true believers of Israel under their rightful leaders. The role for the chorus in the next scene (where they appear as Athalia's followers) is as sharply observed, though quite different. Two brisk and tuneful attempts to dispel the queen's forebodings contrast pointedly with the unsettling blend of recitative and air in which Athalia expresses her fears. Accompanied recitative and arioso passages are of special note throughout the oratorio, quickening the dramatic pace and often creating a sense of physical location. The sequence that opens Act III is especially fine. Joad's arioso:

Ex. 13

evokes the incense-laden atmosphere of the temple, the solemn entry of the chorus brings the ranks of the priests into view, and the whole scene comes before the mind's eye as the chorus join in Joad's ensuing air. Characterization is clear and consistent: the neat sketches of the boy-king Joas and the shifty apostate priest Nathan are as memorable as the broadly drawn portrait of Athalia herself.

### IL PARNASSO IN FESTA

Though Handel can hardly have been unsure of the qualities of *Athalia* he chose not to bring it to London the following season in the form in which it had been composed. Instead he converted it into an Italian serenata on a totally different subject, *Il Parnasso in festa*. (Metastasio would have called it a *festa teatrale*: it was

Handel's only exercise in that form.) Various factors influenced this curious metamorphosis. Having lost most of his singers to the rival Opera of the Nobility, Handel had a new company with two good castratos, Carestino and Scalzi, unfamiliar with the English language. The marriage of the Princess Royal, planned for November 1733, eventually took place the following April and required celebration, but an oratorio dealing with the overthrow of a usurping monarch was not entirely suited to the occasion. Arranging the music to a new Italian text was the logical course. *Il Parnasso* is by no means the hasty pasticcio it has been said to be. The text was prepared with great skill to suit the mood of the *Athalia* items as well as syllabic matching of the notes. It would be hard to say that the exuberant F major chorus representing the attempt of Athalia's attendants to console their queen is not equally suited to the Tritons and Nereids celebrating the marriage of Peleus and Thetis:

Ex. 14

And there is sufficient original music in *Il Parnasso* to justify its occasional performance in its own right. The solo and chorus 'Non tardate, fauni ancora' is the longest and finest of Handel's nostalgic evocations of pastoral contentment, while the finale exhilarates with its mezzo-soprano solos of Paganini-like virtuosity.

*Athalia* came to London during the next season, in March 1735, but in a substantially revised version; many numbers had been reset to compensate for the use of the originals in *Il Parnasso*. With revivals of *Esther* and *Deborah* the performances formed a solid block of Lenten oratorio. A significant innovation was the introduction of organ concertos, usually—but by no means always—placed between the acts. These were immediately popular; from now on advertisements for the oratorios would invariably make special mention of concertos to be played. Later Handel often made deliberate provision for the concertos during composition, and many became specifically associated with particular oratorios.

## VARIETY OF FORMS: 1736–40

With this 1735 season Handel had actually arrived at what would become the standard pattern of his oratorio seasons from 1743 onwards. No such pattern was settled at this moment, however; for the rest of the 1730s Handel continued experimenting with a wide variety of forms. In the 1735–6 season he abandoned opera to his rivals and produced nothing until February, when the new work was a setting of the later and longer of Dryden's two Cecilian odes, *Alexander's Feast*. A new opera, *Atalanta*, designed to celebrate the marriage of the Prince of Wales, did however follow for a short season in May and June 1736. For the next two seasons opera was resumed, and English oratorio took a back seat. The only new non-operatic work in 1737 was a thoroughly recomposed version of Handel's first Italian oratorio *Il trionfo del tempo e del disinganno*,[50] retitled *Il trionfo del tempo e della verità*. *Il Parnasso* reappeared and *Esther* and *Alexander's Feast* were revived, but there were only two performances of *Esther* and a number of Italian arias were incorporated in deference to yet another company of Italian singers. A plan to revive *Deborah* was abandoned. In 1738 no non-operatic works at all were given; instead Handel put on a concert of miscellaneous works and excerpts from *Deborah* and *Athalia*, calling it simply 'An Oratorio'. It was specifically a benefit night for the composer to make up the losses on the operas and, as such, did very well. Subscriptions invited for a further opera season did not materialize. Only this bleak rejection of Handel's normal mode of musical expression for over thirty years seems to have forced him back to oratorio. Happily it also brought a special concentration of mind: the two new works composed at the end of 1738 were *Saul* and *Israel in Egypt*, both powerful masterpieces breaking fresh ground. The lure of the Italian language remained, though: the 1739 season ended with *Giove in Argo*, a semi-staged pastoral described as a 'Dramatic Composition' and mainly a pasticcio from the operas, included the as yet unfinished *Imeneo*, abandoned by Handel in favour of *Saul*. The following year Handel gave two short seasons of English works at Lincoln's Inn Fields (leaving operatic production to a new company under Pescetti at the Little Theatre in the Haymarket). Lacking an Italian company, he kept wholly to English works. On 22 November 1739 (St Cecilia's Day) *Alexander's Feast* was revived with a new setting of Dryden's other Cecilian ode ('From harmony, from heavenly harmony'); *Acis and Galatea*, at last restored to its all-English Cannons version (with one additional chorus) followed to end this pre-Christmas season. In Lent came a new English secular work *L'Allegro, il penseroso ed*

---

[50] See Vol. V, p. 342.

*il moderato*, taking its place with revivals of *Saul*, *Israel in Egypt*, and *Acis*. Still at Lincoln's Inn the next season, Handel made one last attempt at Italian opera with *Deidamia* and the completed *Imeneo*; but two performances of the latter and three of the former were all that could be justified. Stuck with another Italian company, Handel had to resort to giving revivals of *L'Allegro*, *Acis*, and *Saul* bilingually. The writing on the wall was now in sharp focus. At the age of 56 Handel either had to adapt himself to new trends in opera or concentrate on English oratorio. A letter to Jennens suggests he had already opted for the second course before leaving for Dublin in November 1741. The great success of his oratorios in that city, culminating in the première of *Messiah* in April 1742, served to confirm that judgement and set the course for his musical activity for the rest of his life.

## ALEXANDER'S FEAST

The six non-operatic works of the period 1736–40 must all be briefly surveyed; their variety prohibits generalization. In *Alexander's Feast* Dryden avoided the instrumental catalogue of earlier Cecilian odes (including his own) in favour of a vigorous description of a scene from classical antiquity. At the feast celebrating the defeat of the Persians the musician Timotheus shows how he can control the moods of Alexander through his playing and singing. St Cecilia herself appears somewhat belatedly in Dryden's concluding stanzas, more as the patroness of harmony and counterpoint than of music in general; the poet concludes that she should 'divide the crown' with Timotheus. Setting a text shorter than usual Handel, as in *Esther*, occasionally stretches his material more than it will bear (with the repetitions of 'None but the brave' in the first chorus, for example, or the finale of Part 1 with its *da capo* air framed by two performances of a chorus already making very thorough use of its themes). Some airs ('War he sung', 'With ravish'd ears', 'The princes applaud') are perhaps a shade too dependent on sequential repetitions. But there is no denying the quality of the rest, and, as ever, it is those moments where the emotions can be most clearly personalized, as in the lament 'He sung Darius':

Ex. 15

that call out the best in Handel. The orchestral colouring is vivid and apt. A harp concerto[51] imitates Timotheus's lyre-playing after the recitative 'Timotheus plac'd on high'; a solo violin points the tragic fate of Darius, a solo trumpet puts a brilliant edge on the summons to Alexander to avenge the army slain by the Persians: and at least three bassoons delineating eerie harmonies depict the 'ghastly band' of Grecian ghosts rising to demand vengeance:

Ex. 16

---

[51] Brit. Lib. Roy. 20. g. 12, which became the Organ Concerto, Op. 4, no. 6.

Any suspicion of anti-climax in Dryden's conclusion is banished in Handel's setting. In the accompanied recitative 'Thus long ago', eked out by quiet phrases on a pair of recorders, the vision of antiquity is gently allowed to fade. A solemn chorus (marked by a startling suspension to illustrate the harmonic enlargement of 'the former narrow bounds') leads to a well-wrought fugue ('arts unknown before'). All this is capped by an even more skilful display of contrapuntal expertise: a chorus based on four interwoven subjects. Handel expanded the ode slightly with some verses supplied by Newburgh Hamilton (taken from Hamilton's own Cecilian ode of 1720). This additional chorus, ending with a cheerful 6/8 tune, brings down the curtain pleasantly in the manner of an operatic *coro* and is not to be despised.[52]

## IL TRIONFO REWORKED

The 1737 *Il Trionfo del tempo* is a slighter, less spectacular, piece though by no means deserving of the obscurity to which it has been condemned by inadequate publication. Handel thoroughly re-worked the material taken from his 1707 setting of Panfili's libretto[53] and wrote new music for many arias as well as adding choruses. The allegorical characters develop some vestiges of personality, especially the light-headed Bellezza (Beauty), brought by the admonitions of Tempo (Time) and Disinganno (Enlightenment) to a mature consideration of her own transience. Handel maintains a light touch throughout and Beauty's early arias even have a trace of skittishness, a rare but not unwelcome quality in oratorio:

Ex. 17

[52] On Handel's various revisions for later performances, see Donald Burrows, 'Handel and *Alexander's Feast*', *Musical Times*, cxxiii (1982), p. 252, and idem, 'The Composition and First Performance of Handel's *Alexander's Feast*', *Music & Letters*, lxiv (1983), p. 206.
[53] See Vol. V, p. 342.

## SAUL

With *Saul* Handel returned to full-scale drama, producing a tragic epic surpassing *Athalia* in its immediacy and power. Thanks partly to a good libretto by Charles Jennens, whose structural sense compensates for occasional lapses into bathetic verse, Handel was able not merely to make each musical number apt to the dramatic situation but also to show a clear development in the character of Saul. Running in parallel is a depiction of the growing disillusion of the Israelite people, who, impersonated by the chorus, emerge as a character in their own right. An especially effective innovation was the use of carefully placed instrumental symphonies to denote the passing of time; two—the processional 'carillon' symphony and the noisy representation of the battle on Gilboa—are also descriptive. Airs with *da capo* are reduced to four, two of which have middle sections based on new material in contrasting keys and tempos. There are also two strophic songs, one of which is interrupted by a solo for another character, so that the dramatic pace is not relaxed. To his normal orchestral resources Handel added three trombones and *carillons* bring the entire ensemble together just once, at the climax of the scene in which the Israelite women unthinkingly contrast David's ten thousands slain with Saul's thousands. In six bars of accompanied recitative Saul's terrible jealousy rises to the surface, foreshadowing the tragedy to come:

Ex. 18

The ensuing entry of full orchestra and chorus redoubling David's praises is one of the most stunning moments in his dramatic music.

A further feature of *Saul* is its tonal unity. The overture, the symphonies, and the opening and closing choruses are in C major, the main key centre. The gloomy relatives C minor and F minor, hinted at in Ex. 18, dominate the scene at Endor and the start of the Elegy. The latter, however, progresses to the remoteness of E major for the final and most personal section of the lament, 'In sweetest harmony'. This in itself is a skilfully organized blend of solo and chorus. A soprano begins what at first seems like a regular da capo air:

Ex. 19

but at the close of what would be the middle section it is the chorus who take up the threnody in the home key. Suddenly David enters for his own tribute, chilling the music into the minor:

Ex. 20

and poignantly delaying the final choral climax. A few of the airs in *Saul* fall below the level of the best, and the neat characterization of Saul's haughty daughter Merab is not sustained after the first scene, but these are the only weaknesses. With hindsight we can feel that Handel should have settled there and then on the dramatic oratorio as the perfect vehicle for his talents; but there were further paths to explore.

*ISRAEL IN EGYPT*

Just one month after completing *Saul* Handel finished his oddest work, *Israel in Egypt*. This was the first oratorio to be based on a text compiled, anthem-like, from Biblical verses arranged to form a loose narrative. The initial motive for composing it was probably a desire by Handel to make use of the extended anthem he had composed for the funeral of Queen Caroline in December 1737. (He had toyed with the idea of incorporating most of it in *Saul* as the lament for Saul and Jonathan.) The text of the anthem itself was an ingenious compilation from all parts of the Bible. A few adjustments served to turn it into Part 1 of *Israel in Egypt*, with the title 'The Lamentations of the Israelites over the Death of Joseph'. Part 2 (composed last) was called 'Exodus' and dealt with the Ten Plagues and the release of the Israelites from bondage, while Part 3 'Moses' Song', was a setting of their hymn of thanksgiving (Exodus xv, 1–21). Handel followed the example of the anthem in the newly composed parts by concentrating on the chorus, but otherwise there is little attempt at stylistic consistency. The opening chorus of Part 2 ('And the children of Israel sigh'd') is restrained enough to start, restoring the mood of exalted mourning temporarily banished by Handel's performance of the F major organ concerto (no. 2 of the 'Second Set') in the interval; but the gradual division of the chorus into two four-part groups soon hints that the normal vocal deployment of the anthem is to be left behind. Startling confirmation comes with the chorus 'He spake the word'. Here Handel uses, for the first time since his Italian days, a full-scale *cori spezzati* technique. There follows a dazzling display of virtually every kind of choral writing, only seven solos and ducts (apart from plain recitative) being interposed between a total of 28 choral numbers. The latter include highly original choral recitatives, themselves greatly varied in manner. In 'He sent a thick darkness' the terrible night of the ninth plague is graphically depicted by the shifting harmonies on bassoons and low strings and the breaking up of the chorus into individual voices, as if they had lost sight of each other. In 'He rebuked the Red Sea', on the other hand, the full eight-part chorus and orchestra are impacted into mighty declamatory chords. It all proved too much for the public, with the result that the second performance of *Israel in Egypt* was 'shortened, and intermixed with Songs'. Handel gave only two more performances before 1756, when a 'new' first part (largely compiled from *Solomon* and the *Occasional Oratorio*) was provided.

The sudden emphasis on the chorus is not the only remarkable feature of *Israel in Egypt*. There is also the question of the large amount of 'borrowing' or re-use of music by other composers that the work contains. As Handel's borrowings are by no means confined to his oratorios a general discussion of the matter would be out of place here, but *Israel* is a special case. The amount of borrowing (involving sixteen numbers out of thirty-three, discounting repeats and plain recitatives) is itself unusual, but even odder is the comparatively antiquated style of Handel's sources, which gives a

distinct flavour of the antique to the work as a whole. The unaltered choral adaptation of an organ canzona by J. C. Kerll for the
chorus 'Egypt was glad' must have astonished musical connoisseurs
at the first performance, even if they were unaware of the source;
compositions in the pure Dorian mode cannot have been heard
publicly in London for a very long time. Further modally inflected
passages are derived from Erba's Magnificat, and Handel seems to
have allowed his original contributions to be similarly influenced,
notably in 'And the children of Israel', the surprising conclusion of
'But as for his people' and in 'And I will exalt thee', though the last
may be an as yet undetected borrowing. What moved Handel to be
so reliant on the work of others in *Israel in Egypt* remains
mysterious, for there are equally abundant signs that the work was
composed under the influence of urgent inspiration. There is certainly no need for moral indignation, for the finest numbers are
wholly original: the choruses 'I will sing unto the Lord' and 'The
people shall hear' with their perfectly timed climaxes, and among
the solos, 'Thou shalt bring them in', one of Handel's serenest E
major melodies.

THE CECILIA ODE AND *L'ALLEGRO*

Handel's setting of Dryden's shorter *Ode for St Cecilia's Day*
takes only about 50 minutes and hence was always given as part of
a double bill. At the first performance it was paired appropriately
with *Alexander's Feast*; later performances were given with
*L'Allegro* or *Acis and Galatea*. The music is again rather dependent
on borrowings, but as they mostly come from a single source contemporaneous with Handel himself (the *Componimenti* or keyboard suites of Gottlieb Muffat) and are fairly thoroughly recomposed there are no stylistic clashes. Some of the numbers are rather
ordinary, but the final chorus attempts the apocalyptic with some
success (the line mentioning the 'dark and dreadful hour' of the
Last Judgement sets off a chilling set of modulations to remote
keys) and there are two fine soprano solos in praise of the lyre
(imitated by solo cello) and the organ (with suitable obbligato).

With *L'Allegro, il Penseroso ed il Moderato* Handel returned to
original thematic material and created a unique work at once
delightful and profound. The words of Parts 1 and 2 are dovetailed
extracts from Milton's two youthful poems defining the pleasures of
L'Allegro, the 'merry man' and Il Penseroso, the 'thoughtful man',
mirth and melancholy, extroversion and introversion. It was
probably Handel's own idea to use the poems as a basis for a choral

work, doubtless spurred by John Dalton's adaptation of Milton's *Maske presented at Ludlow Castle*, which, under the title *Comus* and with music by Thomas Arne, had had great success since its first performance at Drury Lane in March 1738. It was certainly the case that Handel applied to Jennens for the text of a third part for the work which could reconcile the two aspects of personality by suggesting the idea of a balance between the two. This Jennens supplied, placing the sentiments in the mouth of another 'character', Il Moderato. Jennens presumably helped with the selection from Milton also, modernizing the English in places. The verse of Part 3 is no match for Milton's, of course, but greater poets would have had difficulty in extolling moderation. Originally Handel maintained a loose dramatic form, the 'part' of L'Allegro being divided between three male soloists (boy treble, tenor, and bass) while a single soprano sang Il Penseroso. The solos for Il Moderato are not consistently allocated, however, and the idea disappeared in the 1741 revival when new songs were added for the soprano Maria Monza and the castrato Andreoni. The clear images drawn from all aspects of English life were a direct inspiration to Handel, who could find as much enjoyment in the scenes of rural merrymaking or the bustle of city life as in the 'service high and anthems clear' of a great cathedral or the evening song of the nightingale. Though Handel eventually abandoned Part 3, it is really needed to keep the balance and the music is not vastly inferior to what has gone before. For the final duet (carefully marked 'L'Allegro ed il Penseroso' by Jennens)—it is the only number involving more than one solo singer—Jennens happily looked beyond his own muse for inspiration and chose a simile from one of Prospero's speeches in *The Tempest*. Handel responded with an exquisite setting, oboe and bassoon matching the duetting of the voices over a gently pulsing string accompaniment.

Ex. 21

Just as in Milton the greater length and more exalted imagery of *Il Penseroso* hint that thoughtfulness should be the dominant characteristic of the ideal man, so Handel subtly makes the same emphasis by providing many of the *L'Allegro* quotations with music that could equally well suit *Il Penseroso*. Who ignorant of the poems could be sure that the quiet dying fall of Part 1:

Ex. 22

belonged to *L'Allegro* rather than *Il Penseroso*? *L'Allegro* is both a tribute to the wide sympathies of Handel's own personality and a reflection of the ideals of an era.

### AN ALTERNATIVE TRADITION

Thus by the spring of 1741 Handel, while continuing to write and promote Italian opera, had attempted a range of non-acted choral works of every imaginable variety. Each was motivated as much by circumstances as by artistic prompting, each defines its own terms of appreciation and none can be dismissed as mere imitation of a predecessor. But with the final renunciation of opera Handel needed to settle upon some definite framework that could allow him to utilize within a formal unity all aspects of his talents as a composer of solo vocal, choral, and instrumental music. This was to be the dramatic oratorio, already loosely achieved in *Esther* and *Deborah* and more fully realized in *Athalia* and *Saul*. Only two further works could not be so described, one—the *Occasional Oratorio*—of little importance, the other—*Messiah*—a very special case. Before going on to examine the permanent establishment of Handel's oratorio seasons, however, it will be appropriate to examine the work of other composers up to this point.

Defesch's *Judith*, mentioned earlier, was the only work produced in England in Handel's lifetime that represented a true emulation of the Handelian dramatic oratorio. The oratorios and oratorio-like works of English composers, besides being few in number, are too different in manner to be considered as direct challenges to Handel, though his example stimulated their production. They are more sensibly seen as an attempt by the composers concerned to explore possibilities in their own way. Neither Maurice Greene (1696–1755) nor his protégé William Boyce (1711–79) had Handel's operatic background. They were primarily church musicians. Neither developed connections with the theatre until he had reached his mid-thirties, and neither produced a work that might without qualification be called an opera. It was rather the composition of court and other occasional odes that was their main activity in the secular sphere. This form, with its easy sequencing of short, flexibly constructed solos and choruses often developing the same material, was the foundation of their choral works on sacred subjects.

## GREENE'S *DEBORAH*

The first works which may be considered native English oratorios (though neither was actually so designated) demonstrate their closeness to the ode by being settings of narrative poems. The anonymous libretto of Greene's *The Song of Deborah and Barak* is a verse paraphrase of the victory song of the Israelites preserved in Judges v. Despite occasional use of the first person ('I, Deborah . .') this is primarily a retrospective relation of the event it celebrates, including the gruesome death of the Caananite chieftain Sisera at the hands of Jael. As befits its original production in Greene's

Apollo Academy, mainly comprising the members of the choir of St Paul's, the scoring is for an all-male trio of soloists (alto, tenor, and bass) with the choir and an orchestra of oboes, bassoon, trumpets, and strings. The work opens with a French overture and a pair of choruses framing a brief plain recitative, all in D major and all typical of Greene in their well-crafted working-out of rather short-winded and undistinguished melodic motives. What follows is more exciting: Greene 'dramatizes' his text with a fluid mixture of accompanied recitative, arioso, and formal aria, no item outstaying its welcome. Opportunities for harmonic surprise are seldom lost. The recitative 'They came, they fled':

Ex. 23

a sud-den, sud-den dread through all, through all their host was spread

The Hea - vens this sal - va-tion wrought, the stars, the stars for Is - rael fought.

epitomizes Greene's word-painting and shows a nice transition from accompanied to plain recitative: it leads to a powerful and demanding aria for the tenor. Greene is at his best in the sections dealing with the despatch of Sisera. The recitative 'When Sisera with weariness opprest' is introduced with a short 'slumber' sinfonia, solo oboe and violin over a murmuring accompaniment:

Ex. 24

This, with fuller scoring, returns to form the basis of an arioso. The alto takes up the description of Sisera's mother vainly waiting for her son. The first air, 'Why stays my Sisera', creates a sense of foreboding with its broken vocal line, while in a second air the string phrases rising to high sevenths express the mother's desperation and grief:

Ex. 25

Both Greene and Boyce make use of *affetuoso* style, with prominent appoggiaturas, but the nod in the direction of the new *galant* style (not found in Handel) is only adopted for occasional special effect, and seems not to be an attempt to follow fashion.

### BOYCE'S *DAVID'S LAMENTATION*

Like Greene's *Deborah*, Boyce's setting of *David's Lamentation over Saul and Jonathan* is an ode-like work of some fifty minutes' length, but the constituent numbers are more formally defined, one aria being *da capo*. Accompanied recitatives again make an important contribution to continuity. Despite its title, John Lockman's poem spends over half its length on David's encounter with the Amalekite, the Lamentations proper beginning only at the fourteenth of nineteen numbers. The music, as always with Boyce, is graceful, but the composer is seldom inspired to his characteristic tunefulness and some of the airs are trite. The vocal forces are those of Greene's *Deborah* and for the same reason; the orchestra lacks trumpets but makes use of a pair of flutes. Boyce gathers inspiration as the work progresses. The second chorus 'For Saul, for Jonathan', a moving elegy in E minor, may well have been in Handel's mind when he composed 'Mourn Israel':

Ex. 26

for his own treatment of the same episode in *Saul*. The best of the numbers with solo voices are the duet 'Sad Israel thy beauty's pride', opening with two solo violins without bass, and the *da capo* tenor air 'On thee Mount Gilboa', in which the key of A major has a special eloquence in the prevailing minor key context. Boyce reserves his most original stroke for the final chorus 'How are the mighty fallen', abandoning the elegiac mood in favour of a grim vivace in G minor; the strings maintain relentless double bowing almost throughout, and the violins scud bleakly down to their bottom G at the end.

In these pieces Greene, Boyce, and their librettists were obviously mindful that they were creating works for concert, not theatre, performance. Pictorial images are evoked intermittently and not in a way that would be enhanced by staging. By keeping the musical forms short and fluid, and the moods pleasantly varied, the composers found they could maintain the listener's interest and avoid the confusion that more specifically dramatic works could engender when presented in concert form. The same considerations were applied to the larger works that followed, and indeed it was on these lines that oratorio continued after Handel's death, none of his followers having comparable theatrical experience or vision.

GREENE'S *JEPHTHA*

Though nominally a dramatic oratorio, Greene's *Jephtha* (1737) is extremely static in effect. Part I of John Hoadly's libretto is largely taken up with a lengthy debate between the Israelites and Jephtha on the question of whether he can accept their offer of leadership in view of past humiliations. Eventually he does accept, and the story at last moves forward as he makes his fatal vow to sacrifice 'what first shall meet my eye, of purest Virgin Blood' if he is granted success over the Ammonites. Part 2 jumps immediately to the victory celebrations and the inevitable meeting with his own daughter, and once again the action effectively stops as the situation is slowly explained and the daughter resigns herself to her fate; she is not (as in Morell's libretto for Handel) redeemed from the sacrifice. Greene makes the un-named daughter a soprano (perhaps a boy treble; the part was later revised for alto), Jephtha (tenor) and the First and Second Elders (bass and alto) complete the cast. The orchestral scoring is as for *Deborah*, with a pair of recorders added.

As in *Deborah* Greene begins rather stiffly: a two-movement overture, with a curiously old-fashioned canzona-like Allegro, leads to a chorus whose dactylic rhythm is sustained too monotonously. Again it is with the first accompanied recitative ('O mighty leader', the First Elder's opening address to Jephtha) that the listener becomes involved. Jephtha's scornful reply ('Where are your gods') is a full *da capo* aria. The texture is soon varied by a minuet-like duet for the two Elders. Further pleas, reinforced briefly by the chorus of Israelites, soften Jephtha's heart: his reply begins without ritornello:

Ex. 27

[attacca]

The Israelites in a fine *da capo* chorus, 'Thou universal Lord', assure him they have abandoned their false gods; the middle section, in the relative minor is for altos, tenors, and basses only, allowing a thrilling re-entry for the sopranos in the tonic at the start of the reprise. A short D major air from Jephtha is interrupted by the statement of his vow, and the music then returns to form the basis of the closing chorus of Part I. Greene makes his customary play with such words as 'Strike!' (great choral shouts) and 'mourn'

(a sudden plunge into the subdominant minor). A march with trumpets, presumably signifying the return of the triumphant Israelite army, begins Part II. The victory chorus is enhanced by the use of oboes and bassoons on their own, a colour new to the oratorio. The daughter and her attendants add their welcome, an air leading through a duet to a two-part chorus with recorders. (This, according to the libretto, is sung 'within the House', the only specific hint of stage presentation and a useful explanation of why Jephtha does not see his daughter immediately.) When Jephtha finally blurts out the details of his vow—each painful phrase stretched between string ritornellos in bare octaves—the reaction of the chorus is unexpectedly direct and angry: the arbitrary deity, as in Handel's later treatment, stands accused:

Ex. 28

The daughter's final air, 'Let me awhile defer my fate', is disappointing. Greene perhaps intended to suggest heroic resolution by the four-square dotted rhythms and major key, but pathetic resignation would have been more apt. However, the last exchange of farewells is a marvellously expressive blend of recitative, air, duet, and chorus and there is a moving pianissimo close to the final chorus. Though Greene may not have achieved the highest quality of musical invention throughout, *Jephtha* is a most satisfying work. The development through the music of Jephtha's change of heart in Part 1, and the daughter's growing understanding and acceptance of her fate in Part 2, adequately compensates for the lack of action, showing that the internal conflicts of the mind can be as useful a mainspring for oratorio as external battles.

To what extent Greene managed to overcome the much feebler text provided by Hoadly for his second full-length oratorio, *The Force of Truth* (1744), we cannot tell, as the music is lost. The libretto indicates it was a good deal looser and less dramatic than *Jephtha*. King Darius calls upon three Persian youths to tell him what is the greatest power on Earth. Wine, Darius himself, and the beauty of woman are the answers he is offered, with extensive illustrations. But as soon as the third youth, Zorobabel, has received approval for his answer, he launches unexpectedly into an assertion of the over-riding power of the 'God of Truth', coupling with it an appeal to Darius to restore the temple at Jerusalem and free the Israelites captive in Persia. This Darius promises and the oratorio concludes with a 'Hymn in Grand Chorus, by Zorobabel and Israelites in Captivity'. *The Force of Truth* clearly marks another step away from oratorio as a dramatic form. Evidence that this trend had the approval of English composers is provided by J. C. Smith's setting of a version of the same libretto in the 1760s.

BOYCE'S *SOLOMON*

Boyce's second major choral work outside the categories of liturgy, anthem, and ode is the serenata *Solomon*. It was completed, according to a note on Boyce's autograph, in March 1742 and published in full score the following year. Edward Moore's text is derived from the Song of Songs via a rhymed paraphrase by the Rev. Samuel Croxall, published in 1720 under the title *The Fair Circassian*.[54] Neither author is concerned with interpreting the Biblical book as an allegory of Christ's love for the Church: the interest lies solely in the erotic imagery. This feature of the text helped commit *Solomon* to oblivion in the nineteenth century, though the comparatively small role for the chorus (mostly confined to adding codas to solo numbers) was another inhibiting factor: even a bowdlerized *Solomon* could not have found a place

[54] For comparisons of the Croxall and Moore texts, and different versions of the score, with many other details, see Ian Bartlett and Robert J. Bruce, 'William Boyce's "Solomon" ', *Music & Letters*, lxi (1980), p. 28.

in the mainstream of the choral repertory. A modern audience will find nothing of concern in the eroticism as such, but Moore's verse, teetering precariously between legitimate metaphor and double entendre is still hard to swallow:

*He*: Let me (Love) thy bole ascending
   On the swelling clusters feed
   With my grasp the vine-tree bending,
   In my close embrace shall bleed.

It is redeemed by some delightful music. The overture (republished in 1760 as no. 6 of Boyce's *Eight Symphonies*)[55] retains the French form, in contrast to the more Italianate symphonies Boyce was favouring for his theatre works. The opening chorus is in a surprising stern D minor and unusual in form: a grand homophonic Adagio leads to a fugue which is interrupted by a return of the Adagio. It is the only place where Solomon and the Lord are mentioned. The rest of the work is a dialogue between a man and a woman simply designated He (tenor) and She (soprano), who may be taken as the shepherd and shepherdess of the pastoral convention. Their exchanges in Part 1 follow a fairly regular alternatation of recitative and air, the static nature of which encourages Boyce to some extravagance of musical gesture. When the woman speaks of love's invasion of her heart in the air 'Ah! simple me' the music suddenly transforms itself into a violent accompanied recitative more apt to a description of physical rape. Boyce is in fact at his best in the formal airs. The delectable tune of 'Tell me lovely shepherd, where' was rightfully remembered long after *Solomon* had been forgotten, and 'Balmy sweetness ever flowing' shows the composer capable of a Handelian extension of melody while retaining his own personality:

Ex. 29

HE [ + violins 8^va]

Bal - my sweet-ness ev - er flo-wing from her drop - ping

B.C. *piano* 6 7 6 6

---

[55] See Vol. VII, p. 430.

Parts 2 and 3 taken together are about the same length as Part 1 (about 45 minutes) and by 1749 Boyce had sensibly run them together. A sprightly Italian symphony opens Part 2 and the welcome to spring that follows is an enchanting scene, passing through recitative, duet, and air to a brief concluding chorus. The vernal mood continues through the once famous tenor solo and chorus 'Softly rise, o southern breeze', in which a solo bassoon duets with the voice:

Ex. 30

A moment of real drama comes in a dream sequence at the start of Part 3. Shuddering string figures and dark harmonies depict the chills of winter. 'He' calls to be admitted, 'She' opens the door—but no one is there. A 'chorus of virgins' (high voices unaccompanied) sympathizes. The nightmare swiftly passes, however, and there are a radiant duet and chorus to finish.

*Solomon* remained for Boyce and for English choral music in general a unique work. In its pastoral aspects it may possibly have been influenced by Handel's *Acis and Galatea* or Greene's dramatic pastorals, but it is quite clearly a concert work still maintaining in its linked solo and choral sections the outlines of the ode. It is unhelpful to relate it to the Italian *oratorio erotico*, not merely because Boyce was not likely to have been aware of that tradition but rather because the musical inspiration is not the eroticism but the natural images through which it is expressed. For this Boyce's most probable model was Handel's *L'Allegro*, which itself contains much of that shapely melody and homely sturdiness that became the characteristics of his English contemporaries.

### MESSIAH

A month after Boyce completed the score of *Solomon*, Handel gave in Dublin the first performance of a very different work. He had been in the Irish capital since November 1741 and directed performances of *L'Allegro*, *Alexander's Feast*, the *Ode for St Cecilia's Day*, and *Esther*. On 13 April came *Messiah*. Although 'He was despised and rejected', for instance, is in the form of a conventional *da capo* operatic aria, and although some of the great choruses are dramatic in the sense that those in *Israel in Egypt* are dramatic, it is not a 'dramatic oratorio'; it stands, in fact, in close relation to *Israel*—choral writing predominates, if not to the same extent, and the words are again a compilation of Biblical texts, the great majority from the Old Testament, together with some from the Book of Common Prayer. 'Part the first' is concerned with the promise of a Messiah and the birth of Christ, Part II with the Passion, Christ's ascension, and the going forth of the Apostles, and Part III with Christ the Redeemer. Handel was later to make many changes in *Messiah*, some normal second thoughts, some forced on him by conditions of performance and different soloists —as, for instance, the replacement of Sra.Avolio in 1742 perhaps by Giulia Frasi in 1749:

Ex. 31

Thus no definitive score exists.[56]

However untypical *Messiah* is of Handel's oratorios in general, it is completely typical in its self-borrowings, its Italian-operatic melody (for instance, the *da capo* aria 'He was despised and rejected'), and such tremendous dramatic strokes as 'Wonderful! Counsellor!' which simply by juxtaposition infuse with spiritual ecstasy the empty coloratura of one of his Italian duets, 'No, di voi non vo' fidarmi':

Ex. 32

[56] The most important variants are printed in the vocal score ed. Walther Siegmund-Schultze (Leipzig, 1959). The specialized *Messiah* literature, in addition to the vast general Handel literature, is itself considerable. Among the best later studies are Jens Peter Larsen, *Handel's 'Messiah': Origins—Composition—Sources* (New York, 1957; second ed. 1972), Harold Watkins Shaw, *A Textual and Historical Companion to Handel's 'Messiah'* (London, 1965), Hans Dieter Clausen, *Händels Direktionspartituren* (Hamburg, 1972), and Donald Burrows, 'Handel's Performances of "Messiah": the evidence of the conducting score', *Music & Letters*, lvi (1975), p. 319. The two complete basic scores are London, Brit. Lib., RM20. f. 2, the original autograph (facsimile, ed. Friedrich Chrysander, Hamburg, 1892), and Tenbury, St. Michael's College, a working copy with numerous autograph changes (facsimile, ed. Watkins Shaw, London, 1974).

incongruously borrowed as 'For unto us a child is born'. The wealth
of inspired melody, equalled but never surpassed in his other
scores, and the great choral frescoes, together with a subject that
appeals as strongly to humanistic Christianity as to eighteenth-
century Anglican piety, have combined to make *Messiah* the most
popular of all Handel's works.

Yet even before the first performance of *Messiah* Handel had
composed *Samson* (September–October 1741) in the dramatic
tradition and performed it in London (18 February 1743) before he
gave *Messiah* there (23 March). Indeed *Samson* was at first the
more successful, with eight performances as compared with only
three of 'the sacred Oratorio', as *Messiah* was originally announced
in England. 1743 also saw the first performances of *Semele*, really
an opera but produced, as we have seen, 'after the manner of an
oratorio', and *Joseph and his Brethren*. And then in fairly regular
succession came eleven works, from *Belshazzar* (1744) to *Jephtha*
(1751), mostly based on the Old Testament or Apocrypha and all
except the *Occasional Oratorio* dramatic. The English version of
the 1737 *Trionfo del Tempo e della Verità—The Triumph of Time
and Truth* (1757)—contains little new music.

THE ORATORIO CONCEPT

The librettist of *Samson*, Newburgh Hamilton, defined oratorio in
his preface as 'a musical Drama, whose Subject must be Scriptural,
and in which the Solemnity of Church-Musick is agreeably united
with the most pleasing Airs of the Stage'. But this encompasses
only part of Handel's output of oratorio; his eventual commitment
to that definition was a gradual and initially uncertain development. The new form found a public response, but what Handel's
audiences came to value in oratorio was not fully congruent with
what Handel, for his own satisfaction, wanted to write. For thirty-
six years as a composer of Italian or Italianate *opera seria* he had
demonstrated the intensity that could be obtained by placing
formal arias and ensembles in precise dramatic contexts, and he

had shown that these individual numbers could be united within a broad tonal structure and a careful balancing of mood and style. These features could be transferred without change to oratorio. Though the assistance of visual spectacle in defining dramatic situation was lost, there was more than adequate compensation in the use of an immediately comprehensible English text. On top of this was the musical enrichment provided by the choruses. By no means confined to solemnity, these could be as gay and colourful as any aria, and infinitely more varied in texture. Only through the use of the chorus could a vocal work of a full evening's length be sustained without a dramatic basis, and thus the way had been opened to such works as *Messiah* and *L'Allegro*.

For contemporary listeners the greater involvement demanded by dramatic oratorio was both exhilarating and unnerving. In oratorio Handel could take on weighty subjects from Scripture that could not be tackled on the stage, and in *Semele* and *Hercules* he was able to treat two resonant classical myths more directly and more powerfully than would have been possible with the hackneyed clichés of an Italian libretto. It is a little unfair to condemn the early audiences for reacting unfavourably to those very works which today we especially admire—and which Handel, insofar as can be determined, himself most valued. In 1743 what pleased in *Samson* is easily analysed: the familiarity of the Biblical story and Milton's poem; the dramatic encounters, both personal (Samson/Delila, Samson/Harapha) and national (Israelites/Philistines); and the moralizing apt to the Lenten season. The sexual element was just right: seduction attempted and repulsed. But Handel's next London premières veered wildly either side of this nice compromise. Immediately after *Samson*, in the concerts closest to Easter, came *Messiah*, when the audience found themselves listening in a public theatre to the *comédienne* Kitty Clive announcing the birth of Christ and the notorious adulteress Susannah Cibber reflect on His Passion. At the start of the next oratorio season they were offered in *Semele* the frankly expounded tale of a courtesan seeking penetration by a deity in order to achieve immortality. Mrs. Delany, while reporting her own pleasure in *Semele*, noted 'a strong party against it, viz. the fine ladies, petit maîtres and *ignoramus's*'. The cuts made for the revival the following December (notably in Juno's explanation of how Semele should attain immortality) leave no doubt that the explicit sexual references were cause of offence.

The failure of *Hercules* in 1745 suggests there were other difficulties. On 21 February Charles Jennens reported to his friend Edward Holdsworth on the disastrous start to Handel's new subscription series:

For the last two years he had perform'd Oratorios in Covent-Garden Playhouse on Wednesdays & Fridays in Lent only, when there was no publick entertainment of any consequence to interfere with him: & his gains were considerable, 2100 11. one year, & 1600 11. the other, for only 12 performances. Flush'd with this success, the Italian Opera being drop'd, he takes the Opera-house in the Hay-market for this Season at the rent of 400 11., buys him a new organ, & instead of an Oratorio produces an English Opera call'd Hercules, which he performs on Saturdays during the run of Plays, Concerts, Assemblys, Drums, Routs, Hurricanes, & all the madness of Town Diversions. His Opera, for want of the top Italian voices, Action, Dresses, Scenes & Dances, which us'd to draw company, & prevent the Undertakers losing above 3 or 4 thousand pounds, had scarce half a house the first night, much less than half the second; & he has been quiet ever since.

This was written just before the première of *Belshazzar*, which Jennens, as librettist, doubtless considered a real oratorio, though it was only partly based on the Bible and turned out to be as much a choral opera as *Hercules*. The vivid dramatic nature of these two works, with *Semele*, had come into conflict with their basic function as concert works. The stronger the visual images created, the more intense becomes the wish to see those images realized, and the more frustrating is the denial of that realization. Yet it was precisely that dramatic vividness, played out in the ideal theatre of the mind, which inspired Handel to his best work.

In 1746 Handel compromised with the hasty assembly of his last non-dramatic oratorio, the *Occasional*, and the composition of *Judas Maccabaeus*. The latter, though nominally dramatic, is more in the nature of a celebratory cantata, concerned wholly with anticipation of, and reaction to, events, rather than the events themselves. Two of the leading roles are anonymous Israelites and the named characters are void of life. The piece is entirely appreciable as a concert work and was a great success in the oratorio season of 1747, now prudently restored to Lent. The fact that *Judas Maccabaeus* was conceived as a victory oratorio to celebrate the quashing of the '45 Jacobite rebellion may have given it a head start, but its continuing popularity both in Handel's lifetime and subsequently can only be attributed to the absence of those very elements which had hampered appreciation of the earlier and greater music dramas. By an ironic coincidence it was in these very years that London theatregoers were witnessing a young actor beginning to abandon the old manner of delivering spoken drama in formal set speeches in favour of something more natural and realistic. In the year of the triumph of *Judas Maccabaeus* Handel may well have heard David Garrick proclaim Johnson's famous couplet from the stage of Drury Lane—

The drama's laws the drama's patrons give,
For we that live to please must please to live

—and reflected ruefully that the new freedom and fluidity that had brought audiences flocking to Garrick's performances were just the qualities that had turned them from his.

In his last four oratorios Handel happily allowed his natural bent to reassert itself, perhaps in the hope that his audiences would slowly come with him. But the fundamental conflict of dramatic oratorio could not be resolved. Both *Susanna* and *Theodora* were indifferently received. They may have been Biblical stories but, like *Semele* they were lively dramas with an explicit sexual element, and *Theodora* like *Semele* was heavily bowdlerized at its revivals. The omission of much of the love music from the 1756 revival of *Solomon* suggests that similar considerations accounted for its lack of success, and though a much more static piece dramatically than the others of this period it nevertheless evokes strong visual images. The greyer and more introspective *Jephtha*, on the other hand, was comparatively popular. Meanwhile *Messiah*, which once had so shocked the pious, was beginning its ascendancy and becoming the epitome of what a true oratorio should be; it was a view heavily endorsed in the nineteenth century and for much of the twentieth.

In the latter half of the twentieth century it has just become possible for audiences to perceive the dramatic oratorios in a way much closer to Handel's own. We can accept, not to say admire, the breaking away from formal divisions into air, chorus, and so on. The quiet respect with which live performances are now heard, with applause restricted (mostly) to the ends of clearly defined sections, allows us to absorb Handel's large-scale constructions. The burgeoning of concert performances of operas and complete recordings means that many listeners are used to using their imaginations to supply the visual element, and to following printed librettos, often of pieces which they have never seen on stage. On the other hand, they may well have actually seen a modern stage performance of a dramatic oratorio, or the performers may have had the benefit of taking part in one. Though such stagings generally involve abridgement or some re-ordering and obviously cannot be a true reflection of the works as Handel conceived them, they have been a vital means of bringing out the dramatic element, long obscured by Victorian attitudes. The taboo on complete performances of those works which contain more than about two and a half hours of music remains to some extent sustained by an over-emphasis on dramatic aspects. Performers feel justified in removing those lighter airs (typically *da capo* in form and involving florid writing in triplets) which occur in most of the oratorios. But these too may become acceptable as use of period instruments encourages a lighter and fleeter performing style and if performers, with the help of recordings, can gain the experience of placing such pieces in the context of full-length performances. What Handel was attempting above all in his oratorio concerts was a complete evening's entertainment in which the light and the serious, the abstract and dramatic all commingled. When musicians have the confidence to allow all these aspects to have their place in performance, the result may be found to work far better than has hitherto been allowed.

## HANDEL'S LAST DECADE OF ORATORIO

The works of Handel's last decade of oratorio composition were not all masterpieces, though none is without lovely passages—Cleopatra's 'Here amid the shady woods' in *Alexander Balus*, Joseph's 'The peasant tastes the sweets of life', and in *Joshua* Caleb's 'Shall I in Mamre's fertile plain', with its wonderful treatment of a dropping-fourth motive—and masterly dramatic strokes. But *Semele, Belshazzar, Hercules, Solomon, Susanna, Theodora,* and *Jephtha* are masterpieces indeed. Setting aside as operas in concert disguise *Semele, Hercules,* perhaps *Belshazzar* with its copious stage-directions, and *Susanna* which the Countess of Shaftesbury at once recognized as 'in the light *operatic* style'[57]—with unItalian tunes so popular in both senses that Arne borrowed one for his *Love in a Village* (1762)—we are left with three true 'dramatic oratorios' of the first order. All date from the period 1748–51 and superbly crown Handel's creative career.

*Solomon* (composed in 1748, performed the following year, and drastically revised to its disadvantage in 1759) is remarkable for its choruses—including one of Handel's most beautiful essays in poetic sound, 'May no rash intruder' (see Ex. 33), which draws the curtain

---

[57] Otto Erich Deutsch, *Handel: a Documentary Biography* (London, 1955), p. 657.

on the hero's love-scene with his young queen—and its blissful airs, 'Bless'd the day when first my eyes' and 'With thee th' unshelter'd moor I'd tread'. Few things in Handel are more dramatic than the judgement scene and in none of his scores is the orchestra used more richly and subtly:

Ex. 33

sleep     with their   song,
night- in - gales___   lull them

Whereas Solomon is shown in Act I with his 'wedded love' and in Act II with the quarrelling women, in Act III he entertains yet another female character, the Queen of Sheba, with picturesquely beautiful, powerful, tragic, or splendid choruses. The Queen herself has a remarkable farewell air with *obbligato* for sole oboe and *traversieri tutti*.

Finest of all are *Theodora* (1750), which according to the librettist, Thomas Morell, 'Mr Handell himself valued more than any Performance of the kind',[58] and *Jephtha* (1752). In *Theodora* the choruses are fewer than usual but very striking and extremely varied, with the Purcellian simplicity of 'Queen of Summer' in Act II (where it is followed by an almost equally Purcellian air for Valens), the dramatic expressiveness of 'How strange their ends' in Act III, using a theme borrowed from a vocal duet by Giovanni Carlo Maria Clari, and the sublimity of 'Oh, love divine'—a transformation of Dejanira's 'Cease, ruler of the day' in *Hercules*, its texture tightened and more closely woven—which concludes the tragedy. But, again according to Morell, it was 'the Chorus at the end of the 2nd part', 'He saw the lovely youth', that Handel him-

[58] Deutsch, op. cit., p. 852.

self thought 'far beyond' the 'Grand Chorus in the Messiah'.[59] Equally varied are the numerous airs, of which the heroine's 'Angels, ever bright and fair' only happens to be the best known; her 'Fond, flatt'ring world' in Act I and 'With darkness deep' in II are greater music, only less spiritually beautiful. Her companion Irene also has some lovely things—'Defend her, Heaven', 'Lord, to Thee each night and day'—and Didymus, with 'Sweet rose and lily', perhaps the loveliest of all.

## JEPHTHA

*Jephtha* was Handel's final masterpiece, final because work on it was, as he noted in the score (13 February 1751), 'verhindert . . . . wegen relaxation des gesichts, meines linken auges':[60] within a month he had lost all sight in the left eye. After the Apocryphal heroine of *Susanna* and one from Christian hagiography in *Theodora*, Handel now returned to his favourite field, the Old Testament, and to the 'oratorio concept' of Newburgh Hamilton's definition. It is an uneven work with copious borrowings from the *Philomela pia* (Kraslice, 1747) of Franz Habermann (1706–83), a collection of six Masses, each dedicated to a Czech saint,[61] but its greatest dramatic passages are unsurpassed in Handel's earlier music: Storge's air 'Scenes of horror, scenes of woe' in Act I and her accompanied recitative 'First perish thou, and perish all the world!' in II, Jephtha's 'Open thy marble jaws, O tomb!' and his recitative 'Deeper and deeper still' leading into the chorus 'How dark, O Lord, are thy decrees!'. At the other extreme the protagonist has the idyllic 'Waft her, angels' and the serenely beautiful arioso 'For ever blessed be thy holy name'.

## ARNE'S JUDITH

When Handel died, English oratorio nearly died with him. Life was not extinct, but the pulse was feeble, although there are some fine choruses in Arne's *Judith* (1761), notably the first:

---

[59] Ibid., p. 821.
[60] Ibid., p. 701.
[61] The relevant passages were published by Max Seiffert, 'Franz Johann Habermann', *Kirchenmusikalisches Jahrbuch*, Jg. 18 (1903), p. 81, whence they were quoted incompletely and sometimes inaccurately by Sedley Taylor, *The Indebtedness of Handel to works by other composers* (Cambridge, 1906), pp. 15–27. See also Winton Dean, *Handel's Dramatic Oratorios and Masques* (London, 1959), particularly pp. 603 and 612–3.

# Ex. 34

'Sleep, gentle cherub'[62] is the best of the airs in *Judith* but 'Adorn'd with ev'ry matchless grace', 'Wake my harp', and 'Vain is beauty's gaudy flow'r':

Ex. 35

[62] Ed. Geoffrey Arkwright in his *Old English Edition* (London and Oxford, 1889–1902), ii, p. 47.

also show Arne's considerable melodic gifts.

# II

## SOLO SONG AND VOCAL DUET

### (a) ITALY

#### By HANS JOACHIM MARX

THE CHAMBER CANTATA

THE Italian cantata of the baroque period is chamber music in the original sense of the term. In contrast to the *motetto* with its Latin text and ecclesiastical associations, the *cantata a voce solo* with secular text was intended for the chamber; it was *musica da/per camera*, one of the most polished musical forms of social entertainment within the whole musical culture of the seventeenth and eighteenth centuries. Giovanni Maria de Crescimbeni refers to it as one of the forms of *'nobili conversazioni'*,[1] and members of the aristocracy or princes of the Church frequently had solo cantatas performed in their literary and musical 'academies'.

These audiences expected their music to be such as made the highest artistic demands. This presupposed a type of singer of exceptional technical and musical accomplishment; the cantatas (and duets) of the seventeenth and eighteenth centuries were not written for the dilettante but for the professional singer, the 'virtuoso'. Christoph Bernhard's manuscript treatise *Von der Singe-Kunst oder Manier* (On the Art or Style of Singing) describes what was demanded of such a virtuoso. He must not only have mastered the fundamentals of vocal technique including ornamentation (*canto sodo*), but also be able to convey the emotion delineated in the text (*cantar d'affetto*). Finally he had also to be able to embellish the written voice part (*cantar passagiato*).[2] Castratos (soprano or contralto) were normally the best at meeting these demands and most Italian cantatas of the baroque period were written for them.

The texts of the cantatas and duets are more or less variations on

---

[1] *De Comentari intorno all'Istoria della volgar Poesia* (Rome, 1702), vol. I, lib. IV, p. 241.
[2] See Josef Maria Müller-Blattau, *Die Kompositionslehre Heinrich Schützens in der Fassung seines Schülers Christoph Bernhard* (Leipzig, 1926), pp. 31–9.

a single theme: unhappy love. In this the poets followed the tradition of the love poetry of Tasso, Guarini, and Marini. A historical or mythological subject is very often made the occasion for a lover's description, in narrative or semi-dramatic form, of the pangs of unrequited love, while the beloved is frequently depicted as a cruel, merciless woman who brings about her lover's death. The emotions treated in the cantata texts are matched by the verse forms, which vary from the simple stanza with regular rhyme scheme to complex forms with irregular metrical structures. Sometimes a distinction is made between narrative passages (recitative) and lyrical ones (arias). In general the literary style of the seventeenth-century Italian cantata is marked by graphic imagery and onomatopoeia as well as an abundance of rhetorical figures. It was rare for composers to write their own texts (Domenico Mazzocchi and Loreto Vittori are among those who did). Frequently the poets were cultivated dilettanti who were members of the literary and musical academies or had connexions with them. Beside less well known names—Domenico Benigni, Francesco Balducci, Francesco Buti, and Giovanni Lotti—they included the cardinals Fabio Chigi, Giulio Rospigliosi, Francesco and Antonio Barberini, Benedetto Panfili, and Pietro Ottoboni.[3]

The term 'cantata' itself is seldom found in the printed or manuscript sources before 1650. After Alessandro Grandi's *Cantade et Arie à voce sola* (Venice, 1620) it was more usual for individual compositions in the genre to be given fantasy titles like 'capriccio', 'scherzo', 'spirito affetto', etc. The generic term 'cantata' did not come into general use until the last third of the seventeenth century. From an early date the cantata differed from other kinds of monodic vocal chamber music in presenting a succession of different formal types.[4] Strophic variations over a recurring bass alternated with short song-like ariosos or arias, and later on with through-composed recitatives. By its division into separate movements, above all through the separation of recitative and aria which took place around 1650, the chamber cantatas had from the very first affinities with *dramma per musica*, opera.

Beside opera and oratorio, the chamber cantata was one of the most popular and therefore the most widely diffused musical genres of the time. While cantatas were printed in collections in the first

---

[3] On the texts, see Eugen Schmitz, *Geschichte der weltlichen Solokantate* (Leipzig, 2nd ed. 1955), pp. 26–35, and Gloria Rose, 'The Italian Cantata of the Baroque Period' in *Gattungen der Musik in Einzeldarstellungen* (*Gedenkschrift Leo Schrade*), i (Berne and Munich, 1973), pp. 668–70.

[4] On the early history of the chamber cantata, see Vol. IV, pp. 172–5.

third of the seventeenth century, especially in northern Italy, their diffusion from about 1640 onwards was restricted to manuscript sources. The manuscripts, sometimes illustrated with miniatures, often contain the repertories of particular academies. The quantity and nature of the material is as yet hardly known, even in outline.[5]

## THE CANTATA IN ROME

Of all the musical centres of the seventeenth century, Rome appears to have been the one where the chamber cantata was most intensively cultivated. This was largely due to the closure of the Roman theatres ordered by Pope Innocent X Panfili (1644–55) and renewed several times thereafter; the dramatic nature of many cantatas made them welcome substitutes for the forbidden *dramma per musica*. There was hardly one among the more important *maestri di cappella* or singers in Rome who did not try his hand at composing cantatas. While Stefano Landi (*c*.1586–1639) still devoted himself almost exclusively to the solo madrigal and aria,[6] the chamber cantata was already central to the work of Luigi Rossi (*c*.1597–1653). Nearly 300 cantatas by him survive,[7] demonstrating astonishing formal variety; strophic variations and rondo forms, recitatives moving without a break into ariosos or shorter arias. His dramatic gifts were deployed most tellingly in expressive *lamenti*, notably the often cited 'Un ferito cavaliero' on the death of Gustavus Adolphus of Sweden in 1632.

Prominent among Rossi's contemporaries as composers of cantatas were Marco Marazzoli (*c*.1602 or *c*.1608–62), Domenico Mazzocchi (1592–1665),[8] Antonio Tenaglia (b. *c*.1610–20; d. after 1661), and Carlo Rainaldi (1611–91)—unknown as a composer but one of the most important architects of the High Baroque in Rome. Influenced by Rossi (but also by Carissimi), Rainaldi gave the representation of emotion priority over vocal virtuosity in his

---

[5] A bibliographical listing of part of the cantata repertory is available in the first ten fascicles of *The Wellesley Edition Cantata Index Series*, ed. Owen Jander (Wellesley, Mass., 1964–   ). The volumes are listed individually in the bibliography to this chapter.

[6] One exception is the cantata 'Dammi Lidio tanti baci', in I-MOe Campri 105c. For a modern edition see Silke Leopold, *Stefano Landi. Beiträge zur Biographie, Untersuchungen zur Vokalmusik*, part 2 (*Hamburger Beiträge zur Musikwissenschaft*, 17) (Hamburg, 1976), pp. 27–8.

[7] See the thematic catalogue by Alberto Ghislanzoni, *Luigi Rossi* (Rome and Milan, 1954), pp. 220 ff., and the bibliographical list by Eleanor Caluori, *Wellesley Edition*, iii (Wellesley, Mass., 1965). One of Rossi's cantatas, 'Io lo vedo', a *da capo* aria, is printed in Archibald T. Davison and Willi Apel, *Historical Anthology of Music*, ii (Cambridge, Mass., 1950), no. 203.

[8] See Wolfgang Witzenmann, *Domenico Mazzocchi, 1592–1665. Dokumente und Interpretationen* (*Analecta Musicologica*, viii) (Cologne and Vienna, 1970), especially pp. 172–87.

solo cantatas, some fifteen in number.[9] In the cantata 'Entro a stanze reali' for soprano and *basso continuo*, which is constructed on the principle of repetition of recitative-ritornello-strophic aria, the refrain of the final aria exemplifies the musico-rhetorical means employed by Rainaldi to contrast the *affetto* of joy ('io canti') with that of sorrow ('io piango').[10]

Ex. 36

(Sometimes I think I'll sing – and then I weep.)

Giacomo Carissimi (1605–74), *maestro di cappella* at San Apollinare, was one of the most important composers of secular

[9] See H. J. Marx, 'Carlo Rainaldi als Komponist' in Gerhard Eimer, *La Fabbrica de S. Agnese in Navona. Römische Architekten, Bauherren und Handwerker im Zeitalter des Nepotismus* (*Acta Universitatis Stockholmiensis*, 17), i (Stockholm, 1970), pp. 244–278, with a new edition of the cantata 'Pallido, muto'.

[10] A-Wn, Ms. 17761, fo. 123/124.

chamber music in the middle years of the century. His cantata output (109 solo cantatas, twenty-seven for two voices, and nine for three with *basso continuo*)[11] reaches a high artistic level and served as a model to his contemporaries. The formal variety of his cantatas ranges from simple ariosos and strophic arias to binary and rondo arias. Recitative and aria, or arioso, are not yet separated, but run on without a break.[12] He employed his considerable powers of melodic and harmonic invention in expressive word-painting; hardly one of his contemporaries equals him in finding the right musical expression for a poetic text, grave or lighthearted. As the following example from 'Ferme, lascia ch'io parli',[13] a *lamento* by Mary, Queen of Scots, demonstrates, Carissimi achieved, by his declamation and expressive harmony, an intensity of feeling which still impressed Charles Burney at the end of the eighteenth century:

Ex. 37

---

[11] See Gloria Rose, *Giacomo Carissimi* (*Wellesley Edition*, v), (Wellesley, Mass., 1965).

[12] See Gloria Rose, 'The Cantatas of Giacomo Carissimi', *The Musical Quarterly*, xlviii (1962), p. 204. She has also published six of Carissimi's solo cantatas (London and New York, 1969). Further examples in Lino Bianchi (ed.), *Giacomo Carissimi. Cantate*, i (*Istituto italiano per la storia della musica, Monumenti* III) (Rome, 1960).

[13] Münster, Santini Hs. 868, fo. 155ᵛ.

(Stay, let me speak. But what shall I say?)

Among Carissimi's younger contemporaries, Mario Savioni
(1608–85) is a figure of some importance. He wrote something like
175 solo cantatas, in which word-painting takes second place to
rhythmically varied *bel canto*. The incorporation of melodic
material in the continuo part shows him as a progressive representative of the Roman school.[14]

### VENETIAN AND BOLOGNESE COMPOSERS

Especially after 1637 at the latest, the year when the first public
opera house was opened in the city, Venice was the hub of
dramatic musical creativity in Italy. It is hardly surprising that the
cultivation of the more intimate genres of vocal chamber music was
a relatively peripheral activity. In spite of the restriction of the
field, however, the chamber cantatas of Antonio Cesti (1623–69)
were acknowledged models of the genre.[15] They were still praised
by Giacomo Antonio Perti in 1688, in the preface to his *Cantate
morali, e spirituali*. In Cesti's fifty-five surviving cantatas the arias
with their extended passages of coloratura are especially remarkable, betraying unmistakably the hand of the operatic composer.[16]

[14] See Irving R. Eisley, *Mario Savioni* (*Wellesley Edition*, ii) (Wellesley, Mass., 1964).
[15] See David Burrows, *Antonio Cesti* (*Wellesley Edition*, i) (Wellesley, Mass., 1964).
[16] On Cesti's operas see Vol. V, pp. 22–30.

Cesti made an unusually witty contribution to the solo cantata with his 'Aspetto, adesso canto',[17] in which he parodies the fashionable genre by putting it in the mouth of a singer-composer who consults the audience on its musical preferences. As can be seen from the following example, Cesti amusingly illustrates the devices available to the composer of a chamber cantata about 1660:

Ex. 38

(If you want one stanza to have trills and coloratura, and the next to be chromatically salted with sharps and flats . . .)

Among the contemporaries of Cesti and Francesco Cavalli (1602–76), of whose cantatas only a few survive, Barbara Strozzi (1619–c.1665), the adoptive daughter of Monteverdi's librettist

[17] Brit. Lib., Harl. 1863, fo. 70. The cantata is treated in detail in David Burrows, 'Antonio Cesti on music', *The Musical Quarterly*, li (1965), p. 518.

Giulio Strozzi, made her mark as a composer of cantatas. The ones she published in Venice in 1659 under the title *Diporti di Euterpe overo Cantate et Ariette a voce sola* are particularly remarkable for the expressive power with which she shapes the passages of recitative. The recitative-arioso part of the cantata 'Lagrime mie', which is distinct from the following aria, is a good example:

Ex. 39

(My tears . . .)

Even before the publication of the *Diporti di Euterpe*, Barbara Strozzi claimed to have invented the cantata form made up of recitative and aria.[18] But if she consciously distinguished between

---

[18] See the preface to *Cantate, Ariette e Duette* (Venice, 1651). Cf. Ellen Rosand: 'Barbara Strozzi, virtuosissima cantatrice: The composer's voice', *Journal of the American Musicological Society*, xxxi (1978), p. 241.

recitative and aria-like sections, as in contemporary Venetian opera, the tendency to distinguish between narrative and lyrical sections within the chamber cantata was in fact noticeable earlier still. The principle of alternation of recitative and aria in the cantata can be traced as early as Francesco Negri's *Arie musicali . . . à 1 e 2 voci con alcune Cantate in stile recitativo* (Venice, 1635),[19] but it was to be more than a generation before it became the general rule. It was not until about 1670 that the succession of different formal segments was discarded in favour of separate movements complete in themselves. The standard (not to say schematic) form of the cantata in the last quarter of the seventeenth century consisted of *recitative/aria*, the length and number of the two parts varying according to the text. Johann Mattheson describes the sequence aria-recitative-aria-recitative-aria as the most usual in the early eighteenth century.[20]

Developments in opera also influenced the form of the cantata aria. Around 1700 both the strophic form on the same bass for each strophe and the binary arietta were superseded by the *da capo* aria in *a-b-a* form, with the first section returning like a refrain at the end, in which the *b* section, from Alessandro Scarlatti onwards, if not earlier, was contrasted in beat, tempo, scoring, and expression with the *a* section. It remained the most important form of cantata aria up to the middle of the eighteenth century, but during that period considerable changes occurred in the internal structure of the separate parts of the aria. For instance, Antonio Vivaldi (1678–1741), who wrote some thirty-nine solo cantatas,[21] extended the aria form by the alternation of ritornellos and solo sections, bringing it closer to that of the instrumental solo concerto as he himself had developed it.[22]

Some idea of the scope of the Bolognese cantata can be obtained from the anthology *Melpomene coronata*, published by Giacomo Monti (Bologna, 1685),[23] which includes solo cantatas with thoroughbass by Pirro Conte d'Albergati (1663–1735), Giulio Cesare Arresti (1619–1701), Giovanni Paolo Colonna (1637–95), Giacomo Antonio Perti (1661–1756), and others. Common to them

[19] See Schmitz, op. cit., p. 72.
[20] *Der vollkommene Capellmeister* (Hamburg, 1739), p. 214.
[21] See Peter Ryom, 'Le recensement des Cantates d'Antonio Vivaldi', *Dansk Årbog før Musikforskning*, vi (1972), p. 81, and Michael Talbot, *Vivaldi* (London, 1978), pp. 175–8.
[22] See Walter Kolneder, *Antonio Vivaldi (1678–1741). Leben und Werk* (Wiesbaden, 1965), especially p. 233.
[23] There is a copy in the Royal College of Music Library, London. A short description of the cantatas in Schmitz, op. cit., pp. 132–3.

all is the recitativo-arioso form predominant in the Venetian cantata, with the arioso sections often designated 'aria'. Bologna, like Rome, shows a tendency to dramatize the cantata: the incipient tendency can already be observed in the cantatas published by Giovanni Maria Bononcini in 1677–8. Contemporary theorists used the term *scena da camera* for these dramatized cantatas.[24]

### ALESSANDRO SCARLATTI

The extraordinarily comprehensive cantata output of Alessandro Scarlatti (1660–1725) represents a summit in the history of the *cantata da camera*. Besides a substantial number of serenatas, sacred cantatas, and oratorios, he wrote more than 600 chamber cantatas, mostly for academies in Rome and Naples: 508 of them are for solo voice and *basso continuo*, fifty-four have instrumental accompaniment (*cantate con stromenti*).[25] Scarlatti's chamber cantatas continue the tradition of Rossi and Carissimi. Although in the earlier ones, up to about 1697, the greater variety of stylistic means and the preference for ariosos in 3/2 time, binary ariettas and strophic arias with ostinato bass as well as carefully fashioned recitatives, betray a certain conservatism, their musical language is full of passion. The later cantatas, after 1697, usually observe the principle, predominant in Naples in the early seventeenth century, of alternating recitative and *da capo* aria (mostly in the sequence R-A-R-A or A-R-A-R-A).[26]

The fact that the cantatas most often end with an aria is consistent with Scarlatti's tendency to shift the centre of gravity from the narrative element to the lyrical. The recitatives of the late cantatas (so far as they are dated) are innovatory in their harmonic layout, especially in their modulatory progressions. Scarlatti's use of chromatic inflexions in the representation of strong emotions is illustrated by the following example from the cantata 'Dormono l'aure estive' (dated 10 January 1705), which has an undeniably experimental air.[27]

---

[24] Eugen Schmitz coined the term *Sujetkantate* for cantatas which acquire dramatic character 'through the depiction of a particular situation' (op. cit., p. 64).

[25] See the lists in Edwin Hanley, article 'Alessandro Scarlatti', *Die Musik in Geschichte und Gegenwart,* xi (1963), col. 1488–96, and in *The New Grove,* xvi (1980), pp. 562–5.

[26] An example from 1709, 'Lascia, deh lascia al fine', in which only the final aria is *da capo*, is given in Arnold Schering, *Geschichte der Musik in Beispielen* (Leipzig, 2nd ed., 1955), no. 260. See also Malcolm Boyd, 'Form and style in Scarlatti's chamber cantatas', *Music Review,* xxv (1964), p. 17.

[27] Private collection of Gerald Coke (Bentley, Hants.), Ms. without sig., dated 1711, p. 68/69.

Ex. 40

Dor - mo-no l'au-re e - sti - ve fra i si - len-tii not -
tur - ni agl' ar - bo - scel - li zef-fi - ro lu - sin -
ghie - ro no scuo-te i ra - mi e in cal - ma ne-ghit - to - sa

**Andante**

fat - to im - mo - bil chris-tal - lo il mar ri - po -
- - - - so,
dor - me, dor-me an - cor l'i - dol mi - o

e mes-to in- tan - to    co-sì a des-tar - lo   in - do-len - te  ce - dro

sciol - go  la  vo - ce all' ar - mo - nia    del  pian -

- to,   sciol - go  la  vo - ce, sciol - go  la  vo - ce

(The summer breezes sleep in the silences of night; in the little trees the
fluttering zephyr does not shake the boughs, and in indolent calm the sea,
made motionless crystal, reposes, sleeps. So sleeps my idol and sadly to
wake the sluggard I raise my voice in lamentation.)

Johann David Heinichen censured this harmonic audacity as
'*Extravagant und irregulair*' and called Scarlatti's style violent.[28]

The arias of the late cantatas are almost without exception in *da
capo* form, with the middle section strongly contrasted in key,
beat, and melodic material with the main section. Scarlatti introduces thematic material in the instrumental preludes, particularly
in the *cantate con stromenti*. There is an interesting example in the
cantata 'Ben mio, quel verme', in which the three-part *sinfonia* is a
contrapuntal working of the beginning of the first recitative:[29]

---

[28] *Der Generalbass in der Composition* (Dresden, 1728), pp. 798–836.
[29] Brit. Lib., Add. MS. 31506, and D-Hs, Ms. M A/252, fo. 19.

# Ex. 41

(My dear, that winged worm that in dim light when night rises with a thousand enchantments.)

To his contemporaries, Scarlatti's style appeared too conservative, too academic. Count Zambeccari wrote in a letter in 1709 that Scarlatti's compositions 'are very difficult, and are things for the chamber, which make no effect in the theatre . . . people want *saltarelli* and lively stuff, such as they have at Venice'.[30]

[30] Cf. Edward J. Dent, 'Italian Chamber Cantatas', *The Musical Antiquary*, ii (1910–11), p. 190.

## HANDEL'S ITALIAN CANTATAS

It is in the context of Scarlatti's vocal chamber music that the Italian cantatas of Handel should be examined in that they mostly date from his first stay in Rome (1707–8), a time when Scarlatti was *maestro di cappella* at Santa Maria Maggiore. Handel wrote his secular cantatas for the *conversazioni* of Roman patrons of the arts, particularly the Marchese Francesco Maria Ruspoli and the cardinals Benedetto Panfili and Pietro Ottoboni, the *nepote* of Pope Alexander VIII Ottoboni.

The immediately notable feature of Handel's cantata output is the large number of works with orchestra: of the total of almost 100, no fewer than thirty-one are *cantate con stromenti*;[31] sixty-six are for solo voice and thoroughbass.[32] The relatively large number of cantatas with orchestral accompaniment may well have been in response to his patrons' wish to have larger-scale compositions for larger social gatherings such as the academies of the 'Arcadia'. Another factor was that the young Handel's orchestral writing, with its debt to Reinhard Keiser, was something of a novelty in Rome. His ability to intensify the emotional effect of vocal music by means of the instrumental accompaniment (accompanied recitative, arioso, aria) was astonishing. His *cantate con stromenti* also appear to some extent to have satisfied the general craving for dramatic music, frustrated by the closure of the theatres.

Formally and stylistically, Handel's cantatas combine the German tradition of attention to the meaning of the words with the Italian tradition of emotionally expressive *bel canto*. By employing instruments, often divided into concertino and concerto grosso groups, he was able to construct large-scale aria movements with contrapuntal working. The cantata 'Qual ti riveggio' for soprano, solo violin, two oboes, and strings is a good example.[33] Handel takes Scarlatti as his model in his formal layout (R-A-R-A-R-A with final recitative but no *sinfonia*). Though contrasted in expression, the arias are about the same length, the tempo markings, *poco allegro* for the second aria and *adagio* for the third, making up for the difference in the number of bars. The final aria, 'Empio mare, onde crudeli', strikingly underlines the contrast of different

---

[31] *Georg Friedrich Händels Werke*, ed. Friedrich Chrysander, lii a/b. In addition to the twenty-seven cantatas in that edition, four more have been ed. H. J. Marx, *Hallische Händel-Ausgabe*, v, 3/4.

[32] Ibid., 1, li. On the unpublished cantatas see also Rudolf Ewerhart, 'Die Händel-Handschriften der Santini-Bibliothek in Münster', *Händel-Jahrbuch*, vi (1960), p. 111.

[33] See H. J. Marx, 'Ein Beitrag Händels zur "Accademia Ottoboniana" in Rom', *Hamburger Jahrbuch für Musikwissenschaft*, i (1976), p. 69.

emotions: the first section, illustrating the 'onde crudeli' of the text, is written in the style of the early concerto grosso (Ex. 42 (i) ), while in the middle section, Hero's lament, the forces are reduced to a trio of solo violin, soprano, and *basso continuo* (Ex. 42 (ii) ):[34]

Ex. 42

[34] Description in Georg Kinsky (ed.), *Manuskripte, Briefe, Dokumente von Scarlatti bis Stravinsky, Katalog der Musikautographen-Sammlung Louis Koch* (Stuttgart, 1953), p. 1.

((i) Pitiless sea, cruel waves; (ii) Yet thou art dead and I live still, Leander; faith lives in thee.)

A large number of Handel's solo cantatas with thoroughbass are composed in the customary Neapolitan form R-A-R-A. In these also the structure of the text dictates stylistic variety, ranging from severely contrapuntal arias, such as those of 'Si bel foco e quel che t'arde',[35] to symmetrically constructed, song-like ariettas or pure dance-songs.[36] In some of his solo cantatas—and nowhere is Alessandro Scarlatti's influence more obvious—Handel goes to the very limits of what can be musically represented: in order to paint the terrors of the primeval forest in the bass cantata 'Nell' africane selve', he has recourse to unusual modulations in the recitative, and in the following aria the instrumentally conceived vocal part requires high notes and intervallic leaps that only a bass with a compass reaching from the C sharp below the bass stave to the A above middle C could sing:[37]

[35] *Händels Werke*, li, p. 22. There are similar passages in the cantata 'Occhi miei, lo miraste' by Agostino Steffani, ed. Alfred Einstein, *Zeitschrift für Musikwissenschaft*, i (1918–19), p. 457.
[36] e.g. the dance-song 'Altra spene', *Händels Werke*, 1, p. 152.
[37] Idem, p. 174.

Ex. 43

(Then he stumbles when he strikes the safe tracks.)

Both in choice of text and in musical structure, Handel's cantatas display a strong inclination towards the dramatic *scena*: abrupt alternations of mood in the arias, combined with underlying dance rhythms, vividly suggest mimetic movement and gesture. The stylistic similarity of cantata and opera enabled Handel (and others besides him) to transfer a large number of arias from cantatas to operas.

NEAPOLITAN CANTATAS IN THE EARLY EIGHTEENTH CENTURY

Although we can no longer speak of a 'Neapolitan School', the cantatas written at Naples in the early part of the eighteenth century do display a number of common formal and stylistic characteristics which permit some general observations. The Neapolitan chamber cantata is typified by a formal scheme that as a rule consists of two arias and two recitatives. Consequently double cantatas—that is, cantatas for two solo voices—consist of four arias or of two arias and a duet, so that each soloist has two numbers. Pietro Metastasio defended this arrangement as late as 1755.[38]

A chamber cantata may begin with an aria (A-R-A-R) or with a recitative (R-A-R-A); in the second case, *cantate con stromenti*

---

[38] He wrote to Calzabigi (letter of 14 February 1755): 'a solo cantata . . . with four ariettas is not performable, for no musician has a voice so indefatigable that he can sing four ariettas without a break and recitative as well; and a cantata that cannot be sung is no less reprehensible than a tragedy that cannot be staged' (quoted in Helmut Hucke, article 'Kantate', *Die Musik in Geschichte und Gegenwart,* vii, col. 563).

often begin with an instrumental prelude (*sinfonia* or sonata). The binary *cavata* is considerably less significant than the ternary *da capo* aria. Occasionally *recitativo secco* leads into an arioso. As orchestral cantatas grew steadily in importance, *secco* recitative was often replaced by *recitativo accompagnato*. Cantatas for three voices usually concluded with an ensemble for all three.

The greater emphasis on the aria in chamber cantatas went hand in hand with a greater approximation to operatic aria. With hardly any stylistic differences between the two types, they became on principle interchangeable. As noticed in the case of Handel, eighteenth-century composers frequently included arias from cantatas in their operas. Often, too, popular operatic arias were performed in the *camera*. This is probably the reason why, in the eighteenth century, manuscript anthologies of *aria staccate* (detached arias) replaced the cantata anthologies popular in the seventeenth.

The work of such composers of Neapolitan provenance as Francesco Provenzale (*c*.1626–1704), Leonardo Leo (1694–1744), Leonardo Vinci (*c*.1690–1730), and Domenico Sarro (1679–1744), shows a distinct falling-off of the solo cantata with thoroughbass. The number of cantatas written even by Giovanni Battista Pergolesi (1710–36) is small indeed, compared with Alessandro Scarlatti's output, but musically they are in no way inferior to his other works.[39] The 'Orfeo' cantata ('Nel chiuso centro'),[40] published in 1738, clearly shows how a composer as inventive as Pergolesi was able to avoid schematization of musical forms and genres. The cantata, for soprano, two violins, viola, and *basso continuo*, has operatic traits: the unbroken succession of *recitativo accompagnato*-aria-*recitativo secco*, and echo aria amounts to a complete dramatic scene, especially as the separate forms are linked by the same thematic material. The careful dynamic markings (from *piano assai* to *forte assai*) underline the dramatic character of the cantata. In the *da capo* arias the ritornello-like repetitions of the theme at the end of a section are not the only interesting feature: an apparent innovation in cantata literature is the interruption of arias by recitative interpolations—a practice which became increasingly common in the eighteenth century. The

[39] On the authenticity of the cantatas in Pergolesi's *Opera omnia*, ed. Filippo Caffarelli (Rome, 1938–42), see Helmut Hucke, *The New Grove*, xiv, p. 399.
[40] Modern edition by Hugo Ruf in *Die Kantate*, ed. Richard Jacoby (*Das Musikwerk*) (Cologne, 1968), p. 74.

uniformity of key still observable in Scarlatti and Handel is
abandoned.

The cantatas of Niccolò Jommelli (1714–74) are also dramatic in
conception. The great majority are for solo voice and orchestra (six
solo cantatas with *basso continuo*, five for two voices and
orchestra, five for three voices and orchestra and one serenata;
four of the three-part cantatas have sacred texts). Like Pergolesi,
Jommelli regarded the succession of movements primarily in
dramatic terms. In the cantata 'Giusti numi', for example, he
begins a recitative with *secco*, but as soon as passions are mentioned goes over to an *accompagnato* which sometimes approaches
arioso; in accordance with its narrative tone, the recitative concludes *secco*. Jommelli thus dramatizes the recitative part of the
composition by employing different musical means to depict the
flow and ebb of emotion.

Just how far advanced stylistically Jommelli's cantata arias were,
by comparison with the arias of early Neapolitan cantatas, may be
illustrated by the opening of the aria 'Se parla' from 'Cessa, o
Augusta'. The working of the thematic material in the voice part as
well as the orchestra, the fugal interpolations in the middle section,
and the changes of dynamics and tempo to suit the sense of the
text, all anticipate the Mozartean 'action aria':

Ex. 44[41]

[41] Reproduced from Robert R. Pattengale, *The Cantatas of Niccolò Jommelli* (including a list of works), an unpublished University of Michigan dissertation, 1973, pp. 234–6.

Adagio

chie-de Au-gu-sta dov' ē? Au-gu-sta, Au-gu - sta dov'

Come primo [andante]     Rinforzando

[Rinf.]

ē? l'a il cic - lo, l'a il cic lo di - vi - sa di-

Rinforzando

p

[p]

re - te          da te

p

(If he speaks, if he speaks,
  'Where is Augusta?'
You will say: 'Heaven has separated
  her from you.'
Ah no, say: '[Heaven has] carried her
  only a step away.'
But by leaving she left her heart
  and Elisa. . . .)

The cantatas of Johann Adolf Hasse (1699–1783) are among the
last important contributions to the history of the Italian solo
cantata. Although Hasse was a German by birth, he studied with
Porpora and Scarlatti and married the famous Italian singer
Faustina Bordoni. His *cantate con stromenti*, like all the rest of his

output, belong to the Neapolitan tradition. He was much more prolific in the field of the cantata than Jommelli: seventy-six solo cantatas by him are known, of which forty-two are accompanied by orchestra, and only thirty-four by *basso continuo*.[42] The cantata for soprano 'L'armonica' is in some respects the most remarkable among the orchestral cantatas. Written for Vienna, where he lived for some time during the 1760s, on a text by Metastasio, it calls not only for wind (two oboes and two horns) and strings (two violins, viola, cello, and viola da gamba), but also for such an unusual instrument as the glass harmonica: the Italian cantata was here bowing to German fashion. It is noticeable that Hasse deliberately changed the formal balance of the arias, especially their *da capo* structure; the first aria in 'L'armonica', 'Ah, perchè col canto mio', for instance, has a shortened *da capo*: the repeat, written out in full (without a *dal segno* direction), is only about half the length of the initial section. The shortened *da capo* aria was not unusual, however, in Naples around the mid-century.

The introductory aria from the cantata 'Scrivo in te l'amato nome' (Vienna, 1761)[43] illustrates the inventiveness with which Hasse integrated orchestral passages in the aria structures, and how he overcame the schematic layout of the *da capo* aria—veiling the beginning of the repeat by bringing in the voice on the final cadence of the middle section:

Ex. 45

(I write for thee.)

### THE CHAMBER DUET

Like the solo cantata, the chamber duet was cultivated especially in aristocratic circles and particularly at the Italian courts and

---

[42] See Sven H. Hansell, *Works for Solo Voice of Johann Adolph Hasse (1699–1783) (Detroit Studies in Music Bibliography*, xii) (Detroit, 1968).

[43] Ed. Hansell in *J. A. Hasse: Cantates pour une voix de femme et orchestre, Le Pupitre*, xi (Paris, 1968).

political centres (Rome, Venice, and Naples). Its stylistic history runs parallel to that of the chamber cantata, rising to its highest levels in the second half of the seventeenth century and the beginning of the eighteenth. Both genres share the same fundamental characteristics of style: antithesis of lyrical and declamatory expression, variation of strophes over an ostinato bass, articulation by changes of beat and key, gradual separation of recitative and arioso sections, and so on.[44]

Chamber duets—the term *duetto per camera* first occurs in 1677,[45] that is, at almost exactly the same time as *cantata*—could be composed according to one or other of two distinct principles: either dialogue of short, imitative phrases, of which Mattheson says that it offers 'absolutely nothing, or just occasionally something a little irregular or *concertierend*, creeping one after another', or else more or less severe contrapuntal writing. While the dialogue duet was more suited to dramatically conceived texts, the polyphonic duet tended to comport with lyrical, reflective ones. Moreover, this second type, with its extraordinarily artificial character, presupposed a listener of cultivated literary and musical taste who was seeking intellectual entertainment in the intimacy of chamber music. Thus the chamber duet was of exactly the same social rank as the chamber cantata.

Both forms of duet, the dialogue and the polyphonic, derive from compositional types that had developed from the vocal polyphony of the sixteenth century and were among the favoured genres of early monody: dialogue and madrigal.[46] The dialogue form was particularly popular in Venice in the 1620s and 1630s, for instance, with Francesco Rasi (b.1574) in his *Dialoghi rappresentativi* of 1620, or with Giovanni Valentini (b.1582 or 1583; d. 1649), whose *Musiche a due voci* was printed in Venice two years later.

The polyphonic duet, on the other hand, was cultivated particularly by representatives of the Roman school; early examples appear in collections published by Hieronymus Kapsberger (*Libro secondo d'arie a una e piu voci*, 1623) and Paolo Quagliati (*Sfera armoniosa*, 1623). Besides comparable works by Girolamo Frescobaldi (1583–1643) and Domenico Mazzocchi (1592–1665), there are also the duets of the opera-composer Giuseppe Antonio

---

[44] See Schmitz, 'Zur Geschichte des italienischen Kammerduetts im 17. Jahrhundert', *Peters Jahrbuch*, xxiii (1916), p. 43.

[45] In Maurizio Cazzati's *Duetti per camera*, op. 66 (Bologna, 1677).

[46] See Vol. IV, pp. 181–2.

Bernabei (1649–1732), which survive in manuscript.[47] To take one example, his 'Arietta à 2', 'Tormentato, e afflitto cor'[48] for soprano, tenor and *basso continuo* is symmetrically constructed: two solos (S) are placed between three duets (D)—D-S-D-S-D— but the closing duet is a repetition of the second with new words. The second duet, 'Fuggi cor mio', by its clear key structure and varied working of the initial motive (in which the *basso continuo* joins in bar 14), achieves an emotional effect completely matching the *lamento*-like text.

Ex. 46

[47] Some of Bernabei's duets are preserved in the Library of the Institute of Musicology at Bonn. See Magda Marx-Weber, *Katalog der Musikhandschriften in Besitz des Musikwissenschaftlichen Seminars der Universität zu Bonn* (Cologne, 1971), nos. 64–83.
[48] Bonn, Ms. Ecc. 377. 13. 6 (*Katalog*, no. 80).

(Fly, my heart; cease to love, adore no more him/her who despises thee. I
long to change, ease my suffering; a tyrant deity is Beauty.)

The thirty-four duets of Giovanni Carlo Maria Clari (1677–1754)
are famous examples of the genre in the early eighteenth century.[49]
His *Duetti e Terzetti da camera* printed at Bologna in 1720 were
widely diffused and imitated, on account of their mixture of contrapuntal ensemble sections and soloistic virtuosity. Handel borrowed five of Clari's duets in his oratorio *Theodora* (1750).[50]
Another master of the chamber duet was Agostino Steffani (1654–
1728). His output in the field of vocal chamber music consists

[49] See Colin Timms, article 'Clari', *The New Grove*, iv. p. 428.
[50] *Händels Werke*, ed. Chrysander, Supplement iv.

almost entirely of duets: there survive in manuscript more than 100
with thoroughbass accompaniment and six *scherzi a due voci con
stromenti*.[51] The duets, probably composed for the court of
Hanover between 1688 and 1696, were praised as models of polyphonic chamber music, not only by Steffani's contemporaries, but
even by E. T. A. Hoffmann. Johann Mattheson, in *Der vollkommene Capellmeister* (Hamburg, 1739),[52] wrote that there were
probably no more correctly constructed compositions, no fugues
with more agreeable themes and more skilful answers and imitations, than the duets of Steffani: 'These Italian duets demand far
more skill and thought than a whole chorus in eight or more parts.
At every point a fugal and imitative character is encountered, with
suspensions, displacements and skilful resolutions; without any
noticeable aberration in the harmony. Short imitations, competing
displacements, and unforced suspensions ornament these duets
before everything else. In this Steffani was incomparable.' There
could hardly be a more apposite description of the cantabile polyphony of these works.

## (b) GERMANY

### By HANS JOACHIM MARX

DIFFUSION OF THE ITALIAN CANTATA

THE Italian solo cantata was adopted in Germany relatively late
and enjoyed only a short efflorescence there. It became fashionable
to some extent around 1730, but German composers had long been
familiar with its stylistic bases. Following Schütz's pupil, Johann
Nauwach (*c*.1595–*c*.1630), who studied in Italy, adopted Caccini's
monodic style in his *Arie passeggiate a una voce* (Dresden, 1623),
and employed *stile recitativo* in his *Deutsche Villanellen* of 1627,[53]
the composers of the 1630s busied themselves with intensive exploration of the new types of Italian vocal music. Kaspar Kittel
(1603–39) was another Schütz pupil who studied in Italy. In his
*Arien und Cantaten* (Dresden, 1638), the earliest instance of the

---

[51] Sixteen of the duets were ed. Alfred Einstein and Adolf Sandberger, *Denkmäler der
Tonkunst in Bayern*, vi (2) (Leipzig, 1905); one of these, 'Occhi, perchè piangete', reprinted
in Schering, op. cit., no. 242. See also Colin Timms, 'Revisions in Steffani's Chamber
Duets', *Proceedings of the Royal Musical Association*, xcvi (1969–70), p. 119.
[52] pp. 345 and 349.
[53] See Vol. IV, p. 183.

use of the term 'cantata' in Germany, he developed fairly fully the principle of the through-composed strophic song with ostinato bass. With the *Neue Arien* (1667) of Adam Krieger (1634–66),[54] which are discussed below, conformity with the contemporary Italian solo cantata seems to be complete: the layout in several movements interspersed with instrumental ritornellos and the quasi-arioso lyricism of the strophic song (without recitatives) point clearly to the chamber cantatas of Luigi Rossi and Carissimi.

It was Reinhard Keiser (1674–1739), described as late as 1773 by Johann Scheibe as 'the greatest original genius Germany has ever produced', who, after publishing the German cantatas described below, really naturalized the Italian cantata in Germany.[55] His collection of *Divertimenti serenissimi delle Cantate, Duetti ed Arie diverse senza stromenti* (Hamburg, 1713) contains, in addition to some macaronic compositions on part-German, part-Italian texts, markedly Italian solo cantatas. These, mostly in four movements, conform to the standard scheme of the Neapolitan cantata. The arias generally begin with a 'motto': the voice anticipates its first phrase and then, after a brief instrumental passage, begins again with the identical theme. The lyrical content of Keiser's arias shows the hand of the experienced opera composer who knows how to give pregnant musical expression to the emotion of a character on the stage.

Like Keiser, J. S. Bach wrote only a small number of cantatas on Italian texts.[56] His contemporary, Johann David Heinichen (1683–1729), who was active at the court of Dresden and certainly known to Bach, was much more prolific. Of his approximately sixty Italian cantatas, the majority, as usual in the eighteenth century, are *cantate con stromenti*.[57] Pronounced instrumental effects, achieved by lavish orchestration (in addition to strings he has flutes, *corni da caccia*, oboes, and theorbos) and precise instructions as to performance (*con sordino, pizzicato*, etc.) are typical of Heinichen, and indeed of the Italian cantata in eighteenth-century Germany as a whole. The preference for fuller orchestration in the arias and accompanied recitatives of these cantatas is ascribed by Mattheson to

[54] Krieger's best-known cantata, 'Fleug, Psyche, fleug', is ed. Carol MacClintock, *The Solo Song 1580–1730 (A Norton Music Anthology)* (New York, 1973), p. 258.

[55] See Richard Petzoldt, *Die Kirchenkompositionen und weltlichen Kantaten R. Keisers* (Düsseldorf, 1935).

[56] See Vol. V, p. 762. On the authenticity of 'Amore traditore' (BMV 203) see Robert Donington, '*Amore traditore*: a problem cantata', *Studies in Eighteenth-Century Music*, ed. H. C. Robbins Landon (London, 1970), p. 160.

[57] List of works in Günter Hausswald, 'Heinichen', *Die Musik in Geschichte und Gegenwart*, vi (1957), col. 49–51.

the shortcomings of German singers, whose voices are 'perhaps . . . not so delicate as in Italy, and therefore have more need than Italians of an accompaniment to hide behind a little'.[58]

## GERMAN CANTATA TEXTS

Solo cantatas on German texts did not appear until the end of the seventeenth century. The reasons are primarily literary; until then German poetry, unlike Italian, had only strophic forms of lyric verse. It was only with the imitation and translation of Italian madrigals that a model was created for the recitative style with its metrical and rhythmic freedoms.[59] The poet Georg Philipp Harsdörffer (1607–58) had spoken out in favour of greater flexibility in metrical patterns and claimed the freedom 'to fall into other kinds of rhyming', according to the 'character and suitability of the content'.[60] But it was left to Caspar Ziegler to introduce madrigalian poetry to Germany in his treatise *Von den Madrigalen, einer schönen und zur Musik bequemsten Art Verse* (Leipzig, 1653). He expressly emphasized that 'no single *genus carminis* in the German language is better suited to music than a madrigal', and for that reason he would consider the '*stylum recitativum*, such as the Italians use . . . for a continuous madrigal', which could be interrupted by an arietta or aria.[61] Ziegler's proposed alternation of recitative and aria was taken up by Erdmann Neumeister, the outstanding poet of sacred cantatas. Although initially employed in the Protestant church cantata, it gained acceptance in the secular cantata as well. For Christian Friedrich Hunold, the Hamburg opera librettist, the cantata represented the summit of musical poetics.[62]

The secular cantata with German text was popular enough in the 1730s for Johann Christoph Gottsched to include a chapter 'On cantatas' in his celebrated *Versuch einer critischen Dichtkunst* (Leipzig, 1730), in which he set out both the literary and the musical principles. He recommended the librettist to put 'the gayest, wittiest, and liveliest things into the arias, but the rest, namely narratives and so forth, into recitative'.[63] Following

---

[58] *Neueröffnetes Orchester* (Hamburg, 1713), p. 177.
[59] See Günther Müller, *Geschichte des deutschen Liedes vom Zeitalter des Barock biz zur Gegenwart* (Munich, 1925), especially pp. 116–21.
[60] See Marian Szyrocki, *Die deutsche Literatur des Barock* (*rowohlts deutsche enzyklopädie*, 300–301) (Hamburg, 1968), p. 53.
[61] Modern edition by Dorothea Glodny-Wiercinsky, in the series *Ars Poetica*, xii (Frankfurt/M, 1971), p. 41.
[62] *Die allerneueste Art zur reinen und galanten Poesie zu gelangen* (Hamburg, 1706).
[63] Quoted from Schmitz, *Solokantate*, p. 263.

Gottsched, Johann Adolf Scheibe postulated in *Der critische Musikus* (Leipzig, 2nd ed., 1745) that it was in the nature of the cantata to be epic: either the poet spoke alone, or he introduced 'other persons who likewise spoke'. Neither speech nor dialogue, but description by the poet, was essential in the German cantata.

## THE GERMAN SECULAR CANTATA

During the first half of the eighteenth century the number of cantatas on German texts was modest indeed. In his *Versuch* Gottsched bemoaned German composers' preference for Italian texts and asked whether 'their own mother-tongue (were) not worthy to be set to beautiful music'.[64] Basically it was the lack of German lyrical poetry that hindered a richer flow. It is significant that the German secular cantata first became important in the 1760s with texts by Klopstock, Herder, and others. The Italian solo cantata was largely cultivated in court circles, while the German cantata had first to establish itself in middle-class society. The majority of German cantatas before 1750 are occasional pieces, celebrating private or civic events (birthdays, name-days, weddings, civic elections, etc.). Hence German composers tended to neglect the solo cantata with thoroughbass in favour of the cantata with orchestral accompaniment.

The German cantata first materialized in Keiser's *Gemüths-Ergötzung, bestehend in einigen Sinngedichten* (Hamburg, 1698), whose later Italian publication has already been mentioned. The German collection consists of seven solo cantatas on love poems by Christian Heinrich Postel ('Die bis in den Tod geliebte Iris', 'Die rasende Eifersucht', and others), which derive formally from the Neapolitan *cantata con stromenti*. Beside the *da capo* aria with initial motto, Keiser's invention is at its best in the smaller, song-like forms. The cantata 'Der vergnügte Amyntas', for instance, has an aria headed *Tempo di Courante alla Francese* which, however, has a perceptible struggle at the beginning to fit the metre of the German verse to the French dance rhythm:[65]

## Ex. 47

(How sweet it is, after sharp pain.)

---

[64] *Versuch*, p. 471.
[65] Quoted from Schmitz, *Solokantate*, p. 269.

French influences, particularly Lully's, are also evident in Keiser's collection of cantatas, *Musikalische Landlust* (Hamburg, 1714). The cantata-like anthology *Kayserliche Friedenspost* (Hamburg, 1715)[66] includes fragments from an opera.

Following in the Hamburg tradition, Georg Philipp Telemann (1681–1767) also cultivated the German cantata. As he remarks in the autobiography he wrote for Johann Mattheson's *Grundlage einer Ehrenpforte* (Hamburg, 1740), some of his secular cantatas are occasional pieces written for his friends in Hamburg and circulated in manuscript, others he had printed for a wider public. The occasional character of most of Telemann's cantatas—for instance the *Moralische Kantaten* for solo voice and *basso continuo* (1735–6) or the solo cantata 'Ich kann lachen, weinen, scherzen' from *Der getreue Musicmeister* (Hamburg, 1728)—is obvious. The brevity of the numbers, the rather mannered melodies with innumerable ornaments in the arias, and the expressive weakness of the recitatives, suggest that they were written in haste. Besides the late 'Ino' cantata (1765), the 'Schulmeister-Kantate' is notable for the full development of the comic musical element characteristic of Telemann (cf. his well-known intermezzo *Pimpinone*). The cantata survives in an orchestrated version and is a sort of parody of a school singing lesson.[67]

The joke lies in the schoolmaster's brilliantly represented inability to express himself musically. His inflated opinion of his meagre powers is made clear in the first aria ('Wenn der Schulmeister singet, so klingt es wunderschön'): instead of a well written aria, he produces only a parody of one. As the following excerpt shows,[68] the false modulations and cadences, the primitive harmonies and pedestrian melodies, quite apart from the absurdly constructed *da capo* section, are the comic materials. It is true that understanding of the comedy depends on acquaintance with the background, the Neapolitan aria.

---

[66] For a general study of the cantatas, see Petzoldt, op. cit., especially pp. 42–69.

[67] See Fritz Stein, 'Eine komische Schulmeisterkantate von Georg Philipp Telemann und Johann Adolf Hasse', *Festschrift Max Schneider* (Leipzig, 1955), p. 183.

[68] Ed. Fritz Stein (Kassel, Basel, etc., 1965).

Ex. 48

(How does that sound? Quite bad! I must confess it myself . . . When the schoolmaster sings, it sounds lovely.)


Few composers apart from Keiser and Telemann cultivated the secular cantata with German text. The German cantatas of J. S. Bach, often designated *dramma per musica*, have been dealt with elsewhere.[69] So far as we can judge today from the isolated surviving cantatas of Carl Heinrich Graun (b.1703–4; d.1759), Gottfried Heinrich Stölzel (1690–1749). Johann Heinrich Rolle (1716–85) and others, they hardly reached the artistic standard of Telemann's.[70]

### THE GERMAN CONTINUO SONG

The solo song with thoroughbass takes a subordinate position among the monodic genres of German baroque music (cantata, sacred aria, dance song).[71] Since, for the most part, it was regarded as the music of utility rather than art, and associated with music-making in student and domestic circles, it was often amateur composers (with a few exceptions) who made the running in song composition. The invariably simple structure of these songs, in keeping with the capabilities of amateur performers and reflecting the talents of the composers, seems to have been an aesthetic principle of the age. In the preface to the first volume of his *Arien* of 1638, Heinrich Albert (1604–51) disclaims any aspirations to great art with his *melodeyen*, but hopes only that anyone 'who can sing a little shall easily master a melody or tune which later, with familiarity, will be enjoyed'. Similarly Johann Rist in the preface to his *Galathea* (Hamburg, 1642), describes the simplicity of his songs as a mark of popular singing.[72] The unpretentiousness of the solo song

[69] Vol. V, p. 762.

[70] See Schmitz, *Solokantate*, pp. 301 ff.

[71] See Hermann Kretzschmar, *Geschichte des neuen deutschen Liedes*, I. Teil: *Von Albert bis Zelter* (Leipzig, 1911), and Richard Thomas, *Poetry and song in the German Baroque: a study of the Continuo Lied* (Oxford, 1963).

[72] On the social role of song, see Hans Christoph Worbs, 'Die Schichtung des deutschen Liedgutes in der 2. Hälfte des 17. Jahrhunderts', *Archiv für Musikwissenschaft*, xvii (1960), p. 65.

deprived it of any significance as art music. There is some justice in
Hermann Kretzschmar's description of the seventeenth century as
'Germany's songless age'.

Albert's *Arien*, published in Königsberg in eight volumes between
1638 and 1650,[73] are representative of early German thoroughbass
monody. The 'arias' are strophic songs, some of them based on
French and Polish dances. As 'Der Mensch hat nichts so eigen' in
the second volume makes clear, the restricted tessitura and the
simplicity of the melodic and harmonic development are in accordance with Rist's ideal:

Ex. 49

---

[73] Ed. Eduard Bernoulli, *Denkmäler deutscher Tonkunst*, xii–xiii (1903), rev. ed. Hans
Joachim Moser (Graz, 1958). Another example in Davison and Apel, op. cit., no. 205.

(There is nothing so right for man and nothing becomes him so well as keeping faith and preserving friendship. When he forms a bond with his fellows he promises not to want with heart and life and hand.)

Besides Albert, who was an associate of the Königsberg circle of poets centred on Simon Dach, and the members of the Hamburg school of songwriters—Thomas Selle (1599–1663), Heinrich Scheidemann (*c.*1595–1663), and also Andreas Hammerschmidt (1611 or 1612–75), Theophil Staden (1607–55) *et al.*—the most distinguished composer of German songs was Adam Krieger (1634–66) of Dresden. His *Neue Arien*, published posthumously in 1667,[74] includes (besides ensembles for from two to five voices) secular monodies which, in their artistic simplicity, are among the most beautiful inventions of the time. They are straightforward strophic songs, in which the melodic line is usually developed from a single motive of dancelike rhythmic character. The instrumental ritornellos concluding the separate stanzas are freely composed or borrow isolated motives from the vocal melody. The brevity and musical simplicity of the following example, the aria 'Wer recht vergnüget leben will', suggest that it was intended for social music-making in a students' *collegium musicum*.

Ex. 50

(i)

---

[74] Ed. Alfred Heuss in *Denkmäler deutscher Tonkunst*, xix (Leipzig, 1905), rev. Moser (Graz, 1958), p. 8. Examples in Davison and Apel, op. cit., no. 228, and Schering, op. cit., nos. 209a and b (the last a duet).

(Let him who wants to live contentedly here on earth trust quietly in God above. Let him bear patiently whatever the Almighty imposes on him and, when misfortune strikes, let him not complain.)

While the songs of Albert and Krieger were composed for middle-class circles, the monodies of Philipp Heinrich Erlebach (1657–1714) have more courtly connotations. The preciosity of the melodic style and the fully worked-out instrumental accompaniments of the songs in the collection *Harmonische Freude musikalischer Freunde* (i, 1697, ii, 1710)[75] are clear signs of the influence of Italian operatic arias.

In the first half of the eighteenth century monodic genres such as the secular solo cantata and the operatic aria almost smothered German song. Collections like *Das Ohren vergnügende und Gemüth ergötzende Tafelkonfekt* by Valentin Rathgeber (Augsburg, 1733) and *Die singende Muse an der Pleisse* by Sperontes (Johann Sigismund Scholze) (Leipzig, 1736)[76] had wide circulation, but were of little musical merit. The songs in Sperontes' collection made use of existing instrumental melodies to which new texts were given.

It was not until the middle of the century that the *Berliner Liederschule*[77] around C. P. E. Bach began to take musical advantage of the poetic impulse generated by Lessing and his contemporaries.

## (c) ENGLAND

### By Ian Spink

DECLAMATORY AND TUNEFUL AYRES

No book of solo songs was published in England from 1622 until 1652, when the music publisher John Playford (1623–86) brought out his first book of *Select Musicall Ayres and Dialogues*. However, much of the repertoire of the intervening years survives in manuscript. The period saw the rise of a new kind of song in which declamatory elements supplanted melody in the voice part, and a thorough bass (realized on theorbo, lute or keyed instrument, or played on the bass viol alone) provided the accompaniment. Declamatory features have already been noted in some of the lute-songs of Alfonso Ferrabosco II and John Dowland,[78] particularly in

---

[75] Ed. Otto Kinkeldey, *Denkmäler deutscher Tonkunst*, xlvi–xlvii (1913), rev. Moser (Graz, 1959). Examples in Davison and Apel, op. cit., no. 254, and Schering, op. cit., no. 262.

[76] Examples in Schering, op. cit., no. 289.

[77] See Vol. VII, pp. 345–7.

[78] See Vol. IV, pp. 211–15.

those written for masques, but the earliest song to establish the type clearly is 'Bring away this sacred tree' 'made and exprest' by Nicholas Lanier (1588–1666) for Campion's *Maske . . . at the Marriage of the . . . Earle of Somerset* in 1613.[79]

Ex. 51

[79] For a more detailed treatment of the stylistic development which English song underwent during the period see Spink, *English Song: Dowland to Purcell* (London, 1974), pp. 38–127, which also lists printed and manuscript sources and provides an extensive bibliography up to 1973, which should be consulted for the writings of J. P. Cutts, Vincent Duckles, McDonald Emslie and others who have worked in this field. *English Songs, 1625–1660*, ed. Spink, *Musica Britannica*, xxxiii (1971) provides a selection of 124 songs of the period: those of Robert Johnson are available in *Robert Johnson, Ayres, Songs and Dialogues*, ed. idem, *The English Lute-Song*, 2nd ser., xvii (2nd ed., 1974).

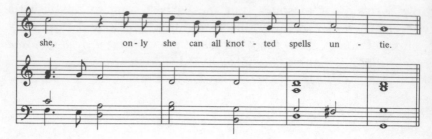

she,    on - ly   she   can   all   knot - ted   spells   un - tie.

The contrast with the older lute-song is striking. Tuneful or polyphonic elements are absent; instead there is declamation based on rhetorical principles and an accompaniment that is to all intents and purposes a continuo realization, though in this case printed in tablature. What this style of song owed to Italian influences (if anything) is difficult to say, but it is at least possible that it developed independently as a kind of English *stile rappresentativo* designed for the court masque.

Lanier, travelling in Italy probably in 1610 and again between 1625 and 1628, certainly had experience of Italian music at first hand. It is assumed that his famous recitative *Hero and Leander* dates from the late 1620s, yet a hundred years later Roger North was moved by the way it expressed 'passion, hope, fear, and despair, as strong as words and sounds can bear'.[80] The whole piece is worthy of comparison with the great laments of Monteverdi and d'India on account of its remarkable breadth and intensity of expression, and the psychological truth of its emotions.

Ex. 52

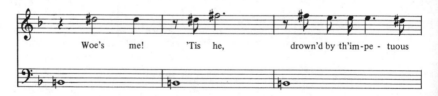

Woe's   me!    'Tis   he,     drown'd by th'im-pe - tuous

[80] John Wilson (ed.), *Roger North on Music* (London, 1959), p. 265. See Duckles 'English song and the challenge of Italian monody' *Words to Music: Papers on English Seventeenth-Century Song* (Los Angeles, 1967), p. 3; also Emslie, 'Nicholas Lanier's innovations in English Song', *Music & Letters*, xli (1960), p. 13.

The only other work by an English composer at all comparable with this recitative is 'Ariadne's Lament' by Henry Lawes (1596–1662), although by no means as successful. Lawes was at his best in setting the lyrics of the 'cavalier poets' who frequented the court of Charles I where he himself was employed—among them Carew, Herrick, Lovelace, Suckling, and Waller.[81] His output was enormous; over 430 songs survive, more than 150 of them in three books of *Ayres and Dialogues* (1653, 1655, and 1658).[82] Milton, whose songs he set in *Comus* (1634), eulogized him thus:

*Harry*, whose tunefull and well measur'd song
First taught our English Music how to span
Words with just note and accent . . .
      . . . the man
That with smooth Aire couldst humour best our tongue.

and it is from the point of view of 'just note and accent' that his declamatory songs deserve attention.

[81] W. McC. Evans, *Henry Lawes, musician and friend of poets* (New York, 1941) is a general treatment. Studies of Lawes' songs include Eric Ford Hart, 'Introduction to Henry Lawes', *Music & Letters*, xxxii (1951), p. 217 and 328, and R. J. McGrady, 'Henry Lawes and the Concept of "Just Note and Accent" ' *Music & Letters*, 1 (1969), p. 86; see also Pamela Willetts, *The Henry Lawes Manuscript* (London, 1969), pp. 5–27, which includes an annotated list of the contents of his large autograph songbook.
[82] His autograph manuscript (Brit. Lib. Add. MS 53723). contains 325 songs.

Compared with his contemporaries he brought a much more subtle awareness of the inflections and accents of the English language to his word setting, combined with a richer and more expressive harmonic vocabulary. The opening of 'Whither are all her false oaths blown?' (Herrick) provides a characteristic example of his technique. The question, itself rhetorical, is made doubly so by exaggerating the natural speech rhythm and inflexion of the words, the voice rising over an octave and expressing the idea of 'false oaths' through the hollow sound of an augmented chord.

Ex. 53

Too many of Lawes's declamatory songs depend on such details without achieving a completely convincing synthesis of words and music. Not only is his word-setting sometimes less than 'just'; in general the problem of reconciling the natural speed of spoken verse with music's own natural speed of progression is not comfortably solved. Thus, words at the beginning and in the middle of a line are delivered fairly rapidly but drawn out at cadences for musical reasons in a way which is fundamentally incompatible with the idea of 'just note and accent'. Furthermore, the subordination of elements of musical structure often causes a rambling effect, especially in longer, through-set songs. These weaknesses, attributable to the style rather than the man, do not, of course, disfigure Lawes's tuneful ayres or ballads, many of which are in triple time and based on dance rhythms. Burney was sufficiently impressed to refer to one such (Herrick's 'Among the myrtles') as 'pleasing psalmody', though he had little to say in favour of the declamatory songs.

In the lighter style Lawes's contemporaries were less obviously his inferior. Indeed, a setting of Herrick's 'Gather ye rosebuds' by Henry's brother William (1602–45) was one of the most popular songs of the time, while many of the *Cheerfull Ayres or Ballads* (1660) published by John Wilson (1595–1674) were reprinted again and again both in solo versions and as glees for three voices with continuo.[83] Though less successful in the declamatory style, songs such as 'In the merry month of May' and 'From the fair Lavinian shore' testify to Wilson's popular and attractive melodic gift.

Brief notice should be taken here of the dialogue—a dramatization of a pastoral incident, or one drawn from the Bible or classical mythology, set in declamatory style for one or two singers with concluding chorus. Lanier and the Lawes brothers wrote several attractive pastoral dialogues, and some on biblical and mythological subjects by John Hilton (1599–1657) and Robert Ramsey (*fl.c.*1612–44) show dramatic flair.[84]

## PURCELL AND HIS CONTEMPORARIES

The Restoration period is dominated by Henry Purcell (1659–95) and his songs are undoubtedly among his greatest achievements.[85] Not only did he inherit and enrich the tradition of the tuneful ballad, he developed newer and larger forms more capable—as the ballad was not—of conveying powerful emotion. He made his rather inauspicious debut as a song writer in one of Playford's collections of *Choice Ayres, Songs and Dialogues* (2nd. ed., 1675) — a series whose contents represented the taste of the court and the public theatres and consisted largely of triple-time songs, by Pelham Humfrey (1647–74), William Gregory (*fl.*1651–87), and others a good deal worse. Slightly later, the songs of Thomas Farmer (*fl.*1671–88) and William Turner (1651–1740) reflect a move away from triple-time to common-time tunes in the early 1680s. Turner writes gracefully but rather overdoes the quaver passing notes so that the effect soon palls.

[83] The songs of William Lawes receive due attention in Murray Lefkowitz, *William Lawes* (London, 1960), pp. 149–186; Wilson's in Duckles, 'The "Curious" Art of John Wilson (1595–1674)' *Journal of the American Musicological Society*, vii (1954), p. 93.

[84] On the biblical dialogues, see above, p. 2.

[85] The subject of this section is treated at somewhat greater length in Spink, *English Songs* pp. 151–259. On Purcell's songs see also Jack A. Westrup, *Purcell* (London, 1937, rev. 1968), pp. 153–71; Anthony Lewis, *The Language of Purcell* (Hull, 1968), pp. 17–22; Franklin B. Zimmerman, 'Sound and sense in Purcell's "Single Songs"', *Words to Music: Papers on English Seventeenth-Century Song* (Los Angeles, 1967), pp. 45–78, and Margaret Laurie, 'Purcell's Extended Solo Songs', *Musical Times*, cxxv (1984), p. 19. Purcell's secular songs and cantatas are published in the *Purcell Society Edition*, xxv (London, 1928; rev. ed., 1984): his theatre songs in xvi, xx, and xxi (1906–1917).

Ex. 54

*Choice Ayres and Songs. . . IV (1683)*

Almost without exception the products of this school are blighted by the affectations of gallantry and insipid pastoralism: it is fop's music. Hardly surprisingly Matthew Locke (1622–77) provides stronger fare; for example, his recitative 'In a soft vision of the night' (Flatman) shows the influence of Lawes's declamatory style, but the highly expressive harmonic language is characteristically Locke's own.

Ex. 55

*Choice Ayres and Songs. . . II (1679)*

As a young man Purcell came strongly under the influence of Locke, especially with regard to expressive declamation and affective use of dissonance and chromatic harmony. But, unlike Locke, he was willing to learn from foreigners and saw in the Italian style a way in which he could overcome the limitations of the ballad. In tracing his development as a song writer through the all too short period of his creativity, we can recognise several approaches to the problem of expanding the physical dimensions of song in order to support greater emotional weight. The forms he chose to enlarge for this purpose were the ground bass, the binary air (leading eventually to the *da capo* aria) and the recitative—often linked together in multi-sectional structures analogous to the recitative-aria pair and the Italian cantata.

To some extent he may have been influenced by the songs of the immigrant Pietro Reggio (1632–85), in whose settings of poems by Abraham Cowley we find an ambitious attempt to deal with serious material on a large scale. For all their shortcomings Reggio's *Songs* (1680) open up new horizons, and it is no mere coincidence that one of Purcell's earliest ground-bass songs—his setting of Cowley's 'She loves and she confesses too' (1683)—uses the identical bass that Reggio had used in setting the same text. Purcell's early ground-bass songs take over where Reggio's left off. At first he was content to repeat a bass at the same pitch, disguising the cadences with overlapping phrases in the voice and exploiting the harmonic ambiguities of the ground ever more resourcefully. One of the best examples of this type is his setting of Katherine Philips's 'O Solitude' (1687). But the increased scale he sought was to be achieved by introducing modulation into the ground bass. It brought not only variety; it added a new dynamic element to the structure, and led to increasing freedom in handling the ground-bass form, numerous examples of which occur in the odes and operatic pieces of Purcell's last years. Almost without exception they reveal a superb technique used to great imaginative effect.[86]

[86] See Hugh M. Miller, 'Henry Purcell and the Ground Bass', *Music & Letters*, xxix (1948), p. 340; also McGuinness, 'The Ground Bass in the English Court Ode', *Music & Letters*, li (1970), pp. 118 and 265.

'Music for a while' (1692) is a notable example that has been mentioned in Vol. V,[87] but deserves quotation here not only as an illustration of Purcell's vivid response to Dryden's sinister imagery, but also as an example of his freer handling of the form. Starting with strict repetitions of the three-bar bass in C minor, modifications of the cadential pattern are introduced so as to lead via statements in G minor and Bb major to a cadence in Eb major, and finally back to C minor and a repeat of the opening section. Thus ground bass and ternary form fuse together.

Ex. 56

*Orpheus Britannicus,* II(1702)

---

Large-scale structure without the use of a ground as a prop presented more fundamental problems, but Purcell's study of Italian models enabled him to move towards the more spacious perspectives of the Italian aria. Of course, he continued to write light strophic airs of great charm throughout his life, as 'Fairest Isle' (1691) and 'If love's a sweet passion' (1692) demonstrate; indeed, his continuing popularity as a song writer has largely depended on such songs. But weightier matters needed a different mode of expression, and it was by adapting the techniques of abstract instrumental composition from the sonata (or inheriting them already adapted by way of Italian models) that Purcell was able to create an appropriate vehicle for them. One of the earliest songs in which these new techniques are found is 'I'll sail upon the dog-star' (1688), though they are as yet somewhat compressed. Still, the characteristic elements of motivic imitation, repetition, and extension through sequence are evident, and it was only a matter of time before the dimensions of the binary tonal framework would expand to accommodate them, and lead eventually to adoption of *da capo* form. The best examples are to be found in some of the larger songs in *The Fairy Queen* (1692–3), notably the brilliant trumpet aria 'Hark! the ech'ing air'—though not itself in *da capo* form. Less exuberant in style and on a smaller scale 'Lovely Albina' ('The Last

Song the Author sett before his Sickness') demonstrates the idiom, at the same time reminding us that far from submerging his musical personality in the Italian style, Purcell made it his own.

Ex. 57

*Orpheus Britannicus*, I (1698)

There remains one other type of vocal composition to consider: what, for want of a better word may be called recitative, although Purcell did not distinguish it as such. In some respects it was his most individual and remarkable achievement, as can be seen by comparing the rather cramped style of the elegy on the death of Matthew Locke, 'What hope for us remains' (1677), with the extravagance that characterizes those of his last years; the opening section of 'Sweeter than roses', for example. He set himself to practise the techniques involved in a series of settings of Cowley dating from the mid-1680s, and by the 1690s he was their complete master—truth to tell, they had begun to master him. It was a style ideally suited to depicting states of extreme emotional stress and even mental disturbance, hence its use in 'mad songs' and at moments of deep pathos.

Essentially the technique is one of ornamentation applied to certain emotive or descriptive words and phrases, coloured by discords or chromatic harmony. In the opening bars of 'The fatal hour comes on apace', for example, a sense of dreadful foreboding is conveyed through affective treatment of key words such as 'fatal hour', 'die', 'certain misery', etc. Although by no means an example of Purcell at his most flamboyant, it demonstrates the importance of ornament as an expressive element in his art.

Ex. 58

*Orpheus Britannicus,* II(1702)

So far we have been considering how Purcell developed and enlarged certain types of song as vehicles for the greater expressive
range he sought. Their synthesis came in the multi-sectional song,
or cantata (though the term was not yet used in England). Comprising from two to six sections such songs came to dominate his
mature output. His Cowley settings of the mid-1680s represent an
important early stage in this process, whereby in recognizing and
exploiting the natural divisions of the verse, the argument of the
poem emerges in a series of linked yet contrasting movements. In
practice, the lengthy and powerful recitatives in these cantatas
over-balance the comparatively undeveloped tuneful sections, a
fault which persists to the end, even in such a fine work as 'The
Blessed Virgin's Expostulation' (1693).

Two volumes of Purcell's best songs were published posthumously by his widow in 1698 and 1707 under the title *Orpheus
Britannicus*. The contents reveal the breadth and depth of his
genius, an incredibly fertile imagination, and amazing technique.
His erstwhile teacher John Blow (1649–1708) had a sufficiently
high opinion of his own talents as a songwriter to publish a similar
collection called *Amphion Anglicus* in 1700.[88] The inspiration behind
the title is clear; the inspiration behind the contents less obvious,
for Blow's genius lay in other directions. Hardly able to write even
a shapely tune (though his setting of Waller's 'It is not that I love
you less' is perhaps an exception) his successful songs are few and
far between. Two books of songs by Robert King (*fl.*1676–1728)
published in the last decade of the century contain polished but
innocuous work, openly acknowledging Italian influence and palely
reflecting Purcell.

For a decade or more after his death, Purcell's influence was
inescapable. The work of his brother Daniel (*c.*1660–1717), John

---

[88] Published in *Monuments of Music and Music Literature in Facsimile*, Ser. 1, ii, (New
York, 1965).

Weldon (1676–1736), and William Croft (1678–1727) show it clearly, particularly in their use of florid recitative and ground bass. Others, like John Eccles (c.1668–1735) and Richard Leveridge (b. 1670–71; d.1758)—and the younger generation of songwriters— were less affected, bringing polish, but increasing vapidity, to the ballad style. Most of their songs were published in single sheets, but Eccles, who in many ways was the best composer among them, can be sampled in his *Collection of songs for one, two, and three voices* (1704).

## CANTATA AND BALLAD: 1710-50

Although Italian influences threatened to swamp English song in the years around 1710, it was really only in the cantata that they came to anything. Italianate taste was catered for by Walsh's many publications of favourite opera songs, but it was a taste apart and left the mainstream of English song comparatively untouched—if anything stronger and more self-assured. Indeed, the indigenous tradition emerged triumphant in the 1730s, refined through contact with opera, but essentially unsubverted. Handel himself was not unaffected, and though his authentic English songs are few, it should not be forgotten that the enormous number of songs from operas and oratorios that Walsh published make him, in effect, the most significant song-writer of the time—though having made the point it must be allowed to rest, in order to look more closely at the work of others. Above all it is in the songs of Thomas Augustine Arne (1710–78) that the synthesis of 'polite' and 'popular', 'art song' and 'ballad' finds its most congenial expression.[89]

A generation earlier, however, the Italian style seemed likely to carry all before it. The first cantatas directly based on Italian models were the *Six English Cantatas* (1710) of Johann Christoph Pepusch (1667–1752): 'the first Essays of this kind, written for the most part several Years ago, as an Experiment of introducing a sort of Composition which has never been naturaliz'd in our Language'. The poet and author of the interesting preface was John Hughes who sought to justify the English language as a vehicle for 'the most elegant Stile of Musick'. The method was to treat a pastoral incident, or one drawn from classical mythology, in a manner analogous to an operatic scene, but presented in narrative rather

[89] The song literature of the period has, as yet, hardly been explored except for H. Diack Johnstone, 'English Solo Song, c.1710–1760', *Proceedings of the Royal Musical Association*, xcv (1969), p. 67.

than dramatic form—*secco* recitative carrying the story forward, *da capo* air (with obbligato instrumental accompaniment) conveying the thoughts and feelings of the characters expressed by a single singer, almost invariably a soprano. All but one of Pepusch's first set of cantatas adheres to the recitative-air/recitative-air sequence, and this was to remain fairly standard practice in the works of composers who followed him. Significantly, Handel's first attempt at setting English words was in the cantata *Venus and Adonis* to a text by Hughes, and within a few years collections of English cantatas were published by Daniel Purcell in 1713 and Johann Ernst Galliard (*c*.1687–1749) in 1716, both 'after the Italian manner' and by George Hayden (*fl*.1713–1722) in 1717, more English in tone, with echoes of Purcell. Pepusch published a second set in 1720. Important later collections include six by Thomas Roseingrave (1688–1766), to Italian words, published in 1735, rich in invention and elaborate in execution. In contrast, the two books published by John Stanley (1712–1786) in 1742 and 1748 are more facile in style and show an increasing inclination to dispense with the *da capo* air in favour of binary songs, sometimes strophically treated.[90]

Numerous composers included a single cantata in their song collections as specimens of their competence in a more imposing style. Among them Maurice Greene (1696–1755) deserves attention, for although he wrote a number of light songs, he clearly had serious aspirations. Certainly in setting *Spenser's Amoretti* (1739) his intentions were worthy and the results significant if not entirely successful. His method was to divide each sonnet into sections and set each section as a different movement, rather like a cantata without recitative. But sixteenth-century language and versification in this case presented problems that were hardly capable of a convincing solution. Even in dealing with lyric verse of his own day his vocal writing often sounds forced. The setting of Gay's 'Go, rose' (from *A Cantata and four English songs*, Book I, 1745) may be taken as typical, for, despite a certain rococo charm, its rather stilted verbal repetitions and somewhat obviously contrived sequences create an effect which is too fussy for the words. The ballad style would have suited the poem much better.

---

[90] See Tony Frost, 'The Cantatas of John Stanley (1713–86)', *Music & Letters*, liii (1972), p. 284; also Gerald Finzi, 'John Stanley (1713–1786)', *Proceedings of the Royal Musical Association*, lxxvii (1951), p. 69.

Ex.59

Henry Carey (*c.*1689–1743) and Johann Friedrich Lampe (*c.* 1703–51) are perhaps the best-known ballad composers in the first half of the eighteenth century, although it seems not to have been beyond the skill of dozens of others to write one or two lively or graceful tunes worth printing, either on single sheets or in collections such as *The Musical Miscellany* (1729–31). Most were no more than sixteen bars long and many took their rhythm and phrasing from the minuet. The pastoral convention was, if anything, more prevalent than before and Chloe never more courted by ardent swains. Carey's early reputation was won as a humorous poet but as a musician he was far from being a complete amateur; he had a passable technique and plenty of natural talent. His songs began to be printed from about 1715, one of the earliest being 'Sally in our alley' which soon inspired numerous parodies. In 1724 and 1740 he even published sets of *Cantatas* 'To please my Friends, To mortify my Enemies, To get Money, And Reputation' although it seems unlikely that any of these objectives was achieved. Some, no doubt, were amused by the burlesque cantata on a mare who lost her shoe, 'Compos'd in the High Stile by Sigr. Carini'. The most complete collection of his songs is *The Musical Century* in two volumes (1737 and 1740), comprising 'one hundred English ballads . . . the words and musick of the whole by Henry Carey'.

Lampe was a more polished composer. In 1731 he published a collection of his songs entitled *Wit Musically Embellish'd* in which he defended the ballad from those prejudiced against it: 'notwithstanding the best Modulation & Harmony is compendiously couch'd under that Denomination'. As an example which seems to justify his argument without need of further comment 'The young lover's first address' may be quoted.

Ex. 60

pas - sion    be - cause    it    is    ten - der,
ca - sion'd,    O    pi - ty    my    an - guish,

Think  on  your  charms and  you'll  pi - ty  my  smart.
And   let  your  smiles for  your  ri - gour  a - tone.

Carey and Lampe crystallize the taste of the ascendant middle class. In establishing the musical respectability of the ballad, they helped to re-establish the self-respect of the English tradition and offered a viable context for the work of Arne whose earliest songs date from the 1730s. His first song book was not published until 1745, under the title *Lyric Harmony* (Op. 4): a second volume (Op. 5) came out a year later, 'The words collected from the best Poets, ancient and Modern'—among them Shakespeare's 'Where the bee sucks' etc., and verses by Jonson and Suckling. Most are strophic songs in binary form, tricked out with instrumental ritornellos and accompaniments in which the first violin usually doubles the air. Following his engagement to compose for the Vauxhall Gardens in 1745, and the introduction of vocal items into the concerts there (and soon at Ranelagh and Marylebone) Arne's songs for the gardens began to be issued in numerous collections from 1746 onwards, beginning with four books of *Vocal Melody* (1746–1752), the first of which contains 'Sigh no more ladies' and the cantata 'Fair Celia love pretended' to words by Congreve. A similar collection of songs by William Boyce (1711–1779) was published in six books of *Lyra Britannica* (1747–55), but despite his undoubted talents Boyce lacked Arne's effortless lyric gift, which, at its best, lifted him into another class. The perennial freshness of the Shakespeare songs reveals one side of Arne's genius, while a song like 'The fond appeal' from the first book of *Lyric Harmony* shows at once the perfection of his melody.[91]

[91] See Julian Herbage, 'The Vocal Style of Thomas Augustine Arne', *Proceedings of the Royal Musical Association*, lxxviii (1952), p. 91; also J. A. Parkinson, *An index to the vocal works of Thomas Augustine Arne and Michael Arne* (Detroit, 1972).

Ex. 61

1. Gen - tle youth, O! tell me why
2. Tell me, when th'ap - poin - ted hour
3. Tell me, when the pains I feel

Tears are star - ting from my eye,
Calls us to the sec - ret bow'r,
Pun - gent as the wounds of steel,

When each night from you I part,
Blush - ing, trem - bling, why I run
When I feel the thril - ling smart,

Why the sigh that rends my heart?
Ear - ly as the ri - sing sun?
Why I bless the poin - ted dart?

Why the sigh that rends my heart?
Ear - ly as the ri - sing sun?
Why I bless the poin - ted dart?

Gen - tle youth, O! tell me true,

Is it then the same with you?

Gen - tle youth, O! tell me true,

## (d) FRANCE

### By DAVID TUNLEY

THE SEVENTEENTH-CENTURY FRENCH *AIR*

WHEN Michel Lambert dedicated his volume of *Airs* (1660) to Louis XIV's aging *premier valet de la chambre*, Pierre de Nyert (*c.* 1597–1682), he described him as the 'God of Song to whom France is indebted for the fine and expressive style of singing he introduced into that country'. A gifted singer and lutenist, de Nyert had travelled to Rome with the Count of Crecqui in 1633 where he was deeply impressed by what he heard. On his return to Paris two years later he began to reform French singing along Italian lines, and his protégés were to include some of the foremost French singers of his time: Anne de la Barre, Hilaire Dupuy, La Varenne, and Rayman. Michel Lambert was also his pupil, and he in turn passed the principles on to his own circle.[92] De Nyert's gifts and the

[92] While all seventeenth-century sources praise the singing of both de Nyert and Lambert, Tallemant des Réaux considered that neither had naturally good voices, but that the 'method made everything', *Les Historiettes,* ed. Léon Cerf (Paris, 1929), vi, p. 129.

influence he shed over French singing are amply confirmed from a diversity of seventeenth-century French sources both musical and literary. Sicard, de Chancy, Luigi Rossi, La Fontaine, Tallement de Réaux, Saint-Evremond, Saint-Simon are among those who esteemed him highly, although during the eighteenth century his name became largely forgotten. In *Le Parnasse françois*, for example, Titon du Tillet ascribes to Lambert much that might have been due to Nyert:

Lambert was the first in France to reveal the true beauties of vocal music, its precision and the ornaments of expression. He also composed *diminutions* for most of his airs in order to exploit lightness of voice, vocal ornamentation in various passages, brilliant and graceful roulades, in which he succeeded admirably.[93]

The art of *diminution* or *doubles*, i.e. dissolving a simple line of melody into faster, ornamental notes, referred to by Titon du Tillet had had a long and continuous tradition in France (as it had in Italy), but Bénigne de Bacilly in his *Remarques curieuses sur l'art de bien chanter* claimed that the earlier approach had been to ornament all notes indiscriminately, having little regard for long or short syllables and at the expense of pronunciation (which he claims was evidently held in little esteem).[94] Bacilly points to the singer Henry du Bailly as the one responsible for developing the 'modern' practice of *diminutions*,[95] and it would seem clear that de Nyert and Lambert refined it still further so that (as Bacilly suggests) the ornamentation could also be used to rectify differences between the various verses. Neither de Nyert nor Lambert left any treatises on singing but many of their ideas were probably embodied in Bacilly's *Remarques curieuses*, which is concerned with good pronunciation, correct breathing, finesse and accuracy in executing ornaments through rigorous training comparable to that

[93] *Le Parnasse françois* (Paris, 1732 ed.), p. 391.
[94] *Remarques curieuses sur l'art de bien chanter* (Paris, 1668), pp. 224–5. This important treatise has been translated and ed. Austin B. Caswell, *A Commentary upon the Art of Proper Singing* (New York, 1968), in which the musical examples that Bacilly assumed would be known to his readers (and were therefore not written out) have been located and reproduced. Page numbers in the present chapter however refer to the original pagination. Bacilly's concept of long and short syllables should not be confused with attempts by Baïf and others in the late sixteenth century to apply the rules of classical prosody to French poetry and which, through union with music, gave rise to *musique mesurée* (cf. Vol. IV, pp. 29–31 and 192–3). Bacilly makes it quite clear that he is not referring to any artificial imposition of long and short quantities upon prose or poetic writing, but to the way that syllables achieve a natural weight when properly spoken or declaimed (pp. 328–9). His concern that ornamentation must take this into account is identical with Caccini's ideas in *Le Nuove Musiche* (1602) (cf. H. Wiley Hitchcock's translation, Madison, Wis., 1980), p. 46).
[95] Bacilly, op. cit., p. 225.

undertaken by Italian singers.[96] Yet if clear pronunciation had been the basis of the new method of singing (the second half of Bacilly's treatise is devoted to this matter), it is worth noting that it was precisely this aspect of Du Bailly's singing that claimed the approval of Mersenne.[97] As Du Bailly's career was almost over by the time de Nyert returned to Paris, it would seem that such changes were already in the air.

It is significant that what changes there were in mid seventeenth-century French song were largely in the realm of performance rather than composition. Whereas in Italy new vocal techniques had been intimately associated with new compositional ones, in France musical traits from the earlier period persisted throughout much of the century. Despite the lapse of time between them, the following three melodies published at roughly twenty-year intervals from 1632 (i.e. before de Nyert's return) are very similar in style.

Ex. 62

(i)                                                          Antoine Boësset (1632)

Beau - té dont les ri-gueurs pri-vent d'es-poir mon â - me Et mes sens de plai-sirs,
Hé - las! Jus-ques à quand veux-tu ré - gler ma flam-me Aux lois de tes dé-sirs?

Ah! cru-elle U - ra - ni - e    Je ne sçau-rais ce-ler    Mon a-mour in-fi - ni - e.

(ii)                                                         Michel Lambert (1658)

Pour-quoi faut il, belle in-hu-mai-ne   Que vous so-yez in-sen-si-ble à ma pei - ne,

---

[96] However, whereas in Italy the tenor was trained to sing with a full, natural voice avoiding falsetto (see Caccini, ed. Hitchcock, p. 56), the latter received Bacilly's high praise (Bacilly, p. 45).

[97] Marin Mersenne, *Harmonie universelle* (Paris, 1636), ii, p. 356.

Et que mon cœur soit sou-mis   à vos lois?   lois?   Un autre au-rait re-gret

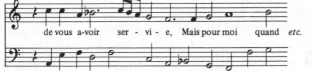

de vous a-voir   ser - vi - e,   Mais pour moi   quand *etc.*

(iii)                                                                Le Camus (1673)

Vous se-rez   les té-moins   de mes vi- ves dou-leurs,   Som-bres dé-serts, fo-rêts ob-

scu - res,   J'i - rai pleu-rer   chez vous   mes tris - tes a-ven-tu - res, Mais

vous ne sçau-rez point le   se-cret de mes   pleurs

(i) (Beauty whose harshness deprives my soul of hope and my senses of pleasures! Alas! How long do you wish to submit by flame to the laws of your desires? Ah, cruel Uranie, I know not how to conceal my infinite love.)

(ii) (Why, cruel beauty, must you be insensible of my pain, and why must my heart be submitted to your laws? Another would regret having served you. But as for me . . . .)

(iii) (Gloomy deserts, dark forests, you will be the witnesses of my acute sorrows; I shall go to you to mourn my sad fortunes, but you will not know the secret of my tears.)

The last of these airs was published in Ballard's monumental series *Airs de différents autheurs à deux parties* which up to as late as 1685 retained the Renaissance practice of notating the parts without bar-lines and placing them on separate pages, although some earlier publications like Lambert's *Airs* of 1660 had been engraved by Richer in score. In the versions quoted here, all three melodies were published with accompaniment for lute.

The use of the lute for song accompaniment—in practice the bass lute known as theorbo—throughout most of the century is usually regarded as a prime example of French musical conservatism, although the preference for that instrument rather than the harpsichord should not necessarily be interpreted merely as a negative response to changes that had long come over Italian and German music. Bacilly claimed that there were good musical reasons for it. Because of its supple, accommodating tone, which did not obscure even the softest voice, he placed the theorbo well ahead of harpsichord and viol.[98] On the other hand, lute tablature began to give way to figured bass in the middle of the century, even though the two methods were practised side by side for some years. The growing popularity of figured bass can be seen from the fact that in the same year as Nicolas Fleury's *Méthode pour apprendre facilement à toucher le théorbe sur la basse continue* (1660), Michel Lambert's *Airs* were published with a note explaining that although the composer could have easily added the theorbo tablature which he had conceived for these pieces, he had decided to provide instead a continuo bass so that, as was customary, the music could be transposed more easily for different voices.

Common to the three airs in Ex. 62 is a melodic style which writers of the day summed up by the word *douceur*. Smooth contours and rhythmic gentleness are obvious traits; a closer study soon reveals also the lack of any of that motivic development which generates many an Italian aria. In place of reiteration and sequential development of small melodic or rhythmic fragments (which in song writing may entail much repetition of words) we see melodic spans embracing whole poetic phrases. If these spans lack the tightly knit unity which follows motivic development, a classical sense of order is gained through their clear-cut juxtaposition. All these features, interacting with a decided penchant for declamation, produced a style of melody characteristically French. Indeed, as we shall see later, so highly prized was this kind of lyricism that

---

[98] Bacilly, op. cit., pp. 17–18.

French composers deliberately retained it in the Italian-inspired cantata of the next century.

Yet it was also in the *cantate française* that French vocal chamber music became more of a composer's art. As we have seen, those who influenced the course of French song in the seventeenth century were essentially singers; their airs were the starting-point for vocal artistry. It was thus almost inevitable that serious song in France did not undergo any radical stylistic development during much of this period. Even if only a relatively small part of seventeenth-century repertoire was written for the highly trained singer, the general conservatism that marks the music of this time could have only been strengthened by the 'occasional' nature of much of the remainder: songs for dancing and drinking. All these factors, allied to the prevailing national taste for elegant expression in both music and poetry led to a repertoire which, although very extensive, was also very stereotyped within the various categories of song. It is hard to escape the conclusion that the *esprit précieux* which pervaded seventeenth-century society was the main influence determining the narrow style of the French air.[99] It was not until social changes came over the country towards the end of the century and a second wave of Italianism, more forceful than the first, washed against French vocal chamber music that it took on a new character. Nevertheless, at its most sophisticated, seventeenth-century French song undoubtedly reached the level of true art, but largely through the artistry of performance—particularly in the mastery of intricate ornamentation. In describing the kind of skill required for his 'new music' Caccini had written 'this art will not suffer mediocrity'.[100] This is perhaps the only real meeting-point throughout much of the century between French and Italian vocal styles.

## CATEGORIES OF SEVENTEENTH-CENTURY SONG

When de Nyert returned to Paris in the 'thirties the main solo vocal form was the *air de cour*,[101] a strophic song either for several voices (with the top voice usually predominating) or for solo song with lute accompaniment; usually the two versions of the same song existed side by side. While at the beginning of the century the *air de cour* was as light-hearted and popular in style as the *voix de ville* which it had replaced, it also began to take on a more serious

---

[99] Théodore Gérold, *L'Art du chant en France au XVII<sup>e</sup> siècle* (Strasbourg, 1921), p. 237.
[100] Caccini, ed. Hitchcock, p. 48.
[101] See Vol. IV, pp. 189–94.

tone evolving the typically French combination of lyricism and gentle declamation mentioned earlier. Of the leading musicians who had cultivated the *air de cour* before 1630 only Antoine Boësset (1586–1643), Étienne Moulinié (d. after 1669), François Richard (1580–1650) and Jean de Cambefort (1605–61) were to publish any more, Cambefort's second volume of *Airs de cour à quatre parties* (1655) being the last. As styles as well as terminology tended to overlap throughout the century, *air de cour*, *air* and *chanson* were terms in common currency at the beginning of the period, although, as we shall see, *chansons* were usually lightweight works associated with dancing and convivial occasions. (A diminutive, *chansonette*, was to appear in the last quarter of the century.) The term *air* eventually became so all-embracing in its stylistic connotations that, like the *air de cour* before it, it could serve as a generic title for virtually all solo and polyphonic songs, so we find *airs sérieux*, *airs à boire*, *airs à danser*, *airs tendres*, and so on. They may, however, be divided into two main categories: serious songs, and songs for dancing and drinking. What was common to most was their bipartite structure, modest proportions, limited range of expression, and conservative idiom, all in striking contrast to the Italian aria of the same period.

POETIC TEXTS

The narrow range of expression characteristic of the seventeenth-century air was primarily due to the conventions of their texts. Bacilly went to some lengths in his *Remarques curieuses* to describe the restrictions which must be placed upon poetic language if the desired goal of 'a marriage between beautiful melody and beautiful words' were to be achieved.[102] His three-volume anthology *Des plus beaux vers qui ont esté mis en chant*, published (anonymously) between 1661 and 1668 and containing 1452 texts, strikingly illustrates how countless variations could be made upon the themes of *beaux yeux*, *mon martyre*, *belle inhumaine*, and other stereotyped phrases. Poetic freedom was found only in poetic form, the *vers libre*. The following text by De La Salle (set to music by Lambert) is typical of the kind of poetry encountered in the *air sérieux* and also the *air à danser*.

Beaux yeux si doux et si charmants,
Sources de lumière et de flamme,
Que j'aurais de contentements

---

[102] Bacilly, op. cit., p. 69.

A vous abandonner l'empire de mon âme!
Mais vos plus doux regards, mortels à mes plaisirs,
Font mourir mon espoir, et vivre mes désirs.

(Beautiful eyes so gentle and so charming, sources of light and flame,
what contentment would I have if I were to surrender the empire of my
soul to you! But your sweetest glances, deadly to my pleasures, would kill
my hope and quicken my desires.)

The names of many of the authors of these verses have long
since sunk into obscurity, but among the better-known literary
figures of the times who contributed to the genre were Corneille,
Molière, Quinault, Benserade, Perrin, Scarron, and Mme. de
Scudéry; and of course the repertoire is liberally sprinkled with
texts from aristocratic circles. Bacilly, Jean-Baptiste Boësset,
Maulevrier, and de Mollier were amongst those who often wrote
both words and music. Only the *air à boire* forsook these precious
poetic groves, exchanging the language of courtly refinement for
that of convivial heartiness and good humour.

### SERIOUS SONGS

Of the countless airs composed during the mid-to-late seventeenth century none were held in higher esteem than those by
Michel Lambert (1610–96), *maître de musique de la chambre du
roi*, whose output of songs was exclusively in the field of serious
song. We have already seen an example of his simpler style (Ex. 62
(ii) ) in an air published in the first volume of Ballard's *Airs de
différents autheurs à deux parties* (37 volumes 1658–93). Lambert
included the same piece in his own collection of 1660 in which
pieces like 'Pourquoi faut-il belle inhumaine' alternated with those
in a more embellished style such as the following:

## Ex. 63

(rev. ed. 1666)

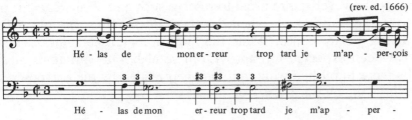

Hé - las de        mon er - reur    trop tard je    m'ap - per-çois

Hé - las de mon    er - reur trop tard    je    m'ap - per -

(Alas, I have seen my error too late. I thought this god would submit to his laws only those who do not well know how to defend themselves; but I feel that, despite myself, my heart is going to yield.)

It was, however, more usual to reserve such embellishments for the second verse of an air, when the art of *diminutions* was introduced into the performance. While the most accomplished singers might have been expected to improvise these elaborate variations, many airs were published with *diminutions* provided by the composer, as in this song by Bacilly.

# Ex. 64

(1668)

Puis-que Phi - lis est in - fi - del - le E - vi-tons le tré -
Puis-que Phi - lis est in - fi-del - le E - vi - tons le tré -

-pas, Mon cœur ré-vol - tons nous contre d'el - le.
-pas, Mon cœur mon cœur ré-vol - tons nous contre d'el - le.

Mais tu n'y con - sens pas, Ah! qu'il
Mais tu n'y con - sens pas, Ah! qu'il est mal - ai -

est mal - ai - sé quand l'A - mour est ex - trê - me De ban-
sé quand l'A-mour est ex - trême est ex - trê - me De ban-nir

-nir de son cœur une in - gra - te qu'on ai - me,
de ban-nir de son cœur une in - gra - te qu'on ai - me.

(Since Philis is faithless, let us not die (on her account). My heart, let us rebel against her. But you don't agree. Ah, how hard it is, when Love is extreme, to banish from one's heart an ingrate whom one loves.
(*Double*) She has changed, this inhuman creature. Let us despise her charms; my heart, let us avenge her hate. But you don't consent. Ah! how hard it is, etc.)

Even the *airs tendres*, more usually known as *brunettes*, simple and unpretentious as they were, were often published with *diminu-*

*tions* for their second verse. Although Christophe Ballard's extensive collection of *brunettes* appeared in the early years of the eighteenth century most of them had been composed very much earlier and so represent a seventeenth-century repertoire. Ballard explains in the Preface to the first book that the name *brunette* stemmed from texts such as that of Ex. 65, which also gives a good idea of the musical style:

Ex. 65

Sont les fleurs qui vont    nais - sant    Des lar - mes que    Tir - cis

jet - te. Ah!    pe - ti - te Bru - net - te, Ah!         tu me fais    mou-rir!

(The handsome shepherd Tircis, seated near his beloved Annette by the banks of the Loire, sang to his pipes: 'Ah, little Brunette, Ah, you make me die.')

This kind of song lasted well past the middle of the eighteenth century, and in so doing reflected, of course, a number of changes that came over French music at that time.

A term frequently encountered in the pages of the serious song is *récit* which, although obviously related to *récitatif*, had several more specific meanings. In the *ballet de cour*, for example, *récits* were generally found at the beginning of each act and provided a narrative element.[103] Often in bipartite structure with double-bar repeats, and with additional verses (some of which were provided with *diminutions*) such *récits* were more akin to the *air* than to the *récitatif* proper which had to wait until the advent of Lully's operas. *Récits* were also composed outside the *ballet de cour*. Some of the earliest examples of these are in fact more dramatic than those written for the ballets of the mid-century, the *récits* of Pierre Guédron (1565–1621)[104] furnishing some of the finest examples of the Italian-influenced declamatory style. As the century wore on, differences between *récit* and *air* became narrower and both terms were applied somewhat indiscriminately. A further blurring of the categories was caused by the fact that the word *récit* acquired the meaning of soloist (or group of soloists).[105] One other use of the term in song repertoire was the *récit de basse*, song for bass voice, usually unaccompanied. An extension of song terminology was *dialogue*, which, in its predominantly pastoral setting and lovers' conversations, contains some of the seeds of later dramatic music.

The solo religious air was a genre which began to appear (at least

---

[103] See James Anthony, *French Baroque Music* (London, rev. ed., 1978), p. 30, and André Verchaly, 'A propos du récit français au début du XVIII$^e$ siècle', *Recherches sur la Musique française classique*, xv (1975), p. 39.

[104] See Vol. IV, pp. 189–90.

[105] See Sebastian de Brossard: 'On appelle aussi Récit en François tout ce qui se chante *seul*, ou *à deux*, *à trois*, *à quatre* Voix seules, et un mot tout ce que les Italiens marquent par *solo & soli*'. *Dictionnaire de Musique* (Paris, 1703), entry 'Recitativo'.

in its solo and duet forms) in the middle of the century with the first volume of *Airs de dévotion à deux parties* (1658), compiled by the Rev. Father Berthod who included in it pieces by Lambert, Bacilly and some anonymous composers.[106] Others who were to cultivate the religious air were Thomas Gobert and Moulinié. Bacilly, who published three books of *Airs spirituels* (1672–88), distinguished betwen this kind of music and works such as motets and *cantiques* (popular hymns in the vernacular), claiming that while the sentiments of the *air spirituel* are religious, the actual style of both words and music should approach the secular air.[107] Accordingly he provided *diminutions* for the second verses of his *airs spirituels*. Despite his distinction between religious airs and *cantiques*, a number of works bearing the latter title did in fact approximate to the style of the former, such as those found in Ballard's collection of *Cantiques spirituels et Noëls de différents auteurs* (1699) but the mediocrity of these and many other similar pieces can only have strengthened what appears to have been a general indifference to religious song in France.[108]

On the other hand the secular air enjoyed increasing popularity as the century drew to its close. Besides those mentioned so far, other composers of the mid-century generation who contributed to the repertoire of the serious song were Lully, Le Camus, Jean-Baptiste Boësset, Hurel, D'Ambruis, Batiste, Charpentier, De La Barre, Maulevrier, Martin, De Mollier, Perdigal, De Sablière. Towards the end of the century the *air sérieux* was most frequently coupled with a genre whose popularity began to reach almost epidemic proportions: the drinking song.

## DANCE SONGS AND DRINKING SONGS

In contrast to the sophisticated serious air with its supple rhythms and often elaborate ornamentation, songs for dancing were unpretentious in the extreme. Normally published as single-line melodies only, they were usually performed *à la cavalière*, i.e. without accompaniment. Early in the century the Caen publisher Jacques Mangeant had issued three volumes of *Airs nouveaux des plus belles chansons à dancer . . . mesurées sur toutes sortes de cadences de branles, voltes, courantes, ballets & autres dances . . .* (1608), the purpose being to provide pieces which could be 'sung

---

[106] Works for four voices had appeared earlier, for example De Gouy's *Airs à quatres parties sur la paraphrase des pseaumes de Messire Antoine Godeau* (1642).
[107] Preface to Bacilly's *Airs Spirituels* (new ed. 1688).
[108] Ibid.

and danced in company'. But it was not until the appearance of
Robert Ballard's twenty-volume series *Chansons pour danser et
pour boire* (1627–1661) that songs for dancing became a regular
feature of seventeenth-century French vocal music. The first composers to publish their own collections were Guillaume Michel
(dates unknown), whose eight books of *Chansons pour danser et
pour boire* began appearing in the 'twenties (the earliest books are
not extant), Louis de Mollier (*c.*1615–1688), and Jean Boyer (dates
unknown). The indefatigable Bacilly also wrote five books of
*Chansons pour danser et pour boire* (1663–67), retaining even at
this late stage the convention of printing only the melody of the
dance songs, while furnishing a bass part for the drinking songs.[109]
In the light of this, it is interesting that the composer suggested that
through the introduction of ornaments and by assuming a certain
rhythmic freedom *chansons pour danser* could serve as songs in
their own right, and not merely as accompaniments for dancing. A
similar point of view had been expressed much earlier by De
Chancy who, in dedicating his third book of *Chansons* (1649) to de
Nyert, wrote '. . . although it seems that *chansons à danser* are
much inferior to *airs de cour*, I assure you that if they were accompanied by lute they would dispute the prize'.

While many *chansons pour danser* were headed by the name of
the actual dance (the most frequent being sarabandes, courantes
and gavottes) others gave no clue beyond the rhythmic character of
the melody. The following, published anonymously in the ninth
book of Ballard's series mentioned above, illustrates the style. The
cross-rhythms in the third 'bar' are quite typical of the pieces in this
collection.

Ex. 66

Prin-ces-se    de ma pen - sé - e   Per-met à mon ju - ge-ment   De te di - re le    tor-ment

De quoi mon âme est bles-sé- e;    Ton bel œil,    Mar-got, Bles - se les cœurs sans dire un mot.

(Princess of my thoughts, allow me to tell you of the torment with which
my heart is wounded. Thy lovely eye, Margot, wounds hearts without
saying a word.)

---

[109] Bacilly's first book of such songs was published as the twenty-second book of Ballard's
*Chansons pour dancer et pour boire* (1663). In accordance with Ballard's custom in this
series, they were published anonymously.

Simplicity of style remained the characteristic feature of the *chanson pour danser*, and gradually these relatively undeveloped songs largely gave way to those with which they had invariably been coupled from the days of the earliest collections: the *chansons pour boire*.

In Ballard's collection of *Chansons pour danser et pour boire* the main feature which distinguished one type from the other was the text, for both were clear-cut and decisive in their rhythmic outlines (in contrast to the *air sérieux*), and in the earliest volumes both kinds of song were published with their melody line only. An example of a drinking song from the same book as 'Princesse de ma pensée' will make their musical similarity obvious.

Ex.67

Sus al-lons, mes chers a-mis, Il faut tous pren-dre le ver-re, Puis-que Bac-chus nous a mis

Tant de vin des-sus la ter-re. Nous en au-rons tant et tant et tant et tant et tant et tant, Que cha-

-cun se - ra con-tent.

(Come, dear friends, we must take up the glass, since Bacchus has given us so much wine on earth. We'll have so very, very much that we'll all be satisfied.)

Gradually, however, drinking songs developed a more sophisticated and imaginative musical style (although their texts remained hearty and were often amusing), and it is not mere coincidence that towards the end of the century they broke their partnership with songs for dancing and were most frequently coupled with the *air sérieux*. By the turn of the century volumes of *airs sérieux et à boire* were tumbling from Parisian presses in extraordinary numbers.

The decade of the 'nineties saw the conclusion of two series by Ballard which had played a significant part in the propagation of vocal music in France during the century: his *Airs de différents autheurs à deux parties*, and thirty volumes of *Chansonettes*. It also saw the beginning of new ones which were to have the same role in the next century as the earlier series had for the seventeenth; in particular, the monumental collection of *Recueils d'airs sérieux et à*

*boire* which, planned by Ballard to appear at the beginning of each
month, ran for more than thirty years. So wide in compass was
this series that it would be difficult to find any composer active at
the time whose songs were not represented in it.[110] The closing
years of the century also saw the beginnings of extensive collections
of similar songs devoted to the works of single composers, Jean
Sicard having set the example slightly earlier in the century with his
seventeen books of *Airs à boire* (1666–83). These represent a significant step in the development of the genre. Sicard's lead was
followed by Dubuisson and Jean-Baptiste Bousset who published
sixteen and forty volumes respectively of *airs sérieux et à boire*.
Others, less prolific, were Brossard, Du Parc, Piroye and Regnault.
An example of the *air à boire* of 1700 is this one by André Campra
(1660–1744):

Ex. 68

[110] Two of François Couperin's *airs sérieux,* 'La Pastorelle' (August, 1711) and 'Les
Pellerines' (February, 1712), *Oeuvres complètes*, ed. Paul Brunold (Paris, 1932), xi, pp. 24
and 38, were afterwards published in harpsichord transcriptions, ibid, iii, pp. 35 and 98.

(Without thee, Bacchus, there's no sweetness in living. Love comes hither, hasten to follow it; if it wishes to charm our hearts, come and redouble its fires. But if it makes us shed tears, O potent god, arm us against its stern power.)

With Campra we encounter the generation of composers who followed that of Lambert, Bacilly, and others mentioned so far; in their *airs sérieux et à boire*[111] is found a range of style that attests the changes that came over French music in the late years of the seventeenth century. Although the later repertoire retains many traits from the past—a preference for short airs in bipartite structure, and the continued cultivation of traditional melodic style, there are also many airs which sound a more fervent and impassioned note, particularly through new-found harmonic warmth, and which display a dramatic element of bravura very different from the intimate art of *diminutions*. This is not to say that the preciosity of the previous era disappeared from French vocal chamber music—indeed it flowered afresh in the environment of eighteenth century rococo—but that the French air now encompassed a range of style and expression far wider than ever before. When its technique includes among other devices strict canonic writing (as can be found, for example, in pieces by Couperin and Rameau) we have a sure sign that French vocal chamber music has moved away from the province of the singer/creator to that of the composer. Nothing could illustrate the new character of French song better than the genre which was to dominate vocal music in France until the middle of the eighteenth century, the cantata.

[111] For a modern anthology of such works see *Airs sérieux et à boire à 2 et 3 voix*, ed. F. Robert (*Le Pupitre*) (Paris, 1968).

ANTECEDENTS OF THE *CANTATE FRANÇAISE*

While the French cantata was essentially an eighteenth-century form, some of its elements can be found in a rudimentary stage in earlier vocal pieces. Its ensemble accompaniment, for example, was not entirely new to French song; Lambert's *Airs à I, II, III, et IV parties, avec la basse continue* of 1689 provided three-part instrumental *ritournelles* for each piece. Similarly, François Martin (dates unknown), in the previous year, had published his *Premier livre d'airs sérieux et à boire, à deux, trois & quatre parties, entre-meslez de symphonies en triots* (sic) *pour les violons et les flûtes, avec des accompagnements dans les récits, le tout propre pour des concerts.*[112] Nor in the later volumes of Ballard's *Airs de différents autheurs* is it uncommon to find pieces with gently flowing bass lines which anticipate to a certain extent the more dynamic style of harpsichord continuo accompaniment featured in cantata composition. On the possible origins of the French cantata, James Anthony has pointed to various short dramatic entities formed by groupings of airs, recitatives and ensembles which are found scattered through the Ballard collections of the later seventeenth century.[113] Standing apart from these short pieces was Charpentier's dramatic work *Orphée descendant aux enfers* (c.1685) for three voices and instrumental ensemble. Here indeed is a work of cantata-like proportions.[114] Yet let us make no mistake: the genre known as the *cantate française* would have emerged precisely in the way it did had Charpentier's work and the other pieces just cited never been written. The *cantate française* was stimulated by musical influences outside France and by social forces within it which had not affected to any great extent the earlier forms of vocal music described so far.

NEW INFLUENCES ON THE CANTATA

Among Ballard's publications begun at the end of the seventeenth century were his *Recueils des meilleurs airs italiens* (1699–1708). What is particularly interesting about these collections is the fact that in addition to works by Scarlatti, Carissimi, and others, they include 'Italian arias' by a number of French composers. Such direct imitation of the Italian style was to have a strong influence

---

[112] Unfortunately some of the part-books of this collection have not survived. The extant volumes are held by the Bibliothèque Nationale, Paris.

[113] Anthony, op. cit., p. 359.

[114] See Henri Quittard, 'Orphée descendant aux enfers', *Revue Musicale*, iv (1904), and Claude Crussard, *Un musicien français oublié—Marc-Antoine Charpentier* (Paris, 1945), pp. 16–18.

on the creation of the eighteenth-century French cantata. French enthusiasm for Italian music (at least in some quarters) at the turn of the century was one of the signs of a new spirit of cosmopolitanism abroad in France, induced in part through the waning influence of Versailles during the long decline of Louis XIV's reign (1661–1715) and the growing importance of Paris as the centre of French thought. In short, a court-dominated art, created for the monarch's taste, was giving way to that of the metropolis. Eighteenth-century Paris was to be the scene of the private and public concert (the most notable being the *Concert Spirituel* from 1725)[115] at which were performed for the first time in France many established vocal and instrumental masterpieces from Italy as well as examples of the newly composed French repertoire of sonatas and cantatas. Both these last mentioned forms emerged through a desire on the part of a number of Parisian composers to *unite* the styles of French and Italian music in such a way as to produce what Couperin optimistically called 'la perfection de la musique'.[116]

So far as the cantata was concerned, Jean-Baptiste Morin (1677–1745) summed up its style in the Preface to his *Cantates françoises à une et deux voix melées de symphonies* (1706) by saying that he wished to retain the sweetness (*douceur*) of French melody, combining it with the harmony (*modulation*), rhythmic character (*mouvement*), and diversified accompaniments of the Italian cantata. Morin's example so fired the imagination of almost every composer of his day that it led to the rapid cultivation of a repertoire which remained popular for some thirty or forty years. As a genre it had a much longer history than this,[117] but the later cantatas and so-called *cantatilles* failed to remain in the forefront of French vocal music after about 1730, although this is not to deny the worth of some of these pieces. The earlier works, however, played a dominant role in helping to fashion eighteenth-century French musical style. The emergence of the *cantate française* was one indication that French music was moving away from its classical tradition towards a truly baroque style.

STYLISTIC TRAITS OF THE *CANTATE FRANÇAISE*

The converging of the French classical style with the Italian baroque is illustrated in the opening work (see Ex. 70) of Morin's

[115] See Vol. V, p. 441.

[116] François Couperin, *Concert instrumentale sur le titre d'Apothéose composé à la mémoire immortelle de l'incomparable Monsieur de Lully* (Paris, 1725).

[117] For a detailed historical and stylistic study see David Tunley, *The 18th Century French Cantata* (London, 1974).

first book of cantatas, 'Euterpe' (1706). Its solo voice part is accompanied by continuo, which Morin explicitly states should comprise harpsichord and bass viol. In the entire repertoire of the *cantate française* there is no instance of lute accompaniment (although fifty years later Pierre de la Garde was to introduce the guitar into some of his *cantatilles*, by which time however the genre had shed most of its baroque features). In any case, the decisive, forward-moving bass, now to be characteristic of most fast cantata airs, was alien to the technique of the theorbo, demanding instead the agility of a keyboard player. Campra was to describe his own cantatas as a bringing together of French *délicatesse* and Italian *vivacité*, and there can be no doubt that the latter was achieved largely through the nimbleness of the bass line. As will be seen from Ex. 69, the third air of *Euterpe*, the relationship of the bass to the melody also exemplifies that 'polarity' between upper and lower parts considered by Bukofzer to be essential to the full baroque style.[118]

## Ex. 69

---

[118] Manfred Bukofzer, *Music in the Baroque Era* (New York, 1947), p. 11.

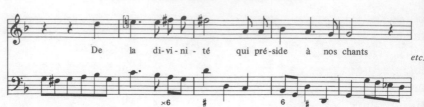

De    la    di-vi-ni-té    qui pré-side    à    nos chants    *etc.*

(Let's sing of victory and celebrate the glory of the divinity who watches over our songs.)

Morin's airs illustrate how French composers were to avail themselves of harmonic resources common in Italian music but until now less frequently found in vocal music of the French school. They include sequences of secondary sevenths and the 'cycle of fifths' (both exemplified in Ex. 69) and a general unfolding of chord progressions through clear patterns of harmonic rhythm. Chromaticism and harmonic intensity became fairly regular features of the French cantata, although only one of Morin's works in his first book, *Circe*, shows this to any extent. Nevertheless it was not so much a matter of wholesale adoption of Italian harmonic practice into French music as a fertilization of one by the other which characterized the new form. This, together with the retention of the French melodic style, effectively prevented the *cantate française* from sounding like a mere imitation of the foreign models which had inspired it.

Yet the retention of the native melodic style posed its own problems for Morin and his followers, for while it was admirably suited to the short, bipartite songs of the previous century, the cantata demanded lyrical movements far more expansive than ever before in French vocal music. We have seen at the beginning of this chapter how the seventeenth-century air was shaped by the sensitive juxtaposition of flowing musical phrases each moulded by the poetic phrase; both the music and the poetry provided the basic elements of its form. The need for purely musical devices to unify and expand the content was thus minimal. How different the situation in the cantata air, especially as its text, modelled on those of the Italian school, was relatively short and, far from contributing an element of form through its own poetic structure, required considerable repetition to embrace the time-span of the melody. In doing so, the new genre, of course, courted the derision of those whose main target of criticism of the Italian style had been the 'endless repetition' of a few lines of poetry, and indeed there is considerable evidence that in its early stages the *cantate française* met a very mixed reception.[119]

Nevertheless, French respect for the text prevented any extreme laceration of the poetry, and so (as in the previous century) cantata airs were shaped by fairly long spans determined by the length of the poetic phrase. Melodic expansion was achieved by repetition of phrases, either exactly, slightly varied, or (more usually) just in their rhythmic outline, and by the inclusion of preludes and interludes, and the adoption of *da capo* form. Motivic development was rare, even though it found an outlet in Morin's air quoted in Ex. 69. A more characteristic approach is illustrated in the opening air of the same cantata:

Ex. 70

[119] See, for example, Jean-Léonor de Grimarest, *Traité de récitatif* (Paris, 1706), pp. 211–212.

(May your brilliant daring lend new grace to our sweet and flattering songs. Give us back our gaiety and cure the sadness that Love spills in our hearts.)

The inclusion of an obbligato instrument opened up further possibilities for expansion through recourse to the ritornello principle, and in the pages of the French cantata may be seen the earliest examples in France of this formal device. The violin obbligato in particular brought yet another italianate element to the *cantate française*, its style of writing often reflecting the influence that Corelli's music was having upon string playing in France at that time.

Italian influence can also be seen in Morin's recitatives, where French declamation of the kind which Lully had developed in his operas gave way to *recitativo secco*. Considered by most Frenchmen to be the perfect matching of word and note, Lully's recitatives, while flowing in measured time, achieved rhythmic suppleness by means of constantly changing time-signatures. Morin's recitatives on the other hand caught something of Italian *parlando* style as illustrated in the third *récitative* of *Euterpe*:

Ex. 71

qui ve-nez nous ap-pren-dre Un art qui des hu-mains fait la fé - li - ci -

-té. Qui nous fait au Des-tin ou-bli-er les ca - pri - ces, Qui calme in-no-cem-

-ment notre es-prit a - gi - té, Qui nous rend les Dieux plus pro - pi - ces, Et qui flé -

-chit les in - jus - ti - ces De la plus in-gra - te Beau - té.

(What reverence, what honours, should one not offer you, O Muse who comes to teach us an art that provides the happiness of the human race, that makes us forget the caprices of Fate, that innocently calms our agitated spirit, that makes the Gods smile on us more, that softens the injustice of the most ungrateful Beauty.)

It was in his recitatives only that Morin did not set the undisputed pattern for the *cantate française*. Although some composers did in fact follow his lead, there were many others who retained the Lullian style—infusing it, however, with greater harmonic warmth than before and exploiting the resources of modulation for dramatic or expressive effect. Divided opinion over the merits of Morin's Italianate recitatives was largely bound up with the question of its suitability to convey the subtleties of French prosody.

CANTATA TEXTS

Amongst the six cantatas which comprise Morin's first book, two of the texts, *Circé* and *L'Amour devoilé*, were by Jean-Baptiste Rousseau[120] (1671–1741) who stands in the same relationship to the poetry of the French cantata as Morin did to its music. Taking the Italian cantata pattern of three recitatives alternating with three arias (which he described as representing the 'body' and the 'soul' of the piece) Rousseau evolved a poetic form, free in its rhyming and metrical scheme, which took as its starting-point a mythological event; from this was extracted a "lovers' maxim or moral". Thus *Circé*, his most admired text, concluded with the warning

Ce n'est point par effort qu'on aime,
L'Amour est jaloux de ses droits;
Il ne depend que de lui-meme,
On ne l'obtient que par son choix . . .

(It's not through effort that you love. Cupid is jealous of his rights; it depends upon him alone; it is gained through his choice . . .)

If this is a rather limp ending to one of the great classical legends Rousseau's poem has in fact some powerfully descriptive lines, such as

Dans le sein de la mort ses noires enchantements,
Vont troubler le repos des Ombres,
Les Manes effrayes quittent leurs monuments,
L'Air retentit au loin de leurs longs hurlements:
Et les vents echappés de leurs cavernes sombres,
Mêlent à clameurs d'horribles sifflements . . .

(In the depths of the Underworld her evil spells disturb the slumber of the Shades, the terrified Manes quit their tombs, in the far distance the air resounds with their long-drawn shrieks, and the winds, escaping from their dark caverns, add to their clamour with dreadful whistlings . . .)

Bacilly once claimed that the expression of anger rarely found a place in the French air.[121] Viewed against the preciosity of most poetry composed for the songs of the previous century, Circe's bitter recriminations against the faithless Ulysses (in Morin's cantata set to music which was reaching towards a new level of intensity) vividly illustrate some of the changes that were coming over French vocal chamber music.

[120] For a modern study of this poet's work see Henry A. Grubbs, *Jean-Baptiste Rousseau—his life and works* (Princeton, 1941). Rousseau's own description of his attempts to give shape to cantata poetry (not included in Grubbs) may be found in the Preface to the 1743 edition of his works.

[121] Bacilly, op. cit., p. 46.

Rousseau wrote twenty-seven cantata texts and in doing so established this kind of poetry as a minor literary form.[122] While the great majority of texts were written anonymously, amongst those well known in their day who cultivated cantata poetry were Antoine Houdar de la Motte, Pierre Roy, and Antoine Danchet. As might be expected the theme of the cantata was almost invariably love, and mythology was ransacked for incidents which could provide an amorous allegory. Yet there were also cantatas inspired by other literature (for example, *Gulliver's Travels*) and contemporary events. The very small number of sacred cantatas (as distinct from Latin motets) attests the essentially secular nature of the *cantate française*.

## DEVELOPMENT OF THE CANTATA

Although the cantata emerged in France during the closing years of Louis XIV's reign its spirit was that of the Regency (1715–25). It is thus no mere coincidence that the earliest exponents of the form, Morin, Nicolas Bernier (1665–1734), and Jean-Baptiste Stuck, more usually known as Battistin (1680–1755), were associated with the household of the Duke of Orleans whose musical tastes inclined strongly to the Italian style and whose pleasure-loving outlook gave the period of his regency a character for ever associated with the *fête galante*. Another circle congenial to cantata composition was at Sceaux where the gardens of the château became the scene of the celebrated *Nuits* (1714–15) devised for the Duchess of Maine. Among cantata composers active at Sceaux were Thomas-Louis Bourgeois (1676–1750 or 1751), Philippe Courbois (*fl.* 1705–30), Colin de Blamont (1690–1754), Jean-Joseph Mouret (1628–1738), as well as Bernier whose fifth book of cantatas is entitled *Les Nuits de Sceaux, Concerts de Chambre ou cantates françoises à plusieurs voix en manière de Divertissements* (1715). Bernier's description of the two long works which comprise his fifth book as being *en manière de divertissement* raises an issue central to understanding of the development of the cantata in France. Unlike any others in the repertoire, these two call for chorus and dancing and were thus closely linked to traditional forms of French dramatic music. Their exceptional nature highlights the fact that the *cantate française* emerged and developed as a reaction to that very tradition which had its source in the entertainment of the court. The cantata, stimulated by forces outside the

[122] The *Mercure de France*, for example, published cantata poetry during a period of sixty years from 1711.

court, found its natural home in the Parisian salon and concert room. It was in every sense of the word chamber music. Its most common scoring was for solo voice and continuo, with or without obbligato instruments (known as *symphonie*), although duo cantatas were also popular. Those for three voices were far less frequent.

If in his own day Morin was appreciated as the initiator of the cantata in France, his contemporaries also recognised his musical limitations,[123] and his works in the genre were soon outstripped by those of Bernier,[124] Battistin, Campra, and above all by Clérambault whose twenty-five cantatas contain some of the finest pages in the repertoire. Louis-Nicolas Clérambault (1676–1749), one of the most accomplished organists of his day, published his first book of cantatas in 1710, amongst which was the work that secured his reputation in this field, *Orphée*, a powerful composition for high voice, violin, flute, and continuo.[125] In it French and Italian styles coalesce into an individual and highly expressive style raising the work to the level of a true masterpiece.

In the course of the cantata's development the relationship between the two national styles varied a good deal. Within a single work, for instance, an Italianate movement might be followed by one more indebted to *le goût français*. Yet it would be true to say that by the 'twenties, Italian traits were being absorbed into a decidedly Gallic expression, but through a language far more assertive than before. The process can be seen in the works of a single composer such as the Tuscan-born Battistin whose cantatas, vigorously Italianate in the first two books (1706–8), gradually acquired more of a French character, so that by his final book (1741) the composer in his recitatives had changed over from the *parlando* style to the Lullian declamation. Something of this general trend is also illustrated in the cantatas of Rameau, Elisabeth Jacquet de La Guerre, Destouches, Colin de Blamont, Boismortier, and Montéclair, to mention only a few better-known names of the many composers who wrote these works.[126]

[123] D'Aquin de Chateaulyon, *Siècle littéraire de Louis XV* (Paris, 1754).

[124] Even though Bernier's early volumes of cantatas bear a *privilège* date three years earlier than that of Morin's volume of 1706, it would seem that Morin's cantatas were composed earlier. He claims that they had circulated in manuscript for a number of years, and all eighteenth-century writers point to Morin as the first in France to attempt this genre.

[125] Performing edition ed. Tunley (London, 1972).

[126] Collection of Montéclair's cantatas ed. James Anthony, Barbara Jackson, and Erich Schwandt (Madison, Wis., 1975). Those of Rameau—with one by Boismortier and another by La Garde—are included in the *Oeuvres complètes*, iii, ed. Malherbe (Paris, 1897); they are studied at length in Cuthbert Girdlestone, *Jean-Philippe Rameau* (London, 1957), pp. 65–73.

Although the history of the cantata in France continues to the Revolution, by 1730 most of the significant works of its repertoire had been composed. Undoubtedly the regeneration of French opera by Rameau, whose *Hippolyte et Aricie* launched his career in this field from 1733,[127] was one of the reasons why the cantata lost its hold. But its further development was also shaped by musical forces which drained the dramatic element from the cantata and reduced its size: through the influence of the rococo style the history of the *cantate française* from about 1730 to 1750 is largely concerned with the *cantatille*.

### THE *CANTATILLE*

While the term *cantatille* had been used occasionally before 1730 to mean a short cantata, after this time it became firmly established and works bearing it rapidly increased in number, eventually almost to oust the earlier term. The *cantatille* usually comprised two airs joined by a brief recitative. Typical titles being *L'Heureux surprise*, *L'Absence*, *L'Espérance*, *La Rose*, etc., it is not surprising that the *cantatille* caught the scorn of Jean-Jacques Rousseau who in his *Dictionnaire de musique* (1768) dismissed it as a 'medium for poetasters and musicians without genius'. It is perfectly true that the repertoire includes much banality, but also works that are charming specimens of the rococo style, especially those by Jean-Joseph Mouret (1682–1738) and Louis Le Maire (1693 or 1694–1750). The third air from Le Maire's *L'Hiver* (1733):

Ex. 72

---

[127] Six years earlier, setting out his qualifications as a dramatic composer to Houdar de La Motte, he had cited his cantatas *L'Enlèvement d'Orithie* and *Thétis* as supporting evidence. The latter is given in full in Louis Laloy, *Rameau* (Paris, 1908), pp. 29–31. More recent research has been undertaken by Mary Cyr in preparation for the New Rameau Edition.

Char-mant A-mour, é-tends tes aî-les sur les plus ten - dre des A-

- mants.

Fl./Vns.

*fort*           *doux*

Voice

Char-mant A-

-mour e-tends tes aî-les sur les plus ten - dre des A-mants, Tu dois gar-

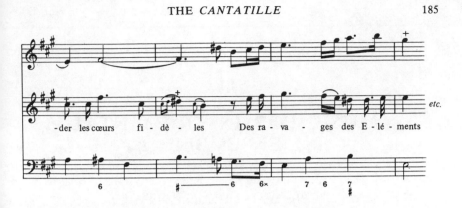

-der les cœurs    fi - dè - les    Des ra - va - ges des E - lé - ments

(Delightful Love, spread your wings over the tenderest of lovers. You must guard the faithful hearts from the havoc of the Elements.)

shows that in the intimate, highly embellished rococo *cantatille*, French song to some extent returned to being the singer's art it had been in the previous century.

# III

## MUSIC FOR INSTRUMENTAL ENSEMBLE: 1630–1700

### By WALTER KOLNEDER

VARIETY OF INSTRUMENTAL FORMS

ABOUT 1630 a point had been reached in the development of music for instrumental ensemble when everything that was to follow in the course of the century was already present in embryo. In the following pages the various forms and types of orchestral music will be treated separately; but it must never be forgotten that the reciprocal influence of one form on another and the elements that are common to all are just as important as the individual forms of expression. The chief difficulty here is one of terminology. It is rarely possible to trace the development of musical forms in terms of precise definition: their first appearance is apt to be uncertain and experimental. We have to deal with idioms that are the product of a personal style, with local variations, with national or regional characteristics. Types of formal structure which had already begun to make their mark were often, for various reasons, abandoned, only to reappear later in different circumstances. This complex interplay of forces is reflected in the terminology of the seventeenth century, which can hardly be applied unequivocally to any single form or category. Terms like *canzon, sonata, sinfonia, concerto,* or *trattenimento* are ambiguous. They are often used synonymously and may refer to similar forms, but at the same time they frequently indicate very different types of structure. Any attempt to deduce definite distinctions from particular works is defeated by the existence of an equal number of examples which prove the contrary. Additions to titles, such as *da camera* and *da chiesa* must be interpreted with caution, nor is it always possible to be certain whether a work is designed as chamber music or intended for performance with more than one instrument to a part.

Of the two principal forms of early instrumental music, the

*canzon* and the suite, the former had the greatest influence on the development of the sonata, the *sinfonia*, and the *concerto grosso*. Until the middle of the century it was the leading form, particularly in Italy, and although it gradually disappeared as an independent form its influence was felt long after. It was originally closely related to the *ricercar:*[1] composers such as Giovanni Gabrieli and later Frescobaldi make hardly any distinction between the two. Properly speaking, however, the *ricercar*, with its linked series of fugal expositions, was nearer to the strict style of church poly- phony, whereas the pattern for the typical *canzon* was the madrigal or the *chanson*. Johann Gottfried Walther in his *Lexicon* (1732)[2] says: '*Canzone* (Ital.), *Chanson* (Fr.) means a musical song, of two kinds: (1) with words . . . (2) without words.' He explains the second type by saying that it is 'constructed with short fugues and pleasant fantaisies, and at the end the first fugue is generally re- peated from the beginning and so brings the piece to a conclusion', and gives a reference to Praetorius's *Syntagma Musicum*, iii, pp. 16 ff., from which his own explanation is paraphrased.

Giovanni Gabrieli's *canzoni* often consist of comparatively short sections, strongly constrasted with each other, which are then re- peated in a different order. In the numerous *canzoni* written by his contemporaries and pupils the form acquired a greater diversity: ten or more sections would be composed, using contrasting ma- terial. The fact that this material was often based on dance rhythms shows the connection between *canzon* on the one hand and the *sonata da camera* and dance suite on the other.

Through the medium of young German composers who had studied in Italy and Italians who were active abroad, the *canzon* soon found its way to the North—to German centres where the influence of Italian music was accepted and to Vienna. There it had to compete with the instrumental suite, which was becoming in- creasingly popular, and so could enjoy only a limited vogue. Beside the works of the Italians we find *canzoni* writted by *oltramontani*, such as Johann Hermann Schein (1586–1630). In Germany the variation suite, which had now come into favour, had a marked effect on the *canzon*, as we see from a *Cantzon* by Johannes Schultz (1582–1653) (no. 53 of his *Musikalischer Lüstgarte*, 1622).[3] The first two sections are related in the same way as a pair of

---

[1] See Vol. IV, particularly pp. 557–8.
[2] Facsimile edition (Kassel, 1953).
[3] Ed. Hermann Zenck, *Das Erbe deutscher Musik, Landschaftsdenkmale Niedersachsen*, i (Wolfenbüttel, 1937), and see Vol. IV, p. 118.

dances, the second of which is based on a rhythmical variant of the
first (*Tanz* and *Nachtanz*):

Ex. 73

In the third section, which is once more in common time, small
groups are constructed from the following motives:

Ex. 74

The piece ends with a short coda in triple time:

Ex. 75

The titles of some works make a distinction between sonata and
*canzon*, but it is much more common to find that works described
as sonata or *sinfonia* or otherwise are in fact *canzoni* in structure,
either throughout or in single movements. This is particularly the
case with music for one or two violins with continuo, which had
begun to appear early in the century on the model of vocal monody
and trios for two voices and bass. It is also worth recalling that the
term 'sonata' arose as an abbreviation of the expression *canzon per
sonar*.

### THE *CANZON* IN ITALY

Particularly important, from the ponit of view of further development, was the type of *canzon* in which composers aimed at

the strongest possible contrast between the sections, in tempo, in rhythm, and in texture (i.e. homophony contrasted with polyphony). The clear-cut division between the sections was probably encouraged by the fact that in the church service—on feast days and other occasions—the complete *canzon* was not always played but only parts of it. Thus the form of such works served a very definite practical purpose, which appears to be overlooked by writers who speak contemptuously of 'patchwork'. When the sections were separated by breaks in performance, the one-movement *canzon* had in fact become a work in several movements. Side by side with this development we find a firmer sense of tonality, which carries with it the possibility of a regular system of modulation. The possibility of creating larger forms (or larger movements) which resulted from this led to a reduction in the number of movements. Wilhelm Fischer[4] drew attention to an early example of this in a trio sonata (or *canzon*) published—1623 by Salamone Rossi (1570–*c*.1630) in which there are only four movements. The scheme:

Slow    C (polyphonic)
Quick   3 (fugal)
Slow    C (homophonic)
Quick   C (homophonic)

anticipates the structure of the much later *sonata da chiesa*.

We also find a gradual reduction in the number of parts. The *canzon* for large instrumental forces becomes increasingly less frequent in Italy: it gives place to works in three and four parts (two upper parts with continuo, as in Rossi's *Varie sonate* Op. 12 (Venice, 1623), or three upper parts with continuo). In 1644 we find Massimiliano Neri (?1615–1666) publishing four-part *canzoni*. The advantage of a smaller number of parts is obvious: it made performance possible when resources were limited. A characteristic detail which sometimes occurs in works in more than three parts is not to write a separate part for the middle voice but to include it in the continuo part. It is impossible to decide whether there should be one or more instruments to a part, though Neri's virtuoso parts could only be soloistic while the more sober ones suggest performance by more than one instrument. Trio sonatas may very well have been performed by more players and this may be the reason why they came to be played in church. The early instrumental *canzon* appears generally to have been performed by solo instru-

---

[4] In Guido Adler, *Handbuch der Musikgeschichte* (2nd ed., Berlin, 1930), p. 548.

ments, since Adriano Banchieri (1568–1634) in his *Moderna armonia di canzoni alla francese* (Venice, 1612) makes a point of adding the indication *a cori*, i.e. with several instruments to a part. About 1670–80 the *canzon* in Italy became obsolete though individual movements of the sonata, and also of the *concerto grosso*, still show the *canzon* structure.

## THE *CANZON* IN THE GERMAN LANDS

In Germany and Austria the development was on quite different lines. At first the *canzon* was not much cultivated, but by the second half of the seventeenth century the contrasts which were one of its characteristics found an echo in the practice of writing for large ensembles. The reason for this was the same as for the growth of the form in Italy: the desire for festal pomp. The splendid instrumental resources of princely courts, which were particularly rich in wind instruments (the trumpet was a symbol of nobility) encouraged the cultivation of a form which owed its origin to contrasts of colour. The prince-bishop of Kroměříž in Moravia established during 1664–95 a very large chapel including thirty-eight string players and eight trumpets.[5] Works of this kind were seldom described as *canzoni* any more but rather as *sinfonie* and *sonate*. A few characteristic examples from the great mass of festal music are:

Antonio Bertali (1605–69) (active in Vienna):
    11 *Sonate con trombe solenni* (13–18 parts).
    17 *Sonate ordinarie per chiesa à 5 e 6*.
Vincenzo Albrici (1631–96) (active in Dresden):
    A MS. sonata (dated *c*.1660 by Schering[6] but almost certainly later) and two *sinfonie*.
Johann Heinrich Schmelzer (b. *c*.1620–1623; d. 1680) (court *Kapellmeister* in Vienna):
    *Sacro-profanus concentus musicus* (Nuremberg, 1662)[7] consisting of 13 sonatas (2–8 parts).

Described as *sinfonia*, the *canzon* occasionally served as part of an opera overture, as in Landi's *Sant' Alessio* (1632):

---

[5] See also pp. 403–6.
[6] *Geschichte der Musik in Beispielen* (Leipzig, 1931; New York, 1950), no. 214.
[7] Published in *Denkmäler der Tonkunst in Österreich*, cxi–cxii (1965).

Ex. 76

It also found its way into the suite both in Italy and elsewhere, as a 'neutral' movement: examples of this are found quite early in the works of English composers like William Brade domiciled in Germany in 1609 and Thomas Simpson in 1617,[8] who occasionally replaced the pavane by a *canzon*. Johann Rosenmüller's dance suites published as *Sonate da camera* (Venice, 1667)[9] began with a *canzon* in four or five sections entitled *sinfonia*. By 1700 the *canzon* had become rare outside Italy. Examples, which are in fact fugues with more than one subject, occur in the sonatas and theatre music of Purcell, e.g. the *canzona* in the symphony to Act II of *The Indian Queen* (1695):

Ex. 77

---

[8] See Vol. IV, p. 590.
[9] Ed. Karl Nef, *Denkmäler deutscher Tonkunst*, xviii (Leipzig, 1904).

### THE *SONATA DA CHIESA*

As the composers of *canzoni* for several instruments came more and more to write movements which were independent of each other and to reduce their number, there came gradually into existence a new form in several movements which later acquired the name *sonata da chiesa*. During the decade when this transition was taking place the term *da chiesa* did not imply any definite form but merely referred to the function of a particular work. As early as the time of Andrea Gabrieli the church was the principal place where the *canzon* was performed. This fact, often recognized by the addition of the word *sacra*, had a considerable influence on the structure of the music. It was presumably in order to make a sharper distinction between works intended for the church and those primarily meant for secular occasions that the Cremonese Tarquinio Merula (1594 or 1595–1665) in 1637 published at Venice a collection entitled *Canzoni overo sonate concertate per chiesa e camera*.[10] Both types of work in this collection, however, were still in the *canzon* form. It seems possible that *chiesa* not only referred to the purpose for which the music was intended but also implied orchestral performance, and similarly that *camera* indicated performance by soloists; but it was the growing distinction of form and content that had the really decisive effect on later developments. The use of dance forms is not necessarily a distinction of this kind. For example, the pavane was a slow and solemn dance which was even used for processions in church; and the Catholic church at the time of the Counter-Reformation had consciously used the achievements and resources of secular music to enrich its services. The presence of dances or movements in dance rhythms in works marked *chiesa* is in line with this attitude. In fact the structure of the *canzon* came more and more to lose its character through the introduction of dance elements and the influence of monodic writing. The *Symphoniae* of the Flemish composer Nicolaus a Kempis (*c*.1600–76),[11] are quite clearly *sonate da chiesa* in form, often with the following sequence of movements: fugato (triple time in dance rhythm), slow transition, fugato with the character of a gigue. It was Giovanni Legrenzi (1626–90) with his Op. 2 (Venice, 1656) who made a definite distinction between the *sonata da chiesa* and the *sonata da camera*.

About the middle of the century this distinction, which extended to other branches of music, was made explicit by writers. Marco Scacchi, in his *Cribrum musicum* (1643), uses the term *stylus cubicularis* for the chamber style; and in 1650 the learned Jesuit Athanasius Kircher, in his *Musurgia universalis*, distinguishes three main categories—*ecclesiasticus*, *theatralis*, and *madrigalescus* (i.e. chamber)—which he further subdivides into nine smaller groups. Kircher's categories were still accepted as valid by Mattheson and Walther. In the final stage of the history of the two forms—for

---

[10] Example from Merula's *Secondo Libro delle canzoni* (Venice, *c*.1631 and reprinted, 1639) in A. Davison and Willi Apel, *Historical Anthology of Music*, ii (Cambridge, Mass., 1946), no. 210.
[11] Op. 1, 1644; Op. 2, 1647; Op. 3, 1649 (all at Antwerp).

instance, in the work of Corelli (1653–1713)—the *sonata da chiesa* generally has four movements:

Slow
Quick (fugal)
Slow
Quick (fugal or in dance rhythm),

in marked contrast to the *sonata da camera*, which was now the Italian name for the suite. During the period when the *canzon* was changing into the *sonata da chiesa* composers like Legrenzi wrote works of both types: the *canzon* in one movement and strongly improvisatory in character, the *sonata da chiesa* in several movements clearly distinguished from each other.

We find examples of the *sonata da chiesa* written for a large variety of instrumental combinations. The following table summarizes the possibilities:

*Sonata a violino solo*
(violin & continuo)
Solo violin (*or* flute, *or* oboe, *or* even cello an octave lower) with a melodic bass instrument *ad lib.* (cello, violone, bass viol, *or* bassoon, *or* trombone) and a harmony instrument (spinet, harpsichord, organ, theorbo, chitarrone, etc.). Performance without a harmony instrument (i.e. only upper part and bass) was possible.

*Sonata a tre*
(two violins & continuo)
1. Two solo violins (the second often replaced by cornett or some other instrument), continuo instruments as above, the harmony instrument being less necessary than in the *sonata a violino solo*.
2. The same, wtih the upper parts each played by two or more instruments.

*Sonata* (*Sinfonia*, etc.) *a quattro* (generally two violins, viola, and bass, i.e. cello & violone)
1. String orchestra with harmony instrument (often organ).
2. Four or (less common) five strings with harmony instrument. In both cases the harmony instrument could if necessary be omitted, but in large buildings two or more harpsichords were used.

*Sonata* (*Sinfonia*, etc.) *a cinque* (generally two violins, two violas, and bass)
String orchestra (less often five or six solo strings) with harmony instrument.

Of works described as *sonata* (with or without the addition *da chiesa*) those marked *a quattro* and *a cinque* were primarily for orchestra. The trio sonata was first and foremost chamber music, the *sonata a violino solo* was exclusively for a solo performer.

In works in several parts the nature of the part-writing, which included little that required virtuosity, made performance possible by any kind of ensemble. Monteverdi in the *Ballo delle ingrate* (1608), after specifying five viole da braccio, harpsichord, and chitarrone, adds: 'Which instruments may be doubled if necessitated by the size of the place of performance'. Later, we know from pictures, from contemporary accounts, from the number of parts to be found in libraries, as well as from lists of payments to musicians, that for great festivals, whether secular or in church, large numbers of musicians were summoned from far and wide. 150 *sonatori* played under Corelli's direction at an 'academy' in the palace of Queen Christina of Sweden at Rome in 1687, and in 1716–17 works by Torelli and Giacomo Perti were performed in the Basilica of San Petronio at Bologna with 123/131 instrumentalists (*musici sonatori pigliati per ripieni*).[12]

As an example of a *sonata da chiesa* (conceived for orchestra, though it can be played by a chamber ensemble) we may consider no. 10 of Giuseppe Torelli's Op. 3 (Bologna, 1687). It is typical of the time that this collection of twelve sonatas should be entitled *Sinfonie*. The work is particularly interesting as showing the development of the form, since the change of tempo which occurs three times in the first movement shows clearly its derivation from the *canzon*. Also the figure ♩ ♩♩♩ ♩ is one that goes back to the very earliest period of the *canzon*. A notable feature of the quick movements is the clearly defined recapitulation, as well as the development of the thematic material in the middle, so that we have examples of ternary form:

Ex. 78

[12] Franz Giegling, *Giuseppe Torelli* (Kassel, 1949), pp. 29–30.

CODA

Adagio

Allegro

CODA

Adagio

In the second half of the seventeenth century the *sonata da chiesa* was one of the most important forms of instrumental music and, together with the suite, the principal form of orchestral music. With the development of the French and Italian types of overture, as well as the emergence of the solo concerto, the *sonata da chiesa* came to occupy a much less conspicuous place in the field of orchestral music. It became in fact a repository for a type of fugal writing which was gradually reserved for church music; yet the form still survived in the newer instrumental style of the *concerto grosso* in the eighteenth century.

### THE *CONCERTO GROSSO*

Any discussion of seventeeth-century music is constantly faced with problems of terminology. The reason is partly that many terms (e.g. *concerto*) have more than one meaning, and partly that those who write about this music do not distinguish sufficiently between form, the number of players required, and instrumentation. *Canzon*, suite, *sonata da chiesa* and solo concerto are forms. Descriptions such as *sonata a violino solo* or trio sonata are primarily indications of the number of players required: works of this kind may be written in the form of a *canzon*, a suite, or a *sonata da chiesa* or be a combination of two different forms. But the term *concerto grosso* is used partly to indicate the number of players and partly with reference to a particular instrumentation. There is no such thing as a *concerto grosso* form.

To make this clearer it is necessary to examine first of all the form of two *concerti grossi* before discussing the origins of this type of music. In 1682 Georg Muffat (1653–1704), who had got to know Corelli's *concerti grossi* in Rome, published under the title *Armonico tributo* a collection, each number of which is headed

Sonata, while the composer in his foreword to the reader speaks also of *sinfonie*.[13] The third sonata has six movements:

| | |
|---|---|
| Grave | 3/2 |
| Allegro | C |
| Corrente | 3/4 |
| Adagio | C |
| Gavotta | C |
| Rondeau | 3/4 |

The first movement leads directly into the second, so that these two form a pair.

The opening Grave (10 bars long) has the character of a solemn introduction: three simple progressions of two chords each, separated by rests, followed by a half-close in *hemiola* rhythm:

Ex. 79

The Allegro which follows immediately consists of nine sections, each ending with a cadence. The key sequence is: A major, F sharp minor, E major, E major, E major, C sharp minor, B major, E major, A major, A major. This systematic scheme is marked by the contrasting minor tonalities, by the strong emphasis on the dominant, and by the return to the tonic through the dominant of the dominant. The first section (bars 11–26) announces the two-bar theme, which is made up of four overlapping motives, the fourth being an inversion of the second:

Ex. 80

[13] Ed. Erich Schenk, *Denkmäler der Tonkunst in Österreich*, lxxxix (Vienna, 1953). The original text of Muffat's foreword is in ibid., xxiii (Jg. 11 (2)) (Vienna, 1904; reprint, 1959), p. 118.

The second section (bars 26–33) uses motive *c* as material for imitation:

Ex. 81

The third section (bars 33–9, 39–43) develops in imitation a new motive, which becomes a counterpoint to the principal theme in bar 36:

Ex. 82

Up to this point the introduction (Grave) and sections I–III of the Allegro follow the pattern of a *canzon*. The development of motive *c* gives the second section very definitely the character of a fugal episode, but unlike a normal fugue the episode is not followed by the immediate entry of the subject. The fourth section begins by treating the theme in stretto (though abbreviated by the omission of the inversion of *b*), together with the other material which has already been heard, and then breaks off into a kind of development:

Ex. 83

The remaining sections develop the material in a similar way, the theme often being abbreviated still further:

Ex. 84

This progressive transformation of the theme recalls the methods of the variation *ricercar*.

The alternation between soli and tutti (indicated in the original by S and T) sometimes has a structural significance; at other times it seems to be fortuitous. In the dance movements of the sonata the division between soli and tutti is generally arranged so that groups of two, four, six, or eight bars are repeated with a different setting.

A contrasting passage occurs more rarely. Two examples from the concluding Rondeau will serve to illustrate both types—first, simple repetition, and secondly contrast:

Ex. 85

Analysis of the whole sonata shows that it is an intermediate form between the *sonata da chiesa* and the suite, with the instrumentation of a *concerto grosso*.

### CORELLI'S *CONCERTI*

Muffat's model, Arcangelo Corelli (1653–1713), had in 1682 published only a collection of trio sonatas. His collection of *concerti*:

> Concerti Grossi / con duoi Violini e Violoncello di Concertino obligati e duoi / altri Violini, Viola e Basso di Concerto Grosso ad arbitrio, / che si potranno radoppiare.

was published—through Matteo Fornari, a pupil of the composer's—by Estienne Roger at Amsterdam in 1714. Corelli had written the dedication on 3 December 1712, a month before his death. This Op. 6 represents the ripest fruits of thirty years' labour. In the thirty years which separate Corelli's work from Muffat's the term *concerto grosso*, which originally referred only to the accompanying orchestra, had come to be the name of a type of composition. The forces required for performance and the nature of the instrumentation had become so important that they were not only noted on the title-page but also had a far-reaching influence on the structure of the individual movements. Furthermore there had been a considerable development in the writing of passages demanding virtuosity, so that the opposition between soli and tutti was more and more a contrast of material, not least in the degree of difficulty involved. From the point of view of form Corelli's first eight *concerti* in Op. 6 are *sonate da chiesa* (no. 8 being described as 'fatto per la notte di natale'), with individual movements in dance rhythm—particularly gigues (though not described as such). The remaining four *concerti* are suites with a prelude (similar to that of the *sonata da camera*) and occasionally the inclusion of movements which are not dances. Two examples will show how the solo instruments are treated—the first from the last movement of no. 1, showing figuration for the soloists alternating with simpler material for the tutti:

Ex. 86

and the second from the Allemanda of no. 11, which revives the old practice of diminution in the bass line, so that we have in effect a miniature cello concerto, with the orchestra playing merely a supporting role:

Ex. 87

Corelli's method of developing a basically simple idea is very characteristic. The first movement of no. 1 is made up of seven sections:

Largo (11 bars), Allegro (7½ bars), Adagio (2 bars), Allegro (6 bars), Adagio (1½ bars), Allegro (7½ bars), Adagio (3½ bars).

Taking an overall view we can say that it consists of a Largo followed by an Allegro, the latter being interrupted by short Adagio passages. The thematic material of the whole movement is developed from the first two bars:

Ex. 88

This group includes two transformations of *a*, the second, by means of the leap of a tenth, turning into *b*. A section of *b* ($b_1$):

Ex. 89

in combination with *b* itself provides the material for a further two bars, which carry the ideas further by means of modulation:

Ex. 90

The first Allegro section begins by using $b_1$:

Ex. 91

but at bar 15 $b_1$ breaks up into $b_2$:

Ex. 92

and this provides the material for the first Adagio:

Ex. 93

The whole movement develops in the same way. The technique of transforming, developing, and breaking up a motive, which later was to provide the basis for the development section of the classical sonata, had thus already been firmly established by Corelli.

### ORIGINS OF THE CONTRAST PRINCIPLE

There are two points to be borne in mind when we turn to the origin of the *concerto grosso*: first the principle of contrast between solo group and tutti, and secondly the application of this principle to the orchestra. In works for two or more choirs in Gabrieli's time it was already the custom for one choir to be composed of solo singers, or of solo singers and solo instrumentalists. This practice of using the so-called *coro favorito* shows that the principle of the *concerto grosso* was already well established. The same idea was adopted in the orchestral *canzon*, where the technique of repeating a passage as an echo favoured the use of a group of solo players. Francesco Vatielli[14] has shown that the reason why the application of the *concerto grosso* principle to orchestral music took place chiefly in the *sonata da chiesa* is to be found in what happened on feast days in North Italian churches. In addition to the regular musicians, some of whom were of outstanding quality, there were others less qualified—civil servants, manual workers, and the like— who played an instrument as a side activity. Anything that was liable to cause technical difficulties was left to be played by the *professori*. Thus the instrumentation of a *concerto grosso* sprang from the practical necessities of performance before it became a principle of composition. The contrast between *concertino* and *concerto grosso* was primarily one of sound and only gradually developed into an element in the structure.

The first composer who consciously used the method of the *concerto grosso* was Alessandro Stradella (1644–82). In addition to using contrasts of groups in his semi-dramatic *Lo schiavo liberato* (1674), in his oratorio *San Giovanni Battista* (1675), he contrasted solo and tutti in purely instrumental works (*sinfonie a più stromenti*), for instance in the opening bars of this *sonata di viole*:[15]

Ex. 94

1682, the year of Stradella's death, was also the date of the publication of Muffat's *Armonico tributo*. It is probable that Corelli got

---

[14] *Arte e vita musicale a Bologna* (Bologna, 1927).
[15] Turin, Bibl.nat., see Owen Jander, *Catalogue of the Manuscripts of Compositions by Alessandro Stradella in European and American Libraries* (Wellesley, Mass, 1960).

ideas from Stradella's work while he was in northern Italy and then developed them independently in Rome, where he made such an impression on the young Muffat. About the same time Lully in Paris had introduced the practice of using a trio of two oboes and a bassoon as a contrast to the string ensemble, particularly in the middle section of a dance movement (which consequently came to be known as the 'trio'). We know from Corelli's last pupil, Geminiani, that Lully had some influence on his master: for instance, the third concerto of Op. 6 begins with two movements which form a typical Lullian overture. It seems quite possible, therefore, that the standard solo trio in Corelli's *concerti grossi* was based on a French model. In any case it was so natural at that time to think of transferring to instrumental music the long-established practice of using a 'chorus' of solo voices (with instruments replacing missing singers if necessary) that the development of *concerto grosso* instrumentation followed as a matter of course. In the suites of Lully's pupils and of composers who came under his influence the woodwind trio is a favourite device which helped to introduce the *concerto grosso* principle into the suite and also did much to produce an intermediate form, half suite and half *sonata da chiesa*. A good example of the widespread influence of the *concerto grosso* principle in the second half of the seventeenth century is a *sinfonia terribile* from the oratorio *Miracolo del Mago* (1680) by Domenico Freschi (d. 1710),[16] where a *concertino* of two cornetts and a bassoon carry on a dialogue with a six-part string orchestra. By the end of the century the *concerto grosso* was, after the suite, the most widely cultivated form of orchestral music. In addition the principles which it employed were introduced into many other forms, such as the suite and *sinfonia*, and even the fugue.

The range of alternatives which composers allowed in its interpretation of their scores is interesting. Muffat gives detailed instructions in the foreword to his *Armonico tributo*:[17]

. . . I have tried to serve your convenience by making it possible for you to perform these sonatas in various ways in accordance with the following instructions:
1. They can be played with only three instruments, i.e. two violins, and a cello or bass viol for the continuo. The two violins must take care to play also the passages in their parts which have the viola clefs; similarly when the bass player has passages with the alto or tenor clef he is requested not to rest but to play (either as written, or in case of difficulty an octave lower), so that the harmony does not lack a bass.

    [16] Arnold Schering, *Geschichte des Oratoriums* (Leipzig, 1911), p. 112.
    [17] Ed. E. Luntz, *Denkmäler der Tonkunst in Österreich*, xxiii (Jg. 11(2)), p. 118.

2. They can be played by four or five instruments. If there are four, the tenor viola will be omitted; if there are five, it will be included. In performances with four or five players the violins will be able to rest where the above-mentioned viola clefs occur.

3. If you want to hear them as full concertos, with a certain fanciful treatment (*con qualche bizzarria*) or variety of harmony, you can organize the players into two groups, one of them a three-part *concertino* of two violins and cello or bass viol, played by soloists and not doubled. These will play throughout. The violins will have to notice when the letter T (meaning *tutti*) occurs, and the same applies to the violins who double them in the *concerto grosso*. The latter will stop playing at the letter S (*soli*) and will leave the *concertino* to continue alone. The violas will be doubled proportionately to the other parts of the *concerto grosso*, with which they will play, except however where the said letter S occurs. Here it will be sufficient for these parts to be played by soloists and not doubled. I have taken all these precautions to ensure this agreeable variety (*laquale commoda varietà*).

6. Finally with regard to doubling, take care that the number of first violins should not be much larger than the number of seconds, and that the basses of the *concerto grosso* should be reinforced by double basses and violoni according to the conductor's discretion.[18]

Muffat's instructions show that in the early years of the *concerto grosso* the new style of instrumentation was designed to produce an 'agreeable variety' rather than as a means of organizing the structure of the music. It is obvious that Corelli's *concerti grossi*, where Muffat's instructions are no longer applicable, represent a higher stage of development.

THE OPERA OVERTURE

It was particularly fortunate for the development of orchestral music that opera, which offered new opportunities for the orchestra, should have arisen at the same time as a typical orchestral idiom began to be established in the *canzon* and the suite. The demands that composers had to face in the way of orchestral invention, instrumentation, and formal organization were unusual and compelled them to make continual experiments. For this reason what may be called *ad hoc* orchestral music in opera came to play quite an important role and to influence music which had no connection with the theatre. Of the purely instrumental movements in opera (*sinfonie* and *ritornelli*) the *sinfonia* which began the work— sometimes known as *sinfonia à prencipio*, *sinfonia avanti l'opera*, or

---

[18] The latter part of this sentence is mistranslated by Schenk in *Denkmäler der Tonkunst in Österreich*, lxxxix, p. xxvi.

*sonata avanti il Prologo*, to distinguish it from entr'actes and other incidental pieces—came to have supreme importance.

Monteverdi's idea of making the opening *sinfonia* an organic element in the work was occasionally imitated by other composers. Domenico Mazzocchi's opera *La catena d'Adone* (1626)[19] includes in Act II an elaborate independent scene (a 'Festa d'Amor'). It begins with a sinfonia ($\frac{3}{2}$), the principal themes of which recur in two following movements for women's and men's chorus respectively. This is followed by a second *sinfonia* (C) which in due course is used for choruses of nymphs and shepherds. Most of the *sinfonie* in the early period of Roman and Venetian opera are *canzoni* in form, the movements being generally reduced to two or three in view of their function in the work. The opening *sinfonia* of Monteverdi's *L'incoronazione di Poppea* (1642), following a precedent by Marenzio,[20] consists of a pavane and galliard (though not actually described as such) of whch the second piece is partly a rhythmic transformation of the first. One finds similar examples in several of Cavalli's operas.

In the second half of the seventeenth century two types of overture were becoming established; but the early history of opera shows several different ways of solving the problem—a problem which affected solo opera on a sacred subject and through it the oratorio. In 1625 Francesca Caccini, daughter of the Florentine composer, wrote for her ballet-opera *La liberazione di Ruggiero dall'isola d'Alcina*[21] the first known overture to have a definite three-movement structure. A substantial first movement (C) is followed by a dance movement ($\frac{3}{2}$) and the work ends with a four-bar coda (C). Opera in Rome had a strong inclination to sacred subjects, elaborate choral writing and carefully worked-out orchestral pieces, and this tended at an early date to establish a particular type of overture. In Michelangelo Rossi's *Erminia sul Giordano*[22] (probably first performed in 1625 in the Palazzo Barberini, though not printed till 1637) three solemn introductory bars are followed by a fugato with quick note-values, providing the basic elements of the later French overture:[23]

[19] See Vol. IV, pp. 838–9.
[20] See ibid., p. 795.
[21] Ed. D. Silbert, *Smith College Music Archives*, vii (Northampton, Mass., 1945).
[22] See Vol. IV, pp. 840–1.
[23] Hugo Botstiber, *Geschichte der Ouvertüre* (Leipzig, 1913), p. 234.

Ex. 95

Sinfonia per Introduzione del Prologo

Stefano Landi's sacred opera *Sant' Alessio* (1632)[24] is also important for the development of the opera *sinfonia*. Each of the three
acts begins with an extended *canzone*, the one before the first act
being in three sections, with the quick section in the middle (as in
Lully's overtures).[25]

The most important composer of opera *sinfonie* in Venice after
Monteverdi's death was Cavalli. Some of these—generally in the
course of an opera—have programmatic titles such as 'Concilio
infernale', 'Sinfonia navale', 'Notte', 'Aurora', 'Tocca di battaglia'.
These established a precedent for much that came after. The idea
of illustrating a programme affected not only the music itself but

[24] See Vol. IV, p. 840, and Vol. V, pp. 3–5.
[25] Hugo Goldschmidt, *Studien zur Geschichte der italienischen Oper im 17. Jahrhundert*, i
(Leipzig, 1901), p. 202.

also the instrumentation. Thematic material for the overture was often suggested by warlike cries such as *all'armi* from the chorus. The trumpet as a symbol of battle not only played its part as an obbligato instrument in arias but was also heard in *sinfonie*. It is significant for the future development of the overture that Cavalli was active in Paris and there came into contact with Lully. Their relationship is made clear by the fact that Lully in 1660 was invited to write ballet music and the overture for a Paris performance of Cavalli's *Xerse*—an overture which Prunières claimed to be the first typical French overture to appear.[26] In his *Ercole amante*, written for Paris in 1662,[27] Cavalli shows a considerable response to French influence.

THE FRENCH OVERTURE

The development which led to the creation of the French overture began in the ballet. As early as the sixteenth century the first known performances of ballet included instrumental introductions, though music was not often specially composed for this purpose. In the succeeding period an introduction consisting of two sections, on the analogy of the pavane and galliard, was provided, the usual practice being to begin with a processional entry (generally a march) and follow this with a dance in duple or triple time. The succession C—$\frac{3}{2}$ ($\frac{3}{4}$, $\frac{3}{8}$) survived as a characteristic feature of the form which developed later, which from 1640 onwards was known as *ouverture*. Equally characteristic is the half close at the end of the march, which serves to link the two sections. The dotted rhythm appeared in 1640 in the *Ballet de Mademoiselle*.[28] Lully became familiar with these mannerisms of the French ballet overture when he was appointed to the court in 1652 as violinist, dancer, and actor. It was not long before he came forward as a composer. In the court ballets which from 1655 onwards were almost exclusively written by him he remained in all essentials faithful to this older type and gave it great musical significance. In the overtures to his ballets *L'amore ammalato* (1657), *Alcidiane* (1658), and *La Raillerie* (1659)[29] we can trace the growing development of the characteristic features of the second section—for instance the fugato, first introduced in *Alcidiane*.

Lully's art was strongly influenced by the traditional repertory of

[26] 'Notes sur les origines de l'ouverture française', in *Sammelbände der internationalen Musikgesellschaft*, xii (1910–11), p. 582.
[27] See Vol. V, pp. 192–4.
[28] Prunières, op. cit., p. 571.
[29] Ibid., pp. 573–7, 580–1.

the *vingt-quatre violons du roi* (*la grande bande* in contrast to the smaller body of sixteen, later enlarged to twenty-two, which was founded at Lully's suggestion in 1656). A close melodic relationship between the upper parts and the bass, including exact imitation, is to be found in the *Ballet de la Raillerie* of 1659:

Ex. 96

In the overtures to *Alcidiane and Xerse* imitation at the octave or fifth appears for the first time at the beginning of the second sections:

Ex. 97

For a long time it was held that this was the result of Italian influence (cf. the *sinfonie* by Landi and Rossi) and that Lully was responsible for uniting French and Italian elements. Nils Schioerring[30] has drawn attention to a possible model in the allemande-courante pair of dances, with its long established tradition of fugato in the allemande. This may explain why Lully's

---

[30] *Allemande og fransk ouverture* (Copenhagen, 1957).

device of transferring the fugato to the courante was so quickly
adopted by others. As early as 1661—the year in which Lully was
appointed *surintendent de la musique de la chambre*—Charles-
Louis Beauchamp imitated Lully's procedure in his overture to
Molière's *Les Fâcheux*:[31]

Ex. 98

Second section

Thus the type of the French overture was established and survived
for roughly a hundred years. It had begun in the ballet but was
soon employed in opera in the overture Lully composed for the
Paris production of Cavalli's *Xerse* (1660).[32] Lully's innovation
spread with remarkable rapidity. French violinists and dance in-
structors, who were in great demand everywhere in Europe at that
time as representatives of *le goût français*, carried the form to
Germany; and as early as 1663 the Grand Duke of Tuscany
ordered works by Lully from Paris. In view of its origin it was
natural that the form should have been more widely used in the
suite than in opera itself.

The Italian opera composers of this period, particularly those
who were active outside Italy, were soon unable to avoid this
French influence, though they generally had their own way of

[31] Paris, Bibl. du Cons., Collection Philidor, Vol. 44. See Prunières, op. cit., p. 583.
[32] See Vol. V, p. 192.

adapting the model. Together with the ballet overture dance movements soon began to appear as well. We find for instance in
Antonio Draghi's *Achille in Sciro* (1669)[33] a *corrente* after the
slow introduction, and in Cesti's *Disgrazie d'Amore* (1667)[34] a
sarabande, which is repeated after the prologue.

The overture came to England with Cambert, who had to leave
France in face of Lully's rivalry. English composers adopted it so
quickly that it came to be regarded almost as the national type
rather than the later Italian form. This is understandable, since
after the Restoration an orchestra of twenty-four string-players was
founded after the French model and English taste was at this time
nearer to the French than to the Italian. John Blow wrote a French
overture for his three-act opera *Venus and Adonis* (c.1682)[35] (described as a masque) and Purcell, in whose work French and English
influences overlap, regularly used the French overture as an introduction to dramatic works and court odes. He showed how the
traditional stiffness of the form could be enlivened in the first
section by introducing elements of the allemande, while the second
(quick) section is often similar to a gigue, which may have suggested to him a very thorough contrapuntal treatment. The overture in G minor which Edward Dent assigned conjecturally to *The
Tempest*[36] shows a subtle use of imitation:

Ex. 99

[33] Botstiber, op. cit., p. 30.
[34] Ibid.
[35] Ed. Anthony Lewis (Paris, 1939), and see Vol. V, pp. 278–81.
[36] *Purcell Society*, xix, p. 112.

## THE THREE-MOVEMENT *SINFONIA*

In the meantime another type of overture had become established in Italy, which was to be of the greatest importance for the further development of instrumental music. It is usually associated with the name of the Neapolitan composer Alessandro Stradella (1644–82) and described as a three-movement form: quick—slow—quick. A much more important element in its origin, however, was the principle of introducing solo instruments. The trumpet as a symbol of nobility or heroism was extremely popular in North Italy throughout the seventeenth century. For obvious reasons the first (slow) section of the old overture came to be restricted, in the trumpet overture, to a few simple chords; the Allegro became the principal movement. Another result of using the trumpet was that both sections were generally very simple in tonality and rarely departed from the basic key of D major. The balance was restored by the middle movement, which generally went further afield and incidentally gave the wind-players a chance to rest. The sequence Allegro—Largo—Allegro (i.e. a *sonata da chiesa* without an introductory movement) occurs already in a *Sinfonia a più istrumenti* by Stradella, equally important as a pioneer of the *concerto grosso* and of the overture: but many of his opera overtures also follow the same plan.

In this period when formal construction and the use of solo instruments were closely linked, Bologna played an important part. In fact it may be said that it was the most important centre for the practice of instrumental music. The *sinfonie* written there by Giacomo Antonio Perti (1661–1756), *maestro di cappella* at the Basilica San Petronio—including the works known as *sinfonie avanti il Chirie*, which were used as preludes to the Mass—are very close to the later Italian overture in form. Alessandro Scarlatti (1659–1725) remained faithful in his early works (after 1679) to the Venetian type of overture (similar to the *sonata da chiesa*), though before long he added a dance movement at the end, perhaps as a result of French influence. The use of such a dance movement became characteristic of the new form, which occurs already in Scarlatti's work before 1690 and for this reason is sometimes known as the 'Scarlatti overture'. Three movements now became the norm, and the incorporation of a style derived from the use of solo instruments may be regarded as typical. Scarlatti's later overtures[37] are, so to speak, *concerti grossi* with the opening

[37] For examples see Robert Haas, *Die Musik des Barocks* (Potsdam, 1934), p. 207 (the opera *Eraclea*. 1700); Botstiber, op. cit., p. 252 (the oratorio *Sedecia, rè di Gerusalemme*, 1706); Davison and Apel, op. cit., no. 259 (the opera *Griselda*, 1721).

movement missing. The new form seems to have quickly spread to other countries. In 1699 André Campra (1660–1744) wrote a little Italian opera, *L'Orfeo dell'inferni*, for insertion in his ballet *Le Carnaval de Venise*, which has an overture consisting of Vivace ($\frac{4}{4}$)—Adagio ($\frac{3}{2}$)—Presto ($\frac{3}{8}$).

With the sequence quick—slow—quick Scarlatti and the composers of his time found a method of organizing a work in several movements which has remained valid down to the present day. About 1700 it was adopted for the solo concerto and later formed the basis for the classical symphony. Rousseau has left us a very exact description of the essentials of the Italian overture. After giving pride of place to the French overture he adds:[38]

The Italians have not been slow to escape from this restriction, and they organize their overtures in a different way. They begin with a gay, lively movement in duple or quadruple time. Then comes a subdued (*à demi-jeu*) Andante, in which they try to exploit all the charm of a fine melody, and they end with a brilliant Allegro, generally in triple time.

The reason they give for this arrangement is that in a crowded theatre where the audience are making a great deal of noise the first thing to be done is to impose silence and to engage their attention by a striking opening. They say that no one hears or listens to the slow introductions of our [i.e. French] overtures, and that our *premier coup d'archet*, about which we make so much fuss, being less noisy than the full chord which precedes it and with which it gets confused, is more likely to prepare the listener for boredom than for attention. They add that after having seized the spectator's attention it is a good thing to interest him with less noise by means of a pleasing and soothing melody which will incline him to the emotional state of mind (*attendrissement*) which it will soon be the composer's object to create in him, and to end the overture with a piece of another character which, since it contrasts with the beginning of the drama, will mark by its noisy ending the silence which the actor who appears on the stage expects of his audience.

The importance of both the French and Italian types of overture in seventeenth-century music need hardly be stressed. Hugo Botstiber summarizes their characteristics:[39]

The French overture and the Neapolitan *sinfonia* have two things in common: their origin and their purpose. Both were written for festival occasions, for the entertainment of the aristocracy, as an introduction

---

[38] *Dictionnaire de Musique* (Paris, 1768), s.v. 'Ouverture'.
[39] Op. cit., p. 59.

o princely performances. The difference between them arises from the way in which the achievement of this purpose was pursued in the two countries: in France with frigid grandeur, in the South with carefree exuberance. One might say that the existence of the two types is due merely to circumstances, that they reflect the characteristics of two different cultures.

## THE SUITE

The practice of writing a set of instrumental dances in the form of a suite, which sometimes consisted of variations on the principal dance, was cultivated particularly in Germany;[40] Karl Nef's list of suites composed in Germany,[41] which does not pretend to be complete, includes the names of seventy-eight composers from Hassler in 1601 to J. C. Fischer in 1708. How international was the influence of the form can be seen from the fact that at the beginning of the seventeenth century we have English composers like William Brade (1560–1630) and Thomas Simpson (1582–after 1625), and later Italians like Biagio Marini (c.1587–1663) and Carlo Farina (c.1600–c.1640) working in this field. An example such as the following[42] gives some idea of the high standard of technical mastery which Brade helped to introduce into the German orchestral suite:

Ex. 100

---

[40] See Vol. IV, pp. 594 ff.
[41] *Geschichte der Sinfonie und Suite* (Leipzig, 1921), pp. 52 ff.
[42] *Newe ausserlesene Paduanen*, etc. (Hamburg, 1609); printed in Bernhard Engelke, *Musik und Musiker am Gottorfer Hofe*, i (Breslau, 1930), p. 209.

He spent many years in Hamburg and wrote a good deal of music for the English companies of actors who visited North Germany. The fact that far fewer suites were written by German composers after 1622–3 (there is a complete gap between 1628 and 1635) is due to the ravages caused by the Thirty Years' War.

When Johann Hermann Schein (1586–1630), in the foreword to his *Banchetto musicale* (Leipzig, 1617),[43] says that the dances are 'so arranged that there is a subtle correspondence between them in key and in thematic material',[44] he is describing the variation suite, which became a standard form in the second decade of the seventeenth century, not only in his own work but also in that of Paul Peuerl and Ignaz Posch.[45] By means of variation or progressive transformation the upper part of the first dance provides the thematic material for the remainder:[46]

[43] Ed. Siegsmund Helme, *J. H. Schein: Neue Ausgabe sämtlicher Werke*, ix (Kassel, 1979).

[44] 'also gesetzet, dass sie beides, in Tono und inventione einander fein respondiren'.

[45] Extracts from Peuerl's *Newe Padouan Intrada Däntz vnnd Galliarda* (Nuremberg, 1611) and *Gantz Neue Padouanen Auffzüg Balleten Couranten Intraden vnd Däntz* (Nuremberg, 1625), ed. Karl Geiringer, *Denkmäler der Tonkunst in Österreich*, lxx (Jg. 36(2)) (Vienna, 1929; reprint, 1960), together with a *balleta* from Posch's *Musicalische Ehrnfreudt* (Regensburg, 1618) and a complete edition of his *Musicalische Tafelfreudt* (Nuremberg, 1621).

[46] Another example from Schein in Vol. IV, pp. 594–5.

## Ex. 101

(i) **Peuerl** (1611), Nos. V—VIII

Padovan

Intrada

Dantz

Galliarda

(ii) **Schein**

Padovana

Gagliarda

Courente

Allemande

Tripla

The composition of suites was actively resumed after 1635, but by this time the variation technique was largely abandoned[47] or treated very casually. The important point was to have all the dances in the same key. In place of the *intrada* we quite often find an introductory movement which is called *sinfonia, sonata, sonatina, praeludium, toccata,* or even *pavane* and is frequently similar to the style of the Italian *canzon*: the use of *pavane* as a title for a piece of this kind is explained by the fact that by this time it had practically ceased to denote a specific dance form. In the contemporary suites by the Paris lutenists it is usual to find a *praeludium*—a type of composition which dates back to a considerably earlier period.[48] These introductory movements prepared

[47] Exceptions will be found in Andreas Hammerschmidt's *Ander Theil neuer Paduanen, Canzonen, Galliarden,* etc. (Freiberg, 1639), ed. H. Mönkemeyer, *Das Erbe deutscher Musik,* xlix (Kassel, 1957).
[48] Adrian Le Roy's *A brief and plaine instruction* (1574), the English version of his lost *Instruction de partir toute musique facilement en tablature de luth,* includes 'a little fantasie for me tunying of the Lute'.

the way for the introduction of the French overture into the suite and so led to the development of the overture-suite. About the middle of the century we begin to find in the works of the French lutenists the four basic dances which were to remain standard for nearly a hundred years: the allemande (C) and its companion the courante ($\frac{3}{4}$), the sarabande ($\frac{3}{2}$), and the gigue ($\frac{6}{8}$ or $\frac{3}{8}$). The show very clearly the cosmopolitan tendencies of the times, since the allemande, as its name implies, came from Germany, the sara bande was probably of Spanish origin, and the gigue had long been familiar in England, as the 'jig', in masques and later in the suite Through Froberger's keyboard suites these sequences of dance became known in Germany and widely accepted there from 1660 onwards; in the process the individual characteristics of each dance became more sharply defined and the contrasts between them more distinct. The basic series could be enlarged at will to include dance such as the gavotte, the bourrée, the polonaise and so on. The most significant of these additions was the minuet, which came in about 1670. When there was a second minuet (or trio) as a middle section, Lully's practice of making a contrast between the *concerto grosso* and a trio of two oboes and bassoon was adopted. The same principle was applied, by analogy, to works which did not include wind instruments.

THE DOMINANCE OF FRENCH INFLUENCE

The popularity which the suite enjoyed at this time, not only in Germany but throughout Europe, was a result of the political supremacy of France, where Louis XIV had ruled as an absolute monarch since 1661. He was himself an accomplished solo dancer (the inscription *dansé par sa Majesté* occurs in many of the scores in the Philidor Collection) and he regarded the ballet not only as a means of providing entertainment of high artistic quality but also as a way of glorifying his régime. The French overture introduced by Lully about the time of the king's accession, with its solemn and stately introduction, was the perfect musical counterpart for the ceremonial proper to a court. The artistic tastes of the French court, and its way of life, became the model for other courts, both large and small, all over Europe, so that the French ballet and music in the style of Lully found ready acceptance. In earlier days German musicians had made the pilgrimage to Italy to study; now it was Paris that was the magnet, more as a centre of taste than as a place where one could learn how to compose. Telemann described the situation of a German court composer very clearly when he said of his employment at Sorau:

The brilliance of this court, which had been newly established as a principality, inspired me to feverish energy, particularly in the field of instrumental composition. I chose for preference overtures with their accompanying movements [i.e. suites], since His Excellency the Count had recently returned from France and so liked this kind of music.[49]

The new French dances in quick tempo were introduced comparatively early into German suites, e.g. in Lüder Knoep's *Erster Theil newer Paduanen*, etc. (Bremen, 1652), Hans Hake's *Ander Theil Newer Pavanen*, etc. (Stade, 1654), Johann Christoph Seyfried's *Erster Theil Neuer Balletten*, etc. (Erfurt, 1656) and *Zweyter Theil neuer Paduanen*, etc. (Erfurt, 1659), Georg Wolffgang Druckenmüller's *Musikalisches Taffel-Confect* (Schwäbisch Hall, 1668), and other publications of a similar kind. Knoep says in a foreword that 'the ballets are composed in the French style and should be played with a lively beat'. Movements directly modelled on Lully's are found for the first time in Georg Bleyer's *Lust-Music, nach ietziger Frantzösischer Manier gesetzet* (Leipzig, 1670). Johann Sigismund Kusser (1660–1727), who lived in Paris for six years as Lully's pupil and there changed his name to Cousser, adopted the type of overture practised by his teacher and used it as the prelude to a suite. His collection entitled *Composition de Musique Suivant la Méthode Françoise contenant Six Ouvertures de Théâtre accompagnées de plusieurs Airs* (Stuttgart, 1682) is of great importance in the history of the suite. Philipp Heinrich Erlebach (1657–1714), who also studied with Lully, uses the term *ouverture* as a synonym for the whole suite in his *VI Ouvertures, begleitet mit ihren dazu schicklichen Airs nach Französischer Art* (Nuremberg, 1693). Rupert Ignaz Mayr (1646–1712), who was in Paris c.1684, indicates in the sub-title of his *Pythagorische Schmids-Füncklein* (Augsburg, 1692) that the contents can be used for many purposes — 'dinner music (*Tafelmusik*), comedies, serenades, and other joyful assemblies'.

By this time the new type of suite was widely practised in Germany: excellent examples are to be found in Georg Muffat's *Florilegium Primum* (Augsburg, 1695) and *Florilegium Secundum* (Passau, 1698).[50] Johann Caspar Fischer's *Jounal du Printems*

[49] From the autobiography contributed to Mattheson's *Ehrenpforte* (1740), reprinted in *Denkmäler deutscher Tonkunst*, xxviii, ed. Max Schneider (Leipzig, 1907; revised ed., Wiesbaden and Graz, 1958), pp. vi–xvii.

[50] Ed. Heinrich Rietsch, *Denkmäler der Tonkunst in Österreich*, ii and iv (Jg. (1) and 2(2)) ) (Vienna, 1894 and 1895; reprint, 1959).

(Augsburg, 1695),[51] Benedict Anton Aufschnaiter's *Concors discordia* (Nuremberg, 1695), and J. A. Schmicorer's *Zodiaci Musici* (Augsburg, 1698).[52] The forewords to Muffat's two collections, particularly the second, offer valuable information about the performance of music in the French style. The titles of many of the pieces derive directly from the French ballet; their original purpose was simply to indicate that a dance was performed by a particular member of the ballet. Such indications gave rise in turn to the use of fanciful titles, which influenced the character of the music and tended to the composition of programmatic pieces, e.g. Muffat's 'Les Cuisiniers' (*Florilegium II*, no. 12), which illustrates the mincing of meat. Ballets in which different countries were represented gave abundant opportunities for a more subtle treatment of idioms and instrumentation. The exploration of the folk music of other countries made German composers aware of the musical traditions of their own, with the result that the suite, in spite of its French origin, sometimes shows strong national traits. It should be noted that the overture-suite as an independent form flourished almost exclusively in Germany; in France it hardly existed outside the theatre, apart from arrangements for chamber ensembles, keyboard instruments, or the lute.

[51] Ed. Ernst von Werra, *Denkmäler deutscher Tonkunst*, x (Leipzig, 1902; revised ed. 1958).

[52] Ibid. Schmicorer also appears as Schmierer and in various other spellings.

# IV

## ORCHESTRAL MUSIC IN THE EARLY EIGHTEENTH CENTURY

### By WALTER KOLNEDER

THE previous chapter has shown how, starting from the transcription and imitation of vocal forms, instrumental music had gradually become independent. Composers had created new forms, had found a stimulus to their invention in the technique of individual instruments, and had experimented with various combinations of instrumental colour. The orchestra had become an instrument which was able to serve the church with simplicity and dignity, to give expression to dramatic tension, and to satisfy the demands of fastidious connoisseurs when employed 'for the permissible recreation of the mind' ('Zu erlaubter Recreation des Gemüthes') at banquets and dances. Finally at the turn of the century we have the solo concerto,[1] the last of the great achievements of the Baroque period. Compared with this abundant activity the early eighteenth century seems to be a period when the grain ripened and was harvested. The works of J. S. Bach may be taken as a symbol of this autumnal fulfilment. His Brandenburg concertos, his orchestral suites, and the considerable part played by the orchestra in his solo concertos, oratorios, Passions, and cantatas, embrace everything that had been discovered by laborious experiment in the previous century. At the same time in the works of composers such as Pergolesi, Monn, Sammartini, and others we find the evidence of a new style, and this is what gives the period a special interest.

### CONDITIONS AND RESOURCES

Conditions could hardly have been more favourable for orchestral music. In Italy the *accademie* had in course of time become important centres for its cultivation. The church provided ample opportunities for purely instrumental music: Tartini, for example, was employed as a solo violinist at the basilica of San Antonio at

---

[1] See chap. V.

Padua. Lastly the so-called *conservatori* of Naples and Venice were the nurseries which produced young and able players to swell the ranks. The fact that the orchestra of the Ospedale della Pietà at Venice was compared to that of the Paris opera (Académie Royale de Musique) gives some idea of the high standard of these institutions. In Venice Vivaldi was able to develop a new orchestral style, brilliant and expressive, which aroused the admiration of all the visitors from abroad who attended the regular services with music on Sundays and feast days.

In Austria and Germany princes and bishops were anxious for their courts to be regarded as important cultural centres: for this reason a large number of ensembles were established, some small, some of medium size, in addition to the larger court orchestras which had a long tradition behind them. All these offered musicians a livelihood and the possibility of further development. When money was scarce, servants, clerks, and footmen were drawn upon as 'extras': there was no better recommendation for employment at court than the ability to play an instrument. It was understood, and sometimes specified in contracts, that anyone appointed as *Kapellmeister* should himself supply any music that was needed; and daily contact with an orchestra gave him a sound, practical basis for his creative work. Much later, Haydn, speaking of his work at Eisenstadt, said: 'As director of an orchestra I was able to experiment':[2] many others had found themselves in the same position. The interest in orchestral music shown by the aristocracy spread to the middle classes. The *collegium musicum* became a new opportunity for people to meet each other and make music together. One was founded at Elbing in 1630. At Hamburg the *collegium* gave public concerts every Thursday from 1660 onwards: in Switzerland the *collegium* at Winterthur gave its first public performance in 1665. In Leipzig it was Telemann, then a law student, who suggested in 1701 that his fellow-students should join him for regular music-making. His *collegium* at times had as many as sixty members. It usually met once a week for public rehearsals, but twice a week when the Leipzig fair was on. When Telemann left, Pisendel sometimes deputized as director of the *collegium*. From 1729 to 1737 and again from 1739 till probably 1744 Bach was in charge. Later on, in Frankfurt and Hamburg, Telemann was able to put to good use the experience he had gained in Leipzig; the

---

[2] Georg August Griesinger, *Biographische Notizen über Joseph Haydn*, ed. Franz Grazberger (Vienna, 1954), p. 17.

enormous amount of music which he wrote is closely connected with these activities.

In France cultural life was mainly confined to Paris and the Court, and this made it difficult for orchestral music to spread further afield. Two institutions in Paris were particularly important, and were to retain their importance for a good many years to come. For some time people had felt it was a pity that there were no theatres or concerts in Lent. It was to fill this gap that the oboist Anne Danican-Philidor (1681–1728) instituted the *Concert Spirituel*. This was originally restricted to performances of sacred music or instrumental music of a religious character in Holy Week. Soon, however, a broader policy was pursued and orchestral music—particularly solo concertos—became more firmly established in the repertory, with the result that the concerts gradually became the chief influence in the development of instrumental music in France. Leclair's rise to fame began when he played a sonata at the *Concert Spirituel* in 1728; and it was in a trio sonata of Leclair's that Pierre Gaviniès (1728–1800) made his début at these concerts in 1741. Orchestral music was also cultivated in noble houses and in well-to-do middle-class circles. A sincere enthusiasm for music often went hand in hand with a desire to cut a figure in society. In 1730 Alexandre-Jean-Joseph Le Riche de La Pouplinière (1693–1762), who as *fermier général*[3] had ample means at his disposal, instituted musical performances under the direction of Rameau at his private residence, and these led to the formation of a permanent orchestra. On the advice of Johann Stamitz (1717–57) horns were introduced into this orchestra for the first time in France in 1748. In 1754–5 Stamitz himself directed Pouplinière's orchestra, which had in fact been playing his compositions for some time before that date.

In England, where John Banister (*c*.1625–79) and the enterprising coal-merchant Thomas Britton (1644–1714) were pioneers of the public concert, orchestral music made a considerable advance in London at the turn of the century, largely through the influence of Italian musicians, such as Francesco Gasparini (1668–1727) and Francesco Geminiani (1687–1762). Popular concerts of a high quality in the public gardens reached large sections of the community, while connoisseurs met in Hickford's Room,[4] where the dancing-master Hickford organized concerts. Orchestral music also

---

[3] Farmer-general of taxes.
[4] Orginally in James St., off the Haymarket, but from 1739 in Brewer Street, off Golden Square.

played an important part in the life of the Court and the nobility, including river parties on the Venetian model. Handel's contributions to the repertory of 'water music' for such occasions are well known.

## CONSTITUTION OF ORCHESTRAS

We have a good deal of information from pictures, written records, account books, lists of payment, and so on about the size of these orchestras, which sprang up all over Europe, and also about their composition. Except as a result of war or other adverse circumstances we find that in general there was a gradual increase in the number of players. In 1712 the King of Prussia's orchestra in Berlin consisted of six first violins, five second violins, two violas, and five cellos and double basses. By 1787 it had grown to twenty violins (first and second), six violas, eight cellos, and four double basses. In 1730 the court orchestra in Vienna had thirty-two string-players. The orchestra of the *Concert Spirituel* in 1751 numbered sixteen violins, two violas, six cellos, and two double basses. The orchestral parts of Telemann's suites in Dresden included three each for first and second violins, two each for violas, double basses, and bassoons, and one each for cellos and the remaining wind. Since violin- and viola-players usually stood in groups of three at a desk, one can assume that there were up to nine first violins. Not all orchestras were as fortunate as this. The Duke's band at Weimar had only four first violins, including J. S. Bach. At Leipzig Bach had to play with the combination 3.3.2.2.1. Graupner at Darmstadt had the same number of strings, plus two flutes, two oboes, four bassoons, two horns, timpani, and harpsichord.

It is often difficult to decide how many players there were for each wind instrument. In the King of Prussia's list of payments for 1712, for instance, there are four oboes and three bassoons. Since wind-players often played more than one instrument, this number includes flutes and later on would include clarinets. Players changed instruments from one work to another, and often in the course of a single work. The number of bassoons employed is striking: their principal function was to support the cellos and basses by reinforcing the continuo line. Trumpeters and timpanists hardly ever appear in the lists of payments; they were listed as soldiers with their regiments and used in orchestras as occasion arose. The figures for orchestral players that have come down to us refer, of course, only to those who were on the staff in that capacity. Other members of the household who were competent musicians also had to do their turn of duty. A late example is the Bishop of Grosswardein's orchestra: in 1765, according to Dittersdorf,[5] it consisted of twelve solo players, nine liveried servants, a valet, a confectioner, seven musicians from the chapter, and four vocalists. On festive occasions musicians were borrowed from neighbouring courts or brought in from the town and the surrounding countryside. Exceptional resources were employed for very special occasions such as coronations. When Charles VI was crowned King of Bohemia at Prague in 1723 Fux's opera *Costanza e fortezza*[6] was performed in an open-air theatre in the Hradčany by 100 singers and 200 instrumentalists: the audience numbered 4,000.[7] Schubart's report that the continuo was played by fifty harpsichords must be an exaggeration, but it gives some idea of the amount of space available. Quantz tells us that the Emperor had summoned to Prague the most famous virtuosos in Europe. He adds: 'only about twenty players came from the Vienna orchestra.[8] The rest of the orchestra was assembled in Prague from students, members of various noblemen's orchestras, and foreign musicians.' The violinists included Tartini and Veracini, Conti and Weiss played theorbo, Graun played the cello, and Quantz himself was one of the *ripieno* oboes.[9]

Quantz makes the interesting observation that Fux's ritornellos, 'which on paper may often look rather stiff and dry, were very effective on this occasion, performed on a grand scale by so many instrumentalists'. When he was in Dresden also he had noticed that 'Lully's rather dry overtures, when played by a large orchestra, sound much better than the more attractive and more *galant* overtures of other famous composers'. This means that the relatively simple melodic lines and straightforward part-writing of the seventeenth and early eighteenth centuries made it possible to increase the number of players at will; so much so that the music sounded better on a large orchestra, without any loss of clarity. In fact, any type of performance was possible—from one instrument to a part up to the enormous forces employed at Prague. The suggestions about the composition of an orchestra to be found in contemporary

[5] *Lebensbeschreibung*, ed. Eugen Schmitz (Regensburg, 1940), pp. 135 and 137.
[6] See Vol. V. pp, 131–2.
[7] See the reproduction in *Denkmäler der Tonkunst in Österreich*, xvii (vols. 34 and 35), ed. Egon Wellesz (Vienna, 1910; reprint, Graz, 1959).
[8] The number was actually thirty-three: ibid., pp. x–xi.
[9] Quantz's account comes from his autobiography, printed in F. W. Marpurg's *Historisch-kritische Beyträge zur Aufnahme der Musik*, i (Berlin, 1754–5), p. 210, modern reprint in *Selbstbiographien deutscher Musiker*, ed. Willi Kahl (Cologne, 1948), pp. 123 ff.

manuals are not based on any specific works or forms but rather on limitations of space and the relative strength of groups within the orchestra. In the seventeenth chapter of his *Versuch, einer Anweisung die Flöte traversiere zu spielen*[10] Quantz summarized the practice of the first half of the eighteenth century. In the first section he begins by discussing how to use the space available and how to seat the players. He then comes to the question of the composition of an orchestra:

13. Finally, the leader must know how to distribute, place, and arrange the instrumentalists in an ensemble. Much depends upon the good distribution and placement of the instruments, and upon their combination in the proper ratio.

16. He who wishes to perform a composition well must see to it that he supplies each instrument in the proper proportion, and does not use too many of one kind, too few of another. I shall propose a ratio which, to my thinking, will satisfy all requirements in this regard. I assume that the *harpsichord* will be included in all ensembles, whether large or small.

With *four violins* use *one viola, one violoncello*, and *one double bass* of medium size.

With *six violins*, the same complement and *one bassoon*.

*Eight violins* require *two violas, two violoncellos*, an *additional double bass*, larger, however, than the first, *two oboes, two flutes*, and *two bassoons*.

With *ten violins*, the same complement, but with an *additional violoncello*.

With *twelve violins* use *three violas, four violoncellos, two double basses, three bassoons, four oboes, four flutes*, and in a pit *another keyboard* and *one theorbo*.

*Hunting horns* may be necessary in both small and large ensembles, depending upon the nature of the piece and the inclination of the composer.

His later sections on *ripieno* violinists, viola-players, cellists, double bass players, and harpsichordists, and on 'The Duties That All Accompanying Instrumentalists in General Must Observe' are a mine of information about methods of performance and the constitution of orchestras from the time of Corelli up to the death of Handel. Matheson's voluminous writings and other theoretical works of the time supplement and develop further what we learn from Quantz.

OUTPUT OF WORKS

With so many orchestras in existence there was a demand for

---

[10] Facsimile ed. (Kassel, 1953); English translation, *On Playing the Flute*, ed. Edward R. Reilly (London, 1966), pp. 211, 214.

music which it is difficult for us to imagine at the present day. Printed music could supply only a fraction of this demand. The greater part of the repertory of any orchestra was the music composed by its *Kapellmeister*. This music generally remained the property of the employer, who not infrequently guarded it jealously, allowing copies to be passed on to his noble friends only as a special favour. The resident *Kapellmeister* was able, in his compositions, to take account of local conditions and to provide special parts for virtuosos on a particular instrument. The peculiar scoring of Bach's Brandenburg concertos, which changes from one number to the next, is a typical example. These conditions made possible an astonishing increase in the composition of orchestral music. Forkel, in a list of contemporary composers in Germany,[11] mentions 340 names: Burney tells us that 'the composers to be found at Milan are innumerable'.[12] The vast number of works written by some composers is explained by the constant obligation they were under to supply the society in which they lived with new compositions. Alessandro Scarlatti is credited with the composition of more than 600 cantatas,[13] and more than 550 keyboard sonatas by his son Domenico are extant.[14] Of more than 450 extant concertos by Vivaldi more than 220 are for the violin. Telemann, in his 1718 autobiography,[15] says of the time he spent at Sorau: 'In two years I produced about 200 overtures [i.e. orchestral suites]'. In 1740[16] he mentions 600 overtures; Horst Büttner[17] estimates the total number at about 1,000. In Frankfurt alone Telemann wrote 800 church cantatas, and 1,300 by Graupner survive. It is obvious, with the production of such a mass of music, that quality could not keep pace with quantity. But by and large this is music of solid workmanship and the average standard is surprisingly high.

## THE SUITE

In Germany the suite was the most popular form of orchestral music around 1700. Since composition was one of the duties of a *Kapellmeister* a great number of suites were, so to speak, written to

---

[11] In *Musikalischer Almanach für Deutschland auf das Jahr 1784* (Leipzig).
[12] *The Present State of Music in France and Italy* (London, 1771), p. 101; modern edition, ed. Percy A. Scholes as *Dr. Burney's Musical Tours in Europe*, i (London, 1959), p. 76.
[13] See p. 106.
[14] See pp. 608 ff.
[15] In Mattheson's *Grosse General-Bass-Schule* (1731); reprinted in *Denkmäler deutscher Tonkunst*, xxviii, ed. Max Schneider.
[16] In Mattheson's *Grundlage einer Ehren-Pforte* (1740); reprinted ibid. and in Kahl, *Selbstbiographien*.
[17] *Das Konzert in den Orchestersuiten Georg Philipp Telemanns* (Berlin, 1935), p. 14.

order. Christoph Graupner, who was court *Kapellmeister* at Darmstadt, speaks with feeling on this subject.

I am so overburdened with work that I can scarcely do anything else. I am constantly having to see that my compositions are ready in time, as Sundays and feast days follow one after the other, not to mention the interruptions that frequently occur.[18]

As we have seen, only a small part of all this music appeared in print, and publishers' catalogues give only an approximate idea of the actual situation. The outstanding composers in the early years of the century were men who had studied with Lully in Paris. The following chronological table lists their names and their published works:

1700 Johann Sigismud Kusser (Cousser) (1660–1727)
   *Apollon enjoué*
   *Festin des Muses*
   *La cicala della Cetra d'Eunomio*
   Johann Fischer (1646–?1716 or 1717)
   *Neu-verfertigtes musicalisches Divertissement*
1701 Johann Joseph Fux (1660–1741)
   *Concentus musico-instrumentalis*[19]
1702 Johann Fischer
   *Tafel-Musik*
1704 Johann Fischer
   *Feld- und Heldenmusik*[20]
   Johann Philipp Krieger (1649–1725)
   *Lustige Feld-Musik*
1706 Johann Fischer
   *Musicalische Fürsten-Lust*
1707 Jakob Scheiffelhut (1647–1709)
   *Musicalisches Klee-Blatt*

A second generation of German composers comprises those who were born c.1680–1700, some of whom lived on into the early years of the classical period. The Bach family is represented by three names: Johann Ludwig (1677–1714), Johann Bernhard (1676–1749), and Johann Sebastian (1685–1750). Composers who began writing suites about 1710 include Johann Friedrich Fasch (1688–1758), Pantaleon Hebenstreit (1669–1750), and Christoph Graupner (1683–1760), together with the Bohemian composer Jan Dismas Zelenka (1679–1745), who spent many years of his life in the service of the court in Dresden. The Graun brothers—Johann

[18] In Mattheson's *Ehren-Pforte* (1740).
[19] Ed. Heinrich Rietsch, *Denkmäler der Tonkunst in Österreich*, xxiii (2) (vol. 47) (Vienna, 1916; reprint, Graz, 1960).
[20] Written to commemorate the Battle of Blenheim; published in 1706.

Gottlieb (1703–71) and Carl Heinrich (c. 1704–59)—Johann Adolph Hasse (1699–1783), and Conrad Friedrich Hurlebusch (1695–1765) form a slightly younger group. The composer whose work is most characteristic of the period is Georg Philipp Telemann (1681–1767).

An indication of what Fux thought about the suite is provided by the first sentence of the foreword to the collection of seven partitas (i.e. suites) which make up the above-mentioned *Concentus musico-instrumentalis*. No doubt because of his obligations to the Palestrina tradition he offers a mild apology for having written works of this kind:

Here, dear reader, is my *Concentus musico-instrumentalis*, which I under-stand is in demand in several places. It has been published not with the object of offering you evidence of great mastery (that must be sought in another kind of music) but in order to satisfy also listeners who have no skill in music—and they are the majority.[21]

The suite was music for entertainment, as suggested by the titles, *Airs pour le souper du Roy*, by Philidor, and *Symphonies de M. de la Lande, surintendant de la musique du Roy, qui se jouent ordin-airement au souper du Roy*. Its artistic level was determined by courtly etiquette and the taste of the upper middle classes. There was, however, one great difference between France and Germany. In France the suite was actually a series of dances written to fit the choreography; concert performances were meant to recall the ballet. Transcriptions for lute, harpsichord, or chamber ensembles were made for the same purpose and were commonly entitled *suite*, *suite de pièces*, and later *ordre*. Works of this kind by Lully, Campra, Colasse, Destouches, and Desmarets are, so to speak, potpourris of the ballet, not independent suites (though this does not imply any judgement of their quality). In Germany, on the other hand, suites were written almost exclusively for concert performance. The dances which occur in them were hardly ever danced, and in fact were highly stylized—*künstlich elaboriert* is Mattheson's phrase. This very different function gave rise to a number of features which played an important part in the future development of the form:

1. The increasing incidence of movements which are not dances, which generally augments the number of movements.

[21] 'Habes, amice Lector, Concentum meum Musico-Instrumentalem, qualem in pluribus locis desiderari deprehendi, non in eum finem editum, ut tibi grandis artificii dem probam (quod in alio Musices genere petendum est) sed ut auditoribus etiam Musices imperitis, quorum maxima pars est, satisfacerem.'

2. The particular attention paid to the overture, which from being a mere introduction to the ballet gradually becomes an independent piece for concert performance.
3. The importation of elements of the *concertante* style, i.e. solo instruments.
4. A distinctive style of instrumentation, which increasingly becomes an important element in the music.

TELEMANN'S SUITES

The title of Telemann's *Musique de table* (after 1721) illustrates the changes that were taking place:

Musique de Table,
partagée
en
Trois Productions,
dont chacune contient
1 Ouverture avec la suite, à 7 instruments,
1 Quatuor,
1 Concert, à 7,
1 Trio,
1 Solo,
1 Conclusion, à 7,
et dont les instruments se diversifient par tout.[22]

This must be the development which Scheibe had in mind when he said of Telemann that 'in this respect too he was so distinguished that, without being guilty of flattery, one can rightly say that as an imitator of the French he ended by writing their national music better than they did themselves.'[23] This helps us to understand how a single German composer could win an international reputation a generation after Lully. Karl Nef points out that the list of subscribers to the *Musique de table* contains 'roughly 200 names, mostly noble lords, ambassadors, ministers, and also prominent musicians'.[24] Among them are subscribers from Paris, which Telemann had visited as early as 1718 and where he had a great reception in 1737–8. The success which his music enjoyed is principally due to his elegant, *galant* melodic invention, which combines the lively rhythms of the dance with a strong feeling for *cantabile* and at the same time shows a well-nigh inexhaustible skill and imagination in writing for instruments. Three short extracts

[22] Facsimile of the engraved title-page of the 1733 edition in Georg Philipp Telemann, *Musikalische Werke*, xii, ed. J. P. Hinnenthal (Kassel, 1959).
[23] J. A. Scheibe, *critische Musikus*.
[24] *Geschichte der Sinfonie und Suite* (Leipzig, 1921), p. 91.

will illustrate this. The first (i) is the Air from the overture in
E minor for two flutes and strings; the second (ii) is the Menuet
from the suite in B flat major for two oboes and strings; the third
(iii) is the Harlequinade from the overture in C major for two
oboes (alternating with two recorders, two flutes, and flute and
piccolo), bassoon, and strings, which is discussed below:[25]

## Ex. 102

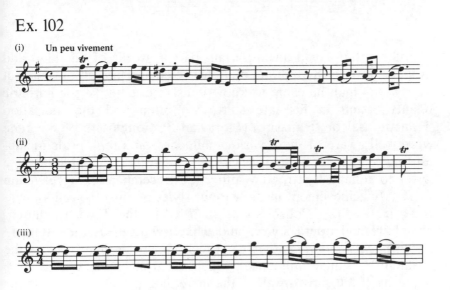

The *Wasser-Ouverture* (Water Overture) in C major, from which
Ex. 102 (iii) is taken is a typical example of a work with imaginative titles:

Ouverture
Sarabande: *Die schlaffende Thetis* (Thetis asleep)
Bourrée: *Die erwachende Thetis* (Thetis waking up)
Loure: *Der verliebte Neptunus* (Neptune in love)
Gavotte: *Die spielenden Najaden* (The Naiads at play)
Harlequinade: *Der schertzende Tritonus* (The frolicsome Triton)
                       *Der stürmende Aeolus* (Aeolus in a fury)
Menuet: *Der angenehme Zephir* (The pleasant Zephyr)
Gigue: *Ebbe und Fluth* (Ebb and flow)
Canarie: *Die lustigen Boots Leute* (The jolly sailors)

The last movement introduces a sailor's call:

[25]  (i) Ed. Max Seiffert, *Denkmäler deutscher Tonkunst*, lxi–lxii (Leipzig, 1927: new ed.,
         Wiesbaden & Graz, 1959), p. 19, and in Telemann, *Musikalische Werke*, xii, p. 23.
     (ii) *Denkmäler deutscher Tonkunst*, lxi–lxii, p. 194.
    (iii) Ed. Friedrich Noack in Telemann, *Musikalische Werke*, x (Kassel, 1955), p. 17.

Ex. 103

Folk music played an important part in works of this kind and influenced both rhythm and melody. Telemann himself tells us that as a young man he came to know Polish music 'in its true barbaric beauty'[26] and in his late suites we often find the indication 'Hanaquoise' or 'Hanasky' (Moravian).[27] Composers of the time were well aware of these various influences and took pride in submitting to them as a sign that they were truly cosmopolitan. In a letter to Johann Gottfried Walther (20 December 1729) Telemann says: 'My achievement in the various styles of music is well known. First it was the Polish style, then came the French, church, chamber, and opera styles, and what is known as the "Italian" style (*nach dem Italiänischen*), which chiefly occupies me at the moment.'[28] Italian influence, which is strongly marked in Fux, made itself felt most of all in the increasing use of the *concertante* style in the suite. Büttner[29] has classified Telemann's suites as follows:

(a) Three-part and four-part suites for string orchestra.
(b) Suites for string orchestra with a group of wind instruments, which are frequently contrasted with the strings (as in Lully and in the *concerto grosso*).
(c) Suites with one or more solo instruments.

Wind instruments were used extensively in suites by Fasch, who was so much admired by Bach. But Telemann, by combining the solo concerto and the suite in a single work (the third group mentioned above), created a new type which had a strong influence on the early classical serenade—an influence which survives in Mozart's youthful works—and on compositions of a similar kind (cassations and divertimenti). When there were several groups of soloists the composer had the opportunity of alternating them in

---

[26] From his autobiography of 1740: see n. 18.
[27] Haná is a district in Moravia.
[28] Kahl, *Selbst-Biographien*, p. 228.
[29] Op. cit., p. 17.

the manner of the earlier Venetian music. Fux often does this, and so does Telemann, e.g. in a suite in A minor[30] where he makes a contrast between three groups of soloists: two flutes and viola, two oboes and bassoon, two violins and continuo. To do this successfully required expert acquaintance with the technique of writing trio sonatas. Fasch, in a suite in B flat major[31] for double orchestra, goes even further: he divides each orchestra into groups and makes three of the six oboists change to flutes and the other three to recorders. This gives him altogether six groups:

|           | *Orchestra I*            | *Orchestra II*         |
|-----------|--------------------------|------------------------|
| 1st group | 3 oboes and bassoon      | 3 oboes and bassoon    |
| 2nd group | 3 recorders and bassoon  | 3 flutes and bassoon   |
| 3rd group | string orchestra         | string orchestra       |

Often we find a change of mood from one group to another, as in the following overture in F major for horns and strings by Telemann:[32]

Ex. 104

[30] Darmstadt, Hessische Landesbibl., Mskr. mus. 3360/30; see Büttner, op. cit., p. 42. Miniature score, ed. Büttner (London and Zurich, 1939).

[31] Dresden, Landesbibl. Cx 262; Büttner, op. cit., p. 48.

[32] Hessische Landesbibl., Mskr. mus. 3360/27; Büttner, op cit., p. 39. Miniature score, ed. Büttner (London and Zurich, 1939).

The dimensions to which the once modest orchestral suite could grow can be illustrated from a suite in B flat major by Telemann[33] which consists of an overture and eight additional movements and lasts as long as a middle-period Beethoven symphony. The scoring is for solo violin, two recorders, one flute, two oboes, bassoon, and strings. The increase in length led to a greater variety in the use of keys. Telemann's practice, based on French models, sometimes goes far afield with a freedom which is not found again until Beethoven. A suite in G minor for strings only[34] has the following key scheme:

| | |
|---|---|
| Overture (La changeante) | G minor |
| Loure | D major |
| Les Scaramouches | B minor |
| Menuet I | E minor |
| Menuet II | E major |
| Menuet I *da capo* | E minor |
| La Plaisanterie | C major |
| Hornpipe | F major |
| Avec douceur | B major |
| Canarie | G minor |

Not much is left of the old dance suite: the road now leads in the direction of programme music. Büttner, however, quite rightly refuses to use the term 'programme music', since it can so easily be confused with music of the time of Berlioz and Liszt, which is based on quite different principles. He suggests that we should use the term *Charaktersuite* for which unfortunately there is no exact English equivalent.[35]

[33] Darmstadt, Hessische Landesbibl., Mskr. mus. 3360/70; Büttner, p. 55.
[34] Idem., Mskr. mus. 3360/2; Büttner, p. 20.
[35] The implications of the term can be understood by comparing the word *Charakterbild*, which means a portrait drawn from life.

## THE *CHARAKTERSUITE*

The aesthetic basis of this kind of music is outlined by the industrious Mattheson in his book *Der vollkommene Capellmeister* (Hamburg, 1739):[36]

The so-called 'text' in vocal music serves in the main to describe emotions (*Affecte*). But it should be realized that even when there are no words, i.e. in purely instrumental music, the intention must always be, in every melody, to present a picture of the dominant mood, so that the mere sound of the instruments speaks to us in terms that we can understand.

By this time dances had become *genre* pieces which expressed definite emotions. Later on Mattheson has this to say about individual dances:

The *allemande* is a serious piece, showing careful workmanship and using broken chords (*eine gebrochene, ernsthaffte und wol ausgearbeitete Harmonie*). It represents a happy, contented mind which delights in peace and good order.

The passion or emotion which should be represented in a *courante* is sweet hope, since in its music there is courage, longing and joy, and these are the characteristics that go to make up hope.

[*In the sarabande*] no other passion should be expressed but reverence. . . . It does not admit any runs (*lauffende Noten*), since *grandezza* abhors them.

The special characteristic of the ordinary (or English) *gigue* is a hasty, transient passion—anger that is quickly over. On the other hand the *loure* (a slow movement in dotted rhythm) has a proud, supercilious character. The *canarie* must express strong desire and move fast, but at the same time it should sound a little artless. Finally the Italian *gigue* which is not used for dancing but only for fiddling (hence perhaps the name),[37] forces itself, as it were, to reach the fastest possible speed, yet for the most part in a flowing, not a vehement, manner—rather like the even current of a brook as it speeds on its way.[38]

Mattheson describes the *menuet, gavotte, bourrée, rigaudon,* and *anglaise* in similar terms, offering suggestions for their interpretation. His remarks on the characteristics of the folk music of other countries include some delightful observations:

If I had to set a text which was marked by a free, openhearted spirit, or had to express such ideas in music, I should choose no other type of melody than the Polish, since to my mind this is its distinctive character and the emotion that it expresses. National character is rarely concealed

---

[36] Facsimile edition (Kassel, 1954).

[37] Mattheson is referring to the etymology, still widely accepted, which derives the name of the dance from medieval French *gigue* (German *Geige*), meaning a fiddle.

[38] Op cit., pp. 228, 231–2.

by the amusements and dances of the people, though of course this may happen on other occasions.

Hornpipes are of Scottish origin. Sometimes their melodies are so extraordinary that one might imagine they were the work of court composers at the North or South Pole.[39]

Mattheson's view that the traditional dance forms were primarily vehicles for musical expression is natural from one who classified the emotions.[40] It led gradually to a transformation of the suite, which had in fact already begun in the French ballet. A small selection of the titles of movements used by Telemann will serve to illustrate the change.

Les Augures; La Bizarre; La Bouffone; Les Boiteux, La Changeante; Le Contentement; Les Capriccieux; La Doute; Les Furies; Les vieilles Femmes; La Galante; La Grimace; Les Gladiateurs; L'Indignation; Irresolute; Pierrot; La Querrelleuse; Le repos interrompu.

From here it is only a short step to the *Ouverture bourlesque de Quichote*:[41]

Ouverture
*Le Reveil de Quichote* (Don Quixote wakes up)
*Son attaque des Moulins à vent* (He attacks the windmills)
*Ses soupirs amoureux après la Princesse Dulcinée* (He sighs with love for Dulcinea)
*Sanche Panse berné* (Sancho Panza tossed in a blanket)
*Le Galope de Rosinante* (Rosinante galloping)
*Celui d'Ane de Sanche* (Sancho Panza's donkey doing the same)
*Couché de Quichote* (Don Quixote goes to bed)

Telemann was also capable of ribaldry, e.g.:

Overture: *La Putain* (The Prostitute)[42]
Loure: *Die Bauren-Kirchweyh* (Peasants' parish fair)
Gasconnade: *In der Läussherberg* (In the lousy inn)

### THE SUITE IN ITALY

The history of the orchestral suite in Italy is quite different. The French and Italian styles were felt to be diametrically opposed, and the composers and theorists of the period were very conscious of this contrast. At the turn of the century the publication of the Abbé Raguenet's *Paralèle des italiens et des françois, en ce qui*

---

[39] Op. cit., pp. 228–9.
[40] On *Der vollkommene Capellmeister* see also p. 284.
[41] Darmstadt, Hessische Landesbibl., Mskr. mus., 3360/80, and other libraries. Ed. Felix Schroeder in *Musikschätze der Vergangenheit* (Berlin-Lichterfelde, c.1963).
[42] Authenticity uncertain; the manuscript score, Hessische Landesbibl., 3360/67, has no composer's name.

*regarde la musique et les opéra* (1702)[43] gave rise to acrimonious
disputes in France which dragged on for several decades, though
they were not always conducted on a purely musical basis and were
sometimes pursued for their own sake. Bukofzer defines the differences as follows:

The harmonic resources of tonality, the concerto style in instrumental and
vocal music, and the concerto and sonata forms of 'absolute' music passed
as the characteristics of the Italian style; the coloristic and programmatic
trends in instrumental music, the orchestral discipline, overture and
dance suite, and the highly florid ornamentation of the melody passed as
the characteristics of the French style.[44]

The strength of Italian music lay in the creation of forms. That is
why in Italy, around 1700, it was the solo concerto and the Italian
overture that became established, whereas French ballet music, still
active after Lully and very successful in Germany, aroused hardly
any interest. Moreover the new forms offered such abundant
opportunities for writing for the orchestra that the suite was treated
almost entirely as chamber music. A list of Albinoni's published
instrumental works (excluding those without an authentic opus
number) will make this clear:

Chamber music:
  Op. 1  *Suonate a tre*
  Op. 3  *Balletti a tré* (suites)
  Op. 6  *Trattenimenti armonici per camera* (sonatas for violin and
         continuo)
  Op. 8  *Baletti e sonate a tré* (sonatas and suites)
Orchestral music:
  Op. 2  *Sinfonie e concerti a cinque*
  Op. 5  *Concerti a cinque*
  Op. 7  *Concerti a cinque*
  Op. 9  *concerti a cinque*
  Op. 10 *concerti a cinque*

We find the same thing in the work of Vivaldi, Benedetto Marcello
(1686–1739), Francesco Maria Veracini (1690–1768), Tartini, and
others. Evaristo Felice Dall'Abaco (1675–1742) is an exception. In
1704 he was in Munich, from 1705 to 1715 in Brussels, and then
returned to Munich as leader of the orchestra. He is an exception
not because he wrote suites in the French style, which he did not,
but because he inserted dances of the French type into the traditional *concerto da camera* or into the type of *concerto grosso* that
included dances.

---

[43] An English translation was published in London in 1709.
[44] *Music in the Baroque Era* (New York, 1947), p. 260.

## THE SUITE IN ENGLAND

In England Lully was at first the dominant influence. This was natural in the case of Louis Grabu, who was a Frenchman. But it is also very apparent in suites by John Banister and Robert Smith (d. 1675), and it is worth noting that Lully's pupil Kusser, who died in 1727, was in Dublin in the latter part of his life. By degrees, however, Corelli came to be the foreign composer most frequently performed in England, and in addition his pupil Geminiani made a deep impression on English instrumental playing, so that French and Italian influences in the suite became evenly balanced. 'Signor Handel, the composer of Italian music' was at the same time a cosmopolitan and was so familiar with the French style that he was able in his two suites of *Water Music* (probably 1715 and 1717)[45] to assemble more than twenty small pieces, chiefly in the French style, with colourful contrasts of orchestration. Works of this kind were not usually played complete at one sitting: they were collections which could be drawn upon as required. Handel's other work of this kind, the *Music for the Royal Fireworks*, was rather different, since it was written to order to celebrate the Peace of Aix-la-Chapelle on 27 April 1749, the main attraction being an elaborate fireworks display. 12,000 people had attended six days previously when the music was rehearsed in Vauxhall Gardens.[46] It consists of an overture and a series of dances, the symbolic centre-piece being a *siciliana* called 'La Paix'. Handel was wonderfully successful in finding the right style for an open-air work of this kind: a broad harmonic scheme, melodies which are simple but cover a wide span, and instrumentation for a wind band—twenty-four oboes, twelve bassoons, nine trumpets, nine horns, three timpani, and side drums (the string parts were added later).

### BACH'S ORCHESTRAL SUITES

Bach wrote only four orchestral suites, but these represent the highest point reached by this form of composition. Each has a different orchestration, but the order of movements is similar and follows the French model, which Bach got to know in Celle when he was a choirboy at Lüneburg. The scheme is as follows:

Suite No. 1 in C major: 2 oboes, bassoon and strings:
     Ouverture—Courante—Gavotte I—Gavotte II—Gavotte I (*da*

[45] On the problems of the *Water Music*, see Basil Lam in *Handel: a Symposium* (ed. Gerald Abraham) (London, 1954), pp. 217–9.

[46] See the contemporary account in Otto Erich Deutsch, *Handel: a Documentary Biography* (London, 1955), pp. 666–9.

*capo*)—Forlane—Menuet I—Menuet II—Menuet I (*da capo*)—
Bourrée I—Bourrée II—Bourrée I (*da capo*)—Passepied I—
Passepied II—Passipied I (*da capo*).

Suite No. 2 in B minor: flute and strings:
Ouverture—Rondeau—Sarabande—Bourrée I—Bourrée II—Bourrée
I (*da capo*)—Polonaise—Double—Polonaise (*da capo*)—Menuet—
Badinerie.

Suite No. 3 in D major: 3 trumpets, timpani, 2 oboes and strings:
Ouverture—Air—Gavotte I—Gavotte II—Gavotte I (*da capo*)—
Bourrée—Gigue

Suite No. 4 in D major: 3 trumpets, timpani, 3 oboes, bassoon and
strings:
Ouverture—Bourrée I—Bourrée II—Bourrée I (*da capo*)—Gavotte—
Menuet I—Menuet II—Minuet I (*da capo*)—Réjouissance.

Suite no. 1 uses the traditional scoring associated with Lully; no. 2
is a solo suite; nos. 3 and 4 are festive music with appropriate
orchestration. It is impossible to determine exactly the date when
they were written. It seems likely that nos. 1 and 2 were written at
Cöthen, between 1717 and 1723, and nos. 3 and 4 at Leipzig. What
is certain is that all four were written after Bach had come to terms
with the form of the Italian concerto: this is clear from the treatment of the overtures. It would have been quite natural for such a
master of fugal writing to develop the quick sections of the overtures as strict orchestral fugues and so impose his personality on
what was conventionally a loose sort of fugato. But since the suite
is meant for entertainment Bach relaxes the fugal structure in no. 1
by writing episodes for the solo trio of two oboes and bassoons.
This practice started with Lully. Agostino Steffani (1654–1728),
who met Lully in Paris in 1678–9, occasionally does the same in his
opera overtures, from *Orlando generoso* (written for Hanover in
1691) onwards.

The Allegro of the overture in Bach's first suite starts with a
19-bar fugal exposition, beginning:

Ex. 105

After a cadence in the tonic we have a solo episode based on the
same subject:

Ex. 106

which modulates to the relative minor. This is followed by further treatment of the subject by the tutti in A minor, which again ends with a cadence. The next section is very ingeniously constructed: violins and violas in unison play the theme while the solo trio discourses in imitative counterpoint:

Ex. 107

In the rest of the movement, where tutti and solo alternate in the manner of a solo concerto and where the key scheme is now firmly established, the solo sections are almost entirely based on the subject, so that this appears altogether more than forty times. Bach seems to have been dissatisfied with this treatment, since in the second suite (which was probably written after no. 1) he based the Allegro of the overture entirely on thematic contrast between tutti and solo. The scheme is as follows:

Ritornello I, bars 1–34: exposition of the subject, B minor:

Ex. 108

Solo I, bars 35–58: modulation to D major:

Ex. 109

Ritornello II, bars 58–74: D major
Solo II, bars 74–82: modulation to E minor:

Ex. 110

Ritornello III, bars 83–99: E minor, modulating to B minor
(Solo) III, bars 99–155: brief solo sections, alternating with tutti inser-
tions (two to eight bars): modulations: B minor—D major—E minor—
B minor.
Ritornello IV, bars 155–77: B minor

What we have here is an Italian solo concerto movement of considerable length sandwiched between two stately sections in the
style of the French overture (marked *lentement*). Telemann sometimes calls movements of this kind *concert en ouverture*. The figuration for the solo flute has nothing to do with the subject of the
ritornello, and its relation to the counterpoint is purely one of
rhythm. Bach makes the contrasts in this overture even stronger by
remodelling the opening 4/4 section of the overture (i) in 3/4, and
dividing it between flute and first violins, when it comes back at the
end (ii):

Ex. 111

These two overtures (no. 1 and no. 2) are splendid examples of the
way in which Bach was working at the problem of finding a satisfactory form. Each of his solutions is strictly speaking unique.

According to his sons he solved a problem of this kind by 'thinking it over' (*eigenes Nachsinnen*)—a method which his predecessors and contemporaries were either unwilling or unable to pursue.

Contrasts are often found in the other movements of the suites. For example, the minuet and bourrée of no. 1 are scored as follows:

Menuet I (tutti)—Menuet II (strings)—Menuet I (tutti)
Bourrée I (tutti)—Bourrée II (2 oboes and bassoon)—Bourrée I (tutti)

Counterpoint and elegant homophony both have their place: compare, for instance, the sarabande of the second suite, with a canon at the fourth below, with the *badinerie* of the same suite. To Bach's almost limitless capacity for sustaining a melodic line we owe the famous air in the third suite, built above a traditional type of bass. In the *double* to the polonaise of the B minor suite the use of variation enables the flautist to show his virtuosity:

Ex. 112

Bach's suites radiate an influence which affects the subtlest details of style—and this is true not only of Bach. Forkel realized this very clearly:

The composers of Bach's time had an admirable opportunity to acquire the due and easy management of the various kinds of rhythm, by the so-called suites, which were then common instead of our sonatas. In these suites there were, between the preludes and the concluding jigs, many French characteristic pieces and dance tunes, in which the rhythm was the most important object. The composers were therefore obliged to make use of a great variety of time, measure, and rhythm (which are now for the most part unknown), and be very expert in them, if they desired to give to every dance tune its precise character and rhythm. Bach carried this branch of the art also much farther than any of his predecessors or contemporaries. He tried and made use of every kind of metre to diversify, as much as possible, the character of his pieces. He eventually acquired such a facility in this particular that he was able to give even to his fugues, with all the intricate interweaving of their single parts, striking and characteristic rhythmic proportions in a manner as easy and uninterrupted from the beginning to the end as if they were minuets.[47]

## THE OPERA OVERTURE

The most significant instrumental event in the development of opera at the turn of the century was the gradual emergence of the Italian overture.[48] But equally important for the future was the gradual introduction of elements of the *concertante* style, which had a precedent in the use of obbligato instruments in arias. In the works of Italian composers after Alessandro Scarlatti, e.g. Fago, Feo, Greco, Leo, Logroscino, Mancini, Orefice, Porpora, Sarro, and Vinci, his three-movement type of overture (Allegro—Andante—Minuetto) was retained with scarcely any change,[49] but in other countries, however much under Italian influence, the Scarlatti type of overture had to compete from the first with the French overture, which was by then a firmly established tradition, demanding, in its fugato section, a high quality of workmanship. The serious character of the first section and the polyphonic treatment of the second, as in Bach's suites, made the French overture particularly suitable for tragic or heroic operas, and even more for oratorio. Sometimes it seems to have been chosen by composers for this reason, but there was no hard and fast rule. In Vienna French and Italian influences intermingled. The inclination towards polyphony, represented by Fux, and the cultivated tastes of the court[50] tended to favour the more serious French overture. Fux and Ferdinand Tobias Richter (1649–1711) generally wrote French overtures for oratorios and Italian ones for operas. The titles *overture* and *sinfonia*, however, were not always used to mark the difference. There were also mixed forms: Fux's *Orfeo ed Euridice* (1728) has a French overture followed by an Adagio and a minuet. A remarkable feature of Fux's work is the elaborate orchestration; as *Kapellmeister* at one of the leading courts in Europe he was able at times to use as many as four trumpets in addition to a very full complement of woodwind players. This made it possible to contrast various groups in the orchestra and often resulted in works for double orchestra. Since the French overture was considered su-

---

[47] Quoted from the English translation (1820) of his *Life of Bach*, as printed in Hans T. David and Arthur Mendel, *The Bach Reader* (New York, 1945), pp. 323–4.

[48] See pp. 217 ff.

[49] On operatic conditions in general see Vol. V, pp. 73 ff. on treatment of the orchestra, ibid., pp. 13–14, 18–19, 28, 49–52, etc.

[50] Between 1637 and 1740 there were four emperors who were composers: Ferdinand III, Leopold I, Joseph I, and Charles VI.

perior to the Italian, the custom developed in Dresden and Vienna of beginning Italian operas with French overtures by other composers, and even commissioning works for this purpose. Fux, for instance, wrote overtures of this kind for operas by Giovanni Bononcini (*Proteo sul Reno*, 1703), Lotti (*Costantino*, 1716), C. A. Badia, and M. A. Ziani. Lotti himself accepted this convention and wrote French overtures for his Dresden operas.

Handel, who came across French music in Hamburg and subsequently studied Italian music so diligently that he became the foremost Italian opera composer of his time, generally used the French overture, particularly in his oratorios. In the opera *Rodrigo* (Florence, 1707), he begins with a complete suite: Ouverture—Gigue—Sarabande—Matelot—Bourrée—Rigaudon—Menuet—Passacaille. Though the addition of dances to the overture was not at all uncommon, a whole series of movements like this was exceptional. In *Rinaldo* (1711), the first opera written for London, he made his bow to the English public with an overture followed by a gigue. Arias with obbligato instruments are frequent. He had used them in his youthful operas in accordance with the tradition established at Hamburg by Kusser and Keiser.[51] He seems also to have learned something from Scarlatti, in whose later operas the orchestra became increasingly important. Arias with trumpet obbligato, on the Ventian model, were popular in England in Purcell's time and remained so after his death. Familiar examples by Handel occur in *Samson* (1743) and *Judas Maccabeus* (1747). In general the orchestra plays a very important part in his operas and oratorios.[52] Quite apart from traditional battle scenes, fights with dragons and so on, he developed a psychological insight into his characters which enabled him to represent states of mind with a subtlety rarely found in opera before his time. In the mad scene in *Orlando* (1733), the poisoning scene in Act III of *Tamerlano* (1724), and the two great monologues in *Giulio Cesare* (1724) the orchestra helps a great deal towards the creation of a new art of expression. In particular *recitativo accompagnato* offered many opportunities for using the orchestra in an original way.

## THE ORCHESTRA IN FRENCH OPERA

In French opera after Lully, too, there were new opportunities for the orchestra. In the works of Destouches and Campra, and even more in Marais, we find more and more examples of instru-

[51] Cf. Vol. V, p. 308.
[52] Cf. pp. 26, 28, 49, 51–2, and 89 ff., and Vol. V, pp. 139 and 142–3.

mental pieces used to intensify the impression made by dramatic incidents on the stage.[53] The age inclined to naturalism and this found expression in scenes involving storms and thunder. The type of music provided for these occasions became the opera composer's stock-in-trade for over a century. The orchestral *tempestes* written by Colasse and Campra excited much admiration; Marais actually studied the sea at first hand before writing *Alcyone* (1706). Rameau was already a mature composer when he embarked on opera: he was turning fifty when he wrote his first work for the theatre, *Hippolyte et Aricie* (1733). He began with overtures in the style of Lully; that to *Hippolyte et Aricie* starts with a slow introduction which is followed by a fugato:

Ex. 113

The fugato, however, is not repeated; instead, scene 1, a 'Choeur des Nymphes', follows immediately; Rameau must have felt that to bring back the slow introduction after the fugato would hinder the progress of the drama and therefore eliminated it. Following these lines, he gradually transformed the overture into a dramatic prelude, which suggested the mood of the opera and often led straight into the first scene. That to *Zoroastre* (1749) is frankly programmatic.[54] Handel actually anticipated these French experiments: in *Riccardo I* (1727) the overture is followed by an orchestral storm incorporating recitative for the singers. In later works (from 1745 onwards) Rameau used a type of overture which combined the French and Italian styles: a slow introduction followed by an Italianate allegro which has few fugal elements or none at all and comes very close to a movement with two contrasting themes. This scheme was used also by Gluck: there is no doubt that it helped to establish the classical first movement with a slow introduction. In his treatment of the orchestra Rameau was far in advance of his contemporaries; he also assigned it a prominent place in his arias and recitatives. Like Wagner he had to endure the reproach that his orchestra would drown the singers. Rousseau maliciously re-

[53] Cf. Vol. V, pp. 236, 239, and 257 ff.
[54] Ibid., p. 257.

ferred to the singers in Rameau's operas 'who provide the accompaniment to the orchestra'.

In the hands of gifted composers Lully's type of overture had proved to be an excellent vehicle for music in which ingenious contrasts between solo and tutti, skilful part-writing, and colourful orchestration all played a part; but once it had become simply the prelude to an opera it gradually went out of fashion. Johann Adolph Scheibe was obliged to admit in 1745 that 'today many connoisseurs regard overtures as old-fashioned and ridiculous'.[55]

## THE NON-OPERATIC OVERTURE

Two important types remain to be considered: the overture to a play, and the 'independent' overture, having no connection with an opera or oratorio. Scheibe tells us that it was the custom to perform *sinfonie* before a play began and in the intervals. There is nothing surprising in this, since both in Italy and in countries which admitted Italian influence *sinfonia* meant the same thing as overture. For a long time past *sinfonie* published in instrumental collections had been used as introductory music for a variety of occasions. But music chosen in this way might not be suitable for a particular play; the only solution would be 'to prepare for each play its own music, exactly suited to that same play only'.[56] Scheibe himself composed 'symphonies [in these cases, entr'actes as well as overtures] for that admirable tragedy *Polyeukt*, and shortly afterwards symphonies for the tragedy *Mithridat* which were performed in 1738 here in Hamburg and later in Leipzig and Kiel.'[57] He thought these were the first examples of their kind, evidently not realizing that incidental music for the theatre was a long-standing tradition in England. Purcell and his contemporaries wrote quantities of music of this kind, both for revivals of Shakespeare and for plays by their contemporaries.[58] Italian composers of the eighteenth century were also very active in writing 'independent' overtures. A spurious 'Op. 4' (c.1736) attributed to Carlo Tessarini (c.1690–after 1766) by the Amsterdam publisher Le Cène clearly distinguishes in its title between overture, *sinfonia*, suite and concerto:

La Stravaganza, divisa in quattro parti, e composta d'Ouverture, di Concerti con Oboe, di Partite, Concerti a due Violini obbbligati, Sinfonie

---

[55] *Der critische Musikus*, (rev. ed. Leipzig, 1745; reprinted Hildesheim, 1970).
[56] Ibid., Section 67.
[57] Idem.
[58] See, for instance, Ex. 77 for the 'symphony' to Act II of Purcell's *The Indian Queen*.

e Concerti Con Violino obligato a cinque: cioè trè Violini, Alto Viola e Basso.

Pietro Locatelli (1695–1764) is even more precise in describing the six overtures of his Op. 4 (Amsterdam, 1735), as *Introduttioni teatrali*. The overtures in this collection are in three movements, like the Neapolitan opera overture, but very close to the *concerto grosso* in style, a string quartet often being used as a contrast to the tutti. Tessarini also used the term *Introducioni* for a collection of overtures published as Op. 11 (Paris, 1748).

It was probably in England that opera overtures were first published separately. Walsh in 1733 issued 'Bononcini's overtures for violins in all their parts . . . in the operas of Astartus, Croesus, Camilla, Hydaspes, Thomyris and Elpidia'. (The title is incorrect, since only *Astarto* w.s by Bononcini.) The tradition was carried on by Francesco Barsanti (1690–1772), who played the flute, oboe, and viola in London and lived for a time in Edinburgh, and by Giuseppe Sammartini (1695–1750) (brother of Giovanni Battista of Milan), who was director of chamber music to the Prince of Wales. Barsanti published *Nove Overture a quattro* (Edinburgh, c.1743) and Sammartini *Eight overtures op. VII in 8 parts for violins, hoboys, French horns, with a through bass for the harpsichord or violoncell* (London, 1752). William Boyce (1710–79) also played an important part in this development. He continued to write French overtures till the end of his life, but also wrote some Italian overtures in three movements, in which, perhaps under the influence of Johann Christian Bach, he occasionally came near to the form of the classical symphony.

## THE *CONCERTO GROSSO*

When Handel came to Rome in 1707 Corelli was still alive. The *concerto grosso*, which had reached the peak of its popularity, made a deep impression on him. He originally wrote a French overture for his cantata *Il trionfo del Tempo e del Disinganno* (1707) but replaced it by a *concerto grosso* very closely modelled on Corelli's practice. His enthusiasm for the new style of instrumentation led him to write a new kind of aria, which might be described as a *concerto grosso* for voice and instruments. In nos. 14 and 15 of *Il trionfo del Tempo* obbligato instruments combine with the voice to form a *concertino*—a method which had some kind of precedent in the work of Stradella, Steffani, and Scarlatti. In the first part of the same work there is also a 'sonata' with parts for solo violins, oboes, and organ (fully written out) which is actually a *concerto grosso* movement.

In Germany Georg Muffat's *Armonico tributo* (1682)[59] had introduced the technique of the *concerto grosso* at the same time that Lully's use of a woodwind trio became fashionable in the suite. But it was not until he published his *concerti grossi* (Passau, 1701), with a title-page in four languages,[60] that he stimulated other composers to follow his example. It will be noticed that the date of publication is close to the time when Handel's interest in the form was awakened in Rome. During this period the solo concerto was also being developed. It is some indication of the vague terminology of the time that Torelli's famous collection Op. 8 (published in 1709, the year of his death by his brother, the painter Felice Torelli) was entitled *Concerti grossi*, in spite of the fact that it consists of six violin concertos and six concertos for two violins.[61]

In the feverish exploration of new instrumental forms which was taking place at this time the solo concerto was regarded as the more modern type. This explains why it so soon had such a strong influence on the *concerto grosso*, an influence that eventually led to a mixture of the two forms. If we study the solo concerto and the *concerto grosso* merely from the point of view of scoring, it is easy to keep them apart. But if we feel that the essential difference lies in the actual form of the solo concerto, we are faced with the paradox that there are movements in the form of a solo concerto for two or more solo instruments (double or triple concertos), while the continuo group in the *concerto grosso*, influenced by the *concertante* style, is so often broken up into solo parts that very little remains of the old *concerto grosso* scoring. The same thing happened with the suite. Nos. 9–12 of Corelli's *Concerti grossi*, Op. 6, are suites, and the suites of Fux, Telemann, Graupner, Fasch, and others, as we have seen already,[62] are very strongly affected by the spirit of the *concerto grosso*. All these ramifications make it very difficult to distinguish clearly between the various types. Needless to say, the titles used by composers do nothing to help us; it was the music that mattered to them, not what it was called. The titles they chose were often dictated by local tradition.

---

[59] See pp. 206 ff.
[60] Nos, 1, 3, 6, 7, 8 and 9 are ed. Schenk in *Denkmäler der Tonkunst in Österreich*, lxxxix (Vienna, 1953). Nos, 2, 4, 5, 10, 11 and 12, id., xxiii, Jg. 11 (2), ed. Luntz (Vienna, 1904; reprint, Graz, 1959). The German title-page reads: *Ausserlesene mit Ernst- und Lustgemengter Instrumental-Music*.
[61] See pp. 354 f.
[62] See pp. 240 ff.

THE HANDELIAN 'GRAND CONCERTO'

It often happens that the individual movements of a work which is called a *concerto grosso* by the composer belong to different types. Some examples from Handel's *Twelve Grand Concertos* Op. 6 (1740), will make this clear. No. 5 in D major begins, like Corelli's Op. 6, no. 3, with a French overture. In the Allegro section of this movement a three-part fugal exposition (tutti) is followed by a solo episode which derives its material from the subject. The subsequent alternations of soli and tutti have mostly no structural significance: the tuttis are neither ritornellos nor do they develop the subject. The other movements can be briefly summarized:

2nd movement: Presto (a passepied, though not so called):
binary form, only incidental solo passages.

3rd movement: Largo (in the style of a *sonata da chiesa*):
alternations of soli and tutti, with regular cadences.

4th movement: Allegro:
tutti throughout, in the style of a *concerto ripieno* [63] movement.

5th movement: Menuet, un poco larghetto:
binary form with variations (though not so called), six sections in all (each repeated), tutti throughout.

The complete concerto is thus a mixed form, consisting of an overture-suite, with one movement in the style of the orchestral concerto and another in the style of the *sonata da chiesa*. Of the five movements only the first two make use of the essential soli-tutti contrasts of the *concerto grosso*; the last two are purely orchestral pieces.

No. 6 is also made up of different types of movement. The first and third movements treat the solo trio as a *concertino*; the second and fifth (the latter in only three parts) are purely orchestral; the fourth is a solo concerto movement for violin, with ritornellos after Vivaldi's model. Of the remaining concertos, no. 7 is an orchestral concerto without soloists; in no. 4 the soloists have very little to do; no. 10 has a French overture and is similar in structure to no. 5. The third movement of no. 3 is probably the best illustration of the combination of solo concerto and *concerto grosso*. It has the structure of a solo concerto, the ritornello, like Vivaldi's, being made up of several motives. The solo episodes are played by a concertino of two violins and cello, but they are relatively short (the longest is only six bars), and the first violin is so much in command that one

---

[63] See p. 276.

might also call it a solo concerto, with the soloist accompanied by the other two members of the *concertino*. Of the sixty-eight bars in this movement fifty-four are taken up by the ritornello and only fourteen by the solo episodes, so that it is also very like a *concerto ripieno*.

It is obvious then that Handel's *concerti grossi* belong to various types (some of them are not strictly *concerti grossi* at all) and also that the individual works are by no means uniform in themselves. This is only partly explained by the variety of influences which helped to form Handel's style. We need to know how he actually used these works (and his solo concertos as well) when he was organizing and directing performances. We have seen already how *Il trionfo del tempo* had a *concerto grosso* as overture, to be followed later in the work by another instrumental piece with parts for solo instruments. When Handel performed his setting of *L'Allegro* (1740), which has no overture, he used a *concerto grosso* as an introduction; during a change of scene in *Ottone* (1723) he used a *sinfonia* afterwards published as the first movement of Op. 3, no. 6; and organ concertos, with the composer as soloist, were regularly played as interludes in the oratorios.[64] On such occasions it was probably unusual for all the movements of a concerto to be played: extracts would have been used to suit the particular performance and the soloists available. Writing a *concerto grosso* did not mean for Handel the creation of a unified work in a specific form but rather the preparation of something which he could fall back on when he needed it. This is what Bukofzer meant by saying that 'Handel raised the Italian concerto grosso to the highest level of baroque entertainment'.[65]

## BACH'S BRANDENBURG CONCERTOS

With Bach's Brandenburg concertos we are in a different world, a world where virtuoso solo music is combined with a strong feeling for architectural form. In his dedication to the Margrave of Brandenburg Bach calls these works, written presumably at Cöthen between 1718 and 1721, *Six Concerts/Avec plusieurs Instruments*. The question whether these are chamber music or orchestral works has often been debated; since the Prince of Anhalt-Cöthen had

[64] Handel's practice of using *concerti grossi* as overtures has a parallel in Fux's oratorio *La donna forte nella madre de' sette Macabei* (1715). This work begins with a *concerto grosso* which must also have been performed as a separate piece. *La donna forte* is published in *J. J. Fux: Sämtliche Werke*, iv 2, ed. H. Federhofer and O. Wessely (Graz and Kassel, 1976).

[65] Op. cit., pp. 342–3.

nine regular musicians in his employment, and the Margrave of Brandenburg only six, the argument that the concertos were originally performed as chamber music is a strong one. (Extra players would have been needed for no. 1.) This does not mean, however, that they are not true *concerti grossi*, since the character of the form is determined by the contrast between a solo group and the orchestra. The mistake has too often been made of regarding the restrictions from which Bach suffered all his life as a valid basis for first principles. The two concertos without soloists, no. 3 and 6, are presumably intended to be performed by one player to a part. The scoring of the remaining concertos is as follows:

No. 1 Two horns, three oboes, bassoon, *violino piccolo*; first and second violins, viola, cello, double bass, continuo.

No. 2 Trumpet, recorder, oboe, violin; first and second violins, viola, cellos, double bass, continuo.

No. 4 Violin, two recorders; first and second violins, viola, cello, double bass, continuo.

No. 5 Flute, solo violin, solo harpsichord; violin, viola, cello, double bass.

The first concerto is a splendid example of Bach's power of organizing his material. It begins with three large-scale movements:

| | |
|---|---|
| Allegro (not so described) | 84 bars |
| Adagio | 39 bars |
| Allegro | 124 bars |

The first and third are held together by the recurrence of a ritornello and are therefore in the form of a solo concerto. There is, however, a difference in the treatment of the solo episodes. In the first movement the solo instruments enter mostly in groups, in the style of the *concerto grosso*, whereas in the third the *violino piccolo* is on the whole more important than the others. Together, the first three movements make up a *concerto grosso*, the outer movements being constructed on the model of a solo concerto. We then have a group of dances:

| | |
|---|---|
| Menuet | Tutti |
| Trio | Two oboes and bassoon |
| Menuet (*da capo*) | Tutti |
| Polacca | Strings and continuo (*without violino piccolo*) |
| Menuet (*da capo*) | Tutti |
| Trio | Two horns and three oboes (in unison) |
| Menuet (*da capo*) | Tutti |

This arrangement is like a rondo, with the minuet acting as the refrain. The two trios and the polacca offer an opportunity to make a contrast between various instrumental groups. A detail worth noticing in the minuet is the way in which it begins in the sub-dominant, giving the music a curiously Mixolydian flavour: this creates the impression that it is not so much the beginning of a new movement as a link with what has gone before, and so serves to connect it not only with the preceding movement but with the other members of the rondo cycle of which it forms a part. The concerto as a whole bears witness to the two foreign influences which enriched Bach's work: it is an Italian concerto joined on to a French suite. At the same time it is far more than a mere imitation. The invention displayed here, the mastery of structure and the contrapuntal elaboration are Bach's and his alone.

Nothing could better illustrate the difference between his skill in development and the empty routine work of most of his contemporaries than the masterly first movement of the second concerto. The eight-bar ritornello consists of four groups (*a*, *b*, *c*, *d*), each of two bars, which are related to each other, as shown by the arrows in the following example:

Ex. 114

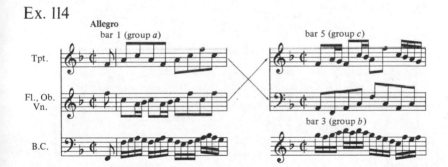

This ritornello occurs seven times:

| I | bars | 1–8 | F major | *a b c d* |
|-----|------|--------|----------|-----------|
| II | | 23–8 | C major | *b c d* |
| III | | 36–9 | D minor | *c d* |
| IV | | 56–9 | Bb major | *c d* |
| V | | 80–3 | G minor | *c d* |
| VI | | 99–102 | A minor | *c d* |
| VII | | 103–18 | F major | *a b c d* |

The scheme is made more complex by the facts that the tutti sometimes break into solo sections (bars 11–12, 15–16, 19–20, 48–9) and the final ritornello is interrupted by a passage for solo instruments (bars 107–14). The normal scheme of keys, as found in Vivaldi, is here very much extended: it will be noticed that all the first six degrees of the scale are used as key centres. The reason why the ritornello is shortened when it occurs within the movement is clear when we look at the solo sections. The first of these (bars 9–22) has its own theme, which from bar 13 is presented in three-part counterpoint:

Ex. 115

When this reappears later (bar 60) a fourth part, like a sigh, is added (bar 64):

Ex. 116

The latter part of Ex. 115, Ex. 117 (i), is clearly related to the ritornello (ii):

Ex. 117

and does much to unify the movement. The solo sections which begin at bars 31 and 68 respectively are not designed to contrast with the ritornello but to develop the preceding material, particularly *a* of the ritornello, which with its succession of semiquavers ensures continuity of movement. Since the counterpoint derived from *a* is also closely related to *b*, both these groups are omitted from ritornellos III–VI. The part-writing has now become so elaborate that the solo group is not sufficient to carry the development: for long stretches it is accompanied by the orchestra, which is far from having a merely subordinate function. In this part of the movement, therefore, the contrast between soli and tutti largely disappears, so much so that it is doubtful whether one should refer to 'solo sections' at all in this kind of development. What Bach is writing here is much more like a symphony (in the classical sense) than a *concerto grosso*. It is perhaps not entirely beside the point to wonder what course the history of music would have taken if Haydn and Mozart, in their prentice days or even as mature composers, had known the Brandenburg concertos.

Bach solved the problem of writing a fugal movement with parts for solo instruments—a problem which he also had to face in his suites—in two different ways. In the finale of the second concerto both the subject and the counterpoints to it are in a virtuoso style, and the exposition is assigned to the *concertino*:

Ex. 118

In the last movement of the fourth concerto the exposition of the subject, which is in an earlier style:

Ex. 119

is entrusted to the tutti: the soloists do not emerge until the episodes, in which fragments of the subject are also heard. In the first movement of the sixth concerto the normal relationship between soli and tutti is reversed. The ritornello is a two-part canon played by the two violas, with the other instruments (two bass viols, cello, double bass and harpsichord) merely supplying the accompaniment. What would normally be the solo sections are treated as material for elaborate development, in which all the instruments have approximately an equal share.

OTHER MASTERS OF THE *CONCERTO GROSSO*

So far we have been concerned with the *concerti grossi* of four leading composers: Corelli, Muffat (in the preceding chapter), Handel, and Bach. Their works not only illustrate the tremendous developments that took place in the space of roughly fifty years but also indicate how many different ways there were of handling the form. It may be convenient to attempt a classification of these methods:

1. Dance movements in which alternative sections are played by the *concertino*.
2. Dance movements in which the *concertino* is contrasted with the *concerto grosso* in the form of an echo, or a series of *repetitions* or a group with different material.
3. *Sonata da chiesa* movements in the form of a *canzon*, with contrast between *concertino* and *concerto grosso* as in 2.
4. *Sonata da chiesa* movements in the form of a fugue, the distinction between *concertino* and *concerto grosso* corresponding more or less to that between episodes and entries with the subject.
5. Structures in several movements:
   (a) suite, with movements as in 1 or 2.
   (b) *sonata da chiesa*, with movements as in 3 and 4.
   (c) a mixture of *sonata da chiesa* and suite (often arranged so that two dance movements follow a pair of *sonata da chiesa* movements).
6. French overture treated in the style of a *concerto grosso*; *concerto grosso* in the form of an overture-suite (or *vice versa*); or overture added to 5a–5c.

7. Fugue for solo instruments and orchestra, the *concertino* dealing either with the exposition (and subsequent entries of the subject) or with the episodes. In the latter case the episodes may either be independent of the subject or be so constructed that the soloists play counterpoints against it.
8. Combination of the solo concerto movement (as a form)[66] with the style of the *concerto grosso*. In this type the members of the *concertino* are often not treated as a group but as individual instruments, as in the solo concerto. Approximations to the double and triple concerto also come under this heading.
9. The development of the material may in certain sections of the work become so prominent that the style is nearer to that of the classical symphony.

A composer writing a *concerto grosso* in the first half of the eighteenth century had all these possibilities at his disposal. His choice depended on a variety of factors: his personal preference for the style of Corelli on the one hand or that of Vivaldi on the other, the purpose for which his work was intended, and the instrumental resources available. In Italy, where the *concerto grosso* originated, it had been the custom, ever since Giovanni Lorenzo Gregori (1663–1745) published his Op. 2 at Lucca in 1698, to mention the scoring in the title: Gregori's title runs:

CONCERTI GROSSI A PIÙ STROMENTI / DUE VIOLINI CONCERTATI, CON RIPIENI, SE PIACE, ALTO VIOLA, ARCILEUTO, Ò VIOLONCELLO, CON IL BASSO PER L'ORGANO / . . . / DA GIO: LORENZO GREGORI, MUSICO DI VIOLINO NELLA CAPPELLA / DELLA SERENISSIMA REPUBLICA DI LUCCA. / . . .

Some indication of the number of Italian composers working in this field may be gathered from a list of the principal names (in alphabetical order):

Tomaso Albinoni (1671–1751):
  Four concertos with two oboes in both Op. 7 (1715) and Op. 9 (1722)
Giuseppe Bergonzi (dates unknown)
  *Sinfonie da chiesa e concerti a quattro*, Op. 2 (1708), with two solo violins
Francesco Antonio Bonporti (1672–1749):
  Ten *concerti a quattro con violino di rinforzo*, Op. 11 (after 1727)
Francesco Geminiani (1687–1762):
  Six *concerti grossi*, Op. 2 (1732)
  Six    ''        ''    Op. 3 (1732)
  Six    ''        ''    Op. 7 (1746)

---

[66] See chap. V.

Twelve   ''      ''   after Corelli's Op. 5 (1726–7)
Six      ''      ''   after his own violin sonatas, Op. 4 (1743)
Pietro Antoni Locatelli (1695–1764):
Twelve *concerti grossi*, Op. 1 (1721)
Six        ''        '' Op. 4 (1735)
Six        ''        '' Op. 7 (1741)
Six        ''        '' Op. 9 (1762)
Francesco Manfredini (1684–1762):
*Concerti grossi*, Op. 3 (1718)
Alessandro Marcello (1684–1750):
Twelve *concerti grossi*: 'La Cetra' (*c*.1740)
Giovanni Mossi (dates unknown):
*Concerti a 6 istromenti*, Op. 3 (*c*.1720)
Artemio Motta (dates unknown):
*Concerti a cinque*, Op. 1 (1701)
Giuseppe Sammartini (1695–1750):
Six *concerti grossi*, Op. 2 (1728)
Six *concerti grossi*, Op. 5 (1747), after his own trios, Op. 3
Alessandro Scarlatti (1660–1725):
Twelve manuscript *sinfonie di concerto grosso* (1715) (Brit. Lib.)
Carlo Tessarini (*c*.1690–after 1766):
Several opus nos. with titles such as 'Contrasto armonico' (*c*.1748)
Giuseppe Torelli (1658–1709):
*Concerti grossi*, Op. 8 (1709) (six solo concertos, six concertos for two violins)
Giuseppe Valentini (*c*.1680–after 1759):
*Concerti grossi*, Op. 7 (1710)
Francesco Venturini (*c*.1675–1745):
*Concerti da Camera a 4–9 instr.*, Op. 1 (*c*.1714)
Antonio Vivaldi (1678–1741):
*Concerti grossi*, Ryom catalgoue, nos, 109–11, 113–15, 117–20, etc.

These composers used either the type derived from the *sonata da chiesa*, with generally rather modest demands on the technique of the soloists, or else the type which was influenced by the solo concerto both in its form and in its treatment of the solo instruments.

In Germany the *concerto grosso* was less popular than the suite and the solo concerto. J. G. Sulzer's *Theorie der schönen Künste* (Leipzig, 1771–4) offers a plausible explanation:

To write concertos of this kind the composer needs all the arts of counterpoint, and since the work involved is difficult and laborious it is rare to find a composer who will take the trouble. For this reason concertos of this kind are rare in Germany.[67]

---

[67] Article, 'Concerto'.

In spite of this Walther Krüger[68] was able to refer to about two hundred examples. Before Muffat introduced the Italian term these works were called by various names: Johann Christoph Pez (1664–1716) uses *Sonate concertate*, and Johann Melchior Molter (1696–1765) *Sonate grosse*. Later on alternative Italian titles occur, such as *Concerto à più strumenti*, *Concerto à 6*, *Concerto à 7*, etc. Where the number of instruments is given it includes the orchestra, i.e. first and second violins, viola and bass (cello, double bass, continuo). The word *concertino*, on the analogy of *concerto*, means music played by a small ensemble or the ensemble itself. Hence it was used not only as a term for the group of soloists in a *concerto grosso* but also as the title of a work for a small number of players. Torelli calls his eleven little suites, Op. 4 (1688) *Concertino per Camera a Violino e Violoncello* (note the singular). In course of time it became the generic term for chamber music written in a *concertante* style—the opposite of *concerto ripieno*. The Blancheton collection in the Paris Conservatoire includes seventy-two works of this kind, about two-thirds of which are trio sonatas. Zocarini used the word *concertino* as the title of works for cello and continuo, in the form of a Vivaldi concerto, with the cello playing both the ritornellos and the solo sections.[69]

It is significant that Italian composers like Dall'Abaco who were working in Germany had hardly any influence on the development of the *concerto grosso* in their adopted country. Many composers in Austria and Germany from Muffat to Heinichen learned the style in Italy itself; others such as Bach, Quantz, and Telemann, studied the Italian *gusto*[70] from works that were readily available, thanks to the activities of publishers, particularly the Amsterdam firm of Estienne Roger. The majority of German composers who wrote *concerti grossi*—men like Telemann, Fasch, Graupner, Pez, and Molter—were also prominent as composers of suites – a further indication of the close connection between the two forms. In spite of the fact that Vivaldi's works had a strong influence in Germany, Graupner, among others, remained faithful to the older type. The eighteen *concerti grossi* by him that survive usually have four movements, beginning with a slow introduction, and little virtuosity is demanded of the soloists. Heinichen, on the other hand, was a follower of Vivaldi: one of his concertos has the note: 'Venetia

---

[68] *Das Concerto grosso in Deutschland* (Wolfenbüttel, 1932).
[69] See p. 276.
[70] *Gusto*, like the French *goût*, means both 'taste' and 'style'. It is used in this sense by Bach in his *Concerto nach Italiaenischen Gusto*.

7.d'ottobre 1715'. But once he was established at the Dresden court he began to introduce French elements into his concertos. As he put it himself: 'a happy mixture of Italian and French styles is certain to make a favourable impression on the ear and to prove superior to any other style in the world'.[71] A peculiarity of German *concerti grossi* was to increase the size of the *concertino* by adding wind players, so that there were sometimes as many as six soloists. This is probably because many of the courts had considerable instrumental resources.

### THE CONCERTO IN ENGLAND

In England Corelli very quickly became the most admired Italian composer of instrumental music. Walsh published an edition of Op. 6 in 1715, and other London publishers followed suit.[72] Arrangements also appeared. In 1720 Walsh & Hare printed *Six Concertos for two Flutes and a Bass, with a Through Bass for the Harpsicord Neatly Transpos'd from y*e *great Concertos*; and twelve years later Pepusch published a full score, with an extra viola added to the *concertino*. In 1714 (the year in which Op. 6 was first printed) Corelli's pupil Geminiani came to England; the success of his own Op. 2 and Op. 3 is a further indication to the popularity of the *concerto grosso* in England. Geminiani also arranged Corelli's violin sonatas, Op. 5, for a string quartet *concertino* and string orchestra (1726).[73] The following example, from the first sonata, will give some idea of the way in which he treated Corelli's text:[74]

Ex. 120

(i) Original

[71] *Der General-Bass in der Composition* (Dresden, 1728).

[72] Benjamin Cooke (active 1726–43) and John Johnson (active 1740–62).

[73] See above, p. 270. An English musician did the same in the same year; *Two Concertos being the first and eleventh solos of . . . A. Corelli as they are made into concerto's by Mr. Obadiah Shuttleworth* were published in 1726.

[74] Modern edition by Virgilio Mortari (Milan, n.d.).

(ii) Arrangement
Fuga

He also adapted his own works to suit the fashion for *concerti grossi*. Six of his violin sonatas, Op. 1, appeared some fifty years after their original publication as

VI Sonatas for two violins & violoncello or a harpsichord with a ripieno bass to be used when the violins are doubled, from the first VI solo's of his Op I with a few additional movements (1757).

The orchestral parts are headed:

The ripieno parts, belonging to the six sonatas composed . . . from the 6 first solos of . . . Opera prima.

Geminiani also arranged his violin sonatas, Op. 4, as *Concerti grossi a due violini, due viole e violoncello obligati con due altri violini, e basso di ripieno . . . composti dalle sonate . . . dell'opera IV* (London, 1743).

Francesco Barsanti (1690–1772) accompanied Geminiani to England. In addition to publishing his own *Concerti grossi*, Op. 3 (Edinburgh, 1742), he also arranged works by other composers. In a note on the title page of his *Concerti grossi*, Op. 6 (London, 1757), he acknowledged the original source: 'Questi concerti sono composti di diversi notturni del St. Martini da Francesco Barsanti'. Among the composers who helped to make Corelli's style familiar in England was Pietro Castrucci (1679–1752), for many years the leader of Handel's orchestra in London; his own *Concerti grossi*, Op. 3, were not published till 1736. The fact that Handel, in spite of his early acquaintance with Vivaldi's concertos, tended to favour an older and less virtuoso style, may be attributed to a desire to satisfy the taste of the English public. His love of song-like melodies left its mark on the *concerti grossi* of Pepusch and native composers such as Humphries, Mudge, Corbett, and Babell, who was Handel's pupil. In the works of the younger generation, e.g. John Stanley (1712–86), the old type was modified by the infusion of a rococo kind of melody. The *Six Concerto's in Seven Parts* (1750) of Stanley's pupil John Alcock (1715–1806) mark the complete change to 'sensitive' (*empfindsam*) style.

THE CONCERTO IN FRANCE

In France the importation of music involving soloists had for a long time been hindered by resistance to the Italian style. One consequence of this was the decline in the technical competence of the *24 violons du roi*, who still clung to the old discipline imposed by Lully and were quite unaware of the latest developments in Italian violin-playing. In these circumstances it was natural that the solo concerto should be neglected; but it is not so easy to see why the *concerto grosso* should have been ignored, since there was a precedent in Lully's wind trios for using a solo group. However, in 1725 Philidor was able to start the first meeting of the Concert Spirituel with a *concerto grosso* by Corelli. One of the pioneers of Italian orchestral music in France was Michele Mascitti (*c*.1664–1760), who was born in Naples but settled in Paris and had his first volume of sonatas published there by Foucaut in 1704. It was not until 1727 that he ventured to add four *concerti à 6* to a collection of eight violin sonatas published as Op. 7, and even then the concertos are called sonatas in the part-books. The twelfth sonata (i.e. the fourth concerto) has the notes: 'Questo concerto Si potrà Sonare ancora a Violino Solo col Basso di questo libro' (This concerto can also be played as a violin solo with the bass part of this volume). This was possible because the first violin in these four works is so much the dominant partner that they should rather be reckoned as solo concertos. By the time Italian instrumental music was getting a firm footing in France, in Italy itself the *sinfonia* had become the favoured form. That the French came to enjoy the instrumental contrasts of the *concerto grosso* may be gathered from the fact that Charles-Henri de Blainville (*c*.1710–*c*.1777) published an arrangement of Tartini's violin sonatas, Op. 1, as

> Concerti grossi Con due Violini, Viola e Violoncello di
> Concertino Obligato e due altri Violini e Basso di
> Concerto Grosso Da Carlo Blainville Composti della Prima e
> Seconda parte dell'Opera Prima Di Giuseppe Tartini.

The mosaic of Tartini's melodic lines makes them very suitable for dialogue treatment:

Ex. 121

The practice of alternating soloists and orchestra was commonly adopted by composers whatever kind of music they were writing. But the *concerto grosso* never became a fixed form, and for that reason it was open to the admission of the many new elements of form and style which were gaining ground about 1740 and led gradually to the classical symphony. Once that process was complete the *concerto grosso* ceased to exist.

## THE *CONCERTO RIPIENO*

The word *concerto* never lost its original sense of 'playing together', but as time went on it came also to imply 'contrast between groups', 'competition' and 'solo performance'. To these was added about 1700 the idea of technical difficulty. At that time not only did the *sinfonia* (used mainly as an opera overture) include short solo passages in the style of the *concerto grosso*; the style of instrumental writing itself was based on the assumption that there would be players competent to deal with the technical problems involved. The new style was also to some extent a product of the new urge for emotional expression. The use of characteristically instrumental turns of phrase, whether simple or highly elaborate, affected not only the kind of music written for an ensemble but also the way in which it was written. Corelli did not write solo concertos; but the principal violin part in his *concerti grossi* (sometimes the bass part as well) is so exuberant that in certain movements (e.g. the second movement of Op. 6, no. 12) the result is very much like a concerto for a single soloist.

About 1700 the old *concerto à quattro* underwent a change which was closely related to the changes that were taking place in the opera *sinfonia*. The new form which began to appear was a sort of 'concerto without soloists'. Arnold Schering was the first writer to give it a name: he called it *Konzertsinfonie*.[75] Though the term has been widely accepted, it is not entirely happy, since it combines 'concerto' and 'symphony'—two words which have quite a different meaning today—and can easily cause misunderstanding. Remo Giazotto[76] has suggested 'sonata-concerto', David Boyden[77] proposes 'concerto-sonata'. The obvious term would be 'concerto for orchestra', since we are familiar with this in twentieth-century music. But the problem of finding a name was in fact solved long ago by Vivaldi, who used the designation *concerto ripieno* for certain works of this kind. The term also implies a formal structure: in most of these compositions we have, paradoxical though it may appear, a solo concerto movement written for an ensemble without

---

[75] *Geschichte des Instrumentalkonzerts* (Leipzig, 2nd ed., 1927), p. 24.
[76] *Tomaso Albinoni* (Milan, 1945), p. 98.
[77] *Notes*, xiii (1955–6), p. 330; *Musical Quarterly*, xliii (1957), p. 230, n. 19.

soloists. We have about fifty concertos of this type by Vivaldi, some in three parts and some in four. Some of them exist in copies headed *sinfonia*, a further indication of the relationship between *sinfonia* and concerto. In the four-part works the writing is often in three parts, with the two violins in unison, and in some of the works the upper part looks very much as if it had been written as a study—perhaps for the use of pupils at the Ospedale della Pietà.

There were several ways of adapting the ritornello form to a concerto without soloists:

1. To take the ritornello through the usual keys but to omit episodes: the result is rather like a solo concerto without any solo sections. This was the least interesting method, possible only when there were plenty of contrasts within the ritornello and sufficient variation when it was repeated.
2. Between the ritornellos to insert episodes which either introduce new material or develop the material of the ritornello.
3. To extend the episodes considerably, so that the ritornellos merely form the framework of the movement.

There are examples of all three methods in Vivaldi. The following example, the first movement of a concerto in C,[78] illustrates method 1 (notice how R.IV is so severely compressed that nothing survives except the opening bar, which leads straight into the cadenza):

Ex. 122

---

[78] No. 309 of the edition, ed. Gian Francesco Malipiero *et al.* (Milan, 1947–71); no. 115 in the catalogue of Vivaldi's works by Peter Ryom (*Verzeichnis der Werke Antonio Vivaldis*) (Leipzig, 2nd ed., 1979).

In another example[79] the form is very elastic. The whole of the first movement is in the style of a trio sonata, i.e. the two violin parts are treated as equally important. This affects the character of the ritornello (A), which is not, like most of Vivaldi's ritornellos, a series of short phrases but a complete sentence (a), the violins changing places for the repetition:

Ex. 123

[79] Malipiero, no. 251; Ryom, 128.

In bars 9–13 the initial idea is developed (*a*¹) and the music modulates to F major:

Ex. 124

At this point a new section (B) begins, in marked contrast to the ritornello:

Ex. 125

At first sight this looks like an episode. But it is not a normal episode. It recurs several times in the movement (with minor variations), to which it supplies the concluding bars. In other words the ritornello and the 'episode' are an alternating pair, arranged as follows:

> A   (a: bars 1–8) D minor
> (a¹: bars 9–13) D minor to F major
> B bars 13–23 F major to A minor

A   (a: bars 23–31) A minor
     B bars 31–40 A minor
A   (a¹: bars 40–46) A minor to F major
     B bars 46–9 F major
A   (a: bars 49–53) D minor
     B bars 53–61 D minor

The penultimate movement of Handel's Op. 6, no. 5, is in the form of the first type of *concerto ripieno*; the initial ritornello is made up of three elements which are repeated in different keys and with various modifications and omissions throughout the movement.

Vivaldi's *concerti ripieni* are mostly in three movements, the second movement being Andante, Adagio or Largo, and third Presto or Allegro. The middle movement is sometimes merely a transition, though not quite so brief as the Phrygian cadence in Bach's third Brandenburg concerto; if it is more than this, it is often in ABA form. The finale is generally in dance rhythm, with two repeated sections, the second of which begins with the thematic material in the dominant, proceeds to develop it and leads to a recapitulation. In the *concerto ripieno* the finale is generally in $\frac{2}{4}$ time: in the *sinfonia* it is more often a minuet.

Needless to say, the 'concerto without soloists' is not a fixed form. No. 7 of Handel's Op. 6 illustrates further possibilities. There are five movements:

> Largo
> Allegro (fugue), with 3-bar Adagio coda
> Largo, e piano
> Andante
> Hornpipe

The first two movements are a French overture, and the whole work is more like a suite than a concerto. It is certainly not a *concerto grosso* in the conventional sense. Titles, as we have seen already, were often used in a very casual way. What Vivaldi called *concerto ripieno* was also known as *sinfonia* or *concerto à quattro*, e.g. Op. 7[80] by a supposedly Swiss composer Heinrich Weissenburg, who served as an officer in Holland and called himself Henrico Albicastro (fl. *c*.1700). Towards the middle of the century there was a marked tendency to omit violas and write in three parts: when that happened *concerto à quattro* was also used to mean a solo concerto with orchestra in three parts, e.g. a *Concerto à 4* for recorder, two violins and bass by Johann Adolf Scheibe (1708–76). Bonporti's

---

[80] *Schweizerische Musikdenkmäler*, i (1955).

use of the description *concerti à quattro* for his *concerti grossi*, Op. 12, was quite abnormal.

The finest example of a *concerto ripieno* is Bach's third Brandenburg concerto. The shape of the first movement clearly derives from the third type mentioned above (p. 277); but Bach's imagination was so fertile and his technique of development so economical that the movement will not fit into any watertight category. The framework is a three-part ritornello, corresponding to the threefold division of the nine instruments (three violins, three violas, three cellos):

Ex. 126

The three-part texture makes a wonderful contrast to the subtle and elaborate part-writing of the development. The first statement of the ritornello lasts eight bars. It is repeated in bars 9–15, with the omission of *b*, and modulates to the dominant; *a* is divided up between the three groups. The figure (x) originally assigned to the violas is now taken up by the violins and developed; this development turns out to be very important later in the movement:

Ex. 127

By inventing new material in this way Bach is able to maintain the tension without abandoning the anapaestic rhythm  with which the movement opens. From the end of bar 23 *b* becomes prominent. The first real climax comes at the end of bar 31, where *b*, harmonized in three parts, is combined with *a*:

Ex. 128

The C major cadence which immediately precedes this might lead one to expect the ritornello at this point. It is in fact present in a fragmentary form in the lower parts, but the independent development of the upper parts largely effaces any impression it might make; the ritornello is caught up into this development and loses its independence. It is not until bar 39 that we hear a genuine ritornello—in the tonic, contrary to the normal practice of Vivaldi and of Bach himself. The composer may have felt that his elaborate development was a threat to the formal unity of the movement and decided to re-establish this by emphasizing the principal key. At bar 47 the bowed semiquavers of *b* are detached from their context and used as further material for development:

Ex. 129

A modulation to E minor brings us to the third ritornello, starting at the end of bar 53. The next development section (bars 58–70) is related to bars 16–22 but also introduces the development from Ex. 27. It cnds in B minor, which is also the key of the fourth ritornello (bars 70–77). The tonic key is resumed at bar 78 with a new counterpoint, which reminds us of the E major violin concerto:

Ex. 130

This new figure, however, has no lasting significance and disappears from sight after bar 87. At bar 91 the material of Ex. 129 again returns, beginning on a Neapolitan sixth, which prepares us for a modulation to A minor. A passage similar to bars 31–34 leads to a renewed emphasis of the tonic key (bars 106–7). The material of Ex. 129 is now developed at some length, with subtle changes of harmony, leading eventually to the final ritornello, which appears at the end of bar 125. The whole movement is a striking example of unity achieved by variation.

## THE ORCHESTRA IN CHURCH MUSIC

The great advance made by instrumental music in the early years of the eighteenth century was not without its effect on the church. The rise of opera had forced church music into a secondary role: it benefited from its association with secular music but it had little to offer in return. Fux, in his *Gradus ad Parnassum*, had taken his stand by the sixteenth-century ideal of vocal polyphony and provided an example himself in his *Missa di San Carlo canonica a-cappella* (1718), dedicated, like the *Gradus*, to the Emperor Charles VI. Yet in other works for the church he made substantial use of instruments. It was not that he wanted to reject modern developments: he was much more concerned with creating a synthesis of the new instrumental style of homophonic writing and the spirit of the old polyphony.[81] The opposing claims of the *stile antico* and the *stile moderno* were balanced in the *stile misto*—a union of both, with strong emphasis on instrumental participation.

In the twelfth chapter of Part II of *Der vollkommene Capellmeister* Mattheson[82] analyses the superior position that instrumental music had acquired in the early eighteenth century. He does not deny that his education was founded on vocal music; he admits that vocal music is 'the mother' and instrumental music 'the daughter'. But he thinks that 'instrumental melody has altogether more fire and freedom than vocal', that 'a melody which is sung does not admit the leaps that are possible in one that is played', that 'the limitations of instruments are not so narrow as those of singers'. He ends by asserting that 'singing without instruments has largely fallen into disuse . . . since the human voice is by no means steady, it sounds lost by itself (*einsam klingt*) and is also severely limited'.

The effect of this attitude on church music, with its dependence on the word, is closely related to the change which had taken place in religious experience. In the Middle Ages faith was objective: people felt they were part of a community. But since the Renaissance there had grown up a stronger sense of a personal relationship between man and his Maker. Yet though the indi-

---

[81] See Vol. V, pp. 591–4.
[82] Op. cit., pp. 203 ff.

vidual believer might seek religious experience outside the church sevice, the composer's chief interest had to be the response that could be aroused by the liturgical text. 'Finis primarius', writes Joseph Majer,[83] 'or the first aim, is the glory and praise of God. Finis secundarius, or the second aim, is to move the listener'. In order to awaken in the listener the strongest possible response to the service in church, all the resources of secular music—and particularly dramatic music—were called upon. There was no real division between the opera, the secular cantata, and instrumental music on the one hand and the Passion, the oratorio, and the Mass on the other, since the means they employed were the same.

Ever since the time of the canzone da sonar for groups of instruments, from which the sonata da chiesa originated, the part played by instrumental music in church had grown steadily. The Sinfonie avanti la messa of Giacomo Perti (1661–1756) are examples of instrumental music played before High Mass; Pierre-Antoine Fiocco (c.1650–1714), lieutenant de la musique at the Brussels court, sometimes began a Mass with a French overture. The tradition of having an organ solo 'per l'elevazione' soon had to give way before the desire to hear an expressive violin solo at the most solemn moment of the Mass. A soloist for this purpose was appointed at St Mark's, Venice, as early as 1693. Tartini had a similar position at Padua, with considerable benefit to his work as a composer. As late as 1786 St Mark's had a concertista in the person of Tartini's pupil Antonio Nazari, whose salary was twice that of the average leader of an orchestra. It was not until his death that the post was finally abolished.

It is no coincidence that men like Lotti, Alessandro Scarlatti, Vinci, Leo and Pergolesi were admired for their church music as much as for their operas. The text of the Mass, and of the other offices of the church, invited contrast, which earlier composers were able to use to give a formal structure to their music. Eighteenth-century composers intensified this contrast by treating the words as material for expressive music and so making further divisions in the text. The principal contrast was between soli and tutti—a contrast not merely of dynamics but of style. The introduction of orchestral preludes and postludes, arias, duets, and solo quartets, in addition to choral movements, produced the so-called 'cantata Mass'.[84] In this the orchestra played an important part,

---

[83] Museum Musicum (Schwäbisch Hall, 1732; facsimile, Kassel, 1954).
[84] On the early orchestral Mass, see Vol. V, pp. 359 ff.

particularly in underlining the dramatic significance of the text. The older *Messe pour les instruments au lieu des orgues*,[85] which was still being written by Marc-Antoine Charpentier (d. 1704), grew into the *missa concertata*. The dramatic character of this type of work became intensified as time went on, and increasing emphasis was laid on a symphonic treatment of the orchestra, which often had the principal thematic material, leaving the chorus to declaim the words in a homophonic style. Other liturgical texts were set in the same way. Orchestral effects such as the string tremolo were introduced—there is an example in Johann Caspar Kerll's Requiem Mass (1689)[86]—and passages like 'terra tremuit' and 'quantus tremor est futurus' were treated as opportunities for descriptive writing. A solo violin was indispensable for 'qui tollis peccata mundi' and 'et incarnatus est'. At the same time the fugal style was retained for the choral setting of 'et vitam venturi' and 'Amen'. The old polyphony survived here as it did in the *sonata da chiesa* (fast becoming obsolete); in fact the tradition continued right down to the time of Schubert. We can see at this time two trends. The conservative style is represented by Padre Martini (1706–84) in Bologna: the more progressive composers included Antonio Caldara (c.1670–1736), Johann Georg Reutter the younger (1708–72), Georg Christoph Wagenseil (1715–77) and Florian Leopold Gassmann (1729–74) in Vienna; Johann Ernst Eberlin (1702–62) and Leopold Mozart (1719–87) in Salzburg; and Franz Xaver Richter (1709–89) and Ignaz Holzbauer (1711–83) in Mannheim.

MUSIC OF THE LUTHERAN CHURCH

These developments took place mainly in Italy, France, Austria, and Catholic Germany. But there were also close parallels in the music of the Lutheran church, where the cantata became an essential part of the Sunday services. The Pietist clergy were strongly opposed to the introduction of operatic elements, but this did not prevent Bach from so uniting them with the traditions of Lutheran church music that to us the two appear inseparable. The incorporation of instrumental movements into his cantatas[87] was typical of his approach. He used the first movement of the third Brandenburg concerto, with the addition of two horns and three oboes, as an introduction to BWV 174, 'Ich liebe den Höchsten von ganzem

---

[85] See ibid., p. 461.

[86] Ed. Guido Adler, *Denkmäler der Tonkunst in Österreich*, lix, Jg. (1) (Vienna, 1923; reprint, Graz, 1960), p. 73. The passage referred to is on pp. 78–9.

[87] See Vol. V, 740 ff. On orchestral effects, see ibid., p. 763.

Gemüte' (1729), and the first movement of the first Brandenburg concerto as an introduction to BWV 52, 'Falsche Welt, dir trau' ich nicht' (1726). More remarkable still is the transformation of the fugal section of the overture of the fourth suite in D major into the opening chorus of BWV 110, 'Unser Mund sei voll Lachens' (1725), by superimposing voice parts on a virtually unaltered orchestral texture. Purely orchestral introductions are comparatively rare. When they do occur Bach generally calls them *sinfonia* or *sonata* or *sonatina*, as in BWV 106, 'Gottes Zeit ist die allerbeste Zeit' (1707). The *sonata* which opens BWV 31, 'Der Himmel lacht' (1715, revised 1731), is a concerto movement for three trumpets, timpani, four oboes, bassoon, and strings. The second part of the Christmas Oratorio is introduced by a pastoral *sinfonia* on the lines of a *concerto grosso* movement by Corelli: two oboi d'amore and two oboi da caccia form a *concertino* which alternates with the strings, with two flutes to soften the tone of the violins. The short *sinfonia* which opens BWV 4, 'Christ lag in Todesbanden' (1707–8), is in the old style which had come down from Gabrieli by way of Schütz, Tunder, and Buxtehude. Its use in Bach's time has the air of a deliberate archaism.

More common than independent instrumental preludes are introductory movements in which the orchestra and chorus join forces—for instance, the *ouverture* to BWV 61, 'Nun komm der Heiden Heiland' (1714), which is a French overture for instruments and voices. Another example is the opening chorus of BWV 119, 'Preise, Jerusalem, den Herrn',[88] which is also a French overture, scored for four trumpets, timpani, two recorders, three oboes, and strings. The slow introduction is assigned to the orchestra alone: the voices enter in the fugal section. Bach's method of writing for voices is so elaborate that he has no difficulty in giving them parts which are wholly instrumental in character. Here is the opening of the fugato:

---

[88] Written for the election of the Leipzig town council in 1723.

Ex. 131

A further example of a French overture is the opening chorus of BWV 20, 'O Ewigkeit, du Donnerwort' (1724), where the chorus is restricted to singing the chorale. Finally, special mention must be made of the opening chorus of BWV 11, 'Lobet Gott in seinen Reichen' (1735), which is a full-scale concerto movement, complete with *da capo*, scored for three trumpets, timpani, two flutes, two oboes, and strings, with voices superimposed.[89]

[89] For a detailed study of Bach's cantatas see Vol. V, chap. 9.'

## FROM *SINFONIA* TO SYMPHONY[90]

Our view of the development of music about the middle of the eighteenth century is all too often based on our knowledge of the works of the 'great masters'. We know that *Die Kunst der Fuge* was written in the last years of Bach's life and that Haydn's first string quartet dates from *c*.1755. Consequently we think of these few intervening years as a time of radical change and are led to conclude that there must have been two quite distinct cultures. But if we try to look at the facts through eighteenth-century eyes a very different picture emerges. Bach was appreciated by only a small circle and was better known as an organist and improviser than as a composer; the works of his second-rate and third-rate contemporaries were printed and published, while his own remained virtually unknown outside that immediate circle. The development which led from the *sinfonia* to the symphony had already begun in his lifetime, though he took practically no part in it. It was a steady, gradual development, in which it would be hard to find any abrupt changes of style or revolt against the past. It was almost entirely the minor composers who were responsible for the change—composers who rarely, if ever, could arouse sufficient creative energy to write significant works; possibly this very failing gave them the freedom and innocence of mind to invent and experiment. The widespread habit of looking at this development from the standpoint of the later classical symphony has certain advantages, but it can also be dangerous. The danger lies in misrepresentation. Composers who had their own particular sphere of activity become 'forerunners'; they are allotted 'historical tasks' and blamed if they did not 'fulfil' them, or praised if they have made a solid contribution to the 'direct line of development'. If these mistakes are avoided, it becomes much easier to understand the gradual change of style.

In the classical style the contrast between two groups of thematic material was the decisive element in what we know as 'sonata form'—the form that was assumed by orchestral music, chamber music, and, with certain modifications, the concerto.[91] It is usual

---

[90] The spelling 'symphony' (French *symphonie*, German *Symphonie*) is based on a Latin translation of the Greek symfvnía. It actually occurs as early as 1617 in Biagio Marini's *Affetti musicali, Symfonie, Canzoni* &c., Op. 1, but never became domesticated in Italy. In the late seventeenth and early eighteenth centuries it was common in England and France (though *simphonie* is also found), but in Germany was not in general use before the classical period. In this section *sinfonia* means the early form, 'symphony' the classical form.

[91] The truth of this as a general principle is not affected by the fact that Haydn and others sometimes wrote monothematic movements.

or the contrast to be emphasized by a difference in the expressive
quality of the music, which is not only important as an element in
the structure but often creates strong dramatic tension. This does
not mean that there were no contrasts in Baroque music. But there
the contrasts follow one another in succession, e.g. in the *canzon*
or in combinations of two different dances; they do not occur as
part of material for development. A countersubject in a fugue
obviously offers a contrast to the subject; but at the same time it is
closely related to the subject, since they are both heard together.
From about 1700, however, we find a growing tendency to express
abrupt changes of mood—changes which had always existed in
opera for dramatic reasons. Themes like this:[92]

Ex. 132

become more and more frequent. But it is going too far to see in
such a miniature example of a change of mood the first steps
towards the contrasts which are a feature of sonata form. No doubt
one of the origins of a contrast of thematic material was the alternation of brass and strings in the Bolognese trumpet sonata.
Another was the contrast between solo and tutti in the concerto,
particularly where the composer chose to provide the soloist with a
genuine theme, as opposed to mere figuration. The following example from a violin concerto by J. G. Pisendel (1687–1755):[93]

Ex. 133

[92] First movement of a concerto for two violins in C minor by Vivaldi, Malipiero, no. 48;
Ryom 509.
[93] Ed. Günter Hausswald (Kassel, 1959).

will serve to illustrate this kind of contrast.

### THE *SINFONIA* IN TRANSITION

In the *sinfonia* of the transitional period contrast was expressed in various ways. Sometimes it merely takes the form of an episode marked *p* which has no significance in the subsequent development. At other times it grows out of the original theme and so is itself a form of development. The introduction of a counterpoint to the principal theme occurs frequently, in which case the unity of the movement results from the use of a single theme. An undated *sinfonia* in A major by Tartini is a good example. The movement begins with a strongly marked figure:

Ex. 134

which provides a rhythmical background for the second section:

Ex. 135

Ex. 135 (i) does not recur, but (ii) has an important part to play later in the movement.

Sonata form is obviously derived from the binary form of dance movements, where the first half ends in the dominant (in a major key) and the second half in the tonic. When, as often happens, the thematic material is developed in the second half and when the first half consists of two contrasted paragraphs, one in the tonic and the other in the dominant, we have something very like sonata form. Bukofzer[94] points out that the polonaise in the third of Handel's *concerti grossi*, Op. 6, is in its formal structure a complete sonata movement. Here the contrast is strengthened by the fact that the first group in the exposition is played by the tutti and the second group by the *concertino* (two violins and cello). At the same time it is impossible to say definitely whether the influence of dance movements on sonata form was direct or whether it came by way of the Italian opera *sinfonia*: one may assume that both roads were followed. There is also a connection between the French overture and the classical symphony. In Fasch and other composers we quite often find that the opening section is followed not by a fugato but by an Allegro of the Italian type—an early example of a first movement with slow introduction.

The principle of contrast came to be incorporated in every type of form. It appears in the finale (entitled 'Fuga') of a *Sinfonia da camera*[95] by Franz Xaver Richter, a Bohemian composer who was employed as a violinist and bass singer at Mannheim from 1747, and in 1769 became *Kapellmeister* at Strasbourg cathedral. The movement begins with a traditional type of exposition:

---

[94] Op. cit., p. 361.
[95] Ed. Walter Upmeyer, *Nagels Musik-Archiv*, no. 72 (Celle, 1930).

Ex. 136

A short interlude modulates to the dominant, after which, at bar 26, we have a second group, homophonic in style and unmistakably 'classical' in manner:

Ex. 137

The fugue subject returns, suggesting a closing group, and the exposition ends with a cadence and a repeat sign. Though the composer calls this a fugue it is much more like a movement in sonata form, with the first group in the style of a fugal exposition. The *sinfonia* is typical of music of the transitional period which so often seems to hover between two styles. The finale which, as Marpurg puts it,[96] combines 'the *galant* style with elements of the contrapuntal', is all the more remarkable as the first movement (Allegro moderato) has no clearly marked second group at all.

Before 1750 it is quite unusual to find two distinct groups, together with development section and recapitulation, in spite of numerous examples which point in that direction. An early example is the *sinfonia* to the opera *Pallade trionfante* (1721) by Francesco Conti (1681–1732), composer at the Viennese court.[97] After an opening in the style of the Italian concerto:

Ex. 138

we reach the dominant (F major). The second group, however, begins in F minor, which makes the contrast even stronger:

Ex. 139

The development presents the contrast in a very much condensed form:

[96] *Kritische Briefe über die Tonkunst* (Berlin, 1759–64).
[97] Hugo Botstiber, *Geschichte der Ouvertüre* (Leipzig, 1913), p. 83, was the first to draw attention to this work. It was analysed by Wilhelm Fischer in Adler's *Handbuch der Musikgeschichte*, 2nd ed. (Berlin, 1930), pp. 797–8. The music is printed in Botstiber, op. cit., pp. 258–69.

Ex. 140

but the introduction of such a contrast into this section is an example of classical procedure many years before its time. In the recapitulation the material of the exposition is reduced to essentials. In an age when so many experiments were being made, Conti's *sinfonia* would have been regarded as merely one attempt among many: no one would have thought of it as prophetic. Yet here is the new form long before it became the normal practice of the Mannheim school.

### THE CHANGE IN MELODIC STYLE

The gradual change in melodic style was even more significant than experiments with form, since it was easier for the listener to grasp. The so-called *galant* style, strongly influenced by the French suite and harpsichord music, began to make its mark about 1700 and gradually changed into the 'sentimental' (*empfindsam*) style. Thus a new musical idiom was coming into being at the very time when J. S. Bach was writing his late works; and, as in the early years of the seventeenth century, battle was joined with the contrapuntal style. Rousseau, in his *Lettre sur la musique françoise*, had no doubt which side he was on:

As regards counter-fugues, double fugues, invertible fugues, ostinato basses and other tiresome nonsense[98] which the ear cannot tolerate nor reason justify, these are obviously the remains of barbarism and bad taste, which survive, like the doors of our Gothic churches, only to shame those who had the patience to make them.

Baroque pathos gave way to a simple, 'natural' sensibility. Rousseau's famous *retour à la nature* sums up the aesthetic ideals of

---

[98] 'Contre-fugues, doubles fugues, fugues renversées, basses contreintes et autres sottises difficiles'.

the time. Melody became a matter of neat formulas, grateful both to the player and to the listener, and depending largely for their effect on appoggiaturas and similar graces. Mattheson maintained that he was the first theorist to deal with the invention of melodies: they should be 'light, distinct, flowing and pleasing (to the ear)', and their true beauty lies in their power to excite emotion in the listener.[99] More than a century earlier Johannes Lippius, writing c.1609–12, had clearly recognized that the essence of the homophonic style, then in its infancy, was melody:

Mere melody, with its noble simplicity, clarity, and distinctness, can move the heart so powerfully that it often surpasses all the arts of harmony.

The invention of melodies of this kind was now the principal concern of composers. Telemann confesses that he 'made himself quite exhausted with writing tunes' (ganz maröde melodieret). The new style is most marked in slow movements and in more or less stylized dances, but it also strongly affects allegro movements, replacing the earlier concertante style: we now have the 'cantabile allegro'. Giovanni Battista Sammartini (c.1700–1775), maestro di cappella at the convent of Santa Maria Maddalena in Milan, became the idol of the younger generation and was much respected as a teacher. Quantz made a point of visiting him; he had a profound influence on Johann Christian Bach (1735–82), and Gluck was his pupil. His symphonies, which travelled all over Europe in print and in manuscript copies, made everyone acquainted with the new style.[100] Many of his works reached Austrian noblemen through Count von Harrach, governor of Lombardy, which was at that time a Habsburg province. Haydn knew them well and learned more from them than he was later willing to admit. The opening of a Sammartini sinfonia now in the Paris Conservatoire Library[101] illustrates the new type of Allegro:

[99] Op. cit.
[100] On Sammartini's symphonies, see Vol. VII, pp. 374–8.
[101] Fonds Blancheton, no. 150; miniature score ed. Newell Jenkins (London, 1956). And see Vol. VII, p. 375.

Ex. 141

This style, however, was not peculiar to Sammartini: it is found also in the works of those of his contemporaries who were brought up in the Corelli tradition. A *sinfonia* by Carlo Tessarini (also in the Paris Conservatoire) begins as follows:

Ex. 142

At this stage of development the basses to these melodies are still very much like a continuo part, though the harmony which they support is largely governed by a simple tonic/dominant relationship. Bukofzer neatly described this kind of texture as 'continuo homophony'. But the new desire for expression soon affected the texture as well. The part-writing was loosened to make way for a new clarity. The basic tonic-dominant harmony made it possible to create new patterns of sound by means of a dominant pedal:

Ex. 143 [102]

It was principally the Mannheim composers who developed this method as a basis for orchestration, which became the standard practice of the classical masters. The horn became the 'sustaining pedal' of the orchestra, and the other wind instruments, if they were not being used as soloists, were treated in the same way. Writers of the period were well aware of the important part played

[102] Johann Gottlieb Graun, *Concerto grosso* in C minor (Berlin, Sing-Akademie, DII 1509g). On Graun's concertos, see further Vol. VII, p. 449.

by the horn in this new style of writing. Ancelet observes: 'The Germans have taught us to use horns; it is they who have shown us how these instruments can support and enrich the sound of an orchestra.'[103] Filling up the harmony in this way meant that a keyboard instrument was no longer necessary, though it was retained for a long time in deference to tradition. The fact that it could be dispensed with was a distinct advantage when performances were given in the open air—a practice which became very common, not only at courts but in the social life of the people.

THE MERGING OF STREAMS

Serenades, divertimenti, cassations, in fact all occasional music, played an important part in the change of style since they were not only the successors of the suite but also adopted the popular idioms of the time. Towards the middle of the century all these various streams tended to merge in the symphony, which was now the most important form of orchestral music, not least because amateurs preferred it to the concerto on account of its more modest technical demands. Nef[104] quotes a ruling of the Basel *collegium musicum* for the year 1752, which says that a concert must be in three parts. The first part had to begin 'with a robust symphony with horn(s)' (*mit einer starken Sinfonie mit Waldhorn*), the second part with a symphony without horns and a third part again with a symphony with horns. The great popular demand for symphonies was a strong incentive to composers. After the mid-century, publishers responded by issuing orchestral parts in periodical series, e.g. La Chevardière's *Simfonie périodique* in Paris and Robert Bremner's *Periodical Overture* in London.

It is impossible to survey the various currents that helped to create the classical style, and particularly the classical symphony, without having the impression of a tremendous and exciting activity everywhere in Europe where music was performed. Italy once more had its contribution to make. The influence of Sammartini has already been mentioned and the symphonies of Antonio Brioschi are stylistically close to his. (Both were Milanese.)[105] In Vienna, after the death of Fux in 1741, a younger generation took the field. His pupil Georg Christoph Wagenseil (1715–77) played an important part in the development of symphonic form. Others who were active at the same time included the younger Reutter, Mathias Georg Monn

---

[103] *Observations sur la musique, les musiciens et les instruments* (Amsterdam, 1757), p. 32.
[104] Op. cit., pp. 106–7.
[105] On Brioschi's symphonies, see Vol. VII, p. 378.

(1717–50), and Joseph Starzer (1726–87).[106] Another important centre was the court of Frederick the Great in Berlin. The *Kapell-meister,* Carl Heinrich Graun (b.1703–4; d.1759), and his brother Johann Gottlieb (b.1702–3; d.1771), who led the orchestra, were faithful to tradition in their suites and *concerti grossi* but up-to-date in their symphonies.[107] (Those of Carl Philipp Emanuel Bach (1714–88), for many years harpsichord-player at the Berlin court, belong almost entirely to a later period.) Even more important than Vienna and Berlin was Mannheim, where from 1741 onwards the Elector Karl Theodor brought distinguished musicians to his court. Johann Stamitz (1717–57),[108] the principal violinist, who led the orchestra from 1745, was not only the founder of a new style of performance and an orchestral discipline which was the admiration of all Europe but also the mentor of a generation of young composers in France as well as Germany who more than anyone else created the classical style.

---

[106] On the Viennese symphonists, see ibid., pp. 395–9.
[107] Ibid., pp. 383–4.
[108] On the symphonies of Stamitz and the first generation of Mannheim composers, see ibid., pp. 407 ff.; on their concertos, pp. 456 ff.

# V

# THE SOLO CONCERTO

*By* WALTER KOLNEDER

THE combination of a solo instrument with orchestra led to two different forms: the Baroque solo concerto and the concerto of the Classical and Romantic periods. The latter is basically an adaptation of sonata form—in other words a sonata for soloist and orchestra. The Baroque concerto, on the other hand, is an independent form, using new principles of structure which were also applied to other forms of music. Wilhelm Fischer rightly described the solo concerto as the principal form of the Baroque period:[1] similarly Bukofzer calls it 'the most fertile of the three types of the baroque concerto'[2] (i.e. solo concerto, *concerto grosso*, and orchestral concerto). It is usual to distinguish the solo concerto from the *concerto grosso* by saying that in the former there is only one soloist and in the latter a group of soloists; for this reason German writers often use the term *Gruppenkonzert* for the *concerto grosso*. Closer investigation, however, shows that these two types of concerto frequently overlap and that it is inexact to base the differences between them on the number of soloists employed. The fact is that the form which developed in the solo concerto was also transferred to the 'group concerto', i.e. there are concertos for two or more soloists which are written in the form of the solo concerto. For the sake of clarity I propose to use the term 'solo concerto' for the work as a whole (generally in three movements) and the term 'solo concerto movement' for the very definite form which is mostly found in the first movement. The sonata presents the same problem, as Bukofzer has pointed out: 'The term concerto form presents the same difficulty as the term sonata form. Both are ambiguous because they are used to designate the form as a whole . . . and the form of a single movement.'[3]

---

[1] In *Handbuch der Musikgeschichte*, ed. Guido Adler (Berlin, 2nd., ed 1930), p. 358.
[2] *Music in the Baroque Era* (New York, 1947), p. 227.
[3] Loc. cit.

Many details of the early history of the solo concerto movement and the solo concerto as a whole still need to be clarified. Most of the errors that occur in books on the subject, particularly in works of reference, can be traced to the ambiguity of the word *concerto* in the seventeenth century as well as to a failure to understand the music. We have seen in the previous chapter that before 1700 the word *concerto* might have any number of different meanings other than the principal one which it acquired after 1700, i.e. solo concerto. The earliest information we have about the origin of this form comes from Quantz:[4] 'Concertos started with the Italians. Torelli is said to have been the first to write them.' Elsewhere he says of Vivaldi that he was 'lively, rich in invention, and filled almost half the world with his concertos. Although Torelli, and after him Corelli, was the first, it was he, with Albinoni, who improved the form and provided good models. This won him . . . general renown.'[5] So far as Torelli and Vivaldi are concerned, Quantz's summary is perfectly correct. But before we discuss the development to which he refers, it will be convenient to examine the mature form as we find it in the work of its chief exponent.

## SOLO CONCERTO MOVEMENT AND SOLO CONCERTO IN VIVALDI

As a typical example we may consider the third movement of a concerto for viola d'amore (no. 198; R. 393):[6]

Ex. 144

[4] *Versuch einer Anweisung die Flöte traversiere zu spielen* (facsimile edition, Kassel, 1953), p. 294; English translation, *On Playing the Flute*, by E. R. Reilly (London, 1966).

[5] Ibid., p. 309.

[6] All Vivaldi numbers in this chapter, unless otherwise stated, refer to the edition of his instrumental works, ed. Malipiero (Milan, 1947–71). Ryom or R indicates numbers in Peter Ryom's thematic catalogue (Leipzig, 1974).

Solo II

50

and so on
for 17 more
bars

(ii)

Rit. III

Solo III

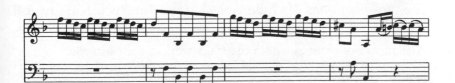

The movement begins with an orchestral ritornello (Rit. I, bars 1–19, D minor), which recurs twice in different keys in a compressed and altered form and ends the movement in the tonic (Rit. II, bars 38–48, F major; Rit. III, bars 67–80, A minor; Rit. IV, *da capo*). Between these appearances there are three solo sections which begin in the key of the preceding ritornello and proceed to modulate. The first and third of these sections (Solo I and Solo III) are accompanied only by the continuo (normally one harmony instrument and one melody instrument); the second section (Solo II), on the other hand, is accompanied by the violins and violas of the orchestra. The thematic material of Rit. I consists of five segments (A–E). In Rit. II (bars 38 foll.) B and C are eliminated and D and E extensively transformed. Rit. III (bars 67 foll.) has a similar structure, except that D and E reappear in approximately their former shape. The three solo sections show various ways of dealing with the material. Solo I is restricted to virtuoso arpeggios without any thematic significance. Solo II borrows its material from section A of Rit. I. Solo III starts off with section E of Rit. I: the further development after bar 87 is related to section C, and at bar 91 we reach a dominant pedal which eventually leads to the reprise of Rit. I.

The movement has the following characteristics which are typical of Vivaldi's solo concertos:

1. A sequence of motives within the framework of the ritornello.
2. A basic tonality which is established by the keys used for the ritornello.
3. The use of the solo sections as a means of modulation.
4. The most important relations possible between the solo and the ritornello.
5. The dominant pedal in the last solo section, with a quasi-cadenza for the soloist, in preparation for the *da capo*.

The pedal point, however, is missing in quite a number of Vivaldi's concertos or is present in only a rudimentary form.

There are about 40 concertos by Vivaldi extant, almost all of which have first movements in the form of the 'solo concerto movement'. The last movements are frequently in the same form, so that altogether we have over 800 examples, not to mention others which may have been lost. With mass production of this kind it was inevitable that the formal scheme should sometimes have become a matter of routine. There are, however, a great number of cases where the solution of the problem is handled with surprising subtlety. What might appear to be a rigid formula did in fact offer plenty of opportunity for variation.

## STRUCTURE OF THE RITORNELLO

Writers on the Baroque concerto often speak of Vivaldi's 'themes'. Bukofzer, for instance, says: 'Vivaldi owed his European fame to the gestic simplicity and precision of his themes . . . An examination of Vivaldi's tutti and solo themes reveals that, while the two ideas are distinctly independent of each other, they are not dramatically contrasted but actually unified by key and the uniform rhythms of the concerto style.'[7] But if we look at Vivaldi's solo concerto movements we do not often find themes, in the generally accepted sense of the word. The ritornello quoted in Ex. 144 is not complete in itself; it has no organic unity. Hans Mersmann, in the course of an analysis of a sonata by Handel,[8] has some pertinent things to say about the idea of a 'theme' in pre-classical music:

The concept of a 'theme', which still needed exact definition in later instrumental music (in the *stile antico* themes properly speaking were found only in fugues), is not applicable to the form of the movement in the sense of an organic growth or a principle of structure, as it is later in the sonata and the symphony.

A theme in the sense of an entity occurs in Vivaldi principally when he begins a ritornello with a fugato, e.g.:[9]

---

[7] Op. cit., p. 230.
[8] *Musikhören* (Potsdam, 1938; 2nd ed., 1952), p. 106.
[9] Third movement of a bassoon concerto in A minor, no. 119; Ryom 500.

Ex. 145

Here A is developed on the lines of a fugal exposition. Notice the very effective countersubject and the lively part-writing when the basses and violas enter. When the exposition is finished the movement is carried forward by groups of motives which are complete in themselves. As often happens, the last group is particularly striking, which is why Vivaldi often uses it in the solo section which follows. But even here it would be incorrect to speak of a ritornello 'theme', since the fugue subject dominates one section only, not the whole ritornello.

Vivaldi's ritornellos are usually distinguished by a great wealth of invention. It is only the individual motives that are strictly speaking developed. When they are eventually linked together one does not always get the impression of a natural organic growth. Frequently they are separated by rests and only occasionally joined together by a transition. The sequence of motives is rarely felt to be inevitable:

Ex. 146[10]

[10] First movement of bassoon concerto in C, no 282; Ryom 471.

Here one could easily imagine the groups in a different order. Experiments of this kind, however, are not mere flights of fancy: they provide the basis for Vivaldi's technique of transforming the ritornello when it recurs. Section E in the example is of particular interest. The indication *piano* generally occurs in a ritornello only for a short echo passage (e.g. second bar of G); but in longer ritornellos one often finds larger sections which are contrasted in dynamics and in expression. This is doubtless one of the many origins of the division of thematic material in the classical sonata; but it would be unwise to speak of a 'second subject group' in the case of Vivaldi.

We also find instances of a thematic connection between neighbouring groups, or even between those which are separated from each other. Thus in Ex. 146 the bass of D is related to the treble of A. The relatively rare occurrence of such a connection running through the entire ritornello may be illustrated from another bassoon concerto (no. 236; R. 487):

Ex. 147

Combining the motives of a ritornello can also lead to a kind of dovetailing, with the use of interchange of parts and inversion, as in the following example:

Ex. 148[11]

[11] Violin concerto, no. 165; Ryom 289.

As a rule ritornellos do not modulate, though they may include harmony related to adjacent keys.

The tonality of the solo concerto movement as a whole can be made clear by the following outline:

*Major Keys*

| | |
|---|---|
| Rit. I | tonic |
| Solo I | tonic → dominant |
| Rit. II | dominant |
| Solo II | dominant → relative minor |
| Rit. III | relative minor |
| Solo III | relative minor → tonic |
| Rit. IV | tonic |
| (*da capo*) | |

*Minor Keys*

| | |
|---|---|
| Rit. I | tonic |
| Solo I | tonic → relative major |
| Rit. II | relative major |
| Solo II | relative major → dominant |
| Rit. III | dominant |
| Solo III | dominant → tonic |
| Rit. IV | tonic |
| (*da capo*) | |

Departures from this scheme are comparatively rare, though occasionally the subdominant replaces the dominant in movements in a minor key.

When Vivaldi extends the form to include five ritornellos the following succession of keys is usually found:

*Major keys*: tonic—dominant—relative minor of the dominant—
relative minor—tonic.
*Minor keys*: tonic—relative major—dominant—subdominant—tonic.

One of the reasons for having more than four ritornellos may have
been the use of a solo instrument whose technical resources were
naturally limited or not fully developed in Vivaldi's day, so that a
greater number of short solo passages became desirable. The first
movement of a flute concerto in G major (Op. 10, no. 4; R. 435)
has the following structure:

| | |
|---|---|
| Rit. I (23 bars) | G major |
| Solo I (21 bars) | |
| Rit. II (9 bars) | D major |
| Solo II (21 bars) | |
| Rit. III (8 bars) | E minor |
| Solo III (14 bars) | |
| Rit. IV (6 bars) | B minor |
| Solo IV (13 bars) | |
| Rit. V*a* (3 bars) | G major |
| Solo V (18 bars) | |
| Rit. V*b* (23 bars) | G major |
| (*da capo*) | |

But it is entirely wrong to regard the presence of five ritornellos as
a hall-mark of the Vivaldi concerto or as a more advanced stage in
the composer's development.[12] In the scheme given above Rit. V is
divided into V*a* and V*b*, both in the same key. The use of dialogue
between solo and tutti, which was so highly developed in the
*concerto grosso*, had its influence on the solo concerto, so that we
find the ritornello broken up into sections and the orchestra inter-
polated into solo passages. If one were to analyse the movement by
counting all these fragments separately, the result would be a
monstrous conglomeration of small units. It is more sensible, and
clearer, to base analysis on tonality and to treat ritornello sections
in the same key as a single unit, as in the following example from
the first movement of a cello concerto in C (no. 204; R. 400):

[12] e.g. Minos Dounias, *Die Violinkonzerte Giuseppe Tartinis*, &c (Wolfenbüttel, 1935;
2nd ed., 1966), p. 20; Bukofzer, op. cit., p. 230.

Ex. 149

First movement, bar 27

## RECURRENCES OF THE RITORNELLO

One of the most interesting things about the structure of a solo concerto movement by Vivaldi is his method of altering the recurrences of the ritornello by means of variation, transformation, curtailment and compression. Since Rit. I and Rit. IV (or V) have the function of providing a framework for the whole movement, the ritornello usually appears here complete (the last appearance generally as a *da capo*). The other appearances are practically always abbreviated. In the third movement of no. 119 (for the opening see Ex. 145) it is the fugal exposition that is shortened; it would hardly be tolerable if it recurred several times. Therefore in Rit. II we find that A is reduced to the length of the theme and immediately followed by C; Rit. III, on the other hand, omits B and C. The complete scheme is as follows:

| | | | |
|---|---|---|---|
| Rit. I: | A (8 bars) | B (2 bars) | C (4 bars) |
| Rit. II: | A (1½ bars) | – | C (4 bars) |
| Rit. III: | A (5 bars) | – | – |
| Rit. IV: | A (8 bars) | B (2 bars) | C (4 bars) |
| (*da capo*) | | | |

The shortening of a ritornello affects mostly the middle groups, so that often only the first and last groups are left. It is obviously unnecessary to have any modification of the tonality in a shortened ritornello, considering that the solo sections on either side will be concerned with modulation. In ritornellos which contain a large number of motives—e.g. Ex. 146, where there are eight—there is a tendency to give them a semblance of novelty by making an appropriate selection at each recurrence; only the concluding formula is constant. The scheme of Ex. 146 is as follows (figures in brackets indicate the number of bars):

| | | | | | | | | |
|---|---|---|---|---|---|---|---|---|
| Rit. I: | A (6) | B (6) | C (2) | D (2) | E (6) | F (2) | G (2) | H (2) |
| Rit. II: | A (3½) | – | C (2) | – | – | – | G (2) | H (2) |
| Rit. III: | A (5½) | B (4) | – | – | E (4) | F (1) | – | H (2) |
| Rit. IV: | – | – | – | – | – | – | G (2) | H (2) |
| (*dal segno*) | | | | | | | | |

Examples of this kind throw a clear light on Vivaldi's conception of form. One has the impression of a highly skilled craftsman fashioning something whose component parts are interchangeable. The order in which these parts occur is virtually a matter of chance and could be changed without any real damage to the structure as a whole. The method of grouping together several motives in a ritornello is a very effective means of keeping the listener's interest alive when the ritornello recurs. It was essential that these modifications should not create any problem of form, which Vivaldi would hardly have had the time to solve. The world in which he lived expected him to produce a great quantity of music, and he was perfectly ready to supply the demand; but this was only possible with a technique which did not have to bother about problems and could work quickly. Not only the structure of the ritornello but the scheme of the whole movement is the outcome of an approach to form which is dictated by the practical requirements of the period.

The relation between the solo and the ritornello also has an influence on the selection of motives. It often happens that the group which is omitted is the one that is used in the preceding or subsequent solo. The opposite, however, also occurs: that is to say, the ritornello ends with the group which is to provide material for the solo that follows. In other words, the object is sometimes contrast, sometimes organic connection.

### RECAPITULATION

At least three times in the course of a solo concerto movement the composer was faced with the problem of the return of the ritornello. Though there is no intrinsic connection between the solo and the ritornello, they are generally linked by the fact that the last note of the solo becomes the first note of the ritornello. The entry of the final ritornello in the tonic, however, is often given special significance by Vivaldi and prepared by means of devices which later played an important part in the classical sonata: Ex. 144 (ii) shows a kind of cadenza for the soloist over a long dominant pedal. Another method was to enrich the harmony by allusions to adjacent keys:

Ex. 150[13]

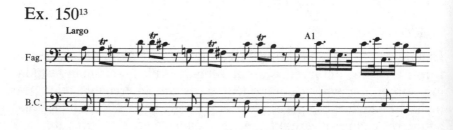

[13] Second movement of bassoon concerto in C, no. 47; Ryom 474.

In the third movement of no. 119; R. 500, the opening of which was quoted in Ex. 145, we find the first three notes of the fugato used as the basis of a harmonic transition to the recapitulation:

Ex. 151

If the preparation for the recapitulation is made by the whole orchestra, the preparation and the recapitulation may be so closely linked together that it is hardly possible to distinguish one from the other, e.g.:

Ex. 152[14]

[14] 'Concerto del Vivaldi' in A (Cambridge, Fitzwilliam; Ryom 342).

SOLO IN THE RITORNELLO

There is nothing unusual in the introduction of the solo instrument in the ritornello, considering that it was contemporary practice for the soloist to play with the orchestra in all ritornellos; in a violin concerto the soloist was generally the leader of the orchestra, who was much too valuable a person to be silent when the ensemble was so small (as was generally the case at that time), quite apart from the fact that it was his duty to ensure that his colleagues kept together. Furthermore, in Corelli's *concerti grossi*, the soloist had brief passages to play in the exposition of the principal motives. These solo insertions in the ritornello are generally of an improvisatory character, though occasionally we find a normal dialogue between soloist and orchestra:

Ex. 153[15]

[15] First movement of bassoon concerto in C, no. 238; Ryom 472.

1.) This half-bar is an editorial insert by Malipiero.

The first five bars are a regular solo theme. When the ritornello returns these are omitted, but the first and second solo sections begin with them and develop them without reference to the ritornello. It is rare, however, to meet with any close interchange of motives between soloist and orchestra as early as the first ritornello, as here:

Ex. 154[16]

---

[16] First movement of flute concerto in A minor, no. 44; Ryom 108.

(ii)      (bar 15)
          Rit. II

This procedure goes a long way to obliterate the contrast between the ritornello and the solo – a practice which was later typical of Bach's treatment of the concerto. Ex. 154 is very similar to Bach's A minor violin concerto, which leads one to suppose that Bach knew Vivaldi's work and got ideas from it.

### THE SOLO SECTIONS

In the key scheme of the solo concerto movement the soloist had the task of effecting the modulations between the ritornellos; hence the solo sections are generally less stable in tonality than the ritornellos. There is usually a difference between the first solo and the third (or last). Whereas the first, following the opening ritornello, begins with a broad affirmation of the tonic key, the final solo, though it soon turns in the direction of the tonic, delays the actual entry of the tonic by a preparation of considerable length; a typical scheme of modulation (from F major to A minor) can be seen in the second solo of Ex. 144. The relation between the solo and the ritornello can take one of the following forms:

(a) The solo is independent of the ritornello.
(b) The opening motive of the ritornello is also the beginning of the solo.
(c) The solo includes other motives from the ritornello.
(d) The solo includes both the opening motive and subsequent motives.

It is comparatively rare to find the solo sections completely independent of the ritornello. In the first movement of the cello concerto in C major, already quoted from in Ex. 149, there may have been a special reason for this: the ritornello is particularly weak in motives, so that the solo sections had to have new material in order to avoid monotony. Ex. 155 (i) shows the opening ritornello and (ii, iii, and iv) extracts from the opening solo sections:

Ex. 155

(i)   Allegro

(ii)  Allegro
      bar 12

(iii)       bar 48

(iv)  bar 59

The development of virtuoso figuration without any reference to the ritornello is found chiefly in violin concertos. It is worth noting that it is generally the second or third section that is treated in this way. The first solo either takes over from the ritornello or embarks on its own characteristic motive—obviously the best way to handle the first section. Once a sufficient number of motives had been dealt with in the course of the movement the way was clear for the second or third solo to exploit figuration which would give the player an opportunity to show off his technique. Ex. 144 is a good example of this.

Solo sections which begin by taking over the opening motive of the ritornello are frequent; this is almost invariably the practice in the first section. Either this is followed immediately by passage work:

## Ex. 156[17]

[17] Third movement of viola d'amore concerto in D minor, no. 196; Ryom 394.

or the opening motive is developed—a process which often shows Vivaldi's melodic invention at its best, e.g.:

Ex. 157[18]

In the following example both the solo line and its bass are neatly developed from the opening of the ritornello:

Ex. 158[19]

A particularly favoured device was to take the concluding motive of the opening ritornello and use it as the starting-point for the first solo section, e.g.:

Ex. 159[20]

[18] First movement of oboe concerto in C, no. 222; Ryom 451.
[19] First movement of concerto in A, no. 229; Ryom 343.
[20] First movement of cello concerto in A minor, no. 205; Ryom 422.

Examples of a more thorough treatment by the soloists of all the
material of the ritornello occur above all in wind concertos. This is
no coincidence. As we have seen, the connection between solo
sections and ritornello is strongest when the technical resources of
the solo instrument are limited. In works for the violin, with their
headlong arpeggios, there was a danger of dissipating the musical
substance in a show of virtuosity; but where wind instruments were
employed the composer was encouraged, not to say compelled, to
find a substitute for such figuration in the development of his ideas.
In the first movement of the flute concerto in F major (no. 46;
R. 434), published as Op. 10, no. 5, the motives are so closely
interwoven that the first solo section is almost like a variation of
the ritornello:

## Ex. 160

There is a particularly close relationship between the ritornello and the three solo sections in the first movement of the bassoon concerto in C, the opening ritornello of which has been quoted in Ex. 146. The letters in the following extracts correspond to those in Ex. 146:

Ex. 161

(ii)

(iii)

Since most of the wind concertos were in a collection (now in the Biblioteca Nazionale, Turin) that was not made available till 1927–30 by Alberto Gentili, it is understandable that until then Vivaldi's treatment of the solo instruments was considered only on the basis of the violin concertos. For instance, Arnold Schering wrote:

[The solo] either confines itself to the usual virtuoso figuration, which has virtually nothing to say, accompanied by triads on the harpsichord, or simply borrows its material from the ritornello, with only the slightest modification, or else it introduces a completely new contrasting theme with a character of its own.[21]

Judgements of this kind, still heard today, lead to the assumption that close thematic connection between solo and ritornello was invented by Bach.[22]

There is naturally a close relation between the solo sections whenever several of them use the same motive from the ritornello. In the first movement of an oboe concerto in D minor (no. 2; R. 454) the opening ritornello is dominated by a syncopated rhythm which is taken up in all the four solo sections:

Ex. 162

---

[21] *Geschichte des Instrumentalkonzerts* (Leipzig, 2nd ed., 1927; reprinted 1965), p. 87.
[22] See p. 360.

The way in which this idea is continually developed into new melodic shapes is an outstanding example of Vivaldi's ingenuity, for monothematic movement can easily become tiring.

### RITORNELLO MOTIVES IN THE ACCOMPANIMENT

Solos are generally accompanied only by the continuo. This practice, besides making a clear distinction between ritornello and solo, was also very convenient from the point of view of performance. The orchestral rehearsal could be restricted to running through the ritornellos, while a short session with an experienced continuo-player was all that was needed for the solo sections. In many works, however, the orchestra takes part in the accompaniment of at least some of the solos. One is tempted to assume that this represents a higher stage of development in Vivaldi's work, but as only a few of his works can be dated there is no proof of this assumption: it is very doubtful whether criteria of this kind are sufficient to establish creative periods in his life. Dialogue between soloist and orchestra had already been fully developed in the *concerto grosso* before the solo concerto came into existence. Which of the two methods was employed must have depended on the time available, the special conditions of a performance, the particular orchestra, and so on.

In the simplest cases the orchestral accompaniment of a solo is merely a continuo part scored for strings, e.g. the second solo of Ex. 144; but more often the accompaniment introduces thematic material that is either new or borrowed from the ritornello. The invention of new motives in the accompaniment may have the object of giving substance to a rather dull solo, e.g.:

Ex. 163[23]

In the first movement of a violin concerto in E minor (no. 164; R. 273) the first and second violins of the orchestra play a rather more important role:

Ex. 164

[23] Third movement of bassoon concerto in A minor, no. 119; Ryom 500. The passage continues in the same style for twelve bars.

Thematic development of a motive in a solo section may involve the isolation of a small fragment as a basis for continuity: e.g.:

Ex. 165[24]

In order to appreciate Vivaldi's position in the history of the concerto it is important to realize that solo sections for development occur as early as Op. 3 (printed in 1712):

Ex. 166[25]

[24]  Third movement of a concerto in C for two flutes, no. 101; Ryom 533.
[25]  Op. 3, no. 12; Ryom 265.

One of the most important works in this respect is a bassoon concerto in C (no. 47; R. 474). The richness of the string texture here
is made possible by the contrast in timbre, which never allows the
soloist to be drowned. In the first movement the motives of the
orchestral accompaniment are mostly new:

Ex. 167

(i)

(ii)
Solo II

(iii)

In the third movement they are consistently taken from the ritornello:

(i) Ex. 168

(ii)
Solo II

The final solo could very well be part of the development section of a Beethoven concerto. Even more polished in its workmanship is the first movement of the flute concerto in A minor, the opening of which has been quoted in Ex. 154. Apart from a few episodes which are definitely solos the whole movement consists of a development in the form of a dialogue:

Ex. 169

bar 18

bar 48

## THE SOLO CADENZA

Quantz tells us that 'it was somewhere between 1710 and 1716 that cadenzas of the kind now customary, where the bass has to wait, became fashionable'.[26] He is referring to those extended improvisations by the soloist, sometimes also called 'fantasia' or 'capriccio', which prepare for the final ritornello and so have a particularly important part to play in the structure of the movement. Their predecessors were Torelli's three *perfidie* (San Petronio, Bologna)——brief solo sections with bustling figuration, for insertion in the *sonate da chiesa*. By 1700 instrumental cadenzas were also common in operatic arias (e.g. Alessandro Scarlatti's *Laodicea e Berenice*, 1701), with obbligato instruments competing with the singers. Quantz has a warning against having too many cadenzas: he says one should not spoil the listener's appetite.[27] C. F. D. Schubart[28] makes the point that 'a long cadenza is a state

[26] Op. cit., p. 152.
[27] Ibid., p. 153.
[28] *Ideen zu einer Ästhetik der Tonkunst*, written in 1784 but published posthumously (Vienna, 1806).

within the state (*ein Staat im Staate*) and is always detrimental to the impression made by the movement as a whole'. Wind-players accepted in principle the old rule of singers that a cadenza should be performed in one breath. In cadenzas for string instruments the numerous technical resources available, such as double stops, arpeggios, &c., soon gave rise to a more extended form.

In Vivaldi's works the place for the cadenza is usually marked: 'Qui si ferma à piacimento' (pause here ad. lib.), and the ritornello which follows immediately has 'poi segue' (continue). In some cases the cadenza is written out, perhaps as a model for pupils or to help a soloist who had only a slender talent for improvization. In one particular concerto, however, the written cadenza is such an essential part of the movement that it must be there by Vivaldi's express intention, since an improvized cadenza would never have achieved the same result. The work in question is a violin concerto in D major (no. 312; R. 212), composed in 1712: the autograph[29] bears the inscription: 'Fatto per la Solemnità della S. Lingua de S. Antonio in Padua'. The first movement has the usual instructions for a cadenza; but the cadenza in the third movement, by Vivaldi himself, makes exceptional demands on the player, who is required to go up to F sharp two octaves above the top line of the treble stave. Though the movement is in 3/4 time the cadenza starts in the 4/4 time of the first movement, from which it quotes motives; it changes to 3/4 time for five bars in order to refer to the third movement, but the remainder of the cadenza—and its most brilliant section—is again in 4/4 time. A cadenza which uses material from two different movements in this way is hardly what one would expect from a composer of Vivaldi's time. The first part is quoted here as it appears in the autograph (see Plate IV); Malipiero's version is not entirely trustworthy:

Ex. 170

Cadenza

---

[29] Dresden, Landesbibl., Cx. 1043.

and so on

## THE MIDDLE MOVEMENT

In the great majority of cases Vivaldi wrote his slow movements in binary form, which had long been used for dance movements and was also customary for the middle movement of the Italian overture. The viola d'amore concerto in A (no. 189; R. 396) is a characteristic example. The first section ends in the dominant and is repeated; the second begins in the relative minor of the dominant and ends with material from the first section in the tonic. This movement is often accompanied only by continuo, so that there is a further contrast of texture with the outer movements. Ritornellos, in the form in which they are found in the first and third movements, rarely occur in a middle movement. In a slow tempo such a procedure would obviously be long-winded, just as rondo form is rare in slow movements of the classical sonata. To shorten the ritornello sections would be no solution, since it would make any extended melodic development impossible. The slow movement of the cello concerto in C minor (no. 19; R. 401)[30] probably represents an early experiment made before experience had taught the composer to prefer a more concise form:

Ex. 171

### EARLY HISTORY OF THE SOLO CONCERTO

As with all forms of this kind, the origins of the solo concerto go back a long way. Two elements are to be distinguished in any study of its early history: (1) instrumentation, i.e. the contrast between a single soloist and the orchestra, (2) form, i.e. the use of a ritornello and the organization in three movements. The combination of these two elements resulted in something that was more important than either by itself.

[30] It is not impossible that Handel heard this concerto in Venice and recalled the first movement when he was writing the trio 'The flocks shall leave the mountains' in *Acis and Galatea*.

There was nothing particularly original in the use of one soloist with the orchestra, considering that in the *concerto grosso* the *concertino* did not always operate as a single unit but often allowed a pair of instruments or only one to play separately. This is clearly the result of reducing the number of upper parts in the *canzon*, which was often written for solo instruments. Solo episodes of a highly emotional character were particularly common in what was known as the *stylo phantastico*. Mattheson tells of a performance at Christian Bernhard's house in 1666, with two violins and bass viol, 'in which each player had eight bars in which to improvise'.[31] A similar example, according to Abraham Veinus,[32] is a sonata by Giovanni Valentini (1639) for violin, cornettino, bassoon, and trombone. It is clear that the violin, the technique of which was considerably enlarged by Marini, Farina, and their contemporaries, soon acquired particular importance as a solo instrument. This is shown, for instance, by a *sonata a 6* written by the Vienna Court Kapellmeister Antonio Bertali (1605–69) and dating from 1663.[33] Most significant of all was the trumpet symphony, chiefly cultivated in Bologna, with its suggestion of heroic, warlike scenes. The influence of the trumpet on violin-playing is shown by the trumpet symphonies of Perti and Torelli, where the solo trumpet plays only in the outer movements and is replaced in the more expressive slow movement, with its wider range of harmonies, by a solo violin.[34] Occasionally the solo violinist took the place of the trumpet, if necessary, throughout the whole work, as in Giovanni Bononcini's *Sinfonie 5, 6, 7 e 8 Istromenti, con alcune à una e due trombe, servendo ancora per violini . . .*, Op. 3 (Bologna, 1685). From works of this kind it was only a small step to the violin concerto.

In the ritornello the age-old idea of a recurring melody was realized anew. The idea was taken up in the early operas as a framework for monody: the ritornello form, together with the ostinato or ground bass and the *da capo* aria, became one of the principal forms of solo vocal music with instruments in the early seventeenth century. The Florentine composers preferred to adhere to the tonic when the ritornello returned, but in the later Venetian opera closely related keys were also used. In this way the older ritornello form was transformed into a kind of modulating

---

[31] *Grundlage einer Ehren-Pforte* (Hamburg, 1740; ed. Max Schneider, Berlin, 1910; reprinted 1969), s.v. 'Bernhard'.
[32] *The Concerto* (New York, 1944), p. 10.
[33] Schering, op. cit., p. 13.
[34] See the example by Torelli, ed. Felix Schroeder (Vienna and Munich, 1975).

rondo. A strikingly early example of a definite key scheme is to be found in the aria 'Son gobbo, son Demo' from Cavalli's *Giasone* (1649),[35] where the ritornello is respectively in D minor, A minor, C major, and D minor. There is also an early example of the introduction of the ritornello into instrumental music: in a *sonata a 3* by Bertali passages for individual instruments are separated by a ritornello.[36]

### TORELLI'S *CONCERTI MUSICALI*

The combination of the *concertante* principle with contrasts of instrumentation and the use of a ritornello was first effected, so far as our present knowledge of the sources goes, by the Bolognese viola-player and violinist Giuseppe Torelli (1658–1709). The work which marks this decisive step is his Op. 6, which was published at Augsburg in 1698 under the title *Concerti musicali*.[37] This series of twelve concertos clearly shows that the composer was chiefly concerned with problems of form, i.e. with the application of ritornello form to orchestral music and the key structure which goes with it. A characteristic example is no. 1,[38] a work in four movements without any soloists. In the first movement, a seven-bar ritornello:

Ex. 172

is followed by an interlude in the *concertante* style:

Ex. 173

[35] Ed. Robert Eitner, *Publikation älterer . . . Musikwerke*, xii (Leipzig, 1883), pp. 42–6. On *Giasone* generally see Vol. V, pp. 17–19.

[36] Schering, op. cit., pp. 13 ff.

[37] See Michael Talbot, 'The Concerto Allegro in the Early Eighteenth Century', *Music and Letters*, lii (1971), pp. 160–2.

[38] Ed. Kolneder (Mainz, 1958).

which modulates to the dominant and cadences in that key. Then follows the second ritornello, which is simply the last five bars of Rit. I (Ex. 172) transposed to D major. In the next interlude the first violin is not so prominent as in the first, though there is a marked contrast of rhythm between it and the rest of the orchestra:

Ex. 174

This interlude modulates to E minor and is immediately followed by Rit. III in G major, consisting this time of only bars 3 and 4 of Rit. I. The third interlude corresponds to the first:

Ex. 175

After Rit. IV (once again the last five bars of Rit. I) the movement ends with a 3½-bar coda (Adagio) introducing the rising fourth which is a feature of the second interlude (Ex. 174):

Ex. 176

What we have here is in fact the form of the solo concerto movement:

Rit. I      D major    (7 bars)
    Interlude I    G major—D major (7 bars)
Rit. II     D major    (5 bars)
    Interlude II    D major—E minor (14½ bars)
Rit. III    G major    (2 bars)
    Interlude III    G major (9½ bars)
Rit. IV     G major    (5 bars)
    Coda    G major (3½ bars)

The use of interludes for modulation and modifications of the ritornello when it recurs created a pattern which was followed in the later development of the form. It is particularly instructive to observe the shape of the first and third interludes (Exx. 173 and 175). The passages for the first violin, at a speed marked 'Presto C', make technical demands which the *ripieno* players of the orchestra would certainly have been unable to meet. One can well imagine that they were glad to leave sections of this kind to the leader, in fact that Torelli played these interludes at Ansbach himself, leaving the rest of the violins to join in at the ritornellos. It is very probable that the solo concerto had actually existed in performances of this kind long before there is any evidence for it in print. In the foreword to his Op. 8 (1709) Torelli confirms that the performance of 'solo' passages by a single player was more or less a precautionary measure:

Please notice that if you wish to play these concertos of mine the violins of the *concertino* must be *soli*, without any doubling, to avoid creating confusion. You may, however, increase the numbers of the supporting parts: in fact, this is how I want the works to be performed.[39]

(One is reminded of Leclair's delightful indication in his opera *Scylla et Glaucus* (1746): 'Pas trop vite, de peur d'une catastrophe!') How seriously Torelli was occupied with the problem of key structure at this time is shown by the second movement of Op. 6, no. 1: a chaconne on a four-bar ostinato which is so arranged that it passes through G major, D major, B minor, E minor, and G major.

The development of the solo concerto from the *concerto grosso* is shown in the first movement of another work, Op. 6, no. 12. The score expressly provides for the performance of certain passages by two solo violins and a solo viola. Since the bass to this group must have been played by a solo cello, we have in fact a

---

[39] 'Avvertendoti, che volendo sonare questi miei Concerti, è necessario, che i Violini del Concertino sijno soli, senza verun radopiamento, per evitar maggior confusione, che se poi vorrai moltiplicare gl'altri Stromenti di rinforzo, questa si è veramente la mia intentione.'

string quartet contrasted with the tutti. Only the first violin, however, has a solo part in the *concertante* style; the other soloists accompany. In the first solo section the second violin and viola merely bridge the gaps in the first violin part:

**Ex. 177**

In the second the first violin is still in command, but the others provide a fragmentary accompaniment:

**Ex. 178**

From the point of view of structure the movement is a solo concerto movement with three ritornellos and two solo sections, the
accompaniment to the soloist being provided not by the orchestra
nor wholly by the continuo but by the other solo instruments. The
instrumentation, however, has no structural significance; it is
merely a way of ensuring that the soloist, particularly if he has only
a small tone, should not be drowned by the orchestra. The third
movement of Torelli's concerto, in the form of a gigue, is quite
definitely a solo concerto movement, with a clear distinction
between solo and tutti. The two brief solo sections, one of ten bars,
the other of six, are developed from the material of the ritornello:

Ex. 179

(iii)
Solo II

In Op. 6, no. 6, the two outer movements are solo concerto move-ments in ritornello form: the first movement has the four ritornellos and the three solo sections (8, 12 and 11 bars) in the manner later favoured by Vivaldi, while the last movement has only two ritor-nellos and two solo sections (8 and 10 bars). So far as we know, this is the first genuine solo concerto ever written. Here is part of the first movement:

Ex. 180

It is curious that here the contrast between solo and tutti is clearly marked, whereas the structure of the movement is not so definite as in no. 1 of the same collection, discussed above. It will be noticed that the second solo section is a kind of free improvization on the opening figure of the ritornello.

### TORELLI IN GERMANY

The fact that the *Concerti musicali* were published at Augsburg in 1698 when Torelli was working in Germany prompted Schering to observe that the concertos 'date from the time when he was employed at Ansbach and resulted from the stimulus which he received from German music and German musicians'.[40] Biographical facts hardly support these claims. Torelli was a member of the orchestra at San Petronio, Bologna, as a *suonatore di violetta* from 1686 to 1689 and as a *suonatore di viola tenore* from 1689 to 1696 when this ensemble was disbanded. He was therefore free to accept the offer of the post of leader of the orchestra at Ansbach, made him by the Margrave Georg Friedrich, who had visited Italy in 1695; but first he went to Vienna in company with Francesco Antonio Pistocchi, who had recently been appointed Kapellmeister at Ansbach. When he did start work at Ansbach, where it was proposed to establish an Italian opera company, his activity was

---

[40] Op. cit., p. 32.

very erratic; in May 1697 he went to Berlin and in 1700 spent a considerable time in Vienna. By 1701 he was back again in Bologna, though it was not until 1703 that he was officially dismissed from his post at Ansbach. Certainly his contacts at Ansbach, and also in Vienna and Berlin, were predominantly with Italian musicians, and the works which he played and heard must have been largely those of Italian composers. It is also doubtful whether the whole of Op. 6 was written at Ansbach. It was customary at that time to publish works of the same kind in collections of twelve, under a single opus number; it is therefore reasonable to suppose that Torelli's were written over a lengthy period and that he brought at least some of them with him from Italy.

An interesting fact emerges from a reprint issued by Roger of Amsterdam in the same year. This publisher realized the importance of precisely indicating where solos were to be played. The Augsburg edition, as was usual at the time, prints the 'Note to the Reader' between the dedication and the first concerto, i.e. inside the orchestral parts; Roger, on the other hand, prints it on the title page:

I must warn you that if you find the word *solo* in any of these concertos the part must be played by a single violin. Elsewhere you may have as many as three or four instruments to a part. In this way you will discover my intentions.[41]

## ALBINONI

Two years after Torelli's *Concerti musicali* Tomaso Albinoni (1671–1751) brought out his Op. 2. This work was first published by Sala in Venice in 1700 under the title *Sinfonie e Concerti a cinque, due Violini, Alto, Tenore, Violoncello e Basso*. In this edition the concertos are orchestral concertos without soloists. A reprint was published in 1701–2 by Roger; there are only minor differences in the text, but the indications 'solo' and 'tutti' are added.[42] It might be supposed that this addition was made by Albinoni himself at Roger's suggestion, if it were not that Sala reprinted the first edition in 1707 without alteration. It is highly probable that the 'solo' and 'tutti' indications were added by Roger and that it was not until his Op. 5 (1707) that Albinoni took an

[41] 'Ti avverto, che se in qualche concerto troverai scritto solo, dovrà esser suonato da un solo Violino; Il Rimanente poi fà duplicare le parti etiamdio trè à quattro per stromento, che così scoprirai la mia intenzione.'
[42] François Lesure, *Bibliographie des Éditions Musicales publiées par Estienne Roger et Michel-Charles Le Cène (Amsterdam 1696–1743)*, (Paris, 1969), p. 57.

active part in the development of the form. Yet the Roger version of Op. 2 would not have been possible unless the structure of the pieces, at least in some of the movements, was near to that of a solo concerto. As we have seen, orchestral works were often performed as solo concertos in North Italy when there was a large orchestra and the leader had to play the more difficult sections by himself 'per evitar maggior confusione', as Torelli puts it, and Albinoni's concertos seem to have been treated in the same way. Although his own share in the development of the form was more modest than has hitherto been assumed,[43] it must not be forgotten that the Roger edition of his Op. 2 had a strong influence on the propagation of the solo concerto whenever this edition was used. It is significant that it was reprinted as early as 1709 by Walsh, Randall and Hare in London.

## JACCHINI'S CELLO CONCERTOS

The first works related to this category to appear in Italy were the *Concerti Per Camera 3 e 4 strumenti con Violoncello obligato*, Op. IV (Bologna, 1701) by Giuseppe Maria Jacchini (*c*.1663–1727), cellist in the orchestra of San Petronio. Jacchini, called by Schering the 'creator of the grand solo',[44] has always been accepted as the first composer to write cello concertos. A study of his Op. 4, however, suggests some reserves. The 'grand solos' mostly consist of only a few bars and never go higher than F sharp above middle C. There are usually three movements (quick—slow—quick), hardly any of them remarkable; occasionally there is an approximation to ritornello form, but without any definite key scheme. These works have little to recommend them, either in invention or in technique. With regard to their instrumentation it is worth noting that 'violoncello obbligato' at that time merely implied that the continuo was doubled by a cello which occasionally played an independent part. The indication 'solo' in the cello part is used for short sections, generally accompanied only by continuo, which either employ figuration or play a modest part in developing the thematic material of the movement. The contrast between solo and tutti has so little structural significance and the use made of a *concertante* style is so naïve that the works are obviously far inferior to Torelli's concerto movements of 1698. They have some importance, however, in the history of solo music, since they are the first compositions in which

---

[43] For a different view see A. J. B. Hutchings, *The Baroque Concerto* (London, 3rd, revised edition, 1973), pp. 156–64.

[44] 'Schöpfer des grossen Solos', op. cit., p. 79.

the cello has an individual part (previously it had done little more than provide the bass of a group of solo instruments). Incidentally there are no violas in these works and the violins are mostly in unison. The opening of the first movement of no. 1 is typical:

Ex. 181

This is obviously merely the embryo of a concerto movement.

### TORELLI'S LATER WORKS

Torelli's later concertos, most of which were presumably written after his return to Bologna, are of some importance for the further development of the form. They include four manuscript works in the Dresden Landesbibliothek and two in the archives of San Petronio and finally Op. 8, published in the year of the composer's death (1709) by his brother under the title *12 Concerti Grossi Con una Pastorale per il Santissimo Natale*. Nos. 7–12 of the latter work are solo concertos,[45] nos. 1–6 are concertos with two solo violins which would be more appropriately described as double concertos. Franz Giegling[46] describes the development of Torelli's work up to Op. 8 in the following terms:

When we look at the violin concertos of Op. 8 we are struck by their comparatively mature invention, particularly by the freedom of the solo sections. Compared with the scanty solo passages in some of the Op. 6 concertos, which it would be more proper to call 'ripieno concertos', the violin concertos in Torelli's last work suggest a rather too sudden advance.

He feels that there should be some clear line of development and concludes that there must have been other composers before Torelli who cultivated this form and whose works have not come to light.

It is probable that a good many of Vivaldi's concertos were written during the ten years between 1698 and 1708, though there are no dated works to prove this. His violin sonatas, Op. 1, the first Italian edition of which (now lost) must be earlier than 1703, are so mature, particularly in their form, that they cannot possibly date from his earliest years as a composer. Also the fact that his *Estro armonico*, Op. 3, was printed by Roger in 1711 suggests that he must have made a reputation as a writer of concertos long before that date. Schering's supposition that Vivaldi came on the scene in 1709,[47] though it neatly provides a line of continuity from Torelli, is certainly wrong.[48]

Torelli's Op. 8 is also of interest from the point of view of ter-

---

[45] Op. 8, no. 7 in Schering, *Geschichte der Musik in Beispielen* (Leipzig, 1931); miniature score of no. 8 ed. Ernst Praetorius (Zürich and London, 1950); Op. 8, no. 9, ed. P. Santi (Milan, 1959).

[46] *Giuseppe Torelli* (Kassel, 1949), p. 71.

[47] Op. cit., p. 84.

[48] See Kolneder, 'Das Frühschaffen Antonio Vivaldis', *Kongressbericht, Utrecht 1952* (Amsterdam, 1953), p. 254.

minology. For him the solo concerto was merely a species of *concerto grosso*, in which the concertino consisted of a single violin. Similarly Giuseppe Matteo Alberti (1685–1751) called his Op. 1 *Concerti per chiesa e per camera, à violino di concertino, due violini, alto viola e basso continuo*. Often the number of instruments is given, as here, and the solo concerto called a *concerto à cinque*, unless the work was given a simple title such as *concerto per violino*. The term *à cinque* had previously been used for a five-part ensemble consisting of two violins, alto viola, tenor viola and continuo, e.g. Artemio Motta's *Concerti à cinque* Op. 1 (1701) are purely orchestral works with two violas. Another method of reckoning was to speak of a *concerto à tre violini*, &c, i.e. a solo violin with first and second violins in the orchestra. Titles are very misleading guides; to decide what any particular work is we need to look at the music.

## THE SOLO CONCERTO IN GERMANY

We have plenty of evidence for the cultivation of the solo concerto in Germany as early as the first decade of the eighteenth century. Johann Georg Pisendel (1687–1755), who is said to have studied with Torelli in Ansbach as a boy, played a violin concerto by Torelli (probably one of the Dresden collection) with Melchior Hoffmann's *collegium musicum* in Leipzig in 1709; and on 27 February 1710 the Provost of Würzburg Cathedral, Johann Philipp Franz, Count of Schönborn, wrote to his agent in Venice, asking him 'to try and obtain some more rare compositions by Vivaldi and to despatch them as quickly as possible'.[49] Shortly after this, Vivaldi's first printed works became known in Germany and made an overwhelming impression. Quantz tells us:

At that time [1714] in Pirna I was able to see Vivaldi's violin concertos for the first time. As a quite new kind of musical piece at that time they made no little impression on me. I did not fail to acquire for myself a fair collection of them. Vivaldi's splendid ritornellos served me as a good model in later days.[50]

Vivaldi's example encouraged a great number of German composers, some of whom actually visited Venice, to write solo concertos. In addition to Pisendel and Quantz the most important were Johann David Heinichen (1683–1729), Johann Gottlieb Graun (c.1703–71), Carl Heinrich Graun (c.1704–59), Christoph

[49] Karl Heller, *Die deutsche Überlieferung der Instrumentalwerke Vivaldis* (Leipzig, 1971).
[50] In *Selbstbiographien deutscher Musiker*, ed. Kahl (Cologne, 1948), p. 112.

Graupner (1683–1760),[51] Johann Friedrich Fasch (1688–1758),[52] Conrad Friedrich Hurlebusch (c.1696–1765), Georg Philipp Telemann (1681–1767)[53] and, above all, Johann Sebastian Bach (1685–1750). All of them wrote suites and *concerti grossi* as well, which meant that all these forms had a considerable influence on each other, as we have seen in the case of certain movements of the Brandenburg concertos.[54] Telemann seems to have been not too happy about writing concertos; he attributes this to his strong susceptibility to the French style. Writing of the period which he spent in Eisenach (1706–12) he says:

Since variety is the spice of life I also tried my hand at concertos. But I must admit that I was never whole-hearted about it, though I wrote a good many of them . . . One of the reasons may be that in most of the concertos which I came across I noticed plenty of difficulties and any number of awkward leaps (*krumme Sprünge*) but little harmony and even less melody. I disliked the difficulties and the leaps as they did not suit my hand or my bow, and since the melody and harmony to which I was accustomed in French music were lacking I could not take to them, much less imitate them.[55]

In spite of this he wrote some 45 solo concertos.[56]

BACH AND THE ITALIAN STYLE

Bach's reaction to Vivaldi's concertos was very different from Telemann's: it led to a radical change of style which is clearly marked in the works written around 1720. Forkel, after telling us that as a young man Bach wrote down more or less what his fingers discovered when improvising, goes on to say:

But Bach did not long follow this course. He soon began to feel that the eternal running and leaping led to nothing; that there must be order, connection, and proportion in the thoughts; and that, to attain such objects, some kind of guide was necessary. Vivaldi's Concertos for the violin, which were then just published, served him for such a guide. He so often heard them praised as admirable compositions that he conceived the happy idea of arranging them all for his clavier. He studied the chain of the ideas, their relation to each other, the variations of the modu-

---

[51] See M. Witte, 'Die Instrumentalkonzerte von Johann Christoph Graupner 1683–1760', (Diss. Göttingen, 1963).

[52] See G. Küntzel, *Die Instrumentalkonzerte von Johann Friedrich Fasch (1688–1758)* (Frankfurt am Main, 1965).

[53] See S. Kross, *Das Instrumentalkonzert bei Georg Philipp Telemann* (Tutzing, 1969).

[54] See pp. 265 and 267.

[55] In Mattheson's *Grosse General-Bass-Schule* (1731), pp. 168 ff; printed in *Denkmäler deutscher Tonkunst*, xxviii (Leipzig, 1907; new edition, Wiesbaden and Graz, 1958), p. xiii.

[56] See Philippa Drummond, *The German Concerto: Five Eighteenth-Century Studies* (Oxford, 1980), p. 189.

lations, and many other particulars. The change necessary to be made in the ideas and passages composed for the violin, but not suitable for the clavier, taught him to think musically; so that after his labour was completed, he no longer needed to expect his ideas from his fingers, but could derive them from his own fancy.[57]

Forkel possibly overestimates Vivaldi's influence on Bach, and he is not quite accurate about his dates; but his account is based on the Bach family tradition and may very well represent what Bach told his sons. Bach was certainly very systematic in his adoption of the solo concerto form: he may have met it for the first time in 1708 when he was at Weimar, encouraged perhaps by Johann Gottfried Walther (1684–1784), who was a keen student of Italian music in the *concertante* style. Altogether Bach transcribed six concertos specially for the organ and sixteen more for keyboard instruments in general. 'Transcription' in this case meant more than mere copying: it implied actual alterations in the structure as well as the adaptation of violin figuration for the keyboard. Of these twenty-two concertos nine come from Vivaldi, one from Alessandro Marcello, one from Telemann, and five from the very talented young Duke Johann Ernst von Sachsen-Weimar (d. 1715), in whose private orchestra Bach had played for a few months in 1703. The origin of the remaining six concertos in unknown. It appears then that Bach's assimilation of the style owed something to German composers who shared his interest in the latest developments of Italian music.

It was probably in 1718, with the sixth Brandenburg concerto and the double concerto for two violins in D minor, that Bach really came to grips with the Italian style. He had recently, at the end of 1717, been appointed Court Kapellmeister at Cöthen, and this obviously encouraged him to write concertos. The following list of his works in this form also includes the many re-arrangements which he made, chiefly when he was at Leipzig and needed a good deal of *concertante* music for the *collegium musicum* of which he was at one time director:[58]

BWV
1041  Violin concerto in A minor, later arranged as harpsichord
       concerto No. 7 in G minor (BWV 1058).
1042  Violin concerto in E major, later arranged as harpsichord
       concerto No. 3 in D major (BWV 1054).

[57] From the English translation of 1820, as printed in Hans T. David and Arthur Mendel, *The Bach Reader* (New York, 1945), p. 317.
[58] BWV = Wolfgang Schmieder, *Bach-Werke-Verzeichnis* (Leipzig, 1950).

1043 Concerto for two violins in D minor, later arranged as concerto
     for two harpsichords in C minor (BWV 1062).
1044 Concerto for flute, violin and harpsichord in A minor, adapted
     from Prelude and fugue for harpsichord in A minor
     (BWV 894) and organ sonata No. 3 in D minor (BWV 527).
1052 Harpsichord concerto No. 1 in D minor, probably adapted from
     a lost violin concerto.[59]
1053 Harpsichord concerto No. 2 in E major.
1055 Harpsichord concerto No. 4 in A major, probably adapted from
     a lost violin concerto.
1056 Harpsichord concerto No. 5 in F minor, probably adapted from a
     lost violin concerto.
1057 Harpsichord concerto No. 6 in F major, arranged from the fourth
     Brandenburg concerto (BWV 1049).
1060 Concerto for two harpsichords in C minor, probably adapted
     from a lost concerto for two violins (or violin and oboe).
1061 Concerto for two harpsichords in C major.[60]
1063 Concerto for three harpsichords in D minor, probably adapted
     from a triple concerto by another composer.
1064 Concerto for three harpsichords in C major, probably adapted
     from a triple concerto by another composer.
1065 Concerto for four harpsichords in A minor, adapted from
     Vivaldi's concerto for four violins in B minor (Op. 3, No. 10).

BWV 1063 and 1064 should probably be omitted from this list,
since there is no certainty that the adaptations are by Bach, and
BWV 1065 should properly be described as Vivaldi-Bach, though it
rarely appears so in concert programmes.

### BACH AND THE CONCERTO FORM

In his concertos, Bach is faithful to the pattern established by
Vivaldi but develops it in a way which illustrates vividly his extraordinary capacity for absorbing the influence of other composers.[61]
The first movement of the violin concerto in A minor (BWV 1041)
is a good example of his art of transformation:

**Ex. 182**
(i)

Ritornello

[59] It has been reconstructed as a violin concerto by W. Fischer in vol. vii/2 (Supplement)
of the *Neue Bach-Ausgabe* (Kassel, 1970); similarly BWV 1055 (for oboe d'amore),
BWV 1056 (for violin), BWV 1060 (for violin and oboe), BWV 1064 (for three violins).

[60] It seems likely that this work was originally written without orchestra, since only the
harpsichord parts exist in Bach's autograph.

[61] See H.-G. Klein, *Der Einfluss der vivaldischen Konzertform im Instrumentalwerk
Johann Sebastian Bach* in *Collection d'étudés musicologiques*, liv (Strasbourg, 1970).

From bar 32 onwards the orchestra plays a significant part in developing the initial fragment of the ritornello. We have already noticed isolated examples of this treatment of a solo section in Vivaldi, but it now becomes a typical method of combining solo and tutti. The ritornello (marked *f*) begins again at bar 39 but at the same time the solo violin continues its figuration. Similar instances occur at bars 51, 101, 122, and 142. The contrast between tutti and solo—the fundamental principle of the form—is here largely abandoned. Some writers have spoken of Bach's 'dissolution' of concerto form, but the term has a flavour of depreciation. Considering his masterly treatment of his material it would be nearer the truth to speak of a further development or the ultimate perfection of the form. At the same time it would be a mistake to suppose that Bach was the sole inventor of this kind of treatment. Though he may not have known the works of Vivaldi which are the most significant in this respect (see Ex. 166–9), he did make a keyboard transcription in C major (BWV 976) of Vivaldi's Op. 3, no. 12 (see pp. 330–1) and so had an excellent opportunity of studying Vivaldi's technique of development.

Bach not only transformed the relationship between solo sections and ritornello; he also gave a new shape to the concerto movement as a whole. A familiar example in tenary form is the first movement of the violin concerto in E major (BWV 1042), which is divided into three quite distinct sections:

A    Bars 1–52
B    Bars 53–122
A    Bars 123–74
(*da capo*)

The opening ritornello (slightly decorated by the soloist in bars 4 and 5) lasts for eleven bars. The remainder of section A is a combined development for solo and orchestra, which is actually nothing but a twofold repetition of the ritornello, though with a good deal of elaboration and variation. The orchestra provides the basic material, while the soloist so to speak improvises above it. The scheme of this section is as follows:

Ritornello, main statement: bars 1–11—orchestra—E major
Ritornello, 1st variation: bars 12–34—solo and orchestra—E major to
    B major
Ritornello, 2nd variation: bars 35–52—solo and orchestra—E major

The technique employed in varying the ritornello may be seen by comparison of bars 1–3 with bars 35–42:

Ex. 183

Section B affords a contrast of tonality to section A by starting in C sharp minor (bar 53) and modulating to F sharp minor (bar 95) and G sharp minor (bar 107). The whole of this 70-bar section is a large-scale development of the basic material. Whenever new material appears it is in the form of a counterpoint to the ritornello motive, e.g. bars 95–7:

Ex. 184

The Adagio cadenza at the end of this section helps to emphasize the fact that bars 123–74 are a recapitulation.

The movement as a whole is a high point which was equalled only by Bach himself. Though it starts on the basis of ritornello form, the ritornello is not merely the framework for a series of solo sections but actually provides the thematic material for the whole movement. The ternary form is derived from the *da capo* aria,

while the development of the middle section looks forward to the
practice of the classical period. The last movement of the concerto
illustrates the close connection between the solo concerto movement and the rondo. There is a clear distinction between solo and
tutti. Only the orchestra plays the ritornello (which does not
modulate). Of the four solo sections the first is accompanied by the
continuo, the others by the orchestra.

### THE KEYBOARD CONCERTO

Bach also played an important part in the development of the
keyboard concerto. Heinrich Besseler[62] maintained that the fifth
Brandenburg concerto was the first concerto to use the harpsichord
as a solo instrument. It is worth remembering, however, that
Handel had used the organ as a solo instrument in a 'sonata' in
ritornello form in the cantata *Il trionfo del tempo* (1707), with two
oboes, two violins and cello as additional solo instruments: the
work is partly a *concerto grosso*, partly a solo concerto.[63] Handel
also used the harpsichord as a solo instrument before Bach did,
e.g. in the aria 'Vo' far guerra'[64] in *Rinaldo* (1711) and again in
*Teseo* (1712). It was only natural that other composers who sat,
like Handel, at the harpsichord should have provided themselves
with solos. Minor German composers who wrote keyboard concertos—some of them even before Bach—included Johann Paul
Kunzen (1696–1757), Johann Mattäus Leffloth (1705–31),[65] and
Michael Scheuenstuhl (1705–70). They were all surpassed by Carl
Philipp Emanuel Bach (1714–88) who wrote his first harpsichord
concerto in 1733 when he was still being taught by his father. In his
extant keyboard concertos—forty-five for one harpsichord, and one
for two harpsichords, and one for harpsichord and fortepiano—he
developed new types of structure and new forms of expression:
these in turn had a strong influence on his younger brother, Johann
Christian (1735–82), who in his numerous concertos written in
London completed the transition to the form of the classical
concerto.[66]

[62] Besseler, ed., *Sechs Brandenburgischen Konzerte: Kritischer Bericht*, Neue Bach-
*Ausgabe*, vii/2 (Kassel, 1956).
[63] Ed. Chrysander, *The Works of George Frederic Handel*, xxiv, p. 33.
[64] Printed in *Arie dell' Opera di Rinaldo* (London, 1711) with the heading: 'With the
Harpsichord peice (*sic*) perform'd by Mr. Hendel': see Chrysander, op. cit., xlviii, p. 206,
and lviii, p. 117. The autograph score merely has the indication 'Cembalo' where the solos
should occur.
[65] D major concerto ed. H. Ruf (Nagels Musik-Archiv, no. 184).
[66] For a discussion of the concertos of C. P. E. Bach and J. C. Bach see Vol. VII,
pp. 453 ff and 483–5.

OTHER MEANS OF CONTRAST

It was the custom in keyboard concertos for the soloists to play continuo in tutti passages, and this practice survived for a considerable time; solo parts were still provided with a figured bass as late as Beethoven's Op. 15. The reason for this was that the soloist generally directed the performance. If there was no orchestra available a soloist could even perform a complete concerto by himself, by playing the tuttis from the score. The Swedish composer Johan Joachim Agrell (1701–65) says of one of his concertos: 'Tal maniera di poterlo suonare anche a cembalo solo senza di altri stromenti'.[67] When Bach wrote his Italian Concerto, where the contrast between tutti and solo sections is represented by a thinner texture and appropriate dynamics, he was following a practice he had already adopted in arranging the works of other composers. It is worth noting here that the form of a solo concerto was often used in works where no contrast between solo and tutti was possible. In the *Concertini* for cello and continuo by Matteo Zocarini both the ritornellos and the solo sections are played by the cellist. Vivaldi wrote a number of chamber works (trios and quartets)[68] in which the first movement is in solo concerto form ingeniously adapted to the resources employed. In works such as Telemann's *Concerto à 4 Violini Senza Basso*, where the four violins have approximately an equal share in developing the material in the manner of a *concerto grosso*, the ritornello disappears completely, so that there is no contrast between solo and tutti. On the harpsichord and organ such a contrast could be represented by a change of manuals or of registration. The advice on registration given by Michel Corrette (1709–95) in his *Concerti a sei stromenti, cimbalo o organo*, Op. 26, should be taken to apply not merely to continuo-playing but to the performance of organ transcriptions of concertos and original compositions in the ritornello form: 'Allegros should be played on the full organ, Adagios on the flutes, and Solos on the Swell cornet'.[69]

The abundance of players at German courts had the result that German composers (e.g. Heinichen, Graupner, and Quantz) showed a certain preference for wind concertos. This has led to the widespread view that the Italians were a nation of string-players, the Germans of wind-players. Quite apart from the numerous

[67] 'It is possible to play it also as a harpsichord solo with no other instruments.'
[68] Nos. 39, 149, 144, 23, 103, 41; Ryom 92, 91, 94, 103, 105, 106.
[69] 'Sur l'Orgue il faut toucher les Allegro sur le grand jeu, les Adagio sur les Flûtes, et les Solo sur le Cornet de Recit.'

works written for the trumpet in Venice and Bologna, a mere glance at the list of Vivaldi's wind concertos should be sufficient to show that this view is mistaken. Of his extant concertos thirteen are for flute, one for two flutes, three for *flautino*, nineteen for oboe, three for two oboes, thirty-seven for bassoon, one for trumpet, and two for two trumpets, in addition to works in which wind instruments form part of a mixed *concertino*.[70]

### QUANTZ ON THE CONCERTO

The popularity of the solo concerto and its intensive cultivation by composers and players is reflected in the literature of the time, particularly in Germany. It produced a 'theory of the concerto' which, so far from being theoretical, was so practical that sometimes it virtually offers recipes for the manufacture of works of this kind. The most thorough discussion of the concerto is to be found in Quantz, who on the strength of his 300-odd flute concertos was well qualified to speak on the subject. He begins by saying:[71]

A *concerto grosso* consists of a combination of various solo instruments, with two or more instruments (sometimes increased to as many as eight or even more) playing together. In a chamber concerto, on the other hand, there is only one solo instrument.§30

He continues:

A serious concerto, i.e. a solo piece with orchestral accompaniment, should have in the first movement: (1) an imposing ritornello, with good part-writing for all the instruments; . . . (4) The best ideas of the ritornello may be split up and combined with the solo sections or played between them . . . (6) One should not write more middle parts than is compatible with the solo part . . . . (7) The movement of the bass and middle parts should neither interfere with the agility of the solo nor drown or suppress it. (8) One must observe due proportion in the length of the ritornello, which should consist of at least two main sections. The second section, since it will be repeated at the end of the movement and so bring it to a conclusion, must have the finest and most imposing ideas . . . (10) Some of the solo writing must be in a *cantabile* style, but it must not all be caressing: there must also be from time to time melodic and harmonic figuration which is brilliant but yet suited to the instrument; and to keep the fire burning brightly right up to the end there must be at intervals short, lively and imposing tutti sections. (11) The *concertante* or solo sections should not be too short, on the other hand the tutti in the middle of the movement should not be too long . . . (17) Finally, in the last tutti, the Allegro should end as briefly as possible with the second section of the first ritornello. §33 . . .

---

[70] Talbot, *Vivaldi* (London, 1978), p. 138.
[71] *Versuch einer Anweisung*, pp. 294 ff.

The Adagio must be quite distinct from the first Allegro—in the way the ideas are put together (*im musikalischen Reimgebäude*), in time and in key. If the Allegro is in one of the major keys, e.g. C major, the Adagio may be written, as you will, in C minor, E minor, A minor, F major, G major or even G minor. But if the Allegro is in one of the minor keys, e.g. C minor, the Adagio may be written in E flat major, F minor, G minor or A flat major. These successions of keys are the most natural.§35

The Adagio offers more opportunity to arouse and calm the passions than the Allegro does.§36

The final Allegro of a concerto must be very different from the first movement, not only in its whole character but also in time . . . The three movements of a concerto must never all be in the same time . . . Though the last movement is in the same key as the first, one should take care when modulating that changes of key do not follow each other so closely as in the first movement, so as to avoid too much similarity.§38 . . .

In order to get the proportions right in a concerto it is useful to look at one's watch. If the first movement takes five minutes, the Adagio five to six, and the last movement three to four, the concerto is the right length. It is better that the listeners should find a piece too short rather than too long.§40

With regard to performance Quantz observes that improvised ornamentation (*Diminution*) is strictly forbidden in the ritornello; it is exclusively reserved for the soloist.

The immense number of concertos that were being written inevitably led to a certain falling off in quality, particularly as the general public was very much inclined to prefer technical tricks and cheap effects from the soloist to solid musical values. The new profession of travelling virtuosos was soon invaded by charlatans, who were ready to offer anything that would create a sensation. At Frankfurt on 9 December 1739 there was advertised a 'concerto for a special kind of jew's harp, with other instruments, composed by Herr Telemann'. Earlier than this, in 1727, also at Frankfurt, a recital was given by a virtuoso who could 'play first and second horn parts, i.e. high and low, at the same time on two horns with ordinary mouthpieces' and promised the public 'the most difficult leaps, runs, *chasses*, solos, overtures, concertos', &c.

## THE SOLO CONCERTO IN FRANCE

The French objection to Italian music, on aesthetic grounds, was particularly strong in the case of the concerto. Rousseau, in his *Dictionnaire de musique* equates 'vocal' with 'natural', and 'instrumental' with 'artificial'. Pure instrumental music seemed tolerable only in opera or ballet, where it could serve the needs of dramatic expression or provide an accompaniment to mime. The concerto was considered an inferior kind of music—mere note-spinning: this is implied by a remark of Pileur d'Apligny: 'It is not enough for the musician to know perfectly the rules of melody and harmony. If Nature has not made him a poet at birth, he will never be able to write anything but good concertos.'[72] It was presumably as a result of the *Affektenlehre*,[73] which had been given a new lease of life by French ballet music, that these ideas also found their way into Germany. J. G. Sulzer considers that 'the concerto has strictly speaking no definite character, since no one can say what it is meant to represent or what the composer is aiming at. It is basically nothing but an exercise for composers and players and a completely vague and unprofitable means of giving pleasure to the ear.'[74]

It is indicative of French taste that the set of violin concertos entitled *I stagioni* (The Seasons) should have been the most popular of Vivaldi's works in France. They were imitated in Germany by Christoph Graupner (1683–1760) with his harpsichord concertos *Die vier Jahreszeiten* (1733), and the idea was carried further by Josephus Gregorius Werner (1695–1776), *Kapellmeister* at Eisenstadt, who wrote a *Musikalischer Instrumental-Kalender . . . in die zwölff Jahres-Monate eingetheilet* (Calendar for musical instruments, divided into the twelve months of the year), which must have been known to Haydn. The first French concertos of any importance appeared relatively late,[75] viz. the Op. 7 (1737) and Op. 10 (1745) of Jean-Marie Leclair (1697–1764), both entitled *Six Concerto a tre Violini, Alto e Basso per Organo e Violoncello*; the composer has a note on Op. 7, no. 3, saying: 'The solos can be played on the German flute or the oboe'. Leclair's work was founded on Italian violin technique which he had learned from his teacher, Giovanni Battista Somis (1686–1763) in Turin; but he was also quick to seize on the innovations of Tartini and Locatelli and develop them further. In this way he became the founder of the great French school of violin-playing. Like other French composers he delighted in *cantabile* melodies, with an abundance of ornaments borrowed from the harpsichord. His form is clearly modelled on Vivaldi's; the concertos are in three movements (quick—slow—quick), and in Allegro movements he prefers a clear distinction between solo sections and ritornellos to any combined develop-

---

[72] *Traité sur la Musique* (Paris, 1779).
[73] Stylized musical representation of codified emotions.
[74] *Allgemeine Theorie der schönen Künste* (Leipzig, 1771–4), article, 'Concerto'.
[75] See J. R. Anthony, *French Baroque Music* (London, 1973), pp. 303–8.

ment of their material. His activity as soloist and composer played an important part in establishing an independent school of French instrumental music. It is true that Jacques Aubert (1689–1753) had already claimed that his Op. 17 (1774)[76] was 'the first work of this kind to come from the pen of a Frenchman'; but these pieces are very modest in invention and part-writing and do little to exploit the possibilities of violin technique. Also, like so many other works of the time, they stand midway between the *concerto grosso* and the solo concerto. Although the title, *Concerto a quatre violons violoncelle et Basse continue*, implies two solo violins, the first violin is much more prominent than the second, which for long stretches merely doubles the first *ripieno* violin. The works of the distinguished violinist Louis-Gabriel Guillemain (1705–70) are on similar lines: *Six concertinos à quatre parties* were published in 1740 as Op. 7; another concerto for four violins and bass survives in manuscript.[77] Aubert, in an announcement in the *Mercure de France*, probably written by himself, explained with charming candour the principles which he had followed in his *Première Suite de Concerts de Symphonies pour les violons, flûtes et hautbois*[78] (1730):

Although Italian concertos have for several years enjoyed some success in France, where justice has been done to all the excellent works of this kind that have been written by Corelli, Vivaldi and others, yet it has been noticed that this music, in spite of the skill shown by some of its interpreters, is not to everybody's taste—particularly the ladies', whose judgment has always determined the amusements of this country . . . It is for this reason that M. Aubert has decided to try his hand at a form of music which is not only more pleasant to the ear but also within the reach of students of moderate ability . . . It has been the author's intention to combine liveliness and gaiety with what we call French melodies.

Three years before Aubert the remarkably prolific Joseph Bodin de Boismortier (1689–1755) had published his Op. 15, 'contenant six concerts pour cinq flûtes traversières ou autres instrumens sans basse', and had drawn attention to their novelty by adding 'ce qui n'avait pas encor été imaginé'. These works already show the adoption of the Italian three-movement form, and from Op. 21 (*Six concerts pour les flûtes traversières, violons ou hautbois, avec la basse*) onwards we find a close approach to ritornello form, though in the French manner this was treated rather as a *rondeau*, with the

[76] H. Brofsky, 'Notes on the Early French Concerto', *Journal of the American Musicological Society*, xix (1966), p. 89.

[77] Agen, Archives Départementales de Lot-et-Garonne.

[78] i.e. orchestral symphonies.

solo sections serving as episodes. Later the wind concerto, particularly the concerto for transverse flute and strings, played an important role in France. Composers who wrote works of this kind included Michel Blavet (1700–68), Pierre-Gabriel Buffardin (c.1690–1768), Michel Corrette (1709–95) and Jacques-Christophe Naudot (c.1690–1762).

Boismortier, Aubert and Leclair had laid such solid foundations that everything was ready for the emergence of genuinely French concertos, particularly for the violin. The works of Jean-Pierre Guignon (1702–74), Michel Corrette, Jean-Baptiste Cupis de Camargo (1711–88), and others show many signs of an inclination to a rococo art of expression. Their concertos, even more than Leclair's, point so strongly towards the early classical form, that only the influence of the Mannheim composers was needed to produce the new type of concerto which had such a pronounced effect on the work of Mozart and Beethoven. French composers generally made a distinction between *concerto*, meaning a type of composition or a form, and *consert* or *concert*, meaning an ensemble or an organization. Until the middle of the century *concert* is used in titles of compositions almost exclusively in the sense of 'ensemble'. Rameau's *Pièces de clavecin en concerts, avec un violon, ou une flûte et une viole ou un violon* (1741) are perfectly defined by their title.

## THE KEYBOARD CONCERTO IN ENGLAND

In England Corelli's immense reputation aroused an enthusiasm for the *concerto grosso* which at first was unfavourable to the cultivation of the solo concerto or to the production of works of this kind by native composers. However, under the influence of Handel, who sometimes used the harpsichord as a solo instrument in his operas and the organ in his oratorios,[79] both keyboard instruments became popular with the public as solo instruments in concertos. Since the English organs of that period, with the exception of the one in St. Paul's Cathedral, had no pedals, scarcely any difference was made in the style of writing for organ and harpsichord, particularly as harpsichord mannerisms had crept into organ music from Italy. Handel's organ concertos (six in Op. 4, six in Op. 7, and four others) appeared in contemporary editions as 'for harpsichord or organ' with a view to attracting a wider circle of purchasers and facilitating performance by amateurs. Handel's

---

[79] See above, pp. 37–8, 45, 55–6.

example was followed by English composers,[80] e.g. William Felton (1715–69), who published no fewer than thirty-two concertos for harpsichord or organ (Op. 1, Op. 2, Op. 4, Op. 5, and Op. 7) between 1744 and 1760. Italian composers living in England, such as Giuseppe Sammartini (1695–1750), helped to satisfy the demand; *G. St Martini's concertos for the harpsichord or organ with the instrumental parts for violins*, Op. 9, were published in 1754. Up to the time when Johann Christian Bach appeared as a composer of keyboard concertos (by that time usually 'for the harpsichord or fortepiano') there are extant as many as three hundred English concertos for keyboard instruments, with an orchestra generally restricted—no doubt for practical reasons—to two violins and bass. As with Handel, great importance was attached to improvised cadenzas: there are many places where even in the course of a movement the solo part is not written out.

## THE ITALIAN SOLO CONCERTO AFTER VIVALDI

It is curious that, so far as concertos are concerned, Torelli and Vivaldi did not have as marked an influence on their successors in Italy as they did in Germany. The reason is probably that so many of Corelli's pupils were active, both as violinists and as composers, and these maintained the Corelli tradition in their playing and in their attitude to the concerto right up to the middle of the eighteenth century. Quite often the new solo concerto form was not adopted as it stood; what usually happened was that individual features of the solo concerto found their way into the *sonata da chiesa* and the instrumentation of the *concerto grosso*. *Concerti grossi* were written in which the first violin of the *concertino* is so much the dominant partner that the works are in fact solo concertos, at least in some of the movements. On the other hand, in many works that are called *concerti* there is hardly any resemblance to the structure of a solo concerto, in spite of the inclusion of a part for solo violin. Titles do not always tell us precisely what kind of work we are dealing with. From the title one would assume that Alessandro Scarlatti's *VI Concertos in seven parts, for Two Violins & Violoncello obligato with two Violins more, a Tenor & Thorough Bass*[81] were *concerti grossi*. In fact, nos. 1, 2, 4, and 5 are Italian overtures with occasional solo passages and cadenzas, no. 3 is a solo concerto, and only no. 6 is a true *concerto grosso*.

---

[80] C. L. Cudworth, 'The English Organ Concerto', *The Score*, viii (1953), 51–60.
[81] Published under this title in England (1740).

Albinoni's twelve *Concerti a cinque*, Op. 5, are overtures with occasional use of a solo violin rather than real concertos. On the other hand Francesco Manfredini (1684–1762) calls his Op. 3 (Bologna, 1718) *Concerti a due Violini e Basso continuo obligati*, though the collection includes four solo concertos, four concertos for two violins, and only four works which are actually *concerti grossi*.

The result of giving prominence to the first solo violin in a *concerto grosso* can be seen in a set of *Concerti grossi à quattro e sei strumenti*, Op. 7, by Giuseppe Valentini (*c*.1680–after 1759). It is clear from no. 9 of the set that the composer did not expect the orchestra to be particularly large, since he describes the work as 'à sei con quattro Violini obligati, potendosi raddopiare tutte le parti de piace'. The vague terminology of the time is also reflected in the *Concerti per Chiesa e per Camera*, Op. 1 (Bologna, 1713), of Giuseppe Matteo Alberti (1685–1751). The title, which must have sounded old-fashioned at the time, conceals the fact that these are solo concertos of the Vivaldi type. Among the works made up of movements of different kinds, and so standing midway between the solo concerto, the *concerto ripieno* and the *concerto grosso*, are the *Concerti a quattro*, Op. 6 (1709) by Luigi Taglietti (1668–1715), and the *Concerti a quattro, Due violini, alto viola e basso, con violino di rinforzo*, Op. 11, by Francesco Antonio Bonporti (1672–1749), as well as the orchestral works of Evaristo Felice Dall'Abaco (1675–1742)[82] and Giuseppe Brescianello (*c*.1690–1758).

This alternation between various forms in a single work, which is also common in Handel, is not a sign of immaturity. If it seems so to us today, that is because the concerto as a form has been firmly established in concert programmes for nearly two hundred years. In the early eighteenth century all orchestral music—whether solo concerto, *concerto grosso*, *concerto ripieno*, suite, *sinfonia* or French overture—was predominantly *concertante* music and was closely associated with the many occasions for public performance offered by contemporary society. It was needed for the overture and entr'actes in opera and oratorio, it was introduced into Mass and Vespers in a similar way, it was required at banquets, serenades and domestic music, and little distinction was made between the various forms. Works which did not belong to any one form of orchestral music must have been more useful for these different

---

[82] Selected works by Dall'Abaco, ed. Sandberger, *Derkmäler der Tonkunst in Bayern*, i and ix(1) (Leipzig, 1900 and 1908).

purposes than those which adhered to a regular pattern.

Of all the numerous Italian composers who wrote concertos, both in Italy and abroad, Pietro Antonio Locatelli had a particularly important influence on the development of the form.[83] Born at Bergamo in 1695, he became one of the greatest virtuosos of his time. After extensive concert tours as a soloist he finally settled in Amsterdam, where he died in 1764. His twelve violin concertos, Op. 3, were published there in 1733 under the title *L'arte del Violino*. The concertos are followed by an appendix of twenty-four *Capricci ad libitum*, consisting of two cadenzas for each concerto, which became standard works for the study of violin technique in the eighteenth century. Rousseau, in his *Dictionnaire de musique* says, 'Today Locatelli's caprices give our violin-players something to work at'. The reason was that they demanded a technical standard far in advance of anything that Vivaldi had asked for, e.g.:

Ex. 185

[83] On Locatelli, see also Vol. VII, p. 441. The best study is Albert Dunning, *Pietro Antonio Locatelli: Der Virtuose und seine Welt* (Buren, 1982).

The whole future development of violin-playing from Tartini, through the French school, right down to Paganini owes an enormous debt to Locatelli. His concertos are much more worthwhile, musically speaking, than the caprices.[84] The principal movements are in ritornello form, the ritornello as a rule being stated four times. Before the final ritornello a caprice is meant to be inserted in place of a solo episode. The prevailing key scheme is tonic—dominant—tonic—tonic, so that the basic structure is ternary, as sometimes happens in Bach.[85]

### TARTINI AND HIS SCHOOL

Locatelli's principal service, both as player and as composer, was to develop the technique of the violin and to enhance its reputation as a solo instrument. It was Giuseppe Tartini who transformed the concerto by releasing it from adherence to current ideals of expression and form. Born in 1692 at Pirano (Istria), he became one of the leading players of his time through his appointment as solo violin at the cathedral of San Antonio, Padua, in 1721. He went to Prague in 1723 to play in Fux's opera *Costanza e fortezza* and remained there for three years in the service of Count Kinsky. In 1726 he returned to Padua and in spite of very favourable offers from England and France remained at his post until his death in 1770. His profound influence on the development of violin-playing was to a large extent due to his private music school, where his pupils not only studied the violin but could also, if they wished, learn counterpoint and composition. Tartini had a great gift for

[84] On his concertos generally see Hutchings, op. cit., pp. 336–42.
[85] See pp. 360–1.

teaching and devoted himself to it with an energy which was indifferent to financial gain. In consequence pupils from all over Europe flocked to his school and he became known as *Maestro delle nazioni*. When in the 70's Leopold Mozart, Charles Burney and other notable travellers visited the main musical centres of Europe they frequently found pupils of Tartini as leaders of orchestras and were able to admire in them the style of playing they had learned from their master.

Tartini's contact with Venice played a significant part in his early development as a composer. There is evidence that this contact was maintained during the time when he was studying law at the University in Padua and subsequently when he became a solo violinist. He was originally attracted by Vivaldi's conception of ritornello form, but very soon developed a markedly different style of his own. A tutti opening like this:[86]

Ex. 186

is built up of two-bar phrases in a way which suggests the early classical style and shows how large a part Tartini took in shaping that style. It is remarkable that this concerto was published as early as 1728 in a collection issued by Michel Charles Le Cène in Amsterdam, incidentally without the composer's permission—a detail which throws some light on publishing in the eighteenth century. Le Cène acquired these works from people who had received copies from Tartini. The title of the collection runs:

Sei Concerti a cinque e sei stromenti a Violino principale, Violino Primo di Ripieno, Violino secondo, alto Viola, Organo e Violoncello, del Signor

---

[86] Minos Dounias, *Die Violinkonzerte Giuseppe Tartinis als Ausdruck einer Künstlerpersönlichkeit und einer Kulturepoche* (Wolfenbüttel and Berlin, 1935), p. 66.

G. Tartini di Padoua. Opera prima, libro primo, Raccolti da me. Amsterdam. Michel Charles Le Cène. No. 536.

In these early concertos Tartini's personal style emerges only in details: the overall impression is that the texture is still modelled on Vivaldi's and the ideas on Corelli's. But towards the middle of the century there is a distinct increase in the use of early classical features, which leads to a complete change of style. Burney says: 'He changed his style in 1744, from extreme difficult, to graceful and expressive'.[87] Dounias, however, has shown that this change occurred as early as 1735:[88] it is therefore closely related to the development that led to the early classical symphony. Openings like the following[89] are typical of the new idiom:

Ex. 187

This *cantabile* Allegro shows Tartini's inclination to vocal expression, which had even more scope in Adagios. 'Many of his adagios', says Burney, 'want nothing but words to be excellent pathetic opera songs'.[90] This close relationship between words and music shows clearly how instrumental music was becoming subject to a form of emotional expression inspired by poetry. Abbate Fanzago[91] relates that before Tartini began a composition he used to read 'some passages from the most passionate poets in order to stimulate his imagination and inspire his soul'. Individual movements are prefaced by lines from Metastasio and other poets, and often Tartini actually writes the beginning of a movement to a text and then goes on to develop the music in the spirit of the poetry, e.g.:[92]

[87] *A General History of Music*, iii (London, 1789), p. 563.
[88] See Vol. VII, p. 442.
[89] Dounias, op. cit., p. 109.
[90] Op. cit., p. 566.
[91] *Elogi di Giuseppe Tartini* (Padua, 1792).
[92] Dounias, op. cit., p. 132.

Ex. 188

Se tutti i ma - li miei io ti po - tes - si dir, di -
- vi - der - ti fa - rei per te - ne - rez - za il cor

With the change in expression came also a change in form. The importance assigned to the key of the dominant, to which reference has already been made, led in Tartini's case to a type of structure which is very near to the formal scheme of the early classical symphony. After the introductory tutti the first solo section (a rudimentary 'second subject') follows in the dominant and the exposition is repeated. After a tutti which develops the thematic material there is a recapitulation of the first solo section (now in the tonic), followed by a sort of coda for the orchestra.

Contrast of expression between ritornello and solo is mentioned by Quantz[93] as one of the many possibilities which should be used only in certain circumstances: 'If the opening idea of the ritornello is not *cantabile* or not quite suitable for the solo, one must introduce a new idea and join it to the other in such a way that no one can tell whether this has been done from necessity or with deliberate intention.' Tartini does not seem consciously to have used this contrast as a structural principle, as the classical composers did. It does occur in some of his works, but his general practice is to have a thematic connection with the ritornello, particularly in the case of the first solo.

Tartini's work as a whole, which exerted a very strong influence on composers writing concertos between the time of Vivaldi and Bach on the one hand and Mozart on the other, occupies an intermediary position. He not only abandoned the current forms of expression; the concertos of his maturity also abandon the form of the earlier solo concerto. When Leopold Mozart wrote his *Violinschule* (1756) he included examples from Tartini but none from Vivaldi—an implication of the extent to which Tartini's senti-

[93] Op. cit., p. 296.

mental, rococo style had driven out the older style. Yet in his old age Tartini had no use for the early works of the classical period which came into Italy from Austria and South Germany. Burney, writing in 1789, was compelled to admit that Tartini's music, so highly esteemed when the early classical style was first emerging, was already regarded as old-fashioned. 'Boccherini, Haydn, Pleyel, Vanhal, and others' were the stars of the new age.[94]

---

[94] Op. cit., p. 567.

# VI

## CONCERTED CHAMBER MUSIC

*By* ERNST H. MEYER

MUSIC FOR THE INDIVIDUAL LISTENER

TOWARDS the middle of the seventeenth century instrumental ensemble music in Europe served a variety of purposes. There was still a great deal of activity in both Catholic and Protestant churches, and in municipal bands. Yet the general tendency in instrumental music at that time was to move away from those services in town and church, which in form and function often bore a resemblance to the medieval guilds, towards the court, theatre, and concert hall with the more brilliant forms associated with them. Amateur music still held its own, but the social status of the amateur was undergoing important changes in all countries, in varying forms and degrees.

More and more closely the composer's creative work became directed to the individual listener, chiefly the middle-class visitor to musical performances. The listener felt that the music was written for him, to express his thoughts and emotions. Subjective elements grew more and more important in later seventeenth-century music, in the same measure as the middle-class mind and philosophy became a vital force in the economic and political make-up of the different countries. The growth of commerce and industry was in most cases the direct cause of the rise of such undertakings as the public concerts organised by Banister and Britton in England, or by Hacquart in Holland. These started in a small way but grew quickly in scope and size.

The new individualist attitude to music completely revolutionized all forms of music, including court and chamber music. On the one hand, with the increase in number of both the concert public and the performers, the first signs appeared of a final split between orchestral and chamber music. Many instrumental works of the second half of the seventeenth century, it is true, could still be played either by single or by massed instruments. However, during the course of this century more and more music was actually based on the alternation of *soli* and *tutti*, thus preparing the way for numerous *concerto* forms. There appeared a gradually increasing number of pieces with indications such as Buxtehude's *Sonata con molti violini all' unisono* (Lübeck, 1705). In opera music, particularly in France and Italy, doubling of single instrumental parts had become a common feature, the way having been led by Monteverdi's *Orfeo*. This development was helped by the tremendous increase in the scope and quantity of music performed at some European courts, with the Paris court of Louis XIV ahead of all the others. In England this movement had already started in performances of masques earlier in the century; but only during Charles II's reign did music begin to be composed specially for larger forces.

On the other hand, the opposite development took place in what was to become genuine chamber music. In non-orchestral music the number of instrumental parts decreased. Teams of two, three, or four replaced the eight- and twelve-part combinations of the Gabrieli era. This tendency was strongest in Italy, France, and England, while in Central Europe chamber music for larger numbers of instrumental parts still flourished up to about 1685. By 1700 solos, duos, and trios constituted by far the greater part of chamber music everywhere. The single parts in these forms, used more and more as solos, are the expression of all the exciting and varied life in late seventeenth-century music. Solo parts became a standard feature in orchestral music too, not only in the *concerti* that appeared towards 1700, but in many other symphonic forms as well. The virtuoso's display of his artistic proficiency (one of the new features arising out of both court function and public concert) was one reason for this development; the demand for subjective, individual and expressive playing was another.

### THE FORMS AND STYLES OF 'ABSTRACT' MUSIC

The general trend in instrumental music was to move away from 'functional' music towards what is now somewhat misleadingly called 'abstract' music, i.e. music which is primarily heard for pleasure, excitement, and emotional enrichment, but not for the fulfilment of non-musical purposes as had been the case in church music. With this change in musical practice came a re-shuffling of forms and styles. This again gradually affected the whole of Europe, even though national differences played an ever-increasing part in shaping the character of instrumental music.

Some of the more conspicuous changes may be outlined here.

First of all, musical works grew in length: individual movements as much as groups of movements such as sonatas and *sinfonie*. It was something new for the composer to be completely free to plan the size and length of a work. In church music, in music at court, in that of the town-band, in music for the theatre, in instrumental music in opera and even in the functional dance, the length was generally determined by factors outside the composer's control. This was changed under the influence of the public concert where the listening appetite of audiences increased, and with it the composer's freedom to spin out his ideas and conceive more extensive and far-reaching forms. There are works such as a *Sonata a 5 parties* (1660) by the German composer Gerhard Diessener[1] which takes more than seventeen minutes to perform.

Another change is visible in formal structure. The public performance of music no doubt led to the emergence of the A-B-A scheme during the second half of the seventeenth century. Nonfunctional music, presented to listeners for pleasurable enrichment of the mind, had to have a much more clearly defined character and emotional quality, whether this was expressed in the jubilant major, e.g. this excerpt from a trio sonata by Alessandro Stradella,[2] *c*.1680:

Ex. 189

[1] See E. H. Meyer, 'Gerhard Diessener', *Zeitschrift für Musikwissenschaft*, xvi (1933–4), p. 405.
[2] Brit. Lib., R.M. 23.f.10.

or the 'tragic' minor as in the *Lamento a 4* by Pierre Verdier (1627–1706)[3] *c*.1680:

Ex. 190

Each instrumental piece had to have some clear-cut original feature of its own, whether in melody, rhythm, harmony, tone-colour, or mood. To define this new quality a piece of music needed as one of its chief requirements a convincing beginning and a convincing end.

The A-B-A principle was rarely found in the sixteenth century. Yet it appeared increasingly often in the first half of the seventeenth, especially in vocal music, and gradually permeated most musical forms as the year 1700 approached. It occurred either in the form of a repeat (a literal *da capo*) or in the form of a restatement at the end of the essential features of the opening part, or again in the vaguer form of a juxtaposition of general types of movements such as Allegro-Adagio-Allegro. In any one of these forms the A-B-A scheme could apply to whole sonatas, to individual movements, or only to parts of movements. Largely based on this formula, the consolidation of certain forms made rapid progress. Distinct types of movement developed, originating in certain countries but soon accepted everywhere.

### METHODS OF UNIFICATION

If the *da capo* principle is an expression of a stricter desire to organize a composition thoroughly, so too are other types of tech-

---

[3] Uppsala, Univ. Bibl., CAPS 9:7.

nique which developed vigorously during the second half of the seventeenth century. In particular, attempts were made to unify a piece of music by thematic reference: a figure recurring several times during the composition. This technique had already been employed by Giovanni Gabrieli (*Canzon a 8 primi toni*) and Monteverdi (*Sonata sopra 'Sancta Maria'*), but it was used much more systematically and frequently later in the century. In a *Sonata a 5 (c.1691)*[4] by Johann Theile (1646–1724) the five movements are built on a variety of themes all traceable to the same basic subject. In Rosenmüller's *Sonata VIII a 4*,[5] consisting of Grave-Allegro-Adagio-Allegro-Adagio-Allegro-Adagio-Allegro, several movements are based on similar or identical thematic material as in the earlier dance-suites of Peuerl and Schein:[6]

Ex. 191

[4] *Organum*, iii, 19 (Leipzig, 1929).
[5] From *Sonate a 2. 3. 4. e 5. stromenti* (Nuremberg, 1682); modern ed. by E. Pätzold (Berlin, 1954–5).
[6] See Vol. IV, pp. 594–5.

(cf. main motives in 5 & 6)

Sometimes movements are held together by unity of technical treatment. Giovanni Battista Vitali (1632–92) in a Sonata a 4 (Bologna, 1669) uses the same canonic technique in all six sections of the piece, which are very different in character yet are kept together by this artifice:

Ex. 192

Yet another method of unifying a work was the grouping of the various movements or sections in distinctive patterns. One sonata by Clemens Thieme (1631–68)[7] consists of movements or sections arranged in the order A-B-C-D-A-B'. Calculated and reasoned structure is often allied to strongly emotional expression, especially among German composers. Unification through contrast was also a favourite seventeenth-century technique. The popularity of this element, far from diminishing, increased in all this music after the beginning of the seventeenth century. The dramatic power of juxtaposition of movements is notable in many works by David Pohle, Gerhard Diessener, and others.

One important factor in this formative period of chamber music was that between 1650 and 1700 dance music became largely absorbed by 'free' (non-dance) music. Suites of dances continued to exist after 1650, but it became more and more the rule to introduce them by 'free' movements, or even to intersperse the two types. The French led the way in this development, to be followed by the Germans and the English. On the other hand dance movements were incorporated in 'free' sonatas and sinfonias. Some composers regularly introduced certain types of dance in their works. Towards 1700 many dance forms, it is true, were still danced to; but wherever they became stylized, the functional differences that had existed at the time when the sonata was divided into *sonata da chiesa* and *sonata da camera* gradually disappeared. The suite of the second half of the seventeenth century was, in fact, basically different from that of the first half. The later suite was much more distinguished and elegant, intended for court or concert performance and no longer merely for dancing. Everything seems to have been drawn into the magic circle of concert music.

If a widening of forms in general has been observed, it is equally significant that single movements also grew considerably. In sonatas, *sinfonie* and concertos the tendency was to concentrate on three or four main and comparatively long movements. Several works consisted of only one extensive movement—a feature which occurred in particular in late seventeenth-century German music. Such movements were sometimes sets of variations, but they might be cast in any other form.

[7] Kassel Landesbibl., Mus. fol. 60 p². See Hans-Joachim Buch, 'Bestandsaufnahme der Kompositionen Clemens Thiemes', *Die Musikforschung*, xvi (1963), particularly p. 369.

### THE FUGAL ELEMENT

Fugue was approached more and more closely. General *fugato* was a technique employed frequently in instrumental ensemble music, especially in opening movements. Themes in 'fugues' or 'fugato' were often composed of corresponding periods, *a* and *b*. This was achieved either within the theme, e.g. in a Sonata a 4 in C major (1654)[8] by Vincenzo Albrici (1631–96):

Ex. 193

or by making the theme itself appear as *a* (*dux*) and the counter-subject as *b*, e.g. in Johann Rosenmüller's Sonata no. 7, a 4 in D minor (Nuremberg, 1682):[9]

Ex. 194

Easy, expressive and singable phrases made up most of the melodic material.

Development after the theme had been stated was quite free. Nevertheless cadences were quite strict; indeed most of them can be reduced to a few basic formulas which were common to seventeenth-century instrumental music of all countries, e.g.:

Ex. 195

---

[8] Uppsala, Univ. Bibl., 1654.
[9] Ed. E. Pätzold (Berlin, 1954–6).

Ex. 196

By 1650 the following melodic structure had become very common: thematic lead—sequences—cadence, e.g. in Rosenmüller's sonata no. 5 a 3 (1682):

Ex. 197

This basic scheme of melody building[10] first developed fully in Italy; however, during the second half of the seventeenth century it became the common property of the music of all nations. Until the time of Bach and Handel, and even later, it remained the basis of instrumental part-writing; in fact, the development of classical symphony and sonata borrowed important elements from this seventeenth-century technique. Arising from it, fugue in its stricter and ultimate meaning appeared quite clearly in some German compositions round about 1670 and 1680, at first without episodes but soon also with them. Fugues could either be parts of sonatas, symphonies, etc., or else complete and independent pieces.

### MELODIC AND HARMONIC STYLE

Together with this consolidation of the technique of contrapuntal composition went a new general instrumental *cantabile* style. We find fiery and expressive melodies full of subjective meaning:

[10] Cf. Wilhelm Fischer, 'Zur Entwicklungsgeschichte des Wiener klassischen Stils', *Studien zur Musikwissenschaft*, iii (1915), p. 24.

Ex. 198 — Matthew Locke, *A Martial Jigge*, from *The Tempest* (London, 1675)

Ex. 199 — Gottfried Finger, *Playhouse Tunes* (London, *c.* 1690)

Ex. 200 — Benedictus a Sancto Josepho, *Orpheus Elianus*, Sonata a 3, No. 5 (Amsterdam, *c.* 1695)

Ex. 201 — Carolus Hacquart, *Harmonia Parnassia*, Sonata a 3, No. 7 (Utrecht, 1686)

Simultaneously thematic invention became very varied. Instrumental figuration was abundant and personal initiative had free play. Towards 1700 melodies were almost everywhere constructed on harmonic bases. In particular the bass line underwent a complete transformation. Semi-ostinato basses, e.g.:

Ex. 202

became common, most of all in the trio sonata, which by this time was the main form of chamber music; ostinato in the strict sense (chaconne, passacaglia) also occurred frequently. In no. 7 of Heinrich Biber's *Sonatae tam aris quam aulis servientes* (1676) three out of four movements are chaconnes.

Harmonic content underwent further changes. Harmonic effects were used for emotional expression, especially the flattened sixth in a major key, e.g. by the Belgian, Carolus Hacquart (*c*.1640–before 1708), in the sonata already quoted in Ex. 201:

Ex. 203

or Giuseppe Torelli (1650–1709), Sinfonia a 4 (Bologna, 1687):[11]

Ex. 204

Sharply dissonant sevenths served for expressive characterization, e.g. Gerhard Diessener's already mentioned Sonata a 5 (1660):[12]

Ex. 205

[11] Foreshadowing his writing in a later concerto (cf. Ex. 174).
[12] Kassel, Landesbibl., Ms. fol. 60 W.

'Dominant' sevenths appeared more and more frequently, e.g.
Francesco Cavalli (1602–76), Canzon a 5 (1656):[13]

Ex. 206

or Johann Wilhelm Furchheim (*c.*1634–82) Sonata a 5 (*c.*1680):[14]

Ex. 207

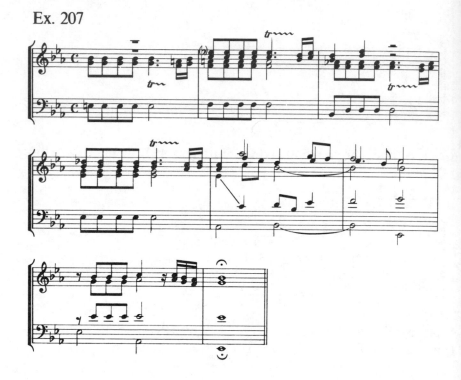

All these changes in practice, style, and form affected instrumental
ensemble music in every European country. Yet special national
developments continued to be of great importance.

ITALY

  During the middle of the seventeenth century Italy still led in the
development of large instrumental forms and of the modern instrumental melody. It is an indication of the degree to which solo

[13] *Musiche sacre* (Venice, 1656).
[14] Uppsala, Univ. Bibl.

melody—fiery or sweetly expressive, excited or restful, tragic or humorous—had gained the upper hand that music for ensembles larger than three instruments became less and less common towards the end of the century. At the same time an ever-increasing number of solos, duos and trios found their way to the printing press:

| *Solos, duos and trios*[15] | *Ensembles larger than three* |
|---|---|
| 1645 Bertali | |
| Uccellini | |
| Pesenti | |
| 1648 Cazzati | Cazzati |
| 1649 Ferro, Uccellini | Ferro, Filippi, Marini |
| 1650 Todeschini, Falconieri | |
| 1651 Merula | Neri |
| 1652 Leoni | |
| 1655 Legrenzi, Gandini | Marini |
| 1656 Cazzati | Cavalli |
| 1657 Giamberti, Carlo Grossi | |
| 1658 Cazzati | Cazzati |
| 1660 R. Mealli (two), Cazzati | |
| 1662 Cazzati | |
| 1663 Legrenzi | Legrenzi |
| 1664 | Fra Sisto Reina |
| 1665 Arresti, Medico, Prioli | |
| 1666 Prattichista, S.B. Vitali, G.M. Bononcini | |
| 1667 Vitali, Uccellini (two) Pistocchi, G.M. Bononcini | Cazzati, Uccellini (two), Placuzzi, G.M. Bononcini, Vitali (two) |
| 1668 Vitali, Colombi, Giuseppe Allegri | Uccellini |
| 1669 Uccellini (two), Cazzati, Vitali, Pizzoni, G.M. Bononcini | Uccellini, S.B. Vitali, Battiferri G.M. Bononcini |
| 1670 Cazzati | |
| 1671 G.M. Bononcini, Piocchi, Legrenzi, Pietro degli Antoni | G.M. Bononcini, Legrenzi |
| 1672 G.M. Bononcini | |
| 1673 Viviani, Guerrieri, Polaroli, Colombi, Bonaventura, G.M. Bononcini, Legrenzi | Guerreri, Penna, Legrenzi |
| 1674 Colombi, Mazzaferrata, Natale | |
| 1675 Piochi, G.M. Bononcini, C. Grossi | G.M. Bononcini |

[15] Most of the items given here are in the Bologna libraries or in Modena. To this list of printed material may be added many manuscripts by Albrici, Bertali, Poglietti, the Bononcinis, Gabrielli, Melani, Steffani, Stradella, Ziani, and others. (Several are mentioned later in this chapter).

| | |
|---|---|
| 1676 Colombi, Pietro degli Antoni | |
| 1677 Cazzati, Bassani, Legrenzi | Cazzati |
| 1678 Mainerio, Mazzaferrata, | P.A. Ziani |
| Bassani, G.M. Bononcini, | |
| Viviani | |
| 1679 A. Grossi, Pasino | Pasino |
| 1680 Silvani | |
| 1681 Piazzi, Motta, Natale | |
| 1682 Manelli, A. Grossi, Albergati, | A. Grossi, Legrenzi |
| Legrenzi | |
| 1683 Albergati, Vitali, Steffani, | |
| Corelli, A. Ziani, Bassani, | |
| Gaspardini, Albertino | |
| 1684 Gabrieli, G.M. Bononcini | Vitali |
| 1685 G.B. Bononcini, Corelli, | G.B. Bononcini, Vitali, Fedeli |
| Fedeli, Albergati, A. Grossi | |
| 1686 Torelli (two), P. degli Antoni, | |
| Monari | |
| 1687 Marino, Albergati, G.M. | Taglietti, Torelli |
| Bononcini, Viviani, | |
| Mazzolini, Taglietti, Torelli | |
| 1688 Borri, P. degli Antoni, | |
| Mazzaferrata, Bassani | |
| 1689 Mazella, Colombi, Zanetti, | |
| Gigli, Corelli, Vitali, Gabrielli | |
| 1691 Laurenti, Belisi, Vannini, | |
| Vitali, Baldassini | |
| 1692 Veracini, B. Bernardi, | Torelli |
| Tocrini, Marino, Vitali, | |
| Boccaletti | |
| 1693 Buoni, Viviani, Albisi, Vitali, | Isabella Leonarda, Brevi |
| Brevi | |
| 1694 Albinoni, Corelli | |
| 1695 Castro, Ariosti (two) | |
| 1696 Taglietti, Migali, Bernardi, | |
| Veracini, Marino | |
| 1697 Avitrano, Bianchi, Jacchini | |
| 1698 Bernabei, Pegolotti | Torelli, Gregori |
| 1699—1700 Fiorè, Baldassini, Caldara | Albinoni, Jacchini |

## VENICE

Venice was the most important place for instrumental music immediately after 1650, with Massimiliano Neri,[16] Gaspare Filippi,[17] Agostino Guerrieri,[18] Pietro Andrea Ziani,[19] Pier

---

[16] *Sonata e Canzone a 2–4*, Op. 1 (Breslau, 1644). *Sonate da sonarsi a 3–12*, Op. 2 (ibid., 1651).
[17] *Musiche* (with nine sonatas a 3–5) (ibid., 1649).
[18] *Sonate a 1–4 violini* (Bologna, 1673).
[19] *Sonate a 3–6* (Freiberg, c.1667).

Francesco Cavalli,[20] and especially Giovanni Legrenzi[21] as the main representatives. Here in this city of opera the influence of vocal music on instrumental was strongest. It worked in two ways. For one thing the expressive *cantabile* style advanced rapidly in instrumental composition; for another, the instrumental works of Venetian composers showed an inclination towards operatic posturing and showmanship—in church sonatas no less than in chamber suites and symphonies. The percentage of large ensembles in mid-seventeenth-century Venice was greater than elsewhere. Yet even in music for more than three parts the influence of the *sonata a tre* grew, as is shown, for instance, by the splitting-up of six-part ensembles into double trios such as are found in works by Legrenzi. Similarly there is a growing number of sonatas and suites for four to eight instruments in which two violins have the chief melodic material, while the middle parts are degraded to mere accompaniment. The bass part is generally very lively, both in trio sonatas and in duos for a treble and a bass instrument, of which there are a large number between 1650 and 1700.

To achieve a full, sonorous sound is one of the main requirements in all this music. Grandiose orchestral chord effects are found frequently, e.g. the conclusion of a Sinfonia a 8 by Neri (1615?–66), in his Op. 2 (Venice, 1651):

Ex. 208

---

[20] *Musiche sacre* (with six sonatas a 3–12) (Venice, 1656).
[21] *Sonate a 2–3*, Op. 2 (ibid., 1655); *Sonate a 2–6*, Op. 8 (ibid., 1663); *Sonate a 2–4*, Op. 10 (Bologna, 1673).

In late seventeenth-century Italy we do not find the intense struggle for form which is characteristic of German music of that time. In the shaping of the three- and four-movement structure Italian composers were far in advance. Often there are three main allegro movements which are connected by short adagio interludes. Four-movement schemes often consist of Adagio—Allegro fugato—Adagio—Allegro fugato. This scheme had already existed in sonatas by Salamone Rossi in 1607 and 1608.[22] Sometimes after 1650 the four movements are Allegro fugato—Adagio—Allegro fugato—dance movement (preferably a gigue) or a free homophonic movement. With apparent ease and logic Italian composers rid themselves of the multitude of sections found in the so-called 'patchwork' *canzona* of 1600,[23] and worked out three- and four-movement schemes. The *fugato* emerges as the standard type of movement. From Corelli's time onward composers were able to reap the fruit of this straight line of development; they built on a firm and secure tradition of musical form. As to the distinction between *sonata da chiesa* and *sonata de camera*, the observer is struck by the indifference with which after 1670 these ostensibly opposite functions were treated by most Italian composers. *Sonate da camera* and *da chiesa* appear together in the same collections, e.g. those by Mario Uccellini (1667),[24] Maurizio Cazzati (1669),[25] Giovanni Maria Bononcini (the elder) (1675),[26] Giovanni Bonaventura Viviani (1678),[27] and others, and dance movements

[22] See above, and Vol. IV, pp. 575–6.
[23] Ibid., pp. 576–7.
[24] *Sinfonici Concerti*, Op. 9 (Venice, 1667).
[25] *Suonate da chiesa e da camera* (also entitled *Varii, e diversi cappricci*), Op. 50 (Bologna, 1669).
[26] *Trattenimenti musicali* (Bologna, 1675), and see n. 38 below.
[27] *Capricci armonici da chiesa e da camera* (Venice and Rome, 1678).

MVSICK.

*Although the Cannon, and the Churlish Drum—
Haue strooke the Quire mute, and the Organs Dumb:
Yet Musicks Art with Ayre and String, and Voyce
Makes glad the Sad, and Sorrow to Reioyce.*

I.  MUSICK
Frontispiece to John Playford's *Select Ayres and Dialogues* (1659)

II.   FROM BLOW'S 'DIALOGUE BETWEEN DIVES AND ABRAHAM'
Published in Henry Playford's *Harmonia Sacra* (1688)

III. COLLEGIUM MUSICUM

From *Musicalischer Arien Erster Theil* (Stralsund, 1647)

IV.   VIVALDI: VIOLIN CADENZA
From the Concerto in D (1712) (Dresden, Landesbibliothek Cx. 1043)

V.   EARLY 18TH-CENTURY GERMAN VIOLINIST
From Johann Christoph Weigel's *Musicalisches Theatrum* (Nuremberg, *c.*1722)

VI. PURCELL'S *LESSONS FOR THE HARPSICHORD* (1696)
(i) *Above*, 'Rules for Graces'; (ii) *Below*, Saraband from the Second Suite

VII.   HARPSICHORDIST OF BACH'S TIME
From Johann Christoph Weigel's *Musicalisches Theatrum* (Nuremberg, *c.*1722)

VIII. ABENDMUSIK

The Jena Collegium Musicum (1744) (watercolour by an unknown artist)

are lightly interspersed among the same types of free movements that are found in *sonate da chiesa*.

## BOLOGNA

After this second heyday of Venetian instrumental music the main activity in this field took place in Bologna (1665–90). Cazzati's work[28] was of decisive importance in that town, and it was followed, imitated and further elaborated by his pupil Giovanni Battista Vitali[29] as well as by Domenico Gabrielli,[30] Petronio Franceschini,[31] Andrea Giosti,[32] Giuseppe Torelli,[33] Giulio Taglietti,[34] and several others. At San Petronio in Bologna, chief centre of instrumental music, this art was not practised on the same scale as at San Marco in Venice. Ensembles rarely exceeded five instruments and they consisted mostly of strings. This music is, on the whole, more elaborate and more in the nature of chamber music than that of the Venetian composers. It is full of delicate artistry, and altogether more stress is laid on detail, unlike the theatrical character of Venetian sonatas. Yet it was the aim of the Bolognese, just as much as of the rest of the Italian schools, to achieve richness, liveliness, and fullness of sound. As a means of building up these qualities *fugato* subjects often had strong and individual countersubjects, e.g. Ziani, Sonata a 5:[35]

[28] *Corenti e Balletti*, Op. 4 (Antwerp, 1651); *Il secondo Libro delle Sonate a 1–4*, Op. 8 (Venice, 1648); *Correnti e Balletti*, Op. 15 (Venice, 1654); *Suonate a tre*, Op. 18 (Bologna, 1656); *Trattenimento per camera*, Op. 22 (Bologna, 1660); *Correnti e Balletti*, Op. 30 (Bologna, 1662); *Sonate a 2–5*, Op. 35 (Bologna, 1665); *Varii e diversi capricci*, Op. 50 (Bologna, 1669); *Sonate a 2*, Op. 55 (Bologna, 1670).

[29] *Correnti, e Balletti da Camera* for two violins and continuo, Op. 1, (Bologna, 1666); *12 Sonate* for two violins and continuo, Op. 2 (Bologna, 1667); *Balletti, Correnti alla francese . . . e Sinfonie da Camera a 4*, Op. 3, (Bologna, 1667); *Balletti, correnti, gighi . . .*, Op. 4 (Bologna, 1668); *Sonate a 2–5 stromenti*, Op. 5 (Bologna, 1669); *Balletti, correnti e capricci a 3*, Op. 8 (Modena, 1683); *Varie Suonate a 6*, Op. 11 (Modena, 1684); *Balli in stile francese a 5*, Op. 12 (Modena, 1685); *Artifici musicali*, Op. 13 (Modena, 1689); *Suonate da camera a tre*, Op. 14 (Modena, 1692).

[30] *Balli, Gighe, Correnti, Alemande, e Sarabande*, Op. 1 (Bologna, 1684); *Ricercari p. violoncello solo*, &c., 1689 (MS., Modena); 6 sonatas a 5–6 (MS., Bologna, San Petronio); *Concerto a 4 viol.* (MS., ibid.).

[31] *Sonata a 7*, 1680 (MS., Bologna), ed. E. H. Tarr (London, 1968).

[32] *Sonate a 3*, Op. 1 (Bologna, 1686); *Sinfonie a 2–4*, Op. 3 (Bologna, 1687); *Sinfonie e Concerti*, Op. 5, 1690 (Bologna, 1692).

[33] *Sonate a 3*, Op. 1 (Bologna, 1686); *Concerti da camera a 3*, Op. 2 (Bologna, 1686); *Sinfonie a 2–4*, Op. 3 (Bologna, 1687); *Concertino per camera*, Op. 4 (Bologna, 1690); *Sinfonie a 3, Concerti a 4*, Op. 5 (Bologna, 1692); *Concerti musicali a 4*, Op. 6 (Augsburg, 1698), *12 Concerti* (Bologna, 1709).

[34] *Sonate da Camera a 3* (Bologna, 1695).

[35] *Sonate a 3–6*, Op. 7 (from the second ed., Venice, 1678; first pub., Freiburg, *c*.1667).

Ex. 209

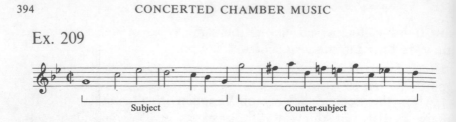

The same dualism appears in freer movements, e.g. Stradella, Sonata a 3 (*c*.1675):[36]

Ex. 210

There are also *fugato* subjects which themselves have several motives, e.g. Cavalli, Canzon a 4 (1656):

Ex. 211

or Legrenzi, Sonata a 6 (1663):

Ex. 212

However, we have here nothing like a return to true polyphony but rather an extension of the *concertante* principle. The ensemble as a whole is conceived primarily in harmonic terms.

36 Brit. Lib., R.M. 23.f.10.

## MODENA

Another school of composers grew up gradually in Modena, where instrumental music was practised not so much in the churches as in the ducal palace of the Este family. Music here was intended for aristocratic listeners and for the well-to-do intelligentsia, who were often well educated in music. A number of these experienced amateurs took part in the performance of the music. Many of the works of the principal composers—Giuseppe Colombi,[37] Giovanni Maria Bononcini,[38] Fra Sisto Reina,[39] Giuseppe Jacchini,[40] Angelo Maria Fiorè,[41] Marco Uccellini,[42] and others, and after 1674 also Giovanni Battista Vitali[43]—show distinct signs of advanced virtuosity, e.g. Uccellini, *La gran Battaglia* (1669):[44]

Ex. 213

[37] *Sinfonie da Camera a 3*, Op. 1 (Bologna, 1668); *La Lira armonica*, Op. 2 (Bologna, 1673); *Balli, Corrente, Gighe &c. a 3*, Op. 3 (Bologna, 1674); *Sonate a 3*, Op. 4 (Bologna, 1676); *Sonata da Camera a 3*, Op. 5 (Bologna, 1689).

[38] *Primi Frutti . . .* (two violins and continuo), Op. 1 (Venice, 1666); *Sonate da Camera e da Ballo a 1–4*, Op. 2 (Venice, 1667); *Varii Fiori . . . overo Sonate da Camera a 2–4 & Basso continuo*, Op. 3 (Bologna, 1669); *Arie, Correnti, Sarabanda a 2* (Violini & violoncello), Op. 4 (Bologna, 1671) and ed. M. Abbado (Milan, 1968); *Sinfonie, Allemande, Correnti e Sarabande a 5–6*, Op. 5 (Bologna, 1671); *Sonate da Chiesa a 3*, Op. 6 (Venice, 1672); *Ariette, Correnti, Gighe, Allemande e Sarabande a 2–4*, Op. 7 (Bologna, 1673); *Trattenimenti Musicali a 3–4*, Op. 9 (Bologna, 1675); *Arie e Correnti a 3*, Op. 12 (Bologna, 1678).

[39] *La Danza delle Voci* (including 1 sonata and 1 *sinfonia* for four violins & continuo) (Venice, 1664).

[40] *Concerti per Camera*, Op. 3 (for violin and cello) (Modena, 1697).

[41] *Trattenimenti da camera* (Lucca, 1698).

[42] *Sonate, Sinfonie e Correnti a 2–4* (Venice, 1639); *Sonate, Correnti, Arie a 1–3*, Op. 4 (Venice, 1645); *Sinfonie i Concerti, &c, a 1–4 per chiesa e camera*, Op. 9 (Venice, 1667); *Sonate, overo Canzoni* (for violin & continuo), Op. 5 (Venice, 1649); *Compositione armoniche a 4–7*, lib 7 (Antwerp, 1668); *Sinfonie Boscareccie a 1 o 3*, Op. 8, (Antwerp, 1669).

[43] See p. 393 n. 29.

[44] From Op. 8.

This is chamber music demanding a well-developed technique, and it is not, on the whole, orchestral. Problems of form or of polyphony are of secondary importance: emphasis is laid on the technique of playing and on effective harmony and tonality. There are many passages in the Modenese works like the following from a sonata by Uccellini (1667):

Ex. 214

After 1675 other centres gained a certain importance, for instance Florence and Rome as well as Venice, where instrumental music was published by Pompeio Natale,[45] Carlo Manelli,[46] Ludovico Baldassini,[47] Antonio Veracini,[48] and Giovanni

[45] *Libro 2 de solfeggiamenti per cantare e suonare* (for flute, violin, cello, &c.) (Rome. 1681).
[46] *Sonate a 3*, Op. 2 (Rome, 1682).
[47] *Sonate a 3*, Op. 1 (Rome. 1691).
[48] *Sonate a 2 violini, violone, arciliuto & basso continuo*, Op. 1 (Florence, 1692).

Buonaventura Viviani.[49] Rome, too, was where Corelli's sonatas were written. (The history of Naples as another centre of great significance for instrumental music belongs to the eighteenth century.) An interesting branch of instrumental group music, practised in Bologna, Modena and elsewhere between 1670 and 1690, is the trumpet sonata and *sinfonia*. Pietro Andrea Ziani,[50] Petronio Franceschini,[51] Domenico Gabrielli,[52] Giuseppe Torelli,[53] Giovanni Battista Bononcini,[54] Cazzati[55] and others wrote trumpet solos and duos which virtually amount to concertos for the instrument, accompanied or opposed by a body of strings. In this field, which is far more than a sideline in the history of Italian music, great artistry was shown. There is no trace of polyphony here; everything points to the style of the solo concerto or the *concerto grosso*.

## CORELLI'S TRIO SONATAS

The trio sonatas of Arcangelo Corelli (1653–1713)—*Sonate da chiesa*, Op. 1 (Rome, 1681) and Op. 3 (Rome, 1689), *Sonate da camera*, Op. 2 (Rome, 1685) and Op. 4 (Rome, 1694)—represent the form in its classic perfection. The impression these works made on his contemporaries may be gathered from the large number of editions published not only in Italy but in Holland, England, France, and Germany. Corelli was proud of his education in Bologna and described himself on the title-pages of Opp. 1, 2 and 3 as 'da Fusignano', his birthplace, 'detto il Bolognese'. He had a considerable reputation as a performer, but the evidence seems to suggest that this was due more to the beauty of his playing than to outstanding virtuosity. It is perhaps significant that his music makes fewer demands on the performers than the works of some of his contemporaries.

The *Sonate da chiesa* (with organ continuo) follow a fairly consistent pattern. The majority are in four movements, alternately slow and fast; and even when this pattern is varied there is a clear differentiation between adjacent movements. The harmony is pre-

---

[49] *Suonate a 3*, Op. 1 (Venice, 1673).
[50] A suonate a 6 with trumpet is in Oxford, Chr. Ch. Ms. 771.
[51] A sonata a 7 for two trumpets and strings (1680) (Bologna, Archivio di S. Petronio), has been ed. E. H. Tarr (London, 1968).
[52] Six sonatas a 5–6 (Bologna, Archivio di S. Petronio); no. 2, ed. Tarr, idem.
[53] Works for trumpets and strings in various printed collections in Brit. Lib., together with works by Bartolomeo Bernardi, Vivaldi, and others.
[54] In *Sinfonie a 5–8*, Op. 3 (Bologna, 1685).
[55] See Don L. Smithers, *The Music and History of the Baroque Trumpet before 1721* (London, 1973), pp. 245 ff. for locations of all these works.

dominantly diatonic, its progression clear and logical. Throughout
the music is kept alive by a contrapuntal treatment which ensures
the individuality of each of the string instruments employed. This is
equally true of fast and slow movements. The following Adagio
from Sonata VII of Op. 3 is typical in its basic simplicity and clear-
cut lines:

Ex. 215

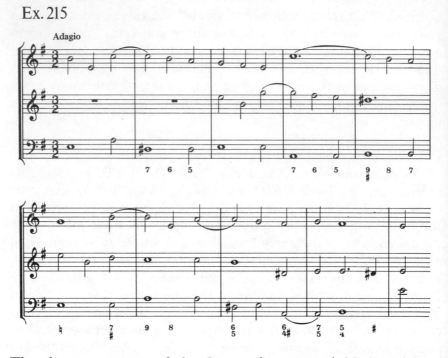

The dance structure of the *Sonate da camera* (with harpsichord
continuo) imposes on the whole a more homophonic texture. But
here too the individual lines emerge distinctly and there are incidental examples of imitation. The Allemanda from Sonata V of
Op. 4, with its athletic bass, is characteristic:

Ex. 216

Corelli's sonatas may not be among the supreme examples of chamber music, but their fertile invention and impeccable craftsmanship command respect.

### CHANGES IN TERMINOLOGY

During the last twenty years of the seventeenth century several terms relating to form assumed new meanings.[56] Up to 1680 there had often been little difference between pieces called concerto, sonata, or sinfonia. (There are also *divertimenti* such as Ariosti's pieces of 1695 and *trattenimenti* as in Bononcini's publication of 1685.) After 1680 'concerto' always means a work in which the distinctive feature throughout its whole length is the juxtaposition of solo (or soli) and tutti.

The concerto as an independent form gradually grew out of the sonata between 1650 and 1680. Alessandro Stradella seems to have been the first to write introductory instrumental pieces in the form of the *concerto grosso*.[57] Jacchini,[58] Gregori, Torelli, and Corelli used the same form and mostly the same name as well. Yet, as has appeared on several occasions during this survey and in Chap. III,

---

[56] See above, p. 186.

[57] See p. 215.

[58] Three *sinfonie* in the form and character of the *concerto grosso* are in Bologna, San Petronio.

elements of the concerto and concerto grosso developed long before the time of Stradella and his successors. Neither was the evolution of this important form confined to Italy—Germany's part in it was of considerable importance, even though the Italians were ahead of their German colleagues in this field, as indeed in so many others. Yet only in the works of Stradella and Torelli did the concerto principle become 'legalized', as it were. The virtuoso solo part countered by the orchestral *tutti* or *ripieni* is in fact the final consequence of Giovanni Gabrieli's principle of playing off different groups of instruments against each other. Thus the concerto took over the tradition of the old ensemble sonata for four and more parts.

Among the great Italians who spread abroad the musical achievements of their country, in Germany, France, England, and elsewhere, were such men as Steffani, Bernabei, Cavalli, and Corelli. Yet after 1700 other countries continued to raise all types of orchestral and chamber music to unexpected heights. Slowly but surely this change in the European scene was prepared for during the seventeenth century by an intensification of musical practice and composition in those other countries which had been learning so much from the Italians.

### AUSTRIA

Italian music had its most marked effect abroad on the Austrian courts; in fact, the imperial chapels of Ferdinand III and Leopold I enabled many a great Italian musician to thrive. A large part of the importance of Vienna in the seventeenth century was due to the fact that it served as an 'entry port' to Central Europe for Italian music. Austrian music has always had a certain international flavour, and at no time more than in the late seventeenth century.

Among Italians working for the Viennese Court either temporarily or permanently were such leading composers as Antonio Bertali (or Bartoli), Mario Antonio Ferro, Giovanni Felice Sances, Marc Antonio Cesti, Alessandro Poglietti, Pietro Andrea Ziani, and Antonio Draghi. Others, such as Francesco Cavalli and later Antonio Maria Bononcini, devoted at least part of their creative work to the musical life of Vienna. All types of Italian styles were practised there, although the Venetian prevailed. Large-scale sonatas, serenades and masques were the commonest; these pieces were written almost entirely for the Court. Particularly in Leopold's time, the Court made it possible for musicians to build up musical life to a very high standard, especially since Leopold was himself a skilled performer and composer. However, music for use at Court did not necessarily mean only music for display or imperial entertainment, although a great deal was written *pro tabula*, to entertain the Emperor and his guests. Such great collections of major instrumental works as Heinrich Ignaz Franz von Biber's *Sonatae tam aris quam aulis servientes* (Salzburg, 1676) and *Fidicinium sacroprofanum* (Zürich, 1680), or Johann Heinrich Schmelzer's *Sacroprofanus Concentus* (Nuremberg, 1662) are proof that composers by no means relied only on imperial commissions to stimulate their imagination. Yet by its very nature Leopold's Court called more often for orchestral than for chamber music. There was also a great variety in the choice of instruments; among many other combinations a sonata by Schmelzer for seven recorders[59] deserves particular mention.

The most significant composers of ensemble instrumental music in Austria in the late seventeenth century were Schmelzer (*c*.1623–80), Biber (1644–1704), Bertali (1605–69), Poglietti (d. 1683), Johann Caspar Kerll (1627–93), Melchior d'Ardespin (1643–1717), Ferdinand Tobias Richter (1649–1711), and Georg Muffat (1645–1704, of Scottish origin).[60] In the works of Schmelzer in particular one can see the influence of two musical worlds, Italian and German, with Vienna as the connecting link. This combination of elements from two different cultures created the soil from which the Viennese classics sprang. Though the Viennese composers of the seventeenth century contributed much to the popularization of Italian music in Germany, they were in turn influenced by German elements of style. In a Sonata a 4 by Schmelzer,[61] for example, we find the kind of string team-work that is more common in the north. A busy viola passage, introduced as a solo:

Ex. 217

is in turn imitated by all the other instruments. After the fourth entry solo passages appear again, changing from instrument to instrument, yet becoming shorter and shorter until all the parts join together and end in an intricate *concertante*:

[59] Uppsala, Univ. Bibl.; ed. Ernst H. Meyer (London, 1948).
[60] For Muffat's sonatas, which are virtually concertos, see pp. 206 ff.
[61] Oxford, Bodl. MS. Mus. Sch. C. 44, fols. 24–34.

Ex. 218

## BOHEMIA AND MORAVIA

There was yet another influence in Austrian (and German) music: that of the Slav countries. The importance of Slavonic instrumental music in the development of seventeenth- and eight-

eenth-century orchestral and chamber music has often been under-
estimated. Apart from Prague (which was in the grip of the
Germans and still feeling the wounds of the Thirty Years' War),
the main centre in Bohemia-Moravia where instrumental music was
cultivated during the second half of the seventeenth century was
the episcopal Church of Kremsier (now Kroměříž).[62] It is evident
that in musical practice as well as in personnel there was close
contact between the Kroměříž and the Vienna Court chapels.
Many of the brilliant masques and serenades of the latter were no
doubt imitated or copied by Kroměříž musicians, yet they made a
significant contribution of their own to the European musical
scene. In many of their pieces the special tone-colours of the
instruments and instrumental groups are subtly exploited, not only
by juxtaposing bands of contrasting instrumental colour but also by
using instruments in a solo manner, as in a Sonata for two violins,
three viols, one violone, two clarini, four trombe, four tromboni,
one tympanum and continuo of 1675 by Philipp Jakob Rittler.

At Kroměříž even percussion parts were quite elaborate, witness
Biber's *Sonata Polycarpi* for eight trumpets, timpani, and continuo
(*c.*1670):

Ex. 219

Strings were graded carefully: violins, violini piffari, viole da braccio, viole da gamba, violette, violone, violoncelli, viola d'amour. The employment of a horn with strings is noteworthy; there is an anonymous Sonata for corno di caccia, two violins, two violette, and violone o cimbalo, almost certainly the earliest known composition for horn in chamber music (the date is approximately 1670). It is elaborately contrived and shows a remarkable sense of balance, with typical horn passages throughout the piece:

Ex. 220

The only other seventeenth-century chamber composition with horn traceable so far appears to be a 'Concerto für Posthorn, zwei Violinen und Bass' of possibly twenty years later by Joh. Baehr (d. 1700), preserved in the Schwerin Library.

The addition of certain instruments of popular provenance to ensembles gives many Kroměříž compositions an especial Slav flavour. Bagpipes are frequently required. 'Piffari' (bagpipes without the drone) are used in an *Aria villanesca* by Rittler (*c*.1675):

Ex. 221

The popular element is also present in Biber's *Serenade with the Watchman's Call*, 'Hört Ihr Herrn und Lasst euch sagen' (1673), where there is much pizzicato (as there is in Johann Valentin

Meder's *Der Polnische Pracher* of the same time, at Danzig). In Biber's *Battallia* (1673) *col legno* is employed.[63]

One of the merits of the episcopal patrons of Court music was that they obviously encouraged their musicians not to rely entirely on Italian models (which at Kroměříž were represented chiefly by Bertali and Poglietti) but to develop their art on the basis of their own local popular tradition. Folk-song-like melodies and episodes of unusual rhythmic interest had been noticeable in Bohemian music much earlier in the century (Otto, Demantius, and others).[64] Striking rhythmic features such as accounts on the 'wrong' beat, as well as the preponderant use of the major key, were conspicuous in this music. A *Villana Hanatica* (approximately 1670) (the Hanakis were Moravians) has rhythms that in later music we recognize as Slav:

Ex. 222

So has another piece from Kroměříž, a *Hanak* for two violins and continuo (on a drone on C):

Ex. 223

[63] 'Das liederliche Schwirmen der Musketiere, Mars die Schlacht und Lamento der Verwundeten mit Arien imitirt und Baccho dedicirt, von H. Biber, anno 1673, a 10, 3 violin, 4 viol., 2 violon, cembalo. NB. wo die Strich seindt, mues man anstadt des Geigen mit dem Bogen klopfen auf die Geigen; es mues wohl probirt werden; der Mars ist schon bekant, aber ich hab ihm nicht boesser wissen zu verendern; wo die Druml geth im Bass, mues man an die Seiten ein Papier machen, das es einen Strepitum gibt, in Mars aber nur allein.' Programme music was cultivated in Moravia as elsewhere in the seventeenth century. There are *battaglie* by Czech composers as there are by the Italians Uccellini and Banchieri, and the Germans Wilche, Hainl, Clamor Heinrich Abel, Johann Fischer, and others, as well as Biber's *Biblical Sonatas*, Locke's *Curtain Tune*, Merula's *T'hane en henne gekrey* from Matthysz *T'uitnement cabinet*, Steffano Pasino's *Sonata all' imitazione diversi che sogliono fare diversi animali brutti* from his work of 1679, Theodor Schwartzkopff's *Sonata a 5 alla imitazione della Rossignole e Cucco* (MS Rostock), etc.

[64] See Vol. IV, p. 601.

Popular melody reappears in all its grace and freshness in instrumental music written on a larger scale and more elaborate in structure, as for example in many works of P. J. Rittler, Jan Tolar, Eusebius Bohemus,[65] Pavel Josef Vejvanovský (*c.* 1640–1693), and others.[66]

Such gay confident openings as that of the Allegro in Rittler's Sonata a 7:

Ex. 224

or the cheerful triadic melodies in Vejvanovský's trumpet sonatas:

[65] Five attractive instrumental movements by this unknown Czech composer are preserved in the Proske Library, Regensburg.

[66] Compositions by Tolar, ed. Jan Racek, *Musica Antiqua Bohemica*, xl (Prague, 1959), and Jaroslav Pohanka, *Dějiny české hudby v příkladech* (Prague, 1958), no. 110; by Vejvanovský, ed. Racek, ibid., xxxvi, xlvii, xlviii and xlix, and Pohanka, ibid., no. 111.

Ex. 225

are near to folk music. Among the notable musicians born and brought up in that area were Heinrich Biber and Gottfried Finger of Olomouc (1655—after 1723), to say nothing of such lesser-known men as Pavel Konwalinka of Skalice who published a work for two violins, two viole da braccio, two bass viols, and continuo in 1673, who owed their success to their melodic heritage. The special gift of Bohemian musicians for popular melody is apparent also in a suite for two violins and bass (the violins are in *scordatura*, i.e. tuned in intervals other than fifths) by Daniel Woita or Voita Pragensis (*c*.1688), included in Sebastian Brossard's collection of instrumental pieces;[67] this is full of fluent melody in the bright key of D major, and there is a note that 'The second part might be taken over by a Viola da braccio (*brazza*) for its greater loveliness'.

There is further evidence of the activity of Bohemian composers in the field of instrumental composition in a list of musical works at one time in the archives of the cloister chapel at Osek; among the names are the above-mentioned Voita and Dolar (no doubt Tolar) with ballets and sonatas (a work by Voita is called 'Parthia amabilis'); there are also pieces by Wentzl[68] (four-part ballets), Kalažka (*Parthia a 5*), Miška (*Parthia a 3*), Finger (ballets), Heinenski (*Parthia*), and others.[69] At Osek music was not on the Kroměříž scale, but then there was only a cloister chapel there, whereas Kroměříž had a Court with all the display of an ambitious Prince Bishop.

### INSTRUMENTAL MUSIC IN POLAND

Instrumental activity had developed in other Slav countries, too. Recent research has thrown light on seventeenth-century instru-

---

[67] Paris, Bibl. Nat., Vm. 7, 1099.

[68] Probably Mikuláš Wentzely (*c*.1642–1722).

[69] See Paul Nettl, *Musikbarock in Böhmen und Mähren* (Brno, 1927); Vladimír Helfert *Hudební barok na českých zámcích* (Prague, 1916), and E. H. Meyer, 'Die Bedeutung der Instrumentalmusik am fürst-bischöflichen Hofe zu Olmütz und Kremsier', *Aufsätze über Musik* (Berlin, 1957).

mental music in Croatia and Dalmatia,[70] and instrumental music was cultivated in Poland. At the Polish Court, among the aristocracy and in other educated circles, the non-Polish element generally predominated in the seventeenth century owing to the engagement of Italian and German musicians. One finds long canzonas reminiscent of Gabrieli and of the early seventeenth-century German type. Italian influences helped to advance *cantabile* melodic writing and to replace the old polyphonic conception of part-writing by an emotional harmonic style. This was considerably helped along by Marco Scacchi, one of the most important members of the Warsaw Court chapel. Yet Italianate melody was modified in Poland as elsewhere in Eastern Europe by folk-song.[71]

Some native Polish musicians, for instance Marcin Mielczewski (d. 1651), using foreign models, injected Polish elements. Mielczewski's works include several compositions for two violins and bass and a canzon for the same combination, which are extremely lively, containing such passages as:[72]

Ex. 226

[70] Dragan Plamenac, 'An unknown Violin Tablature of the Early 17th Century', *Papers of the American Musicological Society, 1941*, and his *Toma Cecchini, Kapelnik stolnih crkava u Splitu i Hvaru u prvoj polovini XVII stoljeca* (Zagreb, 1938); Hellmut Federhofer, 'Vincenz Jelich', *Archiv für Musikwissenschaft*, xii (1955), p. 215.

[71] See Vol. IV, pp. 599–601.

[72] Ed. Adolf Chybiński, *Wydawnictwo dawnej muzyki polskiei*, vi (Warsaw, new edition, 1961); another canzona, ed. Zygmunt Szweykowski, ibid., xxix (Warsaw, 1961).

A number of compositions by Polish musicians, chiefly or even solely based on Polish folk music, are of great originality. Pointed dance rhythms, flexible little figures, turning and twisting in sequences and repetitions, and, as in other early Slav melodies, in gay major keys—such are some of the characteristics of seventeenth-century Polish instrumental music. They appear in sonatas by Cajetan Wutky, in a sonata dated 1706 by Stanisław Szarzyński,[73] and in such imitations of Polish folklore as the portrait of a Polish vagabond, *Der Polnische Pracher*, for five stringed instruments and continuo by Johann Valentin Meder (1649–1719) (1682),[74] or Schmelzer's *Polnische Sackpfeiffen* (*c*.1670) for two violins and bass:[75]

Ex. 227

The opening of one tune in this curious medley, played in octaves by all instruments:

Ex. 228

[73] Ed. Chybiński,. ibid., i (1928).
[74] Bibl. Gdansk, MS Joh. 190.
[75] Published complete in Lavignac and La Laurencie, *Encyclopédie de la Musique*, 1re. partie, 2, pp. 992–8.

is practically identical with the first phrase of a paduana 'Soldat'[76] in the first collection of the *Paduanas et Galliardas* (Leipzig, 1616) of Georg Engelmann (d. 1632), and with the opening of a dance-tune known in England as 'Parson's Farewell'.[77]

The krakowiak and polonaise were well known in the seventeenth century. A *Bransle da Polion*, based on an old Polish dance, is part of a Suite for four instruments by Andreas Kertzinger (choirmaster in Prague from 1658):[78]

Ex. 229

Another old dance tune appears in Jakob Kremberg's (*c*.1650–1718) Concerto for three violins and bass:[79]

Ex. 230

A supplement of *Polnische Däntzen*, arranged for three and four instruments, was added to the *Tafel-Musik* (Hamburg, 1702) of Johann Fischer (1646–*c*.1716). In the Polish dances of the *Delitiae Musicae* (Rostock, 1656) by Nikolaus Hasse (*c*.1617–1672) both trumpets and *clarini* (high trumpets) co-operate with pairs of *Heerpauken* (timpani). A number of compositions on similar lines may be found in German and other works: e.g. a *Kosakenballett* and *Ungarische und Griechische Balletten* are contained in *Musikalisch-Türkischer Eulenspiegel*, a very colourful collection of international dances of 1688.[80] The *Kosakenballett* has a clearly marked *accelerando*.

---

[76] Ed. Hugo Riemann, *Old Chamber Music*, ii (London, n.d.), p. 47.
[77] See John Playford, *The English Dancing Master* (London, 1651; ed. Margaret Dean-Smith, London, 1957), fo. 6.
[78] Kroměříž, St. Maur. Arch.
[79] Bibl. Uppsala.
[80] See *Monatshefte für Musikgeschichte*, xiv (1882), p. 1.

The fine melodic qualities of popular music in Eastern Europe are referred to in a seventeenth-century publication. Konrad Hagius (1550–1616), a German composer, in the preface to his *Newe Künstliche, Musikalische Intraden, Pavanen*, etc. (Nuremberg, 1616), says that he travelled through Austria, Bohemia, Hungary, Poland, Prussia, and Lithuania, and found many dances, especially of such a nature as he would call pavans and galliards, the soprano and bass parts of which were always correct and beautiful though the middle parts were faulty (*vitiosae*).

### GERMANY

The musical situation in Germany during the second half of the seventeenth century was confused. Not only did it reflect the changing styles and practices that existed in the surrounding countries, but the Empire itself, after the Thirty Years' War, continued to consist of a bewildering multitude of autonomous grand-duchies, duchies, counties, and free cities. It was partly her geographical position in the heart of Europe and in the path of many international trade routes which exposed German lands to a great variety of foreign influences. An even more important cause of the preference for foreigners in German musical life was the fact that in 1648 she was herself weakened and split politically, socially and economically no less than spiritually and morally. She was deprived of any national culture. Her musicians looked round eagerly at other nations' achievements. There had been an intense musical life at the beginning of the seventeenth century; now, owing to the war, a whole generation had been lost; there was a terrible breach in tradition. Considering these disadvantages, it is surprising how German music revived during the second half of the century. This was, in fact, a germinating period in German music. Creative activity rallied within twenty years, indeed in many places it became most intense.

It was concentrated round countless local Courts, in a large number of municipal bands, in some churches and among an increasing number of amateur bodies such as students; orchestras and *collegia musica*.[81] Many small-scale amateur groups sprang up as material conditions improved, and as more and more people could afford to buy instruments.

During these years Court chapels increased in size, and several new ones were founded; the most important were those at

---

[81] Regular meetings of musical amateurs or professionals, either vocal or instrumental.

Dresden, Stuttgart, Cologne, Berlin, Kassel, Weimar, and Weissenfels. So far as music in churches was concerned, numerous titles of collections of printed music as well as old inventories of archives show that instrumental music continued to be required in the service. There are many examples of organ music—particularly introductory pieces—having been played by instrumental ensembles. However, Andreas Hammerschmidt's *Kirchen- und Tafelmusik* (1662) was specially written for instrumental ensembles—it contains sonatas on melodies derived from Lutheran hymnody—as were works by the already mentioned Johann Fischer and others.

In some towns, attendance at religious functions was part of the regular work of the *Stadtpfeiffer*, or waits, who in many cases were wind players. Such municipal bands were often the centres of musical activity during the later seventeenth century. Among their duties were short performances from the tower of the town hall (*Turmmusik*) at certain hours of the day (cf. Pezel's *Hora Decima*, 1670, and *Musica vespertina*, 1669), entertainment of people on market days, performing at official receptions, festival occasions, and so on. Some towns also employed string orchestras. The musical standard in some of these bands must have been extremely high, notably in those at Leipzig, Berlin, Ulm, Bremen, Stade, Wernigerode, Jena, and Stuttgart.

The composer for wind bands was undoubtedly Johann Pezel of Leipzig whose music[82] is as refreshing in its melodic vitality as in its contrapuntal interest. Yet more *Turmmusik* of high accomplishment was produced by Gottfried Reiche (1667–1734),[83] Johann Georg Christoph Störl (1675–1719),[84] Andreas Hammerschmidt (1612–75),[85] Johann Melchior Gletle (1626–84),[86] Daniel Speer (1636–1707),[87] and Johann Philipp Krieger (1649–1725).[88] Works for wind band by the famous Wolfgang Carl Briegel (1626–1712) and by many other composers are lost.

The *collegia musica* were of special importance for instrumental ensemble music as they could count on the active support or par-

[82] *Turmmusiken*, ed. Schering, *Denkmäler deutscher Tonkunst*, lxiii.
[83] *24 Neue Quatricinia* (Leipzig, 1696); ed. G. Müller (Berlin, 3rd ed. 1958).
[84] Six sonatas for cornetto and trombones, ed. Helmut Schultz, *Erbe Deutscher Musik*, xiv.
[85] *Kirchen- und Tafel-Musik* (Zittau, 1662), twelve trumpet pieces ed. Willi Schuh (Zürich).
[86] In *Musica Genialis Latino-Germanica* (Augsburg, 1675); twelve trumpet pieces ed. Willi Schuh (Zürich).
[87] *Recens Fabricatus Labor* (1685); seven pieces ed. Schultz, op. cit.
[88] *Lustige Feld-Music* (Nuremberg, 1704); various modern editions of separate suites.

ticipation of large numbers of amateur players and listeners. The most influential of these bodies was that at Hamburg which a Schütz pupil, Matthias Weckmann (1621–74), directed for a number of years. Student orchestras existed in Rostock, Tübingen, Leipzig, Nuremberg, and other towns.

The amount of music composed in Germany rose steadily between 1650 and 1700. Judging from the size of lists from some Court chapels many composers must have been commissioned by their aristocratic masters to write new works at least once a week if not every day. Hundreds of printed collections of music in two to eight parts were issued during those fifty years. There is much great and much small art embodied in this output; yet one thing is certain—that the tradition established at that time was maintained in Germany at a high level for centuries.

As musical life in Germany was so dispersed, and many types of practice and function existed, there was immense variety in the actual work produced. It is difficult to introduce a semblance of order into this creative chaos; yet certain schools and structural principles emerge on closer study.

First of all, as regards form the process of development from multiplicity of movements to standardization was much slower and less direct in Germany than in any other country. Even towards the end of the century seven or eight movements in sonatas are by no means exceptional. On the other hand, a number of works composed around 1650 have only three or four movements. The most varied types of formal structure can often be found in the output of one and the same composer. The restriction to three or four movements developed slowly.

Yet in other aspects of form the line of development agreed with that in other countries. As elsewhere the formal structure as a whole was energized, balanced, unified, planned and no longer strung out piecemeal by linking up any number of sections. This principle can be seen in the above-mentioned works by Thieme, Theile, and Rosenmüller; a *Sonata a 4*[89] by Philipp Friedrich Buchner (1614–69) is a simple example. It has three movement-sections: the first calmly flowing and moderately slow, in triple rhythm—expressive, tuneful, semi-homophonic:

---

[89] From *Plectrum Musicum* (Frankfurt, 1662).

Ex. 231

The second is in sharp contrast to the first—fast, energetic, rhythmical, exciting, and almost entirely homophonic:

Ex. 232

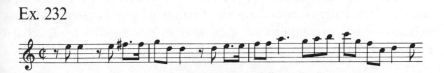

The third movement resumes the character, rhythm, and style of the first but the thematic material is somewhat different:

Ex. 233

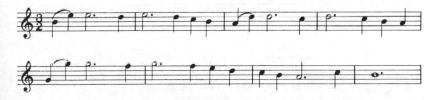

yet when this last movement is finished the listener is left with the impression that he has heard a work of great unity and finality.

One-movement pieces abound and are often in calm triple time (3/2) throughout, e.g. this *Sonata a 3* in C minor (*c*.1665) by Caspar Förster (1616–73):[90]

Ex. 234

---

[90] MS. Uppsala Univ. Bibl.

Less often one-movement pieces are completely *fugato*. In two-movement pieces the second movement is often in the nature of a coda dramatically overtopping the first, as exemplified impressively in the second movement of a *Sonata a 6* (*c*.1660)[91] by Gerhard Diessener:

Ex. 235

[91] Kassel, Landesbibl., Ms. 2° 60 Y.

The gradual consolidation of form in German sonatas and symphonies—the *canzon* disappears in the second half of the seventeenth century—was assisted by the formulation of a definite order of movements within the dance suite. There was always a large variety of these dances throughout the seventeenth century. Yet even as early as the beginning of the century definite sequences of dance types were put together, a practice that became general after 1650 when publication was resumed after the war. Among the types represented, allemande, courante, sarabande, and gigue became the most frequent. There are published collections of this all-dance type of suite by Clamor Heinrich Abel, Johann Heinrich Beck, Johann Philipp Beck, Dietrich Becker, Georg Bleyer, Werner Fabricius, Nikolaus Hasse, Johann Caspar Horn, Lüder Knoep, Johann Neubauer, Johann Rosenmüller, Johann Christoph Seyfried, and Gregor Zuber. These suites are sometimes interspersed with ballets, gavottes, intradas, masquerades, and other types, and the gigues are occasionally omitted.

About the middle of the century non-dance movements (preludes, sonatinas, sonatas, symphonies, and so on) were first added to dance suites as introductory movements by Adam Drese (1620–1701) in 1646 and Martin Rubert (1615–80) in 1650. Under the powerful influence of the French practice these introductory movements were supplanted by large-scale *ouvertures* by Gerhard Diessener (c.1672), Benedict Anton Aufschnaiter (1695), Johann Sigismund Kusser (Cousser) (1682–1700), Philipp Heinrich Erlebach (1693), Johann Fischer (from 1700 onwards), Johann Caspar Ferdinand Fischer (1695), Rupert Ignaz Mayr (1692),

Joseph Schmicerer (1698), and others. Several of these works include in their titles references to their French models (*nach frantzoesischer Art*).

In all this music, four- to six-part combinations are most frequent, but works for seven or eight instruments, too, were still being composed at the end of the century. Solos and trios (two violins and bass) became more and more frequent toward the end of the seventeenth century but not dominant as in other countries.

Two extremes in style may be recognised: constructionist, speculative, polyphonic expressionism, and sensuous, emotional *cantabile*. The first was based on native German as well as some early seventeenth-century Italian elements; there was also some influence from the English polyphonists. The second derived from Italy and Vienna.

### THE NORTH GERMAN SCHOOL

The first school developed chiefly in northern Germany. A typical example may be found in a collection of ten sonatas for violin, cornettino, trombone, bassoon, and continuo by Matthias Weckmann, written about 1670 for the Hamburg *Collegium Musicum*. Weckmann's work is player's rather than listener's music. Being a pupil of Schütz he inherited a great deal from Gabrieli. The combination of instruments gives a clue to the general style; precisely the same combination had appeared in works by Viadana and Giovanni Valentini[92] at the beginning of the seventeenth century. The underlying principle is related to the 'split-sound' (broken consort) technique of the kind encountered in Thomas Morley's *First Book of Consort Lessons*.[93] Great contrast in tone quality, yet equal balance between all participating instruments, these were in Weckmann's mind just as they had been in that of the earlier seventeenth-century English polyphonist.

Looking at Weckmann's counterpoint one can easily understand why. There are instrumental lines of extreme liveliness, ruthlessly kept and identical in all the parts. Thematic material such as:

Ex.236

92 See Vol. IV, p. 579.
93 Ibid., p. 583.

first given to a violin, is repeated literally by trombone and bassoon. All instruments have always the same independence; what results is often a truly fantastic sound picture:

Ex. 237

The thematic material itself is non-sensuous and non-*cantabile*; it is composed of a multitude of motives and much sequential work. Sequences are built up without any consideration for elegance:

Ex. 238

The bass and continuo provide no harmonic consistency; the bass part stumbles on, following the basic notes of whichever happens to be the lowest part of the score. There are long solo passages but also long stretches of full four-part teamwork.

There are elements of experiment and improvisation in this music. Mattheson called it *stilo fantastico*. The same style is mani-

fest in some works by Albrici, Düben, and others. These have long
sections in which bass lines alone are given and upon these, instrument after instrument had to improvise its entire part. In this music
which—like Schütz's instrumental introductions to his vocal
works—relies in this extraordinary way on linear combinations,
much of the figuration of the later concerto is anticipated. In its
radicalism and uncompromising constructivism this music ranks
among the most original manifestations of seventeenth-century art.

A number of composers worked on lines similar to Weckmann's,
notably Caspar Förster, Johann Jakob Loewe von Eisenach (1629-
1703), and David Pohle (1624–95). Pohle was an excellent musician
whio left many sonatas for three to eight parts. He sometimes
builds whole movements on minute thematic subjects; the first part
of one five-part Sonata by Pohle[94] is entirely based on a single
motive; the effect is one of great virtuosity of composition:

Ex. 239

### CENTRAL AND SOUTH GERMAN COMPOSERS

The other main school of composition in late seventeenth-
century Germany is chiefly represented by central and south
German musicians who were in closer touch with contemporary
Italian and Viennese developments. It is in many respects diametri-
cally opposed to the Weckmann school, as the music of Johann
Rosenmüller, another of the major German composers before
Bach, shows clearly. Rosenmüller's music is meant for the listener

[94] Copy in Uppsala Univ. Bibl.

rather than the player. Combinations of instruments are devised
not on the 'split-sound' principle but unified in tone-colour with
strings as the sole or main body in the majority of cases.

Each movement in Rosenmüller is purposeful; the movements
are connected logically and functionally. Harmonies are emotionally expressive and aim at clear and smooth cadences from phrase
to phrase and movement to movement. The melodies themselves
are of great unity in spite of their extended length:[95]

Ex. 240

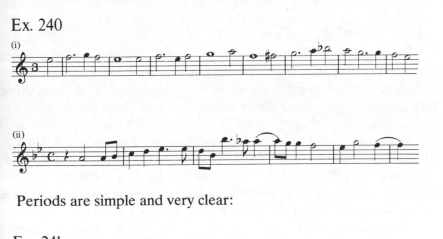

Periods are simple and very clear:

Ex. 241

In Rosenmüller's texture there is always one main strand,
wandering from one instrument to another, which reduces the
others to the function of harmonic accompaniment:

Ex. 242

[95] Exx. 240–2 are taken from *Sonate a 2, 3, 4 e 5 Stromenti* (Nuremberg, 1682).

The top part is generally the most important melodically, and there are often long stretches which are almost entirely homophonic.

During the second half of the seventeenth century more and more composers were drawn into the orbit of this school, notably Philipp Friedrich Buchner (1614–69), Wilhelm Furchheim, Dietrich Becker (1623–79) and Johann Caspar Horn (c.1630–c.1685). However, the majority of German composers combined elements of both the constructionist Weckmann and the emotionalist Rosenmüller styles. This group is extremely large. Best known among them are Dietrich Buxtehude, Johann Pachelbel, Esaias Reusner, Johann Theile, Clemens Thieme, Christoph Friedrich Witt, Johann Jakob Walther, and Friedrich Wilhelm Zachow. The work of Gerhard Diessener,[96] one of the greatest exponents of seventeenth-century German instrumental music, is in many respects that of an outsider. In his music are highly original features, a boldness of expression, a sense of dramatic and harmonic adventurousness such as may be found in the works of few seventeenth-century composers:[97]

Ex. 243

[96] See p. 379, n. 1 and Meyer, *Die mehrstimmige Spielmusik des 17. Jahrhunderts in Nord- und Mitteleuropa* (Kassel, 1934), p. 196.

[97] Exx. 243 and 245 are from a *Sonata a 3* in Brit. Lib., Ex. 244 from a *Sonata à 5 Parties*, dated 1600, at Kassel.

Key-relationships are handled with great freedom:

Ex. 244

Yet it is in the field of melodic expression that Diessener is strongest. Here there are highlights of seventeenth-century expression and of true instrumental pathos:

Ex. 245

With the exception of the ever-popular *sonata a tre* the German ensemble sonata became out of date about 1700. In one direction it developed into the concerto. The solo-tutti division could already be found in many German ensemble pieces as early as 1660, and there was an element of concerto virtuosity in Weckmann's thematic developments and *stilo fantastico*. Pieces named 'concerto', either for solo instruments with orchestra or for groups of solo instruments with orchestra, appeared more and more frequently in works of late seventeenth-century composers—Johann Christoph Pez (1664–1716), Theodor Schwartzkopff (1659–1732), Samuel Baehr, Johann Hieronimus Gravius, Johann Philipp Kaefer, Reinhard Keiser (1674–1739)—including some men who lived abroad, such as Gottfried Keller and Gottfried Finger (*c*.1660–after 1723). In another direction the great German ensemble tradition merged with new foreign forms, the Italian sinfonia and the French overture, both of which progressively influenced German development.

Seventeenth-century German ensemble music, having attained such heights, lived on in many instrumental introductions and preludes to cantatas, Passions, and other vocal works. And the foundations of a new era of chamber music which was to flourish in Germany in the eighteenth century had been laid in the instrumental masterpieces of the men working during the fifty years after the Thirty Years' War.

### SWITZERLAND AND SCANDINAVIA

In a number of countries bordering on Germany a roughly parallel development occurred. A number of Swiss composers of this time belonged to the Viennese and South German schools: notably Henrico Albicastro,[98] Jakob Banwart (1609–*c*.1657),[99] Johann Andreas Baentz,[100] Constantin Steingaden (d. 1675),[101] and

---

[98] See Meyer, *Die mehrstimmige Spielmusik*, p. 178.
[99] Pseudonym 'Jakob Avia'. *Teutsche Tafelmusik (auf neu ital. Manier)* (with twelve dance movements) (Konstanz, 1652).
[100] *Vier Decades newer Arien und Couranten* (for five instruments) (Augsburg, *c*.1670).
[101] *Flores Hyemales* (including two Sonatas a 4, 5) (Constance, 1666).

Romano Weichlein (1652–1706),[102] all of whom worked within or near the Swiss borders. A collection of twelve trio sonatas (Berne, 1680) by Nicholas Pfleger 'Helveticus' has not been preserved.

In Sweden there was great activity in the field of instrumental ensemble music, especially at the Court whose cultural ambitions grew with the tremendous rise of Sweden's political and economic power. Gustaf Düben (c.1628–90), *Hofcapellmästar* from 1663 until his death, was sent to other countries to collect the best specimens of instrumental music for use in Sweden; his vast collection—including many *unica*—is preserved in the University Library at Uppsala.

Musical composition in Stockholm was of an entirely international character. Düben himself and his father Andreas (c.1597–1662) made several contributions to chamber music, and a Parisian, Pierre Verdier (1627–1706), a leading player in Queen Christina's band and called *Musicien du Roi de Suède* in a manuscript at Uppsala, left some highly important ensemble works. There are also instrumental pieces by Johan Celcius, Olav Belgrot and others. Copenhagen, however, was even more important, in that native musical activity was stronger. Several Danish composers produced sonatas, sinfonias, suites, etc.: e.g. Friedrich Erhardt Niedt (1674–1708), Jacob Corvinus (d. 1663), and Andreas Kirchhoff, whose sonatas for four to six instruments (1664)[103] are related to Weckmann's.

## THE NETHERLANDS

Ensemble music in the Netherlands was enthusiastically cultivated between 1650 and 1700. There are many traces of German and French influence; but in its main features it is original in style and based on interesting local musical conditions. The Netherlands in the second half of the seventeenth century were in many respects no longer the homogeneous country of one hundred years earlier. Economic, religious, and political differences existed in plenty between the north (roughly, modern Holland) and the south (large parts of Belgium), yet these differences were less important that the common bonds which united the north with at least the Flemish parts of the south. The influence of sea trade had replaced the clericalism and feudalism left over from the Middle Ages; a new nationalism and the parallel rise of Calvinism were the

---

[102] *Encaenia musices* (twelve large ensemble sonatas) (Innsbruck, 1695).
[103] Uppsala, Bibl. Univ.

spiritual expressions of this change, and in the Netherlands they effected a drastic change in musical practice and tradition.

This new life was perhaps based more on amateur activities than anything else. Playing of instruments must have been widespread not only in large places such as Amsterdam and Antwerp but also in the villages. It was the common people quite as much as well-to-do citizens who were responsible for this. The popular *Muziek Herbergen* (musical inns) were veritable bee-hives of musical activity, the playing and singing of dances and popular songs. Popular melodies like those gathered and published in plenty in such collections as *Hollantsche Schowburg* were the very life-blood of instrumental music. Sonatas and suites abounded in themes which quoted or imitated popular melodies as in the *Ballo Rustica* from *Balletti, Allemande*, etc. (1672) by P. F. Munninckxs (Ex. 246) and the *Quatorze Sonate* (sic) (Amsterdam, 1691) by Carl Rosier (1640–1725)[104] (Ex. 247):

Ex. 246

Ex. 247

[104] On Rosier, see Ursel Niemöller, Carl Rosier (*Beiträge zur rheinischen Musikgeschichte*, xxiii) (Cologne, 1957) and ed. idem, *Ausgewählte Instrumentalwerke* (*Denkmäler rheinischer Musik*, vii) (Düsseldorf, 1957).

Similar themes occur even in the numerous highly developed polyphonic works, especially those by Carolus Hacquart (*c*.1640– *c*.1730) and Benedictus a Sancto Josepho: for instance, an old Dutch and German nursery tune in a *sonata a 4* in Hacquart's *Harmonia Parnassia sonatarum* (Utrecht, 1686):

Ex. 248

The same clarity and popular simplicity prevails in form. Elaborate experiments like those in the works of contemporary German composers will be looked for in vain; there is a certain happy-go-lucky attitude to the way problems of form are dealt with. The same applies to unity of key. Benedictus a Sancto Josepho, for instance in his *Orpheus Elianus* (Amsterdam, 1699) starts a Sonata in F sharp minor and ends it in E flat major. Yet great importance attaches to unity of character in a piece. Many of the best works are most impressive in their big-scale emotional developments, and few countries produced works of such intense joy or of such deeply tragic character as did the best Netherland masters of that time.

In Amsterdam concerts with professional artists, open to all who paid the entrance fee, were introduced in the late 'seventies by Carolus Hacquart, and the virtuoso playing which was stimulated by the institution of the public concert quickly affected the style of the music itself. Even before this the three collections of Italian-influenced *Symphoniae* for one to five instruments (Antwerp, 1644, 1647, and 1649), by Nicolaus a Kempis, require a high standard of technical proficiency:[105]

Ex. 249

Such works became very numerous in the second part of the century when such editions as *Antwerpesche Vrede-Vreught* (1679) appeared—pieces for three violins or other string combinations without continuo, by Pieter Piccaert and Carl Rosier—and Elias Broennemüller's Sonatas for oboe, violin and flute solo in *Fasciculus Musicus* (Louvain, 1710), Jan de Haze's *Clio* (Middelburg, 1681), David Petersen's *Speelstukken* (1683), Johannes Schenck's *Suonate a Violino e Violone*, Op. 7 (Amsterdam, 1693), the *Vrede Triomph*, with three violins in *scordatura*, of Dirk Scholl (1641–1727) (Delft, 1678). Towards the end of the century the viola da gamba became even more popular than the violin, and some works written for one or several gambas were very advanced in their technique, notably the Op. 2, 6, 8, 9 and 10 also by Johannes Schenck (1660–after 1712), published at Amsterdam during 1688–1706, and Jan Snep's *Sonatas* (1700). The flute (recorder) figures prominently in Nicolas Derosier's *La fuitte du roi d'Angleterre* (Amsterdam, 1689; modern edition, London,

---

[105] A heavily edited version of a *symphonia* for solo violin and continuo from the first set was published by Riemann in *Old Chamber Music*, iv.

1959) for two flutes and *basse de viole*, Jacob van Eyck's pieces in *Der fluyten lust-hof* (1646; modern edition, Amsterdam, 1957–8); in Servaes van Koninck's sets of trios (Amsterdam, 1696 and c.1700), and sonatas for one and two flutes,[106] and Vincenz Lambert's *Pièces en trio*, for flute, violins, or oboes (c.1700), Sybrandus van Noordt's *Mélange italien ou Sonates à une Flute ou Violon et une Basse Continue* (Amsterdam, 1690), and Carl Rosier's *Pièces choises* (Amsterdam, 1691).

In addition to the afore mentioned works by Hacquart, B. a Sancto Josepho, Munninckxs and a Kempis, the chief publications of music for trio or larger ensemble are those by Hendrik Anders (*Trios*, Amsterdam, 1696, and *Symphoniae introductoriae* for three and four instruments, Amsterdam, 1698), Elias Broennemüller (*Sonate a due Violini e Violoncelli col Organo, opera Prima*, Amsterdam, 1709), Philipp van Wicchel (*Fasciculus dulcedinis*, for one to five instruments and continuo, Antwerp, 1678), Lothar L. Zumbach van Koesfeldt (*Sonate a 4 Violini e 2 fagotti*, 1690) and Johannes Schenck (*Il Giardino Armonico* for two violins and continuo, Op. 3, 1692).

## FRANCE

French ensemble music did not attain any importance until nearly the end of the seventeenth century. Up to the period of Lully the playing of viols and violins was a secondary matter, as music for harpsichord, lute and guitar completely absorbed the interest of the public for instrumental music. What music for strings can be traced at all was contained (with the exception of Nicolas Métru's Fantaisies of 1642)[107] in theoretical treatises and no doubt served didactic purposes (de la Voye, 1656, Henry Lejeune, 1664, Guillaume Gabriel Nivers, 1667, etc.), or it was produced by composers who were connected in one way or another with other countries. This is true of the violinist Constantyn, a travelling virtuoso; Paulus Matthysz printed some nondescript string pieces by him. This composer is also represented in a collection of suites in the Kassel Landesbibliothek which further contains some more interesting pieces by Guillaume Dumanoir (1615–c.1690) (not to be confused with the works signed 'G.D.' in the same collection which are by the German Gerhard Diessener).[108] The most important composer of symphonies, allemandes, etc., working in Paris

---

[106] Twelve sonatas for flute and continuo (1700) exist in manuscript at Wolfenbüttel.
[107] See Vol. IV, p. 591.
[108] See p. 379, n. 1.

around the middle of the seventeenth century was Henry Du Mont,[109] a Belgian whose music contains the best string work attained in France before Lully.

The rise of the Italian Lully changed the whole aspect of instrumental music in France. In consequence of his musical policy at Louis XIV's court, the violin soon dwarfed every other instrument in royal and public favour, including even the bass viol which had enjoyed some popularity. The function of the violin (or rather violins, for in Lully's music massed violins were almost invariably required) was to achieve drastic characterizations, lively expression, drama, and showmanship. In the instrumental items in his operas Lully used every technical device including *con sordino* and *tremolo*. But the most important influence which French instrumental style exercised internationally in the late seventeenth century lay in the field of the orchestral suite.[110]

An enormous rise in the popularity of instrumental chamber music in France is demonstrated by the sudden appearance of numerous publications. It was the *Sonata a tre* which French composers towards 1700 cultivated more intensely than any other form of chamber music. It is uncertain whether Lully wrote any instrumental music apart from that in his ballets and operas; a collection of *Trios de Violons a Basse de M. Lully* (formerly in Rostock Univ. Lib.) may have contained original instrumental works but is no longer traceable. Various pieces by Michel de Lalande (1657–1726) were written as early as the 'eighties; among them are works of intense passion, e.g. a *Quatuor* (c.1700)[111] which raises Lullyan operatic pathos to new emotional heights:

Ex. 250

[109] See Vol. IV, p. 591.
[110] See p. 230.
[111] Copy in Paris, Bibl. du Conservatoire.

There are many instrumental works by Lalande, including *Symphonie pour les soupers du Roy* and a *Concert de Trompettes et Timballes pour les fêtes sur le canal de Versaille.*[112] An anonymous *Livre de Pièces de Guitarre avec 2 dessus d'instruments et une b.c.* (Amsterdam, 1689) is probably for violins.[113] The *Symphonies De Feu M. Gaultier de Marseille, Divisées par Suites de tons* (Paris, 1707) by Pierre Gaultier (d. 1696),[114] contain five suites for trio combinations probably written in 1687, when the composer was in Avignon gaol. The same composer left another collection of trios. Many of Gaultier's works have characteristic titles; they are full of elegant passages and ornaments—a kind of ornamental polyphony different from both German and Italian styles.

The great time of the French trio sonata began, so far as can be seen, with the *Pièces en Trio pour les flûtes, violon et dessus de viole avec la b.c.* (Paris, 1692) of Marin Marais (1656–1728) and some *sonades en trio* for two violins, *basse d'archet* and *basse chiffrée* composed c.1692–3 but published more than thirty years later by François Couperin (1668–1733).[115] They were followed by

[112] No. 1, ed. A. Cellier (Paris, 1955).
[113] See Guillermo de Morphy, *Les Luthistes* (Paris, 1897).
[114] See Lionel de La Laurencie, 'Un émule de Lully: Pierre Gautier de Marseille', *Sammelbände der internationalen Musikgesellschaft*, xiii (1911–12), particularly pp. 52 ff.
[115] *Oeuvres complètes de François Couperin*, ix and x, ed. Maurice Cauchie (Paris, 1933).

sonatas (including two for two violins and bass) (1695), and a *Minuet, Symphonie pour la Nuit de Noel* for two melody instruments and bass by Sebastien de Brossard (1655–1730); the trio sonatas (1695) and *Recueil de douze sonates à II et III parties* (Paris, 1712) by Jean-Ferry Rebel (1666–1747), Toinon's *Recueil de Trios nouveaux* (Paris, 1699), Freillon-Ponsein's *Les Embaras de Paris* (which also includes *Symphonies et Canons à 6 parties* ), the *Livre de Sonates à III parties* (Paris, 1706) by François Duval (*c*.1673–1728), and an increasing number of works by Jean-François Dandrieu (1682–1738) and other early eighteenth-century composers.

Music for viols, especially the bass viol, was only a sideline compared with the thriving composition of music for violins, yet it benefited from the growing popularity of instrumental music in general. This is impressively shown in a theoretical *Traité de la viole* (Paris, 1687) by Jean Rousseau, interesting for its discussion of ornamental improvisation. In 1685 Le sieur de Machy published a collection of *Pièces de Violle*, but these are solo pieces 'qui, seule, font harmonie'. Marc-Antoine Charpentier (1634–1704), a composer of many overtures and suites, wrote *Préludes* for viols and a *Concerto pour 4 violes*. Some *Pièces de violle* by André Philidor (*c*.1647–1730) in the Bibliothèque du Conservatoire must be dated 1700 at the latest. The greatest bass viol player and composer, however, was Marin Marais whose five books of *Pièces de violes* (for one or two viols) appeared in 1686, 1701, 1711, 1717, and 1725. The whole elegance of French ornamental writing is beautifully illustrated in these collections,[116] the dainty and elaborate style of which had a profound effect on composition for viola da gamba abroad, including Bach's.

ENGLAND

England retained its musical independence longer than any other European country. The great turning point in English music was not reached until 1660–1670. It was caused by changes in the social structure of the nation, comparable with those in the Netherlands. The masters of the Jacobean madrigal and fantasia saw their field of working steadily narrowed down in an increasingly middle-class world. The Royal Court and Anglican strongholds became the chief centres of elaborate musical writing, although the Puritans

---

[116] See the examples quoted by Paul Garnault in Lavignac and La Laurencie, *Encyclopédie*, 2e partie, iii, pp. 1772–7, and Julie Anne Sadie, *The Bass Viol in French Baroque Chamber Music* (Ann Arbor, 1981).

had no objection to the pleasing entertainment provided by instrumental sound:

And all the while harmonious airs were heard
Of chiming strings, or charming pipes
(Milton, *Paradise Regained*, II, 78).

There was a widening rift in style between music intended for
highly skilled professionals and music for amateurs. On the one
hand there was a growing tendency towards more intricate writing
as well as greater technical difficulty; on the other, in the works
produced (and largely issued in print) for the masses who expected
from music simple entertainment, there was a growing trend
towards simplicity and lightheartedness.

Most characteristic of the first school is the work of John Jenkins
(1592–1678) whose creative activity had already born fruit in the
first quarter of the century but reached full maturity only about the
time of the Civil War. The old polyphonic art of the sixteenth
century culminated—and finally expired—in the fantasias, airs,
dances, and In Nomines of this great composer. Jenkins, not unlike
William Lawes, arrived at a very advanced stage of polyphonic
intricacy in which, once again, a horizontal conception of part
writing is prominent. Among his numerous works for two to six
parts[117] those for three and four viols are most lively; his larger
ensembles, full of noble and expressive melody, are more harmonically conceived and there is a certain inclination towards vocal airs
as in this fantasia for five viols (*c*.1630):[118]

Ex. 251

117 *Consort Music of Six Parts*, ed. Donald Peart, *Musica Britannica*, xxxix (London,
1977); *Consort Music in Five Parts*, ed. Richard Nicholson (London, 1971); *Consort Music
of Four Parts*, ed. Andrew Ashbee, *Musica Britannica*, xxvi (second, revised edition, 1975);
*Fancies and Ayres*, ed. Helen J. Sleeper (Wellesley, 1950). Ashbee has also edited for the
Viola da Gamba Society a more complete edition of the four-part consort music (London,
1978), and with Richard Nicholson the six-part (1976). See also Ashbee, 'The Four-Part
Consort Music of John Jenkins', *Proceedings of the Royal Musical Association*, xcvi (1969–
70), p. 29.
118 No. 10 in Nicholson's edition.

In his works of the Commonwealth and Restoration periods
Jenkins's intense polyphony developed virtuoso elements just like
those observed in other countries. Such figuration, it is true, had
largely been prepared for in lute, organ, and virginal music, but it
became an integral part of viol playing too. Here a new Jenkins
shows himself, e.g. this air with variation for violin, bass viol, and
continuo (c.1665):[119]

Ex. 252

[119] Durham Cath. Lib.

This development from intricate and highly developed counterpoint to an ornamental solo or duo or trio style is shared by quite a
number of composers, notably John Hingston (d. 1688)
(Cromwell's musical director), Christopher Simpson (*c*.1605–1669),
Christopher Gibbons (1615–76), John Withie (d. after 1673),
Charles Coleman (*c*.1605–1664), George Jeffries (*c*.1610–1685),
William Gregory the younger (d. 1687 or later)[120] and some lesser-
known men. Instrumental ornamentation and virtuosity reached
astonishing heights especially in the works of Hingston and
Simpson, witness Simpson's fantasia 'January' from his *The
Monthes* (*c*.1650):[121]

Ex. 253

---

[120] See James Riley, 'The Identity of William Gregory', *Music & Letters*, xlviii (1967)
p. 236.
[121] Brit. Lib., Add. 31436.

Yet there is no question of dryness or mere intellectual constructivism; there is real creative genius behind them, in particular behind the work of John Jenkins.

The other type of instrumental ensemble music, light entertainment for the public at large, is mainly represented in publications issued by Playford. A growing tendency to make the fantasia homophonic and thus popularize it could already be observed in the 1620s and 1630s in some works by Michael East,[122] Simon Ives,[123] and others. A great number of composers working about the middle of the century—among them Thomas Brewer (b. 1611), Martin Peerson (d. 1651), Richard Mico (c.1590–1661), Henry Loosemore (d. 1670), John Hilton (1599–1657), John Okeover (d. c.1663), William Young (d. 1662)—followed the same line. If none of these composers can be compared with Jenkins, they are all of some importance in English musical history. Though the changed function of instrumental music and the new outlook towards it made a serious breach in serious musical tradition as a whole, the composers of 'light' fantasias and airs at least represent a connecting link between two ages; they brought enough artistry to the music-loving masses to prevent the musical taste of the public from forgetting all about composed chamber music. Not that this 'music of the people' was devoid of charms and vitality; but it was almost entirely unpretentious. By far the greatest quantity of music performed in England after 1650 was the work contained in Playford's collections: *Music's Recreation on the Viol* (1652), *Courtly Masking Airs* (1662), *Choice Airs and Dialogues* (1676–85), *The Pleasant Companion* (1682), and numerous others.

---

[122] Cf. East's fancy 'Name Right your Notes', in the appendix to Meyer, *English Chamber Music* (London, 1946; rev. ed. 1978).
[123] See Vol. IV, p. 589, Ex. 265.

FOREIGN INFLUENCES

Later seventeenth-century popular instrumental music was more and more often subjected to foreign influences. The incredible number of airs, dialogues, dance types, and so on for (in most cases) only one, two, and three instruments adopted first Italian and later also French and German elements of style, as is shown in most instrumental works from John Banister (d. 1679) to Daniel Purcell (d. 1717). Foreign influences in English music made themselves felt in earnest after the Restoration in 1660. Charles II wanted to augment the splendour of his Court with music, as Louis XIV had so conspicuously succeeded in doing. Thus on the one hand a number of musicians of the old school and of high traditional standards—Jenkins, Hingston, Coleman, and others—were given a new lease of artistic life. And on the other, the King did more than encourage French and Italian music and musicians at his Court. (This was certainly due no less to their more dazzling and showy musical style than to his foreign policy.) Soon after this a new flowering of English music at the Court, and the tremendous advance of the more up-to-date foreign styles, another form of musical activity came into being: public concerts, initiated in 1672—before anywhere else in Europe—by John Banister and continued from 1678 onward by the musical coal-merchant Thomas Britton.

The continued residence of foreign musicians contributed very much to the internationalizing of English music, especially as some of them—Louis Grabu (Master of the King's Music 1666–74), Nicolas Matteis (from c.1672), Finger (from c.1687), and others—were notable composers. At first, however, the old English tradition was still powerful enough to meet foreign music on equal terms and the combination of national elements with international influences proved healthy, as may be seen from the works of various composers from Jenkins to Henry Purcell.

In chamber music, foreign influences worked in three chief directions: final dissolution of the old polyphonic framework, introduction of new forms, and replacement of the viols by the violin family.

Certain episodes, preparing the way for the *concerto*, in which some parts in the ensemble were treated more elaborately and with more figuration than others, are already noticeable at the beginning of the seventeenth century in fantasias by Thomas Lupo[124] and John Ward. Such episodes loosened the tight polyphonic web in which

---

[124] Ibid., p. 585, Ex. 261.

all parts had an equal share. Furthermore the arrangement of parts in the 'trio' style of two treble instruments of equal pitch set against a bass, imitating the Italian *sonata a tre* (first found in fantasias by Orlando Gibbons),[125] became a frequent feature of the instrumental music of the great masters of the second half of the seventeenth century. More significant still, after 1650 harmonic feeling spread in England as it did elsewhere. Accompanied treble melodies such as John Jenkins's 'Air with Variation' for violin, bass viol, and continuo (*c*.1665):[126]

Ex. 254

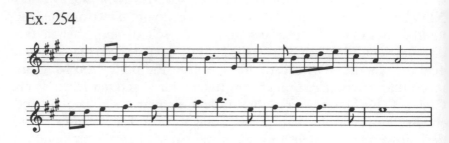

helped more than anything else to loosen the compactness of polyphonic work. Expressive solo passages appear even more convincingly and more frequently in compositions by Matthew Locke (1622–77) who wrote many dance suites and fantasias for concerted chamber music.[127] Eloquent expressive and wide melodic gestures appear in Locke's earliest instrumental pieces:[128]

Ex. 255

In his later compositions *cantabile* is even more fully developed, as in this 'saraband' from the music to Shadwell's version of *The Tempest* (1675):[129]

---

[125] Ibid., p. 586.

[126] MS., Durham, Cath. Lib.

[127] *Locke: Chamber Music*, ed. Michael Tilmouth, *Musica Britannica*, xxxi and xxxii (London, 1971 and 1972).

[128] His first consort music was written in 1651; *Matthew Locke His Little Consort of Three Parts* was published in 1656.

[129] See Ex. 198 for another dance from *The Tempest*.

Ex. 256

Here Italian influence is noticeable, but the earlier English tradition is still alive. Locke's contrapuntal scoring is powerful in its
uncompromising originality.

While Locke, despite his apparent readiness to absorb the most
advanced elements of foreign music, always strongly emphasized
English qualities and tradition in practice as well as theory, the
incidental dances of John Blow (1649–1708) appear more
completely romanized. The same is true of the works of such less
important composers as the amateur James Sherard (1666–1738),
John Lenton (1655–c.1719), Richard Girdler, Thomas Tollett
(d. c.1696), and others.

## PURCELL AND THE *BASSO CONTINUO*

The last and greatest of English seventeenth-century composers,
Henry Purcell (1659–95), frankly announced his intention to
'imitate the Italian way'.[130] Yet, the warm, sweetly emotional
melody of Vitali and Corelli is here allied to English traditional
tunes and harmonies. There is a national as well as a certain international quality in Purcell's melodic and harmonic style which he
treats with such limitless freedom and personal daring.

The same can also be said of his early fantasias (1680) and In
Nomines for three to seven instruments[131]—pieces ostensibly
returning once again to the standard polyphonic type of the
beginning of the seventeenth century. Even these earliest manifestations of Purcell's genius (he was only twenty-two when he wrote

[130] In the foreword to his sonatas of 1683.
[131] Ed. Thurston Dart, *Purcell Society*, xxxi (London, 1959).

them) are full of the 'fire and fury' of Italian music. Intense
emotionalism is shown equally in his melodic and harmonic
elements, especially in the use of major and minor as in the
'Fantasia upon One Note' for five viols:

Ex. 257

The *basso continuo*, the last consequence of harmonic feeling
replacing the earlier polyphonic ideal, had a rough passage in
England. Attempts early in the century, later by John Jenkins,
Christopher Gibbons, Matthew Locke, and others, to introduce it
were mostly little more than short-score arrangements for an organ
optionally accompanying the polyphonic ensemble. Real continuo
parts were first used on a larger scale for vocal music, and only
occasionally for instrumental music; in this they did not really take
over until in Purcell's sonatas[132] the whole style and form were
entirely changed; after Purcell, the *basso continuo* was a regular
feature of English music just as it was on the Continent. The
changes in form, caused by the influx of foreign music, were not

---

[132] The *Sonnata's of III Parts: Two Violins and Basse: To the Organ or Harpsichord*
(1683) ed. J. A. Fuller Maitland, *Purcell Society*, v (1893; rev. ed. 1976); the *Sonatas of IV
Parts* (1697), ed. Charles Stanford, ibid., vii (1896; rev. ed. 1981).

noticeable in English instrumental music until about 1670 when French dance types and the Lully overture were imported into England by Blow, Banister, and their contemporaries. More important still, the polyphonic fantasia with its sectional arrangement had by that time become an introductory movement in dance suites and became more and more assimilated to the one-section fugue of the German type. Christopher Gibbons, Locke, Hingston, Simpson, and the other main composers writing between 1660 and 1680 all cultivated the fantasia as an additional piece in their suites but rarely as an independent form. Much elaborate work, however, was put into the various suite movements, whether dance pieces (chiefly almands, corants, sarabands, jigs, gavots, rants, brawls or bransles, and galliards) or free types (either pieces generally called 'air', which may mean any dance or non-dance composition, or pieces named 'introduction', 'conclusion', 'interlude', 'canon', or 'symphony', this last being a collective name applied to all sorts of long or short pieces). Particularly distinctive were sets of variations, either composed as 'grounds' on ostinato subjects like chaconnes and passacaglias, or else as 'divisions' which often approached the later classical type of *tema con variazioni*. Simpson was the best master of such 'grounds' for chamber music; hundreds of compositions of similar nature were produced by his contemporaries and immediate successors.

The most important newcomer to the field of late seventeenth-century instrumental form in England was the sonata. It had taken the complete re-organisation of musical life to popularize it in England. The polyphonic fantasia was still so alive and strong up to 1660 that the whole conception of the sonata was strange to English minds. Before that year the only Englishman who did try his hand at the sonata was William Young (d. 1662) whose music, faithfully copying German and Austrian models, was published at Innsbruck in 1653.[133] Jenkins seems to have been the first to write sonatas in England, but his pieces bearing the name—at least those which have been traced[134]—are no different in style or form from the fantasia. Only when the expressive Italian style had established itself firmly did composers write sonatas in the Italian and German idiom—Purcell, followed by James Sherard, Raphael Cortevi, Robert King, Daniel Purcell, Solomon Eccles, and others.

---

[133] Ed. William Gillies Whittaker (London, 1930).

[134] His *Twelve Sonatas for Two Violins and a Base with a Thorough Base for the Organ or Theorbo* (London, 1660), mentioned by Hawkins in his *History*, have never been discovered and probably never existed. Durham Cathedral Library possesses some sonatas for two or three viols (not violins).

Ensembles of viols were still played by old-fashioned music-lovers until after the Restoration. In 1676 Thomas Mace mourned their disappearance from the English musical scene. It was largely due to Charles II's personal tastes that violins so very completely conquered the viols in England, but the viols were doomed—even without the King's *coup de grâce*. They had become obsolete by 1675, though the bass viol remained a favourite instrument long after that date either for solo performance or as the bass part in trio ensembles after the Italian manner.

## THE CLIMATE OF THE NEW CENTURY

During the early eighteenth century fundamental changes occurred in every field of European art. Europe needed a new philosophy, new laws of thought, and a new moral code; art demanded new forms of expression. A basic unity of purpose underlies the development of music from the dramatic aspirations of the time around 1600, the monumental fugue and fugato forms of the Schütz-to-Bach period, the 'rationalist' *Lieder* of the Berlin school of the mid-century, the scientific and systematic musical theories of the French *Encyclopédistes* and of Rameau, the eras of *Empfindsamkeit* (sensibility) and *Sturm und Drang* (storm and stress) to the classical age. Through all these periods and styles one traces a common endeavour to emancipate the human mind from outworn forms of thought.

Within this general development two opposite trends can be recognized among musicians. Those who adopted the *style galant*, confining themselves to certain mannerisms of eighteenth-century Rococo, often lacked depth of purpose; tied as they were to absolutist Courts, their music remained superficial in emotional content. Johann Adolph Scheibe (1708–76), in his treatise on musical composition, accuses such composers of 'musical smuggling', specially mentioning Italians in this group.[135] On the other hand, many musicians sought a more profound musical equivalent of the new humanitarian philosophy, and the most important of these rose to true classical greatness. It is true that of the innumerable composers of this age many were torn between the two main trends; their achievement is of unequal value, or in itself contradictory. However, the main interest naturally attaches to the

---

[135] A musician who can only compose in the *style galant* 'ist ein musikalischer Schleichhändler (und das sind die meisten italienischen Komponisten, die auf gut Glück Italien verlassen)' *Über die musikalische Composition* (Leipzig, 1773), p. 10.

second group, who constituted the truly progressive element introducing innovations which proved fruitful and forward-reaching.

In much instrumental music from 1700 to 1750 a regenerated humanist attitude and a new expressive emotional style was gradually unfolded. The new mentality which permeates instrumental music during the first decades of the century is recognizable by certain main features: the evolution of a new clarity and transparency, together with empiricism and new stress on reasoning deduction. Besides this, however, there was a new and passionate searching into the depths of the human soul, a new and intense emotionalism, so that new ranges of human feeling were discovered for music. And composers' attention gradually became focused on the mentality of the ordinary man in accordance with the search for simplicity, genuineness and naturalness.

AESTHETIC CHARACTERISTICS

The French cultivated an art of delicate, distinct, and transparent lines. In the preface to his *Traité de l'Harmonie réduite à ses principes naturels* (Paris, 1722), Rameau expressed the wish to reintroduce 'reason' into music. In Germany we meet not only the unbounded and all-embracing imaginative art of Johann Sebastian Bach but also, in theory as well as in composition, the 'dry tone'— Goethe's Mephistopheles expresses his tiredness of it[136]—those sober and didactic qualities which are directed as much against speculative and mystical tendencies as against courtly pomp. The element of improvization lost importance—if we except the art of ornamental improvization which flowered in some types of music during the whole century. If the importance of the *basso continuo* was gradually declining, one of the reasons for this was the growing desire to note down all details of the music as it was to sound, unequivocally and unmistakably. It must be remembered, however, that such rationalist and precisionist tendencies were often bound up with the *style galant* of Rococo, especially in France.

The desire to be explicit and distinct is also reflected in the widespread custom of providing compositions with titles or programmatic headings. Although this habit started in French harpsichord music, it was soon taken over in chamber music, as we see in the works of Couperin, Marais, and Rameau, and also those of Telemann, Christoph Graupner, and others. At the same time we

---

[136] 'Ich bin des trocknen Tons nun satt,
Muss wieder recht den Teufel spielen.'

observe an increasing tendency towards programme music or 'tone-painting'.

## NEW EMOTIONALISM

As rational thought and empirical understanding assumed more importance, the desire for freedom of emotional expression also became more powerful. It would be quite incorrect to understand the effect of Enlightenment only as rationalistic, important as that aspect of eighteenth-century philosophy certainly is; after all, even Rousseau said about 1750 that in discussing any problem he first and foremost followed his feelings. The element of 'sensibility' became far more influential prior to the Viennese classics than that of mere *galanterie*. Many new terms of expression appear in chamber music, such as *affettuoso* (Franz Xaver Richter), *con spirito* (Ignaz Holzbauer), *amoroso* (Holzbauer), e.g. *lamentabile* in Reinhard Keiser, not to mention innumerable indications in French music—although these are related rather to the *style galant*. Dynamics, too, become more subtle and more detailed long before the Mannheim school made them of overriding importance (but the Mannheim composers transferred them from orchestral to chamber music).

## COSMOPOLITAN TENDENCIES

Ever since the Middle Ages there had been a certain amount of international influence in music. In the seventeenth century German, Austrian, English, and French composers chiefly looked to Italy. But as we have seen[137] there were French elements in Purcell's style, and the French overture penetrated German music; the basic constitution of the late seventeenth-century suite was international co-operation. The allemande was a German dance, the courante originated in France, the sarabande came from Spain, and the gigue from the British Isles; they all became common property. In Georg Muffat's *Florilegium Secundum* (Passau, 1698) there are (after an 'ouverture') an 'Entrée d'Espagnole', an 'Air pour les Hollandois', an 'Air pour des Anglois', a 'Gavotte pour des Italiens', and a 'Menuet pour des François'.

This interchange developed enormously in the eighteenth century. It was assisted by the xenophilism of some Courts, especially in Germany, but to an even greater extent by the numerous travelling composer-violinists such as Ariosti, Locatelli,

---

[137] Above, pp. 437 ff.

Vivaldi, and Veracini who made a variety of styles known to composers and public all over Europe. At the same time the composers themselves found fresh sources of musical inspiration in their travels. Telemann for instance composed whole suites and sonatas in the Polish style;[138] J. S. Bach opened his C minor sonata for violin and keyboard with a 'siciliano'. The Lullyan overture and French dances occur in the works of Handel, Bach, and others; the Italians adopted French dances,[139] and exotic and oriental motives began to appear.[140]

Of deeper significance is the fact that entire national characteristics were taken over by composers of another country: the Italian *cantabile* style, the 'dotted rhythms' of the French overture, harmonic effects such as the 'Neapolitan sixth', French and Italian graces, and so on. Purcell in the preface to his *Sonnatas of III Parts* (1683) claimed that he had 'faithfully endeavour'd a just imitation of the most fam'd Italian masters; principally, to bring the seriousness and gravity of that sort of Musick into vogue and Reputation among our Country-men'. And a decade later François Couperin 'le Grand', 'charmé de celles du signor Corelli', wrote the first of several *sonate da chiesa* or *sonades*, to use the gallicized form he always insisted on—which for years circulated pseudonymously. In 1726 he gave four of them fresh titles—'La Pucelle', for instance, became 'La Françoise' and 'La Visionnaire', 'L'Espagnole'—added a suite of dances to each, and published them as *ordres*, *Les Nations: Sonades et Suites de Simphonies en Trio*.[141] He had already paid public tribute to the Italian master in his 'Grande Sonate en Trio', *Le Parnasse ou l'Apothéose de Corelli* (1724).[142] Although it was a time of sharp controversy in France on the respective merits of French and Italian music,[143] he proclaimed the doctrine of internationalism explicitly in his preface to *Les Goûts-réunis ou Nouveaux Concerts;*[144] to which the *Apothéose de Corelli* was appended:

[138] Cf. K. Wilkowska-Chomińska, 'Telemanns Beziehungen zur polnischen Musik; Beiträge zu einem neuen Telemannbild', *Konferenzbericht der 1. Magdeburger Telemann-Festtage* (Magdeburg, 1963), p. 23.
[139] E.g. in his Op. 2 Corelli introduces gavottes; Veracini and Tartini have menuets.
[140] The *Musikalisch-Türkischer Eulenspiegel* (1668) in the Wolfenbüttel Library is one of the earliest examples.
[141] Ed. Amédée Gastoué, *Oeuvres complètes*, ix (Paris, 1933).
[142] Idem, x.
[143] See, for instance, François Raguenet's *Paralèle des italiens et des françois en ce qui regarde la musique et les opéras* (1702) and Le Cerf de La Viéville's *Comparaison de la musique italienne et de la musique française* (1704–6; reprinted Amsterdam, 1725).
[144] *Oeuvres complètes*, viii.

Le goût Italien et le goût François ont partagé depuis longtems (en France) la République de la Musique; à mon égard, J'ay toujours estimé les choses qui le meritoient, sans acception d'Auteurs, ny de Nation . . .

But Couperin's essential Frenchness is unmistakable. It shows in his employment of fanciful titles and quasi-programmatic plans; the *apothéoses* of both Corelli and Lully have 'stage-directions' which almost suggest ballet scenarios.

He was probably unique at the time in permitting performance of trio sonatas on two harpsichords sharing the two *dessus* parts without string or wind players. He explains in his *avis* to the *Apothéose composé à la mémoire immortelle de l'incomparable Monsieur de Lully* (1725):[145]

Ce Trio, ainsi qui l'Apothéose de Corelli, et le Livre complet de Trios . . . , peuvent s'exécuter à deux Clavecins, ainsi que sur tous autres instrumens. Je les exécute dans ma famille, & avec mes élèves, avec une réussite tres heureuse, sçavoir, en jouant le premier dessus & la Basse sur un des Clavecins; & le Second, avec la même Basse sur un autre à l'unisson.

French concerted music was already beginning to give a new importance to the keyboard partner, who was no longer restricted to a continuo role, witness the *Piecès de clavecin qui peuvent se jouer sur le violon* (1707)—that is, the violin taking over the right-hand part—of Elisabeth Jacquet de La Guerre. It reached a splendid culmination in Rameau's *Pièces de clavecin en concerts avec un violon ou une flûte, et un viole ou un $2^d$ violon* (Paris, 1741).

Of the Germans, Handel was almost invariably faithful to the continuo role of the harpsichord in his chamber music. The trio sonatas which make up the greater part of it are essentially Italianate in the Corelli tradition and his most important sets, the remarkably early (though probably later reworked) sonatas for two oboes and bass, the *VI Sonates à deux Violons, deux haubois ou deux Flutes traversieres & Basse Continue*, Op. 2 (Amsterdam, c.1731) and the *Seven Sonatas or Trios for two Violins or German Flutes with a Thorough Bass for the Harpsichord or Violoncello*, Op. 5 (London, 1739), are often close in style to his other instrumental works,[146] indeed Op. 5 consists largely of adaptations from operas, oratorios and anthems. In his friend Telemann we find not only a combination of German and Italian idioms but strong French influence and, as we have seen,[147] even excursions into

[145] *Oeuvres complètes*, x, p. 51.
[146] See pp. 262–3.
[147] See p. 244.

Polish and Moravian idioms.[148] He seems to have composed his earliest trios at Eisenach in 1708; he had already come under French influence at Sorau, still more at Eisenach, and after his visit to Paris in 1737 he became the leading champion of French music in Germany. A French elegance is detectable, for instance in the third movement of the Trio in the second *production* of his *Musique de Table* (1733):[149]

Ex. 258

[148] Two *Sonates polonaises* have been ed. Alicja Simon in Nagels Musik-Archiv. nos. 50 and 51 (Hanover, 1934).

[149] *Musikalische Werke*, xiii, ed. J. Philipp Hinnenthal (Kassel, 1962).

And a deeper Frenchness naturally informs the *Nouveaux Quatuors en six Suites* which he published in Paris in 1738,[150] as well as the French tempo-markings. The second movement of the first quartet is typical:

Ex. 259

[150] Ibid., xix, ed. Walter Bergmann (Kassel, 1965).

Incidentally, Telemann's quartet is the same here as in the third *production* of the *Musique de Table*: flute, violin, obbligato cello, and continuo. In the second *production* it consists curiously of *flauto dolce* (recorder) *ò Fagotto ò Violoncello*, two *flauti traversieri*, and continuo.

Telemann was the outstanding internationalist among German composers. Bach never really succumbed to French influence, although he was willing to write an *Overture nach Französischer Art* for harpsichord beside a *Concerto nach Italienischen Gust*, and to copy two clavecin suites by Charles Dieupart, apostle of Corelli in England, as well as Dieupart's table of ornamentation, in the same spirit that he transcribed concertos by Vivaldi, but his art was always profoundly German. Even in the mid-century Quantz felt it necessary to advise German musicians to develop 'an artistic taste which selects, by way of adequate appreciation, all that is best from the taste of various nations'.[151]

## NEW NATIONAL CONSCIOUSNESS

Paradoxical though it may appear, there is no contradiction between these internationalist tendencies and the fact that new international interests and individual national elements of style emerged at the same time. The influence of popular music is perceptible in all genres of chamber music. Not only are popular melodies taken over note for note, as they had been in the music of earlier centuries; the general idioms of popular music become part of the melodic fabric of the chamber music of many composers—for instance Bach's sonatas for violin and keyboard:

Ex. 260

(i) Presto (from No. 2: BWV 1015)

(ii) Allegro (from No. 3: BWV 1016)

---

[151] *Versuch einer Anweisung die Flöte traversière zu spielen* (Berlin, 1752; third ed., Breslau, 1789), chapter XVIII. The chapter concludes: 'Denn eine Musik, welche nicht in einem einzelnen Lande, oder in einer einzelnen Provinz, oder nur von dieser oder jener Nation allein, sondern von vielen Völkern angenommen und für gut erkannt wird, . . . muss, wenn sie sich anders auf die Vernunft und eine gute Empfindung gründet, ausser allem Streite die beste syn' (p. 334).

It might be said that the whole of the work of the older Neapolitan school is filled with the charm and fire of Italian popular music.

### THREE STAGES OF DEVELOPMENT

Chamber music during the first half of the eighteenth century shows three stages of development; features belonging to different stages naturally overlapping. The first rises from the firm tradition of seventeenth-century fugal polyphony. Instrumental music largely adheres to the monothematic principle. The *basso continuo* is still a vital part of its structure, and the instrumental style of chamber music (sonatas, trios, etc.) is not yet basically distinguished from that of orchestral music. In the second stage, the firm unity of the older classical age is shaken. Homophonic elements move to the foreground and Mattheson proclaims 'pure melody . . . in its noble directness, clarity and distinction' as against 'the artificial fugues and sophisticated partitas', a remark obviously directed against J. S. Bach, although in Germanic tradition from Fux and Bach to Haydn and Mozart the polyphonic element was never forgotten. The melodic conception is determined by a more sensuous emotionalism which can be grasped immediately by listeners; pleasing qualities, sweeter and more exciting, are more important than monumental content. Scheibe, in 1738, also attacks Bach because of his 'bombastic and confused way of composing, obscured by far too much artificiality';[152] he praises Johann David Heinichen (1683–1729) for his *galante Ausdruck*. Such titles as Guillemain's *Sonates en quatuor ou conversations galantes et amusantes* appear.[153] The art of polyphony is definitely beginning to be neglected; the middle parts of the score are reduced to accompaniment or to a mere filling-in function. Chamber and orchestral music become separated, each developing an instrumental idiom of its own.

The final stage is the 'pre-classical', heralding the age of *Sturm und Drang* and the Viennese classics. Here we find an art of expression foreshadowing Gluck, Haydn, and Mozart, in its search for new emotional qualities and a 'natural' freedom of expression ('. . . dass überall die Natur hervorleuchtet'),[154] introducing, at the same time, quick changes and variability. On the one hand we find in chamber music a new inwardness, on the other new dramatic qualities in melodic life and formal structure, finally leading to the

---

[152] *Der critische Musikus*, I., 6.
[153] See below, pp. 456 f.
[154] Quantz, *Versuch*, Introduction, p. 15.

dualism of 'sonata form' (Stamitz, Wagenseil). The thorough bass becomes less and less important; in many cases (e.g. in the Mannheim school) it becomes redundant altogether.

In the eighteenth century chamber music was no longer the exclusive affair of professional players, a minority of amateur players, and aristocratic audiences. While aristocratic musical centres such as Cardinal Ottoboni's and Prince Ruspoli's palaces in Rome, or the German courts, still retained an important position, the flourishing state of music publishing shows that many more people were prepared to purchase chamber music and play it.

## THE NEW TEXTURES

The distinction between solo and orchestral performance of instrumental music became final. The free and easy practice of the seventeenth century—when the choice of interpretation—solo or doubled or trebled strings—was still frequently left to the players— was superseded by definite indications, especially for the execution of trio sonatas. By around 1750 these almost invariably belonged to the sphere of chamber music. The Op. 1 (Paris, c.1755) of Johann Stamitz (1717–57) is one of the last instances of the older type 'qui sont faites pour exécuter ou à trois ou avec tout l'orchestre'. Around 1700 it was still considered desirable for the bass to be 'doubled at pleasure'. Each sphere of instrumental music henceforth developed independently, chamber music becoming more intimate, more detailed, and more differentiated, even though there are instances of orchestral treatment intruding upon chamber music: e.g. this passage in one Porpora sonata:[155]

Ex. 261

[155] From *Sinfonie da Camera a tre instromenti*, Op. 2 (London, 1736), reprinted as *Sonatas for two Violins with a Thorough Bass* (c.1740); ed. Guido Laccetti (Naples, 1925).

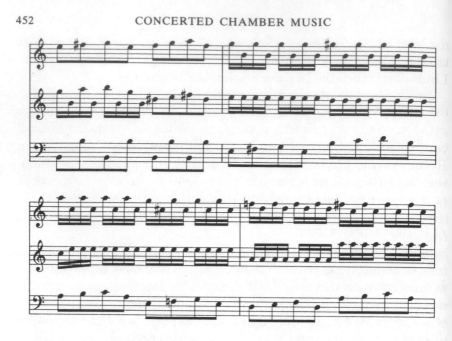

One symptom of the progress of chamber music may be seen in the complete and elaborate keyboard parts in J. S. Bach's sonatas for flute and cembalo (BWV 1030–2) and viola da gamba and cembalo (BWV 1027–9), which replaced the continuo parts of earlier accompaniments. But at the same time he continued to write flute sonatas with continuo (BWV 1033–5) and the great set BWV 1014–9 are described in the autograph as *Sei Suonate à Cembalo certato e Violino Solo, col Basso per Viola da Gamba accompagnato se piace*. Examples of this treatment also occur in sonatas for violin, flute, or oboe with cembalo by William Babell (*c.*1690–1723) and, somewhat later, in six violin sonatas with harpsichord by Christoph Förster (1693–1745). Yet only at the time of the Mannheim composers and Johann Schobert (*c.*1740–1767) did fully written-out keyboard parts in chamber music become the general rule. The more the *basso continuo* lost importance, the more prominent did the keyboard become in chamber music. Indeed it soon took the lead, often relegating the strings to an *ad libitum* role. About 1760 Schobert, a German working in Paris, began to publish *Sonates pour le Clavecin qui peuvent se jouer aver l'acc. du Violon, Sonates en Trio pour le Clavecin avec acc. de Violon et Basse ad Lib.*, and so on.[156] And in England, Charles Avison (1709–70) actually anticipated him with *Six sonatas*

---

[156] See Vol. VII, p. 534.

*for the harpsichord with accompanyments for two violins and violoncello*, Op. 5 (London, 1756); a second set, Op. 7, followed in 1760 and a third, Op. 8, in 1764.

INSTRUMENTS

On the whole, however, stringed instruments—particularly the violin—maintained their hegemony in chamber music. In the early eighteenth century music was still occasionally composed *per ogni sorte d'istromenti*: Franz Weichlein's *Musico-Instrumentalisches Divertissement* (Augsburg, 1705), where there are no indications as to which instruments should be used (*aus drei concertierenden Instrumenten bestehend*). However, around 1700 such instances are isolated. (Bach's *Kunst der Fuge* (1750) is, of course, exceptional for that date; it has indeed been claimed as a keyboard work written in score.) The only choice left to performers of trio sonatas was that one or both treble instruments might sometimes be played either by violins or by flutes or oboes. But around 1730 even this liberty gave way to precise indications for the instruments, since by that time the violin, especially in Italy, was rapidly developing a technique and hence idioms that could not be transferred to wind instruments. About 1740 the first violin became the leading instrument not only in orchestral but also in chamber music.

The bass viol, still a main instrument of chamber music in France (less frequently in Germany) became obsolete in Italian chamber music after 1700. By 1750 it had become an historical instrument used less and less, even for the re-inforcement of the *basso continuo*. Johann Schenk (1656–*c*.1724) was probably the last German composer to write chiefly for bass viol; his *Fantaisies bizarres de la goutte* (*c*.1715), published at Amsterdam where he spent most of his life, represent a last flowering of this formerly very important branch of instrumental composition. In France, Marin Marais (1656–1728) still wrote *La gamme et autres morceaux de simphonie* for *le violon, la viole et le clavecin* (Paris, 1723), while Bach composed his sonatas for viola da gamba and harpsichord at about the same time. But generally the viola and violoncello took the place of the viola da gamba; cello literature spread especially quickly.

All sorts of attempts were made at experiment, such as Bach's *violoncello piccolo*, sometimes described as *viola pomposa*; the quinton, used by Jacques Aubert (1689–1753) among others; as well as the *viola d'amore* which for a time figured quite prominently in chamber music. However, the violin family maintained its decisive influence in chamber music. Flutes were next in frequency (more and more often *traversières*), followed by oboes and bassoons. Interesting wind chamber music was also produced, by Gottfried Heinrich Stölzel (1690–1747), Johann Georg Christian Störl (1675–1719), Anton Wilhelm Solnitz (c.1708–1758), Antonio Vivaldi (1678–1741), Johann Stamitz (1717–57), and others. Solnitz also employed the clarinet in *Parthien* for two clarinets and two horns, and from 1750 onwards numerous composers wrote for it. The popular French *musette* was introduced in chamber ensembles (1726, 1730 and 1734) by Jean-Baptiste Anet (1661–1755), but was never generally accepted.

## VARIED COMBINATIONS

The number of four participants in the chamber ensembles was now rarely exceeded. Carl Heinrich Graun (c.1704–59) composed two quintets; a quintet in B minor for four flutes and bass was written by Jacques Loeillet (1685–1748); and there are some five-part Caprices by Jean-Ferry Rebel (1666–1747) as well as six sonatas for cornetti and trombone by Störl[157]—a late example of the *Turm-Musik* of the waits mentioned earlier in this chapter. The Library of the Gesellschaft der Musikfreunde in Vienna has the manuscript of a septet by Antonio Caldara (1670–1736). François Couperin's *Concerts royaux* for violin or flute, viola, oboe, bassoon and clavecin,[158] are well known, while Telemann and Vivaldi in their prolific output of chamber music experimented with various colourful combinations of string and wind instruments. Shortly after 1700 we further come across non-orchestral music in six to eight parts by Johann Christoph Pez (1664–1716) and Melchior d'Ardespin (c.1643–1717), and a *Musicalische Composition über die weltberühmte Lüneburger Sülze* for violin, four oboes, and bass by Johann Fischer (b. 1646). The six-part ricercar in Bach's *Musicalisches Opfer* (1747) was an exceptional late-comer, reviving an antiquated form.

## THE TRIO SONATA

The trio sonata for two upper parts of equal pitch and one bass, all *concertante*, at first retained its dominating position. Almost every composer from 1700 to 1750 who contributed to instrumental music in any field also wrote trio sonatas. The wealth of artistic content, of means of expression, of styles, of formal structures and

---

[157] Ed. H. Schultz, *Erbe deutscher Musik*, xiv (1941).
[158] *Oeuvres complètes*, vii (Paris, 1933).

(within the limits of this particular combination) of effects of
instrumentation contained in their colossal output is remarkable.
We find lyrical and heroic, dramatic and tragic, playful and sentimental, coquettish and melancholy elements conveyed in strictly
fugal, rhapsodic, or homophonic styles demanding exceedingly difficult and virtuoso-like or easily playable technique. The melodic
lines may be strongly ornamental or elementarily simply. There are
conventional and advanced-experimental types of scoring, with
extremely individual or with neutral and traditional thematic lines
as in the sonatas long attributed to Pergolesi:

Ex. 262

Although the development of this genre gradually moved away from the baroque towards the sentimental (*empfindsam*) style, and later *Sturm und Drang*, several different, even contradictory types of instrumental diction and artistic meaning continued to appear concurrently for a considerable time. The sonata for flute, violin and bass in Bach's *Musicalisches Opfer* dates from 1747, while five sonatas for the same combination but much more 'modern' in style had been written by Carl Philipp Emanuel sixteen years earlier. Johann Stamitz's trio sonatas,[159] again of an entirely different type—optionally for orchestra—were composed only six years after Bach's *Opfer*. From the middle of the century onward the trio sonata was definitely on the decline, although the young Haydn was attracted to it *c*.1750–1765.[160]

## THE STRING QUARTET

The trio sonata retained its vitality for so many decades because it constituted a compromise between polyphonic *concertante* and chiefly harmonic-homophonic *cantabile*. Yet two genres of chamber music which (in addition to the Mannheim piano trios already mentioned) took over this heritage: the solo sonata with *basso continuo* or harpsichord, which is dealt with in the following chapter, and the string quartet.

The string quartet in its final form—for two violins, viola, violoncello without basso continuo—did not arise immediately from its seventeenth-century forerunners such as the four-part sonata with basso continuo, popular in Italy and Germany, or the four-part fantasia in England. It gradually evolved as a new entity, perhaps for the first time in four *Sonate a quattro: Due Violini, Violetta e Violoncello, senza Cembalo* by Alessandro Scarlatti. Six string quartets by Caldara (*c*.1670–1736) are preserved in the Library of the Gesellschaft der Musikfreunde in Vienna, and in 1743 the French violin virtuoso Louis-Gabriel Guillemain (1705–70) published *Six Sonates en quatuor ou conversations galantes et amusantes entre une flûte traversière, un violon, une basse de viole et un violoncelle*, admittedly for the 'wrong' instruments but foreshadowing in its sub-title that which was to be the essence of the true string quartet style: instrumental 'conversation':

---

[159] See Vol. VII, pp. 523–4.
[160] Ibid., p. 526.

Ex. 263

Aria (from Op. 12, no. 1)

The *Sonata à 4* in D minor by Johann Friedrich Fasch (1688–1758)[161] is characteristic of the transition period; 'baroque' themes are treated in a new style:

Ex. 264

[161] Ed. Riemann, *Collegium musicum*, no. 13 (Leipzig, n.d.).

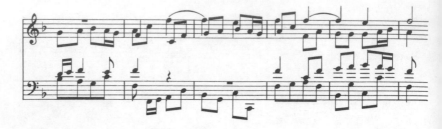

and orchestral performance would be quite possible. It would be equally possibly with Haydn's earliest quartets, Opp. 1 and 2—*divertimenti a quattro* as he called them—the earliest of which dates from *c*.1750; Op. 1, no. 5, actually had parts for oboes and horns and two of Op. 2 had horn-parts. Early publishers sometimes added figures to cello parts. Besides the absence of the thorough bass, the new string quartet was notable for homogeneity of tone-colour among the four instruments, capacity to produce full chords as well as contrapuntal lines, wide compass from C to the top registers of the violin, and unlimited scope for expressive cantilena.

The art of the string quartet is not an art of overwhelming sensuous power, but rather a medium demanding thoughtful, intelligent playing and listening which tends to activize the attention of players and listeners. In spite of the primacy of the first violin, it is egalitarian by comparison with other musical forms, although that equality of treatment of first and second violins characteristic of the trio sonata was lost for the time being.

Closely related to the string quartet were the string trio and string quintet cultivated by Carl Heinrich Graun (*c*.1704–59) and Johann David Heinichen (1683–1729). The *duo* of two instruments of equal pitch (violins, flutes, without bass) received a new stimulus after a long and venerable history since the *bicinia* of the sixteenth century; in the eighteenth the duo took over part of the heritage of the trio sonata. Some composers also wrote for the typically domestic combination of one top and one bottom instrument (violin and viola, violin, and cello) without bass.

### CLASSICAL SONATA FORM

During the first half of the eighteenth century the new type of first movement, 'sonata form' in its classical meaning, was beginning to take shape. Up till then many seventeenth-century structures still survived: the ricercar principle with several (mostly short) fugal developments or non-fugal episodes following each other (containing a variety of ever-changing motives and subjects), or the monothematic fugue which during the age of Bach became particularly common in Germany. In addition the pre-classical concerto (with its 'ritornello form') as it was consolidated by Vivaldi began to play an important part not only in orchestral but also in chamber music. With the new and more nervous and changeable emotionalism which spread during the era of Enlightenment the thematic dualism which was to become one of the main features of the classical sonata evolved more and more distinctly. At the same time the beginnings of sonata 'development' made themselves felt; the tension created by introducing two or more contrasting themes is worked up to a climax in the 'development' and postulates in many cases 'solution'. Thus the function of the new sonata developments is entirely different from that of fugal development.

Early examples of thematic dualism occur in sonatas by Bach (e.g. in his E major and G major sonatas for violin and keyboard, BWV 1016 and 1019). Dall'Abaco, too, and, up to a point, even Corelli show signs of the classical sonata form. But only at the time of the Mannheim school, of the Italians of the Tartini generation (e.g. Carlo Tessarini, c.1690–1766), and particularly of C. P. E. Bach was the new dualistic principle more generally accepted; it may be illustrated by the first and second themes of no. 2 of Stamitz's *Sonates à trois parties concertantes* (Paris, c.1755):

Ex. 265

Movements often grew considerably in length; there are already very long movements among the chamber music of Dall'Abaco. The four-movement-scheme, frequent in seventeenth-century sonatas, had been temporarily reduced to three movements after

1700, but by about the middle of the eighteenth century the four-movement pattern again became predominant, though of a new type, mainly through the activities of the Mannheim school. The anarchy of structures and types was overcome and a sequence of four definite movements established: allegro (mostly cantabile) as the first movement, a song-like slowish second movement, a minuet, and a finale (which might be in sonata form, rondo form, variation form, or extended aria form). This arrangement of movements at the same time served to convey a certain content—translating, as it were, a whole artistic vision into musical reality.

In French chamber music dances and small characteristic movements (often with titles) were very common for a time; such pieces, typical of French rococo, frequently have square metrical schemes and correlative structural periods. This aspect of French instrumental music, by overcoming the seventeenth-century conception of form and melody, constituted an important transitional stage from the colossal melodic lines of the previous century to the highly organised rhythmical and metrical life of the classical age. Yet, after all, the most important achievement of the first half of the century in the melodic field was the 'theme' in its new classical meaning, exemplified in Ex. 265 and in Tartini's *Sonata a tre*, Op. 8, no. 1:

Ex. 266

The strictness and concentration of the older fugal subjects together with the polyphonic structure itself were gradually relaxed. The whole melodic conception became lighter, more flexible, until the former fugue subjects change into replicas of song.

Song-like ideas as main melodic factors of a piece became common by the middle of the century.

The new type of theme was not adopted with a view to a counter-subject joining it, or for a role in a contrapuntal texture; having only harmonic accompaniment, it was intended to absorb the entire attention of the listener. No longer monumental, often decked out with trills, graces, 'sobbing' accents and sentimental suspensions, it was much livelier, more colourful, more character-istic, more sensitive than the old fugal subject, and it was organized in balanced periods. The old formula: 'thematic head—sequences—cadence' was gradually superseded by the principle: 'theme I —transition—theme II' and so on.

Yet certain instrumentalisms were introduced into this cantabile style in the form of octave leaps, broken chords, drumming note repetitions, and so on. The beginnings of themes are often signal-like, frequently sounding a note of optimism in radiant major.[162] As a last remnant of polyphonic procedure, one finds a kind of hidden polyphony in broken-chord figues, as in this passage from Telemann's *XII Fantasien* for solo violin (1735):

Ex. 267

Harmonically it was the relationship of tonic and dominant which became overridingly important. Chords such as the sub-dominant with its parallel, the dominant parallel or even the tonic parallel temporarily lost their importance; they obviously now had a neutralizing effect, tending to make the music appear archaic, remote, or sombre. The reduction of harmonic life to the dominant-tonic relation may appear to us a limitation of harmonic conception; in the eighteenth century it was evidently considered progressive.

[162] Arnold Schering, *Musik-Geschichte* (based on Arrey von Dommer) (6.–8. edition, Leipzig, 1923), p. 593, points out the Mannheim School's preference for major; 95% of their music is in major keys.

# VII

## THE SOLO SONATA

### By CHARLES W. HUGHES

IT was the solo sonata, particularly that for violin, which brought singing melody to instrumental music; indeed it had originated in vocal solo melody.[1] Together with the trio sonata and the *concerto grosso* it also demonstrated the possibilities of a musical structure which, though it absorbed the devices of the *canzon*, used them in a wider plan which balanced movement against movement, which evolved within movements a sense of organic unity, of an articulated whole which was gradually to lose much of its polyphonic character and finally lead to the sonata accompanied by the violin. Yet the *canzon* (later the fugue) was to remain within the framework of the violin sonata to the middle of the eighteenth century. The fugal movements of Corelli, Tartini, and Bach show that the polyphonic impulse remained strong up to the final flowering of the Baroque sonata. The other great impulse came from the dance. The tentative dance groupings – dance and after-dance, pavane and galliard – were amplified into the suite. The relentless repetitions of actual dance music gave birth to a sequence of movements, varied, contrasting in rhythm and mood, intended solely for the pleasure of the listener. The chamber sonata marked the climax of this development. Later violinists preferred the musical variety to be gained by mingling dance movements together with those derived from more purely musical sources. As the solo instrument emerged from the performing group there was also rapid development of technique and of virtuoso effects. This was part of a general development of music as a display art, aspects of which include the gradual extension upwards of the range of the stringed instruments, the development of an elaborate technique of double-stopping and chord playing, the evolution of the bow and the appearance of all the varied articulations of which it is capable. But the human voice was at the heart of things. As Telemann put it:

[1] See Vol. IV, p. 574.

Singen ist das Fundament zur Music in allen Dingen.
Wer die Composition ergreifft, muss in seinen Sätzen singen.
Wer auf Instrumenten spielet, muss des Singens kündig seyn.
Also präge man das Singen jungen Leuten fleissig ein.

(Singing is the foundation of music in all respects. Whoever composes
must sing in his compositions. Whoever plays on instruments must be
experienced in singing. Therefore one should diligently urge young
people to sing.)[2]

The accompanied solo sonata placed a single instrument in relief
as a dominant melodic thread against a harmonic background. This
concept had to emerge gradually in an age in which the polyphonic
interweaving of the madrigal or motet represented the normal way
of making music. Yet a madrigal might be sung by one voice if the
other parts were played by instruments and it could be transcribed
as a solo song accompanied by the lute, and this practice left traces
at a time when the violin was well established in popular favour.
Not only did Biagio Marini include canzonet-like movements in his
first work, the *Affetti musicali* (Venice, 1617), but in no. 21, 'La
Soranza', he even adds the text for the final part. Later examples
may be found in Marco Uccellini's Op. 4, no. 12, from the *Sonate,
correnti et arie* (Venice, 1645), where the words 'Caporal Simon'
are printed wherever the refrain appears, and in Andrea Falconieri's
*Il primo libro di canzon, sinfonie, fantasie, capricci, brandi, cor-
renti, gagliarde, alemane, volte per violini e viole* (Naples, 1650).
Here we find such captions as 'Tiple a Tre', 'Canciona dicha la
Ennamorada'. Such examples, reaching to the mid-century, show
how tardy the instrumental ensemble was in emancipating itself
from the leading-strings of vocal composition; the accompanied solo
sonata had already broken free.

VARIATIONS ON A BASS

Neither the transcription of canzonets nor the embellishment of
madrigals represented an advance in form. Here the string-player
was at most the decorator of a structure which had been established
for other purposes. There were, however, two factors which were
to exert a critical influence on the development of the sonata. One
was the art of variation playing over a repeated bass theme, the
other the *canzon* which, though a vocal form in origin, became
the nucleus from which the church sonata evolved.

---

[2] *Lebens-Lauff mein Georg Philipp Telemann*, in Mattheson, *Grosse General-Bass-Schule*
(Hamburg, 2nd ed. 1731), p. 162. Facsimile reprint in Willi Kahl, *Selbstbiographien
deutscher Musiker des XVIII. Jahrhunderts* (Cologne and Krefeld, 1948), p. 217.

The art of playing extempore variations over a bass theme or 'ground' is very completely described by contemporary authors. Diego Ortiz, in the *Tratado*[3], (Rome, 1553) had given many details while Christopher Simpson, who wrote his masterly treatise *The Division Violist* (1659) over a century later, places his main emphasis on this art. The highest art of the gamba-player according to Simpson was the art of improvizing divisions or diminutions on the longer notes of an ostinato bass. One player repeated the ground, the other elaborated it with an artistic discretion summed up in Simpson's maxim: 'If you have anything more excellent than other, reserve it for the Conclusion.'[4] We may regard such improvisations as the source of the varied compositions constructed over a repeated bass which adorn the literature for bowed instruments during the seventeenth and eighteenth centuries. Favourite themes like the *romanesca* and *ruggiero*, which Salamone Rossi varied in his *3 lib. de varie sonate* (1623), were repeatedly used by later composers. The composed variations or 'divisions' which Christopher Simpson included as examples in his treatise, together with other examples in manuscript by William Brade, Daniel Norcome, John Jenkins, Polewheele, Charles Butler, Charles Coleman, and Maurice Webster,[5] represented English practice, e.g.:

Ex. 268[6]

[3] See Vol. IV, pp. 560–1 and 705–6.
[4] *The Division Violist* (2nd ed., 1665 and 1667), p. 57.
[5] New York Public Library, Drexel Ms. 3551.
[6] Ibid., Drexel Ms. 4257.

Third Division

The persistence of the idea on a more popular level is indicated by John Playford's *The Division Violin* (2nd ed., 1685). Corelli's *La Folia* variations, Biber's Passacaglia for unaccompanied violin, and Bach's D minor Chaconne show the gradually unfolding possibilities of this type of variation.

### THE *CANZON*

The form known as the *canzon* or *canzone* played an important part in the evolution of the violin sonata. Frescobaldi had sometimes secured an underlying unity in his keyboard *canzoni*[7] by making later sections fugal expositions on subjects which are variations of the subject of the first section, but violinist composers do not appear to have carried out the idea of the 'variation *canzon*' as consistently as Frescobaldi. However, Tarquinio Merula,[8] Maurizio Cazzati, G. B. Vitali, and Marco Uccellini followed his example. In a Sonata in A major, Op. 5, no. 2 (Venice, 1649), for violin and basso continuo, by Uccellini the last section is based on a variant of the theme used in the first section, thus giving the work something of a ternary character:

### Ex. 269[9]

(i) First section

---

[7] See Vol. IV, pp. 648 ff.
[8] Ibid., p. 578.
[9] Hugo Riemann (ed.), *Old Chamber Music* (London, 1898), iv, p. 135.

(ii) Final section

The prevailing polyphonic texture of the *canzon* was varied by the intrusion of episodes in triple time, which were often melodious and sometimes homophonic in style, and derived ultimately from Venetian opera. In the simplest possible case such an episode formed a contrasting middle section, preceded and followed by imitative sections based on the *canzon* theme. Where the section in triple time makes two or more appearances we may speak of a 'refrain *canzon*'. Thus a posthumously published Sonata in C major by Giovanni Battista Fontana (d. 1630) begins with an imitative treatment of a *canzon* theme (i); then follows the refrain section in triple time (ii):

Ex. 270[10]

(i) Canzona theme

---

[10] From *Sonate a 1. 2. 3. per il Violino* (Venice, 1641); reprinted in Luigi Torchi, *L'Arte musicale in Italia*, vii (Milan, 1908), p. 92. Torchi's details are unreliable and his continuo realizations should be disregarded.

(ii) Refrain

A new section in duple time starts soberly, then breaks into more rapid figuration. Once more the refrain enters, and the work then closes with a final statement and working out of the *canzon* theme. If *A* represents the *canzon* section and *B* the refrain, we would have *ABACA*.

The number of sections in the *canzon* was not fixed. Some early examples were much subdivided. The patchwork of imitative beginnings, each feebly developed, which we find in Biagio Marini's Sonata in D minor and major from his Op. 22 (Venice, 1655),[11] seems to continue this tendency.

On the other hand a trend in the direction of a form in four

---

[11] Torchi, op. cit., p. 49.

sections was evident at an early date and as the number of sections was diminished each section was better developed. Finally they appear as four detached movements. Though subject to many modifications, a typical order of movements in the *sonata da chiesa* is a Grave introduction, an Allegro chief movement, a sustained lyrical movement, and a rapid and brilliant finale. The early composers named this form *sonata da chiesa* (church sonata), from the *sonata da camera* (chamber sonata), to be discussed later, partly because of the manner in which it was used. In many churches instrumental music played a considerable role; often it was the custom to perform a sonata at the moment when the Host was shown to the worshippers. At St. Mark's, Venice, two violinists were employed for this purpose as late as 1692.[12]

### ELABORATION OF THE BASS

In solo sonatas the continuo elaborating the printed bass-line is essential; in sonatas *à 2* like Corelli's Op. V it is optional as he states on the title page. In the former the continuo provides a harmonic support: in the latter it acts as *basso sequente* following the lowest part of the texture, and usually simplifying it.[13]

Certain compositions, like Frescobaldi's 'Toccata per spinettina e violino, overa liuto e violino',[14] display an elaborate keyboard part; a solo for a *spinettina* was provided with a reinforcing bass part. The violin enters with an elaborate solo by way of interlude and later joins with the other instruments in the final section. More tentative are passages in which a composer has jotted down motives which might be used in accompanying the work. Thus George Jeffries (d. 1685) in the fifth of his six fancies 'of 3 Parts for the Violls and the Virginall'[15] has noted ideas in the autograph score which he must have intended for the keyboard-player. But there is nothing tentative in the organ parts, often independent, to be found earlier in the works of Coprario[16] and William Lawes.[17] Jeffries himself in his 'Fantasia of 2 pts to the Organ For the Violin'

[12] Francesco Caffi, *Storia della musica sacra nella già Capella Ducale di S. Marco in Venezia dal 1318 al 1797*. Two vols. (Venice, 1854–5).

[13] The use of harmonic continuo was by no means as obligatory and omnipresent as is generally supposed. See Peter Allsop, 'The Role of the Stringed Bass as a Continuo Instrument in Italian Seventeenth Century Instrumental Music', *Chelys*, viii (1978–9).

[14] Brit. Lib., Add. 34003; published in the second edition of his *Primo Libro* (Rome, 1628).

[15] Brit. Lib., Add. 10, 338.

[16] E.g. the first suite for violin, bass viol, and organ, *Musica Britannica*, xlvi, ed. Richard Charteris (London, 1980), p. 1.

[17] E.g. *Musica Britannica*, xxi, ed. Murray Lefkowitz (2nd, revised edition, London, 1971), p. 150. See also Vol. IV, p. 588.

elaborately worked out the organ part for the whole piece. As the
title indicates, one of the two parts is for violin; the other, an
undesignated bass instrument, sometimes reinforces the bass of the
organ part, sometimes plays independent phrases. It is described as
'after 1669' in the catalogue of the British Library; if it is autograph
it could not be later than 1685:

Ex. 271

Performers sometimes adapted compositions in three real parts for harpsichord and violin. Not only did composers sometimes indicate that the second violin part of a trio was optional; they also assumed that a trio might be converted into a solo sonata by assigning two of the three *obbligato* parts to a harpsichordist while the solo instrument played the third. Conversely a composition of this kind published as a solo with clavier might also be performed as a trio; Biagio Marini in his Op. 8 (Venice, 1626) includes a sonata composed in imitative style for violin and organ, observing that a violin or descant trombone may play the upper voice of the organ part. Conversely, a century later, Bach utilized a trio for two flutes and continuo (BWV 1039) as the basis for his G major sonata for viola da gamba and clavier (BWV 1027). Solo sonatas with three obbligato parts were sometimes called trios;[18] the D minor sonata attributed to J. S. Bach (BWV 1036) is an example.[19]

## THE *SONATA DA CAMERA*

The word 'sonata' has already been used where the modifications of the *canzon* characteristic of the early seventeenth century were discussed. The terms *canzon* and 'sonata' were used as equivalents in such early collections as Tarquinio Merula's *Canzoni, ovvero sonate concertate* (Venice, 1637), but 'sonata' was destined to be the victorious term. The term *sinfonia* which appears in such titles as Salamone Rossi's *Sinfonie e gagliarde* (Venice, 1607)[20] or Biagio Marini's *Madrigale e symfonie* of the same year is burdened with a superfluity of meanings; it may mean an instrumental piece which is neither a dance nor a paraphrase of a vocal composition; it may mean an introductory movement as in Giovanni Battista Buonamente's *Sonate, Sinfoni, Gagliarde, Corrente, et Brandi* (Venice, 1637); it may mean a *sonata da chiesa*, as it does in the *Symphoniae unius, duorum, trium, IV et V instrumentorum* (Antwerp, 1644) of Nicolaus a Kempis.[21]

The roots of the *sonata da camera*, or chamber sonata, extend back to a period when solo violin literature did not exist. The germ from which it developed was the association of a dance in duple metre with a livelier variant of the same tune in ternary metre. Such pairs might consist of dance and after-dance, pavane and galliard, or various other combinations. Thus in the *balletto* and *cor-*

---

[18] Arnold Schering, 'Zur Geschichte der Solosonate in der ersten Hälfte des 17. Jahrhunderts', *Riemann-Festschrift* (Leipzig, 1909), p. 318.
[19] Mod. ed. Hermann Keller, *Nagels Musik Archiv,* no. 49.
[20] See Vol. IV, p. 575.
[21] One example in Riemann, *Old Chamber Music*, iv, p. 142.

*rente* for two violins and bass called 'Il Priulino' by Biagio Marini
the *corrente* is merely a rhythmical transformation of the *balletto*.[22]
Through the extension of this principle to a series of dance movements the variation suite was evolved in the work of Paul Peuerl
and J. H. Schein.[23] Though this type of suite had little effect on the
*sonata da camera*, we do find examples like a *Partie poure la Fleute
douce* by Johann Fischer (1646–1721), in which the opening phrases
of the allemande, gigue, air, and menuet are all related:[24]

Ex. 272

(i) Allemande

(ii) Gigue

---

[22] *Arie, madrigali et correnti a 1. 2. 3.* (Venice, 1620); mod. ed. in Torchi. op. cit., vii,
p. 10.

[23] See Vol. IV, pp. 594–5.

[24] *Musicalisch Divertissement bestehend in einigen Ouverturen und Suiten mit 2 Stimmen*
(Dresden 1699); mod. ed. in *Vier Suiten für Blockflöte*, ed. W. Woehl (Kassel, 1950).

(iii) Air

Even where this idea is not carried out with such rigour a relationship may sometimes be traced between the allemande and the following courante; thus, in Johannes Schenck's *Scherzi musicali*
(Amsterdam, *c.*1698)[25] these two dances are related in the third
sonata.

## Ex. 273

(i) Allemande

(ii) Courante

(iii) Sarabande

---

[25] Mod. ed. Hugo Leichtentritt (Leipzig, 1906).

(iv) Menuet

Dances appear in the earliest publications for violin though they do not form suites. Thus in Biagio Marini's *Arie, madrigale et correnti a 1.2.3* (Venice, 1620) we find not only the *correnti* of the title but also a *romanesca* followed by its *gagliarda*,[26] the latter based on a variant of the same bass. Fontana's already mentioned posthumous collection of *Sonate a 1.2.3* (Venice, 1641) contains a 'Balletto e Pass'e Mezzo'.[27] Dance movements also appear in Venetian collections by Marco Uccellini (1645) and Martino Pesenti (1645).[28] The term *sonata da camera* was later to become the usual expression for sequences of dance movements. The appearance of the term in Marini's *Diverse generi di sonate, da chiesa, e da camera* (Venice, 1655), is eighteen years later than its appearance on the title-page of a publication by Tarquinio Merula.[29] Any attempt to generalize as to the dances employed in the *sonata da camera* must end in failure. It is true that with the harpsichordist Chambonnières the characteristic movements of the 'classic' suite have appeared, though he does not use the term 'suite'. Froberger favoured the order allemande-courante-sarabande, or allemande-gigue-courante-sarabande. These dances were also employed by violin composers but with great freedom of choice and with the addition of other dances. Giovanni Maria Bononcini (1642–78), who published a volume of violin and violone or spinet in 1671,[30] acknowledges French influence by marking each movement of the sequence *aria, corrente, sarabanda* 'in still Francese'.

[26] *Historical Anthology of Music*, ed. A. T. Davison and Willi Apel, ii (London, 1950), no. 199.
[27] Torchi, op. cit., p. 99.
[28] Ibid. pp. 103 and 284.
[29] Canzon, 'La Strada', from *Canzoni overo sonate concertate per chiesa e camera* in Schering, *Geschichte der Musik in Beispielen* (reprint, New York, 1950), no. 184.
[30] Ed. M. Abbado (Milan, 1968).

Movements of a neutral character had been used to introduce
dance movements by Salamone Rossi in 1607 and by Giovanni
Battista Buonamente in his *Settimo libro di sonate* (Venice, 1637).
Though in many cases the prelude of a chamber sonata seems
merely to borrow the character of the grave opening movement of
a church sonata, almost all the dignified contemporary forms were
used to introduce sequences of dances. In England the imitative
fancy was used to precede a pair of dances, or exceptionally a true
suite. Thus Coprario in the early seventeenth century employed
sequences such as fancy, almaine, galliard.[31] And the fantasias of
Matthew Locke 'for several friends', dating probably from the
1660s,[32] consist mainly of fantasia, pavan, ayre, courante, saraband,
and jigg. Here the dance sequence is extended enough to form a
true suite, though it is strange to see both the ancient pavan (without its usual partner, the galliard) and the more recent saraband in
the same composition. Even more interesting are six sets by Locke's
older contemporary John Jenkins,[33] each consisting of fancy,
almaine, and ayre. These are definitely indicated as 'for a Violin
and a Bass to the Organ'. The fact that the organ is specified shows
that the bass was to be treated as a continuo part. We should
expect this in any case since we have both surviving 'organ books'
and contemporary testimony to show that fancies were so accompanied.

## SOLO MUSIC FOR VIOLS

The most important solo stringed instrument from the late sixteenth century, however, had been not the violin but the *viola da
gamba*, and particularly the bass of the family. The rapid development in the art of violin playing had caused it to lose its popularity
with amateurs, though brilliant players such as Antoine Forqueray
(1671–1745) kept it in the public eye into the eighteenth century,
particularly in France. Such English publications as Playford's
*Musick's Recreation on the Viol, Lyra Way* (2nd ed. 1682), with its
tiny naïve pieces, were obviously designed for domestic music, as
were the song versions for gamba (and a variety of other instruments) in Jakob Kremberg's *Musicalische Gemüths-Ergötzung*
(Dresden, 1689):

[31] John Coprario, *Fantasia-Suites,* ed. Richard Charteris, *Musica Britannica,* xlvi
(London, 1980).
[32] Matthew Locke, *Chamber Music: I and II,* ed. Michael Tilmouth, *Musica Britannica,*
xxxi–xxxii (London, 1971–2).
[33] Two sets in John Jenkins, *Fancies and Ayres,* ed. Helen J. Sleeper (Wellesley, Mass.,
1950).

Ex. 274

wenn schon - bar ge - gen Freund und

Feind _____ be - strei - ten

Unaccompanied works for gamba provide a link between the earlier works for lute and the later compositions for unaccompanied violin. The *viola da gamba* was, as the Sieur de Machy reminds us in the preface to his *Pièces de violle* (Paris, 1685), an instrument of harmony. A whole series of works for unaccompanied gamba illustrate this, e.g. the unaccompanied preludes in Simpson's *The Division Violist* (1659), and the suites in Benjamin Hely's *The compleat Violist* (1699). The Prelude and Gavotte from de Machy's first suite may serve as an example:

Ex. 275

(i)

(ii)

Among the later gambists in France three deserve special mention, Marin Marais, Louis de Caix d'Hervelois, and Antoine Forqueray. Marais (1656–1728), who had a varied career as soloist, composer, and performer in the orchestra of the Académie Royale de Musique and in the Opera where he afterwards became conductor, was one of the great gambists of his day. His pieces, elaborately ornamented, elegant, beautifully adapted to the instrument, were truly French in style.[34] Certain works of his as well as those of Caix d'Hervelois (c.1670–c.1760) were provided with charming poetic titles in the manner of Couperin. Only one volume remains to tell us of the art of Antoine Forqueray (1671–1745)[35] and of that of his son Jean-Baptiste (1700–1782). Daquin de Chateaulyon gives a curious account of the development of Forqueray's playing:

One can say that no one has surpassed Marais: only one equalled him, that is the famous Forqueray. . . . Forqueray appeared in society at the moment when the Italians aroused in France an astonishing desire to imitate them towards the year 1698. He tried to do everything on his viol that they did on the violin and he succeeded in his endeavour.[36]

The compositions of Forqueray did indeed demand a degree of virtuosity which was characteristic of his playing. A contemporary expressed this by saying that Marais played like an angel, Forqueray like a devil.

The gamba developed in an individual fashion in England. Here we find many famous players, but much of their work was concerted music.[37] One branch of the solo literature was that for lyra viol, a small bass instrument often tuned to the notes of the major or minor chord ('harpway sharp' or 'harpway flat'). In Holland Johannes

---

[34] Six Suites for Viol and Thoroughbass, ed. Gordon J. Kinney (Madison, 1976).
[35] Pièces de Viole Avec La Basse Continue, Composées par Mr. Fourqueray le Père. J. G. Prod'homme, 'Les Forquerays', Rivista musicale italiana, x (1903), p. 687.
[36] Siècle littéraire de Louis XV (Paris, 1752), i, p. 142; quoted by Prod'homme, op. cit.
[37] See pp. 433 ff.

Schenck (1660–after 1712) left a voluminous collection of works for gamba, the *Konst-oeffeningen*, Op. 2 (Amsterdam, 1688), *Scherzi musicali*, Op. 6 (Amsterdam, c.1692), *Le nymphe di Rheno* for two gambas and continuo, Op. 8, and *L'echo du Danube*, Op. 9[38] (both Amsterdam, undated). A curious medical item is *Les fantaisies bisarres de la goutte*, Op. 10 (Amsterdam). Certain pieces in the *Scherzi musicali* impress one by their dimensions, their technical demands, and their largeness of style. Occasionally, as in the French overture (no. XIII), the music suggests the force of the string orchestra rather than that of a solo instrument. In the German-speaking countries we may note August Kühnel (1645– c.1700) whose graceful sonatas and other works show an appealing if minor talent.[39] Konrad Höffler (b. 1647), who published his *Primitiae Chelicae*[40] at Nuremberg in 1695, was a fine virtuoso player delighting in fantastic toccata-like runs and in elaborate chordal passages.

The greatest masters were not attracted by the instrument. The gamba sonata formerly attributed to the young Handel is almost certainly the work of the Nuremberg composer Johann Matthäus Leffloth (1705–31). Bach's three sonatas for gamba and harpsichord (BWV 1027–29) are genuine, though 1027 seems to be a transcription of one for two flutes and continuo; they were probably written c.1720 at Cöthen for the gambist Christian Ferdinand Abel. The gamba parts are entirely linear, without the double stopping of the 'classical' gamba style.

### EARLY ITALIAN MASTERS OF THE VIOLIN SONATA

The violin was primarily an Italian instrument and solo violin music was born in Italy. It was Biagio Marini (c.1597–1665) who may be said to have founded the Italian school of violinist composers. His *Affetti musicali* (Venice, 1617) include a solo *sinfonia* and a 38-bar solo 'sonata'. A later work, the *Arie, madrigali e correnti* of 1620, contains a 'Romanesca' for violin with bass *ad lib.* which at one time was claimed as the first solo for the instrument. In his Op. 22, *Diversi generi*[41] (1655), he makes no distinction between types of sonata. A truly singing style was achieved only by

[38] Op. 6, ed. Leichtentritt (Leipzig, 1906); Op. 8, ed. Karl-Heinz Pauls, *Das Erbe deutscher Musik*, xliv (Kassel, 1956); *Gambenkompositionen*, ed. Pauls, ibid., lxvii (1973).

[39] See his 'Preluda' and two sonatas in Einstein, *Zur deutschen Literatur für Viola da gamba im 16, und 17. Jahrhundert* (Leipzig, 1905), pp. 63 ff.

[40] Suite no. 1 in F, ed. Robert Eitner, *Monatshefte für Musikgeschichte*, xxvii (1895), pp. 117 ff.

[41] Examples in *Hortus musicus*, cxxix and cxliii (1955–7).

a later generation, and Marini's music is not without a certain awkwardness. Nevertheless in his perpetual-motion effects, in his experiments with the *tremolo* and with double stops, this Brescian virtuoso shows himself eager to exploit the possibilities of his instrument. Marini spent some years (from 1623) at Neuburg in Bavaria and his works demanding chord-playing were composed at this time. Perhaps the most important of his experiments along this line is the *Capriccio per sonare il Violino con tre corde à modo de Lira* from Op. 8 (Venice, 1629):[42]

Ex. 276

Ottavio Maria Grandi also employed double stops in his Op. 2, no. 1 (Reggio, 1628):[43]

Ex. 277

---

[42] See also the 'Sonata . . . con due corde', Op. 8, no. 4, in Schering, *Geschichte der Musik in Beispielen*, no. 183.

[43] Gustav Beckmann, *Das Violinspiel in Deutschland vor 1700* (Leipzig, 1918), Anhang no. 4.

Uccellini (*c.*1603–80) published compositions in which he explored the upper register, reaching the sixth position in Op. 5, no. 8 (Venice, 1649):[44]

Ex. 278

The range thus established was rarely exceeded until the time of Locatelli. A later device was *scordatura*, the use of varied tunings, which facilitated effects which were impossible or difficult with the normal tuning; examples occur in the Op. 4 (Bologna, 1671) of Giovanni Maria Bononcini (1642–1678), possibly a pupil of Uccellini, and his German contemporary Biber (see below, p. 499). Maurizio Cazzati (*c.*1620–77) deserves mention as the founder of the Bolognese school and the teacher of Giovanni Battista Vitali (1632–92) as well as the composer of one of those miscellaneous collections typical of the period, the *Sonate à due, trè, quattro, e*

---

[44] Beckmann printed this sonata in his companion volume, *Das Violinspiel . . . 12 Sonaten für Violine und Klavier* (Leipzig, 1921).

*cinque, con alcune per Trombe* (Bologna, 1665).[45] In the sonata *A Calva*, which consists of Allegro, Vivace, a transitional Grave followed by another Allegro, and an Allegro e Presto, the subject of the final section is a very free variant of the opening melody. Most interesting of all are Cazzati's 'solo' sonatas, Op. 55 (Bologna, 1670).[46]

Giovanni Battista Vitali has sometimes been confused with his son Tomaso (1663–1745). The father's work combined a perfection of style, grandiose and vivacious by turns, with a taste for musical learning which sometimes manifested itself in compositions of a curious kind. Born near Cremona, he became *suonatore di violino da brazzo* (i.e. violinist) in the church of San Petronio at Bologna, and later *maestro di cappella* of the Duke of Modena. His only two solo violin sonatas are printed in his *Artificii musicali* (Modena, 1689),[47] which also includes a *Capriccio primo* which is really a miniature étude based on the development of a single rhythmic figure, and a very long *Passagalo per Violino che principia per B molle e finisce per Diesis* beginning in E flat major though with a B flat signature, modulating by fifths to B flat, F, C, and so on, 'finishing with sharps', as the composer says, in the key of E major. The famous violin *Ciaconna* attributed to Tomaso Vitali is almost certainly not by him; he published only trio sonatas.

CORELLI AND HIS INFLUENCE

Of much greater importance in the history of violin music and of the sonata was Arcangelo Corelli (1653–1713), 'detto il Bolognese' according to his early publications, Opp. 1, 2, and 3. Actually he studied at Bologna only as a boy, from 1666 to 1671. He would have known there, among others, an older man, Pietro degli Antoni (1648–1720),[48] who published sets of sonatas for solo violin and continuo in 1676 and 1686. A rather younger man than Corelli, Giovanni Battista Bassani (c.1657–1716), published trio sonatas at Bologna in 1683. Corelli did not, it is true, originate a style, but he expressed it in a way that seemed the height of perfection to his contemporaries. He treated the violin with a perfect knowledge of its possibilities; he possessed perfect taste, lyric sweetness, and a grave and aristocratic dignity; with rare exceptions, he kept within

---

[45] On Cazzati, see Newman, *The Sonata in the Baroque Era*, pp. 134–5, and Henry G. Mishkin, 'The Solo Violin Sonata of the Bologna School', *Musical Quarterly*, xxix (1943), pp. 101–3.

[46] Op. 55, no. 1, in *Historical Anthology*, ii, no. 219.

[47] The sonatas and other pieces in Torchi, vii, pp. 179 ff.

[48] See Mishkin, op. cit., pp. 103–9.

the first three positions. Of his small sheaf of works, only one collection concerns us here, his Op. 5 (Rome, 1700), consisting of six
church and six chamber sonatas.[49] In the former he does not adhere
to the four-movement scheme—slow, fast, slow, fast—which was
common at this time. He begins with a slow introductory movement, though this may be (as in the first sonata) interrupted by
brief episodes in rapid movement. The second and principal movement is fugal or at least imitative in style and rapid in tempo. This
is sometimes followed by another movement in perpetual motion.
The slow movement follows and then the brilliant finale which may
be followed by a gigue (as in no. 5) or may lead into a movement in
the manner of a gigue (as in no. 3). All the church sonatas thus
conform to a five-movement rather than a four-movement plan.
The fifth movement follows the first Allegro or is added at the end.
We may also note the mixture of styles, the intrusion of the gigue
in a church sonata, the sarabande-like quality of certain slow movements (as in no. 3).

The second half of Op. 5 consists of chamber sonatas, mostly
dance-movements though no. 11 contains only one acknowledged
dance movement, the final gavotta. The movements are less developed than in the church sonatas and are arranged in a carefree
fashion which is different for each sonata:

    no. 7:   Preludio—Corrente—Sarabanda—Giga.
    no. 8:   Preludio—Allemanda—Sarabanda—Giga.
    no. 9:   Preludio—Giga—Adagio—Tempo di Gavotta.
    no. 10:  Preludio—Allemanda—Sarabanda—Gavotta—Giga.
    no. 11:  Preludio—Allegro—Adagio—Vivace—Gavotta.
    no. 12:  La Folia (23 variations)

It was Corelli's Op. 5, which remained in print for a hundred years
after its publication, that began the popularization of the solo
sonata, hitherto less than that of the trio.

Through his pupils the Corelli style spread over all Europe, acting
as a stimulus particularly in England and in France, where a lower
level of technical achievement had prevailed. Thomas Dean is said
to have given the first public performance of a Corelli sonata
in England in 1709, nine years after Op. 5 was published,[50] and
Obadiah Shuttleworth (d. 1734) was able to support his family in
part by making manuscript copies of Corelli's music before it was

[49] On his other works, see pp. 210 ff. (concerti) and pp. 397 ff. (trio sonatas).
[50] Burney, *A General History of Music*, iv (London, 1789), p. 634.

published in England.[51] A testimony to the extent to which Corelli became popular with all classes in England may be gleaned from a passage in Hawkins; in a brief account of Charles Dieupart, violinist, harpsichordist and composer (d. c.1740), the historian remarks that in his later years he frequented alehouses where he played solos by Corelli.[52] Corelli's pupils were to raise the level of violin-playing all over Europe. In addition to Geminiani (see below, p.490) the list includes Albinoni,[53] Anet, Carbonelli, Castrucci, Locatelli,[54] Mossi, and Giovanni Battista Somis.[55] Many musicians of the next generation were content to repeat with little change but with diminished intensity the style that was Corelli's.

## VIVALDI

The Venetian master Antonio Vivaldi (1678–1741), most famous for his innumerable concertos, was certainly influenced by Corelli[56] though not actually his pupil. As a young man he played in the orchestra of San Marco under Giovanni Legrenzi (1629–90), himself a composer of sonatas. But Legrenzi's are mostly early works and conservative in style; none is a solo sonata. On the other hand Vivaldi preferred the solo form, composing forty for violin, nine for cello, twelve for various wind instruments. He published two sets of violin sonatas, Op. 2 (Venice, 1709) and Op. 5 (Amsterdam, 1716), and there are manuscript collections in the Dresden Landesbibliothek and Manchester Public Libraries. Six cello sonatas were published by Le Clerc of Paris in 1740 and it is these, with the manuscript ones in the Naples Conservatorio, which have won most favour among his chamber compositions. As Talbot has put it:

In the entire Italian baroque repertoire of sonatas for cello perhaps only the sonatas of Benedetto Marcello, harmonically and technically less resourceful and far narrower in their range of mood, can stand comparison with these masterly works. . . . Vivaldi's cello has a double character: generally, it confines its utterances to the tenor register and becomes, as it were, a deeper version of the violin: but at others (and by no means only at cadences) it descends to the bass register, doubling or perhaps slightly elaborating the continuo part.[57]

---

[51] Hawkins, *A General History of the Science and Practice of Music*, v (London, 1776), p. 181.

[52] Ibid., p. 70.

[53] E.g. his Sonatas, Op. 6, nos. 1–4, ed. Michael Talbot (London, 1981).

[54] On Locatelli, see Albert Dunning, *Pietro Antonio Locatelli*, two vols. (Buren, 1982).

[55] G. B. Somis (1686–1763) has often been confused with his brother Lorenzo (1699–1775). Sets of sonatas by both have been published by Michelangelo Abbado (Milan, 1976).

[56] See Michael Talbot, *Vivaldi* (London, 1978), p. 126.

[57] Idem, *Vivaldi (BBC Music Guide)* (London, 1979), p. 69.

DALL' ABACO

The music of Evaristo Felice dall' Abaco (1675–1742) has much more of the lyric sweetness and the elegant vivacity of the masters of the golden period than of the striving for effect, the broadening of forms and the emotionalism of those who were to come. He was evidently proud of his birthplace for we find the phrase *Cittadino Veronese* on his title pages, but his masters Torelli and Tomaso Vitali were of the Bolognese school. Adolf Sandberger, who edited a selection of his works,[58] pointed out similarities between his compositions and Vitali's. Curiously, his appointment to the court music of Max Emmanuel II of Bavaria was as *suonatore da camera di violoncello* though it seems likely that he must also have been a fine violinist. Only his Op. 1 and Op. 4 are solo sonatas; they show the mingling of dances and abstract movements typical of his period. Dall' Abaco was fond of writing movements in which a persistently moving bass part has something of the character of an ostinato. Signs calling for certain effects appear in his works for the first time: the vertical line used to indicate a down bow, and the direction *spiccato*, used here, however, in the sense of *détaché*. The following examples, from Op. 1, no. 4, show how the composer presents and imitates his theme at the opening of a movement and how selected elements of this theme furnish the material for later developments. It is masterly both in the way the possibilities of the theme are exploited and in the fact that this is done without interfering with the natural flow of the movement:

Ex.279

[58] *Denkmäler der Tonkunst in Bayern*, i (1) (Leipzig, 1900).

## VERACINI

Francesco Maria Veracini (1690–1768) was a performer of such brilliance as to cause Tartini to retire for an extended period of study after the two met in Venice. From Venice he went to England, where he arrived in 1714, a year also signalized by the appearance of Geminiani there. His vivacity and brilliance were combined with a broader development of his musical forms and harmony which was bold for his period. These differences were sufficiently obvious at the time to cause Burney to say that his compositions were 'too wild and flighty for the taste of the English at this time', a comment softened by the admission that Veracini was 'the greatest violinist in Europe'.[59]

[59] Burney, op. cit., p. 640.

During the period 1717–22 Veracini was in Dresden, where in
1721 he published the first edition of his solo sonatas, Op. 1,[60] and
where in a fit of insanity the following year, said to have been
brought on by a malicious trick, he threw himself from an upper
window and fractured one foot and his thigh.[61] From Dresden
Veracini went to Prague, where he played for Count Kinsky, who
was later to attract Tartini to his service, and thence to Italy. He
was in London again in the years 1733–45 and spent the greater
part of his remaining years in Florence composing and conducting.

The Dresden Op. 1, later reprinted at Amsterdam, was not
Veracini's earliest set of sonatas for he had composed twelve *Sonate
a Violino, o Flauto solo, e Basso* in the *chiesa* form at Venice in
1716, though they appear not to have been published in his lifetime.[62] Op. 1 consists of six *sonate da camera* in minor keys and six
*da chiesa* in major ones. But Veracini's masterpieces are the twelve
*Sonate Accademiche*, Op. 2, for violin and bass (London and
Florence, 1744), which alarmed Burney. They are big bravura show-
pieces, equally bold in imagination and in technical demands; some
of them are essays in Scottish, Polish and Croatian ('Schiavonna')
styles. Most curious of all are the unpublished *Dissertazioni del sg
Franscesco* [sic] *Veracini sopra l'Opera Quinto* [sic] *del Corelli*,[63] a
free re-writing of the whole of the older master's Op. 5.

## TARTINI

Giuseppe Tartini (1692–1770) forms a second culminating point
in the development of Italian violin music and at the same time,
through his pupils perhaps more than his own public performances,
a means of spreading the fully developed Italian style over all
Europe. His school of violin playing and composition at Padua
(*c*.1727 or 1728 until his death) became known as the 'Scuola delle
Nazioni'. Unlike Veracini, he was very prolific as a composer.[64] He
published his first set of six sonatas *a violino e violone o cimabalo*
at Amsterdam in 1732 and he soon adopted the plan of one slow
movement followed by two fast ones.

The centre of gravity of the three-movement sonata, as of the
Italian overture, was the first Allegro; with the four-movement

---

[60] Ed. W. Kolneder (Leipzig, 1958–9). See John Walter Hill, 'Veracini in Italy', *Music &
Letters*, lvi (1975), p. 272, n. 49, and on Veracini generally Hill's *The Life and Works of
Francesco Maria Veracini* (Ann Arbor, 1979).
[61] Mattheson, *Critica Musica* (Hamburg, 1722), i. p. 152.
[62] Ed. Walter Kolneder (Leipzig, 1959–61).
[63] RISM I: Bc, KK 271.
[64] *Le Opere di Giuseppi Tartini*, ed. Eduardo Farina and C. Scimone (Milan 1971– ).

church sonata it had been the second movement. With Corelli, Tartini, and Geminiani, the principal Allegro frequently retains the polyphonic texture and imitative character which it inherited from the *canzon*. With Tartini, however, we sometimes find instead of principal allegros in a fugal style, the type of movement which, emerging from the simple binary dance form, was to lead to the classical sonata. As in contemporary keyboard sonatas, the movements divide normally into two sections, the first terminating with a cadence in the dominant key, the second traversing a path from dominant to tonic. The evolution of sonata form was largely a result of increased length and the consequent need for variety and differentiation to sustain the hearer's interest.

One common result was a parallelism of beginnings and endings. The cadences at the end of each section were expanded and took on a more or less distinctive melodic character which foreshadowed the closing theme. The beginning was usually the most salient and characteristic part of a movement and composers frequently used it, transposed to the dominant, at the beginning of the second section. Thus we have the principal melodic idea, the 'first theme', stated at the beginning of the movement in the tonic and reappearing in a transposed and perhaps altered form at the beginning of the second section. So far the movement is still obviously binary in character. The composer, however, modulates back to the tonic in the course of the second section. The introduction of the first theme in the tonic at this point dramatizes and emphasizes a feature which previously had had no outstanding importance. This results in two entries of the first theme in the second half of the movement, one in the dominant, the other in the tonic. The result in the long run was a blurring or omission of the statement in the dominant, leaving the tonic entry as a crucial point of the movement, a point carefully led up to by prolonged harmonies of suspense. This change, once achieved, underlined the character of the middle section or 'development' as an episode of contrast giving the movement a ternary character. Frequently the modulation to the dominant took place relatively early in the first section. The dissolution of the first theme and the march of harmonies towards the dominant are features which were to characterize the bridge passage. Once the movement had attained a certain duration the dominant key was likely to be differentiated into material accompanying its attainment and material associated with its concluding phase or, in the terminology of classical sonata form, second theme and closing theme.

Tartini was famous for the pathetic and emotional character of his slow movements; it is said that he put himself in the mood for composing them by reading poetry—Metastasio's plays or Petrarch's sonnets[65]—but such titles as *Didone abbandonata* for Op. 1, no. 10, are fictitious. Tartini's allegros assume a more organic character in contrast to the somewhat dry and étude-like aspects of certain rapid movements by Corelli. Gian-Rinaldo Corli in a letter to Tartini states that the latter 'had recognized that he should use thicker violin strings and lengthen the bow'.[66] Another doubtful work, *L'Arte dell'arco* (Paris, 1758), a set of thirty-eight variations—later augmented to fifty—on the gavotte in Corelli's Op. 5, no. 10, may be considered a summary of the styles of bowing which Tartini employed.

Quiet, retiring (at least in later life), profoundly religious, but continually troubled by family difficulties, Tartini shows in his music a fire and a virtuoso temperament not evident in his daily life. His devotion to Padua and to the orchestra of Sant' Antonio dates from his appointment in 1721, though his contract was so phrased as to permit him to travel to fulfil concert engagements. His only considerable absence abroad was in Prague (1723–6), where he played on the occasion of the coronation of the Emperor Charles VI as King of Bohemia. It was here that Quantz heard him and received the impressions recorded in his autobiography.[67] It is stange that it denies to Tartini precisely the qualities that most critics claimed for him and emphasizes others; it may be that Tartini felt this special occasion called for the utmost brilliance in performance:

He produced a beautiful tone. He showed equal mastery of finger and bow. He executed the greatest difficulties very purely without particular trouble. He played trills, even double trills, equally well with all fingers. He introduced many double stops in fast as well as in slow movements; and he liked to play in the highest register (*auf ersten Höhe*). But his performance did not move one, and his taste was not elevated, on the contrary quite the opposite of a good singing style.

## LOCATELLI

Pietro Antonio Locatelli (1695–1764)[68] after allegedly studying with Corelli in Rome became a musician in a court where Vivaldi

[65] F. Algarotti, *Saggio sopra l'Opera in musica* (Leghorn, 1764), pp. 281–2; F. Fanzago, *Elogi di Giuseppe Tartini e del Padre Francisco Antonio Vallotti* (Padua, 1792), p. 32.
[66] 21 August, 1743: printed in his *Opere*, xiv (Milan, 1786).
[67] *Lebenslauf*, in Marpurg, *Historisch-kritische Beyträge zur Aufnahme der Musik*, i (Berlin, 1755), p. 221; reprinted in Kahl, op. cit., p. 128.
[68] A standard work on Locatelli is Arend Koole, *Leven en werken van Pietro Antonio Locatelli da Bergamo* (Amsterdam, 1949); see also n. 54.

had served, that of Prince Philip of Hesse-Darmstadt at Mantua. After a period of restless concert-giving he settled in Amsterdam in 1729; there he was active till his death as violinist, composer, teacher, and publisher of his own works. These include solo sonatas for flute and bass, Op. 2 (1732), and for violin, Op. 6 (1737) and Op. 8, nos. 1–6 (1744). He was not only a bold innovator in violin technique, climbing to an extremely high register and exploiting all manner of difficult leaps and double notes, but also a composer whose harmonic daring shocked his contemporaries. One of the Op. 6 sonatas is a quasi-programmatic 'Pianto d'Arianna'. He included *XXIV Capricci* in his *Arte del violino*, Op. 3 (1733),[69] one of which—entitled 'Il Laberinto armonico'—bears the motto *Facilis aditus, difficilis exitus*. He has sometimes been called the Paganini of his day and Burney wrote that he had 'more hand, caprice, and fancy than any violinist of his time' and was a composer of 'Music that excites more surprise than pleasure'.[70] This passage, the first movement of his Op. 6, no. 2, is typical of Locatelli's florid writing:

Ex. 280

---

[69] Facsimile edition, with introduction by Paul van Reijen (Amsterdam, 1981).
[70] Op. cit., ii, p. 454.

## THE VIOLIN IN ENGLAND

In England the traces of local colour survived two waves of Italian influence. The earlier was produced by the advent of Corelli's music, the later by that of Handel and the violinists of his circle, notably Geminiani and Pietro Castrucci (1679–1752). Violin music in England emerged imperceptibly from that for treble viol. The sonatas of William Young (d. 1662),[71] the first English compositions specifically so called, though not solo works are notable because they are for violins, not viols.[72] The earliest English sonata for solo violin and bass appears to be Purcell's in G minor. By that time, the 1680s, Italian influence was spreading apace and, with it, cultivation of the violin. Characteristic of the time were the little volumes addressed to the amateur: Playford's *Apollo's Banquet* (1669) and his *Division Violin* (2nd edition, 1685), John Fenton's *The Gentleman's Diversion or the Violin Explained* (1693), Peter Prelleur's *The Art of Playing on the Violin* (c.1730), and Robert Crome's *The Fiddle New Model'd* (c.1740).

Among the earlier English violinists were the expatriate William Brade, Davis Mell, Paul Wheeler (Polewheele), John Banister and Young. Mell (1604–62), was regarded as the finest English violinist of his time until the arrival of Thomas Baltzar (c.1630–63), a virtuoso born in Lübeck. Anthony Wood says:

The company did look upon Mr. Mell to have a prodigious hand on the Violin, and they thought that no person, as all in London did, could goe beyond him. [After they heard Baltzar] they had other thoughts of Mr. Mell, who, tho he play'd farr sweeter than Baltzar, yet Baltzar's hand was more quick, and could run it insensibly to the end of the Fingerboard.[73]

The arrival of Veracini and Geminiani in London in 1714 was to turn English taste in a new direction. Burney could say of the period following that year:

The compositions and performance of Nicola Matteis had polished and refined our ears, and made them fit for the sonatas of Corelli; and many of our young nobility and gentry who travelled in Italy during his life, were ambitious of hearing and taking lessons of this great master on the violin, which became so much in favour, that the English were said to

---

[71] See Walter Senn, *Musik und Theater am Hof zu Innsbruck* (Innsbruck, 1954), p. 262. The William Young who died in 1671 was an English court flautist and violinist.

[72] *Sonate a 3, 4, 5 voci con Allemande, Correnti, etc.* (Innsbruck, 1653); modern ed. by W. G. Whittaker (London, 1930).

[73] *The Life and Times of Anthony à Wood*, ed. A. Clark (Oxford, 1891–1900), i. p. 257. Thomas Baltzar had been in England since 1656; see Evelyn's Diary, 4 March 1656, where he appears as 'Luciber' and is also compared favourably with 'Mr. Mell'.

have stripped Italy, not only of many of its best pictures and statues, but of all its valuable violins.[74]

GEMINIANI

Francesco Geminiani (1687–1762) was one of the major figures in the musical world of London, yet it was his fate to be described by those who were hostile to him. Burney could not endure his enthusiasms when they wandered from the Italian style: 'One day he would set up French Music against all other; the next English, Scots, Irish—any. thing but the best compositions of Italy or Handel'.[75] He would hardly have been better pleased with Geminiani's *Rules for playing in a True Taste on the Violin, German Flute, Violoncello and Harpsichord . . . Exemplified in a variety of Compositions on the Subjects of English, Scotch and Irish Tunes* (London, 1739). Nevertheless Geminiani's music was predominantly Italian. After studying with Carl' Ambrogio Lavati in Milan, he had become a pupil of Corelli in Rome. His residence in London was interrupted by visits to Paris during 1749–55, and to Dublin where his devoted student Matthew Dubourg (1703–67) had settled in 1728. The sonatas of his Op. 1 (London, 1716), which contain fugues of formidable difficulty, e.g. no. 6:

Ex. 281

---

[74] Op. cit., p. 640.
[75] Ibid., p. 645.

were published in 1739 with fingering and elaborate ornamentation for the slow movements. The sonatas of Op. 4 (London, 1739), on the other hand, are decidedly Handelian in character with scarcely any polyphonic passages. His treatise, *The Art of Playing on the Violin*[76] marks an advance in several specific points. The frontispiece of the French edition of his treatise (1752) shows the chin resting nearly over the tailpiece, slightly to the left;[77] he was also the first to publish definite instructions as to the manner of holding the bow.

Burney's criticism of Geminiani[78] as a poor time-keeper is based partly on his own experience and partly on information transmitted by the Neapolitan violinist composer, Emanuele Barbella (1718–77), who was hardly a friendly witness. The fault seems to have lain in his fondness for unexpected rubatos. The dramatic fire of certain of his compositions, such as the principal Allegro from the Sonata in D major, Op. 4, no. 6:

Ex. 282

does suggest the temperamental and impetuous player. Geminiani formed a number of students including Matthew Dubourg (1703–67), Charles Avison (1709–70), and Michael Festing (1680–1752), the last of whom published four sets of solo sonatas during the decades 1730–50.

---

[76] First published anonymously in Peter Crellen's *The Modern Musick Master* (London, 1731); modern edition by David Boyden (London, 1952).

[77] See Boyden, 'The Violin and its Technique in the 18th Century', *Musical Quarterly*, xxxvi (1950), p. 17 and plate II (4).

[78] Op. cit., pp. 641, 644.

OTHER SONATA COMPOSERS IN ENGLAND

Pietro Castrucci (1679–1752), said to have been a Corelli pupil, who arrived in London a year later than Geminiani, was a violinist and performer on the *violetta marina* whose capabilities may be measured by the fact that he was for some time the leader of Handel's orchestra. He inevitably fell under the dominating influence of that composer. His Op. 2 contains two sonatas for muted violin in imitation of the *viola d'amore*. His penchant for self-advertisement found a more than sufficient reply when his announcement in February 1732 that he would play 'twenty-four notes with one bow' was answered by another promising that the 'last violinist' of the Goodman's Field Playhouse (a disreputable resort) would play twenty-five notes with one bow.[79] Castrucci ended his days miserably in a London madhouse.

Other composers of solo sonatas active in England during this period were John Humphries (d. 1730), William Babell (c.1690–1723), and the blind John Stanley (1713–86). John Humphries published 'the first fruits of a young Gentleman now not above 19' in 1726. His music evidently formed a middle ground between the elaborately spun virtuoso sonata and the frankly popular violin music which will be discussed next. Hawkins observes that his compositions were 'of a very original cast, in respect that they are in a style somewhat above that of the common popular airs and country-dance tunes . . . and greatly beneath what might be expected from the studies of a person at all acquainted with the graces and elegancies of the Italians. . . . The sonatas of Humphries were the common practice of such small proficients in harmony, as in his time were used to recreate themselves with music at alehouse clubs, and places of vulgar resort in the villages adjacent to London'.[80]

POPULAR VIOLIN MUSIC

There was also a popular style of violin-playing cultivating forms simpler and less developed than those of the sonata, yet worth mentioning here because of a certain mutual influence between the popular art and that of the sonata players of the period. There is a passage where Hawkins discusses the music played at houses of entertainment: 'If at any time a bass instrument was added, it was only for the purpose of playing the ground-bass to those divisions on old ballad or country-dance tunes which at that time were the

---

[79] Burney, op. cit., p. 353.
[80] Hawkins, op. cit., p. 366.

only music that pleased the common people.'[81] The speciality of a certain John Ravenscroft (d. *c*.1745)[82] was the playing of hornpipes 'in which he had a manner that none could imitate'. Perhaps the folk influence was most pronounced in Scottish music. There we find the elder Niel Gow (1727–1807) who grew up in Perthshire largely self-taught but with some instruction from a John Cameron. He became the ideal player of strathspeys and reels and was much in demand for London balls. He published five collections of music which appeared from 1784 to 1808. Collections were also issued by William MacGibbon (1742, 1746, and 1755), William Marshall (1781 and 1821) and others.

## VIOLIN MUSIC IN FRANCE

Three characteristics of French instrumental music are noticeable. One is the use of the dance rhythms which passed from the ballet to the music-desk of the solo performer; thus the *tambourin* was frequently introduced by French violin composers, as were other dances such as the gavotte and bourrée. A second characteristic was delight in fanciful titles and descriptive musical details. In a few instances this seems almost a borrowing from the tone-painting of the operatic orchestra, as in Michele Mascitti's 'Les Vents' in his Op. 5, no. 12 (Paris, 1714) with its upward rushing scales:

Ex. 283

Mascitti (*c*.1664–1760), Neapolitan by birth, naturalized French in 1739, published nine books of solo sonatas combining Italian and French elements during the years 1704–38. 'Les Caquets' by the flautist Michel Blavet (1700–68) reminds one of Couperin, since an animated musical idea is illustrated by an appropriate title seasoned by a faint sting of satire:

---

[81] Ibid.
[82] Not to be confused with a namesake (d. *c*.1708), possibly a pupil of Corelli, who published a set of trio sonatas in Rome in 1695. Another appeared in London after his death.

Ex. 284

and Rebel's *Gavotte Rondeau* ('Les Cloches'), Op. 1, no. 3, is a typical example of French composers' interest in bells:

Ex. 285

Jean-Ferry Rebel le Père (1666–1747) was the most important among the pioneers of the French violin sonata. He was a child prodigy who played before Louis XIV, a pupil of Lully, and later a performer in the intimate concerts of high society under the Regency where we may still see him as portrayed by the pencil of Watteau. His *Pièces pour le violin* (1705), from which Ex. 285 is taken, were followed by *Sonates à violon seul Mellées de Plusieurs Récits pour la Viole* (comp. 1695; pub. Paris, 1713), six of the *chiesa* type, six *da camera*. Here the viola da gamba sometimes takes an independent part in the *récits* of the title, sometimes merely embellishes the bass. In the earlier publication the praeludium which begins each suite contains double notes; he was in fact the first French composer to employ double-stopping. Though his *Recueil de Douze Sonates à II et III* appeared in 1712–13, a caustic note by the librarian Boisgelou seems to establish that these sonatas, published after Duval's, were composed much earlier: 'These sonatas were composed from 1695. The composer sold them for up to 15 and 16 livres. A copy now would not bring 2 sols.'[83] François Duval (*c.*1673–1728), a member of Louis X1V's *Vingt-quatre violons*, produced a series of seven publications beginning in 1704 which place him with Rebel as a pioneer French sonata composer; all but one of his sets are solo sonatas. With François Couperin, he took part in Louis XIV's intimate concerts, of which we may gain some idea from Couperin's *Concerts Royaux*.

Jacques Aubert (1689–1753) published a *Livre I* of ten solo sonatas in 1719; *Livres II–V* followed during 1721–1739. He had an

[83] L. de La Laurencie, 'Une dynastie de musiciens aux XVII<sup>e</sup> et XVIII<sup>e</sup> siècles: Les Rebel', *Sammelbände der Internationalen Musikgesellschaft*, vii (1905–6), pp. 253–307.

'allegro temperament' and was even willing to replace a slow movement by a gavotte (*Livre II*, nos. 2 and 6). The sonatas in *Livre IV*
show an extensive use of double stopping. But his chief claim to
fame is as the first French composer of a *concerto grosso* (1735).

Jean-Jacques-Baptiste Anet (*c*.1661–1755), often simply called
'Baptiste', was, like Aubert and Duval, a member of the *Vingt-
quatre violons*. He was a pupil of Corelli and is said to have so
moved his teacher that he embraced him and presented him with
his own bow. Anet published two sets of suite-like sonatas in 1724
and 1729. Moser singles out the brisk downward-sweeping arpeggios
of *Les forgerons* (from the fifth sonata) for special praise.[84]

The music of Jean-Baptiste Senallié le Fils (sometimes spelt
'Senaillé') (1687–1730), who published five books of sonatas from
1710 to 1727, was strongly influenced by the Italian style. The
Allegro of the sixth sonata in G major from his fourth book is
interesting for the kind of approximation to sonata form which
should be expected in a period of transition. The vigorous opening
theme (i) is followed by a plaintive second subject (ii) which is,
however, in G minor instead of D major:

Ex. 286

The middle section hardly has the character of a true development,
but it is followed by a clear restatement of the principal themes.

[84] Hans Joachim Moser, *Geschichte des Violinspiels* (Berlin, 1923), p. 178.

There were several important violinists named Francœur: Louis ('*l'aîné*') (1692–1745), his brother François (1698–1787), and Louis's son Louis-Joseph (1738–1804). A curious technical trick practised by both brothers is the use of the thumb in playing certain chords: the effect is indicated by the words *le pouce* under the chord which requires its use. The following example is from Louis Francœur's *Premier Livre de Sonates* (1715):

Ex. 287

They continued worthily the 'mixed style' which had resulted from the fusion of French and Italian traits. Some critics have traced the influence of Tartini in François Francœur's sixth sonata from his *IIe Livre* (after 1730). Certain it is that the two had met in 1723, with Rebel and other prominent musicians at the performance of Fux's *Costanza e Fortezza* on the occasion of the coronation of the emperor Charles VI at Prague.

Outstanding among these French violin-composers was Jean-Marie Leclair (1697–1764). A dancer in his youth, he was *maître de ballet* at Turin for some time and returned there in 1726, when he studied the violin with a Corelli pupil, Giovanni Battista Somis (1686–1763). But he had already published his *Ier Livre de Sonates a violon seul avec la Basse* (Paris, 1723). This First Book is remarkable for the number of dance movements—gavottes, gigues, sarabands; they almost disappear from the *2e Livre* (*c.*1728) of solo sonatas but return, though in smaller quantity, in the Third and Fourth (*c.*1734 and 1738). Most of the sonatas follow the pattern slow-fast-slow-fast, sometimes omitting the initial slow movement, but with marked contrasts of rhythm as well as tempo. Leclair's early work was inevitably rather Italianate[85]—one movement of the third sonata of the First Book is unashamedly borrowed from the gavotte of Corelli's Op. 5, no. 10—but the delicacy and precision of his carefully marked ornamentation is typically French; violinistic as his solo writing is, he observes in his First Book 'Il y a quelqu'unes de ces Sonates qui peuvent se jouer sur la Flûte Traversière'. His basses are lively and flexible; like Rebel and Couperin, he sometimes writes a string bass part—for viol or cello—more ornamental than that of the keyboard continuo. (It should be noted, in passing, that the great Couperin—though a pioneer of the *sonade*, as he insisted on calling it, in France—wrote no solo sonatas; his only composition for solo viol and bass is the *Suite de viole* published in 1728.) In one instance, the musette in his *Ier Livre*, Leclair writes out the keyboard part in full.

Jean-Joseph de Mondonville (1711–72) shows in his Op. 3, *Pièces de Clavecin en Sonates avec accompagnement de Violon* (Paris and Lille, c.1734)[86] early examples of a genre popular after the mid-century. Mondonville's Op. 5 (1748) displays the same characteristics. *Les sons harmoniques*, Op. 4 (Paris and Lille, c.1735), was designed to employ single and double harmonics as frequently as possible to help the novice to master this effect. The use of harmonics had been known earlier—indeed *tromba marina* players produced only harmonics—but this work was a remarkable early attempt to exploit the effect on the violin.

Louis-Gabriel Guillemain (1705–1770) was described by Daquin as 'the most rapid and the most extraordinary violin that can be heard'.[87] This characterization is confirmed by such a work as Op. 1, no. 11 (1734):

Ex. 288

[85] On the influences of Corelli, Tartini, Somis, Locatelli, and Vivaldi, see Marc Pincherle, *J.-M. Leclair* (Paris, 1952), pp. 73–5.

[86] Ed. Pincherle (Paris, 1935); no. 5 in Giegling, *Die Solosonate, Das Musikwerk*, xv (Cologne, 1959), no. 11.

[87] L. de la Laurencie, *L'École Française de violon de Lully à Viotti* (Paris, 1922–24), ii, p. 15.

More important from the point of view of the development of the accompaniment is his Op. 13 (1745), the *Pièces de Clavecin en Sonates avec accompagnement de Violon*, which follows the example of Mondonville in its completely worked-out keyboard part.

### THE SITUATION IN GERMANY

In spite of the varied influences which affected German string-playing it maintained a certain independence until that of Italian opera became dominant. English players like William Brade (1560–1630) and Thomas Simpson (1582–after 1630) were important in North Germany in the early seventeenth century.[88] Uppsala contains a work for violin by Brade, the *Coral: del Sr. Wilhelm Brad: Violino solo col Basso*, which has been claimed[89] as the oldest set of variations for violin on a ground. Brade's pupil Nicolaus Bleyer (1591–1658) left manuscript variations on an English march: *English Mars Engl. Nicolai Bleyers, Violista bei dem Herzog Schauenberg*. Our knowledge of the repertory of the German violinist at this period is rounded out by the popular songs, as well as the selections from Hassler's *Lustgarten*, contained in Johann Wolff Gerhard's violin *tablature* of 1613.[90]

Italian influence became more important in the German lands during the following period. Marini was active at Düsseldorf from 1641. Dresden became a great centre of violin playing; Carlo Farina was there from 1625 to 1629 under Schütz. Nevertheless German violin playing maintained a certain local character which Quantz much later characterized concisely if incompletely as 'virtuoso variations and chord playing'.[91]

The first of the Hamburg violinists was Johann Schop (*c*.1590–1667) whose compositions in the '*t Uitnemend kabinet* of the Dutch publisher Paulus Matthysz (Amsterdam, 1646) demand trills in thirds and sixths. The remarkable skill of Nicolaus Adam Strungk (1640–1700) led to his appearance in Vienna before the Emperor who gave him a golden chain with his portrait as a pendant; a later performance was similarly rewarded. Mattheson remarks that 'Biber had three of them, Strungk two'. Strungk was active chiefly in Hanover and Hamburg. He was one of those who cultivated *scordatura*, though it is not employed in either of his two surviving sonatas, one for four instruments plus bass, the other for two.

[88]  See Vol. IV, p. 590.
[89]  Moser, op. cit. (Berlin, 1923).
[90]  Nuremberg, Nationalmuseum, Ms. 14976.
[91]  *Versuch einer Anweisung die Flöte traversiere zu spielen* (Berlin, 1752).

FRENCH INFLUENCE IN GERMANY

The influence of French architecture and literature on the Germans was paralleled by the influence of the orchestra of Lully on German string players. For example, Johann Fischer (1646–1721), who spent some time as a copyist in Paris, must have been one of the intermediaries; Mattheson, who heard him as an old man, was convinced that he must indeed have been one of the greatest virtuosi in his youth. The tale that he played entire trios as solos by using three different instruments tuned in *scordatura* suggests that he had not forgotten how to play in German style. Johann Heinrich Schmelzer (*c.*1623–80), celebrated all over Europe as a performer, was more adventurous in exploring the upper range of the violin than any of his German predecessors. His *Sonatae unarum fidium, seu a Violino solo* (Nuremberg, 1664)[92] is believed to be the earliest German collection of solo sonatas only. Other violinist-composers of the period were Heinrich Weissenburg, a Swiss who was also known as Albicastro, Philip Friedrich Buchner (1614–69), the composer of a *Plectrum Musicum* (Frankfurt, 1662), and Johann Wilhelm Furchheim (1634–82), whose works have almost entirely vanished.

BIBER

Far more important than these was Heinrich Ignaz Franz von Biber (1644–1701). His reputation as a composer—he was also a virtuoso performer—rests on his solo works. A set of solo sonatas, *Mysterien Mariae* (*c.*1674), associated with fifteen mysteries in the life of the Virgin Mary and written for performance in church at the Solemnity of the Most Holy Rosary, is accompanied by illustrations in the form of copper engravings.[93] Programmatic traits are, however, by no means always present. Some of the movements are in church style, some, like the allemande of Sonata II, in chamber style. A sixteenth composition in the collection is a 'Passagaglia' for unaccompanied violin which is a worthy precursor of the Bach Chaconne. A different *scordatura* is employed for each sonata, but the 'Passagaglia' is for an instrument with the usual tuning. The *viola d'amore* partitas of the *Harmonia artificiosa-ariosa* (Nuremberg, 1712) are also chiefly in scordatura; though published posthumously, they may have been composed earlier than the *Mysterien* sonatas. In the eight solo sonatas (Nuremberg, 1681)[94]—

[92] Ed. Erich Schenk, *Denkmäler der Tonkunst in Österreich*, xciii (1958).
[93] Ed. Erwin Luntz, ibid., xxv (Jg.xii(2) ).
[94] Mod. ed. Guido Adler, ibid., xi (Jg.v(2) ).

the year of Corelli's Op. 1—the use of *scordatura* diminishes, but
the difficulties remain. Passages in the seventh position occur; both
left- and right-hand technique is advanced, though this is by no
means mere virtuoso music. Ex. 289, the opening of the fourth
sonata, shows (i) the *scordatura* notation for the player's fingers,
(ii) the actual sounds:

Ex. 289

Biber was first a musician of the Prince-Bishop of Olmütz, later
becoming vice-Kapellmeister, then Kapellmeister at Salzburg. In
1690 the Emperor Leopold I ennobled him as 'von Bibern' 'because
of his accomplishment in music carried to the highest perfection'.

### J. J. WALTHER

Johann Jakob Walther (1650–1717) left two collections which
also reflect the high standard of German violin playing: the *Scherzi
da violino solo* (Frankfurt and Leipzig, 1676)[95] consisting of twelve

---

[95] Mod. ed. Gustav Beckmann, *Das Erbe deutscher Musik*, xvii (Hanover, 1941).

partitas and the *Hortulus chelicus* (Mainz, 1688) which contains twenty-eight suites. Both had to be quickly reprinted. These works combine fresh and folk-like melody with developments presenting great technical difficulties of multiple stopping, shifts, leaps, varied bowings, and so on. The usual order consists of an introductory movement, a melody with variations, and a rapid final movement; the music demands an advanced technique in chord-playing. Perhaps Quantz had Walther's music in mind when he wrote:

The Germans in previous times depended more on difficult than on easy pieces and sought rather to astonish than to please. They endeavoured to imitate animal sounds, for example the Cuckoo, the Nightingale, the Hen, the Quail, on their instruments, nor were the Trumpet and Hurdy-gurdy forgotten.

In fact a *Scherzi d'augelli con il Cuccu*[96] appears in the *Hortulus* as well as a piece with all manner of imitations, two trumpets and drums, the German hurdy-gurdy, and so on—and an imitation of cocks and hens:

Ex. 290

The typical German interest in polyphonic playing is also manifested in the few works of the travelling virtuoso Johann Paul von Westhoff (1656–1705), perhaps the first to make concert tours in the grand manner, tours which included Italy, Austria, France, Holland, and England. His meeting with Bach in 1705 may possibly have suggested the idea of composing for solo violin since Westhoff

[96] Ed. Beckmann, *Das Violinspiel in Deutschland . . . . 12 Sonaten.*

had already published an unaccompanied sonata and suite in the Paris *Mercure galant* in 1682 and 1683 respectively.[97] In addition Westhoff composed six sonatas with continuo which appeared in Paris in 1704. Moser points out his influence on other composers who cultivated the sonata for unaccompanied violin such as Geminiani, Nicola Matteis and Angelo Ragazzi.

### HANDEL AND BACH

The solo sonata does not bulk very large in Handel's vast output nor quantitatively—however remarkable in quality—in that of J. S. Bach. Handel's set of twelve *Sonates pour un Traversiere un Violon ou Hautbois con Basso Continuo* was published in 1722[98] and re-issued *c*.1732 with various alterations and three additional sonatas. (Nos. 10, 12, 14 and 15 are doubtfully authentic.) But some of these are based on earlier compositions; for instance, the first two movements of the oboe sonata, no. 8 in C minor, came from a flute sonata in E minor of perhaps twenty years earlier and the F minor sonata for oboe, no. 6, was originally written for viola da gamba. Other solo sonatas are attributed to him.[99] In the main set he writes simply a figured continuo part; only in a doubtfully authentic gamba sonata in C (*c*.1705) do we find a worked out keyboard accompaniment in two real parts. Handel used the church sonata as the basis for his solo works, sometimes with the addition of dance movements which he generally places at the end; his gigues have a vivacity which is quite his own. Though the technical demands of the violin sonatas are not great, the noble beauty of the slow movements and the drive of the rapid ones place them among the most inspired works of the kind. Perhaps finest of all are no. 3 in A and no. 13 in D.

None of Bach's solo sonatas was published before the mid-nineteenth century; all probably date from *c*.1720. In some of his compositions for violin and clavier (BWV 1014–9) (and in the first three for flute, BWV 1030–2) he prefers to write in trio style with two parts (sometimes three) for the keyboard. Whereas Handel's chamber works are mostly 'chips from the workshop', including adaptations and arrangements, Bach's were an important part of his activities during his Cöthen period where his duties were largely concerned with instrumental performances.

[97] Both ed. ibid.

[98] Ostensibly 'A Amsterdam chez Jeanne Roger' but really by Walsh in London.

[99] On the confusion of Handel's solo sonatas, see Terence Best, 'Handel's Solo Sonatas'; *Music & Letters*, lviii (1977), p. 430, and David Lasocki and Best, 'A new flute sonata by Handel', *Early Music*, ix (1981), p. 307.

The set of sonatas and partitas for unaccompanied violin (BWV 1001–6) together with the comparable set of suites for cello (BWV 1007–12) are the finest of their kind. (The fifth of the cello suites is in *scordatura*, the sixth for the five-stringed *viola pomposa*.) They must be regarded as the culmination of a tradition of harmonic performance which passed from the lute and gamba to the violin and was most intensively cultivated by the violinists of North Germany. This is particularly true of the fugues in the sonatas and of the famous chaconne in the D minor partita, BWV 1004, less so of certain other movements. On the other hand, the prelude in E major in BWV 1006, for example, suggests the style of the future étude.

The sonatas for violin and clavier include movements of deep and moving beauty. In some instances the busy interplay of melody and countermelody gives place to a harmonic figuration allotted to the right hand of the clavier player, e.g. the siciliano of the E flat major flute sonata (BWV 1031), or the Adagio of the fourth violin sonata (BWV 1017). At such moments Bach approaches the harmonic style of the coming period without departing from a three-voice structure. Characteristic, too, is a movement like the Adagio (BWV 1018a) of the fifth sonata with the repeated double stops in the violin part against which the clavier plays animated figuration.

Though Bach did not leave a composition for violin and harpsichord as expressly moulded on the *concerto grosso* as his Italian Concerto for harpsichord solo, the opening Allegro of his G major sonata (BWV 1019) is clearly modelled on the first movement of a concerto. Particularly striking are the opening and closing sections which correspond to the appearances of the 'tutti' at the beginning and end of a *concerto grosso* Allegro. The combination of violin and harpsichord, however, was ill adapted to reproduce the alternation of soli and tutti groups characteristic of the *concerto grosso*. The attractions of the unaccompanied works and those with worked-out keyboard parts have distracted attention from those for violin (BWV 1021, 1023) or flute (1033–5) with figured bass only.

BACH'S CONTEMPORARIES

Two masters with a wide range of interests should at least be mentioned since they both contributed to the literature of the violin. Johannes Mattheson (1691–1764), singer, composer, writer, and critic, published under the title *Der Brauchbare Virtuoso* a set of *XII Sonate per il Violino, overo Flauto traverso*, with continuo

(Hamburg, 1720).[100] Georg Philipp Telemann (1681–1767), a composer of unbelievable fertility, began with *Six Sonates à Violon seul, acc. par le Clavessin* (Frankfurt, 1715) and *Kleine Cammer-music, bestehend aus VI Partien* for unspecified solo instrument and continuo (Frankfurt, 1716) and continued to pour out accompanied and unaccompanied solos. His *Der getreue Music-Meister* (Hamburg, 1728) alone includes ten sonatas for various solo instruments with bass and a gamba sonata without. Especially interesting are his *XII Fantasie per il Violino senza Basso* (Hamburg, 1735).

Johann Georg Pisendel (1687–1755), pupil of Torelli and, later, Vivaldi, and a contemporary of Bach whom he met in 1709, was important as a performer but negligible as a composer. He composed a *Sonata a Violino solo senza Basso* (*c*.1716) and two with continuo. As Court Kapellmeister at Dresden he exerted a wide influence; Quantz said that Pisendel more than anyone else had shown him how to perform an adagio. With Pisendel's pupil Johann Gottlieb Graun (*c*.1703–71), who also studied with Tartini, the Italian influence became stronger. Graun cultivated the trio sonata mainly but also published *Sei Sonate per il Violino e Cembalo* (Merseburg, *c*.1726). His brother, Carl Heinrich (*c*.1704–59) left only a few flute sonatas with continuo but none for violin. The Czech, František (Franz) Benda (1709–86), who was taught the violin by the elder Graun, boasted in his autobiography of 1763 that he had written 'up to eight violin solos . . . and a fair number of capriccios'. These capriccios, composed for the son of a patron, are études at once musical and brilliant. He published a set of solo sonatas as Op. 1 (Paris, 1763) and later sets of 'accompanied' sonatas, but most of them remain in manuscript.[101] The fresh and charming three-movement sonata in A minor (Rust M. no. 82) shows a highly individual synthesis of the singing Italian style—he was particularly renowned for his cantabile performance of adagios—folk traits, and a certain foreshadowing of the emerging classical style. It is easy to see why Burney singled out Benda and Carl Philipp Emmanuel Bach as the two original spirits among the musicians of the Prussian court.

[100] Ed. Ary van Leeuwen (Frankfurt, 1923).
[101] See Newman, *The Sonata in the Classical Era* (Chapel Hill, 1963), pp. 431–5.

# VIII

## KEYBOARD MUSIC: 1630–1700

### By JOHN CALDWELL

INSTRUMENTAL IDIOMS

DURING the late seventeenth century the distinction between music written for the organ and that for other keyboard instruments became more pronounced, particularly in France, where the colouristic possibilities of the organ began to be more widely exploited, and in Northern Germany, where the growth of the pedal organ and of the performing techniques appropriate to it led to the emergence of a grandiose and rhetorical style in which a greater range of pitch and dynamics was exploited than had been heard in any kind of music hitherto. Nevertheless, even in these countries, the separation was far from complete. French organ music, even when most preoccupied with registration, tended to employ the elaborate ornamentation and even the arpeggiated style associated with the harpsichord; while conversely the enlargement of the range and tone-colour of the harpsichord, particularly when provided with a second manual, enabled some of the tonal variety of the organ to be transferred to the domestic sphere, a path which was to be pursued much further in the eighteenth century. In Germany, where the favoured domestic instrument was the clavichord, the contrast between it and the larger types of organ is obviously much greater; yet we find the clavichord in use as a practice instrument, provided with pedals (an addition which can be documented as early as 1460)[1] and a second manual, the whole ensemble consisting in fact of three separate instruments, on which trios and chorale settings as well as preludes and fugues, chaconnes and the like could be played. Nor must we forget the role of the smaller types of organ in a secular context. Thus, although certain external features, such as registration and the use of obbligato pedal, as well as the specifically liturgical context of a great deal of

---

[1] See Susi Jeans in *Proceedings of the Royal Musical Association*, lxxvii (1950–1), p. 2. At this early date, however, the pedals are merely 'pull-downs' operating on the same strings as the manual.

keyboard music, point directly to the organ as the instrument intended, there is little recognition as yet of one of the crucial differences between the organ and other keyboard instruments, namely the sustaining power of the former as opposed to the evanescent character of the latter. The evidence, in fact, points towards a frequent transference of idioms from the organ to the harpsichord or clavichord (between which indeed the distinction is considerable and should not be ignored); and there was still a great deal of music of an instrumentally neutral character being written, even in Northern Germany—toccatas, canzonas, *ricercari*, *capricci*, and the like. The expansion in the printing of keyboard music (except in Italy, where the trade seems to have been more buoyant in the sixteenth and early seventeenth centuries) encouraged composers and their publishers to seek as wide a commercial outlet for their wares as possible, and, following the precedent set by Attaingnant in 1531, to advertise them as being suitable for as many types of keyboard instrument as were currently in fashion: a habit not yet obsolete in the early nineteenth century.

SECULAR FORMS AND STYLES

In addition to neutral forms, the secular keyboard repertory consisted of dances, variations, settings of popular melodies, and arrangements or adaptations of polyphonic vocal works. These categories are far from being mutually exclusive; indeed the variation principle may be said to be common to them all. The very act of transferring a polyphonic work to the keyboard, known as intabulation, nearly always involved a degree of ornamentation in which the principle of variation was in operation. When the canzona emerged from the chrysalis of intabulation as a fully-fledged and independent musical form it did not render obsolete the much older tradition of ornamented transcription. Frescobaldi's version of Arcadelt's 'Ancidetemi pur'[2] in his second book of Toccatas (1627, repr. 1637), doing duty by its position and its style for a twelfth toccata, falls within that tradition, as does the similar setting by the Neapolitan Gregorio Strozzi in 1687. The element of variation is equally apparent in the closely related spheres of popular song and the dance. The lines of derivation are not always clear, but it seems that in the early sixteenth century certain popular tunes gave rise to standard sequences of harmonies in regular rhythm, upon which dance music could be composed or, no

---

[2] *Madrigals*, Book I, no. 5 (*Corpus mensurabilis musicae*, xxxi/2).

doubt, improvised. Thus, in a Venetian keyboard manuscript of *c*.1520, we find a tune called 'Todero' or 'Tuo tene mamina', based on a version of the *passamezzo antico* harmonies (the 'Passo e mezzo', no. 19 in the same manuscript, gives a more standardized version), and 'La cara cossa del Berdolin', giving an early form of the *folia* harmonies. *Passamezzo* and *folia* are, of course, names of dances, but the harmonic sequences came eventually to have a separate identity from that of the parent dances and to become the basis of compositions retaining only a nominal link with them. The early forms of another widespread ground, the *romanesca*, are in duple metre: later versions are generally in triple. All these grounds in their schematic form gave rise to further melodies of which we may name the English 'Fortune my foe' (*passamezzo antico*), the Spanish 'Guardame las vacas', and the English 'Greensleeves' (*romanesca*). By about 1550 another widespread ground, the *passamezzo moderno*, had come into being; a triple-time variant, the 'Tenore de Zefiro', was in use amongst Neapolitan composers. The English tune 'John come kiss me now' is founded upon its harmonies.[3]

This material is an impressive testimony to the continuity of musical thought during the sixteenth and seventeenth centuries; the *folia* material can boast a continuous history of close on two hundred years; the *passamezzo antico*, *passamezzo moderno*, and the *romanesca* very little less. It provided bases for innumerable sets of variations, helping to turn variation technique away from the finely contrapuntal elaboration of melodic material towards the harmonically constant treatment of theme and variations which was to dominate until the end of the nineteenth century. Most of all it was instrumental in establishing a harmonic concept of tonality, partly by enabling composers to dispense with the melodic material hitherto regarded as a definitive indication of mode, and partly by making the triadic idioms associated with cadences the basis of

[3] The Venetian MS is in the Biblioteca marciana, Ital. IV 1227, ed. Knud Jeppesen, *Balli antichi veneziani* (Copenhagen, 1962). For the *passamezzo moderno* (or *nuovo*) bass see Vol. IV, p. 645; a selection of grounds used by English composers, ibid., p. 629. Apel's view of the essentially melodic nature of the *passamezzo antico* and *romanesca* material (*The History of Keyboard Music to 1700*, pp. 236, 263) seems scarcely tenable in view of their early appearances without specific melodic associations. This is not to deny a possible ultimate derivation from melody, nor a subsequent association with standardized melodic formulae, e.g. 'Aria di romanesca' and 'Aria di folia'. The 'romanesca' and 'folia' are nearly always in triple time, and later versions of the 'folia' generally use smaller note-values and often differ in melodic outline:

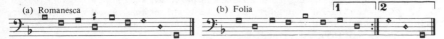

harmonic practice. And while this material was employed in many instrumental media besides that of the keyboard, it is only in the keyboard repertory that all the essential phases of development can be perceived.

Beside the material of purely or largely harmonic foundation there arose in the later sixteenth century a body of themes of vocal origin of which the essence is the melody, the bass, and the harmonies which this polarity implies. The generic name for such themes is *aria*.[4] Some of these are of known origin, and used for variations only by the composer himself; others, whether of known or unknown origin, were used over and over again. To this category belong not only the tunes derived from harmonic grounds and inseparable from them, but such newer items as 'Ruggiero', 'Bergamasca', 'La Monica', 'La Battaglia', the 'Aria detta Balletto', 'La spagnoletta', and others.[5] Frescobaldi's 'Partite sopra l'aria di Fiorenza' was based upon a *ballo* written by Cavalieri for the *intermedi* performed at Florence in 1589;[6] Sweelinck, who also wrote a set of keyboard variations upon it, called it 'Balletto del granduca'. The untitled themes of numerous seventeenth-century sets of variations are in effect arias. It is not surprising that in its instrumental as in its vocal form the aria should have strong connotations of the dance: the association with the *balletto* is paralleled in England by that of the ayre with the alman, a dance virtually identical with the *balletto*.

The dance flourished, needless to say, independently of the aria. Though dance music for the keyboard must normally be regarded as stylized imitation, designed primarily for the recollection in tran-

---

[4] The origin of this term appears to lie in Petrucci's expressions 'aer de versi latini' (*Frottole* Bk. IV), 'aer de capitoli' (*Frottole* Bk. IX), etc., where 'aer', later 'aria', is the equivalent of 'mode', a 'method' of setting standardized verse-forms. The melody-bass polarity, together with a certain regularity and simplicity of construction, is the defining characteristic of the form, valid throughout the seventeenth and eighteenth centuries, the more complex forms associated with opera and oratorio being derived from it, as are its numerous instrumental connotations. The earliest examples for keyboard are in Marco Facoli's *Secondo libro d'intavolatura* (Venice, 1588); see Vol. IV, pp. 644–5.

[5] On the *ruggiero* see ibid., pp. 140–1.

[6] Ibid., pp. 793–5, and Warren Kirkendale, *L'aria di Fiorenza* (Florence, 1972). Frescobaldi's setting is in Rome, Vatican Library, Chigi Q. IV. 25, ff. 1$^r$–5$^r$; the Chigi MSS contain six further sets of variations and the Biblioteca classense at Ravenna, MS 545, yet another. Frescobaldi's *partite* are ed. W. R. Shindle in *Corpus of Early Keyboard Music*, xxx/3, p. 6; other Chigi settings ed. Harry B. Lincoln, ibid., xxxii/2, p. 52; xxxii/3, pp. 26, 31, 32, 33. Kirkendale lists a number of other keyboard settings, two of which (Florence, Biblioteca nazionale, Magl. XIX. 138, ff. 1$^v$–2$^r$, 'Son fonti e fiumi', and Lüneburg K.N. 146, the 'Drallius' MS of 1650, 'Aria grand' duc', ff. 116$^v$–117$^r$) he prints.

quillity of the excitements of the ball-room or the village green, some of its conventions must be closely related to those of the dance itself. Amongst these are the *ripresa* or partial repetition, often in a faster rhythm, of the material of the main dance; another is the grouping together of dances related by tonality if not by actual material, such early seventeenth-century combinations as *corrente—balletto—ciaccona* being but one stage in the evolution from the earliest examples of paired dances in the fourteenth century to the fully-fledged suite of the mid-seventeenth century and later. The *ciaccona*, like the oddly spelt *passacagli*, is a Spanish dance; with the *folia* they powerfully revived in the seventeenth century the principle of *basso ostinato* in the land of its origin. While the *ciaccona* (known in France as the *chaconne*) could and did depart from the ostinato principle while retaining its strongly marked dance characteristics, the *passacagli* (later *passacaglia*, French *passacaille*) was always associated with it. The typical set of 'partite sopra passacagli' of Frescobaldi, Strozzi, or Bernardo Pasquini is based on one or more short and strongly cadential bass themes, in four bars of triple time beginning on the second beat, over which a standard series of harmonies might be varied but never totally denied. The *folia*, though based on a sixteen-bar theme rather than on a four-bar one, came to share both its freedoms and its restrictions. A single *passacaglia (passacaglio, passacaglie*, Sp. *passacalle)* seems to have been, at least as far as its music is concerned, the four-bar phrase on which a complete piece might be built; the plural form *passacagli (passacaglie*, Sp. *passacalles)* indicates one or more such pieces, whether based on one or several four-bar formulae. This could explain much of the linguistic confusion in Italian sources. The expression 'partite sopra passacagli' may imply that the structural divisions (*partite*) of a complete piece normally incorporate several repetitions of the formula, except perhaps in the case of Frescobaldi's 'Cento partite . . .' where in any case the enumeration is inexact. *Ciaccona* (Sp. *chacona*) on the other hand is a complete dance, whatever its structure. The singular 'passacaglia' can imply an introductory or concluding ritornello (or 'ripresa') to a song or another dance as well as the four-bar dance formula itself, the latter based on the sort of music associated with the Spanish custom of promenading while strumming a guitar. It is perhaps not too much to see in the compositions first published by Frescobaldi in 1627 (see below) and others like them a stylization of informal sequences of measures on the dance floor, with their haphazard juxtaposition of *passacagli* and other dances, and their equally unpremeditated changes of tonality.[7]

Yet another dance of Spanish origin, the *sarabanda*, appears to have reached Italy through France; a binary dance like the *corrente* and *alemanda*, it joined them to make up the nucleus of the baroque suite throughout Europe.

### THE LITURGICAL BACKGROUND

While the growth of secular or domestic keyboard music can be related to the increasing prosperity and leisure of the middle classes, enabling them to buy music, pay for instrumental tuition, and, where talent was sufficient and social conditions permitted, to follow the profession itself, the development of church organ music can be seen only in the context of the confessional differences which led to distinctive liturgical practices. The Catholic liturgy continued to permit, and by long-standing custom in many areas to require, the substitution of organ music for specific items of liturgical chant, or to accompany liturgical actions, or both.

The primary method, inherited from the Middle Ages, was that of alternation, in which organ music, based on the portions of plainchant which it replaced, alternated with the choral singing of those which were left. We might more accurately, with reference to other methods yet to be considered, call this 'alternating substitution'. In the course of time it became less obligatory to base the organ music on the plainchant itself, and by the eighteenth century it was possible to hear all kinds of secular idioms pressed into this service. The accurate performance of this kind of music depends not only on an appreciation of its liturgical context but on the careful restoration of the chant in the form current (both as to method of performance and as to musical text) at the time and place when the organ music was composed. In addition to alternating substitution we find total substitution, without any plainsong basis, for such items as the Gradual and Offertory of the Mass. Frescobaldi in his *Fiori musicali* (Venice, 1635) provided for each of the three kinds of Mass at which organ music might be required not only alternating verses for the Kyrie, based on the appropriate plainchant melody, but also an introductory Toccata (substituting for

---

[7] Recent work on the *ciaccona* and *passacaglia* includes Thomas Walker, 'Ciaccona and Passacaglia: Remarks on their Origin and Early History', *Journal of the American Musicological Society*, xxi (1968), pp. 300–320, and Richard Hudson, 'Further Remarks on the Passacaglia and Ciaccona', ibid., xxiii (1970), pp. 302–314, where much emphasis is laid on Spanish and Italian guitar tablatures. See also Hudson, *Passacaglia and Ciaccona from Guitar Music to Italian Keyboard Variations in the 17th Century* (Ann Arbor, 1981).

the Introit), a 'Canzon dopo l'epistola' (substituting for the Gradual and Alleluia) a 'Recercar dopo il Credo' (substituting for the Offertory) and a 'Canzon post il Comune' (substituting for the Communion antiphon and probably intended to provide a musical accompaniment to the rest of the Mass).[8] In addition there are the elevation toccatas, corresponding to no musical chant, unless indeed the Sanctus and Benedictus were to be recited silently against the music. Other composers (e.g. Girolamo Cavazzoni, Claudio Merulo, and Andrea Gabrieli) had provided alternating sections for the entire Ordinary of the Mass: Kyrie, Gloria, Credo, Sanctus, and Agnus. Collections of canzonas, *ricercari, capricci,* toccatas, and the like, may be thought of as providing material suited to the various 'Proper' (i.e. variable) portions of the Mass, or as free introductions and postludes to the service. The evening service, Vespers, was provided with alternate organ verses for the hymn and the Magnificat.[9]

The Lutheran rite was much more variable than the Catholic and the degree of congregational participation differed from place to place. In addition, the service might be entirely in German, or entirely in Latin, or in a combination of the two. Lutheran organ music reflects this lack of uniformity. It is not uncommon to find *alternatim* settings with Latin titles of the Kyrie and Gloria of the Mass, and of hymns and the Magnificat for Vespers, in the Lutheran sphere.[10] In addition we find settings of the melodies of the German metrical hymns used as substitutes for these items of the Latin service, as well as of those for the Credo, Sanctus, and Agnus, and of large numbers of hymns not directly related to any of these items. When an organ setting has a large number of 'verses' it is often difficult to determine the precise function of the composition in relation to the stanzas of the hymn as sung.[11] In any case, the congregational singing of hymns was nowhere neglected, and single-stanza settings are often manifestly (and sometimes explicitly) designed as preludes to such performance, enunciating not only the melody of the hymn, often highly elaborated, but setting the appropriate mood and perhaps symbolizing the text.

[8] Vol. IV, pp. 655–6.

[9] Elevation toccatas, hymns and Magnificats are included in Frescobaldi's second book of toccatas (1627: see below and Vol. IV, p. 655). Information on liturgical practice is given in Banchieri's *L'Organo suonarino* (1605 and later editions) and Arnold Schering, 'Zur Alternatim-Orgelmesse', *Zeitschrift für Musikwissenschaft*, xvii (1935), p. 19.

[10] E.g. by Scheidt in the third part of his *Tabulatura nova* (1624).

[11] Actual substitution for any part of the sung text seems unlikely, though this does not rule out various types of *alternatim* performance.

Large-scale toccatas, passacaglias, and the like, may be thought of as voluntaries in a more general sense.

The Calvinist service strictly speaking disallowed the use of the organ altogether. But in the Netherlands it was customary to play before and after the lengthy sermon which formed the staple diet of the Calvinist regimen, at the expense not of the Church but of the municipal authorities who were also responsible for the upkeep of the instruments.[12] The chorales of Sweelinck were apparently intended for the use of, or as models for imitation by, his German pupils; his few settings of Calvinist melodies, like those of Henderick Speuy (*De Psalmen Davids*, 1610) were presumably intended for informal use as voluntaries.

### TONALITY

These differing liturgical traditions have a bearing on certain aspects of tonal organization in baroque keyboard music. The Lutheran tradition was in some ways more conservative than the Catholic in this respect, probably because the growth of a specifically Lutheran body of hymn-melodies from the early sixteenth century onwards amounted to a national heritage in which the German composer could take a justifiable pride. Since many of the oldest tunes are in fact adaptations of plainsong melodies which are much older still, there was a considerable amount of archaic material embedded in the Lutheran melodic stock, much of which was still actively cultivated in the eighteenth century. It was a challenge to the composer to assimilate this material into his own musical style while preserving its melodic integrity. No one was more successful in doing so than J. S. Bach, and it is fascinating to watch his creative imagination at work on a mode 3 melody like 'Aus tiefer Noth' or the still older 'Kyrie Gott Vater in Ewigkeit', a sixteenth-century adaptation of the tenth-century plainsong Kyrie 'Fons bonitatis'. His transpositions of these melodies in the third part of the *Clavier Übung*, and the key-signatures with which his settings are provided, testify to his grasp of sixteenth-century modal theory and to his ingenuity in applying it to his own eminently practical needs. Not all composers were as acutely conscious of their heritage as Bach, but he is nevertheless the culminating point of a continuous tradition which can be firmly linked to its medieval past.

While the composers of the Lutheran tradition rarely indicated

---

[12] Alan Curtis, *Sweelinck's Keyboard Music* (Leiden and London, 1969), pp. 6–7.

the modality of their settings, Catholic organists and others falling
within that general sphere of influence employed a terminology
based on, but by now only tenuously related to, the system of eight
(later twelve) church modes. Its origin however lies not only in the
modes themselves (in the sense of scales defined by range, *finalis*,
*tenor*, and interval structure) but also in the so-called 'tones' of the
psalms and canticles.[13] Both Catholic and Lutheran organists when
composing *alternatim* verses to the Magnificat indicated the tone to
which they were intended to conform and usually incorporated its
salient melodic ideas into their settings. But in the Catholic
countries the convention went a good deal further than this. While
their technique could always embrace the polyphonic elaboration
of a plainsong melody labelled according to its mode, they
extended the terminology to include freely composed pieces, and in
doing so came to define the character of a tone not by its melodic
material but by the harmonic conventions associated with it. To a
certain extent this was already true of vocal music: not only in the
conventions associated with *falsobordone*, the harmonized
chanting of psalms, but in larger works such as Masses identified by
their 'tone'. Although Tinctoris and Glareanus had stated that the
mode of a polyphonic composition was to be defined by the range
and *finalis* of its tenor part, it is evident that by the end of the
sixteenth century the harmonic conventions associated with the
'tones' were firmly established. In free-textured keyboard music
(without a specific number of voice-parts) these conventions were
of paramount importance. They may be said to have been largely
established in the *Intonationi* of Andrea Gabrieli (known to us only
in a posthumous edition of 1593 but apparently first published in
the 1570s),[14] and may be summarized as follows:[15]

Tone  1 :  D min. (no sig.), (*D*)*F*—*d"*(*f"*), perf. D
      2 :  G min. (1 flat), (*F*)*G*—*d"*(*f"*), plag. G.
      3 :  E phryg. (no sig.), (*E*)*A*—*d"*, plag. E.
      4 :  E phryg. (no sig.), (*G*)*A*—*e"*(*g"*), plag. E.
      5 :  C maj. (no sig.), *F*—*g"*, plag. C.
      6 :  F maj. (1 flat), *F*—*f"* (*g"*), plag. F.

[13] Modern English usage tends to prefer 'mode' for the scale-forms and 'tone' for the
recitative-like melodies of the psalms and canticles, whereas the continental custom was to
use 'tone' ('Ton', 'tono', etc.) for both.
[14] Joseph von Wasielewski, cited by Howard Mayer Brown (*Instrumental Music Printed
Before 1600*, Cambridge Mass., 1965), mentions an edition of Gabrieli's sixth book in 1571;
the *Intonationi* are the first volume of the series published in 1593–1605.
[15] Italicized letters indicate the overall range of the pieces, exceptional notes outside the
normal range being bracketed. The last item of information refers to the type and pitch class
of the final cadence in each case.

7 :   G maj. (no sig.) *G—g"* (*a"*), perf. G.
8 :   G maj. (no sig.) *G—d"* (*a"*), plag. G.

Though these conventions are certainly related to the Gregorian psalm-tones, particularly in the emphasis accorded to the Gregorian tenor in each piece,[16] it would be a mistake to explain them entirely in this way. Gabrieli's nephew, in the *Intonationi* added to the edition of 1593, modified them in various respects, particularly in the matter of overall range, never a very stable factor. Giovanni's cadence in tone 2 is perfect; he writes only one piece for tones 3 and 4; his 6th tone has no key-signature; his 7th tone has a plagal cadence. He also adds, under the direct or indirect influence of Glareanus, four more tones:

9 :   A min. (no sig.), *A—a'*, perf. A.
10 :   A min. (no sig.), *D—e'*, plag. A.
11 :   F maj. (1 flat), (*G*)*c—f"* (*g"*), perf. F.
12 :   C maj. (no sig.), *C—g"*, perf. C.

All eleven works were duplicated in a transposition by a fourth or fifth.

These conventions could be, and were, transferred to larger forms of keyboard music. Indeed, the terminology was widely established in keyboard publications by the third quarter of the sixteenth century and the system exerted a profound influence on large-scale tonal organization in the seventeenth and early eighteenth centuries, not only in organ music but in the ordering of pieces in innumerable collections of secular keyboard works for domestic use, though tonality was gradually orientated towards the exclusive use of major and minor at any pitch.

With these general considerations in view, we may turn to the development of keyboard style in different regions, starting in the Catholic south and proceeding to the largely Protestant north.

## FRESCOBALDI

The outstanding innovator of the seventeenth century was Girolamo Frescobaldi,[17] who transferred the discoveries of the *Camerata* and of Monteverdi to the keyboard and in doing so forged a unique personal style for the instrument. If his *Fiori musicali* (1635) represent the final distillation of that style, the two books of *Toccate* (1615–1627; published for the last time in 1637[18]),

---

[16] The tenor of each mode (after the appropriate transposition in the case of 2 and 5) is: *a, b* flat, *c, c', g, a, d', c'*.

[17] For a more detailed appraisal see Vol. IV, pp. 646–56.

[18] This is the edition followed by Pidoux in his modern reprint (Kassel, 1949–56).

exhibit his brilliance and variety and are a better symbol of his popularity and influence. The toccatas themselves are profoundly diverse in manner, particularly those of the Second Book, ranging as they do from the austerity of no. 8 ('di durezze e ligature', i.e. exploiting suspended dissonances) to the brilliance of no. 9, with its demanding proportional changes of rhythm, and including the two protracted elevation toccatas, the two which are composed over long-held pedal notes ('sopra i pedali e senza', which means that the pedal notes may be omitted) and the elaborate intabulation (or ornamented transcription) of Arcadelt's madrigal 'Ancidetemi pur'. The remaining contents of this Second Book—canzonas, liturgical verses (here for hymns and the Magnificat), variations and dances—are less interesting than some of his other examples in these forms. The *Partite sopra ciaccona* and *Partite sopra passacagli* of the first edition of Book II (1627)[19] are omitted as being more fully represented in the *Aggiunta* (additions) to the 1637 edition of Book I. This latter reprints from the second edition of 1615–16 the enlarged versions of his 'Romanesca', 'Monicha', and 'Ruggiero' variations, the 'Folia' variations, and four *correnti*;[20] the *Aggiunta* consist of three balletti, each with 'Corrente' and 'Passacagli', 'Cento partite sopra passacagli', and some further pieces of various kinds.[21] It cannot be said that the variation sets are particularly successful as complete works of art—they are greatly inferior in overall design to those of some of the English virginalists, in particular Byrd—but they are a milestone in the road along which the harmonically conceived variation technique of the sixteenth century passed into the *lingua franca* of baroque style; and the 'Romanesca' set at least contains some marvellous moments of introspection. The manuscript sources contain numerous additional works by Frescobaldi,[22] including several toccatas. Some of these, such as the works over sustained pedal, are similar in style to those of the Second Book. Others have a thinner texture and that more regular

[19] Modern edition of these versions in *Corpus of Early Keyboard Music*, xxx/3, pp. 44–9.

[20] The 'Romanesca', 'Monicha' and 'Ruggiero' variations first appeared in 1615 in shorter and otherwise different versions from those of 1615–16 and 1637 (modern reprint of the 1615 versions in *Corpus of Early Keyboard Music*, xxx/3, pp. 23–44). The 'Folia' variations (based on an otherwise unknown sixteen-bar ground) and *correnti*, which also appeared in 1615–16, were unchanged in 1637.

[21] The 'Cento partite' intersperse the 'passacagli' with sections marked 'corrente' (1) and 'ciaccona' (3). While much of the material of the 1627 'Ciaccona' and 'Passacagli' is found here in a greatly extended and elaborated form the correspondence is not so close as to make this work a true substitute for those of 1627.

[22] One important source, Vatican MS Chigi Q. IV. 25, headed 'Suonate d'intavolatura del Sig. Girolamo Frescobaldi', has already been mentioned (n. 6). All are included in *Corpus of Early Keyboard Music*, xxx.

rhythmic construction which relates them to what Apel has called 'the musical discourse of the middle Baroque'.[23]

FRESCOBALDI'S CONTEMPORARIES

These features are further developed in the toccatas of Frescobaldi's pupil Michelangelo Rossi, who also revived the technique, frequent in the printed toccatas of Merulo (Rome, 1657) but scarcely evident in Frescobaldi's, of introducing imitative or fugal sections into works of this kind. Rossi is a somewhat ambivalent figure; at times he emulates and even exceeds Frescobaldi in the wildness of his rhythm and the extravagance of his chromaticism which may be illustrated by the opening and close of his seventh toccata, perhaps the finest of the printed works:[24]

Ex. 291

(i)

---

[23] *History of Keyboard Music to 1700* (London, 1972), p. 482.

[24] Ed. John R. White in *Corpus of Early Keyboard Music*, xv. The left-hand chord in bar two was playable without pedals in those days on the usual 'short-octave' keyboard, which appeared to descend only to note *E*; this and the next five notes however actually sounded as follows (apparent note in brackets): *C* (*E*), *F* (*F*), *D* (*F* sharp), *G* (*G*), *E* (*G* sharp), *A* (*A*).

(ii)

But in truth he lacked both the inventiveness and the poise of his master, and the apparently later manuscript toccatas (added to a copy of the 1657 edition in 1700 and 1701) show the weakening of rhythmic interest characteristic of the mid-seventeenth century without the compensating virtue of tonal and structural clarity.[25]

[25] The very fine toccata ascribed to M. Rossi in one manuscript (Brit. Lib. Add. 31446) and to Purcell in another (ibid., Add. 34695) is as far from Rossi's usual style as it is from Purcell's. See Gloria Rose, 'Purcell, Michelangelo Rossi and J. S. Bach: Problems of Authorship', *Acta Musicologica*, xl (1968), 203.

Rossi's ten *correnti* are likewise pale reflections of Frescobaldi's, lacking their melodic and contrapuntal interest, while the 'Romanesca' of the manuscript additions cannot fairly be compared with Frescobaldi's at all; it is to be seen rather in the tradition of straightforward settings by Valente, Mayone, and others.

Another purveyor of dance music was the Venetian Martino Pesenti, who published four books of *correnti* and other dances from some time before 1630 (the first edition of Book I is lost) to 1645. Most of his pieces are as suitable for instrumental ensemble as for keyboard, as his title-pages avow; apart from *correnti* he published *balletti* (which are duple-time dances), *gagliarde*, and *passamezzi*. These works are greatly inferior to the similar examples of his Venetian compatriot Legrenzi for instrumental ensemble, though the tonal experiments of the fourth book, in which such keys as A flat minor and A sharp major appear, are worth mentioning. The few genuine keyboard works of Tarquinio Merula (c.1590–1665) do not add significantly to our knowledge of this gifted composer of ensemble music.[26]

## SOUTHERN ITALIANS

A more consistently interesting group of composers were the Southern Italians, who inherited a continuous tradition of inventive keyboard writing stemming from Valente and Rodio in the sixteenth century and continuing with Giovanni de Macque, Mayone and Trabaci in the early seventeenth. Its chief representatives in this period with their keyboard publications are Giovanni Salvatore (*Ricercari*, 1641), Bernardo Storace (*Selva di varie compositioni*, 1664), and Gregorio Strozzi (*Capricci*, 1687). In addition a Sicilian composer called Gioanpietro del Buono published at Palermo in 1641, as an appendix to a large collection of vocal canons on the hymn 'Ave maris stella', a collection of fourteen *Sonate di cimbalo* on the same theme.[27] There is in the music of the first three of these composers a touch of pedantry and a considerable dependence on Frescobaldi. The pedantry is evident in the *ricercari* of Salvatore on the eight tones, with their precise indications of the tone and transposition, and of the number of subjects in each. A

---

[26] Modern edition by Alan Curtis, *Composizioni per organo e cembalo* (Brescia, 1961); *Monumenti di Musica Italiana*, i/1.

[27] Discussed by William S. Newman, 'The XIIII Sonate di Cimbalo by Giovanni Pietro Del Buono, "Palermitano" (1641)', *Collectanea Historiae Musicae*, ii (1957), pp. 297–310, and *The Sonata in the Baroque Era* (Chapel Hill, 1959; rev. ed. 1966), pp. 126–7. The works of Salvatore, Storace, and Strozzi are in *Corpus of Early Keyboard Music*, vols. iii, vii, and xi respectively.

freer style is evident in the canzonas, toccatas and versets for the Mass added to the 1641 publications. Some of the canzonas are designated as being equally suited to performance by 'il Concerto di Viole'. Not only are these works, being evidently intended for the *viola da brazzo* or violin family, among the earliest examples of genuine string quartet writing; they also exemplify the incipient breakdown of the traditional distinction between keyboard and ensemble style in the contrapuntal genres. This is the beginning of the path which was to lead, through many vicissitudes, to the orchestrally inspired keyboard-writing of J. S. Bach and of the Viennese classical composers.

Storace in his *Selva* included a large number of pieces based on traditional material: settings of the *passamezzo moderno* (eight variations in A major of which the fifth and sixth are marked 'gagliarda' and the seventh and eighth 'corrente'), *passamezzo antico* (sets of variations in C minor and E minor each following the same plan as the *passamezzo moderno* set) and *romanesca* (six variations in A minor); pieces based on the 'Spagnoletta', 'Monica', 'Ruggiero', *cinque passi*,[28] and 'Folia' material; several sets of *passacagli*, a 'Ciaconna', six variations on a 'Balletto', and the 'Ballo della Battaglia'. A few *correnti*, toccatas, canzonas, and *ricercari*, with a 'Pastorale', conclude the volume. Almost every form used can be traced back to Frescobaldi and Storace's Neapolitan forebears. The 'Folia' setting is closer to the traditional harmonic foundation than is Frescobaldi's, though it is not precisely identical to the version so conspicuously revived by Corelli.[29] The *passacagli* are interesting in that they demonstrate a more stable tradition than is evident in the comparable works of Frescobaldi. The variations are not interrupted by other dance measures, and the overall structures are clearer. The *partite* here are not single statements of the four-bar ground but larger units defined by a single rhythm or tempo. In the two sets in which modulating passages occur the *partite* and the individual variations are re-numbered from each change of key. The schemes of these interesting works are as follows:

[28] The *cinque passi* ('five steps') was in origin a quick galliard; it became in English— through the French—'sink-a-pace' and other locutions. On some aspects of the English usage see Sternfeld, *Music in Shakespearean Tragedy* (London, 1963), pp. 252–3. Storace's 'Partite sopra il cinque passi' is a set of fifteen variations on one of the simplest of harmonic grounds: a major-key tonic-dominant-tonic-dominant progression.

[29] See p. 481.

*No. 12*

| Section-title | Variations | Bars | Key | Time sivnature |
|---|---|---|---|---|
| Prima partita | 1–13 | 1–52 | D major | 3/2 |
| Seconda partita, modo pastorale | 14–27 | 53–108 | D major | (3/2) |
| Passa ad altro tono | – | 109–112 | – | (3/2) |
| Prima partita, modo pastorale | 1–4 | 113–128 | A major | (3/2) |
| Seconda partita, altro modo | 5–11 | 129–156 | A major | (3/2) |
| Terza partita, vario | 12–16 | 157–176 | A major | (3/2) |
| Quarta partita, ordinario | 17–24 | 177–208 | A major | (3/2) |
| Passa ad altro tono | – | 209–212 | – | (3/2) |
| Prima partita | 1–11 | 213–256 | E major | (3/2) |
| Seconda partita, altro modo: pastorale | 12–20 | 257–274 | E major | 12/8 |
| Passa ad altro tono | – | 275–276 | – | (12/8) |
| Prima partita: a tempo | 1–11 | 277–320 | B minor | C3/2 |
| Seconda ed ultima partita | 12–20 | 321–356 | B minor | (3/2) |
| [Coda] | – | 357–364 | B minor | C |

*No. 13*

| | | | | |
|---|---|---|---|---|
| – | 1–21 | 1–84 | F minor | C3/4 |
| Passa ad altro tono | – | 85–88 | – | (3/4) |
| – | 1–15 | 89–148 | B flat minor | (3/4) Grave |
| Passa ad altro tono | – | 149–152 | – | (3/4) |
| – | 1–36 | 153–298 (including 2 bar coda at end) | E flat major | (3/4) Allegro |

The broad structural scheme of the second work, with its contrasts of tempo, is particularly noteworthy. Two quotations will
illustrate, first Storace's harmonic range and his simple but
effective technique of modulation and, second, his method of
improving the sense of continuity in the Allegro section by
grouping pairs of variations together:

Ex. 292

(i) bars 137–153 [Grave]

Passa ad altro Tono

Allegro

(ii) bars 173-189 [Allegro]

The last of these Neapolitans, Gregorio Strozzi, abbot, doctor of civil and canon law, and apostolic protonotary, displays more pedantry than imagination in his *Capricci* of 1687. The various *capricci, ricercate*, canzonas (here called 'sonatas'), and toccatas, down to the 'Ancidetemi diminuito', recall Frescobaldi; the 'Romanesca con partite, tenori e ritornelli' attempts to outdo him. In its great length, its strange chromaticism and its addiction to trills, lombardic rhythm, and other Frescobaldian devices, it represents the extremes of this style. The *tenori* are sustained chromatic variants of the old ground:

Ex. 293

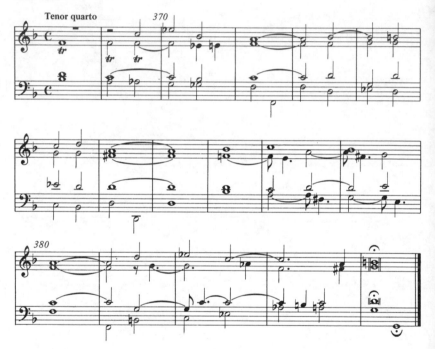

His dances are often scarcely in the keyboard idiom at all; the 'Gagliarda terza' is marked 'per concerto di viole', while the eleventh and twelfth variations of the 'Romanesca' set are marked 'per Arpa, Viola ecc.' and 'per Arpa' respectively; the trills in the 'Gagliarda terza' very possibly indicate vibrato rather than genuine trills, which raises the question whether they do not have that significance in passages like Ex. 293. In some cases Strozzi's dances are amplified as to harmony by a curious and perhaps unique system of figuring in which intervals are denoted downwards from the top part as well as upwards from the bass. If the claim represented by the title of one piece, 'Mascara sonata e ballata da più cavalieri napolitani nel regio palazzo' is true, we have a rare glimpse into the social background of these picturesque, if sometimes musically flimsy, works.

## ITALIAN ORGAN MUSIC

The continuous tradition of Italian liturgical organ music for the Mass and Offices[30] was followed in the *Ricercari Canzoni francesi, Toccate et Versi per rispondere nelle Messe con l'Organo al Choro* (Naples, 1641) of Giovanni Salvatore, the *Frutti musicali de Messe tre ecclesiastiche* (Venice, 1642) of Antonio Croci, and the *Annuale che contiene tutto quello che deve far un Organista per rispondere al Choro tutto l'Anno* (Venice, 1645) of Giovan Battista Fasolo, as well as in the *Modulazioni precettive sopra l'Hinni del Canto fermo gregoriano con le Risposte intavolate in sette righe* (Bologna, 1664) of Giulio Cesare Arresti. There is also the manuscript liturgical music included in the seventeenth-century Chigi MSS Q IV 24, 27, and Q VIII 206.[31] Much of this, apart from some works by Frescobaldi in the manuscript sources, is of only slight musical interest, the restrictions of the *alternatim* structure providing little scope for expansion. The Chigi manuscripts as a whole (Chigi Q 24–29, VIII 205–6), dating from around 1650, in addition to being a major source of unpublished music by Frescobaldi, contain an interesting collection of canzonas, *ricercari*, toccatas, dances, and variation-sets which throw an additional light on the conventions of the time.

## BERNARDO PASQUINI

The principal figure of the later seventeenth century, if only by virtue of the bulk of his surviving music, is Bernardo Pasquini (1637–1710)[32]. He is perhaps the sole Italian representative of that important group of later seventeenth-century composers whose contribution lay, if not exclusively, at least largely and most significantly in the sphere of keyboard music. Though he wrote many operas, his chief importance is as the principal keyboard composer

[30] See Vol. IV, pp. 602–611.
[31] Edited in *Corpus of Early Keyboard Music*, xxx (Frescobaldi), xxxii (anonymous compositions). See Alexander Silbiger, *Italian Manuscript Sources of 17th Century Keyboard Music* (Ann Arbor, 1980), pp. 116–134.
[32] *Collected Works for Keyboard*, ed. Maurice Brooks Haynes, 7 vols., *Corpus of Early Keyboard Music*, v. Unfortunately the edition is marred by numerous misprints and failure to discuss sources properly.

to participate in the middle baroque 'settlement', as it might be called, achieved by Corelli, Torelli, G. B. Vitali, and others in the sphere of instrumental ensemble music. Though there is a certain amount of old-fashioned, post-Frescobaldian music—canzonas, *ricercari*, some of the toccatas, and so on—the bulk of it conforms to the clear, simple, outlines of the newer style. Even the variations on the *folia* and *bergamasca*, and the various *passacagli*, reveal the newer idiom. Particularly noteworthy are the numerous suites and sets of variations, in which the simple binary forms are articulated within a straightforward tonal scheme. In the majority of these the first section will move to a related key without any intermediate modulatory cadence: to the dominant in the case of major keys, to the relative major, dominant, or to an imperfect cadence in the case of minor keys. The second section, usually slightly longer, normally has a point of repose in a different related key: the relative or supertonic minor in the case of major keys, the relative or other close major in the case of minor keys. The structure however is rarely completely straightforward in the second half, a common device being the deprivation, by harmonic means, of the tonal force of the melodic cadence (the so-called 'interrupted cadence' of conventional terminology) as in the following Aria in C major:[33]

Ex. 294

[33] Ibid., v/2, pp. 52–3.

Pasquini might indeed be said to have given the old concept of the aria a new lease of life by making it an original instrumental form, and most of his suite-movements and variation-themes, even when they do not actually bear the title, conform to its spirit. His suites vary in the number and order of their movements—allemanda, corrente, giga is a common sequence—but they are noteworthy for their melodic simplicity and charm, owing little to the conventions established by the French lutenists and transferred to the keyboard by Froberger and Chambonnières. The Italians remained faithful to their old concept of the *corrente* as a quick 3/4, or at the most a 6/4 movement, ignoring its development in the hands of the French as a 3/2 movement with occasional reference to the older 6/4 metre. Though they may have borrowed the names of the *allemanda* and *giga* (as of the *sarabanda* and *gavotta*, hardly found in Pasquini but familiar from the violin works of Corelli) from the French, they owed little to them in point of style: the *allemanda* is little different from the older *balletto*, and the other dances have a similar native background. The history of the Italian baroque suite has received little attention compared with that of the French; yet it developed early and remained a vital force in the early eighteenth century, as a glance at the relevant works of Bach and Handel will show.

## PASQUINI'S VARIATIONS AND TOCCATAS

Pasquini was instrumental in developing the concept of variations on a newly invented theme as opposed to the older idea of using a pre-existent melody (or treble-bass entity or harmonic ground), familiar from the English virginalists and Lutheran organists as well as from the Italians with their more fashionable choice of material. In Italy, the term *partita* generally signifies the older concept, *variatio* the new;[34] but in the seventeenth century terminology was

---

[34] In the *Fitzwilliam Virginal Book* we already find the Italian word *variatio* used to indicate a varied repetition of a complete movement, as in the 'Pavana—Varatio—Galiarda—Variatio' by Richardson *alias* Heybourne, nos. 4–7.

muddled, and Pasquini uses the words interchangeably though nearly always starting the numbering *after* the initial statement of the theme. He also expanded the notion of the 'character' variation, at any rate by changing speeds and metres more thoroughly than had been done hitherto in the works of composers already discussed. The last word in this, as in so many other aspects of variation technique, was to be uttered by Bach in the 'Goldberg' variations. Neither of Pasquini's sets of variations on the *folia* theme quite conforms to the standard harmonic pattern, but they are close to Corelli in spirit by virtue of their inexorable tread. The four sets of 'passagagli' (*sic*) are fine works strongly unified in key and in style, but only the first appears to be complete: the final chord in the other three is missing in the autograph and Pasquini may have intended to finish them later.

Pasquini's toccatas, sometimes called 'tastata' or 'sonata', are on the whole disappointing, though they contain picturesque moments: indeed the 'Toccata con lo scherzo del cucco' is a pure genre-piece of a not particularly tasteful kind. Many of them rely on the arpeggiated openings and jerky rhythms of the traditional type, often welded not too satisfactorily on to the more regular metre of the newer style. Sustained pedal-note technique is employed in two works, of which the second is much the better since the technique is confined to an introductory rhapsody which is followed by a pair of thematically linked canzona-type movements, and these by a short coda in which the pedal is reintroduced for the final cadences. The numerous 'sonatas' for one and for two harpsichords, in which only the figured basses are written out, are curiosities of composition on which perhaps not too much emphasis need be placed.

### ALESSANDRO SCARLATTI

The next major figure in the history of Italian keyboard music, and the last to be considered here, is Alessandro Scarlatti (1660–1725). We may pass over such minor but sometimes interesting men as Francesco Pistocchi, Luigi Battiferri, Fabritio Fontana,[35] Giulio Cesare and Floriano Arresti, Pietro Andrea Ziani, Giovanni Paolo Colonna, Giovanni Battista Bassani, Monari da Bologna, Carlo Francesco Pollarolo, the brothers Pietro and Giovanni Battista degli Antoni, Alessandro Stradella (1644–82) (the impor-

---

[35] Battiferri's *Ricercari* (1669), which include works in five and six parts, have been ed. G. G. Butler in *Corpus of Early Keyboard Music*, xlii (1981). Fontana's *Ricercari per organo* (1677) have been ed. Gerhard Doderer (Milan, 1975).

tant Venetian composer who wrote a single but lengthy keyboard toccata), and Domenico Zipoli (1688–1726), a pupil of Alessandro Scarlatti who died only a year later than his master.[36] But the elder Scarlatti was a startling innovator who not only united the Roman and Neapolitan traditions but exerted a noteworthy influence on later baroque composers: both on Handel, who as 'il Sassone' appears in one source of Scarlatti's keyboard music, and even perhaps on the J. S. Bach of the Chromatic Fantasia and Fugue:

Ex. 295

[36] Ziani, Pollarolo, Bassani, Giustiniani, Monari, and G. C. Arresti, with one or two others, are represented in the important collection of *Sonate da organo di varii autori*, compiled by Arresti and published at Bologna *c*.1700. On Zipoli see below, pp. 604–5.

The work from which this passage is taken[37] falls outside the chronological limits of this chapter, but it is worthy of attention as summing up Scarlatti's historical position at the gateway to the late baroque style. With its steady harmonic rhythms, its recitative-like passages of declamatory *fioriture*, its loosely imitative moto perpetuo in the 'Fuga', and its thoroughly idiomatic harpsichord figuration throughout, the work points decisively to the future; while the twenty-nine variations on the *folia* bass with which it concludes are perhaps the very last word in the long tradition inaugurated in the 1520s. In its enigmatic conclusion on the dominant chord (Scarlatti ignores the 'second-time bar' in calling merely for an exact repetition of the traditional eight-bar strain in each variation) he appears to be symbolizing the dichotomy of his artistic nature. There is a chronological difficulty in establishing the toccata's influence on Bach's Chromatic Fantasia and Fugue. A common influence on both composers is possible; or the date and place (Naples) in the Higgs manuscript, occurring as it does at the end of the volume, might be that of the copying. Handel presumably became familiar with Scarlatti's keyboard music (though not necessarily this work) during his Italian period (1706–9); it is a dominant factor in the style of his *Suites de pièces pour le clavecin*, (London, [1720]).

SPAIN AND PORTUGAL

After the death of Antonio de Cabezón (Cabeçon) in 1566, the tradition of contrapuntal keyboard writing in the spheres of cantus-firmus setting, *tiento* (= fantasia or *ricercare*) and intabulation, but only rarely in variation, was continued by such composers as his son Hernando (d. 1602), the brothers Jerónimo and Francisco Peraza, Bernardo Clavijo del Castillo (d. 1626), Sebastian Aguilera de Heredia, and Francisco Correa de Arauxo. In Portugal the only composer of note was Manuel Rodrigues Coelho (*c*.1555–1635).[38] After Coelho and Correa there was a further decline until in Spain there arose the commanding figure of Juan Cabanilles (1644–1712).[39] One minor predecessor of Cabanilles deserves attention:

[37] Ed. R. Gerlin, *I classici musicali italiani*, xiii, no. 7, pp. 77, 87, from MS Naples, Bibl. del R. Conservatorio, 34.6.31. The work was also edited by J. S. Shedlock (London, 1908) from a manuscript then in the private possession of H. M. Higgs, in which it is dated 1723.

[38] On these composers see Vol. IV, pp. 677–82. For a useful survey of the source material, see José Maria Llorens Cisteró, 'Literatura Organistica del Siglo XVII.', *Actas del I Congresso Nacional de Musicologia* (Zaragoza, 1981), pp. 29–130.

[39] One of the most important sources of Portuguese organ music of this period is MS Braga 964. See Doderer, *Orgelmusik und Orgelbau im Portugal des 17. Jahrhunderts. Untersuchungen an Hand des Ms 964 der Biblioteca Pública in Braga* (Tutzing, 1978).

José Ximenez (Jimenes), who became organist at Saragossa cathedral in 1654 and died in 1672.[40] In his settings of 'Pange lingua' (not one of the traditional plainsong melodies but an old Spanish tune in triple time), and in his fugal compositions including those calling for an organ with divided stops, Ximenez seems at first to be little more than an imitator of Aguilera de Heredia. Yet a closer examination reveals a remarkable capacity for motivic development. This is apparent in each of the four D major settings of 'Pange lingua', for example in the middle section of the last of these:[41]

Ex. 296

If the opening of his 'Dos vajos de 8° tono' is compared with that of the identically entitled work of Aguilera, the charge of plagiarism leaps to mind:[42]

[40] Works ed. Willi Apel in *Corpus of Early Keyboard Music*, xxxi (American Institute of Musicology, 1975).
[41] Ibid., p. 12.
[42] *Corpus of Early Keyboard Music*, xiv, p. 116; ibid., xxxi, p. 80. The tonality of both works is D mixolydian.

## Ex. 297

(i) AGUILERA

(ii) XIMENEZ

At the same time, a greater sense of continuity is found in Ximenez, and a superior handling of the material is apparent throughout his composition. Though his range is small, there is genuine mastery within his distinctive idiom.[43]

---

[43] The names of some contemporaries of Ximenez in the Escorial manuscript of his music include Perandreu, Bruna, Diego de Torrijos, Joan Sebastian and Gabriel Sinxano.

# JUAN CABANILLES

Cabanilles was born in Algemesí near Valencia in 1644; in 1665 he became organist of Valencia Cathedral, a post which he held until his death in 1712. The corpus of his extant keyboard music, surviving in nineteen or so manuscripts and published in part by Anglès in four volumes (1927–1956),[44] presents a strange and forbidding appearance to modern taste. There are 70 *tientos* and twenty-six other pieces in the edition; innumerable 'verses' and other liturgical works remain unpublished. The traditional side of the composer's nature is revealed in the strict part-writing of all this music, a convention unchanged since Cabezón, and the adherence to modal terminology. These traditions, however, are more apparent than real. The strictness of the part-writing derives from the notation in open score which had superseded the equally rigid numerical tablature of Cabezón; but much of the keyboard writing, as with such composers as Frescobaldi and Scheidt, is highly idiomatic. The modal terminology is often merely a façade for a fully-formed sense of major-minor tonality, though it would be wrong to suggest that this is characteristic of his music as a whole.

A closer examination of his music suggests that Cabanilles was both a child of his time and the conscious inheritor of the tradition of Cabezón, and that in his hands this tradition found its last and fullest expression. He can be both dull as in the more conven tional of the *tientos*—and trivial, if picturesque, as in the first of the two *batallas*. He makes use, like his contemporaries, of the divided manual, sometime distributing the four voices into $2 + 2$ rather than $1 + 3$ (treble solo) or $3 + 1$ (bass solo). This device enabled the music to be played on a small instrument, but much of what he wrote can be fully appreciated only in the context of the larger type of instrument found in Spanish cathedrals in the seventeenth century. The Epistle organ built at Seville cathedral in 1673 had three manuals and a pedal organ; in 1703 the third manual was enclosed in a swell-box and a small echo organ was added. With its enormous battery of reeds, including 32' reeds on both great and pedal organs, its 'lleno de 8 hileras' (eight-rank mixtures) and other mixture stops, and its array of quints on the pedal, its superfluity of resource reminds one of the gastronomic excesses of a royal

---

[44] *Johannis Cabanilles Opera Omnia*, in *Biblioteca de Catalunya, Publicaciones del Departamento de Música* (later *Biblioteca Central, Publicaciones de la Sección de Música*), iv, viii, xiii, xvii.

banquet.[45] It is hard to imagine all the stops ever being used together, but the specification allows one to appreciate the possible grandeur of a work like *tiento* 38 'de contras', using the pedal-point technique familiar from the works of Frescobaldi and Pasquini. In its great length (328 bars), arising from the sequential repetition of a relatively short section,[46] however, it goes far beyond such models.

*Tiento* was by now a word covering not only ricercare- and fantasia-like pieces but the techniques of canzona, capriccio and toccata. At their best, such works can approach the organizational and contrapuntal integration of the toccatas of Froberger; at their worst, they can be overlong, formless, and uneven in their figuration. A striking example of a solidly constructed and yet daringly imaginative composition is provided by *tiento* 37. It is not exactly a variation-toccata, but the several sections have a general family likeness, and the work, though lengthy, has both variety and an overall quality of structural unity. A series of short extracts will give some idea of both.[47]

Ex. 298

---

[45] Gonzalo Silva y Ramón, *Die Orgelwerke der Kathedrale zu Sevilla* (Mainz, 1939), cited by W. L. Sumner, *The Organ* (3rd edn., London, 1962), pp. 97–8. There is a more critical discussion in Peter Williams, *The European Organ 1450–1850* (London, 1966), pp. 249–50.

[46] Apel, *History,* p. 773.

[47] *Opera omnia*, iii, p. 48: bars 1–10, 24–7, 58–62, 75–9, 135–7.

(ii)

(iii)

(iv)

(v)

Some of the *tientos* are settings of *cantus firmi*, either plainsong (e.g. no. 4 on 'Ave maris stella', a somewhat rambling right-hand solo in which the melody is very freely treated) or otherwise (no. 17, based on the 'Pange lingua' theme met with in Ex. 296). Cabanilles also uses the technique of 'falsas'—augmented and diminished triads rather than mere chromaticism—as in no. 53, the opening of which is startling enough although much of the continuation is devoted to an exploitation of a cadential figure which Orlando Gibbons would not have thought outlandish:[48]

Ex. 299

Although the *tientos* are so varied, some other types of work are found, not all necessarily for organ, though most pieces could be played on it. The five sets of 'pasacalles' are all sets of variations on

---

[48] Ibid., p. 196.

short bass themes, though only the first is wholly in triple time; all
are founded on the old I—IV—V bass-pattern except no. 4, which
uses phrygian instead of perfect cadences. The four *paseos* are
similar works, though still more refined in contrapuntal technique.
There is little here of a dance-like character, though this can be
seen in the admirable 'Diferencias de folias', which like the second
and fourth *paseos* begin on the second beat of the triple bar. But
the pieces called 'gallardas', again, show no connection with the
familiar galliard, being duple-time sets of variations on themes with
a fairly strong harmonic framework. It cannot be said, however,
that a strong sense of structural harmony is at all characteristic of
Spanish keyboard music from Cabezón to Cabanilles. Variation
technique is often little more than the contrapuntal elaboration of
the given melodic material, even when this is in the bass. The very
fine *pasacalles* no. 2 is strikingly reminiscent both of Cabezón and
of the English virginalists (with its plethora of 'false relations'
amongst other characteristics). The end of this piece, a rare
example of five-part writing in Spanish keyboard music deserves
quotation for its grandeur and its sense of continuity:[49]

Ex. 300

[49] Ibid., ii, p. 47.

Cabanilles stands head and shoulders above his contemporaries and successors, whose works exist beside his in the manuscripts cited by Anglès—though where so much is unpublished it would be wrong to be dogmatic. In particular the five volumes entitled *Flores de musica*, copied by Fray Antonio Martin y Coll between 1706 and 1709, appear to deserve publication: nearly all the music is anonymous (though a few works of Cabanilles and Aguilera can be identified) except for the fifth volume, containing the works of Martin himself.[50] Not all the music appears to be idiomatically conceived for the keyboard. The few modern editions of works by Gabriel Menalt, Juan Bazea, Pablo Nassarre[51] and others reveal only slender talents. Nassarre, for example, though of significance as a theorist, was totally unimaginative as a composer, carrying to excess a penchant for sequence which even in the case of Cabanilles could be overdone.

FRENCH KEYBOARD MUSIC

It is customary to divide French composers for keyboard instruments rather sharply into *organistes* and *clavecinistes*, though many of them (d'Anglebert, Louis and François Couperin, Lebègue, Dandrieu, and others) wrote for both harpsichord and organ. We have already noted that the organists' style tended to be infiltrated by that of the harpsichord; and as the latter in France was of a distinctive and ultimately very influential kind it will be as well to discuss it first.[52] It is usually, and correctly, described as being based on the *style brisé*, or 'broken style' of the lute. In this, what in other idioms would consist of plain chords were arpeggiated in a

---

[50] Madrid, Bib. Nacional, 1357–60, 2267. Described by Anglès in *Johannis Cabanilles Opera omnia*, i, pp. lviii–lxii, the contents of the first four being listed in full. See also the *Catálogo musical de la Biblioteca Nacional de Madrid*, i (Madrid, 1946), pp. 295 ff.

[51] Editions of Menalt, Bazea, and others, in Anglès, *Antología de Organistas Españoles del siglo XVII*, 4 vols. (Barcelona, 1965–7); of Nassarre by J.-M. Llorens (Barcelona, 1974). For an account of some of this music see Apel, *History*, pp. 774–5, 778–80; and for a discussion of contemporary Portuguese music, pp. 775–8.

[52] The fundamental work of reference is Bruce Gustafson, *French Harpsichord Music of the 17th Century*, 3 vols. (Ann Arbor, 1979).

fashion which enabled them to be assimilated rhythmically with the figuration prevailing elsewhere, for example in the ornamented resolution of suspensions. No doubt this was done in order to counteract the evanescence of the tone of the lute, though it is not found in sixteenth-century lute idioms. It has to be seen, however, in the context of the growth of classical culture in seventeenth-century France, in which the lute had to occupy the place of the lyre in ancient and mythological Greece. In these circumstances its downward range was increased and a rhetorical and leisurely style, a counterpart to Caccini's 'certain noble neglect of the song',[53] was cultivated. The beginnings of this style can be seen in lute publications from early in the century, such as Francisque's *Trésor d'Orphée* (1600) and Besard's *Thesaurus* (1603), and it reaches its apogee in Denis Gaultier's manuscript *Rhétorique des dieux*, the title of which is a sufficient indication of the prevailing ethos.[54] The broken style, the rubato and an approximation to the ornamentation were all transferred to the keyboard, both in transcriptions such as those of Gaultier's pieces by the lutenist Perrine (1679), who abandoned tablature for ordinary notation, and the rather later ones by d'Anglebert from various composers, as well as in original works for the keyboard. In this way godlike qualities were made more widely accessible, though at the cost of some loss of finesse. The *rubato*, except in unmeasured preludes, settled down to a fairly uniform use of *notes inégales*, which in written-out transcriptions (such as Perrine's) creates a more rigid impression than should perhaps be the case. The unmeasured preludes themselves, cultivated both by the lutenists and by such keyboard writers as Louis Couperin, d'Anglebert, and even Rameau, are of course the acme of arpeggiation as well as of 'noble neglect'. Taken *en masse*, they appear tedious, but individually they make an effective introduction to a sequence of more formalized dances.[55]

The French suite of this period, like the harpsichord style itself, is derived from the lutenists, and through them from the conventions of the *ballet de cour*. Neither source provided a precedent for a highly integrated sequence of movements, and in French hands the form rarely achieved the compactness that it did with Froberger and his German successors. Indeed the term itself was

[53] See Vol. IV, p. 157.
[54] See ibid., pp. 695 ff., and Bukofzer, op. cit. pp. 164–8. *The Rhétorique des dieux* is published in facsimile and transcription by André Tessier, *Publications de la Société française de musicologie*, vi–vii (Paris, 1932–3).
[55] On these curiously notated pieces, see Davitt Moroney, 'The performance of unmeasured harpsichord preludes', *Early Music*, iv (1976), p. 143.

not often used in France;[56] publications were simply entitled 'Pièces de clavecin' or the like, and the subdivisions according to key either unmarked or announced as 'Ordres', a term devised by François Couperin. Performers were free to make their own choice of movements, which could include transcriptions as well as original works.

## CHAMBONNIÈRES AND LOUIS COUPERIN

Among a number of composers represented in manuscripts of the middle and later seventeenth century Jacques Champion de Chambonnières (c.1602–c.1672) and his pupil Louis Couperin (c.1626–1661) stand out both by the quantity and the quality of their work. The works of Chambonnières have been edited mainly from the 'Bauyn' manuscript and the two printed volumes of 1670; and while a number of additional manuscript sources have since come to light the existing edition will serve very well as an overall guide to his output.[57] The printed source alone goes some way to justify his position as 'father of French harpsichord music': here are the groups of pieces arranged by key; the conventional sequences of allemande, courante and sarabande with the occasional gigue, pavanna, gaillarde, or other movement; the ornamented *doubles*; the descriptive or otherwise allusive titles;[58] in these and other ways the two books provide the pattern for practically every subsequent publication of French harpsichord music. If there were nothing more to be said for their contents, the very fact of publication would make them a landmark. As it is, Chambonnières can be credited with having firmly established the conventions of the style in terms of keyboard texture and ornamentation, and in the clear-cut forms and measured tread of his dance movements. These aspects are interrelated, for it is the profusion of ornamentation and the richness of the arpeggiation which determine the slow, inexorable harmonic tread and the basically very straightforward tonal procedures of his movements.

If Louis Couperin appears to us nowadays as a more 'original' composer it is largely a result of a difference in temperament, of a more romantic outlook—for want of a better word. He had not the same instinct for creating a durable model, so that while in some

---

[56] For an exception see Lebègue, *Second livre de clavessin* (see below).

[57] Paul Brunold and André Tessier, *Oeuvres complètes de Chambonnières* (Paris, 1925). A facsimile of the 1670 edition has appeared in *Monuments of Music and Music Literature in Facsimile*, Series I (Music), iii. The Bauyn MS (Paris, Bibl. nat., Rés. Vm⁷ 674–5) has also been published in facsimile (Geneva, 1977).

[58] Such as 'L'Entretien des Dieux' quoted in Ex. 315.

works he comes very close to Chambonnières there is more variety in his work as a whole.[59] It tends to be lighter in texture, less trammelled by a weight of decoration, more experimental in harmony and form. Unlike Chambonnières, he cultivated the unmeasured prelude, sometimes with a measured middle section. Although his movements are arranged according to their key in both the Bauyn and the Parville manuscripts[60] he travelled less far along the road to the suite than Chambonnières. As an example of his imaginative approach to harmony and texture we may cite the grand *couplet* (refrain) of his remarkable Passacaille in C major:[61]

Ex. 301

Fin

---

[59] Couperin's harpsichord music has appeared in editions by Brunold, rev. Thurston Dart (Monaco, 1959), and Alan Curtis (Paris, 1970). Neither is complete: Curtis makes use of the recently discovered Parville manuscript at Berkeley, California (see *Revue de Musicologie*, p. 123, 1970) but makes only a selection from the pieces ascribed to Couperin in the Bauyn manuscript. He does however include as a work of Couperin the well-known Chaconne in F (reproduced in Davison and Apel, *Historical Anthology of Music*, ii, no. 212), ascribed to Chambonnières in the Bauyn manuscript and found anonymously with two additional couplets in the Bibl. Ste. Geneviève, MS 2348, 'on the overwhelming evidence of style'.

[60] The unmeasured preludes, however, are grouped together in the Bauyn manuscript. Curtis in his edition mixes up movements from Parville and Bauyn 'to form suites of a pleasing variety and size'.

[61] Ed. Curtis, no. 26 (cf. Brunold, no. 27).

The final repetition of this refrain is marked 'Grand Couplet par b mol' though the precise application of the accidentals is uncertain.

One of Couperin's preludes is headed in the Parville source 'Prelude de M. Couperin a limitation de M. Froberger en a la mi'; and although it is uncertain exactly what model he had in mind[62] it seems from this and also from his cultivation of the *tombeau* (lament for the departed) that like some of his contemporaries he was familiar with Froberger's music. *Tombeaux* on the death of the lutenist Blancrocher were composed by Froberger, Couperin, and the lutenists Du Faut and Denis Gaultier. Blancrocher met his death in a fall after dining with Froberger at the house of a lady whose morals, it appears, were not beyond question; and Couperin's piece can be interpreted as a not entirely humourless characterization of the event.[63] It has also been suggested that the Pavane in the unusual key of F sharp minor might be a *tombeau* for the lutenist Ennemond Gaultier.[64]

### LEBÈGUE AND D'ANGLEBERT

Passing over such minor figures as Henry Du Mont, Thomelin, Hardel, and the La Barre family,[65] mention must be made of Nicolas Lebègue (1631–1702), Couperin's junior by five years, who published two books of keyboard pieces, in 1667 and 1687 respectively.[66] Lebègue seems to combine the lighter textures and moderate ornamentation of Couperin with the greater formal and tonal predictability of Chambonnières. In some ways, indeed, he anticipates the textural clarity and rhythmic simplicity, derived from Italian models, of the early eighteenth century. However one interprets his historical position, he was a consummate musician; even when it is not consistently interesting, his music has a natural inevitability. He cultivated the unmeasured prelude but gave it a more specific notation that the undifferentiated semibreves of Couperin. Each of the principal sections, unified by key, of his first book, begins with one; but these lengthy sequences of movements do not yet qualify as suites. It is his second book, divided into groups of movements actually called 'suite' (or 'suitte'), which pro-

---

[62] Curtis suggests the 'Plainte faite à Londres' (see below), though the notation of this, if not the execution, is measured.

[63] The details are given by Curtis. For the composition by Froberger, who seems to have taken a more serious view of the affair, see below.

[64] Dart, cited by Curtis.

[65] Du Mont, ed. Jean Bonfils in *L'Organiste liturgique*, xiii; Thomelin, ibid., xviii; for Nicolas Monnard, Étienne Richard, and Pierre La Barre, also in xviii, see Vol. IV, pp. 675–7.

[66] New edition by Norbert Dufourcq, *Oeuvres de Clavessin* (Paris, 1956).

vides the exception to the general rule. The first suite, in D minor, consists of five short movements: *allemande, courante, sarabande grave, gigue*, and *menuet*. Though most of them are rather longer than this, none is unwieldy or otherwise unsuited to complete performance.

The fourth major figure to be considered here is Jean-Henri d'Anglebert, whose *Pièces de clavecin* appeared in 1689.[67] A pupil of Chambonnières, he is much closer to him in spirit than was either Couperin or Lebègue. Indeed he goes a long way beyond his master in the richness of his textures and the profusion of his ornamentation, and this is his chief claim to originality, for it cannot be said that he was a striking melodist or in any significant sense a formal innovator. He was however a masterly harmonist, though his mastery was generally employed to suggest wider tonal vistas rather than for the sake of the unexpected. It is this quality which rescues him from any tendency to predictability, as may be illustrated by the first section of the allemande in G major:[68]

Ex. 302

[67] Modern editions by M. Roesgen-Champion in *Publications de la Société française de Musicologie*, Series I, viii (Paris, 1934), and Kenneth Gilbert in *Le Pupitre*, liv (Paris, 1975).
[68] Roesgen-Champion, p. 4; Gilbert, p. 4.

The telling allusion to D minor and the balancing imperfect cadence in E minor, in the context of a normal tonic-to-dominant progression, scarcely require comment, any more than the contrapuntal intricacy and elaborate embellishment shown in this passage. An unusual example of a pungent discord may be cited from the noble *Gaillarde* beginning as follows:[69]

Ex. 303

[69] Roesgen-Champion, p. 145; Gilbert, p. 157.

The importance attached by d'Anglebert to the decorative aspects of music may be inferred from his initial table of 29 ornaments or combinations of ornaments, and from his embellished transcriptions of, and *doubles* based on, other composers' works. His transcriptions from orchestral movements by Lully are a pioneering achievement and prepared the ground for the transfer of orchestral idioms to the harpsichord in the eighteenth century, especially among German composers such as Böhm and, later, Bach. Equally noteworthy—if the attribution to him of the anonymous works in Paris, Bibl. nat., MS Rés. 89ter can be sustained— are his transcriptions of lute music by 'Vieux Gautier' (Jacques), 'Gautier le Jeune' (Denis), René Mézangeau, and (Étienne) Richard.[70]

D'Anglebert's published transcriptions are incorporated in the key-related sections of his edition,[71] and these sections are even further removed from the ideal of the suite than are those of Chambonnières and Lebègue. Though his oeuvre is rightly regarded as the crowning achievement of the seventeenth-century harpsichord school, it is also in many ways a dead end. His passion for embellishment led to a mania for repetition which is exemplified in his frequent instruction to repeat an entire movement (presumably, though not necessarily, without repeats the second time). When the *petite reprise*—the additional repeat of the last few bars of a section—is incorporated into such a scheme, and the entire work ornamented in a *double* of precisely similar design,[72] the dangers of the procedure become apparent. Another illustration of the tendency is to be found in the 22 *couplets*, amounting to 352 bars, of his 'Variations sur les folies d'Espagne'.[73] No doubt such works may be, and perhaps were, shortened in performance; but it is also possible, and perhaps more likely, that the hypnotic effect of incessant repetition is a legitimate part of the D'Anglebert aesthetic, an inherent tendency of the baroque here carried to an extreme.

---

[70] Included by Gilbert but omitted by Roesgen-Champion. The manuscript Rés 89ter is supposed by Gilbert to be an autograph of d'Anglebert; hence his inclusion of its anonymous contents.

[71] This order is retained by Roesgen-Champion but not by Gilbert.

[72] As in the courante of the G major 'suite'.

[73] From the D minor 'suite': Roesgen-Champion, p. 93, Gilbert, p. 64. Each sixteen-bar *couplet*, based on the old ground with its two-fold repetitive structure, is itself marked to be repeated.

FRENCH LITURGICAL MUSIC FOR ORGAN

French music for the organ at this period was even more closely
bound up with the liturgy, and devised with its specific needs in
mind, than elsewhere in Catholic Europe. The place of the organ
in the liturgy was rigidly prescribed: a recent list of ceremonials
referring to the use of the organ includes eighteen between 1628
and 1700.[74] The *Caeremoniale Parisiense* of 1662 specifies the use of
the organ at Matins, Lauds, Terce, Mass, Vespers, 'Salut'
(Benediction of the Blessed Sacrament), and Compline. The function of the organ, in France as elsewhere, was to substitute for
portions of the text which would have been otherwise sung, and we
may assume that the great organists of the day habitually improvised on the appropriate plainchant or at least in the appropriate
mode. (The Offertory of the Mass, however, was the opportunity
for a lengthy display without reference to any plainsong.) Their
publications (of which at least fifteen appeared between the first
book of Guillaume Nivers in 1665 and the second book of Jacques
Boyvin in 1700)[75] enabled the less gifted to emulate their style and
to accompany the services in a fashionable manner without unduly
disastrous results. The range of techniques catered for was wide: in
his *Meslanges* of 1657 (primarily a collection of vocal music) Henry
Du Mont included a series of instrumental preludes in two parts, of
which some 'serviront aussi pour les Dames Religieuses qui
touchent l'Orgue en façon de Duo'.[76] At the other end of the scale,
many of the works published by Nivers, Lebègue, Nicolas Gigault,
Boyvin, Nicolas de Grigny, and others call for a finished technique
as well as an insight into the finer points of style. Such works were
intended to ring out from the tribune or west-end organ gallery of
the larger churches, the organ in choir serving to accompany the
voices; though in smaller establishments a single instrument might
have had to suffice.

[74] See Edward Higginbottom, 'French Classical Organ Music and the Liturgy', *Proceedings of the Royal Musical Association*, ciii (1976–7), p. 19.
[75] They are (composers and dates only): Nivers (1665, 1667, 1675), Lebègue (1676,
1678/9, *c.*1685), Gigault (1683, 1685), Raison (1688), Boyvin (1689, 1700), Jullien (1690),
François Couperin (1690), Chaumont (1695), and de Grigny (1699, repr. 1711). For titles
and modern editions see Bibliography. In addition there are the organ pieces in d'Anglebert's
*Pièces de Clavecin* (1689) and the substantial manuscript collections of Jean-Nicolas
Geoffroy, Marguerite Thiéry, and Louis Couperin (see below). Raison published a second
book in 1714; and of course the first half of the eighteenth century is equally rich in such
publications.
[76] The fashion for duo playing in France can be traced to the examples by Charles
Racquet in Mersenne's *Harmonie universelle* (1636); there is a collection in Bibl. Ste.
Geneviève MS 2348 (*L'Organiste liturgique*, xxxi), and the published volumes are full of
them.

There is very little documentation to enable us to trace the development of French organ style from Titelouze to the fully-formed idiom which springs upon us in the first publication of Nivers. There must have flourished a tradition of rather archaic contrapuntal writing of a type represented by the *Fantaisie* by Charles Racquet found in Mersenne's own copy of his *Harmonie universelle*, in one of the two so-called 'Preludes' by Étienne Richard,[77] and in François Roberday's *Fugues et caprices* of 1660, by which time the idiom seems to have been virtually extinct. Roberday (1624–80) published his collection (which includes works by Frescobaldi, Wolfgang Ebner, and Froberger) in open score, flying in the face of accepted French convention and showing himself at odds with the underlying trend of history. More interesting are the hymn-verses from Paris, Bibl. Ste. Geneviève, MS 2348, of which the seven versets on 'Ave maris stella' display among other features the beginnings of an interest in registration.

In some ways a more helpful approach to the style may be made through the vocal religious repertory of the mid-seventeenth century. The *Meslanges* of Du Mont (1610–84) are important here, since they illustrate the transition from a predominantly contra-puntal style to one in which the treble-bass polarization is para-mount. Indeed the organists' repertoire needs to be seen in the context of the entire range of liturgical music: plainsong (in the corrupt versions then employed), *plain-chant musical, chant sur le livre*, and figured music both *a cappella* and with instruments.[78] The organ music can then be understood as just one instance of the gradual subservience of older ideas of tonality, melodic and rhythmic movement, and harmony to those of the full baroque style. Much of the fascination of the style derives from the fact that traces of these older elements still remain, though greatly trans-muted. Another aspect, distinguishing it from secular music, is its sectional nature, derived from liturgical requirements. These and other characteristics are found in the sacred music of this period in all countries, including those of Lutheran protestantism; the individual character of the French repertory stems from the nature of developments in the secular sphere and the point at which they

---

[77] On Racquet and Richard see Vol. IV, pp. 675–6, and the volumes entitled *Les préclassiques françaises* in *L'Organiste liturgique*, xviii, xxxi, lviii, lix.

[78] *Plain-chant musical* is a kind of latter-day plainsong of the type represented by Du Mont's *Messes royales*; *Chant sur le livre* is polyphony improvised above the plainsong; *a cappella*, at this period, accompanied by the organ only. Certain vocal verses in Du Mont's *Cantica Sacra* are designated 'pro organo'.

impinge on the traditional techniques considered appropriate to the church.

Something of the character of an organist's actual needs can be gleaned from the manuscript collection formerly attributed to Jean-Nicolas Geoffroy (1633–94), a pupil of Lebègue and organist first of St.-Nicolas du Chardonnet at Paris and subsequently at Perpignan Cathedral. Whoever the compiler may have been, however,[79] it is probable that the manuscript was written by or for an amateur, since there is much here that a professional player would hardly need to have written down. Here are settings of *noëls*, preludes to motets, continuo realizations, Offertories, versets for the Mass and Magnificat, hymns, and so forth; and transcriptions from the stage works of Lully. The settings of Ps. 131 and of the Magnificat are particularly interesting, for the verses intervening between the organ settings appear in the form of accompaniments to *falsobordone* settings. The volume seems to have been devised for the use of an organist in a small establishment in which only a single instrument was available.

Most of the material for the study of the organ repertoire is now available in modern editions, though a significant body of works by Louis Couperin remains unpublished.[80] The material is too extensive to permit a detailed consideration of each composer here. Although it is possible to distinguish between the extravagant, rather flashy idioms of (say) Gigault and Boyvin on the one hand and the more restrained manner of Nivers and Lebègue on the other, there is enough common ground between them to warrant a general discussion based on prevailing forms and styles. Practically every composer wrote at least some music based directly on plainchant themes, many of them on the selection of chants for the Ordinary of the Mass assigned to 'feasts of the first class' in the then current editions of the *Graduale romanum*: Kyrie, Gloria, Sanctus, and Agnus IV of the modern Gradual with Ite II 'secundum communiorem usum' (but in F) and the Easter week Ite of Mass I as an alternative (but in a modified form, again in F). A frequent method was to present the plainsong in the tenor on a reed-stop of the pedal organ ('Plein chant en taille'). Gigault pro-

---

[79] This attribution is regarded as doubtful by Apel, op. cit., p. 746. The volume has been edited by Bonfils as *Le Pupitre*, liii (Paris, 1974), who also suggests that the attribution is without foundation.

[80] See G. Oldham in *Recherches sur la musique française classique*, i (Paris, 1960), pp. 51–9.

vides alternative pieces to those requiring pedals, in the form of
'contrepoint simple':[81]

Ex. 304

[81] Ed. Guilmant, *Archives des maîtres de l'orgue*, iv (Paris, 1902), pp. 6–7.

Here the bass follows exactly the current version of Kyrie IV. The counterpoint, though certainly simple, is far from neutral in character: its freedom with regard to fourths, sevenths, and diminished triads, reflects the growing importance of harmony in French musical thought and its emancipation from conventional contrapuntal practice. The beginning of Gigault's next movement illustrates fugal treatment of the same theme (cf. Couperin, 1690).[82]

Ex. 305

The G minor Mass, on the other hand, is based on Nivers' *plain-chant musical* from his *Graduale romanum . . . cujus modulatio concinne disposita* (1687).[83] The arrangement in the same manuscript of a motet by Nivers, 'Veni de Libano' (*Motets à voix seule*, 1689), reveals the source of another frequent organists' idiom, the *récit*, since it is nothing but an embellished form of Nivers' vocal line. Such transcriptions could be, and no doubt were, readily improvised; and they gave rise to one of the most characteristically French types of organ composition. Since the French solo motet was closely related to Italian monody of the early seventeenth

[82] Ibid., p. 7.

[83] Other masses on Nivers' *plain-chant musical* are in Paris, Bibl. nat., fonds du Cons., Rés. 2094, published as *Le livre d'orgue de Marguerite Thiéry*, ed. P. Hardouin as *L'organiste liturgique*, xxv (Paris, 1956). Further on the manuscript collections of the period see Apel, op. cit., pp. 746–7.

century, the same may be said of this type of organ piece. The accompaniment to a right-hand solo on the cromorne, cornet, tierce, or similar stop might be for manual alone, or with the bass on a pedal flute stop. The pedal became *de rigueur* for the 'tierce [or cromorne, etc.] en taille', in which the solo part is the tenor; but the extended range and extravagant embellishments of many such pieces put any thoughts of a vocal model out of mind.

Two-part counterpoint continued to fill many pages of these publications; trios, generally for manuals alone, the left-hand acting as a soft accompaniment, were also popular. Both types could be varied to form right-hand or left-hand solos (tierce, cromorne, trompette, etc.) or the two in alternation. Left-hand solos could also be accompanied by free part-writing in the right-hand, and vice versa. Solo parts were not, apparently, normally played on single stops but on recognized combinations such as the 'gros jeu de tierce', 'petit jeu de tierce', 'jeux d'anches', etc., though the cromorne 'se peut bien jouer seul'.[84] Similarly the 'grand jeu', 'plein jeu', 'petit plein jeu', and 'jeu doux' (and also the various types of 'jeux d'anches'), used for fugues and other contrapuntal forms, were regulated by convention. The resource of a large organ of the period was considerable, for in addition to the great organ and positive organ it would have at least a few pedal stops (but no sixteen-foot), a 'cornet séparé' on its own manuals and perhaps also a 'cornet d'Echo', again on its own manual— these in addition to the grand cornet (from $c'$) of the great organ. Joseph Sauveur even mentions a fifth manual, with a reed stop such as a 'petite trompette'. The organ literature abounds with 'dialogues' and similarly-entitled pieces, in which these devices are used either with taste and discrimination, or with a notable lack of such qualities. Another trick was to play a four-part piece on four different manuals, or at any rate on three manuals and pedals. Less frequently used chants (for example, the Gradual and Alleluia of the Mass, which are 'Proper' and consequently change as to text and music at each Mass) were nevertheless used as a basis for improvisation, as we know from surviving manuscripts of such chants destined for the use of the organist (see Higginbottom, op. cit.). At the same time, the interchangeability of music not based on specific chants is well illustrated by Raison's remark, in the

---

[84] Nivers, Introduction to Book III; Joseph Sauveur, *Application des sons harmoniques à la composition des orgues* (Paris, 1704), both cited by Bonfils, *Livre d'orgue attribué à J.-N. Geoffroy* (*Le Pupitre*, liii). Others, such as Boyvin and Gilles Jullien (d. 1703), also gave attention to such matters in the prefaces to their publications.

preface to his *Premier livre*, that the movements of his tonally unified Masses might serve equally well for the Magnificat; he also draws attention to the dance-like elements and characteristic genres of his versets, warning only that in church such types of piece should be played more slowly (cited by Apel, op. cit., p. 731).

In addition to pieces designated for the Mass, and, occasionally, commonly used hymns such as 'Pange lingua' and the Te Deum, there are many sets of pieces for the Magnificat in each of the eight tones. Such sets, comprising the six odd-numbered verses of the canticle, form attractively varied suites. Still more common are undesignated strings of movements unified by key and capable of serving any liturgical purpose. The largest form to be found, and the one in which the composer's talents are most vividly exposed, is the Offertoire, often in several contrasting sections. Here Lebègue in his third book provides the classical examples, including a pair based on the measured tunes of 'Stabat mater' and 'O filii et filiae' for Passiontide and Eastertide respectively, the latter no doubt serving as a model for the rather grander versions by Pierre and Jean-François Dandrieu.[85] Again from Lebègue's third book comes that charming series of *noëls*, or popular Christmas songs, which together with those of Gigault, influenced the later settings of Raison, the Dandrieus, and Daquin.[86]

No account of French organ music of this period, however generalized, can fail to refer to the remarkable book containing two Masses by the twenty-two-year-old Couperin 'le grand'. Their 'publication' in 1690 took the form of manuscript copies masquerading under an engraved title-page: 'Pièces d'orgue consistantes en deux Messes'.[87] Though these works adhere to established conventions they transcend them in many ways, above all in the eloquence of their 'récit en taille' and bass solos, and in the powers of organization demonstrated in the two Offertoires, particularly that from

[85] Jean-François Dandrieu's setting is an expansion of that of his uncle Pierre (for the editions see following note); it was reprinted in his *Premier livre de Pièces d'orgue* (1739), no. 1 (ed. Guilmant, *Archives*, vii, p. 7), possibly reprinted from his 1715 publication (see n. 86).

[86] Gigault, *Livre de musique dédié à la Très Sainte Vierge* (1683); Raison, *Second Livre* (1714); Pierre Dandrieu, *Noëls, O filii, Chansons de Saint Jacques* . . . (c.1710, rev. J.–F. Dandrieu, c.1721–33); Daquin, *Nouveau livre de noëls* (c.1745; ed. Guilmant, *Archives*, iii). Apel incomprehensibly regards Gigault's *noëls* as earlier than Lebègue's.

[87] Guilmant for his edition (*Archives*, v), used three late manuscripts of limited value, one being a nineteenth-century copy of a lost example of the original 'edition', noted by Fétis as being in the Bibliothèque nationale. In 1929 in the *Revue de Musicologie* André Tessier was able to report the discovery of an example of the original 'edition' in the library at Carpentras; this was used as the basis of the edition by Paul Brunold in the *Oeuvres complètes*, vi (Monaco, 1932; now ed. by Kenneth Gilbert and Davitt Moroney, 1982).

the first Mass. This latter piece, indeed, in its grand tripartite structure is one of the masterpieces of French organ literature, in which the organ for once reveals itself capable of a passionate intensity of expression. In the first Mass as a whole, the young composer's feeling for the traditional tonal structure of ecclesiastical music and his assimilation of it into a personal style is particularly impressive; the second Mass attempts no such amalgam, but is full of felicitous touches of melody and harmony. The volume is at once a fitting memorial to the *grand siècle* and a worthy initiation into the mind of the greatest French composer of his generation.

## AUSTRIA AND SOUTHERN GERMANY

Italian influence when combined with that of France was to make a profound and lasting contribution to the German artistic make-up. The key figure in this development was Johann Jakob Froberger (1616–67), who was court organist at Vienna from the accession of Ferdinand III as Emperor in 1637 until 1657, though he spent most of the years 1637–1641 in Italy as a pupil of Frescobaldi.[88] In his later years he travelled widely, visiting Paris and London among other places; and he finally settled at the castle of the Dowager Duchess of Württemberg at Héricourt (near Montbéliard), where he died. A touch of personal interest emerges from the account of his robbery on his journey to London and the 'Lamentation' he composed on the occasion;[89] his nature is also revealed in the range of his personal friendships (including Denis Gaultier, Chambonnières, and Louis Couperin) and in his composition of laments on the deaths of Ferdinand III, Ferdinand IV, and Monsieur Blancrocher (see below, p. 555), and even on his anticipated demise.

[88] The exact dates of his appointment as court organist ('Römisch Kayserliches Cammer-Organist') as given by Guido Adler in his Froberger edition (see n. 90) are: 1.1.1637–30.9.1637; 1.4.1641–October 1645; 1.4.1653–30.6.1657.

[89] This journey is assigned by Mattheson in his *Grundlage einer Ehrenpforte* (Hamburg, 1740, pp. 87 ff.) to the year 1662. This is the source of the familiar story of Froberger's employment as organ-blower to Christopher Gibbons at Westminster Abbey before being recognized as an organist in his own right. But Ulf Scharlau has established, from correspondence in the Athanasius Kircher archives in the Università Gregoriana at Rome, that Froberger visited England in the early 1650s (*Die Musikforschung*, xxii (1969), p. 47); this does not entirely rule out the possibility of a second visit a decade or so later, but it is more likely that Mattheson mistook the date and added some circumstantial details. The inscription on the manuscript of the 'Plainte faite à Londres pour passer la Melancholie' (Suite XXX), which unfortunately is not autograph, refers to a robbery on the journey and to his employment as an organ-blower, but gives no date and mentions no names.

FROBERGER'S MUSIC

Froberger is practically unique among major composers in having confined himself (even more thoroughly than the nineteenth-century piano virtuosi) to keyboard composition: only two motets are known to have been written apart from this. He published no editions of his music, and the only works printed in his lifetime were a hexachord fantasia in Kircher's *Musurgia Universalis* (Rome, 1650) and a ricercare in Roberday's *Fugues et caprices* (1660). His fame during his lifetime was considerable, though it may have been based largely on his powers as a performer. After his death, however, when manuscript copies of his works began to multiply, his music came to be more fully appreciated and his style imitated. In 1693 and 1696 two volumes of a selection of his works were printed at Mainz.[90]

The major sources of Froberger's music are three volumes in the Vienna National Library (MSS 18706, 16560, 18707), the supposed books II–IV of his autograph collection. Book I of this series is nothing but a nineteenth-century copy by Aloys Fuchs from various seventeenth-century sources, and has no independent value (MS 16550, Adler's Source 'A'). MS 18706 is labelled 'Libro secondo' (Adler 'B') in Froberger's hand and is dated 29 September 1649; MS 18707 (Adler 'D') is labelled 'Libro quarto' and is dated 1656 (unnoticed by Adler): it bears a dedication to Ferdinand III. MS 16560 (Adler 'C') is marked 'libro terzo' but in a later hand; and as it bears a dedication to Leopold I (1658–1705) it must, as Adler pointed out, be later than MS 18707. MS 18706 contains toccatas, fantasias, canzonas, and suites; MS 16560 has *capricci* and *ricercari*; MS 18707 has toccatas, *ricercari*, *capricci*, and suites. Between them, therefore, the autograph volumes represent all the forms cultivated by Froberger.

In all except the suites the major formative influence is that of Frescobaldi, and nowhere more so than in the toccatas. It has been pointed out that in their organization into a smaller number of more extended sections, including fugal as well as improvisatory passages, his toccatas resemble those of Michelangelo Rossi more closely than Frescobaldi's;[91] but Froberger's highly disciplined approach to composition makes a strong contrast to Rossi's

[90] The first volume was reprinted in 1693, 1695, 1699, and 1714, the second in 1699. These are Adler's sources E and F (*Orgel- und Klavierwerke*, 3 vols., *Denkmäler der Tonkunst in Österreich*, iv(1) (vol. 8), vi(2) (vol. 13), x(2) (vol. 21), Vienna, 1896–1903, repr. Graz, 1959). The printed sources were used by R. Walter in his edition (Altötting, 1967). For other editions of music by Froberger see Bibliography.

[91] Apel, op. cit., p. 552.

rambling extravagance (cf. Ex. 291). In fact he probably became acquainted with a wide variety of printed Italian music and may well have been influenced by the toccatas of Merulo, which in their published form also include fugal sections. But in any case all of Froberger's music has a much stronger sense of tonality than any of the Italian styles deriving from Frescobaldi, while he rarely lapsed into the triviality all too familiar from some late Italian composers. Even the pronouncedly Frescobaldian idiom of the 'elevation' toccatas is modified by a more disciplined tonal structure. Froberger's strongly unified thematic and tonal idiom may be illustrated by the very fine second toccata, in which the chromatic subject of the quasi-fugal sections serves only to underline the fundamental D minor tonality:[92]

Ex. 306

[92] *Denkmäler*, iv(1) (vol. 8), pp. 5–7; 1693 edn. (followed by Walter), no. 8.

The same points may be made about the fantasias, canzonas, *capricci*, and *ricercari*. All extend the Italian formal principle of the sectional variation (each section making use of a transformation of the original fugal material) by imposing on it a greater regularity of tonality and rhythm and in most cases a broader structural design. There is in fact little difference in Froberger between a fantasia and a ricercare, or between a capriccio and a canzona: the former are slower, the latter faster in pace. These two fundamental types, together with the freer idiom of the toccata, were of paramount importance in the development of organ music in central and northern Germany after Froberger's death.

In his suites, in which the idiom is derived from French sources, Froberger may be said to have created the 'French suite' so far as the German-speaking world was concerned, though not quite in the form with which he was later credited. In his autograph manuscripts the gigue generally comes in second place, before the courante, whereas in later sources, which in this respect were followed by Adler, it is transferred to the end of the four-movement scheme.[93] This transfer of the gigue may have been due to an assumption that the sarabande, which in the authentic form usually comes last, was necessarily the *sarabande grave* distinguished as such by some French composers, whereas in Froberger it is by no means always a slow dance. While Froberger's idioms are French (though deriving from the lutenists' rather than the keyboard

---

[93] The exceptions are Suites 1 and 3–6, which lack the gigue altogether; in no. 2 it comes last in the autograph itself. Nos. 13–30 do not survive in autograph.

composers' repertoire), his highly uniform conception of the overall form appears to be his own creation,[94] as is his more consistently polyphonic interpretation of the *style brisé*. Another feature is the frequent allusion, amounting in some cases to thorough-going variation, between the allemande and courante, though it is rare for this to involve any other movement. In Suite VI ('Auff die Mayerin') the courante (with *double*) and sarabande continue the variation scheme initiated by the six *partite* which in effect are the allemande of this suite.

Froberger's sarabandes are generally in a moderate 3/2 or perhaps rather faster 3/4 measure, though a few—such as the sarabande from Suite XII—appear to demand the measured tread of the *sarabande grave*. His courantes employ the usual 6/4 3/2 (or 6/2 3/1) dichotomy characteristic of the French version of the form, though with rather less emphasis on the hemiolia and a good deal less weight of ornamentation and other detail. His gigues are either in 6/8 (6/4) or quite commonly in 4/4, a feature borrowed from the French lutenists although the quadruple jig is much older than they.[95] Two of them change metre and one has a passage marked 'avec discrétion'. But it is his allemandes which are Froberger's most individual creation. He seems to have conceived the form as a receptacle for his innermost thoughts, and its conventions as almost infinitely malleable for the purpose. This is illustrated above all by the lament on the death in 1654 of Ferdinand IV, King of the Romans,[96] a title which might well be taken to refer to the whole of Suite XII, at the head of which it occurs; but it is particularly applicable to the first movement, a richly expressive piece of the allemande type. A later source miscalls it 'Doloroso pianto fatto sopra la morte di Signoris Giovanni Giacomo Froberger', a confusion resulting perhaps from the fact that Froberger did, apparently, write a 'meditation' on his future death, the allemande from Suite XX.[97] To the same general category belong the 'Plainte faite à Londres pour passer la Melancholie' (Suite XXX, and in particular the allemande), the 'Tombeau fait à Paris sur la mort de Monsieur Blancheroche' and the lament on the death of Ferdinand III. This, like the meditation on his own death, is to be played

[94] See however the remarks below, pp. 580 ff., on the origin of the suite in England.
[95] See, for example, such pieces as 'Nobodys Jig' in the *Fitzwilliam Virginal Book*. Bach's quadruple-time *gigues* (Partitas I and VI, French Suite I) are derived, directly or indirectly, from the Froberger model.
[96] Ferdinand never became Emperor.
[97] This bears the title 'Meditation faict sur ma mort future' in the Hintze manuscript, New Haven, Yale University, School of Music, MS M 1490 H 66 (see Apel, op. cit., p. 560).

'lentement avec discrétion'; that on Blancrocher, perhaps the most deeply felt of them all, is to be played 'fort lentement à la discrétion sans observer aucune mesure'. This work comes very close to the French type of unmeasured prelude; and it is possible, from the example of the latter by Louis Couperin headed 'in imitation of Froberger' that he was accustomed to improvize in this manner to his friends.

FROBERGER'S CONTEMPORARIES AND SUCCESSORS

A number of contemporaries and successors of Froberger— Wolfgang Ebner, Kerll, Poglietti and others[98]—would qualify for extended treatment in a longer survey than this. Johann Caspar Kerll (1627–93) in particular, who was active at Munich as well as Vienna, cultivated many of the same forms as Froberger, mostly in a thoroughly Frescobaldian manner. His *Modulatio organica* of 1686[99] presents versets for the Magnificat in the eight tones—*Fiori musicali* for the Office, as it were. Alessandro Poglietti (d. 1683) is known chiefly for a number of rather extravagant programme pieces though he also wrote more conventional toccatas, canzonas and *ricercari*. To a later generation belong Franz Matthias Techelmann (*c.*1649–1714), Ferdinand Richter, (1649–1711), Georg Reutter (1656–1738), and Nicolaus Adam Strungk (1640–1700), the son of the north German organist Delphin Strunck (1601–94).

The suite with other secular forms was cultivated towards the end of the century by Fux in Vienna and by Johann Caspar Ferdinand Fischer (d. 1746), who was active at Schlackenwerth and Rastatt.[100] The state of organ music in the German-speaking Catholic sphere can be observed in several printed editions from the latter part of the century, all with grandiose titles: Sebastian Anton Scherer's *Tabulatura in cymbalo et organo intonationum*

[98] Ebner's *Aria . . . Imperatoris Ferdinandi III, 36 modis variata* (Prague, 1648) was included in Adler's *Musikalische Werke der Habsburgischen Kaiser* (Vienna, 1892); some of Kerll's keyboard music was published in *Denkmäler der Tonkunst in Bayern*, ii(2), ed. Adolf Sandberger (Leipzig, 1901); some of Poglietti, with music by Ferdinand Tobias Richter and Georg Reutter the elder, in *Denkmäler der Tonkunst in Österreich*, xiii(2) (vol. 27), ed. Hugo Botstiber (Vienna, 1906). On all three composers see Apel, op. cit., pp. 560–72; but much of the music formerly ascribed to Reutter has been discovered to be by Nicolaus Adam Strungk: see Davitt Moroney, ed., *John Blow's Anthology* (London, 1978), p. 61.

[99] Ed. R. Walter (Altötting, 1956).

[100] Fischer's first keyboard publication, *Les Pièces de Clavessin . . Oeuvre II* appeared at Schlackenwerth in 1696; it was reprinted as *Musikalisches Blumen-Büschlein*, at Augsburg (1699 ?). His other keyboard publications, apart from *Ariadne musica* (see below, p. 569), were *Blumen-Strauss* (Augsburg, after 1732), and *Musikalischer Parnassus* (Augsburg, 1738); all are ed. Ernst von Werra, *Sämtliche Werke fuer Klavier* (Leipzig, 1901).

*brevium per octo tonos*, published in one volume together with his
*Partitura octo toccatarum usui apta cum vel sine pedali* (1664);[101]
Georg Muffat's *Apparatus musico-organisticus* (1690);[102] Johann
Speth's *Ars magna consoni et dissoni* (1693);[103] and Franz Xaver
Murschhauser's *Octi-tonium novum organicum* (1696),[104] succeeded
by the two parts of his *Prototypon longo-breve organicum* (1703,
1707).[105] The first three of these composers were much addicted to
pedal-points. Scherer (1631–1712), who was organist of Ulm
Cathedral, provided short suites of four movements each (of which
the first is always a pedal-toccata), followed by eight toccatas, one
for each tone, again over held pedal notes. Both Speth (1664–after
1719, organist of Augsburg Cathedral) and Murschhauser (1663–
1738, active at Munich) in his first publication included a set of
Magnificat versets comparable to Kerll's in his *Modulatio organica*:
that is, six versets followed by a seventh piece replacing the concluding antiphon. Speth's volume also includes toccatas, but on a
more liberal plan than Scherer's. But the prince of these toccata
composers is a composer Georg Muffat (1653–1704), organist to
the Archbishop of Salzburg, who works the pedal-point technique
into a closely integrated yet varied and large-scale structure. In fact
the use of held pedal notes is largely confined to arresting introductions and dominant preparations of the kind made familiar in
later idioms; elsewhere the pedals may move more freely. Fugal
sections are frequent, and a pair of them may be based on similar
material, as in the last two sections of the eleventh toccata, in C
minor. Still more ingenious is the combination of four different
themes in the final fugue from the splendid seventh toccata. A
passage like the Adagio immediately preceding it lends substance
to the composer's claim that these works were 'stylo recentiore
concinnatae':

---

[101] Ed. Guilmant, *Archives*, viii (Paris, 1907).
[102] Ed. S. De Lange (Leipzig, 1888); R. Walter (Altötting, 1957). Walter unfortunately
omits an aria and a set of variations from his edition, presumably on the ground that they
are not for organ.
[103] The toccatas in E. Kaller, *Liber Organi*, ix, ed. G. Klaus (Mainz, 1954).
[104] Ed. R. Walter (Altötting, 1961) and ed. Seiffert, in *Denkmäler der Tonkunst in
Bayern*, xviii.
[105] Ibid.

Ex. 307

The most impressive feature, perhaps, is the consistent use of motives to give a sense of continuity to these lengthy pieces. A motive like the one which unifies the extended Grave of the first toccata, cited by Apel as an example of 'disturbing passages, which announce the decadence of organ music with sequential or modulatory repetitions of cheap formulae', must be seen in its context, in which its gradual transformation into something quite new lends added point to its eventual return in its original form.

Equally noteworthy is the fine passacaglia from the same collection, in which the rondeau and ostinato principles are ingeniously combined. Muffat's work, far from showing decadence, exhibits a strong artistic personality characterized by an ability to weld the old and the new into a distinctive and a satisfying whole. Only in the North, with its incomparably superior instrumental resource, could his rhetorical conception of the toccata be exceeded and so provide the impetus for still further developments.

NORTHERN AND CENTRAL GERMANY:
TREATMENT OF THE CHORALE

The general pattern of confessional distribution, confirmed in 1648 at the conclusion of the Thirty Years' War, makes this a natural geographical area so far as organ music is concerned, though it is not a hard-and-fast one, and has little or no relevance to the stylistic aspects of secular keyboard music. Even in organ music, the influence of Italianate idioms and formal procedures still played a large part, reaching the north Germans partly through the medium of Sweelinck and his German pupils, and partly through Froberger and such figures as Christian Michael (d. 1637), Johann Klemm, (c. 1593–after 1651) and Johann Erasmus Kindermann (1616–55), all of whom were active in central Germany. Nevertheless the composers of this area had at their disposal two unique possessions: a highly developed type of church organ and the priceless heritage of the Lutheran chorale. So far as the former is concerned, its principal distinction was a pedal organ capable of sustaining the bass-line as a normal practice, and even of executing brilliant and difficult solo passages. In the organ music of Sweelinck, Samuel Scheidt and Michael Praetorius the pedal is needed, if at all, only for *cantus firmus* purposes, whereas in Tunder, Pachelbel, Buxtehude and Böhm it functions regularly as a bass line as well. The new technique greatly enhanced the possibilities available in the treatment of chorale melodies. The latter are of course cognate with Lutheranism itself, but in the early seventeenth century its treatment as a form of organ music was a novelty. Sweelinck's type of chorale variation-set[106] was passed on to his German pupils, but we should not forget the indigenous school represented by the Celle tablature of 1601, the work of the

[106] See Vol. IV, p. 640.

southerner Johann Ulrich Steigleder, Christian Michael, Hieronymus and Jacob Praetorius, or indeed of Samuel Scheidt himself who although a pupil of Sweelinck was far from being a mere imitator.[107]

The wide variety of liturgical practice permitted under Lutheranism, and indeed the whole ethos of the confession, prevents any rigid interpretation of the function of the organ chorale. The continued use of Latin made available to composers such forms as the Magnificat and Te Deum in a treatment resembling that of Catholic organists, while the German repertory itself was greatly enhanced by adaptations of the pre-Reformation melodies. The distinction between the preludial function of certain types of short setting and the free-voluntary character of longer ones is sufficiently obvious; but what is one to say of variation-sets, whether the number of statements of the theme corresponds to the number of stanzas in the hymn, or is fewer or more than that? All that can be said with confidence is that organ 'substitution' is alien to the Lutheran concept of liturgy.[108] The performance of a chorale by an organist, whatever the context, is a bonus, not a replacement for anything that might have been sung. For completeness one should mention the accompanimental function (so it would appear) of Scheidt's *Tabulaturbuch* (Görlitz, 1650).[109]

The division into variations, lengthy settings, and short settings is basic, even though there are relationships across the divisions and some borderline cases. A short setting may be a plain harmonization, an ornamented harmonization, an ornamented statement with interludes, or a fughetta. A long chorale may be a motet-like setting without *cantus firmus*, a *cantus firmus* setting in long notes with more or less lengthy interludes, or in some freer form. As for variations and other cyclic works, the possibilities are infinite. Since they are the oldest form, being historically linked with Catholic *alternatim* practice, they may be considered first.

In the works of Heinrich Scheidemann (*c.*1596–1663), chorale variations of two, three or four 'verses', rather than single preludes, are still the norm: the only two single short settings of

---

[107] Celle tablature, ed. Apel, *Corpus of Early Keyboard Music*, xvii; Steigleder, *Tabulaturbuch darinnen das Vatter unser 40mal variiert wird* (1627), ed. Apel *et al.*, ibid., xiii(1). For a discussion and further references see Vol. IV, pp. 661–70. There are still earlier chorale-settings in Elias Nicolaus Ammerbach's *Orgel oder Instrument Tabulatur* (Leipzig, 1571, expanded Nuremberg, 1583).

[108] See Friedrich Blume, *Protestant Church Music* (London, 1975), pp. 105–13, 245–50.

[109] Gottlieb Harms, *Scheidts Werke*, i (Hamburg, 1923); see Vol. IV, p. 670. Some of Bach's simplest settings appear to have been intended for accompanimental purposes.

chorales probably originally belonged to complete sets.[110] As a pupil of Sweelinck, his idiom is related to that of his master, but is more harmonically conceived, less aggressively linear. While his two- and three-part settings of chorales (*bicinia* and *tricinia*) do not significantly advance beyond Sweelinck's methods, the four-part settings, and particularly those in which the melody in the top part is embellished, apart from their more functional harmony helped to pioneer a new kind of organ texture. In this, the melody in the right hand is entrusted to the *Rückpositiv* (behind the organist, played on the lower manual), accompanied by soft stops on the *Oberwerk* (the main organ above the player, operated from the upper manual) and on the pedal. While there is nothing particularly noteworthy about the exploitation of the two manuals, the use of the pedal as a continuous soft bass was an important development. The considerable dynamic range now available on the German pedal-organ enabled it to fulfil this function in all contexts, including those in which the manuals were employed for antiphonal effects. Scheidemann was not an innovator in this respect, but he was perhaps the first composer in which the bass function, as opposed to *cantus firmus* function, of the pedal organ was paramount and consistently exploited in a variety of forms.

The chorale-variation form—with and without the textural innovation just discussed—was cultivated by Sweelinck's pupils Paul Siefert (1586–1666), Andreas Düben (*c*.1590–1662), Melchior Schildt (*c*.1592–1667), and Gottfried Scheidt (1593–1661), as well as by Peter Hasse (*c*.1585–1640), Delphin Strunck (1601–94), and Matthias Weckmann (1619–74);[111] but it was a dying form, only exceptionally and anachronistically revived in later years.[112] Anthologists of the mid-seventeenth century selected individual

---

[110] Scheidemann, *Orgelwerke*, ed. Gustav Fock, 3 vols. (Kassel etc., 1967–71). See Vol. IV, pp. 671–2, and, for a thorough discussion, Werner Breig, *Die Orgelwerke von Heinrich Scheidemann* (*Beihefte zum Archiv für Musikwissenschaft*, iii, Wiesbaden, 1967).

[111] Siefert's variations on 'Puer natus in Bethlehem' in Deutsche Staatsbibl., MS Lynar B1 (unpublished); the same manuscript contains twenty variations on 'Allein Gott in der Höh sei Ehr' by Sweelinck, Düben, Gottfried Scheidt and Peter Hasse, ed. H. J. Moser and T. Fedtke (Kassel and Basel, 1953; mostly also in Sweelinck, *Werken*, i, ed. Max Seiffert, Amsterdam, 1943). A further selection is *46 Choräle für Orgel von J. P. Sweelinck und seiner deutschen Schülern*, ed. G. Gerdes (Mainz, 1957). Chorales, with other works, are in the volume devoted to Delphin Strunck and Peter Morhardt (d. 1685), *Corpus of Early Keyboard Music*, xxiii, ed. Apel; Morhardt's, however, are not genuine sets of variations, although in some of them the theme is stated twice. Seven of Weckmann's nine sets of chorale variations are edited by R. Ilgner, *M. Weckmann: Gesammelte Werke* (Leipzig, 1942); one other in Fritz Dietrich, *Elf Orgelchoräle des 17. Jahrhunderts* (Kassel, 1932; this is the musical supplement to his *Geschichte des deutschen Orgelchorals im 17. Jahrhundert*, Kassel, 1932, which may be consulted for many aspects of this subject); and the last in Karl Straube, *Choralvorspiele alter Meister* (Leipzig, 1907).

[112] See, however the remarks below on the chorale partita.

variations for their manuscripts, and these formed the stylistic basis for numerous single-statement chorales of the later seventeenth century. Indeed, Buxtehude's chorale preludes hardly depart at all from the pattern laid down by Scheidemann in his ornamented four-part settings.

Cycles of Magnificat verses were composed by Scheidemann in much the same way as his chorales: there are four-verse settings in every tone except VII.[113] An important precursor here was Hieronymus Praetorius (1560–1629), who wrote three verses on each of the eight tones.[114] The regularity of these structures suggests a conventional *alternatim* method of performance, though not necessarily involving substitution for the text. In much the same way, as Apel points out,[115] Pachelbel's well-known Magnificat verses consisted originally of two cycles of four verses on each tone, sixty-four verses in all, the present total of ninety-four resulting from later discoveries in additional manuscripts.[116] As these works are short fugues employing the tonality but not the melodic material of the eight tones, they are only doubtfully to be considered as 'chorale variations'. A set of six verses on the eighth tone was included in a publication by an earlier Nuremberger, Kindermann's *Harmonia organica* (1641).[117] Quite different are the three verses, comprising six statements of the melody, by Delphin Strunck. Here the work is given a German title, 'Meine Seele erhebet den Herrn' and is based on the 'ninth tone' or *tonus peregrinus* (cf. n. 114).

Johann Pachelbel (1653–1706), who held posts at Vienna, Eisenach, Erfurt, Stuttgart, Gotha and, from 1695 until his death, as organist of the Sebalduskirche at Nuremberg, wrote only a few sets of chorale variations; but he cultivated the single prelude extensively.[118] Two- three- and four-part settings are found, usually with the chorale in unornamented minims. The pedals are hardly ever specified, but Pachelbel employs and usually extends the tech-

[113] Ed. Fock, op. cit., ii.

[114] Ed. C. G. Rayner, *Corpus of Early Keyboard Music*, iv; see Vol. IV, p. 664, for an excerpt from the first verse on Tone I. Cf. Samuel Scheidt, *Tabulatura nova*, pt. iii, in which the scheme is enlarged by the addition of the *tonus peregrinus* or 'nonus tonus' traditionally associated with the German version of the Magnificat until the time of Bach.

[115] Op. cit., p. 654.

[116] Ed. Botstiber and Seiffert, *Denkmäler der Tonkunst in Österreich*, viii(2) (vol. 17). Vols. vii–viii of the *Ausgewählte Orgelwerke* (see n. 118) contain 95 Magnificat verses.

[117] Ed. R. Walter (Altötting, 1966). Kindermann's *Ausgewählte Werke* are ed. Felix Schreiber and Bertha Wallner, *Denkmäler der Tonkunst in Bayern*, xxi–xxiv.

[118] *Orgelkompositionen*, ed. Seiffert, *Denkmäler der Tonkunst in Bayern*, iv(1); *Ausgewählte Orgelwerke*, 8 vols., ed. Karl Matthaei, W. Stockmeier, and Támas Zászkaliczky (Kassel, 1926–82).

nique, also found in Scheidemann,[119] called in German *Vorimitation*: the more or less extensive imitative treatment of the thematic material of each line in turn, before the latter enters as *cantus firmus*. Pachelbel, like his forerunner Kindermann, also cultivated the chorale fugue or fughetta, based on the first line of the tune only; sometimes a work of this kind is immediately followed by one of the more usual type (which Seiffert calls 'combination form').

## CHORALE FANTASIA AND FREE FORMS

The most impressive type of chorale treatment in the seventeenth century, however, is the large-scale fantasia, a term denoting a variety of different forms. The old type of extended contrapuntal treatment without *cantus firmus*, never extensively employed, virtually died out after Michael Praetorius and Samuel Scheidt; it was replaced by the *cantus firmus* type known in modern literature (somewhat unhappily) as the chorale motet. This differs only in scale from the shorter type of quiet *cantus firmus* setting, and it merges imperceptibly into those varieties in which a more florid type of accompaniment, and perhaps a degree of embellishment in the *cantus firmus*, are introduced. Finally there are those extravagant forms in which every kind of device—fugue, echo effects, fragmentation and embellishment of the *cantus firmus*, repetition of each line in turn—is used to prolong the composition. All these varieties can be traced in a line extending from Jacob Praetorius (1586–1651, son of Hieronymus, unrelated to Michael), Scheidemann, Delphin Strunck, Franz Tunder (1614–1667), Jan Adam Reincken (1623–1722), the Dane Dietrich Buxtehude (1637–1707),[120] and through a host of lesser figures to J. S. Bach himself. Buxtehude exhibits many of the types in his work: in the solemn harmonies of 'Ich dank dir schon durch deinen Sohn', which is a motet-like setting without *cantus firmus*, the sparkle of 'Wie schön leuchtet der Morgenstern' and in the grandeur and ever-increasing brilliance of 'Nun freut euch lieben Christen g'mein'.[121] His 'Te

---

[119] Indeed, its roots go back to the early sixteenth century. See Vol. III, pp. 286–7.

[120] Jacob Praetorius: chorales in *46 Choräle*, ed. Gerdes; Scheidemann (see n. 110); Delphin Strunck in *Corpus of Early Keyboard Music*, xxiii; Tunder, *Sämtliche Choralbearbeitungen für Orgel*, ed. R. Walter (Mainz, 1959) and in Straube, op. cit. and the same editor's *Alte Meister des Orgelspiels, Neue Folge* (Leipzig, 1929); Reincken, ed. Apel, *Corpus of Early Keyboard Music*, xvi; Buxtehude, ed. Seiffert, 3 vols. (Leipzig, 1903–4 and 1939), and J. Hedar, 4 vols. (Copenhagen, 1952, see esp. vol. iii). Scheidemann and Tunder also ed. Jerzy Golos and Adam Sutkowski, *Corpus of Early Keyboard Music*, x/2 (chorale settings from the Pelplin tablature: see below).

[121] Ed. Hedar, nos. 3, 8, 6.

Deum' is an extended treatment of a selection of verses of the chant in five sections: Preludium, 'Te Deum laudamus', 'Te martyrum', 'Tu devicto' and 'Pleni sunt caeli'.[122] The changed order of the verses reveals Buxtehude's modern attitude to tonality: it enables him to end in G major instead of the Phrygian E of the latter part of the chorale melody.

It is not surprising that these same masters were in the forefront of the most arresting developments in the free forms of organ music. While Pachelbel's preludes, toccatas, fantasias, fugues and *ricercari*,[123] even if the terminology differs in part, rarely stray beyond the traditional Italian and South German models, his Northern contemporaries created something radically new and fruitful. Even so, their forms were not new inventions: it was their handling of older types that was novel. The first of these was the prelude (*praeludium* or *preambulum*), a designation used in Germany from the fifteenth century, but now widened to incorporate fugal elements into the design. Indeed the three *preambula* by Jacob Praetorius, together with one by Scheidemann,[124] are nothing but short preludes-and-fugues. It is curious, but significant, that the term 'fugue' (*fuga*) does not appear in the titles of these works, since the term was available in Germany in its present-day sense and had been used by German scribes to denote self-standing fugues at least from the early sixteenth century. While this usage continued in the seventeenth and eighteenth centuries, the word is scarcely, if ever, used of the multi-partite works which we are now considering. (It is, however, used to denote a subsection of a *praeludium*, the latter still serving as a title for the whole work.) The terms *preambulum* or *praeludium* reinforce the unified nature of the entire composition, while perhaps also asserting an age-old preludial function in the liturgy. Two of Scheidemann's preludes add a free postlude to the fugal section, as do those of Tunder;[125] others, however, entirely lack fugal material. The point is that fugal procedures gradually infiltrated an existing type without changing its essential character. The modern term 'prelude and

---

[122] Ibid., no. 7. In spite of its Latin title, the 'Te Deum' uses a Lutheran adaptation of the melody: cf. Tunder's 'Herr Gott, dich loben wir'.

[123] *Denkmäler der Tonkunst in Bayern*, iv(1).

[124] The preludes of Jacob Praetorius are printed in *Orgel-Meister I*, ed. Seiffert (= *Organum, Reihe IV*, ii). Of the fifteen works by Scheidemann printed by Seiffert in *Organum, Reihe IV*, i, eleven are 'preludes' and four are purely imitative pieces (*fuga, canzone, fantasia*). The prelude and fugue is in Davison and Apel, *Historical Anthology*, ii, no. 195.

[125] Tunder's preludes are printed in *Organum IV*, ed. Seiffert; one is reprinted in *Historical Anthology*, ii, no. 215.

fugue', still used for example by Buxtehude's most recent editor, however appropriate for J. S. Bach's separable entities, is unsuited to the works of Buxtehude and his predecessors.

The toccata is a similar case. Here the ultimate model is the Italian form, transmitted through Sweelinck and (rather more importantly) Froberger. Again fugal elements made a gradual appearance. In a famous composition by Delphin Strunck, the lengthy 'Toccata ad manuale duplex', imitative passages are infrequent. Instead there is an extensive use of brilliant echo effects, derived from Scheidt rather than Sweelinck, but transformed through the continuous use of obbligato pedal to provide the bass. Later the five-section toccata, in which the second and fourth sections are fugal, became usual (Weckmann, Reincken,[126] Buxtehude). As in many of Froberger's toccatas, the two fugal sections are often linked thematically. In the later seventeenth century two important stylistic innovations occurred: the use of lively fugue-subjects involving running semiquavers and brilliant repeated-note effects, and the virtuoso use of the pedal in a solo-toccata idiom as well as to play its part in brilliant fugal writing. The new fugal idiom is related to the style of the canzona, a form still cultivated by Buxtehude and his contemporaries although its most significant application is to the development of the toccata. The enormous extension of pedal-technique hardly requires comment: it is the most immediately striking and potentially far-reaching of all the North German developments.

Scribes in the late seventeenth and early eighteenth centuries did not always distinguish carefully between preludes and toccatas; and most of Buxtehude's works in this style actually carry the designation *Praeludium* (or *Preambulum*). A few which are for manuals only point to the subsequent cultivation of the harpsichord toccata by Bach and are comparable to other seventeenth-century works for no specific keyboard medium. The majority are brilliant works with pedal obbligato, and even those with slow, rather archaic fugal sections contain lively figuration in the other parts. Buxtehude's F sharp minor toccata[127] illustrates his original cast of mind as much as his indebtedness to Froberger. Apart from the general conception, the latter is shown in the fourth, toccata-like section, where the jerky rhythms clearly go back to the older master:

---

[126] Weckmann's preludes, fugues and toccatas are in *Organum IV*, iii; those of Reincken in *Corpus of Early Keyboard Music*, xvi.

[127] Ed. Hedar, ii, no. 13.

Ex. 308

A part of the originality lies in the detailed plan, in which the two fugal sections are consecutive instead of being separated by toccata-like material. The relationship between these two sections is ingenious, the subject of the one being ornamented to provide the countersubject of the other, and vice versa:

Ex. 309

Elsewhere the work consists largely of 'motoric' semiquaver figuration of great brilliance. The episode quoted in Ex. 308 is followed by a lengthy and vivacious coda in which the tonal instability of the former is counterbalanced by a more regular harmonic tread, culminating in the vast plagal cadence, extending over nineteen bars of 4/4 time, with which the work ends. The whole piece is dominated by Buxtehude's extravagant rhetoric, characterized by sudden halts in the rhythm and outbursts of demisemiquaver movement; and by his individual harmonic style in which his penchant for emphasising the sharpened sixth and (to a lesser degree) the flat seventh of the minor key may be particularly mentioned.

Buxtehude's Praeludium in C[128] ends with an ostinato section marked 'Ciacona' to provide a lively and metrically straightforward conclusion. Buxtehude was one of the few Northern composers for organ to write, in his passacaglia and two chaconnes, entire pieces based on the ostinato principle, though Pachelbel wrote three with organ pedals and three without. In their simple grandeur these works make an immediate impact and perhaps more than any others reveal their composer's heroic cast of mind. Deleterious comparisons with Bach's great work are as misconceived here as in any portion of his output; Buxtehude's achievement is nearly always complete and satisfying on its own terms.

## SECULAR GERMAN KEYBOARD MUSIC

Secular keyboard music in Central and Northern Germany stems from the work of Froberger and of some of his lesser contemporaries. A number of later seventeenth-century publications provide a parallel to those of J. C. F. Fischer: Johann Krieger's *Sechs musicalische Parthien* (Nuremberg, 1697) and *Anmuthige Clavier-Übung* (Nuremberg, 1698), Johann Kuhnau's *Neue Clavier Übung* (two parts, 1689 and 1692), *Frische Clavier Früchte* (1696), and *Musicalische Vorstellung einiger biblischer Historien* (1700), and Pachelbel's *Hexachordum Apollinis* (1699). There are also numerous manuscript survivals from Kindermann and Pachelbel to Buxtehude and Georg Böhm (1661–1733).[129] The dominant form is the suite, generally in the form allemande, courante, sarabande, gigue; but a prelude is sometimes added, and other movements may be inserted before the gigue. The importance of these extra dances—the *galanteries* derived from French theatrical convention—came to be such that it was possible for Böhm to write a suite consisting exclusively of an overture and a string of such dances: the so-called ballet-suite of which Bach was to provide very

---

[128] Ibid., no. 1.

[129] The two printed works of Johann Krieger, together with some manuscript survivals of works by him and his elder brother Johann Philipp Krieger, ed. Seiffert, *Denkmäler der Tonkunst in Bayern*, xviii; further works by Johann are in *Organum IV*, xvii, and in *Die Orgel II*, iii, ed. F. W. Riedel (Leipzig, 1957). Kuhnau's *Klavierwerke* have been ed. Karl Päsler, *Denkmäler deutscher Tonkunst*, iv; there is a more recent edition of the *Biblische Historien* by K. Stone (New York, 1953), and a facsimile (Leipzig, 1973); numerous editions of separate works have appeared. Keyboard music by Kindermann is ed. Schreiber, *Denkmäler der Tonkunst in Bayern*, xxi–xxiv and ed. R. Baum, *Tanzstücke für Klavier* (Kassel etc., 1950); by Pachelbel, ed. Seiffert in *Denkmäler der Tonkunst in Bayern*, ii(1); by Böhm in his *Sämtliche Werke*, ed. J. Wolgast (Leipzig, 1927); and by Buxtehude in his *Klavervaerker*, ed. Emilius Bangert (Copenhagen, 1941) and *Vier Suiten für Clavichord oder Laute*, ed. B. Lundgren (Copenhagen, 1955). A suite in A flat by Pachelbel is in Davison and Apel, op. cit., ii, no. 250.

much more sophisticated examples in his fourth Partita and the *Overture nach Französischer Art* in the *Clavier Übung*. The term partita or *Parthie* now comes to mean a complete suite or set of variations, as opposed to the single movement or variation which was its original connotation. That there is a close connection between the suite and the variation-set we have seen in the case of Froberger, whose variations 'Auff die Mayerin' consist of a six-part allemande with courante and sarabande to form a three-movement suite, and who frequently made allusions from one movement to another in his regular suites. The six works in Pachelbel's *Hexachordum Apollinis* are all variation-sets; the themes are called 'Aria' and are probably original (with the possible exception of the *Aria Sebaldina*); the treatment resembles that of Froberger in the allemande of his 'Mayerin' set. Also indebted to Froberger are Pachelbel's three authentic suites, which are in the usual three- or four-movement form; others doubtfully assigned to him add 'ballet-movements' or *galanteries* to the scheme.

The term 'partita', or 'partite diverse', came to be applied to certain kinds of chorale-variations, usually somewhat secular in idiom and owing their method of treatment to the types of variation just mentioned rather than to the traditional but virtually extinct chorale-variation method. Three such sets by Pachelbel have survived, perhaps representing in part the contents of his lost *Musicalische Sterbensgedancken* (1683). Others were written by Georg Böhm. Such pieces were apparently intended for domestic rather than church use. In their essentially harmonic treatment of the material they differ from the traditional organ chorale-variation set, with its emphasis on contrapuntal manipulation; but the former came to influence the latter so that the distinction between the two became blurred: nor can terminology in the later seventeenth and early eighteenth centuries be said to be very precise on this point. Secularization, however, was carried to such lengths that we occasionally find a chorale-partita in traditional suite form, as in Buxtehude's well-known work in E minor.

The fantasia, toccata, and fugue (with or without a self-standing prelude), were all transferred to the harpsichord or clavichord. The preludes and fugues of J. C. F. Fischer's *Ariadne musica* (first published in 1702 but surviving only in a reprint of 1715) were intended for the use of organists, though not necessarily for the organ; and as a clear prototype of Bach's *Wohltemperirtes Clavier* they occupy an important position in the history of music for stringed keyboard instruments. Much the same may be said of the *ricercari* and fugues in Johann Krieger's *Anmuthige Clavier-Übung* of 1698, though Krieger's arrangement, unlike Fischer's, is tonally haphazard and the material is interspersed with pieces in other forms. His *Sechs musicalische Partien* (1697) consist of conventional four-movement suites, most of which are followed by groups of lighter dances. The fourteen suites ('Partien') of Kuhnau's *Neue Clavier Übung* add a prelude to the usual four-movement scheme, the gigue being sometimes replaced by another dance and in one instance preceded by a gavotte. All these works in their different ways, together with those of Froberger, Pachelbel, Böhm, and others, exerted a profound influence on Bach in the first part of his own *Clavier Übung* as well as in his 'English' and 'French' suites. Kuhnau's additional fame as 'inventor' of the keyboard sonata in the *Sonate aus dem B* in his *Neue Clavier Übung*, ii (1692), followed by his *Frische Clavier Früchte oder Sieben Suonaten* (1696), and the even greater notoriety of his *Biblische Historien* of 1700, are hardly justified by the quality of his musical thought. The harp-like music with which David soothes Saul is prolonged enough to send a sane listener mad, while the 'Story of Jacob' has all the tedium which must have attended Jacob's fourteen-year courtship of Rachel. The best of these works is probably the 'Mortal Illness and Recovery of Hezekiah', with its effective use of 'Herzlich tut mich verlangen' in the first two movements.

THE EUROPEAN PERIPHERY

In Eastern Europe as in Germany the distinction between Catholic and Protestant areas is important in the history of keyboard music. The largest number of sources is in Catholic Poland, where a strong tradition of both sacred and secular keyboard music had existed from the early sixteenth century.[130] The most important source here is the tablature of Jan of Lublin.[131] Polish manuscripts of the later sixteenth and early seventeenth centuries contain a repertory similar to that of contemporary German manuscripts, with which they share the 'new German tablature' consisting of

---

[130] To the sixteenth-century sources may be added the fifteenth-century sources from Breslau (Wrocław), first described and published by Fritz Feldmann (see Vol. III, p. 426). All are now assembled by Apel in *Corpus of Early Keyboard Music*, i.

[131] Kraków, Biblioteka Polskiej Akademii Nauk, MS 1716; see Vol. III, pp. 300–1. Facsimile and indices in *Monumenta Musicae in Polonia*, series B, i (1964); complete edition ed. J. R. White, *Corpus of Early Keyboard Music*, vi; description by White in *Musica Disciplina*, xvii (1963), p. 137. There are a single facsimile page and some rather faulty transcriptions in the anthology *Muzyka polskiego odrodzenia* (Kraków, 1953); and a selection of pieces (nos. 13–28) in *Muzyka w dawnym Krakowie*, ed. Zygmunt M. Szweykowski (Kraków, 1964).

letters and rhythmic signs only.[132] Dances and intabulations form the bulk of the repertoire. There are also Polish dances in the German tablatures of Christoph Löffelholtz (1585) and Augustus Nörmiger (1598).[133] Rather more significant are the contents of a tablature of about 1580 containing 74 liturgical pieces by Krzysztof Klabon, Marcin Leopolita, Marcin Wartecki, Jakub Sowa, and unnamed composers.[134] The music is in a late-Renaissance style without written ornamentation but with some fast-moving, structurally integral passages. A manuscript from Gdańsk, dated 1591 and initialled 'P.W.S.P.' on the parchment cover, contains intabulations and a series of fantasias which are chordal rather than imitative in style.[135] The tablature of Johannes Fischer Morungensis,[136] who was active in Poland and northern Prussia, is dated 1595 and includes some music by Diomedes Cato, the Italian-born lutenist who achieved fame in Poland.[137]

A series of early seventeenth-century manuscripts now in Warsaw, Cracow, and Pelplin[138] preserve an enormous repertory of intabulations. Some later additions to the Pelplin manuscripts are a valuable source of North-German chorale-settings, including splendid fantasias by Scheidemann and Tunder.[139] Finally one should mention two later seventeenth-century Polish sources: a tablature once belonging to the historian Aleksander Poliński but destroyed in World War II, and some fragments recovered from the binding of a Missal and containing a fantasia by one Piotr Zelechowski.[140] The Poliński manuscript (c.1660) had been tran-

[132] A manuscript formerly in Wrocław, Biblioteka Uniwersytecka, but now lost, could be dated c.1565 and contained a repertory of anonymous Magnificats, psalm-tones, the Te Deum and a setting of 'Wir glauben all' an einen Gott'. Fritz Dietrich, *Geschichte des deutschen Orgelchorals im 17. Jahrhunderts* (Kassel, 1932), p. 14, cited by Apel, op. cit., pp. 97–8.

[133] See Vol. IV, pp. 617–8.

[134] Formerly Warsaw, Music Society, MS I/200. Complete edition in *Antiquitates Musicae in Polonia*, xv; selection ed. Jerzy Golos and Adam Sutkowski, *Corpus of Early Keyboard Music*, x/4; descriptions by Golos in *Muzyka*, iv (1963), vi (1965), and in *L'Organo*, ii (1961).

[135] Gdańsk, Wojewódzkie Archiwum Państwowe 300, R (Vv, 123); ed. idem, *Corpus of Early Keyboard Music*, x/3.

[136] Bydgoszcz, Archiwum Wojewódzkie, Oddziat w Toruniu, XIV 13ª; *Corpus of Early Keyboard Music*, x/4. See A. Osostowicz in *Muzyka*, iii.

[137] See Vol. IV, p. 697.

[138] Kraków, Bibl. Jagiellońska, 24; Warsaw, Bibl. Narodowa, 4577, 4579. These are the MSS 101, 98, and 100 respectively from the former Ritter-Akademie at Lignica. See Pfuhl in *Beilagen zu Monatshefte für Musikforschung*, xix; Golos in *L'Organo*, iii (1962?). Pelplin, Bibl. Seminarium, 304–8, 308a: facsimile in *Antiquitates Musicae in Polonia*, ii–vii; selection of transcriptions ibid., viii–x; inventory ibid., i; see also Sutkowski in *Muzyka*, v; *Die Musik in Geschichte und Gegenwart*, x, s.v. 'Pelpliner Orgeltabulatur'.

[139] *Corpus of Early Keyboard Music*, x/2.

[140] Ibid., x/4.

scribed by Adolf Chybiński in 1924; it contains preludes (one by Jan Podbielski),[141] canzonas, toccatas, fugues, and a few oddments, mostly in the style of Italy or southern Germany.

Hungarian dances are included in the tablatures of Jan of Lublin and Nörmiger, and in the printed collections of Bernhard Schmid the elder (Strasbourg, 1577), Jakob Paix (Lauingen, 1583) and Giovanni Picchi (Venice, second edition 1621).[142] The tradition of Catholic organ music was strong in Hungary, but there are no musical survivals, although we have the names of several organists. Hofhaimer and his pupil Wolfgang Grefinger were prominent at the court of the Jagiełło kings, while Girolamo Diruta's *Il Transilvano* (Venice, I, 1593: II 1609),[143] dedicated to Prince Sigismund Báthory of Transylvania,[144] includes a toccata by Antonio Romanini, organist of the princely cathedral at Gyulafehérvár (Alba Julia). A sixteenth-century manuscript from St. Egidi in Bártfa indicates the use of the organ in alternation with voices in liturgical works by Isaac and others; but for actual written keyboard music we have to wait until the seventeenth century, when a series of manuscripts from the same centre emerges.[145] Written in part by Zakariás Zarewutius (1625–1665), organist at Bártfa, these sources carry a cosmopolitan repertory of Netherlands, German, and Italian music, together with anonymous pieces that may be at least to a certain extent Hungarian. Manuscript collections of definitely Hungarian keyboard music are the *Organo-Missale* (1667) of the Transylvanian Franciscan János Kájoni,[146] his temporarily lost collection of equally primitive little secular pieces, known as the Kájoni Codex, and the Codex Vietórisz, compiled about 1680 by two anonymous musicians—one perhaps named Kádár—which contains Hungarian, Slovak, and Wallachian dances in organ tablature.[147]

[141] Ed. Chybiński, *Wydawnictwo dawnej muzyki polskiej*, xviii.

[142] See Vol. IV, pp. 646 and 781–2.

[143] Ibid., p. 611.

[144] See Carl Krebs's extended study in *Vierteljahrsschrift für Musikwissenschaft*, viii (1892) for lists of compositions (pp. 344–5 and 352) and four of Diruta's own compositions (pp. 383–8).

[145] Budapest, National Library, Bártfa 28, 26, 27, 25, dating from 1649 to c.1680. See F. W. Riedel, *Quellenkundliche Beiträge zur Geschichte der Musik für Tasteninstrumente in der 2. Hälfte des 17. Jahrhunderts* (Kassel and Basel, 1960); L. Schierning, *Die Überlieferung der deutschen Orgel- und Klaviermusik aus der 1. Hälfte des. 17. Jahrhunderts* (Kassel and Basel, 1961); and Sweelinck, *Werken*, i, ed. Seiffert (Amsterdam, 1943), including music ascribed to Sweelinck but reckoned as unauthentic by his more recent editors.

[146] See Vol. V, p. 413.

[147] 56 pieces from the Kájoni and Vietórisz codices have been transcribed by Bence Szabolcsi, *A magyar zene évszázadai: a középkortól a XVII. századig*, i (Budapest, 1959), pp. 292–335 and 358.

As for keyboard music in other areas of Eastern Europe, the earliest to survive is a fragment in Italian tablature from Moravia probably dating from the late fifteenth century.[148] Also in Italian tablature is a collection of anonymous organ pieces preserved in the Moravian Museum at Brno.[149]

Scandinavia is in a similar case. The few manuscripts of Scandinavian origin from before 1700 contain a repertory of German, Netherlands and even English music.[150] Although Buxtehude was of Scandinavian birth, his musical culture was that of North Germany.

## THE NETHERLANDS

The Netherlands produced no one of the stature of Sweelinck in the later seventeenth century, though there is much that is far from contemptible. The successor to Henderick Speuy's *De Psalmen Davids* (Dordrecht, 1610) was Anthoni Van Noordt's *Tablatuur Boeck van Psalmen en Fantasyen* (Amsterdam, 1659).[151] Van Noordt, who was organist of the new 'Side' Chapel in Amsterdam, provided ten psalm-settings of from one to eight verses, and six fantasias. His relation to Sweelinck parallels that of Scheidemann; like Scheidemann he uses the two-manual and pedal-bass combination frequently. The opening of the third verse of his setting of Psalm 7 illustrates his deceptively simple art: the cunning overlap between the end of the first line of the *cantus firmus* with the prior imitation of the material of the second line in the other parts will be noted:

---

[148] Printed in editorial notes to Jaroslav Pohanka, *Dějiny české hubdy v příkladech* (Prague, 1958), p. 28.

[149] Hudební Archiv, A8762. Toccata and Versetto in Pohanka op. cit., no. 98.

[150] These include the Tablature of Elisabeth Eysbock, *c*.1600 (Stockholm, Kungl. Mus. Akad. Bibl., Tabl. no. 1: see Thurston Dart, 'Elisabeth Eysbock's Keyboard Book' in *Svensk Tidskrift för Musikforskning*, xliv (1962), pp. 5–12; a manuscript of *c*.1626–1639 (Copenhagen, Kon. Bibl., 376: see Povl Hamburger in *Zeitschrift für Musikwissenschaft*, xiii (1930–1), pp. 133–40); a manuscript insertion in a copy of Gabriel Voigtländer's *Oden*, 1642, owned by the same library; and the addition made 1655–66 by Johan Bahr, organist of Visby Cathedral, to the tablature of Berendt Petri (written at Hamburg in 1611) and now in the Chapter Library at Visby.

[151] Speuy, ed. Fritz Noske (Amsterdam, 1962); Van Noordt, ed. Seiffert, *Vereniging voor Nederlandsche Muziekgeschiedenis*, xix (Utrecht, 1896); Anthoni van Noordt, *Psalmenbearbeitungen für Orgel*, ed. Pidoux (Kassel, 1954).

Ex. 310

All Van Noordt's music is distinguished by sound craftsmanship and a sense of proportion.

Secular Dutch keyboard music is documented in the later seventeenth century by a small number of sources which continue the modest tradition initiated by Susanne Van Soldt's book of 1599 or earlier. These are, in chronological order so far as can be ascertained, the Dutch section of a manuscript now in Leningrad—two privately-owned sources which have been named the 'Camphuysen' and 'Gresse' manuscripts; the G. H. Brockhuijzen manuscript (1668–9); and the keyboard book of Anna Maria Van Eijl (1671).[152] Towards the end of the century sources become more frequent, the printed suites of Pieter Bustijn (Middelburg, ? 1710)[153] being perhaps typical of a by now very French-influenced art. In the middle of the century French influence, largely filtered through Froberger, contended with a post-Sweelinckian idiom. The Leningrad manuscript actually contains three short pieces by 'Mr. Jan Pijtters', believed to be Sweelinck himself; much of the rest is in that very straightforward rather neutral idiom which through Sweelinck's simplest secular style can be traced back to the English virginalists. Actual English tunes still appear: 'Rosemont' (= 'Rosasolis' set by Farnaby and others), 'Enghels Voishe', and Sweelinck's own 'Malle Sijmen' (the 'Mall Sims' of the *Fitzwilliam Virginal Book*). In much the same way the Camphuysen manuscript has 'De Engelsche Fortuijn' ('Fortune my foe') and 'Daphne', the latter a rather ambitious set of three variations. The Gresse manuscript includes simple rather Frobergian suites ascribed to 'Jb. Gresse', who probably compiled the manuscript himself, perhaps for a pupil. Similarly the Eijl book was compiled by Gisbert Steenwick for his pupil Anna Maria Van Eijl. Steenwick, organist of Arnheim from 1665 to 1674, is the most considerable of this not very considerable group of composers. His attractive variation-sets are a not unsuccessful adaptation of Sweelinckian counterpoint to the more harmonically conceived notions of the mid-century. The other named Dutch composers are one Barend Broeckhuisen and Georg Berff, organist at Deventer.[154]

The keyboard music of the Catholic Netherlands, consisting largely of fantasias, fugues, and other 'neutral' forms, together with liturgical versets and a small amount of domestic music in various dance-rhythms, may be studied in a number of early seventeenth-

---

[152] The Suzanne Van Soldt book (London, Brit. Lib., Ref. Div., Add. 29485), with extracts from the Leningrad, Camphuysen and Gresse manuscripts, has been edited by Alan Curtis as *Monumenta Musica Neerlandica*, iii (Amsterdam, 1961). The Van Eijl book is edited in the same series, ii, by Noske (1959); it supersedes an earlier edition by Julius Röntgen (Amsterdam and Leipzig, 1918).

[153] Three suites ed. Curtis in *Exempla Musica Neerlandica*, i (Amsterdam, 1964).

[154] An 'Allemand Tresoor' in this manuscript is presumably by the Jonas Tresure who appears in English sources (see below p. 580).

century sources:[155] the 'Liber Fratrum Cruciferorum'; a lost manuscript formerly in the Berlin Staatsbibliothek; two collections largely of liturgical music; and the Messaus manuscript compiled apparently from the papers left by John Bull (1628). The anonymous music in the Christ Church manuscript is conjectured to have been composed by the Englishman Richard Deering, who was organist of the convent of English nuns at Brussels before returning to England in 1625; but it may possibly be by William Brown or indeed a Belgian composer, though the scribe was certainly English. Not enough is known at present about the various stylistic traits of the Catholic Netherlands repertory, which in any case contains English elements through the medium of John Bull and Peter Philips, to be certain about the origin of this collection. Just as problematic are the attractive Masses and Magnificats from the British Library source, which has indeed been assigned to France. The presence in it of music by Giovanni Gabrieli and Sweelinck, combined with registration indications in French, suggests rather an area of French-speaking Belgium, but it is impossible at this stage to be certain. The most important named Belgian composer of this era was Pieter Cornet, whose small surviving output reveals sensitive musicianship and a good sense of overall design.

Much the same may be said of Abraham Van den Kerckhoven, organist of the Royal Chapel at Brussels from 1656 to 1668 at least. His music is preserved, along with works by Poglietti, C. Vaes, A. Kolfs, 'L.F.', (Pierre de) Paepen, and much that is anonymous, in a late seventeenth- or early eighteenth-century manuscript now in Brussels.[156] Kerckhoven clearly inherits the tradition of Cornet and his contemporaries: his numerous versets in the eight tones, his 'Missa Duplex', various 'Salve Regina' settings and a number of fantasias are scarcely distinguishable from similar pieces in the Liège and Berlin sources. The pieces called 'fuga' are in an

[155] 'Liber Fratrum Cruciferorum': Liège, University Library, MS 153 (olim 888), ed. Guilmant, Archives des maîtres de l'orgue, x (Paris, 1909–11); see Dart in Revue Belge de Musicologie, xvii (1963), pp. 21–28. The lost manuscript from Berlin bore the number Mus. ms. 40316: the music by Cornet in it was printed in Guilmant, op. cit. and, more completely, by Apel in Corpus of Early Keyboard Music, xxvi; photographs of the manuscript are extant. The collections of liturgical music are Brit. Lib. Add. 29486, possibly of French but more likely of Belgian origin, dated 1618, and Oxford, Christ Church, Mus. 89 (see Dart in Music & Letters, lii (1971), p. 27). The Messaus MS is Brit. Lib. Add. 23623; a lost companion volume was described by John Ward, Lives of the Professors of Gresham College (London, 1740). Music by the Belgian composer Samuel Mareschal survives in a group of four manuscripts at Basel (Universitätsbibl., F. IX. 47–50, dated 1638–40): a selection is given in Corpus of Early Keyboard Music, xxvii.

[156] Bibl. Royale, 3326 II, containing 364 pieces in all. A large selection (137), consisting of those by or presumed to be by Kerckhoven, has been edited by J. Watelet, Monumenta Musicae Belgicae, ii (Berchem-Antwerp, 1933).

Italianate canzona style already absorbed into the Belgian idiom. But in some of his works Kerckhoven shows a sense of overall structure which was beyond many of his predecessors. A 'Fantasia pro duplici organo'[157] is a resourceful piece involving echo effects and working up to a satisfying conclusion; the pedals are mentioned, but were used apparently only for sustained notes (the few directions in the printed edition appear to be misplaced). Still more impressive are two preludes and fugues (the two sections being thus distinguished in the manuscript), in which the short preludes are followed by lengthy and on the whole well-designed fugues on interesting subjects. The opening of the D minor work will illustrate his manner:[158]

Ex. 311

---

[157] Ibid., no. 130.
[158] Ibid., no. 136.

It must be admitted, however, that there is a tendency in his fugal writing, inherited from the previous generation, to lapse into a merely decorative texture as in bar 91–6 of the work just quoted from.

ENGLAND

With the notable exception of the later works of Thomas Tomkins, keyboard music in England suffered a steep decline with the passing of the great age of the English virginalists, three of whom—Byrd, Gibbons, and Bull—died within a few years of each other in the 1620s. All important artistic developments are preceded by an age of uncertainty; but it has to be admitted that the great achievements of the middle and later seventeenth century were not in keyboard music at all, and that the apparent weaknesses of the 1630s and 1640s are not the prelude to anything very spectacular. The most one can claim for the voluntaries and suites of Locke, Blow, Purcell, and Croft is a lively charm or a dignified pathos. But within these limits a distinctive style was cultivated, and the boundaries occasionally transcended.

The keyboard music of Tomkins himself,[159] though he remained

[159] Ed. Stephen D. Tuttle, *Musica Britannica*, v (London, 1955, 2nd edn. 1964).

a great composer to the last, can have reached few ears outside
those of his gradually diminishing circle of friends. That circle
included his half-brother John Tomkins (c.1586–1638), a composer
called Nicholas Carleton (d. 1630), and Arthur Phillips (1605–95),
organist first of Bristol Cathedral and then of Magdalen College,
Oxford, where he also became the University's second Professor of
Music (1639–56). All composed for the keyboard in a small way.[160]
Another traditionalist was John Lugge, organist of Exeter
Cathedral from 1602 to 1645 at least. His fine voluntaries and *cantus
firmus* pieces deserve to be more widely known.[161] Benjamin
Cosyn, organist at Dulwich College, 1622–4, and later at the
Charterhouse, was a somewhat extravagant imitator of Bull. Much
of his keyboard music survives in his hand in a manuscript which
once belonged to Bull and which Cosyn finally indexed in 1652.[162]
A few voluntaries in a quieter style, labelled 'B.C.', are also
generally taken to be his work.[163] Only Tomkins however succeeded in making a perfect amalgam of the stylistic dichotomy
represented by Byrd and Bull. The exceptional technical difficulty
of some works from the 1630s gives place to recollection of past
glories. Not that this latest music is lacking in vigour or imagination. The fascinating holograph of his later music shows the
composer at work, constantly polishing until he is satisfied, penning
the last examples of 'In nomine', 'Miserere', pavan and galliard,
and variations in the tradition of his predecessors. Most of them
bear precise dates within the period 1647–54, the period—as it
happens—between Charles I's surrender to the Scots and
Cromwell's assumption of the Protectorate. The 'Sad Pavan for
these distracted times' is dated 14 February 1649, which, if Tomkins
was then employing 'new style' (an assumption that cannot be
proved) would place its composition a fortnight after the king's
execution.

[160] Some of their music is published by Frank Dawes, *Schott's Collection of Early
Keyboard Music*, iv (London, 1951). A duet by Carleton is printed in the same editor's *Two
Elizabethan Keyboard Duets* (London, 1949); a second Ground by Phillips in New York,
Public Library, Drexel 5611, remains unpublished.

[161] The voluntaries of Lugge have been printed by Susi Jeans and John Steele (London,
1956); the same editors have given us his *Two Toys and a Jigg* (London, 1958). The *cantus
firmus* pieces, which like the voluntaries survive in Oxford, Christ Church, Mus. 49, remain
unpublished.

[162] Paris, Bibl. Nat., fonds du Conservatoire, Rés. 1185. Only marginally less important
as a source of Cosyn's music is his own fine virginal book of 1620 (London, Brit. Lib., R.M.
23.1.4), from which three pieces by Cosyn himself were included in J. A. Fuller Maitland
and W. Barclay Squire, *Twenty-five pieces for keyed instruments from Cosyn's Virginal Book*
(London, 1923). Most of Cosyn's music, however, is still unpublished.

[163] Oxford, Christ Church, Mus. 1113. Three of these eight pieces have been edited by
Steele (London, 1959).

THE SUITE IN ENGLAND

The greatest composer of the Caroline court by a very long way was William Lawes (1602–45); but it is unlikely that any of the keyboard music surviving under his name was originally for that medium. However, his music in the form of what appear to be transcriptions and (probably) scribal arrangements of the material into specific groupings of movements, plays a part in the evolution of the suite in England, an umbrella under which virtually all forms of domestic keyboard music can be considered. In the Bull manuscript already mentioned is a three-movement suite by Lawes,[164] and at least six other three-movement suites and one two-movement suite, the other named composers being 'Mr. Formiloe', William Young, Simon Ives, and La Barre (the composer of the two-movement work).[165] That the Lawes work is an arrangement is clear from the subscription 'Finis B.C.' at the end of the first and third movements. But the indexing of all this material in 1652 provides a convenient starting-point from which to consider the development of the suite in England. Two other important manuscripts of the 1650s contain suites. Christ Church 1236, compiled by William Ellis, organist of St. John's College, Oxford, before the Commonwealth, includes suites, or suite-like groupings, by John Ferrabosco, William Ellis, one 'Moulin' or 'Molin', Lawes, 'Mr. Roberts', Mercure, Tresure, and Benjamin Rogers (two suites of which the second has four movements).[166] The work by Lawes consists of a piece called 'The golden grove' followed by 'The corant to y$^e$ golden grove' and 'The Country Dance', all in A minor and anonymous. A manuscript of comparable date, Christ Church 1003, substitutes a saraband for the 'Country Dance' and specifies Lawes as the composer of the first movement (which it calls 'Allemande: Goden Grove'), though not

---

[164] Ed. Murray Lefkowitz in *Trois Masques à la Cour de Charles I$^{er}$ d'Angleterre* (Paris, 1970).

[165] Formiloe is otherwise unknown. On Young see p. 441. Ives (Yves, 1600–62) was prominent at the court of Charles I. La Barre (whose name appears as Beare, Bare, Labar, etc. in English sources) is apparently Pierre Chabanceau de la Barre (1592–1656).

[166] Moulin is otherwise unknown. Roberts is presumably the John Roberts of *Melothesia* (see below). Mercure (or Merceur) is known only from English sources and is apparently French; Treasure is mentioned in the Dutch Van Eijl book (see n. 154) and in the Hintze manuscript of French origin (New Haven, Yale University Library, M. 1490. H 66), as well as in English sources, and was almost certainly himself Dutch or Belgian. The keyboard works of Rogers are edited by Richard Rastall (London, 1969). The 'Sambonier' of this manuscript is evidently Chambonnières; another Frenchman represented is the lutenist Du Faut.

of the two others. *Musicks Hand-maide* (1663),[167] has a different corant (ascribed to Lawes) but with the saraband of Christ Church 1003; two non-keyboard sources, *Courtly Masquing Ayres* (1662) and *Musick's Delight on the Cithren* (1666) have just the alman and the corant of *Musicks Hand-maide*.

This complex situation illustrates the way in which scribes might select material to form suites (though the term itself was not yet used) of their own compiling, unified by key and more or less standardized in overall form but not necessarily intended by the composer to form a self-sufficient entity. In the present case the diversity no doubt reflects the origin of all this music in some private entertainment in which the dances were not intended to form a unified sequence.

The third principal source, the Elizabeth Rogers 'Virginall Booke' dated 1657, has suites by Thomas Strengthfeild, La Barre, and Mercure, with several anonymous groupings including one (Nos. 50–53) in four movements.[168] To this very early group of sources may be added *Musicks Hand-maid* itself, which in its first edition (1663) included, as well as its version of 'The Golden Grove', yet another suite by Lawes, two by Rogers and a four-movement suite by Benjamin Sandley which reappears (copied from an independent source) in the Gresse manuscript.[169] This source, like the others, raises the question of which movements actually belong together. Rogers' 'Jigg' in D is the third of a sequence of twelve movements in the same key which can hardly be taken to be a single work; though modern editors have ascribed the preceding 'Saraband' to Rogers as well, it is quite uncertain whether this is justified or whether, conversely, further movements ought to be added to the pair.

In spite of such uncertainties there is an overwhelming preponderance of works by single composers employing the formula alman—corant—saraband (to adopt a standardized English orthography), a fourth movement being occasionally added. The precise origin of the form in England is somewhat mysterious. It is hardly conceivable that the English would have hit upon a form identical

[167] Modern edition by Dart (London, 1969), with a valuable account of its publishing history. 'Golden Grove' was the Welsh seat of the Earl of Carbury, whose wife, Lady Alice Egerton, had been the 'Lady' of Milton's *Comus*, performed with music by Henry Lawes at Ludlow Castle in 1634.

[168] London, Brit. Lib., Add. 10337. The date 27. ii. 1656 implies 1657 new style. Complete edition by George Sargent, *Corpus of Early Keyboard Music*, xix; a selection ed. Dawes in *Schott's Collection*, v (London, 1951). Thomas Strengthfeild is otherwise unknown.

[169] See above, p. 575. It is not included in Curtis's edition.

to that of Froberger's simplest works independently; yet there is no evidence of English contact with Froberger (or any German composer) by 1652[170] nor is their style directly imitated. We are driven to assume a French model for both the German and the English forms of the suite—not, of course, the greatly extended *ordre* of Chambonnières and D'Anglebert but an unfortunately undocumented type which seems to have existed in the 1630s and 1640s. But the situation is complicated by the evident prior existence, in England at least, of a two-movement form (alman—corant) and by the doubt as to when, and where, courtly dancing conventions as to movement-grouping were first transferred to the keyboard. Although several of the French composers represented in English manuscripts were primarily lutenists, it is not yet quite clear to what extent the lute repertory influenced such conventions.

The next stage in the history of the suite is represented by the work of Albert Bryne, Matthew Locke, and the lesser composers included in Locke's *Melothesia* (1673).[171] Three works by Albert Bryne (or Bryan) are in a Bodleian manuscript which may be autograph;[172] each contains an alman, a corant, a saraband and a fourth movement called 'Jigg Allmaine', this being a quadruple-time jig similar to the last movement of the four-movement suite by Rogers in Christ Church 1236. As we have seen, Froberger knew the quadruple-time jig, and there are examples of quicker, duple-time, jigs earlier in English music; but the type now being considered, which has its parallels in the consort repertory, is probably again of direct French influence. Two further suites by Bryne (one in the usual three movements and one having only an 'Ayre' and 'Saraband') were included in the third edition (1678) of *Musicks Hand-maid* (to give it its new spelling), together with three alman—saraband pairs by Locke. Two of the Locke almans (actually called 'Ayre') are transcriptions from his masque *Cupid and Death*, and his contribution to the suite is better exemplified by the work copied rather haphazardly into the 'Heardson' manuscript around 1660 and[173], much more significantly, by the four works in

[170] Even the advancement of Froberger's London visit to the early 1650s (see n. 89) would scarcely account for a tradition flourishing by 1652.

[171] Modern edition of the suites by Locke by Dart (London, 1959), and of a substantial proportion of the remainder by A. Kooiker (Pennsylvania University, 1968). Facsimile in *Monuments of Music and Music Literature in Facsimile*, Series II, xxx.

[172] On Bryne and his suites see Barry Cooper in *Musical Times*, cxiii (1972), p. 142, and also the same author's 'The Keyboard Suite in England before the Restoration', *Music & Letters*, liii (1972), p. 309.

[173] New York, Public Library, Drexel 5611, pp. 139–41 (ed. Dart, op. cit.). The same section of this manuscript also has a suite by Rogers (ed. Rastall, op. cit.).

*Melothesia*. These represent a significant advance in the history of the form, with their many additional movements and their awareness of a more recent style of French harpsichord music than had obtained hitherto. The *style brisé* is by now fully understood, and the prelude to the third suite comes close to the French unmeasured type though the notation is fully mensural. On the other hand the movements entitled 'Country Dance', 'Virago', 'Roundo', and 'Rant' betray Locke's very English sense of forthright tunefulness. Some of the sources of his inspiration may be gleaned from a passage in his polemical *Observations upon a Late Book . . .* (London, 1672), pp. 35–6, in which, after mentioning with approval the keyboard music of Bull, Gibbons, Bryne, and Rogers, he goes on to refer to 'Senior *Froscobaldi* (*sic*) of St. *Peter's* in *Rome*, Senior *Froberger* of the Christian Emperial Court, Monsieur *Samboneer* of the *French*, or any other Eminent Author'.

None of his lesser contemporaries approaches Locke's combination of a vivid imagination and formal discipline, though the suites in *Melothesia* by Christopher Preston, John Roberts (possibly the 'Mr. Roberts' of Christ Church 1236), Will Gregorie (d. 1663), Robert Smith, John Moss, and others, include many inventive movements. Indeed the suite in F by John Moss is a remarkable affair, with its elaborate embellishment and ingenious harmonic style. This might be illustrated by the vivid concluding 'Jig-Almain' or by the first section of the corant, in which an imperfect cadence in the tonic key derives a new significance from the actual modulation to the dominant which precedes it:

Ex. 312

## PURCELL, BLOW, AND CROFT

The final stage in the development of the suite includes the work of Purcell, Blow, and Croft (1678–1727), together with many minor composers represented in contemporary sources.[174] The suite as a form, indeed, hardly undergoes any development; it is the style of its constituent movements which deepens and intensifies. We still find, even in the early eighteenth century, such features as movements doing duty in more than one work, different selections of movements for the 'same' suite, the inclusion of transcriptions of theatre airs and like, and even composite authorship. On the whole Purcell, whose suites exhibit fewer of these characteristics than those of most of his contemporaries, is the most distinguished advocate of the suite *per se*, though the overall quality of the eight suites published by his widow in 1696 in *A Choice Collection of Lessons for the Harpsichord or Spinnet*[175] is disappointing compared with his output as a whole. The mannerisms of the traditional movements (as with his contemporaries) are apt to become a little wearisome, and some of the most enjoyable moments occur in the short preludes, such as the charming and very subtle prelude to the second suite (possibly the most satisfying of the suites taken as a whole) or the vigorous (and again subtle) prelude to the fifth suite.

Although John Blow published four suites in his similarly entitled *A Choice Collection . . . Containing four Sett's* (*c*.1698, reissued 1704)[176] it seems that he was less committed than Purcell to

[174] One of these is Francis Forcer, by whom as Apel has pointed out (op. cit., p. 752) there are three suites and some separate pieces in Washington D.C., Library of Congress, M 21. M. 185, together with two pieces by the Italian-born Giovanni Battista Draghi, whose *Six Select Sutes of Leszons for the Harpsichord* were published in London around 1700. References to 'Senior Baptist', etc., in other manuscripts are almost certainly to Draghi. Forcer and Draghi, with John Blow, Richard Motley, Henry Purcell, Moses Snow, William Turner, and 'Verdier' are represented in *The Second Part of Musick's Hand-maid* (London: Henry Playford, 1689; modern edition by Dart, London, 1958, revised 1962).

[175] Good modern edition by Howard Ferguson (London, 1964).

[176] Modern edition by Ferguson (London, 1965), with two other suites from contemporary printed sources.

the suite as a form. Although two more suites can be extracted from contemporary printed anthologies and others from manuscript sources, there are many fine works right outside the context of the suite.[177] Unlike Purcell he applied his skill in ground-bass and chaconne writing assiduously to the keyboard, producing many fine examples of both. While in some works the boldness and originality of his harmonic thought result in stylistic anomalies when placed in the context of more conventional passages, in others there is a consistency of style throughout, as in the very fine G minor Ground, which appears to be a comparatively late work.[178] Its austere simplicity may be illustrated by the last four variations:

Ex. 313

[177] Some of these have never been published; some have appeared in older editions— Ernst Pauer, *Old English Composers* (London, 2nd edn. 1879; the works of Blow reprinted as *Popular Pieces*); Fuller Maitland, *Contemporaries of Purcell*, 7 vols. (London, n.d.), which includes a certain amount of otherwise unobtainable music by Barrett, Clarke, Coleman, Diessener, Eccles, King, Piggot, Daniel Purcell, and Turner from various manuscript and early eighteenth-century printed sources—but these employ out-dated editorial methods and a complete edition of his harpsichord music is a great desideratum.

[178] Fuller Maitland, op cit., ii, p. 16; corrected text here from Oxford, Christ Church, Mus. 1177.

    With Croft, on the other hand, the suite was the principal means
of expression in his harpsichord music. The complete edition has
produced seventeen suites and about twenty single pieces, many of
them arranged from his theatre music.[179] Some of the suites, too,
contain arranged music—no. 12 in F is entirely based on his tunes
for Steele's play *The Funeral, or Grief a la Mode*—but most of
them consist largely or entirely of fine, serious, original music.
Several are unusual in overall form. Even with Croft the perpetual
use of *notes inégales* and of certain conventional ornaments in the
standard dances can be tiresome, and one tends to look for the
short, lighter airs, the grounds, the preludes and so on for evidence
of originality. Yet beneath the conventional mask, if it can be penetrated, his individuality and integrity can still be discerned. The
sombre, tragic sixth suite, in D minor, consists only of the conventional three movements, the 'Almand' and 'Sarabrand' both

   [179]  Ed. Ferguson and Christopher Hogwood, 2 vols. (London, 1974).

marked 'slow'; yet it is finely drawn throughout, a model of restraint and sober dignity:

Ex. 314

Sarabrand: **Slow**

Croft represents the summit in the long rise of the English suite from the first tentative experiments in the 1650s. Although a few of his contemporaries, notably Jeremiah Clarke, possessed comparable gifts, none surpassed his achievement. Clarke's suites, published posthumously in 1711, look forward in some ways to the more Italianized idiom of the later eighteenth century. The rest of them—Daniel Purcell, Eccles, 'Wood', Barrett, Piggot, Weldon, Courtivill, 'Mr. Henry Hall of Hereford'[180], and 'Mr. Richardson of Winton', survive, if at all, by an attractive turn of melody or a touch of whimsicality. Two others—Philip Hart and Antony Young—published collections in 1704 and 1719 respectively, the former a rather pedantic figure, the latter the final representative of the form in its pre-Handelian stage.

[180] Hall (d. 1707) was organist of the Cathedral, where two manuscripts associated with him are still preserved. See Barry Cooper, 'Keyboard Sources in Hereford', *Research Chronicle of the Royal Musical Association*, xvi (1981), p. 135.

ENGLISH ORGAN MUSIC

English organ music may be dealt with more briefly. The omnibus word under which all may be subsumed is 'voluntary': though 'verse' is sometimes used for shorter works and 'fugue' for fugues, there is no doubt that 'voluntary' could mean both of these and much more besides. Before the Commonwealth, organ music was written in as late-Renaissance style. A very few extant works utilize the two manuals which many English organs by then possessed; one by Orlando Gibbons, apparently in a transformation by Ben Cosyn, and three by Lugge. A much-mentioned but little-known 'double voluntary', as such pieces were called, by Richard Portman is probably post-Restoration.[181] The church organ was of course silenced during the interregnum, and its repertory had to be re-created at the Restoration. A voluntary by Ben Rogers, who returned to his post at St. George's Windsor in 1662, survives in an autograph dated 1664:[182] it has the virtues and faults of its time, the solid counterpoint and the rhythmic inconsistency. The voluntaries by Locke, on the other hand, which were printed in *Melothesia*, have both consistency and invention.[183] Even the shortest of them—and none is long—are carefully polished little masterpieces. The only double voluntary shows a resourceful use of the two manuals in the context of a double fugue followed by a free coda. John Blow's organ music is harder to assess.[184] The best of it—like the superb voluntary in D minor on a chromatic subject, no. 18—has all the virtues of Locke combined with its own powerful individuality. At other times we wonder if we are looking at the music of the same composer, so trivial or hopelessly inconsistent in style is some of it. But the manuscript preservation of his music is so chaotic that, expertly though it has been sifted, we cannot be at all certain that we know which pieces bearing his name are really his or how much that is lost or preserved anonymously might be attributed to him. The texts are hideously faulty and incomplete, and we have virtually no picture of the chronology.

---

[181] The manuscript in which it occurs, from the library of Wimborne Minster in Dorset, dates probably from around 1670.

[182] Brit. Lib., R.M. 21. d.8, ff. 65$^r$–66$^r$. Ed. Rastall, op. cit., no. 16, and in a separate edition by Jeans (London, 1962).

[183] Modern editions by Dart (London, 1957) and Gordon Phillips (London, 1957). Phillips preserves the original ornament-signs.

[184] Ed. H. Watkins Shaw, *Thirty Voluntaries and Verses* (2nd edn., London, 1972). Minor additions to the canon have been edited by Phillips, *Three Voluntaries* (London, 1962: the three works are by Blow, Barrett, and John Reading) and by Hugh McLean, *Two Voluntaries from the Nanki Manuscript* (London, 1971).

Blow's teacher was Christopher Gibbons, who was organist of Westminster Abbey from 1660 to 1666. A much less good composer than Blow, he was capable of the most appalling triviality.[185] His successor Albert Bryne, organist from 1666 to 1668 (the probable date of his death) has left very little organ music; the nineteen-year old Blow followed at the Abbey until he too was succeeded by Henry Purcell in 1679, resuming on Purcell's death in 1695.

Purcell too composed very little organ music,[186] but his sense of structure appears to have been stronger than Blow's and his voluntaries in D minor and G major are, in their small way, masterpieces. He also seems to have been responsible for a version for single-manual chamber organ of a voluntary on 'The Old Hundredth', elsewhere attributed to Blow.

Around the turn of the century English organists cultivated a richly embellished and full-textured style of playing exemplified in the manuscripts of John Reading (c.1685–1764), who was more important as a copyist than as a composer, and in the music of Philip Hart (c.1676–1749), whose voluntaries are preserved in manuscript and in his keyboard publication of 1704.[187] But Purcell's real successor was Croft, who took his departure not so much from his keyboard idiom as from the general qualities of his style.[188] In particular, Croft introduced into the voluntary something of the more recent Italianate manner which Purcell had already cultivated in his instrumental and vocal works. They exhibit little trace of English renaissance polyphony, of the French or German middle baroque style, or of the earlier Italian baroque, that curious mélange on which Locke and Blow had subsisted; on the contrary, they are the forerunners of the Italian late baroque idiom cultivated by Greene, Stanley, Boyce, Travers, and others in their voluntaries.

[185] His keyboard music has been edited by Clare G. Rayner, *Corpus of Early Keyboard Music*, xviii.

[186] It has been ed. McLean (London, 1957, rev. 1967).

[187] The manuscript is an autograph section of London, Brit. Lib., Add. 32161. On Hart see Dawes, *Proceedings of the Royal Musical Association*, xciv (1967–8), p. 63.

[188] Ed. Richard Platt, *Complete Organ Works* (2nd edn., London, 1982). The principal source is a section of Brit. Lib. Add. 5336, a late eighteenth-century source which gives the impression of a fair copy drawn up in connection with a projected (but never undertaken) edition. The music is here anonymous, but Croft's authorship is confirmed by concordances in manuscripts written by John Reading (Dulwich College, MSS 92a, 92b, 92d, and Manchester, Henry Watson Library, BRm. 7105. Rf. 31).

# IX

## HARPSICHORD MUSIC: 1700–1750

### By PHILIP RADCLIFFE

INTRODUCTORY

THE first half of the eighteenth century is a period of the greatest importance in the history of keyboard music; France, Germany, and Italy all played a significant part in its development. In France the pioneer was Jacques Champion de Chambonnières (*c.*1602–*c.*1672), who had published two books of *Pièces de Clavecin* in 1670.[1] These consist of dance movements on a small scale, suggestive in their texture of strings rather than a keyboard instrument. In some of them, e.g. the pavane 'L'Entretien des Dieux':

Ex. 315|

the counterpoint looks back to an earlier generation. There is no sign of this in the work of the younger composers, whose music appeared mainly after 1700. The dance forms become increasingly clear-cut, often with the ends of the two halves corresponding; and

---

[1] See chap. VIII. p. 538.

the most sectional of musical forms—the *rondeau*—is often found.
Sometimes the texture is purely harmonic; at other times it conveys
the impression of part-writing, but of a kind that is conceivable
only with a keyboard instrument in mind. 'Les Tourterelles', an
attractive if over-long piece by François Dagincour (1684–1758), is
typical:[2]

Ex. 316

It is undeniable that much of the music of these composers is very
similar in style; but it is equally true that there is a good deal that is
fresh and likeable. The two suites, one in C major, the other in C
minor, which make up the *I^er Livre de Pièces de Clavecin* (1704)[3] by
Louis-Nicolas Clérambault (1676–1749), are particularly remarkable; the allemande of the C major suite may serve as an example:

Ex. 317

[2] *Pièces de clavecin* (Paris, 1733); ed. Howard Ferguson (Paris, 1969).
[3] Modern ed. by Paul Brunold (Paris, 1938); rev. Thurston Dart (Monaco, 1965),
restoring the correct order of the *pièces*.

Another fine piece of non-descriptive music is the chaconne:

Ex. 318

in the *Pièces de clavecin* (1707)[4] of Elisabeth-Claude Jacquet de La Guerre (*c*.1666–1729). Both Clérambault and Jacquet de La Guerre were attracted by the *goût de la musique italienne* fashionable from the late seventeenth century onward. Of the other minor masters, Louis-Claude Daquin (1694–1772) is best known by 'Le Coucou', which deserves its popularity. 'L'Hirondelle' is an equally lively bird portrait, but 'La Ronde Bacchique' hardly lives up to its title, though it is an amusing exhibition of genteel gaiety, emphasized by innumerable mordents.[5]

Bird pieces were a favourite genre. Dagincour suggested the cooing of turtle-doves, Daquin the cuckoo and swallow, but Jean-François Dandrieu (*c*.1682–1738) had already provided a whole 'Concert des Oiseaux' in his *Premier Livre de Pièces de Clavecin contenant plusieurs divertissements dont les principaux sont les caractères de la Guerre, ceux de la Chasse et de la Fête du Village* (1724). A second book followed in 1728 and a third in 1734. Dandrieu's

---

[4] Modern edition by Brunold (Monaco, 1938); rev. Dart (Monaco, 1965).
[5] All in his *Pièces de clavecin* (1735); modern ed. by Brunold and H. Expert (Paris, 1926).

other effective character pieces[6] include a well-known 'Les Tourbillons', while 'Les Tendres reproches' suggests its title by a type of figuration common among the French composers of the period—it appears also in Rameau's 'Les Soupirs'—and 'Le Caquet' uses repeated notes and suspensions with piquant effect.

## FRANÇOIS COUPERIN

Titon du Tillet remarks in his *Parnasse françois* (1732) that Dandrieu's *clavecin* pieces are 'assez dans le caractère du fameux François Couperin'. Important as Louis Couperin is in the history of French keyboard music,[7] it is his nephew François (1668–1733) who has justly earned the epithet 'le Grand' and although his compositions for harpsichord are only a part of his considerable output they have probably contributed most to his fame and lasting popularity. He published four *Livres* (1713, 1717, 1722, and 1730), the first containing 5 *ordres*, the second and third 7 each, and the fourth 8, and in 1716 a treatise *L'Art de toucher le clavecin* which also includes eight preludes and an allemande.[8]

Couperin's *ordres*[9] are not suites, though the earlier ones begin with suite-like successions of allemande, two courantes, and one or two other dances. They are collections of pieces, sometimes related in mood or character, generally on a fairly small scale, and with little formal variety, most of them being either in binary or in *rondeau* form. There is much elaborate ornamentation, to the correct rendering of which the composer attached much importance. But the superficial impression of over-precise elegance is misleading. It is inevitable that in so large a mass of work certain moods should recur from time to time; but there is great imaginativeness and subtlety of detail, and sometimes an unexpected breadth and dignity of style. An examination of the first *ordre*, in G minor and major, will reveal a far greater variety of mood than is usually associated with Couperin. It opens with an allemande, followed by two courantes, a sarabande, a gavotte, a gigue and a minuet; after this there is a series of pieces with descriptive titles, including a second sarabande and a second gavotte. The contrast

---

[6] The collections published by Dandrieu in 1724, 1728 and 1734 have been re-published in one volume by P. Aubert and B. François-Sappey (Paris, 1973).

[7] See above, pp. 538 ff.

[8] Printed in *Œuvres complètes de François Couperin*, i, ed. Maurice Cauchie (Paris, 1932); rev. Dart (1968); English translation by Margery Halford (Port Washington, N.Y., 1974).

[9] Ibid., ii, V.

between the two sarabandes is striking. The first, which has the subtitle 'La Majestueuse', is sombre and dignified:

Ex. 319

with a startling dissonance shortly before the end. The second, 'Les Sentiments', in G major, is far more tender and lyrical:

Ex. 320

The following piece, 'La Pastorelle', is a transcription of a song.[10] Some of the movements illustrate Couperin's love for the tenor register of the keyboard, notably 'Les Sylvains' and 'L'Enchanteresse'.

Such titles for *clavecin* pieces were in a tradition going back to Chambonnières and, as we have seen, followed by all his successors. But Couperin's were not merely fanciful or descriptive; they were frequently enigmatic[11] but never meaningless. In the preface to the *Premier Livre* he makes this clear:

J'ay toujours eu un objet en compassant toutes ces pièces: des occasions différentes me l'ont fourni. Ainsi les Titres répondent aux idées que j'ay eues; on me dispensera d'en rendre compte; cependant, comme, parmi ces Titres, il y en a qui semblent me flater, il est bon d'avertir que les pièces qui les portent sont des espèces de portraits qu'on a trouvé

[10] See p. 170 n. 110.
[11] For solutions of many of the enigmas, see Jane Clark, 'Les Folies Francoises', *Early Music*, viii (1980), p. 163.

quelques fois assés ressemblans sous mes doigts, et que la plûpart de ces Titres avantageux sont plutôt donnés aux aimables originaux que j'ay voulu representer, qu'aux copies que j'en ay tirées.

The second *ordre* is similar to the first in general character, though rather less varied. 'La Garnier'[12] is a quietly flowing piece of great distinction, and the closing bars of 'Les Idées heureuses' are worth quoting for their subtle harmonic details:

Ex. 321

The third *ordre*, in C minor, includes the allemande 'Le Ténébreuse' and the sarabande 'La Lugubre'—sombre and impressive pieces in Couperin's grandest manner. Less majestic but equally imaginative is the chaconne in *rondeau* form, 'La Favorite'. 'Les Pélerines' is another song transcription.[13] The fourth *ordre* is of a far lighter character and omits all dances:

'La Marche des Gris-vêtus' (March of the Grey Coats, a French regiment)
'Les Baccanales':
  1ère partie: 'Enjoumens bachiques'
  2e partie: 'Tendresses bachiques'
  3ème partie: 'Fureurs bachiques'

---

[12] 'La Garnier' would seem to be the wife of Gabriel Garnier, one of the organists of the French Chapel Royal; but Wilfrid Mellers, *François Couperin and the French Classical Tradition* (London, 1950), p. 356, suggests that the feminine article in such cases implies 'La [pièce] Garnier', i.e. a portrait of the organist himself.
[13] See p. 170 n. 110.

'La Pateline'[14]
'Le Réveil-matin'

The fifth *ordre* in A major, includes a fine sarabande, 'La Danger-euse', and an allemande bearing the name of a distinguished family 'La Logiviére', perhaps one of his pupils. The second of the two courantes asserts at one point the conflict between threes and sixes common to the French form of this dance:

Ex. 322

The sixth *ordre*, is entirely in B flat, the first in the *Second Livre*, includes four *rondeaux*: the lively 'Les Moissoneurs', 'Le Gazouil-lement', 'Les Baricades mistérieuses' (which is particularly notable for the rich, quasi-contrapuntal keyboard writing and the long-drawn sequence in the last episode), and 'Les Bergeries', characteristic of Couperin in his most elegant vein. Cauchie has identified 'La Bersan' as Suzanne, daughter of the Seigneur de Bersan. In the next *ordre* we have an odd little set of movements called 'Les Petits âges': 'La Muse naissante', 'L'Enfantine', 'L'Adolescent' and 'Les Délices'. The last of these is interpreted in a curiously demure manner, the melody never rising into the treble stave. There are many good things in the eighth *ordre*, among them the opening 'La Raphaèle' with its finely sustained peroration and the sarabande 'L'Unique' with its unexpected interruptions. But all these are overshadowed by the great Passacaille, which is arguably the finest movement that Couperin ever wrote for the harpsichord. It is in

[14] Presumably a reference to the crafty 'hero' of *La Farce de Maître Pathelin* (*c*.1470), which had been adapted as a comedy in 1706.

the form of a spacious *rondeau*, in which a short but impressive main theme is contrasted with very varied episodes. The seventh episode will give some idea of the richness and dignity of the style:

Ex. 323

It is a movement of considerable length and never goes further from its key (B minor) than the relative major, but its rhythmic variety and wealth of detail prevent it from ever becoming monotonous. It is followed by a short piece 'La Marinéte', perhaps a daughter of the composer Jean-Baptiste Marin or Marin himself.

The ninth *ordre* opens with an allemande for two harpsichords. Of the other pieces, 'La Séduisante', another example of a deep-voiced female portrait, is followed by the well-known short *rondeau* 'Le Barolet-flotant'. The tenth *ordre* begins with 'La Triomphante', a set of three pieces separately entitled 'Bruit de guerre' (with a *couplet* marked 'Combat'), 'Allégresse des vainqueurs' and 'Fanfare', probably a *baccanale* rather than a battle,[15] and ends with 'Les Bagatelles', a kind of *moto perpetuo* for a two-manual harpsichord or two separate harpsichords which, as Couperin points out, can equally well be played by two viols, two violins or two flutes. The eleventh *ordre* begins demurely with four female portraits, but ends with a riot of programme music entitled 'Les Fastes de la grande et ancienne Mxnxstrxndxsx', the x's barely concealing the fact that the word is 'Ménestrandise'. This is a satire on the Paris guild of *ménestrels*, bitterly disliked by other musicians on

[15] See Clark, op. cit., p. 164.

account of a royal privilege dating back to 1659. They enter pompously with a march (*Ier Acte*) and are followed by a procession of beggars and hurdy-gurdy players (*Second Acte*), who parody the tune of the march in a transposed version in the minor. After a dance of jugglers, tumblers and mountebanks, complete with bears and monkeys (*Troisième Acte*), we are shown in the *Quatrième Acte* the invalids who have been crippled in the service of the fiddlers; they enter in a limping rhythm:

Ex. 324

Finally in the *Cinquième Acte* everything is thrown into confusion by drunkards, with the assistance of the bears and monkeys. The whole scene is portrayed with remarkable gusto. The remaining *ordre* in this book begins in E major and ends in E minor. It is far more subdued than its predecessor, but is memorable for the grave beauty of the first piece, 'Les Juméles'.

The main feature of the thirteenth *ordre* (the first in Book III), in B minor, is a set of variations called 'Les Folies Françoises, ou les Dominos'. All the variations have descriptive titles such as 'La Virginité sous le Domino couleur d'invisible', 'La Pudeur sous le Domino couleur de Roze', and so on. 'La Coquéterie sous diférens Dominos' is depicted by constant changes of time, 'Les Vieux galans et les Trésorieres suranées sous des Dominos Pourpres et feuilles mortes' by a pompous rhythm, and 'Les Coucous Bénévoles sous des Dominos jaunes' by a figure which begins by imitating the bird but soon stretches to a wider range. The final variation, 'La Frénésie, ou le Désespoir sous le Domino noir', is followed by the remarkably poignant 'L'Âme-en-peine'. The earlier part of the fourteenth *ordre* is concerned with a series of bird sketches, of which the most distinguished are 'Le Rossignol-en-amour'—Couperin remarks that this 'reussit sur la Flute Traversiere on ne peut pas mieux, quand il est bien joué'—and 'Les Fauvétes Plaintives', a very gentle representation of warblers. There is also another piece for two harpsichords, 'La Julliet', like 'Les Bagatelles' in the tenth *ordre*—what Couperin calls a *pièce-croisée*. The fifteenth *ordre* is remarkable for its variety. A dignified portrait of 'La Régente, ou la Minerve' is followed by 'Le Dodo ou L'Amour au berceau', another *pièce-croisée*, in which a traditional nursery tune, also used by later French composers, is made to assume an air of eighteenth-century graciousness. As in so many of Couperin's harpsichord works this piece never rises above the middle register of the key-board. Several other pieces in the same *ordre* show a similar preoccupation with the sombre colouring that can be obtained from the lower octaves of the instrument. Drone basses figure prominently in this *ordre*. Both the musettes have one, and there is another in the second part of 'Les Vergers fleuris', marked 'dans le goût de Cornemuse' (in the style of a bagpipe). The most striking feature of the sixteenth *ordre* is 'La Distraite', particularly as it comes immediately after the robust humour of 'Le Drôle de corps'. 'Les Petits Moulins à Vent' and 'Les Timbres' in the seventeenth *ordre* are pretty exercises in tone-painting. The eighteenth is distinguished chiefly by the Allemande 'La Verneuil' and 'L'Atendris sante'. The latter has a surprising harmonic quirk in the closing bars, where the ear expects to hear A flat, not A natural:

Ex. 325

The moods of the nineteenth *ordre* range from the acrobatic humour of 'Les Culbutes Jxcxbxnxs' (Jacobin friars) to the pathos of 'La Muse-Plantine' (perhaps the harpsichordist, Mme. de la Plante).[16]

In a note prefixed to his *Quatrième Livre* (1730) Couperin explains that he had completed the pieces about three years earlier but increasing ill-health had obliged him almost to give up work. The twentieth *ordre* opens with 'La Princesse Marie', that is Marie Leszczyńska, wife of Louis XV, and the piece ends with an 'Air dans le goût polonois'. The fourth piece, 'La Croûilli ou La Couperinéte', which has an optional viol part in its second section, is presumably a portrait of his second daughter. The very tender 'La Reine des cœurs' of the twenty-first *ordre* is probably another family portrait, as is certainly 'La Couperin'; marked 'D'une vivacité moderée', its style, so nearly akin to Bach, suggests that she was a musician. The twenty-second *ordre* opens brilliantly with 'Le Trophée' and the amusing 'L'Anguille' is almost equally lively, and the twenty-third includes some vivid character sketches, such as 'Les Tricoteuses'—which ends humorously with 'loose stitches' (maîlles-lâchées)—'L'Arlequine' (grotesquement) and 'Les Satires Chevre-pieds' with a second part *dans un goût burlesque*. The twenty-fourth *ordre*, which is one of the most interesting, contains a large number of movements that are very varied in character. It opens with the 'grave and noble' saraband 'Les vieux seigneurs'; 'Les jeunes seigneurs', who follow, are lively but less distinguished. The first part of 'Les Guirlandes' is notable for its persistent rhythm and unusual design; it is akin to a *rondeau* but not strictly a *rondeau* in form. The four *parties* of 'Les Brinborions' are, as their title suggests, amusing trifles. Very different in character is the long-sustained 'L'Amphibie', *mouvement de Passacaille*, with which the *ordre* ends. This has not quite the richness or the intensity of the B minor Passacaille, but is remarkable for the abundance and variety of its ideas, its admirably balanced design, and particularly the very effective return of the first theme.

There are also striking things in the twenty-fifth *ordre*. The first piece, 'La Visionaire', is in the form of a French opera overture, with an imposing introduction:

---

[16] Ibid.

Ex. 326

and an almost Handelian Allegro section:

Ex. 327

'Les Ombres errantes' is notable for delicately expressive harmony, resulting largely from suspensions.

The two remaining *ordres* contain less that is remarkable, though they both open with finely sustained allemandes. 'La Pantomime', from the twenty-sixth *ordre*, looks back to some of the earlier character pieces, and 'Les Pavots', from the twenty-seventh, has some unusual five-bar phrases at the beginning of the second section. In the later *ordres* there are fewer movements in the traditional dance forms, and the overall structure is sometimes unusual. On the whole, however, there is no noticeable change of outlook. The melodious grace of the more lyrical pieces is immediately apparent; but there are other qualities, less obvious perhaps but equally valuable. Couperin's mastery can be seen in the gradual increase of intensity that is found in so many of the binary movements as the second section draws to its close. This produces an effect of sustained, cumulative emotion which inevitably makes one think of Bach; indeed it is remarkable how closely Couperin's best work does often approach Bach's in spirit.

### RAMEAU

The *clavecin* works of Rameau (1683–1764)[17] have been said to represent 'a later stage than Couperin in the growth of French keyboard music',[18] and this is broadly true although his *Premier Livre de Pièces de Clavecin* was actually published in 1706, seven years before Couperin's. It is virtually a loose suite in A minor, beginning with a prelude of the partly unbarred type common in the works of Louis Couperin and others. There are two contrasted allemandes, the first deliberately flowing, the second brisker and more dance-like type. The courante is in the ambiguous triple time with which this dance was usually associated in France. The only non-dance movement is entitled 'Venitienne'. At the time when these pieces were published Rameau was still a young man and it is hardly surprising that they do not strike a very individual note. Even his second set, *Pièces de clavecin, avec une méthode pour la mechanique des doigts* (1724; rev. 1731), predates all the music by which he is best known. Here, after an introductory minuet which is merely an exercise, we have two groups of pieces—one in E minor and major, the other in D minor and major. The E minor 'Tambourin' is familiar even to those who know nothing else of Rameau's music, but equally characteristic are 'Le Rappel des oiseaux' and 'La Villageoise', both of which manage to suggest their titles without caricaturing, and the delightful 'Musette en rondeau':

Ex. 328

It is the pieces in *rondeau* form that give most scope to Rameau's melodic gift, which, if less elegant than Couperin's, is often simpler

[17] Modern ed. by Erwin R. Jacobi (Kassel, 1961).
[18] Cuthbert Girdlestone, *Jean-Philippe Rameau: His Life and Work* (London, 1957), p. 16.

and more direct. Side by side with purely lyrical pieces like
'L'Entretien des Muses'[19] we have the curiously laconic little
minuet 'Le Lardon', on which in 1903 Dukas was to compose a
monumental set of piano variations, and 'Les Cyclopes', a broadly
designed *rondeau* which has something of Domenico Scarlatti's
brilliance and includes some angry explosions.

Rameau's third book, *Nouvelles suites de pièces de clavecin*,
appeared *c.*1728. Like the second, it can be divided into two
groups, each centring on a single key. The movements in dance
form include a sarabande of great beauty and dignity, a pair of
minuets, the first of which was used in the prologue to *Castor et
Pollux* (1737) and 'Fanfarinette', a frivolous piece in the rhythm of
a gigue. Others show Rameau's increased interest in the possibilities of the keyboard, particularly the A minor gavotte with
variations, 'L'Égyptienne' and 'Les Trois mains'—an ingenious
piece of two-part writing in which the left hand is continually crossing over the right so as to create the illusion of a third part. Very
different in character is 'Les Triolets', with its delicate colouring
and fluid rhythms. The robust humour of 'La Poule' is well known,
but more subtle is 'L'Enharmonique', where patches of expressive
chromaticism:

Ex. 329

alternate with diatonic passages directed to be played 'hardiment,
sans altérer la mesure'.

The last significant composer of French keyboard music in this
period was a disciple of Rameau, Jacques Duphly (1715–89) who
published collections in 1744, 1748, 1758, and 1768.[20]

---

[19] Like the 'Tambourin' and 'Musette en rondeau', this was orchestrated by Rameau in
his ballet *Les Festes d'Hébé* (1739). A number of the pieces were published *en concerts* with
parts for one or two strings. Conversely Rameau published *c.*1735 keyboard transcriptions
of the instrumental music in *Les Indes galantes*; see Graham Sadler's study in *Early Music*,
vii (1979), p. 18.
[20] Modern edition by Françoise Petit (Paris, 1967).

ITALY

In Italy the heirs of Pasquini[21] were the Sienese Azzolino Bernardino Della Ciaja (1671–1755) and a group of younger contemporaries: the Neapolitans Domenico Scarlatti (1685–1757), son of Alessandro, and the church-composer Francesco Durante (1684–1755), the Tuscans Lodovico Giustini (1685–1743) and Domenico Zipoli (1688–1726), and a Venetian, Benedetto Marcello (1686–1739). Although Scarlatti was by far the most important, he was the last to enter the field and Marcello, better known for his oratorios and religious music and his satire *Il teatro alla moda*, may be said not to have entered it at all since his *Suonate per il cembalo*, probably written between 1710 and 1720 were never published in his lifetime.[22] He is heard at his best in the Largo which opens his ninth sonata:

Ex. 330

Zipoli, a more accomplished technician, published at Rome in 1716 *Sonate d'intavolatura per organo, e cimbalo*,[23] and then went to South America as a Jesuit missionary. His collection is in two parts, the first made up of versets and liturgical music for organ, the second of suites and partitas for harpsichord—each suite consisting of a *preludio* followed by three or four dances, *allemande, correnti, gighe, gavotte*. The *preludio* of the second suite, in G minor, is typical of his full, well-wrought textures:

[21] On Pasquini see Vol. IV, p. 641, n.1.

[22] Ed. *Le Pupitre*, xxviii (Paris, 1971), And see William S. Newman, 'The Keyboard Sonatas of Benedetto Marcello', *Acta Musicologica*, xxix (1957), p. 28, with thematic index, and xxxi (1959), p. 192; and *The Sonata in the Baroque Era* (Chapel Hill, 1959; rev. 1966), pp. 174 ff.

[23] Ed. Luigi Tagliavini (Heidelberg, 1959).

Ex. 331

Invention of a very different kind characterizes Della Ciaja's *Sonate per cembalo* (Rome, c.1727).[24] The first two movements of each sonata are a toccata and a fugal canzone;[25] these excerpts are from Sonata II:

Ex. 332
(i)

[24] Nos. 1–3, ed. Giuseppe Buonamici (Florence, 1912).
[25] See Adolf Sandberger, *Ausgewählte Aufsätze zur Musikgeschichte* (Munich, 1921), pp. 175 ff.

(ii)

In each Sonata the shorter third and fourth movements are marked 'Tempo I' and 'Tempo II'.

In strong contrast are the transparent elegance and neat but facile sequences of Durante, who published *Sei Sonate per cembalo divisi in studi e divertimenti* (Naples, *c*.1732)[26] and left *Toccate per il Cembalo solo*[27] and other pieces in manuscript. The sonatas are two-movement works, each *studio* being followed by a *divertimento*. *Studi* 3 and 5 are marked *fuga* but no. 4 is more typical:

[26] Ed. Bernhard Paumgartner (Kassel and Basel, 1949).
[27] Ed. Guido Pannain (Milan, 1932).

Ex. 333

Lodovico Giustini, probably an amateur, has only one claim to distinction—he published the earliest music specifically for the pianoforte: *Sonate da cimbalo di piano e forte detto volgarmente di martelletti*, Op. 1 (Florence, 1732).[28] Beyond the close juxtaposition of different dynamic markings, as in this passage from the curious *gavotta* of his tenth sonata:

Ex. 334

[28] Complete facsimile edition by Rosamond Harding (Cambridge, 1933). See Harding, 'The Earliest Pianoforte Music', *Music & Letters*, xiii (1932), p. 195, and A. B. Caselli, 'Le "Sonate da cimbalo di piano, e forte" di Lodovico Giustini', *Nuova rivista musicale italiana*, xii (1978), p. 34.

Giustini's music is of little interest.

## SCARLATTI

Unlike these composers, Domenico Scarlatti was extraordinarily prolific. He had composed fourteen operas and numerous cantatas and *serenate* before going to Portugal in 1720, first as master of the royal chapel, then as music-master to the king's daughter who in 1729 married the future Ferdinand VI of Spain. The princess was a particularly gifted harpsichordist and Scarlatti's 550 or more harpsichord pieces seem to have been the fruit of this master-pupil relationship; all the later ones are said to have been composed expressly for her. They were certainly influenced by the country of her adoption. The musical traditions of Spain are closely connected with the rhythms of the dance, the background to which is the guitar, whose incisive tone-colour undoubtedly contributed much to the formation of Scarlatti's style.[29] It could be vividly suggested by the harpsichord, which had little capacity for sustaining a broad and simple melodic line but could produce a strongly rhythmical and percussive sonority. Many of the characteristics of Scarlatti's music which make it sound different from that of his contemporaries can be explained by his Spanish surroundings and by the peculiar nature of his approach to composition.

A short analysis of his D major sonata (K 29)[30] will illustrate some of his most characteristic traits. The opening is simply a brilliant flourish, which has no thematic importance but may well have served the purpose of loosening the performer's fingers and perhaps interrupting the conversation of the audience:

---

[29] See Jane Clark, 'Domenico Scarlatti and Spanish folk music', *Early Music*, iv (1976), p. 19.

[30] K = the classification in Ralph Kirkpatrick, *Domenico Scarlatti* (Princeton, 1953; rev. ed. 1968). Complete edition by Kenneth Gilbert (Paris, 1971–8). Kirkpatrick has edited a selection of 60 sonatas (New York, 1953).

Ex. 335

In a few bars it draws to a half close and gives place to a mass of new material, announced in the key of the dominant:

Ex. 336

The term 'second subject', which later textbooks would have applied to this, is far from adequate in view of its length and importance. Beginning with a brief reference to the opening, it expands into a wealth of very lively and effective passage work, full of original and characteristic keyboard writing. This, however, is twice interrupted by a more lyrical phrase:

Ex. 337

which provides a strong contrast in mood and texture. In the second half of the piece a few bars of rather perfunctory development lead to a recapitulation in the tonic of nearly all the material that was announced in the tonic in the first half.

There is much in this scheme that is not only very characteristic of Scarlatti himself but could also be regarded as prophetic of later stages in the development of the sonata. The theme which has just been quoted makes a more vivid contrast with its surroundings than would be found in a binary movement by any other composer of the period. The major and minor tonalities were still comparatively young, and contrasts of mood associated with them were by no means taken for granted as they were in later years, but in this sonata, and in many others by Scarlatti, a sudden digression to a minor key—usually at this stage in a movement—suggests a touch of pathos that is particularly effective against the glittering brightness of its surroundings. Furthermore, the striking contrasts of mood to be found in the first half of so many of Scarlatti's sonatas make it natural and desirable that a considerable proportion of them should be recapitulated in the second. There is also a much stronger emphasis on tonality than in the more continuous and polyphonic music of the period. The opening bars of a sonata are often built round the notes of the tonic chord in a manner which is more common in the latter half of the century:

Ex. 338

Towards the end of each half it is common to find passages consisting of a short phrase, often built entirely on tonic and dominant harmony, reiterated several times and leading eventually to a well-marked cadence, after which the whole passage may be repeated note for note. Often the effect of this is to suggest a cheerful and argumentative insistence but sometimes, when the music is in a minor key, passages of this kind may have an unexpected pathos, particularly when the reiterated phrase is built, not on tonic and dominant, but on dominant and subdominant harmonies, as in the following examples:

Ex. 339

The first of these shows how little Scarlatti was worried by consecutive fifths. The colouring of both examples is strongly suggestive of the Phrygian mode, which has been a characteristic of
Spanish music from the sixteenth century to the present day. In the
second example the exotic effect is emphasized by the curious dissonance in the second bar, which may be compared with the
similar, though less aggressive, instance in Ex. 337. Harmonic
clashes of this kind often occur in Scarlatti's music; they are, in
fact, written out examples of the acciaccatura, the dissonant grace
note being struck (literally 'crushed') at the same time as the chord
which it decorates. In their simplest form they appear in places
where a chord like

Ex. 340

is used instead of an expected major or minor triad: there is an
admirable example in the exhilarating C major sonata (K 487):

Ex. 341

Such sounds must have been familiar to Scarlatti as he listened to
guitar-players tuning their instruments. Thanks to the percussive
quality of the harpsichord he could use them with energy, and
sometimes, as in the D major sonata (K 119), in a ferocious
manner. Sometimes, too, not only the harmony but also the figuration vividly suggests the guitar:

Ex. 342

Often, as might be expected, original harmonic effects arise from
the persistence of pedal notes, either in the bass or in an inner
part, e.g.:

Ex. 343

Later in the same sonata Scarlatti amuses himself by repeating an
insignificant phrase of two notes nine times against a similar
rhythmic background, with a new harmony each time. Persistent
rhythms of this kind emphasize his essentially instrumental
approach to music: his E major sonata (K 380) contains passages of
this kind built on a rhythm commonly associated with the *bolero*:

Ex. 344

Scarlatti's harmonic adventurousness is shown not only by his use of dissonance but by his remarkable range of modulation. The rich and concentrated chromaticism, sometimes temporarily obscuring the tonality, which gives so personal a flavour to Bach's music, hardly ever appears here, for mystery did not appeal to Scarlatti's Latin temperament. But though the tonality is always perfectly clear, it often makes the most surprising digressions. The development at the beginning of the second half of a sonata may lead to very remote keys, and sometimes in the first half the music may go from tonic to dominant by a roundabout route. The choice of complementary key is sometimes unusual—for instance, the relative or mediant minor. Although binary form is prevalent, the treatment is very varied: the opening phrase may count for everything or nothing. The recapitulation, too, is sometimes remarkably free, and there are one or two sonatas, e.g. the E major sonata (K 162), which have themes in strongly contrasted tempi. In the sonatas in D major (K 214) and B flat major (K 202) the second section begins with a completely independent episode, in both cases with results which involve adventurous modulation. In a few cases binary form is abandoned altogether: the sonata in G major (K 284) might almost be called a *rondeau*, and the A minor sonata (K 61) is a set of variations. There are several fugues: one in C minor (K 58) has a chromatic subject and an almost Bach-like texture:

Ex. 345

(i)          Subject:

The slow sonatas vary considerably in character. Some are buil
on very simple themes of a popular nature:

Ex. 346

Others are more suggestive of Italian opera; he had composec
fourteen of them in his earlier years and would have had difficulty
in escaping their influence in Spain.[31] Some of these are rathei
insipid; but the F minor sonata (K 481) has great beauty anc
pathos, the E major (K 206) a surprising harmonic scheme:

Ex. 347

<hr>

[31] See Vol. V, p. 165.

and the sonatas in D major (K 277) and A major (K 208) an almost
Mozartean tenderness. Still more striking are certain other slow
movements, notably those in B minor (K 87) and D minor (K 52),
which show the composer in quite a different light. Here the
texture is far more contrapuntal and continuous, and though both
sonatas are divided into the usual two sections there is a regular
recapitulation. Both are of magnificent quality, with a depth of
emotion far removed from the popular conception of Scarlatti as a
brilliant but shallow virtuoso. His old trick of repeating a short
phrase is still in evidence:

Ex. 348

but of his interest in brilliant keyboard effects there is not a trace.
With these two masterpieces may also be classed the sonatas in D
minor (K 92) and F minor (K 69).

Isolated at the Spanish court during his later years, Scarlatti
seems to have exercised no influence on his younger compatriots:
Platti, G. B. ('Padre') Martini, Galuppi, Paradisi.[32] And there is
not much evidence of it in the harpsichord sonatas of his
Portuguese colleague Carlos de Seixas (1704–42)[33] though more in
those of his Spanish pupil, Antonio Soler (1729–83).[34] But he had
champions in England, notably Thomas Roseingrave (1688–1766)
who had been a personal friend of Scarlatti's in Italy and published
in 1728 *Voluntaries and fugues made on purpose for the organ or*

[32] On these composers see Vol. VII, pp. 574–7 and 581.
[33] Ed. Santiago Kastner, *Portugaliae Musica*, x (Lisbon, 1965).
[34] On Soler, see Vol. VII, p. 579.

*harpsichord* marked by Scarlattian traits. It was probably Roseingrave who instigated the publication of thirty *Essercizi per Gravicembalo* (London, 1738), apparently the earliest printed edition of Scarlatti, and it was certainly he who was responsible for the revised and enlarged edition—*XLII Suites de Pieces Pour le Clavecin*—of the following year. But it was Joseph Kelway (*c*.1702–82)[35] who was described by Burney[36] as 'the head of the Scarlatti sect in London'. However, English composers for the harpsichord had another model before their eyes.

## HANDEL

Although Handel's main activities were in other fields, his harpsichord music is by no means negligible. Of the two collections of suites that were published in his lifetime the first is the more important. Handel issued it in 1720 because, as he says in a foreword, 'surrepticious and incorrect copies . . . . had got abroad'. An incomplete copy of an earlier, and obviously pirated, edition does in fact survive in the Bodleian Library at Oxford;[37] the contents are not exactly the same as in Handel's authorized edition. In the absence of any copyright law the least he could do was to make a slightly different selection. Handel's title is *Suites de Pieces*, but as with other titles used by composers at this period it does not accurately describe the contents. Two of the suites, nos. 1 and 4, consist wholly of dance movements preceded by a prelude; nos. 3, 5, 7 and 8 are mixed; no. 6 has only one dance movement; and no. 2 consists simply of Adagio-Allegro-Adagio-Allegro: in other words, it is a sonata. Two of the suites (nos. 3 and 5) include an air with variations and one of them (no. 7) begins with a French overture. The allemandes are intimate and polished pieces which represent an unfamiliar side of Handel. The courantes have neither the elaborate cross-rhythms of the French type nor the *bravura* character of the Italian; they are altogether simpler and, in spite of their name, should certainly not be played too fast. The sarabandes are less complex than Bach's, but often have beauty of a simple and unassuming kind, e.g. the one in Suite no. 4, which has close affinities with the style of Handel's slow arias:

---

[35] See Vol. VII, p. 580.
[36] *A General History of Music from the Earliest Ages to the Present Period*, iv (1789), p. 665.
[37] Published by Jeanne Roger, Amsterdam, presumably in 1719.

Ex. 349

Of the lively gigues, the one in F minor (Suite no. 8) begins with a fugato which is inverted in the second half, as often happens in Bach. Fugues also appear among the 'neutral' movements. The E minor one (Suite no. 4) is based on one of those apparently intractable subjects to which Handel was addicted, perhaps because of the challenge which they offered to his invention:

Ex. 350

Other striking movements are the slow and heavily ornamented Adagio which opens Suite no. 2 (a worthy companion to the slow movement of Bach's Italian Concerto), the bustling Allegro which follows it, rather like the solo sections of a concerto without the orchestral ritornello, the sombre F minor prelude of Suite no. 8, and the Passacaglia of Suite no. 7. There are some interesting examples of thematic connection between movements similar to those to be found in some of Kuhnau's suites[38]—a curiously old-fashioned device at the time when Handel was writing. Thus the allemande, courante, and gigue of Suite no. 1 all end with the same cadential figure; the Andante and Allegro of no. 7 begin with slightly different versions of the same melody; and there is a close relationship between the openings of the allemande and courante of no. 4. Furthermore the allemande and courante of no. 5 both proceed to the dominant by the same rather unusual harmonic progression, and in both there is a place in the second half where the music seems for a moment to anticipate the first variation on the air known as 'The harmonious blacksmith':

Ex. 351

The second set of suites, published in 1733, is on the whole of less interest. The most remarkable piece is no. 6 in G minor, consisting of three spaciously designed movements, of which the courante is a variant of the allemande, and the gigue is the longest and most exuberant of Handel's movements in this form. Thematic connections are also found in both the D minor suites (nos. 3 and 4). Of the two chaconnes in G major the second (no. 9) which has 62 variations, is a monument of dullness: the first (no. 2), with a mere 22 variations, is on a higher level. In addition to these collections a large number of other harpsichord pieces have been published during the last two centuries.[39] Particular mention may be made of a little three-movement suite in C minor, a sarabande in E major which has a strong resemblance to the third movement of the *concerto grosso* in B minor (Op. 6, no. 12), a sonata for a two-manual harpsichord, and an extended chaconne in C major with some chromatic variations. But the finest of all Handel's keyboard works are undoubtedly the *Six Fugues or Voluntarys for the Organ or Harpsichord* (1735). Like all Handel's best fugues they have striking and original subjects. The first, in G minor, is a double fugue of great dignity which was later used, in a more aggressive form, for the chorus 'He smote all the first-born of Egypt' in *Israel in Egypt*. The third, in B flat major, occurs in the overture to the setting of Brockes' *Passion* (1717), from which presumably it was taken. The second and fourth are rather less successful: they are vigorous enough but rather too long, and the sequences are apt to become mechanical. On the other hand, in the sixth fugue, in C minor, which also appears in the trio sonata in G minor, Op. 5, no. 5 (1739) these have great nobility:

Ex. 352

Most striking of all is the fifth, in A minor:

Ex. 353

which shows how skilfully Handel could use a colour more sombre and chromatic than was his custom. He could hardly have chosen anything more appropriate for the chorus 'They loathed to drink of the river' in *Israel in Egypt*.

[39] See the *Gesamtausgabe der Klavierwerke G. F. Händels*, ed. Walter Serauky and F. von Glasenapp (Halle, 1951), and *Hallische Händel-Ausgabe*, iv, 1, 5, 6, 17, ed. R. Steglich *et al.* (Kassel, 1955–75).

Handel was a fine performer on the harpsichord, but his music for it does not suggest that the actual sound of the instrument was as strong a stimulus to him as it was to Scarlatti. It is perhaps significant that when he is most preoccupied with virtuosity, as in most of the variations and some of the more improvisatory of the preludes in the suites, his music is most empty. Generally speaking, the finest movements are those that are least obviously keyboard music; it is not surprising that several of the six fugues—and the best—were very successfully arranged by the composer himself for other media.

### HANDEL'S CONTEMPORARIES

Of Handel's German contemporaries, besides Bach, both Johann Mattheson (1681–1764) and Gottlieb Muffat (1690–1770), son of Georg Muffat, wrote suites for the harpsichord. Mattheson's appeared in two editions, both published in London in 1714, the first with the German title *Harmonisches Denckmahl*, the second called simply *Pièces de clavecin*. He also published two sets of *Wolklingende Finger-Sprache in Zwölff Fugen* (Hamburg, 1735 and 1737) and re-issued these also with a French title, *Les Doits parlants* (Nuremberg, 1749). They are fluent and ably written works but do not show any marked individuality. Muffat's *Componimenti Musicali per il Cembalo* (Augsburg, 1736)[40] have considerably more character. Handel thought sufficiently well of them to borrow extensively from them. A comparison between the Adagio section of the Fantaisie which opens Muffat's sixth suite and the tenor solo 'When Nature underneath a heap of jarring atoms lay' in Handel's *Ode for St. Cecilia's Day* (1739):

Ex. 354
(i) MUFFAT

[40] Printed in *Denkmäler der Tonkunst in Österreich*, vol. vii, Jg.3(3), ed. Guido Adler (Vienna, 1896; reprint ed. Graz, 1959). See Susan Wollenberg, 'The Keyboard Suites of Gottlieb Muffat (1690–1770)', *Proceedings of the Royal Musical Association*, cii (1975–6), p. 83.

(ii) HANDEL

will show how Handel has copied the outlines of Muffat's passage, making the harmony move at half the pace, scored it for orchestra, added a voice part, and perpetrated a very skilful and artistic piece of burglary. Similarly the march in *Joshua* (1747) is borrowed from the *rigaudon* in Muffat's first suite, and the introduction to Part I from the Adagio of the same suite; there are several other instances.[41] Muffat's suites combine a German richness and solidity of texture with a melodiousness that sometimes suggests Italian in-

[41] See Sedley Taylor, *The Indebtedness of Handel to Works of other Composers* (Cambridge, 1906), pp. 1–14.

fluence. They all include a substantial number of movements, some of which have fanciful titles such as 'La Hardiesse' and 'La Coquette'. 'La Hardiesse' (from the fourth suite) is a lively and wayward piece; its opening phrase bears a striking resemblance to the bourrée in Handel's B flat organ concerto, Op. 7, no. 1.

There is a considerable variety of style in Muffat's work. Sometimes we seem almost to be in the world of Haydn, e.g. the finale of the third suite:

Ex. 355

At other times, particularly in the sarabandes, there is a wealth of intimate detail which recalls the keyboard music of Bach, e.g. the sarabande from the same suite:

Ex. 356

The courantes are mostly of the Italian type, with many rapid passages. On the other hand several of the opening movements of the first suite have stately introductions in the style of the French overture. The six suites are followed by a chaconne in G major with variations, similar to Handel's two and certainly superior to his second and longer example. Muffat was, like Handel, thoroughly cosmopolitan. His fugues are not as compelling as those in Handel's suites, but in general the texture is more substantial and more varied.

Apart from the work of the most distinguished composers, the first half of the eighteenth century produced a vast amount of agreeable keyboard music without strongly marked individuality. The style of Couperin at his simplest is recalled in the *Six Suittes de clavessin* (Amsterdam, 1701)[42] by Charles Dieupart (d. 1740), a French composer who spent most of his life in England. Like Rameau in his *Pièces de clavecin en concerts*[43] he made his pieces available also as chamber music by adding a part for violin or flute. Bach evidently admired Dieupart's work since he made a copy of two of the suites and in the prelude of the first of his *Suites anglaises* (in A major) borrowed an idea from the gigue in Dieupart's no. 1 in the same key (see Ex. 369). Couperin's more ornate, courtly manner reappears in some of the movements in the *Pièces de clavecin* (Brussels, 1730) by Joseph-Hector Fiocco (1703–41),[44] the son of an Italian father who had settled in Brussels before the end of the seventeenth century. Fiocco's work also betrays the influence of Handel. The final movement of his first suite, in G major, recalls Handel's keyboard writing at its emptiest, and earlier in the same suite we have an Adagio and Allegro which are remarkably like the first two movements of Handel's suite in F major: in both cases the slow movement is more distinguished in quality than the quick one. Fiocco's movements are for the most part in binary or *rondeau* form, but the Allegro just mentioned is in the form of a *da capo* aria, as in the preludes of most of Bach's *Suites anglaises*. This principle is used with curious results in *Fantaisies pour le clavessin: 3 Douzaines* (Hamburg, 1733) by Georg Philipp Telemann (1681–1767).[45] Each set contains twelve pieces, and in all of them each odd-numbered fantasia is directed to be repeated after its successor, i.e. no. 1 is repeated after no. 2, and so on. The fantasias of the first and third sets each have two movements, the first of which is repeated after the second. In the second set the repetition of the first movement is followed by a third movement of a lively and popular character. The movements

---

[42] Modern ed. by Brunold (Paris, 1934).
[43] See p. 446.
[44] Ed. Watelet, *Monumenta Musicae Belgicae*, iii (Antwerp, 1936).
[45] Ed. Seiffert (Frankfurt, 1923; reprinted New York, n.d.).

are usually in a simple binary form, though often without any double bar in the middle, or else in the *da capo* form, a form which seems to have had a particular fascination for Telemann. The textures are very slight, being mainly in two parts; but the themes are often robust in character and sometimes, e.g. in the third movement of no. 9 of the second set:

Ex. 357

or the third movement of no. 6 of the same set:

Ex. 358

frankly popular.

Telemann also published *XX kleine Fugen so wohl auf der Orgel, als auf dem Claviere zu spielen* (Hamburg, 1731),[46] six *Fugues légères* (Hamburg, c.1738),[47] and other pieces for the amateur. But his most important keyboard works are his *VI Ouvertüren nebst zween Folgesätzen bey jedweder, Französisch, Polnisch oder sonst tändelnd, und Welsch* (Nuremberg, c.1745)[48] and other overtures and concertos for solo harpsichord. The overtures are typical 'French overtures'—fugal *allegro* introduced and concluded by a *grave* in dotted rhythm, with a suite of dances (e.g. courante, two rigaudons, and a hornpipe)—and may well have been suggested by Bach's *Overture nach Französischer Art* (BWV 831) in the Second Part of his *Clavier Übung* (Nuremberg, 1735) (see p. 634). Similarly Telemann's concerto in B minor[49] may be regarded as a reply to the challenge of Bach's *Concerto nach Italienischen Gust* (BWV 971) which follows the overture in the *Clavier Übung*. The opening of Telemann's finale shows how he contrasts 'tutti' and 'solo':

[46] Ed. W. Upmeyer, *Nagels Musikarchiv,* no. xiii (Hanover, 1928).
[47] Ed. Martin Lange (Kassel, 1929).
[48] Ed. F. Oberdörffer, *Deutsche Klaviermusik der 17. und 18 Jahrhunderts,* iv–v (Berlin, 1940).
[49] Ed. Werner Danckert, *Unbekannte Meisterwerke der Klaviermusik* (Kassel, 1930).

Ex. 359

Another composer of the same generation, Christoph Graupner (1683–1760), was, like Telemann, enormously prolific in other fields, and also like Telemann produced harpsichord music for amateurs and beginners: *Monatliche Clavier-Früchte, bestehend in Praeludien, Allemanden, Couranten, Sarabanden, Menuetten, Giguen etc.* (Darmstadt, 1722) for beginners,[50] and *Vier Partien auf das Clavier, unter der Benennung der Vier Jahreszeiten Winter, Frühling, Sommer, Herbst*, also consisting of dances and non-programmatic pieces (Darmstadt, 1733) for amateurs.

## SUITE AND SONATA

In the *Eight Sonatas or Lessons for the Harpsichord* (1756)[51] by Thomas Augustine Arne (1710–78) the binary movements mark an interesting stage in the development of the sonata. In general they have much in common with Bach's or Scarlatti's but with the important difference that towards the end of the second half the opening theme returns to the tonic. Examples of this in the older composers are not unknown, e.g. Scarlatti's C major sonata (K

[50] No. 1, 'Januarius', ed. A Küster (Wolfenbüttel, 1928).
[51] See Vol. VII, p. 580.

159) and the D major prelude in the second book of Bach's *Das wohltemperirte Clavier*, but they are by no means common.[52] Arne's fourth sonata, which is his finest, contains a fugue which is more consistently contrapuntal than the average keyboard fugue of the period. Some of Scarlatti's fugues, e.g. the D minor (K 417), tend to become less and less fugal as they proceed, and this is still more true of those by composers such as Durante and Dell Ciaja, which often employ a brilliant but wholly uncontrapuntal figuration.

Until well into the eighteenth century the suite and the sonata had continued to exist side by side, with varying results. Before long the form of the sonata became more clearly defined than it had been, for example, in the works of Kuhnau.[53] But the familiar four-movement scheme, alternating quick and slow movements, is far less common in keyboard music than in the sonata for strings and continuo. In binary movements the recapitulation of the first theme in the tonic, already noticed in Arne's sonatas, becomes more common. Generally speaking the keyboard sonatas of this period illustrate the gradual turning away from a contrapuntal texture to the elegant, stylized melodic idiom which eventually found its fullest expression in the music of Haydn and Mozart. The most important ot these transitional works were written by Bach's sons.[54] Meanwhile the suite was continuing on more conservative lines, but with considerable vitality. Those by Roseingrave have points of interest but have none of the strange and sometimes tortured chromaticism of some of his already mentioned fugues and voluntaries. The Swedish composer Johan Joachim Agrell (1701–85) sometimes employs a compromise between the sonata and the suite, the usual sonata movements being followed by short dance movements. As a rule virtuosity does not play much part in any of these works, except in the so-called *Suits of the Most Celebrated Lessons* (1717) by William Babell (*c*.1690–1723), which consist mainly of extravagantly florid transcriptions of operatic arias.

BACH'S VARIATIONS

Attempts have been made to divide J. S. Bach's keyboard works, other than those for organ, into two groups—those written for the harpsichord and those written for the clavichord—but the distinction, even if valid, is of minor importance. Combining all the finest qualities of the German temperament with a strong vein of

[52] For another example see Handel's D major concerto, Op. 6, no. 5, mentioned on p. 262.
[53] See pp. 568 and 570.
[54] See Vol. VII, pp. 581–96.

eclecticism, he was able to evolve an idiom that was unlimited in its power of destroying the barriers between vocal and instrumental, harmonic and contrapuntal, ecclesiastical and secular. He was always ready to adapt his works for a different medium. The most definite statement that can be made about his keyboard music is that the more massive works, which show the more obvious concern for instrumental effect, must be played on a two-manual harpsichord. Bach himself must have realized that the clavichord, for all its delicate beauty of tone, would be audible only in a small room.

It may be convenient to consider first those works which may have been intended for public performance and to discuss later those of a more intimate character. The form that lent itself most readily to the display of virtuosity was the air with variations. Rameau's well-known Gavotte in A minor[55] is a good example of the average treatment of the form at this period—a lively and vigorous piece which shows considerable inventiveness in exploiting the characteristics of the instrument, but little subtlety or variety of treatment.Couperin's 'Les Folies françoises',[56] intimate and fanciful, are superior in this respect, as Handel's are not. There is little deviation in Handel's variations, either in harmony or in melody, from the outline of the theme, except occasionally in the Passacaglia of the G minor suite (1720, no. 7), and it is not unfair to say that, after hearing the opening bars of each variation, it is generally fairly easy to predict what will follow.

Of Bach's three sets of variations the 'Aria variata alla maniera italiana' in A minor (c.1709, BWV 989)[57] is unpretentious and slight in texture, but its methods are a decided advance on Handel's. Instead of taking some rather obvious figure and working it through a variation without any attempt at melodic continuity, Bach gives to several of his variations individual melodic lines. The figuration is generally more inventive, and there are occasional unexpected touches, such as the sudden outburst of triplets for one bar only in the third variation:

[55] See above, p. 603.
[56] *Ordre* no. 13.
[57] BWV = Wolfgang Schmieder, *Bach-Werke-Verzeichnis* (Leipzig, 1950).

Ex. 360

The final variation rounds off the set admirably with a return to the mood and texture of the theme, but with subtle differences both in melody and in harmony. Considerably more interesting is the 'Sarabande con Partite' (BWV 990) in C major, which seems almost like a sketch for the Goldberg Variations—an impression which is heightened by the similarity of the basses of the two themes. Here there is more variety than in the 'Aria variata'. The thirteenth, fourteenth, and sixteenth variations are respectively an allemande, a courante, and a *giguetta*, the last of which has a foretaste of the seventh of the Goldberg Variations. Equally prophetic is the tenth variation, in which scale passages cross over and under a persistently maintained rhythm:

Ex. 361

The texture is richer and more contrapuntal than that of the A minor set, and here and there are unexpected harmonic details, such as the sudden change to the minor that comes twice in the seventh variation.

The theme of the 'Aria mit 30 Veränderungen' (BWV 988), popularly known as the Goldberg Variations, is also a sarabande, of the more florid type found in the Partitas; it was composed originally for Bach's second wife. It owes its particular character to the contrast between its delicate melodic decorations and its slowly moving bass. It is the latter that is the essential feature of the variations: it is maintained with only slight modifications throughout the work, and apart from three variations in the tonic minor the key of G major remains unaltered. In no other work does Bach combine such unity with so much variety. Within the apparently rigid limits of the form every aspect of his personality finds the most spontaneous expression. For the greatest writers of variations the form has been a stimulus, not only to thematic development and harmonic imagination but also to melodic invention, and this is as much in evidence here as in any work by Bach. The opening phrases of four of the variations will serve to illustrate this:

Ex. 362

All these quotations seem to have this indefinable quality of spontaneity, in spite of their similarity of outline; and it is worth noting that three of them come from canonic variations. It is superfluous to comment on the ingenuity of the canons, which occur in every third variation, each time at a different interval.[58] Variations 3, 9 and 24 have been quoted for their melodic invention. Equally remarkable, in very different moods, are the two in the tonic minor. No. 15, a canon at the fifth in the contrary motion, is the most

[58] Fourteen more canons have been discovered and published by Olivier Alain (Paris, 1976). See his 'Un supplément inédit aux *Variations Goldberg* de J. S. Bach', *Revue de Musicologie*, lx–lxi (1974–5), p. 244, and Nicholas Kenyon, 'A newly discovered group of canons by Bach', *Musical Times*, cxvii (1976), p. 391.

austere of all, with a rather angular melodic line, the severity of
which seems to be emphasized in its inversion:

Ex. 363

On the other hand no. 21, a canon at the seventh, though equally
serious, is far smoother and has a peculiar tenderness which derives
from the chromatic interpretation of the bass. The non-canonic
variations include another strikingly contrasted pair—no. 13 and
no. 25. These both show Bach at his most florid, but they are
widely different in mood. No. 13 is deeply thoughtful, but with a
certain ceremoniousness in its rhythm. No. 25, in G minor, though
it keeps to the outline of the theme, is luxuriantly rhapsodic, with
harmonies of singular poignancy:

Ex. 364

Many of the variations show a wealth of brilliant keyboard writing worthy of Scarlatti, often involving his favourite device of the rapid crossing of hands. Tovey has pointed out in his analysis of the work[59] how so many of these quick variations acquire a particular urgency through the introduction of new ideas towards the end of the second half, which is particularly effective when they are built on figures rather than on continuous melodies. It would be unsafe to predict, after hearing a few bars, the course of any of these variations. Particularly remarkable is no. 14, which, though in only two parts, has an astonishing sonority and wealth of ideas; and the keyboard effects in nos. 28 and 29 are very different from the normal run of baroque music. Among the variations are a *fughetta* (no. 10), a French overture (no. 16) and a *quodlibet* on popular German songs (no. 30). In spite of the convivial character of its material the last of these is a dignified piece and makes an admirable transition from the exuberance of its immediate predecessors to the final repetition of the theme. Nothing so comprehensive had been attempted in variation form before.

## BACH'S MISCELLANEOUS WORKS

The early Capriccio in B flat major 'sopra la lontananza del suo fratello dilettissimo' (BWV 992) was written about 1704 to commemorate the departure of Bach's elder brother Johann Jakob (b. 1682) who entered the service of Charles XII of Sweden as an oboist. It is Bach's only attempt at programme music and is obviously modelled on Kuhnau's *Biblische Historien*.[60] He is most successful when portraying the emotions of the friends who at first try to dissuade the traveller from his journey and then, over a ground bass, express their grief at his decision to leave. By comparison the final fugue on the posthorn's call is rather heavy-handed. The impulsive, adventurous side of Bach's personality finds its most exuberant outlet in the *Fantasia cromatica e fuga* in D minor (BWV 903), a close relative of the organ Toccata and Fugue in the same key (BWV 565). The fantasia bears, even more unmistakably than Scarlatti's sonatas, the stamp of improvisation, but its adventurousness is not epigrammatic like Scarlatti's, but wildly romantic, with magnificently bold modulations and an unbroken impetus throughout. The fugue makes a perfect counterpart, though here modulation is inevitably more controlled. The complete freedom with which Bach approached fugal writing is shown by the

---

[59] *Essays in Musical Analysis: Chamber Music* (London, 1944), p. 28.
[60] See p. 570.

way in which the subject is frequently modified—a feature which occurs elsewhere in his work.

Two works in A minor are entitled Fantasia and Fugue (BWV 944 and 904). In the first of these the fantasia consists of only ten bars of arpeggios: the subject of the fugue, which Bach later remodelled in a work for the organ (BWV 543²), is a sequence of rushing semiquavers. This is essentially a concert piece and contains passages which are harmonic rather than contrapuntal in effect, e.g.:

Ex. 365

The final stages, though exciting, are thoroughly unfugal. The other work is very different. The fantasia is a fully developed movement in a massive contrapuntal style. The fugue has an unusual scheme: halfway through there is a well-marked cadence in the tonic followed by a new chromatic theme which brings a completely different atmosphere into the music and is eventually combined with the very diatonic first subject:

Ex. 366

(1st Subj.)

Of the two works this is the less immediately impressive but possibly the more subtle and distinguished.

The toccata had grown considerably during the seventeenth century, and usually contained several contrasted sections,[61] some brilliant and others of a more solid character. Bach's examples, though not all of equal value, show that he was anxious to give as much unity as possible to a form which could easily become shapeless and incoherent. In the toccata in E minor (BWV 914) the first three sections all contain melodic figures which seem, perhaps unconsciously, to anticipate the subject of the concluding fugue. In the G minor toccata (BWV 915) the descending passages in the lively opening movement have their counterpart in the subject of the fugue. The toccata in D minor (BWV 913) has a remarkably beautiful Adagio section which, in its imaginative treatment of a single short phrase, anticipates some of the preludes of *Das wohltemperirte Clavier*. More important than any of these are the toccatas in C minor and F sharp minor (BWV 911 and 910). The first opens with a magnificent bravura flourish, which soon leads to an equally fine Adagio. A powerful and elaborately developed fugue follows: it is interrupted and concluded by reminiscences of the impulsive mood of the opening. The whole work is strongly unified. The F sharp minor toccata begins in the same way with a bravura passage leading to an expressive slow section; but here there are two fugues, one aggressive and the other looking back to the chromaticism of the slow section. Between these there is a remarkable sequential passage with some surprising modulations:

Ex. 367

---

[61] See, for instance, p. 516.

Of all the harpsichord toccatas this is the most imaginative.

Very different in character is the *Concerto nach Italienischen Gusto* (BWV 971), which was published together with the *Overture nach Französischer Art* (BWV 831) as part II of the *Clavier-Übung* (1735). Here Bach conveyed on a single instrument an impression of the contrast between a soloist and an orchestra. The texture is less contrapuntal than in the majority of the keyboard works. The brilliance of the first and third movements is akin to the vivacity of the quick movements of the Brandenburg concertos; on the other hand the Andante is deeply emotional.

## THE PARTITAS

The six Partitas (BWV 825–30) were originally published separately between 1726 and 1730 and then issued together as Part I of the *Clavier-Übung* in 1731 (Op. 1). Like the two works in Part II they seem to have been written with a view to public performance. They are remarkably varied in their keyboard writing and between them they exhibit most of the different aspects of Bach's personality. The general plan of the suite was considerably more regular in Bach's work than in either Couperin's or Handel's. As in the suites of Mattheson and Muffat, the allemande, courante, sarabande, and gigue occur almost invariably. In the partitas and the so-called *English Suites* the allemande is preceded by a prelude of varying character, while between the sarabande and the gigue come various other dances such as the gavotte, minuet, bourrée, and others less familiar. The character of the first partita, in B flat, is immediately indicated by its prelude, which is on an unusually small scale. The courante, of the lively Italian type, and the discreetly florid sarabande provide an excellent contrast, without spoiling the intimate character of the work as a whole, while the gigue, with its passing touches of minor tonality, has a subtle fluidity.

The second partita, in C minor, opens with an elaborate *sinfonia*, in which an impressive introduction in the style of the French overture is followed by a florid Andante leading to a two-part fugue. Instead of the usual gigue the work ends with a capriccio in 2/4 time. The *rondeau* which precedes it is notable for the very subtle returns of the refrain, which soften the outlines of the form in a manner very characteristic of Bach. The next two partitas are strongly contrasted in mood. No. 3, in A minor, is on the whole the severest of the set: the most expansive movement is the allemande and the liveliest the scherzo. No. 4, in D major, on the other hand, is the most vividly coloured. The overture, in which a stately introduction leads to a freely fugal movement, is in Bach's grandest manner, and the exceptionally beautiful allemande illustrates magnificently his power of devising long unbroken melodic paragraphs. The rhythmic ambiguity of the French courante is here treated with great spontaneity. No. 5, in G major, is in a lighter vein, with a very gay *préambule*. The most serious movement, curiously enough, is the gigue, which is elaborately fugal in texture: a new theme introduced at the beginning of the second half is ingeniously combined with the opening subject. No. 6, in E minor, provides a magnificent climax to the series. The opening toccata is more unified than the separate works for harpsichord bearing that title. A rhapsodic introduction leads to a fugue, during the course of which subsidiary material from the introduction is used as an episode. Finally the opening theme returns and holds the stage until the end but without a single bar of exact repetition. The allemande, courante, and sarabande are all on a broad scale and full of elaborate detail; in the sarabande the rhythm of the dance is completely submerged in a flood of expressive arabesques. The last two movements are both unusual: the 'Tempo di Gavotta' has so many triplets that it might well be mistaken for a gigue, while the gigue itself, though it combines binary form with fugal texture, is in common time and has no suggestion of the dance. The separate partita in B minor (*Overture nach Französischer Art*), to which reference has already been made, has no allemande, and the gigue is followed by a lively piece entitled 'Echo'. The sarabande is one of Bach's finest:

Ex. 368

## THE ENGLISH SUITES

Compared with the Partitas the six *English Suites* (BWV 806–11)[62] show certain obvious differences. There is less variety, both in

---

[62] Forkel explained the title, which is not Bach's, by saying that the suites were made 'for an Englishman of rank' (*The Bach Reader*, ed. H. T. David & A. Mendel (New York, 1945), p. 343). There is, however, no certain confirmation of this suggestion. Nor is the fact that Bach remodelled the gigue of Dieupart's first suite as the prelude of no. 1 strictly relevant. Dieupart, as Bach must have known, was not English, though he lived in England for some 40 years.

the texture of the keyboard writing and in the choice of movements, the extra movements being confined to a pair of gavottes,
bourrées, minuets, or passepieds. The prelude of no. 1, in A major,
is in a pastoral vein very similar to the prelude in the same key in
the second part of *Das wohltemperirte Clavier*. Though it is based
on a gigue by Dieupart,[63] the borrowed ideas are merely the
starting-point for a wholly original development:

Ex. 369 (i) DIEUPART

(ii) BACH

The preludes of the other five suites are on a much larger scale and
sometimes (e.g. no. 2 in A minor, and no. 3, in G minor) suggest
an alternation between soloist and orchestra, as in the Italian Concerto. No. 6, in D minor, begins, unlike the others, with a rhapsodic introduction. The courantes are of the more austere French
type: no. 1 has two, the second followed by two variations. The
courante of no. 6 has more urgency than the others owing to its
moving bass and the rising chain of trills at the end of each half.
The sarabandes are all of fine quality and suggest the dance more
decisively than those in the Partitas. The stately sarabande of no. 1
has an undercurrent of agitation which twice surges up in the bass

[63] See p. 623.

and makes a striking contrast to the prevailing good humour of the rest of the suite. The sarabandes of nos. 2, 3 and 6 are not only magnificent in themselves but are followed in each case by a decorative variation. The quasi-contrapuntal writing of the variation in no. 6 is particularly effective:

Ex. 370

The gigue in the same suite, with its menacing trills, is the most original of the series. Indeed the D minor suite as a whole is the finest of the six; Bach may have intended it, as with the E minor partita, to form a climax.

### THE FRENCH SUITES AND INVENTIONS

The six *French Suites* (BWV 812–17), so called, according to Forkel,[64] 'because they are written in the French taste', are similar in quality but smaller and lighter, though no. 5, in G major, and no. 6, in E major, have an unusually large number of movements. There are no preludes. In view of the title by which the suites are known it is curious that the French type of courante occurs more frequently in the *English Suites*, that the *passepied*, a dance of obviously French origin, is found in the *English Suites* and Partitas but not here, and that the only appearance of the *anglaise* is in a *French Suite* (no. 3, in B minor). There are several other separate suites (BWV 818–24, 831–3), including one in E flat major (BWV 819) which is similar in mood to no. 4 of the *French Suites* in the

---

[64] *The Bach Reader*, loc. cit. nos. 1–5 (with missing pages in nos. 1–3) are in the *Clavier-Büchlein vor Anna Magdalena Bachin* (1722), printed in the *Neue Bach-Ausgabe*, v, 4, ed. Georg von Dadelsen (Kassel, 1957).

same key. A suite in E minor (BWV 996), written in an unusually low register, is described in a manuscript copy as 'aufs Lauten Werck', i.e. for a keyboard instrument designed to imitate the sound of the lute.[65]

Bach's devotion to his family is further shown by the *Clavier-Büchlein vor Wilhelm Friedemann Bach*,[66] which includes, in addition to variants of several of the preludes in the first part of *Das wohltemperirte Clavier*, the original versions of the two-part and three-part Inventions (BWV 772–86, 787–801), here called respectively *praeambula* and *fantasie*.[67] The *Clavier-Büchlein*, partly in Bach's writing and partly in Wilhelm Friedemann's, was begun at Cöthen in 1720. Three years later Bach wrote out a definitive version of the Inventions, in which he re-arranged the order:[68] the title runs:

A straightforward introduction [to study], in which lovers of the keyboard, particularly those who are eager to learn, are shown a clear way, not only (1) of learning to play cleanly in two parts, but also, with further progress, (2) to deal correctly and well with three *obbligato* parts, and at the same time not only to have good ideas but also to develop them well, but above all to acquire a singing style of playing and in doing so to get a strong foretaste of composition.[69]

No pedagogic work has ever shown more skill in composition or a more obvious intention to make learning a pleasure. Bach's final arrangement was according to keys, as in *Das wohltemperirte Clavier*, but here he avoids those that might present difficulties for young players: C sharp major and minor, E flat minor, F sharp major and minor, A flat major and minor, B flat minor, and B major. Bach's mastery of imitation is as evident here as in any of his more ambitious works, and his art of expression ranges from the simple charm of the three-part inventions[70] in E major and G minor (nos. 6 and 11) to the more sombre chromaticism of no. 9, in F minor.

[65] Bach is known to have possessed two instruments of this kind: see Charles Sanford Terry, *Bach's Orchestra* (London, 1932), pp. 144–5.

[66] Facsimile edition by Ralph Kirkpatrick (New Haven, 1959); modern edition in the *Neue Bach-Ausgabe*, v, 5, ed. Wolfgang Plath (Kassel, 1962).

[67] Part of the D major three-part invention and the whole of the C minor are missing.

[68] Facsimile edition by Georg Schünemann (Leipzig, 1942).

[69] 'Auffrichtige Anleitung, Wormit denen Liebhabern des *Clavires*, besonders aber denen Lehrbegierigen, eine deutliche Art gezeiget wird, nicht alleine (1) mit 2 Stimmen reine spielen zu lernen, sondern auch bey weiteren *progressen* (2) mit dreyen *obligaten Partien* richtig und wohl zu verfahren, anbey auch zugleich gute *inventiones* nicht alleine zu bekommen, sondern auch selbige wohl durchzuführen, am allermeisten aber eine *cantable* Art im Spielen zu erlangen, und darneben einen starcken Vorschmack von der *Composition* zu überkommen.'

[70] Published in 1801 as *XV Simphonies pour le Clavecin* and often known by this title.

## DAS WOHLTEMPERIRTE CLAVIER

The keyboard works by Bach which have so far been discussed date from very different periods in his life. The B flat major Capriccio dates from 1704, when he was at Arnstadt. The toccatas were probably written at Weimar about 1710. Part I of the *Clavier-Übung* (the six Partitas) was published in 1726–31; Part II, containing the Italian Concerto and the French Overture in B minor, appeared in 1735; Part IV (the Goldberg Variations) was probably issued in 1742, though the theme, which may not be by Bach himself, appears in Anna Magdalena Bach's *Clavierbüchlein* of 1725. Between 1710 and 1726 there is a large mass of work, including the *Fantasia cromatica e fuga* in its original form, the English and French Suites, the Inventions, and Part I of *Das wohltemperirte Clavier* (BWV 846–69). The last of these was completed in 1722[71], though versions of some of the preludes are found earlier in Wilhelm Friedemann Bach's already mentioned *Clavierbüchlein*, and other pieces in the collection may be older still.

The term *wohltemperirt* had been used some 35 years earlier by Andreas Werckmeister (1645–1706), who wrote: 'If we have a well-tuned keyboard, we can play in all keys, (starting) from any note.'[72] He did not, however, advocate equal temperament, nor is there any evidence that Bach had any such intention. According to Kirnberger, as reported by Friedrich Wilhelm Marpurg,[73] Bach insisted on the thirds being tuned sharp, but this does not necessarily imply equal temperament. Forkel, who got much of his information from C. P. E. Bach, says that Bach could tune a harpsichord in fifteen minutes,[74] and it is by no means impossible that he made minor modifications in the tuning when playing in extreme keys.[75] Even if this supposition is rejected, we are not entitled to do more than assume that he adopted a tuning which made all keys tolerable. The title of Part I of *Das wohltemperirte Clavier* merely indicates that the pieces are in all the major and minor keys and are designed 'for the profit and use of musical young people who are eager to learn, and also for the special enjoyment of those who are

---

[71] Facsimile of the autograph, Deutsche Staatsbibl., Mus. MS autog. Boch P415, Leipzig, 1962).

[72] 'Wenn wir . . . . ein wohl temperirtes Clavier haben können wir aus jeglichen Clave alle modos haben' (*Musicae mathematicae Hodegus curiosus* (Frankfurt and Leipzig, 1686), p. 120).

[73] *Versuch über die musicalische Temperatur* (Breslau, 1776), p. 213.

[74] *The Bach Reader*, p. 312.

[75] For a full discussion see J. Murray Barbour, 'Bach and *The Art of Temperament*', in *The Musical Quarterly*, xxxiii (1947), p. 64.

already accomplished musicians'.[76] Though more ambitious than the Inventions, the collection had a similar purpose—to teach students how to play and to give pleasure. In exploring keys outside the normal range Bach had a precedent in a collection of organ preludes and fugues by Johann Caspar Ferdinand Fischer (c.1670–1746), entitled *Ariadne Musica, Neo-Organoedum . . . é difficultatum labyrintho educens* (Augsburg, 1715),[77] which uses all but five of the possible keys. It is clear that Bach knew this work, since he borrowed the subject of Fischer's E major fugue[78] for his own fugue in the same key in Part II of *Das wohltemperirte Clavier*. In Bach's work no instrument is specified, though it is obvious that an instrument with pedals is needed for Fugue no. 20 in A minor. The player can make his own choice between clavichord and harpsichord.

To no composer was the fugue so spontaneous a means of expression as it was to Bach. Even the most obviously brilliant of his fugues, such as the one in A minor, from which a few bars were quoted in Ex. 365, would be easier to score in separate parts than the keyboard fugues of Handel or Scarlatti, who found it harder to resist the temptation to fill out the texture now and then by purely harmonic methods. For Handel, great contrapuntist though he was, a fugal texture tended to be associated with certain well-defined moods, usually involving some degree of tension: for Bach it could express anything, from the tragedy of fugue no. 24, in B minor, to the brilliant gaiety of the gigue from no. 5 of the French Suites. In *Das wohltemperirte Clavier*, despite the great variety of mood, the general tone is intimate; and there are some fugues, particularly in Part II, in which the texture is so smooth and flowing that an unaccompanied chorus would seem to the ideal medium.

The first four preludes and fugues of Part I at once show the range of expression. The serene pair in C major (no. 1) are perfect specimens of the development of a single idea—in the prelude by harmonic, in the fugue by contrapuntal, means. The prelude, in spite of its persistent figuration, is prevented from stagnating by the subtle gradations of the harmony and the gradual but deliberate

---

[76] 'Zum Nutzen und Gebrauch der lehr-begierigen Musicalischen Jugend, als auch derer in diesem *studio* schon *habil* seyenden besonderem Zeitvertreib'.

[77] According to J. G. Walther's *Musicalisches Lexikon* (Leipzig, 1732) this was published in 1702 but it is now known only by an edition of 1715. Modern ed. in *Sämtliche Werke für Klavier und Orgel*, ed. Ernst von Werra (Leipzig, 1901). The title refers to the legend that Ariadne helped Theseus by means of a thread to find his way out of the Minotaur's labyrinth in Crete.

[78] Davison and Apel, *Historical Anthology of Music*, ii (London, 1950), no. 247.

descent of the bass to the low C. In the fugue details like the prepared cadences in A minor (bars 12–14) and D minor (bars 18–19)
illustrate the extraordinary richness of colour that arises in Bach's
counterpoint. The C minor prelude (no. 2), like the C major, is
built on a single figure but is richer in texture, with a dramatic
outburst at the end which recalls the toccata in the same key. In
the C sharp major fugue (no. 3), which is on a larger scale than
either of its predecessors, episodic material plays an important part
in providing contrast to the subject without interrupting the prevailing gaiety. The C sharp minor prelude and fugue (no. 4) are
very different in character. In particular the fugue (in five parts) is
an imposing structure with three strongly contrasted themes. Its
continuity is remarkable: in spite of its length there is only one
cadence, in the relative major (bars 34–5), during the course of its
development. When, after an orgy of triple counterpoint, the final
cadence seems to be approaching, it is continually postponed and is
eventually interrupted by a dissonance resolving on to a brief coda
over a tonic pedal. All the best of Bach's fugues show this continuous urge, which is why the final entries of the subject are so
striking in effect.

Three other pairs have a tragic power similar to that of the C
sharp minor. The E flat minor prelude (no. 8) recalls the mood of
the slow movement of the Italian Concerto; the fugue[79] (in three
parts) employs innumerable academic devices with an air of complete inevitability. The B flat minor prelude and fugue (no. 22) are
movements unified in the same way as those in C major, the prelude growing from a single rhythmic figure and the fugue from the
first two notes of the subject. The B minor prelude (no. 24) is a
trio in which two voices discourse quietly over a perpetually moving
bass, and the fugue has one of the most striking of all Bach's subjects:

Ex. 371

Although it is in four parts, they seldom all play simultaneously. A
recurring episode, with close imitation:

[79] Bach wrote the fugue in sharps, in D sharp minor.

Ex. 372

recalls a passage in Scarlatti's sonata in D minor (K 417). The F minor fugue (no. 12) also has a chromatic subject, but by comparison with the B flat minor seems rather square and angular. The A minor fugue (no. 20) is the only one that seems too large for the medium and to demand the greater resources of the organ, for which indeed it may originally have been written. Its many academic devices seem less spontaneous than those of the D sharp minor fugue, but it is massive, serious music, with some notable harmonic clashes and an effective climax at the end.

The preludes vary considerably in their methods. The use of a single figure, as in nos. 1 and 2, is common, and sometimes, as in nos. 6 and 22, results in a remarkable intensity. Some of them are purely lyrical, e.g. the E major (no. 9), the G minor (no. 16), and the G sharp minor (no. 18), while in others the texture is elaborately contrapuntal, as in the long and rather laboured prelude in E flat major (no. 7), which is followed by a short and very graceful fugue. There are one or two other strongly contrasted pairs, such as the F sharp minor (no. 14), where a brisk prelude is joined to a reflective and melancholy fugue. For the most part, however, there is a close unity of mood, e.g. in the preludes and fugues in F sharp major (no. 13), A flat major (no. 17), and G sharp minor (no. 18). In the case of the pair in B major (no. 23) there is the suggestion of a thematic connection which may have been intentional:

Ex. 373

(i)   Prelude                                    (ii)   Fugue

There is also considerable variety in the fugues, both in their structure and in the character of their subjects, which may be long or short, melodic or primarily rhythmic, smooth or angular. Sometimes, as in C major (no. 1), everything grows from the subject; in others the episodes are of great importance. The modulations, though they are seldom remote, are planned in a variety of different ways. When the subject enters in a comparatively distant key, e.g. the entry on the supertonic at bar 66 of the C sharp minor fugue (no. 4), the effect is very striking. Devices traditionally associated with the fugue, such as stretto, are often dispensed with. Bach may, if so inclined, introduce them at an earlier stage in the composition than is usually prescribed by theorists. In these matters, as indeed in everything, he was a law unto himself.

We do not know when Bach compiled the collection of twenty-four preludes and fugues commonly known as Part II of *Das wohltemperirte Clavier*. An incomplete fair copy in his handwriting[80] dates from 1739–42), and many of the pieces may have been written a good deal earlier; for instance, the fugue in A flat (no. 17) had originally been a much shorter fughetta in F (BWV 901). Altnikol's copy of 1744, 'Des wohltemperirten Claviers Zweyter Theil', shows that Bach designed it as a companion to Part I. Forkel declared roundly that it consisted entirely of masterpieces, in contrast to the signs of immaturity which he detected in Part I.[81] This opinion may be generally endorsed at the present day. The most noticeable difference is in the preludes, which are more highly organized. The continuous treatment of a single figure occurs only once—in the prelude in C sharp major (no. 3),[82] and there it is abandoned towards the end for a fugal passage. On the other hand the binary form found in the Suites and Partitas, which occurs only once in Part I—the B minor prelude (no. 24)— is relatively common in Part II, and the D major prelude (no. 5) is virtually in sonata form.[83] The texture is generally richer than in Part I, the keyboard writing suggests a greater sonority, and the compass is sometimes larger. Contrasts between prelude and fugue are also more common: the thoughtful and organ-like prelude in F major (no. 11) is followed by a fugue similar in mood to the gigue of no. 5 of the French Suites. A still more striking contrast is to be found between the mysterious and chromatic prelude in A minor (no. 20)

---

[80] Brit. Lib., Add. MS 35–012; reproduced in *British Library Music Facsimiles* I (1980), with an introduction by Don Franklin and Stephen Daw.

[81] *The Bach Reader*, p. 342.

[82] An earlier version in C major (BWV 872a), in which the first section consists of minim chords marked 'arpeggio', exists in two manuscript copies: see Paul Kast, *Die Bach-Handschriften der Berliner Staatsbibliothek* (Trossingen, 1958), pp. 15, 36 (P 226, P 550 Mbg).

[83] Cf. p. 626.

and the very powerful fugue which follows it, founded on a 'neutral' subject which was the common property of eighteenth-century composers:

Ex. 374

It is not only the subject that recalls Handel, but also the strongly contrasted countersubject. The same is true of the G minor fugue (no. 16), though the texture here is more elaborate than in the average Handel fugue.

Several pieces have obvious counterparts in Part I. The pastoral grace of the E major and F sharp major preludes (nos. 9 and 13) in Part I reappears in the E flat major and A major preludes (nos. 7 and 19) of Part II. The D sharp minor fugue (no. 8) of Part II has something of the pathos of the G sharp minor (no. 18) of Part I, but it is more massive and rises to a climax in which the subject and its inversion are heard simultaneously:

Ex. 375

The F sharp minor fugue (no. 14) had three subjects treated in a manner reminiscent of the C sharp minor (no. 4) of Part I, but with a clearer texture. The first subject, with its rising minor sixth:

Ex. 376

is very characteristic: compare the B minor (no. 24) of Part I (see Ex. 371).

The vocal character of some of the fugues has already been mentioned. One of the most closely wrought is the D major (no. 5), where a phrase of four notes taken from the subject contrives to insinuate itself into almost every bar of the piece. It has a serene profundity which is more characteristic of Part II than of Part I. Rather similar in mood is the broad and triumphant E flat major fugue (no. 7), with its simple but effective stretti. The E major fugue (no. 9), on the subject from J. C. F. Fischer's *Ariadne*, is the most deeply contemplative of all, and the various stretti, diminutions and inversions serve to intensify its solemnity. Two pairs call for special mention: those in G major (no. 15), the most ethereal, and those in B flat minor (no. 22), the most massive. The prelude of the latter is a sustained and serious contrapuntal movement, with one point of curious and almost certainly accidental thematic resemblance to the prelude in the same key in Part I:

Ex. 377

The fugue has a long and distinguished subject which is equally effective when inverted; the chromatic countersubject is also inverted, and the subject is treated in stretto in both its original and inverted forms, with the latter answering the former at bar 96 (six bars before the end). The result of all these ingenuities is a movement of remarkable power and beauty, rising at the end to a magnificent climax. It has the same continuity and emotional urgency as the fugues in C sharp minor and B minor in Part I. All three may be regarded as among Bach's greatest inspirations.

## MUSICALISCHES OPFER AND DIE KUNST DER FUGE

Two other works must be included in this chapter although one consists only partly of keyboard music and the other was not specified as such: *Musicalisches Opfer* (Leipzig, 1747) (BWV 1079) and *Die Kunst der Fuge* (Leipzig, late 1750 or early 1751) (BWV 1080). The history of the *Musical Offering* has often been told. On 7 May 1747 Bach was taken to see Frederick the Great who gave him a theme on which to extemporize a fugue on one of the royal Silbermann fortepianos; Frederick was so impressed that the following day he asked for a fugue in six parts which Bach proceeded to extemporize on a theme of his own. Two months later he sent the king a collection of contrapuntal pieces, mainly on versions of the royal theme, which he described as a 'musical offering' and in a prefatory acrostic as a 'Ricercar' (Regis Iussu Cantio Et Reliqua Canonica Arte Resoluta). The *Opfer* consists of a three-part fugue (*ricercar a 3*) for keyboard only, probably a revised version of the original improvization; 'VIII Canones diversi' which have to be solved in contrary motion, contrary motion and augmentation, and so on; a 'Fuga canonica in epidiapente'; a six-part fugue (*ricercar a 6*) for keyboard, this time on the royal theme; a four-movement trio sonata for flute, violin, and continuo in which the royal theme plays a secondary role or is skilfully disguised; and a 'Canon perpetuus' also for trio. Most of the original autograph has been lost and it has been persuasively argued[84] that the order in the original edition has been garbled and that Bach intended the *Ricercar a 6* to be placed at the end. The two ricercars, a 3 and a 6, are the only unequivocally solo keyboard pieces in Bach's own hand, despite the fact that the six-part one was published in score, presumably for study. It is certainly one of his most masterly fugal compositions.

There is no indication of the medium for which *Die Kunst der Fuge* (The Art of Fugue) was composed, but there can be little doubt that, though written in open score, it was intended as key-

---

[84] See Hans Theodore David, *J. S. Bach's 'Musical Offering': History, Interpretation, and Analysis* (New York, 1945), pp. 34 ff and 89 ff, and Ursula Kirkendale, 'The Source for Bach's *Musical Offering* ', *Journal of the American Musicological Society*, xxxiii (1980), p. 88.

board music.[85] It has already been pointed out that a keyboard fugue by Bach will go into open score more easily than one by Handel or Scarlatti, but even Bach occasionally allowed himself some licence. In the final bars of the fugues in E minor (no. 10) and A flat major (no. 17) of Part II of *Das wohltemperirte Clavier* an extra part is introduced. There are several places in *Die Kunst der Fuge*[86] where extra parts are introduced in a way that would be unlikely to happen except in keyboard music. As Tovey very rightly pointed out,[87] the whole work is no less grateful to play on a keyboard instrument than *Das wohltemperirte Clavier*. The fact that all the movements are built on variants of the same not particularly distinguished theme has misled many into regarding it purely as an intellectual *tour de force*, while others have sought to introduce variety by a changing scheme of orchestration. There is no justification for either of these attitudes.

The first two fugues use the theme in its simplest form; but whereas in the first the counterpoint is smooth and flowing, in the second it has a persistent dotted-note rhythm against which the subject is constantly thrown into relief. In the third the subject is inverted and accompanied by a chromatic countersubject. In the fourth the subject is still inverted, but the treatment is more lively and adventurous, with prominent episodes and a more spacious design. The work is not all on an equally high level. The canons are rather dry, the sixth and seventh fugues are overburdened with elaborate stretti, and the two invertible fugues are ingenious rather than inspired. But the remaining fugues continually reveal new points of interest, which are none the less valuable for not always standing out obviously from their context. The eight and eleventh fugues are of particularly fine quality. The eighth has three subjects:

[85] See Gustav M. Leonhardt, *The Art of Fugue: Bach's Last Harpsichord Work* (The Hague, 1952). The edition in score by Donald Francis Tovey (London, 1931) includes suggestions for distributing the parts between the two hands, as well as a completion of Contrapunctus XIV (which Bach left unfinished) and an invertible fugue on four subjects by the editor. Helmut Walcha has shown that it can be performed on the organ; see his editon (Frankfurt, 1967).
[86] See the final bars of Contrapunctus V, VI, VII and XI.
[87] Op. cit., preface.

Ex. 378

The third of these is an inversion of the subject of the whole work, which in its original form is as follows:

Ex. 379

All three subjects are eventually combined in triple counterpoint, and the general scheme is similar to that of the C sharp minor fugue (no. 4) from Part I of *Das wohltemperirte Clavier* and the F sharp minor fugue (no. 14) from Part II. The eleventh fugue is built on the same material but inverted and introduced in a different order. There is less contrapuntal ingenuity but richer and more varied colouring; it is in fact the emotional climax of the whole work. Hardly anywhere else does Bach indulge in such luxurious chromaticism as here. The following brief extract (bars 43–7) may serve as a specimen:

Ex. 380

The bass here is an inversion of the first subject of the eighth fugue (Ex. 378, III).

*Die Kunst der Fuge*, composed in the last year of Bach's life and published about six months after his death, ends with a vast unfinished fugue, which has three new subjects, the third being a

translation into notes of the letters B A C H.[88] Schweitzer[89] suggested that this was possibly intended as an appendix to *Die Kunst
der Fuge*, since it does not include the original subject. On the
other hand Gustav Nottebohm had shown that the original subject
could be combined with the other three,[90] and it seems very
probable that this was Bach's intention. C. P. E. Bach says that his
father was prevented by illness from finishing the work.[91] The unfinished fugue is certainly of magnificent quality, and we could
hardly end our examination of Bach's keyboard works with a more
fitting subject for contemplation. Bach had a unique power of
adapting his idiom to varying conditions; he could be as brilliant as
Scarlatti and as intimate as Couperin. Though he wrote also in a
contrapuntal texture which was becoming less and less fashionable
during his lifetime, the very qualities for which he was once
criticized seem now to connect in an astonishing way the traditions
of the past with the adventures of the future.

[88] In English, B flat A C B natural.
[89] *J. S. Bach*, trans. Ernest Newman (London, 1911), p. 426.
[90] In *Goldsteins Musikwelt* (1880), nos. 21–2.
[91] *The Bach Reader*, p. 221.

# X

# ORGAN MUSIC: 1700–1750

## By WALTER EMERY

### THE INSTRUMENT

THAT eighteenth-century organs were very different from those of today is clear from the reports of those who have played them. The diapason stops, which are to the organ what the strings are to the modern orchestra, were quieter and flutier than those now familiar; they spoke more promptly, and the ensemble was surprisingly clear. Hardly any variety of effect could be obtained, except by changing manuals. Swell-boxes were in use in England from 1712 onwards, and in Spain perhaps from an earlier date; but they can hardly have been common in either country, and were not readily accepted elsewhere. Further, stops were difficult to change. J. M. Duncan[1] thus described his experiences with an organ built by Silbermann in 1714:

The drawstops are formidable objects . . . fixed to baulks of timber about an inch square, which need to be hitched down after being drawn. It is a greater physical effort to prepare for a fugue than to play it; and at the end of a loud piece . . . it comes as a shock to realize that one must now face the exertion of pushing the stops home.

He speaks of 'the difficulty of moving the clumsy stops while a performance was in progress' as 'prohibitive, except on a small scale', even if the player had two assistants, one on each side, to work the stops for him. As organists who have been thus assisted are well aware, the English objection to the idea is not simply another manifestation of the sporting spirit; and it is reasonable to conclude that, even on the Continent, stops were not usually changed during a movement.

These expressive limitations, great as they seem, were hardly greater than those of a harpsichord with the same number of manuals. Indeed, the eighteenth-century organ was, if anything, better than the harpsichord as a medium for the earlier music of

---

[1] *Musical Times*, lxvi (1925), p. 342.

the period, since it could sustain any note to any length and provide a greater dynamic range and more variety of colour. In some countries it had a further advantage in the pedal-board. At the beginning of the century, therefore, the organ was at least as attractive to composers as any other keyboard instrument; but this did not last long, for the development of classical homophony soon led to a demand for expression of a kind that the organ could not supply.

## CHANGES OF STYLE

By the beginning of the eighteenth century the conception of Christianity current among educated men had become unfavourable to the development of church music, which was affected not only because such men might be patrons, whose tastes had to be respected, but also because their ideas spread to the classes from which sprang the composers themselves. The laws of nature were beginning to be discovered; and this led to a conception of God as the supreme principle of order, and to that conception of the universe which was satirized by Voltaire: 'All is for the best in the best of all possible worlds'. The idea may now seem absurd, and revolting in its complacency; but it was acceptable enough to men who felt that they, and a select few with them, were thinking on new and inspiring lines.

The majesty of the Divine Organiser may be a proper subject for philosophical contemplation, but has proved a singularly intractable one for artistic treatment. Sin and hell have been far more inspiring. Once the Fall of Man had been relegated to the background of religious thought, organ composers must have found it difficult to set the chorale 'Durch Adams Fall' with conviction; and, in general, they began to take their mission less seriously. They turned more and more to the entertaining type of music that was already satisfying secular patrons. Moreover, it was at this time that the transition to classical homophony took place; by the middle of the century the influence of the new style can be seen in almost all organ music. Unfortunately, it did not suit the organ, on which a thin texture, such as was then current, is apt to sound flimsy, and a melody of the homophonic type may easily sound weak because it cannot be given expression.

In the early years of the century organ composers were greatly influenced by Italian chamber music, and to a smaller extent by French harpsichord music; which meant that, whenever the composer was capable of original thought and had some feeling for the organ, his music gained in fluency, coherence, and a sense of style. But in the Catholic countries and England no great progress was made, and signs of degeneration soon appeared. In the former, homophony was quickly accepted. The liturgy does not seem to have given organists much scope; and the habit of setting liturgical *canti fermi*, which might have maintained dignity, had almost died out.

In England, composers had never been fond of setting hymn-tunes, and there is some reason to think that the social and religious background was exceptionally unfavourable. (Bach's Rector thought music-making a disreputable occupation; Locke and Chesterfield added scorn to disapproval.) Protestant Germany, perhaps the last area to be affected in this way, was also that which made most progress; and the progress was not entirely due to the individual genius of Bach. Here new ideas were slow to filter through—which in the circumstances was an advantage. A tradition of solid craftsmanship had been preserved, to some extent, by comparatively medieval conditions of life: organists were often employed by councils, who had at any rate to pretend to want edification; and furthermore, there were the chorales. Being metrical, they were easier to handle than plainsong; they were popular, and habitually used as bases for composition: they were supremely dignified, and often expressed intense feeling—whether introspective, as in 'Von Himmel hoch', or militant, as in 'Ein feste Burg'. Thus they not only stimulated composers, but also enabled them to appeal to their audiences without condescending to triviality, which would have suited neither the tunes nor the inflexible austerity and religious associations of the organ; and it was in this spirit that the German Protestants approached organ composition of other kinds.

ITALY

In Italy interest in organ music had declined after the death of Frescobaldi in 1643. Composers of merit devoted most of their energies to opera and concerted music, and came to think of the organ as a continuo instrument. Privately-owned chamber organs were built for this purpose, but the instrument did not develop on solo lines; pedalboards, for instance, must have been smaller and more primitive than in Protestant Germany. Perhaps the reasons for this were partly financial. In Italy, as in Catholic Germany, there was much church-building in the seventeenth century and early in the eighteenth; but in Protestant Germany there was little. One may therefore suppose that in the latter area more money was available for church fittings, such as organs.

Continuo-writing had already concentrated interest in the outer obbligato parts; and at the beginning of the eighteenth century there appear liturgical interludes with such titles as 'Elevazione' or 'Offertorio', clearly meant to be tuneful and to make a popular appeal. An 'Elevazione' by Floriano Arresti (c.1660–1719)[2] is a rambling piece of little interest; but a Larghetto of this type by Giovanni Battista Bassani (c.1657–1716), edited to an unspecified extent by Bossi,[3] modulates widely and effectively and has a good deal of expressive power, despite its undistinguished thematic material and loose construction. Fugal movements by Carlo Francesco Pollarolo (c.1653–1723)[4] and Marc' Antonio Ziani (c. 1653–1715) are mainly in three parts. The writing is often harmonic rather than contrapuntal; episodes are short and weak; and in their search for an instrumental style the composers rely too much on repeated notes in their subjects and conventional changing-notes elsewhere.

Alessandro Scarlatti (d. 1725) did not distinguish himself in his keyboard works. Some of his toccatas show the usual mixture of block chords and passage work, with scraps of imitative writing here and there; occasional cadences outline a hazy scheme of modulations, but there is no coherence in the thematic material and the general effect is thin. In others there are long bass notes, perhaps for pedals, over which the hands play in thirds and sixths. His fugal writing, though no more substantial than that of Pollarolo or Ziani, is more contrapuntal, especially in the more old-fashioned quasi-vocal movements.

A slightly later group of composers is formed by Azzolino Bernardino Della Ciaja (1671–1755), Giuseppe Bencini (dates unknown), Giovanni Maria Casini (1652–1719), and Domenico Zipoli (1688–1726). The organ works of Della Ciaja consist of a few short interludes *di largo e grave stile Ecclesiastico per grandi organi* appended to the set of harpsichord sonatas referred to on pp. 605–6, published in 1727; in a solid vocal style, they are of some harmonic interest. Bencini was perhaps the best of the fugue-writers; he could invent a significant subject of Handelian freshness:[5]

---

[2] In *L'arte musicale in Italia*, ed. Luigi Torchi, iii (Milan, n.d.), p. 405.
[3] *Sammlung von Stücken alter italienischer Meister*, ed. Enrico Bossi (Leipzig, 1908), no. 1.
[4] Torchi, op. cit., p. 341.
[5] Ibid., p. 409, and in *Classici italiani dell' organo*, ed. I. Fuser (Padua, 1955), no. 63.

Ex. 381

and he knew the use of a regular counter-subject. His episodes are of reasonable length, and recognizably based on fragments of the subject. Casini published his twelve *Pensieri* (Op. 3) at Florence in 1714.[6] Laid out in open score, like *Die Kunst der Fuge*, they are among the few works of the period that are strictly in four parts. Most of them consist of two or three fugues on variations of the same subject, canzona-fashion. Sometimes the variant forms of a subject prove to be unworkable, or there are lapses into thin conventionality; but there is real organistic dignity in even the most instrumental movements. They have well developed episodes, and there are striking chromaticisms in no. 10:

Ex. 382

Zipoli's organ works, published in *Sonate d'Intavolatura per organo e cimbalo* (Rome, 1716),[7] are liturgical interludes—toccatas, brief versets, canzonas, 'Elevazioni', and so forth. The toccatas are of the usual type. The 'Elevazioni' have clear-cut sections and hint at recapitulation but are not very expressive. A three-section Pastorale has some striking chromaticisms, emphasized by the thinness of its texture:

---

[6] Modern ed. in *Archives des maîtres de l'orgue*, ed. Alexandre Guilmant and André Pirro, x (Paris, 1910). And see G. Giachin, ' I "Pensieri per l'organo" di Giovanni Casini', *Rivista musicale italiana*, x (1976), p. 185.
[7] Modern ed. by Luigi Tagliavini (Heidelberg, 1959).

Ex. 383

The best of the versets are neatly-turned fugato miniatures. The canzonas, with one exception, are ordinary fugues—loosely constructed, but vigorous: best of all perhaps is the only one (in G minor) that lives up to its title.

More important than any of these works are the *12 Sonate d'intavolatura per l'organo e 'l cembalo*[8] by Giambattista Martini (1706–84) published at Amsterdam in 1742 (a second set of six appeared at Bologna in 1747).[9] Each has five movements: a prelude, which may use the dotted rhythms of the overture or consist of arpeggio figuration; a fugato; a slow movement, generally with a treble melody of the arabesque type; an allegro, more or less in a dance style; and either an air with variations or a dance. The writing is seldom in more than three parts, but is fluent and well-knit; and the first three movements, usually the only ones that need to be taken seriously as organ music, are often of considerable merit. The following passage from the Prelude of the eleventh sonata is a typical example of his style:

Ex. 384

[8] Modern ed. by M. Vitali (Milan, n.d. *c*.1927).
[9] Ed. L. Hoffmann-Erbrecht (Leipzig, 1954).

## SPAIN

Spanish pedal boards were of limited compass (perhaps a dozen notes) and of primitive construction; some are described as looking like a row of metal doorknobs set in the floor; they seem to have been used only occasionally for sustaining long notes. Organ-builders were lavish with mixtures and reeds. Each stop-knob controlled pipes covering only half the keyboard; thus, a solo could be accompanied on the same manual. In a toccata by Juan Bautista José Cabanilles (1644–1712)[10] the bass (which is soloed) never rises above middle C, and the upper parts never descend below middle C sharp.

It is easy to compile long lists of Spanish and Portuguese organists; but quite another matter to obtain access to their works. According to Anglès, organ pieces were regarded as of no interest to anyone but their composers; much organ music has probably been lost, and much of what remains is still unpublished. From the available editions of the works of Cabanilles[11] and Miguel López (1669–1723)[12] one can see that, at the beginning of the century, Spanish organ music was technically less advanced than Italian music of the same period, but more organistic and (at least in intention) more expressive. López left some Fantasias (llenos), but most of his works are versets. Some are based on fragments of plainsong; others are free three-part movements, in which the left hand often imitates the treble, and was probably soloed. Like Cabanilles, he crossed parts with some freedom, was liberal with the $^{\#}_{3}6$ on the dominant in minor keys, and juxtaposed major and minor sevenths, e.g.:[13]

---

[10] Modern ed. by Higini Anglès, ii (Barcelona, 1933), no. 26.
[11] See chap. 8, p. 531, n. 44.
[12] Modern ed. in *Música Instrumental*, ed. David Pujol, ii (Montserrat, 1934).
[13] Op. cit., p. 47 (*Primera coleccíon, verso* xii, bars 8–13).

Ex. 385

The last feature reappears in versets by José Ximenez (1601–72) and Francese Llusá (d. 1738). The latter shows an addiction to sequences that is also noticeable in the works of Joaquin de Oxinagas (1719–89), José Elias (d. after 1751) and Juan Moreno y Polo (d. 1776), some of whose fugues have persistently sequential treatment of subjects that are themselves sequential. One of the generally very fine fugues by Oxinagas is intolerable for this reason; but a fugue and some versets by Moreno show some imagination and contrapuntal ingenuity. Elias, a pupil of Cabanilles, was not remarkably successful in any of the styles he used. His prelude and fugue on 'Salve Regina' is excessively severe, his homophonic prelude in D major vulgar, and the double fugue of his ambitious 'Intento cromático' an interminable series of commonplaces in thin harmonic figuration. His constructional methods are of some interest; both the preludes have clear-cut sections, and the introduction to the 'Intento' has two entries of the fugue subject for its bass.[14]

## FRANCE

French organ music was a product of Paris and the Court. It developed rapidly in the second half of the seventeenth century in the hands of such composers as Gigault, Lebègue, de Grigny and Raison.[15] By 1700 its characteristic methods appear fully established and, on the whole, applied to the best advantage. This music

[14] Examples of Spanish organ music are in *Antología de organistos clásicos españoles*, ed. Felipe Pedrell, 2 vols. (Madrid, 1905–8; second ed. 1968).
[15] See chap. 8, pp. 544 ff.

is thoroughly instrumental. Though it may sometimes appear better suited to the harpsichord, it is likely to have been effective on the Parisian organs of the day, which were highly specialized, with a number of manuals, a distinct type of reed tone, and pedal boards of adequate compass though primitive in construction. Sixteen-foot pedal stops were not numerous, for the pedals were used rather as an additional solo keyboard of tenor pitch than as the regular bass to manual writing. Double pedalling appears occasionally, and the quatuors require elaborate thumbing—a technique that even Bach hardly used. Perhaps a second player was sometimes called upon for such movements. Much more than other composers of the period, the French exploited the colouristic possiblities of the organ: they specified stops and changed manuals frequently.

François Couperin (1668–1733), the outstanding harpsichord composer of his time,[16] left only a modest amount of organ music, consisting of two sets of pieces to be performed during Mass, one described as 'à l'usage ordinaire des Paroisses, Pour les Festes Solemnelles', the other as 'propre pour les Covents de Religieux, et Religieuses'.[17] They were issued in a set of manuscript copies with an engraved title page in 1690 and are thus among the composer's earliest works. In the first Mass Couperin follows tradition in using the liturgical plainsong[18] as a *cantus firmus* in some of the interludes (or *couplets*) and in others accepting it as a starting point for free invention. The dignity of style, the skill in handling the material, and the variety of treatment are all remarkable for a young man of 22. Even when the music suggests secular parallels, as in the eighth *couplet* of the Gloria:

Ex. 386

[16]  See chap. 9, pp. 593 ff.
[17]  Printed in *Oeuvres complètes de François Couperin*, vi, ed. Paul Brunold (Paris, 1932). See Beverly Scheibert, 'Couperin's Masses, the Italians and inégalité', *Musical Times*, cxxiii (1982), p. 499.
[18]  Of the Mass 'Cunctipotens Genitor Deus' (no. IV in the *Liber Usualis*.)

it is no sense inappropriate to its environment. Couperin's harmony also shows a considerable range of imagination. In the Benedictus he pursues a form of progression similar to that found in Frescobaldi's toccatas, but with a surer sense of direction. One is reminded of Purcell's harmonic adventures withn the framework of tonality:

Ex. 387

The second Mass is on the whole simpler in style but without any loss of dignity and with equal evidence of resourcefulness.

Couperin's contemporary, Louis Marchand (1669–1732), also an

organist in Paris, was hardly more prolific as a composer for the
organ. A slender volume of pieces was published after his death;
others survive in manuscript.[19] A contemporary poet described him
as 'brillant Orphée, illustre Maître', but the claim seems a little
excessive for a composer who, though not lacking in resource (even
to the extent of writing for double pedal), could not match his
initial ideas with the sustained invention that one finds in
Couperin. It was to Marchand that Jean-Adam Guillaume Guilain
(d. 1739) dedicated four suites of versets for the Magnificat, published in 1706.[20] Though the composer seems to have been of
German origin, his music is typically French. The third suite consists of an introduction in the *durezza* style—rich in dissonant suspensions; a still fugal *quatuor* for three manuals and pedals; a tuneful gavotte-like dialogue, with alternating solos for the two hands; a
*basse de trompette*, in which left-hand trumpet solos and right-hand
cornet solos are accompanied by block chords and some of the left-
hand figuration is purely harmonic; an expressive duo; a neat fugal
*grand jeu*, with effective episodic echoes, beginnng:

Ex. 388

and a *petit plein jeu* which consists of only a few chords and scales.
Another of Marchand's pupils, Pierre du Mage (1674–1751), published in 1708 a *Livre d'orgue*, actually a single suite[21] similar in
style but rather more imaginative. It includes a very expressive *récit*
which recalls the style of the opera air:

Ex. 389

[19] L. Marchand, *L'oeuvre d'orgue, édition intégrale*, ed. Jean Bonfils (Paris, 1970– ).
[20] Ed. Guilmant and Pirro in *Archives des maîtres de l'orgue*, vii (Paris, 1906; rev. 1971).
[21] Ed. Raugel (Paris, c.1952).

and an effective final *grand jeu*—a three-part fugato preceded and followed by sections that owe something to the French overture.

Louis Nicolas Clérambault (1676–1749) published two suites in 1710.[22] He was a pupil of Raison, to whom he dedicated his work, and also of Jean-Baptiste Moreau, who wrote incidental music for the theatre. His music has some Italianate turns of phrase and a good deal of grace and fluency, though there are weak passages where upper parts wander in thirds over a slow-moving bass. He had a firm grasp of tonality, as is evident from his fugue subjects and the dominant answers in his expositions. Another of Moreau's pupils was Jean-François Dandrieu (*c*.1682–1738), whose *Pièces d'orgue*, consisting of six suites, appeared in 1739.[23] Italian influence is obvious in his music; but his conceptions of 'the noble and elegant simplicity proper to the organ' and 'the majesty of the place where it is used' generally enabled him to attain fluencey without flippancy. He used the sequences stepping in fifths which, having been developed by Corelli and others, became universal in the eighteenth century; and the *Gravement* of his Offertoire in D minor might come from any continuo movement of the more homophonic type:

Ex. 390

---

[22] Ed. Norbert Dufourcq (Paris, 1954).
[23] Ibid., modern ed. in *Archives des maîtres de l'orgue*, vii.

It is followed by a spirited fugue, with well-developed episodes that remind one of Bach. He wrote some solid fugues on plainsong, and his solo movements are unusually well knit. Dandrieu also published a collection of *Noëls* (*c*.1720) based on well-known melodies, though some of the pieces may be by his uncle, Pierre Dandrieu (d. 1733) who had already published a volume of *noëls* and other compositions a few years before.[24]

Louis-Claude Daquin (1694–1772) is known by his *Nouveau Livre de Noëls*, published about 1740.[25] The practice of writing variations on *noëls* had been established by Lebègue and Gigault, followed by Raison and Dandrieu's uncle Pierre; but such works had not previously formed so important a part of a composer's output, and Daquin's book may reflect a demand for less serious music. Such charm as his *noëls* have is mainly due to the tunes themselves; his treatment of them is thin, and not in the least organistic. His title-page allows not only the customary harpsichord, but also violins, flutes, and oboes, as alternative instruments; and it is difficult to understand Rameau's remark that Daquin had always treated the organ with due dignity.[26] Michel Corrette (1709–95) published four Magnificats (second edition, 1737), under the title *Premier livre d'orgue*, Op. 15.[27] They are degenerate works. An *offertoire* consists of a few aimless chords followed by a thin concerto-like movement. In a trio the upper parts do little but wander in thirds and sixths—a weakness of which Clérambault had shown signs; and the six-part writing in a *plein jeu* for double pedal is a mere clumsy pretence.

---

[24] Pierre Dandrieu's *Noëls variés* have been ed. R. Hugon (Paris, 1979), his nephew's *Livre de noëls* by Jean Bonfils (Paris, 1952–5). On the problem of attributions, see Hugon, François-Sappey, and Dufourcq, 'Le Livre de Noëls de Pierre Dandrieu. Une énigme', *Recherches sur la musique française classique*, xix (1979), p. 103.

[25] Ed. Guilmant and Pirro, *Archives des maîtres de l'orgue*, iii (Paris, 1901); also ed. Dufourcq, *Orgue et Liturgie*, xxvii–xxviii (Paris, 1956).

[26] J.-B. de La Borde, *Essai sur la musique ancienne et moderne* (1780), iii, p. 377.

[27] Ed. Gwilym Beechey (Madison, 1974).

ENGLAND

Towards the middle of the eighteenth century organ music de-
generated all over the Continent; and there is no doubt that it
would have done so in England as well, even if Handel had never
been heard of, for the social and religious background was certainly
no more favourable in England than elsewhere, perhaps even less
so. As Purcell's prefaces show, the English had come to suspect
what they called the levity of French methods—a foretaste, perhaps,
of the anti-French tendency that Nikolaus Pevsner sees in the rejection of the French relationship between house and garden[28]—they
regarded Italy as their best master, and, at the beginning of the
century, they were right. When presently they found among them a
composer who understood the Italian style better than the Italians
themselves, they naturally imitated him—unfortunately without
realizing that with an unsystematic composer like Handel only the
least valuable elements of his style are imitable: his mannerisms
and mere fluency.

The title 'voluntary', very common at this time, had many meanings. At first it meant a single movement—in the *durezza* style or a
fugue; then, and most commonly, a two-movement work; and later
a three-movement sonata. The two-movement works may begin
with a *durezza*, an introduction and duet, or an overture-like prelude, and conclude with a duet or trio, or sometimes a fugue. The
duets and trios—the notorious cornet and trumpet voluntaries—are
arias for the right hand, full of echoes. It is noticeable that whereas
the French treated the trumpet simply as a solo organ stop, and
often made some pretence at a contrapuntal accompaniment, the
English gave it figuration suitable for the orchestral instrument,
and provided a more homophonic background. Much of this music
is tuneful in a way that one thinks of as typically English; but the
tunefulness is apt to run thin. Italian or Handelian mannerisms are
everywhere; fugues often have two simultaneous subjects and end
with block chords. Contrapuntal writing is generally loose, and in
not more than three parts. The *durezza* movements do not show
the full quasi-vocal severity of the type; they are usually more or
less instrumental in style, with recognizable main themes. Pedals
were not altogether unknown in England; but they must have been
extremely rare, for only Handel seems to have used them.

The best-known composers were Philip Hart (d. 1749), John
Reading (d. 1764), William Croft (1678–1727), Thomas Roseingrave

[28] *An Outline of European Architecture* (London, 4th ed. 1953), p. 238.

(1688–1766), Maurice Greene (1696–1755), John Travers (c.1703–1758) and John Stanley (1712–86). The later composers seldom rise above fluency, though there are occasional flashes of vitality, particularly in Travers and Stanley.[29] But it is only the earlier composers who show anything approaching individuality: Greene occasionally, despite the influence of Handel;[30] Croft, despite his comparative lack of technical accomplishment;[31] and—without qualification—Roseingrave. The last was out of England, at Dublin and in Italy from 1709 until at least 1713; and it is tempting to connect the unconventionality of his music with his foreign upbringing and his admiration for the highly characteristic work of his friend Domenico Scarlatti.[32] At all events the *Six Double Fugues* of 1750 are much less striking than the *Voluntaries and fugues* of 1728.[33] The latter, with one exception, are single movements: most of them fugal, but some in a modified *durezza* style. Roseingrave was an unsystematic writer; but his fugue subjects have character, his harmony—'intolerably harsh' according to Burney—is often original, and his best works are highly expressive and show a command of rhetoric that carries all before it. The following example[34] gives some idea of his style:

Ex. 391

[29] Quasi-facsimile ed. of Stanley's three sets of voluntaries (1748, 1752, and 1754) by D. Vaughan (London, 1957).

[30] *Voluntaries and Suites for Organ and Harpsichord* by Greene have been ed. Beechey (Madison, 1975).

[31] Croft's *Complete Organ Works*, ed. in two vols. by Richard Platt (London, 1976–7).

[32] Cf. pp. 615–6.

[33] Ten organ pieces of Roseingrave, ed. Peter Williams (London, 1961).

[34] Closing bars of Voluntary no. 8 from *Voluntaries and fugues*.

## CATHOLIC GERMANY

It is convenient to divide the composers of the German area into Catholics and Protestants. The former worked mainly in Southern Germany, Austria, and Bohemia, the latter in Northern and Central Germany. The Catholic composers owed something to France and much to Italy. They neglected the pedals and seldom wrote at length. They were not recitalists—display passages are feeble and somewhat uncommon—they strove rather to produce neat and graceful service interludes. Nevertheless, they seldom set liturgical melodies; and when they did, they worked on purely musical lines, not attempting to intensify the expressiveness of the melodies in accordance with the words. They seem to have meant their non-fugal movements to be capable of standing alone.

At the beginning of the century the chief composers were Franz Xaver Anton Murschhauser (1663–1738)[35] and Johann Speth (1664–c.1720).[36] Like the French and Zipoli, they wrote suites of interludes in various keys; a typical suite would consist of a non-fugal introduction, several tiny fughettas, and perhaps a non-fugal finale. The movements are often thematically related. These composers also wrote, on a larger scale, the usual *durezza* movements, toccatas, and fugues: the last may stand alone, or be preceded by non-fugal sections, or be sandwiched between two such sections, with or without thematic resemblances. The preludial movements

---

[35] Modern ed. of his *Octo-Tonium novum Organicum*, (1696) and *Prototypon Longo-Breve Organicum* (1703 and 1707) in *Denkmäler der Tonkunst in Bayern*, xviii (1917), ed. Seiffert.

[36] Modern ed. of 10 toccatas from his *Ars magna consoni et dissoni* (Augsburg, 1693), ed. G. Klaus, *Liber organi*, ix (Mainz, 1954).

suffer from weak construction and indefinite themes; the fugues escape these defects to some extent, and at their best, as in Murschhauser's *Prototypon* of 1703 and 1707, show some command of rhetoric, e.g. the third F major fugue from Part II of this work:

Ex. 392

Gottlieb Muffat (1690–1770) published *72 Versetl sammt 12 Toccaten*[37] at Vienna in 1726. French influence, to be expected in a son of Georg Muffat,[38] may account for the dense ornamentation

[37] Ed. Walter Upmeyer (Kassel, 1952).
[38] For whom see chap. 8, pp. 557–9.

and good keyboard writing, which nevertheless often suggests the harpsichord. The toccatas have some coherence and passages of concerto-like texture; two of the *Versetl* (or fugues) announce two subjects simultaneously. Johann Ernest Eberlin (1702–62) also published a set of toccatas and fugues[39] (Augsburg, 1747). He neglected the pedals, and often failed to write strictly in even three parts; but he had a real grasp of organ style, and is the only composer of this group whose works are at all comparable with Bach's. Like the first prelude of *Das wohltemperirte Clavier*, though with a wider range of modulation, the toccata in D major works out a half-bar motive, which, however, is too elaborate to stand sixty-odd repetitions. Other toccatas develop one or more short figures contrapuntally, with constant use of the ubiquitous sequences stepping in fifths; the development usually runs thin. Eberlin was more successful in his fugues, some of which are in pairs, like Pachelbel's ricercars: the first independent, the second with a new subject presently combined with that of the first fugue. There remain some minor composers: Franz Anton Maichelbeck (1702–50), Carlmann Kolb (1703–65), Marianus Königsperger (1708–69), Johann Baptist Anton Vallade (d. *c*.1780) and Johann Kaspar Simon (1701–76). Their works include the usual suites of versets, preludes and fugues, which bear the marks of this transition period in their thin unorganistic texture, with chordal writing and running thirds instead of counterpoint, and excessive use of sequences.

## BOHEMIA

The Bohemian group of composers was an offshoot of the Catholic German school. It included Bohuslav Černohorský (1684–1742), Jan Zach (1699–1773), and Josef Ferdinand Norbert Seger (1716–82). Černohorský studied in Italy. Most of his music was destroyed in a fire,[40] and he is now chiefly important for his influence. Zach[41] and Seger[42] were among his pupils. These composers wrote preludes and fugues that were fairly organistic and on a reasonably large scale. They were bold harmonists but in some ways rather old-fashioned. Certain pages of Černohorský, Zach, and even Seger look almost like Pachelbel; and in their preludes they, like him, seem unable to strike a balance between shapelessness and

[39] Modern ed. by Hans Ferdinand Redlich (Berlin, 1931).
[40] Modern ed. of seven fugues and a toccata in *Musica Antiqua Bohemica*, iii, ed. František Michálek and Vladimír Helfert (Prague, 1949).
[41] *Musica Antiqua Bohemica*, xii (1953).
[42] Ibid., xii (1953), li (1961) and lvi (1962).

excessive repetition. They were much more successful in their fugues, which are vigorous and expressive; they sometimes handicapped themselves with sequential subjects, but on the other hand they avoided the flimsy harmonic writing of their period.

## PROTESTANT GERMANY

The Calvinists of Holland had used organs almost exclusively for recitals; and the recital habit was firmly established among their neighbours in Northern Germany. The merchants of Lübeck would listen to Buxtehude before they went to work. The most important composers worked in the Hanseatic cities, where there were large organs with adequate pedalboards; and their pedal technique was well developed. They aimed at display and expressiveness, and often achieved both; but their imaginative powers were apt to exhaust themselves in dramatic moments. They arouse interest, but do not maintain it.

Central Germany, on the other hand, was a region of small towns, slow to be influenced by the changes in musical technique and general mental attitude that were taking place in the great centres; and its organists were more conscientious than inventive. Largely neglecting the prelude and fugue, which required original themes, they concentrated on setting chorales; and here the value of the chorales comes out most clearly. Not only did they maintain a serious outlook; they provided pegs on which any organist could hang his performing ability and contrapuntal ingenuity, thus obtaining practice in composition (which otherwise he must have foregone through sheer lack of invention), and contributing his mite to the development of organ music.

### BÖHM

Thuringia, the home of the Bach family, was also the native country of Georg Böhm (1661–1733), who was born near Ohrdruf, the town where J. S. Bach lived with his elder brother from 1695 to 1700. The connection between the two composers was more than merely geographical. When Bach went north to Lüneburg in 1700, as a chorister in the Michaeliskirche, Böhm was already organist at the Johanneskirche, to which he had been appointed in 1698. It is hardly conceivable that the two never met, all the more since Bach is known to have admired the older man's compositions. It has been suggested that he actually had lessons from Böhm, but there is no evidence for this. Indeed, C. P. E. Bach, when sending biographical details of his father to Forkel, crossed out the words 'his teacher Böhm' and substituted 'the Lüneburg organist Böhm'.[43] On the evidence of his preludes and fugues in C major and D minor[44] Böhm must have had a formidable pedal technique. The exuberant virtuosity of these works and their clear-cut fugue subjects obviously had a strong influence on Bach's early compositions for the organ. In Böhm's chorale preludes and variations there is further evidence of his lively imagination, whether, as in 'Allein Gott in der Höh sei Ehr', he is clothing the melody in smooth counterpoint:

Ex. 393

or presenting both the melody and its background in a more elaborate form, as in the second prelude on 'Christ lag in Todesbanden':

Ex. 394

[43] *The Bach Reader*, ed. H. T. David and Arthur Mendel (New York, 1945), p. 278.
[44] Modern ed. of Böhm's keyboard works in *Georg Böhm: Sämtliche Werke*, i, ed. Johannes Wolgast (Leipzig, 1927; new ed. by G. Wolgast, Wiesbaden, 1952).

His delight in his obvious powers as an executant finds particular expression in the variations, which sometimes betray the influence of Italian secular music. Here too the association with Bach's early chorale variations (BWV 766–8, probably written at Lüneburg) is often very close. Compare, for instance, the opening of the third variation of Böhm's 'Auf meinen lieben Gott':

Ex. 395

with the first variation of Bach's 'Sei gegrüsset, Jesu gütig':

Ex. 396

The influence of Pachelbel is obvious in the works of composers who, unlike Böhm, remained in Central Germany: Friedrich Wilhelm Zachow (1663–1712) at Halle, Johann Heinrich Buttstedt (1666–1727) at Erfurt, Andreas Nikolaus Vetter (1666–1734) at Rudolstadt, Johann Bernhard Bach—a third cousin of Sebastian—(1676–1749) at Eisenach (after a short period at Magdeburg), and Georg Friedrich Kauffmann (1679–1735) at Merseburg[45] (whose *Harmonische Seelen Lust* includes some settings which require an oboist to play the melody)—though it became less conspicuous as northern methods filtered through, and Zachow and Kauffmann began to achieve coherence by borrowing the ritornello device or using the chorale as a *cantus firmus* to a fughetta on the first line of the melody. There is, however, no need to discuss the work of these men in detail, for the whole school is summed up in Johann Gottfried Walther (1684–1748), successively organist at Erfurt and Weimar—'a second Pachelbel, if not the first in art'.

[45] For modern eds. see the Bibliography.

### J. G. WALTHER

That description, which is Mattheson's, is incomplete; for Walther knew Böhm's work, was intimate with Bach (his second cousin) and, like the latter, was active in transcribing Italian concertos. Though not the most imaginative, he was one of the most accomplished German organ composers of his time.[46] His preludes and fugues and his concerto (for organ solo) combine northern and Italian elements, and in this respect resemble several of Bach's Arnstadt or early Weimar works. He wrote chorale fughettas, 'Pachelbel' preludes, and many chorale partitas—one movement to each verse of the hymn. The total number of chorales treated is 105 (some more than once), and if we count the separate movements of the partitas we have the impressive total of 286 settings. Many of the movements are for manuals only, but there are plenty of examples with independent pedal parts. Many settings have well-marked ritornelli, e.g. the first verse of the partita on 'Durch Adams Fall':

Ex. 397

Close imitation occurs frequently, e.g. the first verse of 'Allein Gott in der Höh' sei Ehr'':

Ex. 398

---

[46] Modern ed. of his organ works (most of which survive in manuscript) in *Denkmäler deutscher Tonkunst*, xxvi–xxvii, ed. Seiffert (Leipzig, 1906).

Such imitation often develops into canon, either on the chorale melody, as in verse 2 of 'Ach schönster Jesu, mein Verlangen', where the treble entry is decorated and the introduction for the two other parts is treated chromatically:

Ex. 399

or between the accompanying parts, as in verse 3 of 'Wir Christenleut', where the *cantus firmus* is heard on the pedals:[47]

Ex. 400

Throughout, Walther follows consistently the German tradition of chorale treatment, only occasionally breaking into 'French' rhythm, as in the second prelude on 'Mache dich, mein Geist, bereit':

---

[47] See p. 682.

Ex. 401

Though there is sometimes a lack of variety in his settings, there is never any lack of resource; and in his contrapuntal treatment he shows a mastery equalled only by Bach among his contemporaries.

## BACH

Descriptions of Bach's development as an organ composer should be accepted with caution. Most of his works can be dated only by their style—an unsatisfactory method, if only because he revised some of them so thoroughly that they no longer suggest their original early date, and what can be proved in one or two cases may have happened frequently. Biographical facts suggest that he was subjected to certain influences in a certain order, and although the dates at which those influences took effect cannot be stated precisely, the evidence is good enough for an outline.

Born at Eisenach in 1685, he heard as a child the organ music of Johann Christoph Bach (1642–1703), his father's cousin. From 1695 to 1700 he was taught by his eldest brother, who had been a pupil of Pachelbel. At Lüneburg from 1700 to 1703, as we have seen, he must have become acquainted with Böhm's work; he is said to have visited Hamburg (presumably to hear Reincken, Vincent Lübeck, and Kneller) and Celle (where there was a French orchestra). He had not, thus far, had an organ of his own; but he must have had access to one, for in 1703 he was employed as an organ examiner, and his playing satisfied the authorities at Arnstadt. Here until 1707, and at Mühlhausen for another year, he had opportunities for practice, though neither organ was first-rate. In 1705 he went to hear Buxtehude at Lübeck. In 1708 he moved to Weimar, where he was not only Court Organist, but also had much to do with Italian instrumental music. In 1714 he signed a copy of some works by Frescobaldi. Subsequent events are hardly relevant; for he ceased to be a professional organist when he left Weimar in 1717, and it may well be, as the 'obituary' suggests,[48] that by then he had written most of his organ music. No doubt it is true that he studied 'certain good French organists' as well as his German predecessors; but apart from one or two alleged thematic borrowings the organ works show no very clear signs of French influence. For practical purposes it may be said that until 1708 he was engaged in learning all that Germany had to teach him, and that by then the southern bias of his earliest experiences had been corrected by Böhm and Buxtehude. It was only after that date that he became subject to the Italian influences to which his best works owe so much.

CHORALE PRELUDES

The chorale preludes show Bach at his most Teutonic, and technically at his least inventive. Except in the trios, e.g. 'Herr Jesu Christ dich zu uns wend' (BWV 655),[49] there is practically no trace of foreign influences that had not already been digested by German composers; and complete acquaintance with earlier work would probably show that every device used by Bach (again, except in the trios) had already been used by a German. Accordingly, there is little to choose between many of Bach's chorale preludes (particularly the early works) and the best works of his predecessors and contemporaries; but between the latter and his best preludes there is all the difference between incompetence or mere craftsmanship on the one hand, and composition on the other. Bach himself made five collections of chorale preludes: the *Orgelbüchlein* (46 preludes), Part III of the *Clavierübung* (21), the set published by J. G. Schübler (6), the five canonic variations on 'Vom Himmel hoch', and the so-called 'Eighteen Chorale Preludes' (actually 17,

[48] *The Bach Reader*, p. 218.
[49] BWV = Schmieder, *Bach-Werke-Verzeichnis* (Leipzig, 1950).

with the addition of 'Vor deinen Thron',[50] which he dictated during his last illness). He also left fifty-odd uncollected preludes, many of them immature. The Schübler preludes (BWV 645–50) hardly call for discussion here. Published at Leipzig after 1746, five of them are arrangements of cantata movements written some years earlier; so, presumably, is the sixth ('Wo soll ich fliehen hin'). The arrangements are much less effective than the originals, and it is hard to see why Bach published them.

The *Orgelbüchlein*, left unfinished, should have contained 164 preludes grouped on liturgical principles. Bach meant it to provide pedal practice, models for composition, and a prelude for every conceivable liturgical reason. All the evidence goes to show that nearly all the preludes were written between 1714 and 1716, when Bach was still at Weimar,[51] but he may have used the collection for teaching during his years at Cöthen (1717–23) and the title-page, in which he describes himself as 'p.t. (i.e. pro tempore) Capellae Magister S.P.R. Anhaltini-Cotheniensis' must have been added at this time.[52] In its emphasis on a didactic purpose it is very similar to the title-pages of Part I of *Das wohltemperirte Clavier* (1722) and the *Inventions* (1723). The *Clavierübung* preludes are also grouped on liturgical principles. They were published in 1739. Most of the 'Eighteen' preludes were composed at Weimar; then revised, and copied into the same manuscript book, some time between 1744 and 1748.[53] They seem to be a random collection; but Bach may have meant to write more preludes and rearrange the set in accordance with a careful plan.

Bach set chorales in many ways. He probably began with the Central German forms: fughettas on first lines or couplets, 'Pachelbel' preludes, and sets of variations; and some of his early attempts seem to have been preserved among the uncollected preludes. In studying these works one must remember that he generally wrote on two staves; it is therefore sometimes doubtful whether certain bass passages belong to the left hand or to the

[50] An extended and simplified version of the prelude 'Wenn wir in höchsten Nöten sein' (BWV 641) in the *Orgelbüchlein*.
[51] See Georg von Dadelsen, 'Zur Entstehung des Bachschen Orgelbüchleins', in *Festschrift Friedrich Blume* (Kassel, 1963), p. 74.
[52] Sanford Terry's argument, in *Bach's Chorals*, iii (Cambridge, 1921), pp. 19 ff, that 'pro tempore' means that Bach had not yet taken up his appointment at Cöthen is not an admissible interpretation of the words. On the contrary they could be held to imply that Bach had already been appointed Cantor of the Thomaskirche at Leipzig, in which case the title-page dates from the spring of 1723.
[53] See Dadelsen, *Beiträge zur Chronologie der Werke Johann Sebastian Bachs* (Trossingen, 1958), pp. 109–10.

pedals, and it is not safe to date them by the standard pedal technique they would require.

Fugues on a single chorale line present no special problems. If the line does not make a good subject, it can be decorated until it does, or given a countersubject that makes good its deficiencies; the rest is a matter of ordinary fugue technique. Bach can be seen experimenting on these lines in a series of preludes beginning perhaps with 'Gottes Sohn ist kommen' (BWV 703) and 'Nun komm, der Heiden Heiland' (BWV 699) and ending with 'Dies sind die heil'gen zehn Gebot' (BWV 679) and 'Jesus Christus unser Heiland' (BWV 689) from the *Clavierübung*. These works are for manuals alone, and the last is the only one on a large scale. In fugues on two lines of a chorale it is harder to secure coherence. It will not do to write a fughetta on the first line, and then another on the second—especially if the second line is treated in shorter notes than the first (so that it sounds more like a fresh counterpoint than a second subject) and the two fughettas are separated by an irrelevant flourish, as in the spurious 'Der Tag der ist so freudenreich' (BWV 719).[54] Bach himself managed these things rather better, as one can see from 'Herr Christ, der ein'ge Gottes Sohn' (BWV 698) and the third setting of 'Allein Gott in der Höh' sei Ehr' ' in the *Clavierübung* (BWV 677). In both these works (for manuals only) there is a suggestion of *da capo* structure, references to the second line being confined to the middle of the movement, so that there is no break in continuity. Furthermore, in 'Herr Christ' the second line is introduced as a counterpoint to the first:

Ex. 402

A 'Pachelbel' prelude, consisting as it does of a string of fugatos on different subjects, lacks the coherence that even a hint of recapitulation can give; and familiarity with the chorale makes little difference. Furthermore, the successive fugal expositions prevent any continuous growth of interest. Bach nevertheless wrote prel-

[54] Attributed to Bach in *Bach-Gesellschaft*, xl, p. 55, but without any evidence of authenticity.

udes of this type throughout his career, from 'Vom Himmel Hoch' (BWV 700) to 'Vor deinen Thron' (BWV 668). He can be seen disguising the expositions more or less successfully, and realizing that one entry in each fugato must be emphasized by soloing or augmentation;[55] But not even he could make this form satisfying. He was perhaps most successful in the B flat major 'Valet will ich dir geben' (BWV 735), whose vigorous accompanimental parts, if not actually consistent, are at any rate consistently full of conventional figures, and in 'Jesus Christus unser Heiland' (BWV 665), a powerful work whose four sections make no pretence at continuity of any ordinary kind, but are readily acceptable as a set of movements held together by a programme. His most imposing effort, 'Aus tiefer Noth' from the *Clavierübung* (BWV 686), probably owes much of its reputation to the extreme difficulty of making it effective on English organs. As it is seldom heard, it is judged less by its sound than by its appearance; six-part writing with double pedal looks very well on paper.

Bach may have experimented with chorale partitas at a very early date; but 'Christ, der du bist der helle Tag' (BWV 766) and 'O Gott, du frommer Gott' (BWV 767), the earliest that can be attributed to him with any certainty, owe so much to Böhm that they can hardly have been written before 1700. The pedal writing is elementary. In the first movement of each set the chorale is plainly harmonized, and the contrast between these movements and some of the others, with their graceful keyboard writing and bold harmonic touches, e.g. the eighth variation of 'O Gott, du frommer Gott':

Ex. 403

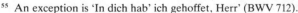

---

[55] An exception is 'In dich hab' ich gehoffet, Herr' (BWV 712).

has been attributed to partial revision; but similar contrasts can be found in Böhm. There seems no reason why Bach's ability should not have revealed itself in moments of grace or audacity at an early date—long before he ceased to be a slavish imitator of his predecessors' structural principles and types of texture. In fact, the chorale partita form does not seem to have attracted him. It was probably at Weimar, under the influence of J. G. Walther, that he completed his most successful essay in this form, 'Sei gegrüsset, Jesu gütig' (BWV 768). But he evidently preferred to elaborate standard partita-types into independent preludes. There is, for instance, a type in which the chorale is stated simply and without interruption. This in itself provides coherence; but the accompaniment contributes by developing one or more independent figures. One figure may be reserved for the pedals, appearing in ostinato-fashion at intervals—an idea hinted at by Böhm. Bach, like Zachow, sometimes achieved still greater concentration by using chorale motives in the accompaniment. There are preludes of these types in the *Orgelbüchlein*, e.g. 'Ach wie nichtig' (BWV 644), 'Heut' triumphiret Gottes Sohn' (BWV 630), and 'Helft mir Gottes Güte preisen' (BWV 613).

Alternatively, the chorale may be worked into an expressive arabesque—again providing adequate coherence, so long as it is not interrupted, although again the accompaniment may be consistently developed from recognizable figures. Bach thus produced such preludes as 'Das alte Jahr vergangen ist' (BWV 614), 'O Mensch bewein' dein' Sünde gross' (BWV 622) and 'Herr Jesu Christ dich zu uns wend' (BWV 709). Longer partita movements, in which the chorale is interrupted, may resemble arias in using an ostinato bass or a rudimentary ritornello. This idea was taken up by Kauffmann and Walther, and developed by Bach on a much larger scale. The recurrent matter may be based on the chorale, as in both settings of 'An Wasserflüssen Babylon' (BWV 653, 653a–b), or independent, as in the first prelude on 'Christ, unser Herr, zum Jordan kam' in the *Clavierübung* (BWV 684):[56]

---

[56] Though some writers see an allusion to the chorale melody in the running semiquavers.

Ex. 404

Bach's method of accompanying a congregation is perhaps exemplified in settings such as 'Lobt Gott, ihr Christen' (BWV 732),
'Allein Gott in der Höh' sei Ehr' ' (BWV 715), 'Gelobet seist du,
Jesu Christ' (BWV 722) and 'Herr Jesu Christ, dich zu uns wend'
(BWV 726). They amount to little more than improvisations, and
he may have written them out only as models for his pupils, though
similar works by Kauffmann were considered worthy of publication.
'Vom Himmel hoch' (BWV 738) and 'In dulci jubilo' (BWV 729)
show that he realized the possiblity, already demonstrated by
Buttstedt, of making interlinear flourishes into something better
than cover for the gasps of the congregation; but movements so

constructed tend to be showy and rhapsodical, and these qualities seem soon to have lost their appeal for Bach. Perhaps this is why Buxtehude's chorale preludes had comparatively little influence on him. The long fantasias left their mark on one or two early works— e.g. 'Christ lag in Todesbanden' (BWV 718) and 'Ein feste Burg' (BWV 720)—and on the later but most exceptional 'In dir ist Freude' from the *Orgelbüchlein* (BWV 615); and among the short preludes on such movements as the A major 'Allein Gott in der Höh' sei Ehr' ' (BWV 662) and, strangely enough, on that supreme achievement, 'Nun komm, der Heiden Heiland' (BWV 659). The latter is pulled together only by the accident that the last line of the chorale is the same as the first; but it was imagination, and no accident, that made the Buxtehudean final flourish into so expressive a coda.

Zachow had hinted at the possiblity of writing a fugue, either on a chorale motive or on an independent subject, against the chorale brought in line by line as a *cantus firmus*; and it was in this way that Bach produced the best of his longer preludes—'Nun komm der Heiden Heiland' (BWV 661), the three pedal settings of the 'Kyrie' and 'Christe' in the *Clavierübung* (BWV 669–71), and 'Komm Heiliger Geist' in F major (BWV 651), a work conceived on the scale of the great preludes and fugues and carried through with tremendous concentration and vigour.

Bach set chorales canonically in two ways. In four of the canonic variations on 'Vom Himmel hoch' (BWV 769) he used the chorale as *cantus firmus* to a canon based largely, or altogether, on independent material. (Walther had used this method in his partita on 'Wir Christenleut'.[57]) In the remaining variation (no. 5 in the original edition) the chorale itself is in canon:[58] here too Walther offers several examples. There are nine canons of this kind in the *Orgelbüchlein*. Comparable with them is the early 'Ach Gott und Herr' (BWV 714); and there are two much longer and more elaborate movements in the *Clavierübung*—'Dies sind die heil'gen zehn Gebot' (BWV 678) and 'Vater unser in Himmelreich' (BWV 682). Written about 1746, to demonstrate Bach's fitness to join Mizler's *Societät der musicalischen Wissenschaften*, the variations are on the whole rather stiff, and the poor tune and didactic words of 'Dies sind die heil'gen zehn Gebot' make uninspiring material. About 'Vater unser' opinions differ, its extreme elaboration making it dif-

---

[57] See Ex. 400.
[58] *Al rovescio*, i.e. by inversion.

ficult both to play and to take in. But there is no doubt about the shorter preludes: they are all successful, and the brilliant 'In dulci jubilo' in the *Orgelbüchlein* (BWV 608) particularly so.

The trios on 'Herr Jesu Christ' (BWV 655) and 'Allein Gott' (BWV 664) are of considerable interest. Texturally Italianate, like the sonatas, they are difficult and cannot be early works; they may nevertheless owe something to a Pachelbel form—that in which a fughetta on the first line precedes a harmonization of the whole chorale. In these trios Bach plays for some time with figures derived from the first line, and then gives the whole chorale, or its first couplet, to the pedal. The five-part fugue on the Magnificat (BWV 733) is somewhat similar in construction.

TRIO SONATAS

The six trio sonatas (BWV 525–30) show the secular and Italianate aspects of Bach. Structurally they closely resemble his own chamber sonatas for two obbligato parts and continuo bass; and in writing for the organ in this style he was breaking new ground. As we know them, they are polished works of about 1730; but the movements may have been written singly over a period of many years, beginning soon after 1708. Two of the movements— the Andante of BWV 528 and Largo of BWV 529—may have been originally intended for the organ, since they are first heard of in association with organ preludes and fugues in G major (BWV 541) and C major (BWV 545);[59] but it is not certain that they all were,[60] and when Bach collected them to form sonatas it is quite possible that he was thinking rather of private practice on a two-manual harpsichord with pedals than of public performance on an organ. Except in cadential chords, the sonatas are strictly in three parts. The upper parts cross freely, and have to be played on separate keyboards. The basses have very little conventional pedal figuration, and look more like cello parts. The sonatas touch no great heights or depths—Bach's works in this style seldom do—but are fascinating to play, and delightful to hear when well played.

PRELUDES, FANTASIAS, AND TOCCATAS

In his other organ works Bach's development can be traced with somewhat greater certainty. It is obviously likely that, after attain-

---

[59] See p. 690.
[60] The Adagio and Vivace of no. 4 appear as an orchestral introduction to the cantata 'Die Himmel erzählen die Ehre Gottes' (BWV 76), which dates from 1723.

ing some proficiency in the Pachelbel or Central German style, he realized that he had much to learn from the North, and began a new course of close imitation. The Fantasia in G major (BWV 572) is decidedly southern in style, with its neat manual passage-work and central *durezza*. So is the Prelude and Fugue in C minor (BWV 549), although no southern or central composer ever equalled its solidity and imaginative power, and there are northern touches in the long subject and showy coda of the fugue.

Direct acquaintance with Böhm and Buxtehude led at first to disastrous results in such works as the Prelude and Fugue in A minor (BWV 551) and the Toccata (BWV 566) which exists in two versions, one in C major and the other in E major. But mere imitation soon gave place to a combination of intensity of expression, which the Northerners had aimed at, with the neatness and consistency that had been the southern ideal: a mixed style in which, thanks to his powers of rhetoric and invention, Bach was able to produce such works as the Toccata and Fugue in D minor (BWV 565) and the Prelude and Fugue in D major (BWV 532), which are neither mere teaching material nor historical monuments but effective recital music. In the Toccata Bach seems to have realized the weakness of Buxtehude's alternations of fugue and display, in which all the sections seem too short to tell; he used three sections only, and emphasized the fugue. Moreover, he found precisely the right effect for the end of the fugue—a point where Buxtehude either destroys all feeling of expectancy with a perfect cadence or breaks continuity by following an inconclusive cadence with an irrelevant chord. The Prelude and Fugue in D major is based on the five-section Buxtehudean type; but here, perhaps for the first time, Bach rejected the fifth section of scales and chords, and the halt that generally precedes it. Instead, he ran the fugue on into a series of brilliant arpeggios, and in the very last bars reverted to material derived from his subject and countersubject.

It is reasonable to suppose that these works were written by 1708, or very soon after. Bach was already writing better than any of his German predecessors; but his acquaintance with Italian instrumental music, which began at Weimar, showed him that there was no further progress to be made. He had yet to write an organized fugue, to explore the possibilities of a slow fugue subject and unconventional figuration, and to write a preludial movement that could stand alone; furthermore, he found himself dissatisfied with the Buxtehudean method of planning a whole work, even when modified as in the works just described.

## FUGUES

The general aspects of his progress in the art of fugue-writing need not be discussed here; but the organ fugues have certain features of their own: rhythmically simple subjects, little contrapuntal elaboration, and a characteristic sectional structure. A pedal entry, sounding as it does, not only at its written pitch but also an octave lower, is more striking than a bass entry on the harpsichord, and should be made with important thematic material. Exceptions to this rule occur only in works such as the fugues in G minor (BWV 578) and E minor (BWV 533/2), written possibly before 1708 and certainly not much later. Furthermore, constant use of the pedals becomes tiresome; they are most effective when they enter after a generous rest. Bach can be seen realizing this in the fugues of the D minor Toccata (BWV 565) and the Passacaglia in C minor (BWV 582); but the fugues in G major (BWV 550/2) and the so-called 'Jig' fugue in the same key (BWV 577) were perhaps the first to show what became a regular feature—an odd number of sections, the even-numbered ones for manuals alone, the others using the pedals almost continuously. The number of sections may be seven, as in the 'Dorian' Fugue (BWV 538/2); five, as in the 'Great' G minor (BWV 542/2); or three, as in the B minor (BWV 544/2). At or near the beginning of each section Bach sometimes introduced a new theme and probably changed manuals, e.g. in the B minor Fugue, bars 58–63:

Ex. 405

The general effect resembles the alternations of solo and tutti in concerto movements.

Bach's earlier fugue subjects tend, like Buxtehude's, to move quickly—to include semiquavers, for instance, if semiquaver movement is maintained in the fugue. Naturally they use conventionally grateful pedal figuration, with its characterless angularity. Bach soon learnt to make the best of it, as in the 'Great' G minor; by mixing it with stringy types of figuration borrowed from the Italian works with which he was becoming familiar; and he made a further advance when he began to use slow-moving subjects and let the countersubjects supply the necessary movement. It is not necessary to suppose that he owed this idea to Italians—to Frescobaldi, whom he imitated in his Canzona in D minor (BWV 588), or to Corelli, from whom he borrowed a subject of this type;[61] for Pachelbel's ricercars and many chorale fughettas might equally well have been his models.

Among the more or less mature works there are two double fugues. That which follows the Passacaglia in C minor is of the type in which the second subject is merely a regular countersubject under another name. The F major (BWV 540/2) is of the other type: the development of the second subject forms a pedal-less middle section. Two fugues have da capos (cf. the finale of Sonata no. 2). In the 'Wedge' in E minor (BWV 548/2) the middle section has passage-work alternating with entries of the subject and countersubject; its great freedom is rather unsatisfactorily balanced by a complete *da capo*. In the C minor (BWV 537/2) the middle section combines a new subject with a motive from the first section, the *da capo* is cut short, and the result is far more effective. The final feminine cadence is perfectly calculated for the organ, whose sustained tone makes the most of the discord. There are two other

---

[61] Fugue in B minor (BWV 579). Both the subject and the countersubject come from the second movement (Vivace) of Corelli's *Sonate da chiesa*, Op. 3, no. 4, (1689).

experimental fugues, both completely successful. In the C major (BWV 547/2) the pedals enter late as a fifth part, as in the early C minor (BWV 549/2), with the subject in augmentation as in the fugue on the Magnificat (BWV 733). The Fugue in E flat major (BWV 552/2) from the *Clavierübung* may owe something to the seventeenth-century strings of fugues on modifications of the same subject, to Pachelbel's ricercars, or to Buxtehude's fugue in F sharp minor;[62] but it is far beyond them in scale, organization, and rhetorical power.

## TYPES OF PRELUDE

The D minor Toccata (BWV 565)[63] and the Prelude and Fugue in D major (BWV 532) are not the only works with Buxtehudean preludes—preludes in a strict sense, since, effectively as some of them set the stage for their fugues, the former at least is too slight for use as an independent movement. The preludes in A major (BWV 536/1), A minor (BWV 543/1) and G minor (BWV 535/1) have fugues that end with display passages (much modified in the A major); and each work, taken as a whole, can be regarded as a development of the Buxtehudean three-section form. Bach seems to have remained satisfied with preludes of this type for some years; and the three fugues show a great advance, with much genuine counterpoint, and in the G minor a most dramatic Neapolitan sixth:

Ex. 406

Bach's last word in rhapsodical prelude-writing was probably the Fantasia in G minor (BWV 542), whose fugue needs no final flourishes, since every pedal entry of its subject is a display of virtuosity. It is quite likely that he played this work to Reincken in

---

[62] *Complete Organ Works*, ed. Josef Hedar (Copenhagen and London, 1952), ii, p. 73.
[63] The authenticity of this famous piece has been challenged by Peter Williams, *Early Music*, ix (1981), p. 330.

1720; but it is by no means certain that he composed it at that comparatively late date, expressly for that purpose. The fugue subject resembles both a tune from Reincken's *Hortus Musicus* and a Dutch folksong (Reincken had worked in Holland); but even if Bach must be supposed incapable of inventing the subject for himself, he is no more likely to have taken a hint from those sources than from Buxtehude's Fugue in F major.[64]

Ex. 407

It may well be that he wrote these movements several years before 1720, basing the fugue on that inferior version of the subject which Mattheson described as well known in 1725;[65] and that the work as known today owes much to a revision after 1720. This Fantasia differs from the preludes just mentioned in having an independent status. It contains violently contrasted textures— recitative, block chords, and close imitative counterpoint—in sharply defined sections, two of which are recognizably recapitulated, while the rest have motives in common. As an example of organized rhapsody it is completely sucessful—it is the sort of music that Reincken and Buxtehude would have written if they had known how to—and the reason why Bach wrote no more in this style must be simply that he came to prefer thematic and textural consistency.

This preference can be seen in his development of the Buxtehudean five-section plan, which probably began before he

[64] *Complete Organ Works*, p. 91.
[65] *Grosse General-Bass-Schule*, 2nd ed. (1731).

wrote the G minor Fantasia. In the D major prelude he had already run the fourth section on into the fifth, to secure continuity; he now began to connect the first and second sections by making the initial display passages announce the motives of the second section. Buxtehude had hinted at this device in his Prelude in E minor.[66] Bach's treatment of it can be seen in the early Prelude in G major (BWV 550) and the Toccata in C major (BWV 564). The Prelude in G major is a failure; but it ranks as a separate movement. The first part of the Toccata is independent and reasonably coherent, and decidedly the best part of the work.

The next step was to combine or develop the initial motives in contrasted short sections and work the latter into patterns. This structural principle, hinted at in the Toccata in C major, is worked out much more clearly in the 'Dorian' and F major toccatas (BWV 538/1 and 540/1), the latter written perhaps for the F pedal board at Weissenfels. In both works the first pages are not display passages so much as enunciations of thematic germs; and neither of the associated fugues ends with passage-work. Unfortunately, the themes are insufficiently contrasted—especially in the 'Dorian', which suffers also from unenterprising harmony and a conventional key-scheme—and dynamic changes are prohibited by the almost continuous use of the pedals, a tiresome feature in itself. The result is that the 'Dorian' toccata is rather dull and the F major too repetitive. But in shorter works, with more suitable themes and freer development, this method was perfectly successful: see the preludes in G major and C major (BWV 541/1 and 547/1). (Both the fugues break off dramatically just before the end; but their codas are strictly thematic. The G major was revised in 1724 or 1725.) In the still shorter Prelude in C major (BWV 545/1) the main theme is hardly ever absent, except from the first three and the last three bars, which may have been an inspired afterthought (the work seems to have been revised about 1730) but a distinct impression of contrasted sections (ABAB) is produced by alternations of holding-notes and movement in the pedal part. The five-part Fantasia in C minor (BWV 562/1) seems to be an isolated attempt to write a non-fugal movement in which coherence is secured by contrapuntal methods. Satisfactory enough in itself, though perhaps a little stolid, it is too much like a fugue to make a good prelude. Perhaps that is why Bach did not complete the fugue (BWV 562/2) that follows it.

[66] Hedar, ii, no. 10.

Having the Buxtehudean third section in mind, Bach was slow to dispense with a link-passage between an organized prelude and a fugue. Thus in the early G major (BWV 550) the prelude and the fugue are separated by a short Grave: the Toccata in C major has an Italianate slow movement as well as a Grave: and the works in G major (BWV 541) and C major (BWV 545) seem originally to have included, as middle movements, borrowings from the fourth and fifth sonatas.[67] But after these, all the preludes and fugues were probably of the familiar two-movement type. The movements are generally united only by similarity of mood; but both the prelude and the fugue in C major (BWV 547) have chordal passages whose resemblance, unlike the resemblances in the G major (BWV 541) and G minor (BWV 535), is significant and probably intentional. Both these passages, in the prelude and the fugue, allow room for improvizational expansion in performance. The Fantasia and Fugue in C minor (BWV 537) is noteworthy because the Fantasia ends on a half-cadence, and cannot therefore be played alone; its last bars are perhaps to be regarded as a built-in link-passage. The ABAB structure of the Prelude in C major (BWV 545/1) reappears more emphatically in this Fantasia, whose sections present different themes, not simply different aspects of the same theme. There are, however, no contrasts of texture like those in the G minor Fantasia (BWV 542); the movement is contrapuntal throughout.

All the preludes so far discussed have more or less continuous pedal parts; but Bach also experimented with discontinuous pedal parts, producing alternations of solo and tutti like those in his mature fugues. The F minor Prelude (BWV 534/1) is perhaps an early experiment, in which he may have tried out various new plans for the first time. The structural principle is competently handled in the vigorous C minor Prelude (BWV 546/1); but even here it is doubtful whether Bach would have emphasized the sectional construction by manual changes in performance. He certainly did so in the Prelude in E flat major (BWV 552/1) from the *Clavierübung*. Here there are sharper contrasts of texture than in the other preludes of this type, and a homophonic passage that shows something very like a change of mood—a rare thing in Bach:

---

[67] See above, p. 683.

Ex. 408

Perhaps he was toying with the 'new music' of his day; but that
would suggest a date contemporary with publication (1739), which
is difficult to reconcile with the clumsy final return to the main
theme. The other concerto-preludes—in E minor (BWV 548/1) and
B minor (BWV 544/1)—are extant in autograph manuscripts of the
1730s. Here Bach treated the ritornello rather freely. In the E
minor there is one complete restatement of it in an unexpected
place (bars 33–51); in the B minor there is none; but in both movements the structural balance is perfect, and the irregularities give
an impression of unusual vitality that is confirmed by the themes
and their working-out. These are among his finest works in any
medium.

## BACH'S PUPILS

Of the German composers born after Bach, the Catholics have
already been mentioned (pp. 665 ff.). Of the rest, Bach's pupils are the
most interesting. Conditions were becoming more and more unfavourable. The sermon grew in importance, interest in organ
music declined, and with it the status of organists. Moreover, Protestant Germany now became subject to the influences that had
already proved harmful to organ music in other areas. It was
Bach's least enterprising pupils (on the whole, the earlier ones)
who wrote the best organ music; those who were more up-to-date
either neglected the organ or mishandled it.

The early group of pupils is formed by Johann Tobias Krebs (1690–1762), Johann Kaspar Vogler (1696–1763), Heinrich Nikolaus Gerber (1702–75),[68] Johann Schneider (1702–88), Bach's eldest son Wilhelm Friedemann Bach (1710–84), and Johann Ludwig Krebs (1713–80),[69] son of Johann Tobias. Johann Peter Kellner (1705–72)[70] was strongly influenced by Bach, whom he describes as 'dieser vortreffliche Mann', but not actually a pupil. All imitated his earlier works; Vogler's 'Jesu, Leiden, Pein und Tod',[71] exaggerates the arabesques and chromaticism of 'O Mensch, bewein' (BWV 622):

Ex. 409

and J. L. Krebs sometimes borrowed both themes and structure not from Bach in general, but recognizably from individual works. Krebs nevertheless wrote some creditable trios and preludes and fugues, and Kellner some agreeable chorale preludes. Friedemann Bach, a notable performer and improviser, was disappointingly stiff and inexpressive in his few compositions.[72]

    [68] *Four Inventions*, ed. Susi Jeans (London, 1975).
    [69] *Ausgewählte Orgelwerke*, ed. Karl Tittel (Lippstadt, 1963–75).
    [70] *Ausgewählte Orgelwerke*, ed. Georg Feder (Lippstadt, 1958).
    [71] Attributed to Bach in some sources. Modern ed. in *Choralvorspiele alter Meister*, ed. Karl Straube (Leipzig, 1907), p. 136.
    [72] *Complete Works for Organ*, ed. E. Power Biggs and G. Weston (New York, 1947). Two chorale preludes in *Das Erbe deutscher Musik, Reichsdenkmale*, ix, ed. Gotthold Frotscher (Brunswick, 1937).

None of Bach's younger sons took any serious interest in the organ. Carl Philipp Emanuel Bach (1714–88) wrote six of his seven undistinguished Sonatas (*c*.1755–8) for manuals alone, and had forgotten the use of the pedals long before Burney visited him.

## CONCLUSION

If the first half of the eighteenth century must be set down as a period of decline in organ music, that is because the decline, once it started, was so rapid. The latter part of the period was nevertheless illuminated by Martini, Dandrieu, Krebs, and Eberlin; and during its earlier years there was a technical advance both in composition and in organ-playing. This advance took place in all areas, as one can see by comparing the works of Clérambault, Roseingrave, and Walther with those of their predecessors. The main reason why it is most conspicuous in Protestant Germany is simply that Bach had worked there.

# BIBLIOGRAPHY

*Compiled by* DAVID BLACKWELL

## GENERAL

**(i) Modern Anthologies**

DAVISON, ARCHIBALD T. and APEL, WILLI: *Historical Anthology of Music*, ii (Cambridge, Mass., 1950).
PARRISH, CARL: *A Treasury of Early Music* (New York, 1958).
—— and OHL, JOHN F.: *Masterpieces of Music before 1750* (New York, 1951).
SCHERING, ARNOLD: *Geschichte der Musik in Beispielen* (2nd ed., Leipzig, 1955).

**(ii) Books and Articles**

ANTHONY, JAMES R.: *French Baroque Music from Beaujoyeulx to Rameau* (London, 1973; 2nd rev. ed., 1978).
BASELT, BERND: 'Verzeichnis der Werke Georg Friedrich Händels (HWV)', *Händel-Jahrbuch 1979*, xxv, pp. 9–139.
BRAUN, WERNER: *Die Musik des 17. Jahrhunderts* (Wiesbaden, 1981).
BUKOFZER, MANFRED F.: *Music in the Baroque Era* (New York, 1947).
BURNEY, CHARLES: *A General History of Music*, i–iv (London, 1776–89; ed. F. Mercer in 2 vols., London, 1935; repr., New York, 1957).
—— *The Present State of Music in France and Italy* (London, 1771; ed. P. A. Scholes, *Dr. Burney's Musical Tours in Europe*, i, Oxford, 1959).
CARSE, ADAM: *The Orchestra in the Eighteenth Century* (Cambridge, 1940; repr., 1950).
CLERCX, SUSANNE: *Le Baroque et la musique* (Brussels, 1948).
D'APLIGNY, PILEUR: *Traité sur la Musique* (Paris, 1779).
DAVAL, PIERRE: *La Musique en France au XVIIIe siècle* (Paris, 1961).
DE LA BORDE, J. -B.: *Essai sur la musique ancienne et moderne* (Paris, 1780; repr., 1972).
DONINGTON, ROBERT: *Baroque Music: Style and Performance* (London, 1982).
EINSTEIN, ALFRED: *A Short History of Music* (5th ed., London, 1948).
HAAS, ROBERT: *Die Musik des Barocks* (Potsdam, 1928).
HAWKINS, JOHN: *A General History of the Science and Practice of Music*, i–v (London, 1776; 2nd ed., 2 vols., London, 1853; repr., New York, 1963).
HEINICHEN, JOHANN DAVID: *Der General-Bass in der Composition* (Dresden, 1728).

KAHL, WILLI: *Selbstbiographien deutscher Musiker des XVIII Jahrhunderts* (Cologne and Krefeld, 1948; repr., 1972).

LAVIGNAC, ALBERT and LA LAURENCIE, LIONEL DE: *Encyclopédie de la Musique* (Paris, 1920–31).

MARPURG, FRIEDRICH WILHELM: *Kritische Briefe über die Tonkunst* (Berlin, 1760–4; repr., 1973).

MATTHESON, JOHANN: *Das neu-eröffnete Orchestre* (Hamburg, 1713).

—— *Der vollkommene Capellmeister* (Hamburg, 1739; repr., 1954; revised translation with critical commentary by E. C. Harriss: *Johann Mattheson's Der vollkommene Capellmeister*, *Studies in musicology*, xxi, Ann Arbor, 1981).

—— *Grosse General-Bass-Schule* (Hamburg, 1731; repr., 1968).

—— *Grundlage einer Ehren-Pforte* (Hamburg, 1740; ed. M. Schneider, Berlin, 1910; repr., 1969).

MEYER, ERNST HERMANN: *Musik der Renaissance—Aufklärung—Klassik* (Leipzig, 1973).

PALISCA, CLAUDE V.: *Baroque Music* (Englewood Cliffs, 1968; 2nd ed., 1981).

ROUSSEAU, JEAN-JACQUES: *Dictionnaire de musique* (Paris, 1768; repr., Hildesheim, 1969).

SASSE, KONRAD: *Händel Bibliographie* (Leipzig, 1967).

SCHEIBE, JOHANN ADOLPH: *Über die musikalische Composition* (Leipzig, 1773).

SCHMIEDER, WOLFGANG: *Thematisch-systematisches Verzeichnis der musikalischen Werke Johann Sebastian Bachs: Bach-Werke-Verzeichnis* (Leipzig, 1950; 3rd ed., 1966).

SULZER, JOHANN GEORG: *Allgemeine Theorie der schönen Künste* (Leipzig, 1771–4).

TOVEY, DONALD FRANCIS: *Essays in Musical Analysis* (London, 1935–9; repr., 1972).

WALTHER, JOHANN GOTTFRIED: *Musicalisches Lexicon, oder Musicalische Bibliothec* (Leipzig, 1732; facs. ed., Kassel, 1953).

WILSON, JOHN, ed.: *Roger North on Music* (London, 1959).

## CHAPTER 1

### ODE AND ORATORIO IN ENGLAND

#### (a) DIALOGUE AND ODE

**(i) Modern Editions**

(*a*) *Anthology*

PLAYFORD, JOHN: *The Treasury of Musick* (London, 1669; repr. Ridgewood, N. J., 1966).

(*b*) *Works by Individual Composers*

BLOW, J.: *Amphion anglicus*, *Monuments of Music and Music Literature in Facsimile*, ser. 1, vol. ii (New York, 1965).

—— 'Begin the song', Ode for St. Cecilia's Day, 1684, ed. W. Shaw (London, 1950).

—— *Ode for St. Cecilia's Day, 1691*, ed. M. Bevan (London, 1981).

GIBBONS, O.: 'Do not repine, fair sun', ed. P. Brett (London, 1961).

HANDEL, G. F.: *Ode for the Birthday of Queen Anne*, ed. F. Chrysander, *Georg Friedrich Händels Werke*, xlviA (Leipzig, 1887); ed. W. Siegmund-Schultze,

*Hallische Händel-Ausgabe. Serie I: Oratorien und grosse Kantaten*, vi (Kassel, 1962).

PURCELL, H.: *Birthday Odes for Queen Mary, part 1*, ed. G. E. P. Arkwright, *Purcell Society Edition*, xi (London, 1902).

—— *Birthday Odes for Queen Mary, part 2*, ed. G. Shaw, *Purcell Society Edition*, xxiv (London, 1926).

—— *Duke of Gloucester's Birthday Ode*, ed. W. H. Cummings, *Purcell Society Edition*, iv (London, 1891).

—— *Miscellaneous Odes and Cantatas*, ed. A. Goldsbrough, *et al.*, *Purcell Society Edition*, xxvii (London, 1957).

—— *Ode on St. Cecilia's Day, 1692*, ed. P. Dennison, *Purcell Society Edition*, viii (London, 1978).

—— *Sacred Music, part 6*, ed. A. Lewis and N. Fortune, *Purcell Society Edition*, xxx (London, 1962).

—— *The Yorkshire Feast Song*, ed. W. H. Cummings, *Purcell Society Edition*, i (London, 1878).

—— *Three Odes for St. Cecilia's Day*, ed. G. E. P. Arkwright, *Purcell Society Edition*, x (London, 1899).

—— *Welcome Songs for Charles II and James II*, ed. R. Vaughan Williams, *Purcell Society Edition*, xv, xviii (London, 1905 and 1910).

**(ii) Books and Articles**

*(a) General*

HUSK, WILLIAM HENRY: *An Account of the Musical Celebrations on St. Cecilia's Day* (London, 1857).

LAFONTAINE, HENRY CART DE: *The King's Musick* (London, 1909; repr., 1973).

McGUINNESS, ROSAMOND: 'A Fine Song on Occasion of the Day was sung', *Music and Letters*, l (1969), pp. 290–5.

—— *English Court Odes, 1660–1820* (Oxford, 1971).

—— 'The Ground Bass in the English Court Ode', *Music and Letters*, li (1970), pp. 118–40, 265–78.

—— 'The Origins and Disappearance of the English Court Ode', *Proceedings of the Royal Musical Association*, lxxxvii (1960–1), pp. 69–82.

PULVER, JEFFREY: *A Biographical Dictionary of Old English Music* (London, 1927; repr., 1969).

SHUSTER, GEORGE NAUMAN: *The English Ode from Milton to Keats* (New York, 1940).

SMALLMAN, BASIL: 'Endor Revisited: English Biblical Dialogues of the Seventeenth Century', *Music and Letters*, xlvi (1965), pp. 137–45.

SMITHER, HOWARD E.: *A History of the Oratorio*, ii (Chapel Hill, 1977).

—— 'The Baroque Oratorio: A Report on Research since 1945', *Acta musicologica*, xlviii (1976), pp. 50–76.

—— 'The Latin Dramatic Dialogue and the Nascent Oratorio', *Journal of the American Musicological Society*, xx (1967), pp. 403–33.

SPINK, IAN: 'English Seventeenth-Century Dialogues', *Music and Letters*, xxxviii (1957), pp. 155–63.

TILMOUTH, MICHAEL: 'A Calendar of References to Music in Newspapers Published in London and the Provinces (1660–1719)', *Royal Musical Association Research Chronicle*, i (1961).

*(b) Individual Composers*

**Blow**

CLARKE, HENRY L.: 'John Blow: A Tercentenary Survey', *Musical Quarterly*, xxxv (1949), pp. 412–20.

EVANS, DAVID R.: 'Blow's Court Odes: a new discovery', *Musical Times*, cxxv (1984), pp. 567–9.

McGUINNESS, ROSAMOND: 'The Chronology of John Blow's Court Odes', *Music and Letters*, xlvi (1965), pp. 102–21.

SHAW, H. WATKINS: 'Blow's Use of the Ground Bass', *Musical Quarterly*, xxiv (1938), pp. 31–8.

—— 'The Secular Music of John Blow', *Proceedings of the Musical Association*, lxiii (1936–7), pp. 1–19.

**Clarke**

TAYLOR, THOMAS F.: *Thematic Catalog of the Works of Jeremiah Clarke* (Detroit, 1977).

**Draghi**

BRENNECKE, ERNEST: 'Dryden's Odes and Draghi's Music', *Proceedings of the Modern Language Association*, xlix (1934), pp. 1–36.

**Humfrey**

DENNISON, PETER: 'Pelham Humfrey 1647–74', *Musical Times*, cxv (1974), pp. 553–5.

**Locke**

HARDING, ROSAMOND E. M.: *A Thematic Catalogue of the Works of Matthew Locke* (Oxford, 1971).

LEWIS, ANTHONY: 'Matthew Locke: a Dynamic Figure in English Music', *Proceedings of the Royal Musical Association*, lxxiv (1947–8), pp. 57–71.

**Purcell**

HARLEY, JOHN: *Music in Purcell's London* (London, 1968).

WESTRUP, J. A.: *Purcell* (London, 1937; 4th ed., 1980).

ZIMMERMAN, FRANKLIN B.: *Henry Purcell, 1659–95: an Analytical Catalogue of his Music* (London, 1963).

—— *Henry Purcell, 1659–95: his Life and Times* (London, 1967; 2nd rev. ed., Philadelphia, 1983).


(b) ORATORIO AND RELATED FORMS

**(i) Modern Editions**

GREENE, M.: *The Song of Deborah and Barak*, ed. F. Dawes (London, 1956).

HANDEL, G. F.: *Georg Friedrich Händels Werke*, ed. F. Chrysander (Leipzig, 1858–1902).

—— *Hallische Händel-Ausgabe. Serie I: Oratorien und grosse Kantaten*, ed. M. Schneider, *et al.*, (Kassel, 1955–  ).

—— *Messiah*, ed. W. Siegmund-Schultze (Leipzig, 1959).


**(ii) Books and Articles**

*(a) General*

See **(ii)** *(a)* above

(b) *Individual Composers*

**Boyce**

BARTLETT, IAN: 'Boyce and Early English Oratorio', *Musical Times*, cxx (1979), pp. 293–7 and 385–91.

—— and BRUCE, ROBERT J.: 'William Boyce's "Solomon"', *Music and Letters*, lxi (1980), pp. 28–49.

**Defesch**

BREMT, FR. VAN DEN: *William de Fesch (1687–1757?), Nederlands componist en virtuoos: leven en werk* (Louvain and Brussels, 1949).

**Greene**

WALKER, ERNEST: 'The Bodleian Manuscripts of Maurice Greene', *The Musical Antiquary*, i (1910), pp. 149–65 and 203–14.

**Handel**

BURROWS, DONALD: 'Handel and "Alexander's Feast"', *Musical Times*, cxxiii (1982), pp. 252–5.

—— 'Handel's Performances of "Messiah": the evidence of the conducting score', *Music and Letters*, lvi (1975), pp. 319–34.

—— 'The Composition and First Performance of Handel's "Alexander's Feast"', *Music and Letters*, lxiv (1983), pp. 206–11.

CLAUSEN, HANS DIETER: *Händels Direktionspartituren* (Hamburg, 1972).

COOPER, BARRY: 'The Organ Parts to Handel's "Alexander's Feast"', *Music and Letters*, lix (1978), pp. 159–79.

DEAN, WINTON: *Handel's Dramatic Oratorios and Masques* (London, 1959).

—— 'How should Handel's Oratorios be staged?', *Musical Newsletter*, i/4 (1971).

DEUTSCH, OTTO ERICH: *Handel: a Documentary Biography* (London, 1955; rev., 1974).

GUDGER, WILLIAM D.: 'A Borrowing from Kerll in "Messiah"', *Musical Times*, cxviii (1977), pp. 1038–9.

—— 'Skizzen und Entwürfe für den Amen-Chor in Händels "Messias"', *Händel-Jahrbuch 1980*, xxvi, pp. 83–114.

HERBAGE, JULIAN: 'The Oratorios', *Handel: a Symposium*, ed. G. Abraham (London, 1954), pp. 66–131.

HICKS, ANTHONY: 'Handel's *La Resurrezione*', *Musical Times*, cx (1969), pp. 145–8.

HUDSON, FREDERICK: 'Das Concerto in Judas Maccabaeus identifiziert', *Händel-Jahrbuch 1974*, xx, pp. 119–33.

LARSEN, JENS PETER: *Handel's 'Messiah': Origins, Composition, Sources* (London, 1957; 2nd ed., 1972).

LEWIS, ANTHONY: 'Some Notes on Editing Handel's "Semele"', *Essays on Opera and English Music in Honour of Sir Jack Westrup* (Oxford, 1975), pp. 79–83.

LINCOLN, STODDARD M.: 'Handel's Music for Queen Anne', *Musical Quarterly*, xlv (1959), pp. 191–207.

MYERS, R. M.: *Handel, Dryden and Milton* (London, 1956).

SHAW, HAROLD WATKINS: *A Textual and Historical Companion to Handel's 'Messiah'* (London, 1965).

SOLOMON, JON: 'Polyphemus's Whistle in Handel's "Acis and Galatea"', *Music and Letters*, lxiv (1983), pp. 37–43.

TAYLOR, SEDLEY: *The Indebtedness of Handel to Works by other Composers* (Cambridge, 1906).

TROWELL, BRIAN: 'Congreve and the 1744 Semele Libretto', *Musical Times*, cxi (1970), pp. 993–4.

YOUNG, PERCY M.: *The Oratorios of Handel* (London, 1949).

## CHAPTER II

### SOLO SONG AND VOCAL DUET

**(i) Modern Anthologies**

JAKOBY, RICHARD, ed.: *Die Kantate, Das Musikwerk*, xxxii (Cologne, 1968).
MACCLINTOCK, CAROL, ed.: *The Solo Song 1580–1730* (New York, 1973).
NOSKE, FRITS, ed.: *Das Ausserdeutsche Sololied 1500–1900, Das Musikwerk*, xvi (Cologne, 1958).

**(ii) Book**

STEVENS, DENIS, ed.: *A History of Song* (London, 1960).

### (a) ITALY

JANDER, OWEN, gen. ed.: *The Wellesley Edition Cantata Index Series* (Wellesley, Mass., 1964– ). *Antonio Cesti*, ed. David Burrows, i (1964); *Mario Savioni*, ed. Irving R. Eisley, ii (1964); *Luigi Rossi*, iii (1965); *Alessandro Stradella*, ed. Owen Jander, iv (1969); *Giacomo Carissimi*, ed. Gloria Rose, v (1966); *Antonio Tenaglia*, ed. Eleanor Caluori, vi (in prep.); *Alessandro and Atto Melani*, ed. Robert L. Weaver, viii–ix (1972).

**(i) Modern Editions**

*(a) Anthologies*

JEPPESEN, KNUD, ed.: *La Flora, arie & antiche italiane*, i–iii (Copenhagen, 1949).
LANDSHOFF, LUDWIG, ed.: *Alte Meister des Bel Canto; Eine Sammlung von Arien*, i–v (Frankfurt and New York, 1912–27).
—— *Alte Meister des Bel Canto; Italienische Kammerduette des 17. und 18. Jahrhunderts* (New York, London, etc., 1955).
PARISOTTI, ALESSANDRO, ed.: *Arie antiche*, i–iii (Milan, 1887–1900; repr., 1947).
PRUNIÈRES, HENRY, ed.: *Les Maîtres du chant*, i, iii, v *Airs italiens* (Paris, 1924–7).
TORCHI, LUIGI, ed.: *L'Arte musicale in Italia*, v (Milan, c.1905).

*(b) Works by Individual Composers*

CARISSIMI, G.: *Cantate*, i, ii (*Istituto italiano per la storia della musica*, Monumenti iii) ed. L. Bianchi and F. Luisi (Rome, 1960–80).
—— *Six solo cantatas for high voice and keyboard*, ed. G. Rose (London, 1969).
CESTI, A.: *Four chamber duets*, ed. D. Burrows, *Collegium Musicum*: second series, i (Madison, Wisc., 1969).
HANDEL, G. F.: *Georg Friedrich Händels Werke*, l–lii a/b, ed. F. Chrysander (Leipzig, 1887–9).
HASSE, J. A.: *Cantates pour une voix de femme et orchestre*, ed. S. H. Hansell, *Le Pupitre*, xi (Paris, 1968).
LEGRENZI, G.: *Cantatas and Canzonets for Solo Voice, Recent Researches in the Music of the Baroque Era*, xiv–xv (Madison, 1972).
LEO, L.: 'Ahi! che le pena mia', ed. L. Bettarini, *Collezione settecentesca Bettarini*, viii (Milan, c.1974).

PERTI, G. A.: *Tre cantate morali e storiche per voci e archi*, *Bibliotheca musica bononiensis, sezione 4*, lxxxv (Bologna, 1969).

QUAGLIATI, P.: *La sfera armoniosa* and *Il carro di fedeltà d'amore*, ed. V. Gotwals and P. Keppler, *Smith College Music Archives*, xiii (Northampton, Mass., 1957).

SAVIONI, M.: *Six cantatas for one and three voices with continuo*, ed. I. Eisley, *Series of Early Music*, iii (Pennsylvania, 1970).

SCARLATTI, A.: 'Bella Madre dei fiori' and 'Correa nel seno amato', ed. L. Bettarini, *Collezione settecentesca Bettarini*, viii (Milan, c.1974).

—— *Cantate ad una voce* ed. A. Toni, *I Classici della musica italiana*, Quad. 120–5 (Milan, 1920).

—— *Due cantate per soprano, archi e basso continuo*, ed. L. Bettarini, *Collezione settecentesca Bettarini*, ii (Milan, 1969).

STEFFANI, A.: *Duetti*, ed. A. Einstein and A. Sandberger, *Denkmäler der Tonkunst in Bayern*, xi (Leipzig, 1905).

—— 'Occhi miei, lo miraste' ed. A. Einstein, *Zeitschrift für Musikwissenschaft*, i (1918–19) pp. 457–66.

STROZZI, B.: *Ariette di Francesca Caccini e Barbara Strozzi*, ed. A. Bonaventura (Rome, 1930).

VALENTINI, G.: *Musiche a due voci*, ed. O. Wessely, *Denkmäler der Tonkunst in Österreich*, cxxv (Graz, 1973).

VIVALDI, A.: *Cantatas for solo voice*, ed. M. Dunham, *Recent Researches in the Music of the Baroque Era*, xxxii–xxxiii (Madison, 1979).


**(ii) Books and Articles**

*(a) General*

DENT, EDWARD J.: 'Italian Chamber Cantatas', *The Musical Antiquary*, ii (1910–11), pp. 142–53 and 185–99.

FERAND, ERNEST T.: 'Embellished "Parody Cantatas" in the Early 18th Century', *Musical Quarterly*, xliv (1958), pp. 40–64.

HAMMOND, FREDERICK: 'Musicians at the Medici Court in the Mid-seventeenth century', *Analecta musicologica*, xiv (1974), pp. 151–69.

KAST, PAUL: 'Biographische Notizen zur römischen Musikern des 17. Jahrhunderts', *Analecta musicologica*, i (1963), pp. 38–69.

MÜLLER-BLATTAU, JOSEPH MARIA: *Die Kompositionlehre Heinrich Schützens in der Fassung seines Schülers Christoph Bernhard* (Leipzig, 1926; 2nd ed., Kassel, 1963).

PRUNIÈRES, HENRY: 'The Italian Cantata of the Seventeenth century', *Music and Letters*, vii (1926), pp. 38–48 and 120–32.

ROSE, GLORIA: 'The Italian Cantata of the Baroque Period', *Gattungen der Musik in Einzeldarstellungen, Gedenkschrift Leo Schrade*, i (Berne and Munich, 1973).

SCHMITZ, EUGEN: *Geschichte der weltlichen Solokantate* (Leipzig, 1914; rev. and 2nd ed., 1955).

—— 'Zur Frühgeschichte der lyrischen Monodie Italiens im 17. Jahrhunderts', *Jahrbuch der Musikbibliothek Peters für 1911*, pp. 35–48.

—— 'Zur Geschichte des italienischen Kammerduetts im 17. Jahrhundert', *Jahrbuch der Musikbibliothek Peters für 1916*, pp. 43–60.

TORCHI, LUIGI: 'Canzoni ed arie italiane ad una voce nel secolo XVII', *Rivista musicale italiana*, i (1894), pp. 581–656.

(b) Individual Composers

**Albinoni**

TALBOT, MICHAEL: 'Albinoni's Solo Cantatas', *Soundings*, v (1975), pp. 9–28.

**Carissimi**

ROSE, GLORIA: 'The Cantatas of Giacomo Carissimi', *Musical Quarterly*, xlviii (1962), pp. 204–15.

**Cesti**

BURROWS, DAVID: 'Antonio Cesti on music', *Musical Quarterly*, li (1965), pp. 518–29.

**Handel**

EWERHART, RUDOLF: 'Die Händel-Handschriften der Santini-Bibliothek in Münster', *Händel-Jahrbuch 1960*, vi, pp. 111–50.

HARRIS, ELLEN T.: 'Handel's London Cantatas', *Göttinger Händel-Beiträge*, i (Kassel, 1984), pp. 86–102.

HERBAGE, JULIAN: 'The Secular Oratorios and Cantatas', *Handel: a Symposium*, ed. G. Abraham (London, 1954), pp. 132–55.

MARX, HANS JOACHIM: 'Ein Beitrag Händels zur "Accademia Ottoboniana" in Rom', *Hamburger Jahrbuch für Musikwissenschaft*, i (1974), pp. 69–86.

**Hasse**

HANSELL, SVEN HOSTRUP: *Works for Solo Voice of Johann Adolf Hasse (1699–1783)*, Detroit Studies in Music Bibliography, xii (Detroit, 1968).

**Landi**

LEOPOLD, SILKE: *Stefano Landi: Beiträge zur Biographie: Untersuchungen zur weltlichen und geistlichen Vokalmusik*, i–ii, Hamburger Beiträge zur Musikwissenschaft, xvii (Hamburg, 1976).

**Leo**

DENT, EDWARD J.: 'Leonardo Leo', *Sammelbände der internationalen Musik-Gesellschaft*, viii (1906–7), pp. 550–66.

PASTORE, GIUSEPPE A.: *Leonardo Leo* (Galatina, 1957).

**Mazzocchi**

WITZENMANN, WOLFGANG: *Domenico Mazzocchi, 1592–1665, Dokumente und Interpretationen*, Analecta Musicologica, viii (1970), (whole volume).

**Pergolesi**

RADICIOTTI, GIUSEPPE: *Giovanni Battista Pergolesi* (2nd ed., Milan, 1945).

**Rainaldi**

MARX, HANS JOACHIM: 'Carlo Rainaldi als Komponist', in: *La fabbrica di S. Agnese in Navona*, i, G. Eimer (Stockholm, 1970), pp. 244–78.

**Rossi**

GHISLANZONI, ALBERTO: *Luigi Rossi: biografia e analisi delle composizioni* (Rome and Milan, 1954).

PRUNIÈRES, HENRY: 'Notes bibliographiques sur les cantates de Luigi Rossi au Conservatoire de Naples', *Zeitschrift der internationalen Musikgesellschaft*, xiv (1912–13), pp. 109–11.

**Scarlatti**

BOYD, MALCOLM: 'Form and Style in Scarlatti's Chamber Cantatas', *Music Review*, xxv (1964), pp. 17–26.

DENT, EDWARD J.: *Alessandro Scarlatti: his Life and Works* (2nd ed., Frank Walker, London, 1960).

EDMUNDS, JOHN: 'Chamber Cantatas: the Mastery of Alessandro Scarlatti', *Tempo*, xlii (1956–7), pp. 24–30.

**Steffani**

TIMMS, COLIN: 'Revisions in Steffani's Chamber Duets', *Proceedings of the Royal Musical Association*, xcvi (1969–70), pp. 119–28.

**Strozzi**

BONAVENTURA, ARNALDO: 'Un'arietta di Barbara Strozzi', *Nuova musica*, x (1905).

ROSAND, ELLEN: 'Barbara Strozzi, *virtuosissima cantatrice*: The Composer's Voice', *Journal of the American Musicological Society*, xxxi (1978), pp. 241–81.

**Vittori**

ANTOLINI, B. M.: 'La carriera di cantante e compositore di Loreto Vittori', *Studi musicali*, vii (1978).

**Vivaldi**

KOLNEDER, WALTER: *Antonio Vivaldi (1678–1741)*. *Leben und Werk* (Wiesbaden, 1965; Eng. trans., 1970).

RYOM, PETER: 'Le recensement des cantates d'Antonio Vivaldi', *Dansk aarbog for musikforskning*, vi (1972), pp. 81–100.


(b) GERMANY

**(i) Modern Editions**

(a) *Anthologies*

MOSER, HANS JOACHIM, ed.: *Alte Meister des deutschen Liedes. 46 Gesänge des 17. und 18. Jahrhunderts* (Leipzig, 1931).

REIMANN, HEINRICH, ed.: *Das deutsche Lied*, i–iv (Berlin, 1892).


(b) *Works by Individual Composers*

ALBERT, H.: *Arien*, ed. E. Bernoulli, *Denkmäler deutscher Tonkunst*, xii–xiii (Leipzig, 1903; rev. ed., Wiesbaden and Graz, 1958).

—— *Ausgewählte Arien für 1 oder 2 Singstimmen*, ed. M. Seiffert, *Organum*, ser. 2, no. 6 (Leipzig, 1929).

—— *Weltliche und geistliche Arien*, Zeitschrift für Spielmusik, ccxxviii (Celle, 1958).

ERLEBACH, P. H.: *Ausgewählte Arien und Duette*, ed. M. Seiffert, *Organum*, ser. 2, no. 8 (Leipzig, 1929).

—— *Harmonische Freude* und *Musikalischer Freunde*, ed. O. Kinkeldey, *Denkmäler deutscher Tonkunst*, xlvi–xlvii (Wiesbaden and Graz, 1959).

KRIEGER, A.: *Arien*, ed. A. Heuss, *Denkmäler deutscher Tonkunst*, xix (Wiesbaden and Graz, 1958).

—— *Ausgewählte Arien für Sopran*, ed. M. Seiffert, *Organum*, ser. 2, no. 7 (Leipzig, 1929).

—— *Lied*, ed. A. Einstein, *Beispielsammlung zur älteren Musikgeschichte* (Leipzig and Berlin, 1917).

TELEMANN, G. P.: *Ausgewählte Lieder für eine Singstimme und Generalbass*, ed. M. Seiffert, *Organum*, ser. 2, no. 12 (Leipzig, 1929).

—— *Der Tag des Gerichts, Ino*, ed. M. Schneider, *Denkmäler deutscher Tonkunst*, xxviii (Leipzig, 1958).

—— 'Der Weiberorden', ed. W. Hobohm (Leipzig, 1966).

—— 'Die Tageszeiten', ed. A. Heilmann (Kassel, 1934).

—— Four Secular Cantatas, ed. W. Menke (Kassel, n.d.).

—— 'Ha ha! Wo will wi hut noch danzen', ed. W. Hobohm (Leipzig, 1971).

—— 'Kleine Kantate von Wald und Au', ed. R. Ermeler (Kassel, 1943).

—— 'Lustig bei dem Hochzeitsschmausse', ed. H. Leichtentritt, *Deutsche Hausmusik aus vier Jahrhunderten* (Berlin, 1905).

—— *Schulmeister-Kantate*, ed. F. Stein (Kassel, 1956).


**(ii) Books and Articles**

*(a) General*

BRESLAUER, M.: *Das deutsche Lied* (Berlin, 1908; repr., 1966).

CALLENBERG, E. -F.: *Das obersächsische Barocklied* (Freiburg, 1952).

FRIEDLAENDER, MAX: *Das deutsche Lied im 18. Jahrhundert* (Stuttgart, 1902; repr., 1962).

GOTTSCHED, JOHANN CHRISTOPH: *Versuch einer critischen Dichtkunst für die Deutschen* (Leipzig, 1730).

KRETZSCHMAR, HERMANN: *Geschichte des neuen deutschen Liedes* (Leipzig, 1911; repr., 1966).

MÜLLER, GÜNTHER: *Geschichte des deutschen Liedes vom Zeitalter des Barock biz zur Gegenwart* (Munich, 2nd ed., 1959).

SCHMITZ, EUGEN: *Geschichte der weltlichen Solokantate* (Leipzig, 2nd ed., 1955).

THOMAS, RICHARD HINTON: *Poetry and Song in the German Baroque: a Study of the Continuo Lied* (Oxford, 1963).

VETTER, WALTHER: *Das frühdeutsche Lied* (Münster, 1928).

WORBS, HANS CHRISTOPH: 'Die Schichtung des deutschen Liedgutes in der zweiten Hälfte des 17. Jahrhunderts', *Archiv für Musikwissenschaft*, xvii (1960), pp. 61–70.


*(b) Individual Composers*

**Albert**

MÜLLER-BLATTAU, JOSEPH: 'H. Albert und das Barocklied', *Deutsche Vierteljahresschrift für Literaturwissenschaft und Geistesgeschichte*, xxv (1951).

**Bach**

DONINGTON, ROBERT: ' "Amore traditore": a problem cantata', *Studies in Eighteenth-Century Music: a tribute to Karl Geiringer*, ed. R. E. Chapman and H. C. Robbins Landon (New York and London, 1970), pp. 160–76.

**Keiser**

KÜMMERLING, HARALD: 'Fünf unbekannte Kantaten in R. Keisers Autograph', *Festschrift Max Schneider* (Leipzig, 1955), pp. 177–81.

PETZOLDT, RICHARD: *Die Kirchenkompositionen und weltlichen Kantaten Reinhard Keisers* (Düsseldorf, 1935).

**Krieger**

OSTHOFF, HELMUTH: *Adam Krieger* (Leipzig, 1929; repr., 1970).

SCHIØRRING, NILS: 'Wiedergefundene Melodien aus der verschollenen Adam-Krieger-Ariensammlung 1657', *Festschrift für Walter Wiora* (Kassel, 1967), pp. 304–12.

**Rist**

KRABBE, WILHELM: *Johann Rist und das deutsche Lied* (Diss., Berlin, 1910).

**Stölzel**

HENNENBERG, FRITZ: *Das Kantatenschaffen von Gottfried Heinrich Stölzel* (Diss., Leipzig, 1965; rev., abridged, Leipzig, 1976).

**Telemann**

MENKE, WERNER: *Thematisches Verzeichnis der Vokalwerke von Georg Philipp Telemann,* ii (Frankfurt, 1983).

PETZOLDT, RICHARD: *Georg Philipp Telemann: Leben und Werk* (Leipzig, 1967; Eng. trans., 1974).

STEIN, FRITZ: 'Eine komische Schulmeisterkantate von Georg Philipp Telemann und Johann Adolf Hasse', *Festschrift Max Schneider zum achtzigsten Geburtstage,* ed. W. Vetter (Leipzig, 1955), pp. 183–90.


(c) ENGLAND

**(i) Modern Editions**

*(a) Anthologies*

POTTER, FRANK HUNTER, ed.: *Reliquary of English Song,* i, ii (New York, 1915–16).

RIMBAULT, EDWARD FRANCIS, ed.: *The Ancient Vocal Music of England* (London, 1874).

SPINK, IAN, ed.: *English Songs 1625–1660, Musica Britannica,* xxxiii (2nd rev. ed., London, 1977).

WHITTAKER, WILLIAM GILLIES, ed.: *The John Playford Collection of Vocal Part Music* (London, 1937).


*(b) Works by Individual Composers*

ARNE, T. A.: *Six Songs,* ed. G. E. P. Arkwright, *The Old English Edition,* ii (London, 1890).
—— *Twelve Songs,* ed. M. Pilkington (London, 1979).

BLOW, J.: *Amphion anglicus, Monuments of Music and Music Literature in Facsimile,* ser. 1, vol. ii (New York, 1965).
—— *Six Songs selected from the Amphion anglicus, 1700,* ed. G. E. P. Arkwright, *The Old English Edition,* xxiii (London, 1900).
—— *Three Songs from 'Amphion anglicus',* ed. A. C. Lewis (Paris, 1938).
—— *Ten Songs,* i–ii, ed. M. Pilkington (London, 1979).

BOYCE, W.: *Ten Songs,* ed. M. Pilkington (London, 1979).

HILTON, J.: *Ayres or fa las, Musical Antiquarian Society,* xiii (London, c.1840–8).

JOHNSON, R.: *Ayres, Songs and Dialogues,* ed. I. Spink, *The English Lute-Song,* ser. 2, xvii (London, 1961; 2nd rev. ed., 1974).

LANIER, N.: *Six Songs,* ed. E. Huws Jones (London, 1976).

LAWES, H.: *Dialogues for two voices and continuo,* ed. R. Jesson, *The Penn State music series,* iii (University Park, Pa., 1964).
—— *Ten Ayres for Contralto (or Baritone) and Keyboard,* ed. T. Dart, *English Songs,* i (London, 1956).

LAWES, W.: *Dialogues for two voices and continuo,* ed. R. Jesson, *The Penn State music series,* iii (University Park, Pa., 1964).

LOCKE, M.: *Three songs,* ed. A. Lewis (Paris, 1938).

PURCELL, H.: *Catches, rounds, 2-part and 3-part songs,* ed. W. Barclay Squire and J. A. Fuller Maitland, *Purcell Society Edition,* xxii (London, 1922).

—— *Dramatic Music, parts 1–3*, ed. A. Gray, *Purcell Society Edition*, xvi, xx, xxi (London, 1906–17).

—— *Secular Songs for a single voice*, rev. M. Laurie, *Purcell Society Edition*, xxv (London, 1984).

—— *Six songs selected from the Orpheus Britannicus*, ed. G. E. P. Arkwright, *The Old English Edition*, xxiv (London, 1901).


**(ii) Books and Articles**

*(a) General*

BOYD, MALCOLM: 'English Secular Cantatas in the Eighteenth Century', *The Music Review*, xxx (1969), pp. 85–97.

COLLES, HENRY C.: *Voice and Verse: a Study in English Song* (London, 1928).

CUDWORTH, CHARLES: 'Songs and Part-song Settings of Shakespeare's lyrics 1660–1960', *Shakespeare in Music*, ed. P. Hartnoll (London, 1964), pp. 51–74.

DAY, CYRUS LAWRENCE and MURRIE, ELEANORE BOSWELL: *English Song-books, 1651–1702* (London, 1940).

DUCKLES, VINCENT: 'English song and the challenge of Italian monody', *Words to Music: Papers on English Seventeenth-Century Song* (Los Angeles, 1967), pp. 3–25.

—— 'The Gamble Manuscript as a Source of *continuo* Song in England', *Journal of the American Musicological Society*, i/2 (1948), pp. 23–40.

HUGHES, CHARLES W.: 'John Gamble's Commonplace Book', *Music and Letters*, xxvi (1945), pp. 215–29.

JOHNSTONE, H. DIACK: 'English Solo Song, c.1710–1760', *Proceedings of the Royal Musical Association*, xcv (1969), pp. 67–80.

NORTHCOTE, SYDNEY: *Byrd to Britten: a Survey of English Song* (London, 1966).

SPINK, IAN: 'English Cavalier Songs', *Proceedings of the Royal Musical Association*, lxxxvi (1959–60), pp. 61–78.

—— *English Song: Dowland to Purcell* (London, 1974).


*(b) Individual Composers*

**Arne**

FARISH, STEPHEN THOMAS: 'The Vauxhall Songs of T. A. Arne', *Dissertation Abstracts*, xxiii (1963), pp. 4375–6.

HERBAGE, JULIAN: 'The Vocal Style of Thomas Arne', *Proceedings of the Royal Musical Association*, lxxviii (1952), pp. 83–96.

PARKINSON, JOHN A.: *An index to the vocal works of Thomas Augustine Arne and Michael Arne*, *Detroit Studies in music bibliography*, xxi (Detroit, 1972).

**Croft**

ROE, LUCY: 'A Note on Croft's Secular Music', *Musical Times*, cxix (1978), pp. 501–4.

**Lanier**

EMSLIE, MCDONALD: 'Nicholas Lanier's innovations in English Song', *Music and Letters*, xli (1960), pp. 13–27.

**H. Lawes**

EVANS, WILLA MCCLUNG: *Henry Lawes, musician and friend of poets* (New York, 1941).

HART, ERIC FORD: 'Introduction to Henry Lawes', *Music and Letters*, xxxii (1951), pp. 217–25 and 328–44.

MCGRADY, R. J.: 'Henry Lawes and the Concept of "Just Note and Accent" ', *Music and Letters*, l (1969), pp. 86–102.

WILLETTS, PAMELA: *The Henry Lawes Manuscript* (London, 1969).

**W. Lawes**

LEFKOWITZ, MURRAY: *William Lawes* (London, 1960).

**Locke**

HARDING, ROSAMOND E. M.: *A Thematic Catalogue of the Works of Matthew Locke* (Oxford, 1971).

**Purcell**

LAURIE, MARGARET: 'Purcell's Extended Solo Songs', *Musical Times*, cxxv (1984), pp. 19–25.

LEWIS, ANTHONY: *The Language of Purcell* (Hull, 1968).

MILLER, HUGH M.: 'Henry Purcell and the Ground Bass', *Music and Letters*, xxix (1948), pp. 340–7.

WESTRUP, JACK A.: *Purcell* (London, 1937; 4th ed., 1980).

ZIMMERMAN, FRANKLIN B.: 'Sound and sense in Purcell's "Single Songs"', *Words to Music: Papers on English Seventeenth-Century Song* (Los Angeles, 1967), pp. 45–83.

**Reggio**

ROSE, GLORIA: 'Pietro Reggio—a Wandering Musician', *Music and Letters*, xlvi (1965), pp. 207–16.

**Stanley**

FINZI, GERALD: 'John Stanley (1713–1786)', *Proceedings of the Royal Musical Association*, lxxvii (1951), pp. 63–74.

FROST, TONY: 'The Cantatas of John Stanley (1713–86)', *Music and Letters*, liii (1972), pp. 284–92.

**Wilson**

DUCKLES, VINCENT: 'The "Curious" Art of John Wilson (1595–1674): An Introduction to his Songs and Lute Music', *Journal of the American Musicological Society*, vii (1954), pp. 93–112.

(d) FRANCE

**(i) Modern Editions**

*(a) Anthologies*

PRUNIÈRES, HENRY, ed.: *Les Maîtres du chant*, iv, vi *Airs français*, (Paris, 1924–7).

ROBERT, FRÉDÉRIC, ed.: *Airs sérieux et à boire à 2 et 3 voix (1694–1724)* (Paris, 1968).

VERCHALY, ANDRÉ, ed.: *Airs de cour pour voix et luth (1603–1643)*, Société française de musicologie, 1st sér.: *Monuments de la musique ancienne*, xvi (Paris, 1961).

WECKERLIN, JEAN-BAPTISTE T., ed.: *Échos du temps passé*, i–iii (Paris, c.1865–75).

*(b) Works by Individual Composers*

BERNIER, N.: 'Les Forges de Lemnos', ed. D. Tunley, *Studies in Music*, ser. 2, no. 1 (1967).

BOËSSET, A.: *Airs de cour*, ed. H. Expert, *Chants de France et d'Italie*, ser. 2 (Paris, 1904).

―― 'Je voudrois bien ô Cloris', ed. A. Cohen, *Notations and Editions: a Book in Honor of Louise Cuyler* (Dubuque, Iowa, 1974), pp. 61–8.

CLÉRAMBAULT, L. -N.: 'Orphée', ed. D. Tunley (London, 1972).

―― *Two cantatas for soprano and chamber ensemble*, ed. D. H. Foster, *Recent Researches in the Music of the Baroque Era*, xxvii (Madison, 1979).

COUPERIN, F.: *Musique vocale, Oeuvres complètes de François Couperin*, xi, ed. M. Cauchie *et al.* (Paris, 1932).

LAMBERT, M.: *2 airs*, ed. F. Delsarte, *Archives du chant*, iv, xvi (Paris, 1856–61).

―― *5 airs*, ed H. Expert, *Chants de France et d'Italie*, i (Paris, 1910).

LULLY, J. -B.: *Airs*, ed. H. Prunières, *Les Maîtres du chant*, ii (Paris, 1924–7).

MONTÉCLAIR, M. P. DE: *Cantatas for one and two voices*, ed. J. R. Anthony and D. Akmajian, *Recent Researches in the Music of the Baroque Era*, xxix–xxx (Madison, 1978).

RAMEAU, J. -P.: *Cantatas*, ed. C. Malherbe, *J. -P. Rameau: Oeuvres complètes*, iii (Paris, 1897).

### (ii) Books and Articles

#### (a) General

ANTHONY, JAMES R.: *French Baroque Music from Beaujoyeulx to Rameau* (London, 1973; 2nd rev. ed., 1978).

BACILLY, BÉNIGNE DE: *Remarques curieuses sur l'art de bien chanter* (Paris, 1688, repr., 1971; English translation by Austin B. Caswell: *A Commentary upon the Art of Proper Singing*, New York, 1968).

BENOIT, MARCELLE: *Musiques de cour: chapelle, chambre, écurie, recueil de documents, 1661–1733* (Paris, 1971).

CAMMAERT, GUSTAVE: 'Les brunettes', *Revue belge de musicologie*, xi (1957), pp. 35–51.

COHEN, ALBERT: '*L'Art de bien chanter* (1666) of Jean Millet', *Musical Quarterly*, lv (1969), pp. 170–9.

DUFOURCQ, NORBERT: *La musique française* (Paris, 1949; 2nd ed., 1970).

FLEURY, NICOLAS: *Méthode pour apprendre facilement à toucher le théorbe sur la basse continue* (Paris, 1660).

GÉROLD, THÉODORE: *L'Art du chant en France au XVIIe siècle* (Strasbourg, 1921).

GRIMAREST, JEAN: *Traité de récitatif* (Paris, 1707).

JONCKBLOET, W. J. A., and LAND, JAN PIETER: *Musiques et musiciens au XVIIe siècle* (Leyde, 1882), pp. 70–90.

JURGENS, M.: *Documents du minutier central concernant l'histoire de la musique (1600–1650)* (Paris, 1967).

LABORDE, L. E. S. J. DE: *Musiciens de Paris, 1535–1792*, ed. Y. de Brossard (Paris, 1965).

LEVY, KENNETH: 'Vaudeville, vers mesurés et airs de cour', *Musique et poésie au XVIe siècle* (Paris, 1954), pp. 185–99.

MACCLINTOCK, CAROL, ed. and trans.: *Readings in the History of Music in Performance* (Bloomington and London, 1979).

MASSON, PAUL-MARIE: 'Les Brunettes', *Sammelbände der Internationalen Musik-Gesellschaft*, xii (1910–11), pp. 347–68.

MERSENNE, MARIN: *Harmonie universelle* (Paris, 1636–7; repr., Paris, 1963).

PIRRO, ANDRÉ: *Descartes et la musique* (Paris, 1907).

SEARES, MARGARET: 'The French Part-Songs of the late sixteenth and early seventeenth centuries', *Studies in Music*, xv (1981).

SCHMITZ, EUGEN: *Geschichte der weltlichen Solokantate* (Wiesbaden, 1955), pp. 191–235.

SCHWANDT, ERICH: 'L'Affilard's Published "Sketchbooks" ', *Musical Quarterly*, lxiii (1977), pp. 99–113.

SPINK, IAN: 'The Musicians of Queen Henrietta-Maria', *Acta musicologica*, xxxvi (1964), pp. 177–82.

TITON DU TILLET, EVRARD: *Le Parnasse françois* (Paris, 1732–43; repr., Geneva, 1971).

TUNLEY, DAVID: 'An Embarkment for Cythera—Social and literary aspects of the Eighteenth-Century French Cantata', *Recherches sur la musique française classique*,vii (1967), pp. 103–14.

—— 'Couperin and French Lyricism', *Musical Times*, cxxiv (1983), pp. 543–5.

—— *The Eighteenth-century French Cantata* (London, 1974).

—— 'The Emergence of the Eighteenth-century French Cantata', *Studies in Music*, i (1962), pp. 67–88.

VERCHALY, ANDRÉ: 'A propos du récit français au début du XVIIe siècle', *Recherches sur la musique française classique*, xv (1975), pp. 39–46.

—— *La Métrique et le rythme musical*, *Report of the Eighth Congress (International Musicological Society)* (New York, 1961), pp. 66–74.

VOLLEN, GENE E.: *The French Cantata: A Survey and Thematic Catalog* (Ann Arbor, Michigan, 1982).

WALKER, D. P.: 'Joan Albert Ban and Mersenne's Musical Competition of 1640', *Music and Letters*, lvii (1976), pp. 233–55.

—— 'The Influence of *musique mesurée a l'antique*, particularly on the *airs de cour* of the Early Seventeenth Century', *Musica disciplina*, ii (1948), pp. 141–63.

## (b) Individual Composers

### Bacilly
PRUNIÈRES, HENRY: 'Un maître de chant au XVIIe siècle: Bénigne de Bacilly', *Revue de musicologie*, iv/8 (1923), pp. 156–60.

### A. Boësset
COHEN, ALBERT: 'A Study of Notational and Performance Problems of an early *Air de cour: Je voudrois bien ô Cloris* (1629) by Antoine Boësset (*c.*1586–1643)', *Notations and Editions: a Book in Honor of Louise Cuyler* (Dubuque, Iowa, 1974), pp. 55–68.

### J. -B. Boësset
DUFOURCQ, NORBERT: *Jean-Baptiste Boësset, surintendant de la Musique du Roi* (Paris, 1963).

### Brossard
COMBARIEU, JULES: 'Compositeur français du XVIIe siècle: Sébastien de Brossard', *Revue d'histoire et de critique musicales*, i (1901), pp. 20–5.

### Cambefort
PRUNIÈRES, HENRY: 'Jean de Cambefort, surintendant de la musique du Roi (. . .–1661) d'après des documents inédits', *Année musicale*, ii (1912), pp. 205–26.

### Charpentier
CRUSSARD, CLAUDE: *Un musicien français oublié—Marc-Antoine Charpentier, (1634–1704)* (Paris, 1945).

HITCHCOCK, H. WILEY: *Les Oeuvres de Marc-Antoine Charpentier—catalogue raisonné* (Paris, 1982). (In English and French).

QUITTARD, HENRI: 'Orphée descendant aux enfers', *Tablettes de la Schola (Cantorum)*, vi (1904), pp. 3–4.

**Clérambault**

TUNLEY, DAVID: 'The Cantatas of Louis-Nicolas Clérambault', *Musical Quarterly*, lii (1966), pp. 313–31.

**Collin de Blamont**

MASSIP, CATHERINE: *François Collin de Blamont: musicien du roi* (Diss., Paris Conservatoire, 1971).

**Jacquet de la Guerre**

BORROFF, EDITH: *An Introduction to Elisabeth-Claude Jacquet de la Guerre* (Brooklyn, N.Y., 1966).

**La Barre**

TIERSOT, JULIEN: 'Une famille de musiciens français au XVIIe siècle: Les De La Barre', *Revue de musicologie*, xi (1927), pp. 185–202; xii (1928), pp. 1–11 and 68–74.

**Lully**

BORREL, EUGÈNE: *Jean-Baptiste Lully* (Paris, 1949).

ELLIS, HELEN MEREDITH: 'The Sources of Jean-Baptiste Lully's Secular Music', *Recherches sur la musique française classique*, viii (1968), pp. 89–130.

**Mangeant**

VERCHALY, ANDRÉ: 'A propos des chansonniers de Jacques Mangeant', *Mélanges d'histoire et d'esthétique musicales offerts à Paul-Marie Masson*, ii (Paris, 1955), pp. 169–77.

**Montéclair**

ANTHONY, JAMES R.: 'French Binary Air within Italian Aria da capo in Montéclair's Third Book of Cantatas', *Proceedings of the Royal Musical Association*, civ (1977–8), pp. 47–56.

**Mouret**

VIOLLIER, RENÉE: *Jean-Joseph Mouret, le musicien des grâces* (Paris, 1950; repr., 1976).

**Piroye**

BOUVET, CHARLES: 'Un musicien oublié; Charles Piroye', *Revue de musicologie*, ix (1928), pp. 225–34.

**Rameau**

CYR, MARY: 'A New Rameau Cantata', *Musical Times*, cxx (1979), pp. 907–9.

——— 'Performing Rameau's Cantatas', *Early Music*, xi (1983), pp. 480–9.

GIRDLESTONE, CUTHBERT: *Jean-Philippe Rameau: his Life and Work* (London, 1957; 2nd ed., 1969).

LALOY, LOUIS: *Jean-Philippe Rameau* (Paris, 1908).

**Richard**

DUFOURCQ, NORBERT: 'Notes sur les Richard, musiciens français du XVIIe siècle', *Revue de musicologie*, xxxvi (1954), pp. 116–33.

**Stuck**

BARTHÉLEMY, MAURICE: 'Les cantates de Jean-Baptiste Stuck', *Recherches sur la musique française classique*, ii (1962), pp. 125–37.

MILLIOT, SYLVETTE: 'Jean-Baptiste Stück', *Recherches sur la musique française classique*, ix (1969), pp. 91–8.


CHAPTER III

MUSIC FOR INSTRUMENTAL ENSEMBLE 1630–1700

**(i) Modern Editions**

*(a) Anthologies*

RIEMANN, HUGO, ed.: *Old Chamber Music*, i–iv (London, 1898–1902).
WASIELEWSKI, WILHELM JOSEPH VON, ed.: *Instrumentalsätze vom Ende des XVI. bis Ende des XVII Jahrhunderts* (Bonn, 1874; reprinted with new introduction and notes by John G. Suess, as *Anthology of Instrumental Music from the end of the sixteenth to the end of the seventeenth century*, New York, 1974).


*(b) Works by Individual Composers*

BANCHIERI, A.: *Opera Omnia*, ed. G. Vecchi, *Antiquae musicae italicae, Monumenta bononiensia*, xii (Bologna, 1963).
BLOW, J.: *Venus and Adonis*, ed. A. Lewis (Paris, 1939).
BRADE, W.: *Neue auserlesene Paduanen, 1609*, ed. B. Engelke, *Musik und Musiker am Gottorfer Hofe*, i (Breslau, 1930), pp. 199–282.
CACCINI, F.: *La liberazione di Ruggiero dall'isola d'Alcina*, ed. D. Silbert, *Smith College Music Archives*, vii (Northampton, Mass., 1945).
CAVALLI, F.: *Scipione Africano*, one sinfonia ed. H. Becker, *Das Musikwerk*, xxiv (Cologne, 1964), p. 37.
CORELLI, A.: *Les oeuvres de Arcangelo Corelli*, ed. J. Joachim and F. Chrysander, *Denkmäler der Tonkunst*, iii (Bergedorf, 1871).
ERLEBACH, P. H.: *VI Ouvertures, begleitet mit ihren dazu schicklichen Airs nach Französischer Art*, two ed. in *Organum*, ser. 3, nos. 15–16 (Leipzig, 1926).
FISCHER, J. C.: *Orchestermusik*, ed. E. von Werra, *Denkmäler deutscher Tonkunst*, x (Leipzig, 1902; rev. ed., 1958).
HAMMERSCHMIDT, A.: *Instrumentalwerke zu fünf und drei Stimmen*, ed. H. Mönkemeyer, *Das Erbe deutscher Musik*, ser. 1, xlix (Kassel, 1957).
KUSSER, J. S.: *Ouvertüre, C-Dur, für Streichorchester, Consortium, eine Spiel- und Kammermusik- Reihe* (New York, 1964).
—— *Ouverture IV aus 'Composition de musique' (1682)*, ed. H. Osthoff, *Nagels Musik-Archiv*, c (Hanover, 1933).
LANDI, S.: *Il Sant' Alessio*, ed. in *Bibliotheca musica bononiensis. Sezione 4*, xi (Bologna, 1970).
—— *Il Sant' Alessio*, one sinfonia ed. H. Becker, *Das Musikwerk*, xxiv (Cologne, 1964), p. 37.
LEGRENZI, G.: *Sonate (libro terzo)*, four ed. F. Lesure, *Le pupitre*, iv (Paris, 1968).
—— *Sonate da chiesa e da camera (libro secondo)*, six ed. F. Lesure, *Le pupitre*, iv (Paris, 1968).
—— *Sonate für vier Violinen mit Basso continuo*, ed. K. G. Fellerer, *Hortus musicus*, lxxxiii (Kassel and Basle, 1951).
—— *Sonate für Violine und Violoncello mit Basso continuo*, ed. K. G. Fellerer, *Hortus musicus*, lxxxiv (Kassel and Basle, 1951).
—— *Triosonate*, ed. W. Danckert, *Hortus musicus*, xxxi (Kassel and Basle, 1949).

LULLY, J. -B.: *Les ballets*, i, ii, *Oeuvres complètes*, ed. H. Prunières (Paris, 1931–3).

MAZZOCCHI, D.: *La Catena d'Adone*, *Bibliotheca musica bononiensis*. *Sezione 4*, ix (Bologna, 1969).

MERULA, T.: *Il primo Libro delle Canzoni*, ed. A. Sutkowski, *Opere complete di Tarquinio Merula*, I/i (Brooklyn, 1974).

MONTEVERDI, C.: *L'incoronazione di Poppea*, ed. G. F. Malipiero, *C. Monteverdi: Tutte le opere*, xiii (Asolo, 1931).

MUFFAT, G.: *Armonico tributo*, ed. E. Schenk, *Denkmäler der Tonkunst in Österreich*, lxxxix (Vienna, 1953).

—— *Florilegium primum*, ed. H. Rietsch, *Denkmäler der Tonkunst in Österreich*, ii (Jg. i(2) ) (Vienna, 1894).

—— *Florilegium secundum*, ed. H. Rietsch, *Denkmäler der Tonkunst in Österreich*, iv (Jg. ii(2) ) (Vienna, 1895).

PEUERL, P.: *Instrumental- und Vokalwerke*, ed. K. Geiringer, *Denkmäler der Tonkunst in Österreich*, lxx (Jg. xxxvi (2) ) (Vienna, 1929; repr., 1960).

POSCH, I.: *Instrumental- und Vokalwerke*, ed. K. Geiringer, *Denkmäler der Tonkunst in Österreich*, lxx (Jg. xxxvi (2) ) (Vienna, 1929; repr., 1960).

PURCELL, H.: *The Indian Queen and the Tempest*, ed. E. J. Dent, *Purcell Society Edition*, xix (London, 1912).

ROSENMÜLLER, J.: *Sonate da camera*, ed. K. Nef, *Denkmäler deutscher Tonkunst*, xviii (Leipzig, 1904).

ROSSI, M.: *Erminia sul Giordano*, *Bibliotheca musica bononiensis*. *Sezione 4*, xii (Bologna, c.1969).

ROSSI, S.: *Sinfonie, Gagliarde, Canzone, 1607–1608*, i, ii, ed. J. Newman and F. Rikko (New York, 1965–6).

—— *Sinfonie, 1607–1608*, iii, ed. J. Newman and F. Rikko (New York, 1971).

SCARLATTI, A.: *Sinfonien für Kammerorchester*, nos. 1, 2, 4, 5, 12, ed. R. Meylan, *Hortus musicus*, cxxv, cxlvi, xlviii, cxvi, clxviii (Kassel and Basle, 1950– 60).

SCHEIN, J. H.: *Banchetto Musicale 1617*, ed. A. Adrio, *Neue Ausgabe sämtlicher Werke*, ix (Kassel, 1979).

SCHMELZER, J. H.: *Sacro-profanus concentus musicus*, ed. E. Schenk, *Denkmäler der Tonkunst in Österreich*, cxi–cxii (Graz, 1965).

SCHMICORER, J. A.: *Orchestermusik*, ed. E. von Werra, *Denkmäler deutscher Tonkunst*, x (Leipzig, 1902; rev. ed., 1958).

SCHULTZ, J.: *Musicalischer Lüstgarte, a 2–8*, ed. H. Zenck, *Das Erbe deutscher Musik*, *2nd ser.*, *Landschaftsdenkmale Niedersachsen*, i (Wolfenbüttel, 1937).

STRADELLA, A.: *Sonata di viole*, ed. E. H. Tarr, *Archives de la musique instrumentale*, ix (Paris, 1968).

## (ii) Books and Articles

### (a) General

ADRIO, ADAM: *Die Anfänge des geistlichen Konzerts* (Berlin, 1935).

APEL, WILLI: 'Studien über die frühe Violinmusik', *Archiv für Musikwissenschaft*, xxx (1973), pp. 153–74 and xxxi (1974), pp. 184–213.

BONTA, STEPHEN: 'A Formal Convention in 17th-century Italian Instrumental Music', *International Musicological Society Congress Report*, xi, *Copenhagen 1972*, pp. 288–95.

BOTSTIBER, HUGO: *Geschichte der Ouvertüre und der freien Orchesterformen* (Leipzig, 1913; repr., 1969).

DELLI, B.: *Pavane und Galliarde: zur Geschichte der Instrumentalmusik im 16. und 17. Jahrhundert* (Diss., Berlin, 1957).

FISCHER, WILHELM: 'Instrumentalmusik von 1600–1750', *Handbuch der Musikgeschichte*, i, ed. G. Adler (Frankfurt, 1924; 2nd ed., Berlin, 1930, repr., 1961), pp. 540–73.

FISKE, ROGER: *Chamber Music* (London, 1969).

GOLDSCHMIDT, HUGO: *Studien zur Geschichte der italienischen Oper im 17. Jahrhundert*, i (Leipzig, 1901–4; repr., 1967).

JANDER, OWEN: 'Concerto Grosso Instrumentation in Rome in the 1660's and 1670's', *Journal of the American Musicological Society*, xxi (1968), pp. 168–80.

LIESS, ANDREAS: *Wiener Barockmusik* (Vienna, 1946).

MEYER, ERNST HERMANN: *Die mehrstimmige Spielmusik des 17. Jahrhunderts in Nord- und Mitteleuropa* (Kassel, 1934).

—— *Early English Chamber Music* (London, 2nd rev. ed., 1982).

NEF, KARL: *Geschichte der Sinfonie und Suite* (Leipzig, 1921).

NETTL, PAUL: 'Die Wiener Tanzkomposition in der zweiten Hälfte des siebzehnten Jahrhunderts', *Studien zur Musikwissenschaft*, viii (1921), pp. 45–175.

OBERST, G.: *Englische Orchestersuiten um 1600* (Wolfenbüttel, 1929).

PRUNIÈRES, HENRY: 'Notes sur les origines de l'ouverture française', *Sammelbände der internationalen Musikgesellschaft*, xii (1910–11), pp. 565–85.

SCHERING, ARNOLD: *Geschichte des Oratoriums* (Leipzig, 1911; repr., 1966).

SCHIOERRING, NILS: *Allemande og fransk ouverture* (Copenhagen, 1957).

SCHLOSSBERG, A.: *Die italienische Sonata für mehrere Instrumente im 17. Jahrhundert* (Paris, 1935).

SELFRIDGE-FIELD, ELEANOR: *Venetian Instrumental Music from Gabrieli to Vivaldi* (Oxford, 1975).

VATIELLI, FRANCESCO: *Arte e vita musicale a Bologna* (Bologna, 1927; repr. 1969).

WASIELEWSKI, WILHELM JOSEPH VON: *Die Violine im 17. Jahrhundert* (Bonn, 1874).

### (b) Individual Composers

#### a Kempis

MEYER, ERNST HERMANN: 'Die Vorherrschaft der Instrumentalmusik im niederländischen Barock', *Tijdschrift van de Vereniging voor Nederlandse muziekgeschiedenis*, xv/1 (1936), xv/2 (1937), xv/4 (1939).

#### Campra

BARTHÉLEMY, MAURICE: *André Campra* (Paris, 1957).

—— 'L'orchestre et l'orchestration des oeuvres de Campra', *La Revue musicale*, (1955), no. 226, pp. 97–104.

#### Corelli

HARRIS, SIMON: 'Lully, Corelli, Muffat and the 18th-Century Orchestral String Body', *Music and Letters*, liv (1973), pp. 197–202.

#### Hammerschmidt

KÜMMERLING, HARALD: 'Über einige unbekannte Stimmbücher der "Paduanen, Galliarden etc." von Andreas Hammerschmidt', *Die Musikforschung*, xiv (1961), pp. 186–8.

#### Landi

SARTORI, CLAUDIO: 'Stefano Landi uno e due. Ma di chi sono le canzoni strumentali?', *Nuova rivista musicale italiana*, ix (1975), pp. 3–9.

**Lully**

HARRIS, SIMON: 'Lully, Corelli, Muffat and the 18th-Century Orchestral String Body', *Music and Letters*, liv (1973), pp. 197–202.

**Marini**

ISELIN, DORA: *Biagio Marini: sein Leben und seine Instrumentalwerke* (Hildburg-hausen, 1930).

**Muffat**

HARRIS, SIMON: 'Lully, Corelli, Muffat and the 18th-Century Orchestral String Body', *Music and Letters*, liv (1973), pp. 197–202.

SCHERING, ARNOLD: 'Georg Muffat: "Ausserlesene mit Ernst und Lust gemengte Instrumental-Musik" 1701', *Zeitschrift der Internationalen Musik-Gesellschaft*, v (1903–4), pp. 365–8.

STOLLBROCK, L. VON: 'Georg Muffat und sein "Florilegium" ', *Monatshefte für Musikgeschichte*, xxiii (1891), pp. 37–48.

**Peuerl**

NOACK, ELISABETH: 'Ein Beitrag zur Geschichte der älteren deutschen Suite', *Archiv für Musikwissenschaft*, ii (1920), pp. 275–9.

**Purcell**

WESTRUP. J. A.: *Purcell* (London, 4th ed., 1980).

ZIMMERMAN, FRANKLIN B.: *Henry Purcell, 1659–95: his Life and Times* (London, 1967; 2nd rev. ed., Philadelphia, 1983).

**Scarlatti**

DENT, EDWARD J.: *Alessandro Scarlatti: his Life and Works* (2nd ed., Frank Walker, London, 1960).

**Stradella**

JANDER, OWEN: *A Catalogue of the Manuscripts of Compositions by Alessandro Stradella found in European and American libraries* (Wellesley, Mass., 1960; rev. 2nd ed., 1962).

MCCRICKARD, ELEANOR F.: 'Temporal and Tonal Aspects of Alessandro Stradella's Instrumental Music', *Analecta musicologica*, xix (1979), pp. 186–243.

**Torelli**

GIEGLING, FRANZ: *Giuseppe Torelli* (Kassel, 1949).

## CHAPTER IV

### ORCHESTRAL MUSIC IN THE EARLY EIGHTEENTH CENTURY

For a full bibliography and list of modern editions of the early symphony, see NOHM vol. VII, pp. 666–72.

### (i) Modern Editions

(a) Anthologies

ÉCORCHEVILLE, JULES, ed.: *Vingt suites d'orchestre du XVIIe siècle français*, ii (Paris and Berlin, 1906; repr., 1970).

SCHERING, ARNOLD, ed.: *Perlen alter Kammermusik deutscher und italienischer Meister* (Leipzig, n.d.).

(b) Works by Individual Composers

ALBICASTRO, E.: Zwölf Concerti a 4, Schweizerische Musikdenkmäler, i (Basle, 1955).

ALBINONI, T.: Gesamtausgabe der Instrumentalmusik, Orchesterwerke, ed. W. Kolneder (Zurich, 1974–     ).

—— Op. 1, Sonata a tre, no. 3, ed. W. Upmeyer, Nagels Musik-Archiv, xxxiv (Hanover, 1929); no. 6, ed. E. Schenk, Diletto musicale, cdxvi (Vienna and Munich, 1969).

—— Op. 2, Sonate, no. 3, ed. R. Giazotto, Antica musica strumentale italiana (Rome, 1959); no. 6, ed. F. Giegling, Nagels Musik-Archiv, clxxxix (Hanover, 1956).

—— Op. 3, Balletti, nos. 1–3, ed. W. Kolneder, Antiqua: eine Sammlung alter Musik (Mainz, 1964).

—— Op. 5, Concerti a cinque, no. 1, ed. G. Piccioli, Somma. musiche vocali e strumentali sacre e profane, Sec. XVII–XIX, xxiv (Rome, 1952); no. 4, ed. R. Cumar, Antica musica strumentale italiana (Rome, 1965); no. 5, Für Kenner und Liebhaber, iii (Basle, etc., 1954); nos. 8 and 10, ed. M. Shapiro, Series of early music, x (Ann Arbor, Mich., 1976).

—— Op. 7, Concerti a cinque, nos. 1–4, ed. W. Kolneder (Zurich, etc., 1975–6); no. 5, Für Kenner und Liebhaber, iv (Basle, etc., 1954); no. 7, ed. M. Shapiro, Series of early music, x (Ann Arbor, Mich., 1976); no. 9, ed. B. Paumgartner, Diletto musicale, ccclxviii (Vienna and Munich, 1971); no. 10, ed. M. Shapiro, Series of early music, x (Ann Arbor, Mich., 1976); no. 12, ed. B. Paumgartner, Diletto musicale, ccclxix (Vienna and Munich, 1971).

—— Op. 8, Balletti e sonate a tre, no. 4 a–b, ed. E. Schenk, Diletto musicale, cdxlvii–cdxlviii (Vienna and Munich, 1975).

—— Op. 9, Concerti a cinque, nos. 2 and 7, Für Kenner und Liebhaber, vii and xlix (Basle, etc., 1955 and 1973); nos. 9–10, ed. R. Giazotto, Antica musica strumentale italiana (Rome, 1959–61).

—— Due sinfonie per archi, ed. R. Giazotto, Antica musica strumentale italiana (Rome, 1961).

BACH, J. B.: Three overtures, ed. K. Geiringer, Music of the Bach Family (Cambridge, Mass., 1955).

BACH, J. C.: Sechs Sinfonien, op. 3, ed. E. G. S. Smith, Diletto musicale, ccclxxix–ccclxxxiv (Vienna and Munich, 1975).

BACH, J. S.: Sechs Brandenburgische Konzerte, ed. H. Besseler, Neue Ausgabe sämtlicher Werke, ser. 7, vol. ii (Kassel and Leipzig, 1956).

—— Vier Orchestersuiten, ed. H. Besseler, Neue Ausgabe sämtlicher Werke, ser. 7, vol. i (Kassel and Leipzig, 1967).

BONPORTI, F. A.: Concerti, op. 11, nos. 3–4, ed. G. Barblan, Antica musica strumentale italiana (Rome, 1959–61).

BOYCE, W.: Overtures, ed. G. Finzi, Musica Britannica, xiii (London, 1957).

CORELLI, A.: Concerti grossi, op. 6, ed. R. Bossard, Historisch-kritische Gesamtausgabe der musikalischen Werke, iv (Cologne, 1978).

—— Les oeuvres de Arcangelo Corelli, ed. J. Joachim and F. Chrysander, Denkmäler der Tonkunst, iii (Bergedorf, 1871).

DALL'ABACO, E. F.: Ausgewählte Werke. Teil 1–2, ed. A. Sandberger, Denkmäler der Tonkunst in Bayern, i (Jg. i(1) ) and xvi (Jg. ix(1) ) (Leipzig, 1900–8).

—— Ausgewählte Werke, Teil 3, ed. H. Schmid, Denkmäler der Tonkunst in Bayern, new ser., i (Wiesbaden, 1967).

DESTOUCHES, A. C.: Première suite des Éléments, ed. J. Feuille, Les Cahiers de plein jeu, xviii (Paris, 1973).

EBERLIN, J. E.: Masses, ed. W. Furlinger, Süddeutsche Kirchenmusik des Barock, i, ii, v (Altötting, 1970–8).

FISCHER, J.: *Tafelmusik*, ed. H. Engel, *Hortus musicus*, xvii (Kassel and Basle, 1951).

FUX, J. J.: *Concentus musico-instrumentalis*, ed. H. Rietsch, *Denkmäler der Tonkunst in Österreich*, xlvii (Jg. xxiii (2) ), (Vienna, 1916; repr., Graz, 1960).

—— *Constanza e Fortezza*, ed. E. Wellesz, *Denkmäler der Tonkunst in Österreich*, xxxiv–xxxv (Jg. xvii) (Graz, 1959).

—— *Mehrfach besetzte Instrumentalwerke*, ed. G. Adler, *Denkmäler der Tonkunst in Österreich*, xix (Jg. ix (2) ), (Vienna, 1902).

—— *Orfeo ed Euridice*, ed. H. M. Brown, *Italian opera 1640–1770*, xix (New York, 1978).

GASSMANN, F. L.: *Kirchenwerke*, ed. F. Kosch, *Denkmäler der Tonkunst in Österreich*, lxxxiii (Jg. xlv) (Graz, 1960).

GEMINIANI, F.: *Concerti grossi, op. 2*, nos. 4–6, ed. H. Moser, *Das Musikkränzlein*, viii–x (Leipzig, n.d.).

—— *Concerto grosso, op. 7 no. 1*, ed. E. Platen, *Nagels Musik-Archiv*, ccii (Hanover, 1960).

—— *Twelve Concerti grossi after Corelli's op. 5*, no. 3, ed. H. Ruf, *Nagels Musik-Archiv*, ccxi (Hanover, 1963); nos. 5 and 12, ed. M. Abbado and R. Fasano, *Antica musica strumentale italiana* (Rome, 1967–8).

GRAUPNER, C.: *Ouverture, F-Dur*, ed. K. Hofmann, *Nagels Musik-Archiv*, ccxx (Hanover, 1968).

HANDEL, G. F.: Instrumental-Concerte; Instrumental Musik; 12 Grosse Concerte, op. 6; Wassermusik und Feuerwerkmusik; ed. F. Chrysander, *Georg Friedrich Händels Werke*, xxi, xlviii, xxx, xlvii (Leipzig, 1865, 1894, 1869, 1886).

—— Sechs Concerti grossi, op. 3; Zwölf Concerti grossi; Wassermusik, Feuerwerkmusik; *Hallische Händel-Ausgabe*, iv/11, iv/14, iv/13 (Kassel and Leipzig, 1971, 1961, 1962).

HEINICHEN, J. D.: *Concerto a 8*, *Moecks Kammermusik*, lxix (Celle, 1961).

KERLL, J. C.: *Requiem*, ed. G. Adler, *Denkmäler der Tonkunst in Österreich*, lix (Jg. xxx (1) ) (Graz, 1960).

LOCATELLI, P. A.: *Sei introduttioni teatrali*, ed. A. Koole, *Monumenta musica neerlandica*, iv (Amsterdam, 1961).

—— *Twelve Concerti grossi, op. 1*, no. 2, ed. C. Abbado, *Antica musica strumentale italiana* (Rome, 1961); nos. 5 and 12, ed. B. Paumgartner, *Diletto musicale*, ccclxxxviii and ccclxxxvi (Vienna and Munich, 1977 and 1975); no. 11, ed. O. Géczy (Zurich, etc., 1973).

MANFREDINI, F.: *Concerto grosso, op. 3 no. 11*, ed. W. Upmeyer, *Nagels Musik-Archiv*, cliii (Hanover, 1941).

MARCELLO, B.: *Concerto a 5, op. 1 no. 4*, ed. M. Zanon, *Antica musica strumentale italiana* (Rome, 1960).

MUDGE, R.: *Six Concertos in 7 parts*, nos. 1, 4, and 6, ed. G. Finzi (London, c.1954).

MUFFAT, G.: *Ausserlesene Instrumental-Musik*, ed. E. Luntz, *Denkmäler der Tonkunst in Österreich*, xxiii (Jg. xi (2) ) (Graz, 1959).

—— *Concerti grossi*, ed. E. Schenk, *Denkmäler der Tonkunst in Österreich*, lxxxix (Vienna, 1953).

PERGOLESI, G. B.: *Masses*, ed. F. Caffarelli, *Opera omnia*, vi, xv/2, xviii (Rome, 1932–42).

PEZ, J. C.: *Ausgewählte Werke*, ed. B. A. Wallner, *Denkmäler der Tonkunst in Bayern*, xxxv (Jg.xxvii, xxviii) (Augsburg, 1928).

RAMEAU, J.-P.: *Hippolyte et Aricie*, ed. C. Saint-Saëns, *et al.*, *Oeuvres complètes*, vi (Paris, 1900).

—— *Zoroastre*, ed. F. Gervaise (Paris, 1964).

REUTTER, J. A.: *Kirchenwerke*, ed N. Hofer, *Denkmäler der Tonkunst in Österreich*, lxxxviii (Graz, 1952).

RICHTER, F. X.: *Sinfonia da Camera*, ed. W. Upmeyer, *Nagels Musik-Archiv*, lxxii (Hanover, 1930).

SAMMARTINI, G.: *Concerto grosso, op. 3 no. 6*, ed. K. Schultz-Hauser, *Musikschätze vergangener Zeiten* (Munich, etc., 1965).

SCHEIBE, J. A.: *Concerto a 4, Moecks Kammermusik*, xli (Celle, n.d.).

SCHEIFFELHUT, J.: *Siebente Suite aus dem 'Lieblichen frühlings Anfang'*, *Musik-schätze der Vergangenheit* (Berlin, n.d.).

STANLEY, J.: *Six Concerto's in 7 parts*, ed. G. Finzi (London, 1949).

TARTINI, G.: *Concerti a 5*, no. 1, ed. J. Brinckmann and W. Mohr; no. 2, ed. F. Nagel and W. Radeke, *Ars instrumentalis*, xix and lxviii (Hamburg, 1954 and 1973).

—— *Sinfonie, D-Dur*, ed. H. Erdmann, *Antiqua: eine Sammlung alter Musik* (New York, 1956).

—— *Sinfonie*, ed. H. Erdmann, *Hortus musicus*, liii (Kassel and Basle, 1950).

TELEMANN, G. P.: Four symphonies and two divertimenti, ed. in *Musikschätze der Vergangenheit* (Berlin, 1936–7).

—— *Ouverture bourlesque de Quichote*, ed. F. Schroeder, *Musikschätze der Vergangenheit* (Berlin, c.1963).

—— Sechs ausgewählte Ouvertüren; Tafelmusik; *Musikalische Werke*, x, xii–xiv (Kassel and Basle, 1955–63).

—— Suite in A minor, ed. H. Büttner (London, 1947).

—— *Tafelmusik*, ed. M. Seiffert, *Denkmäler deutscher Tonkunst*, lxi–lxii (Wiesbaden and Graz, 1959).

TORELLI, G.: *Gesamtausgabe der gedruckten Instrumentalmusik*, ed. W. Kolneder (Vienna, 1965–    ).

—— *Concerti musicali, op. 6*, no. 1, ed. W. Kolneder (Mainz, 1958).

—— *Concerti grossi op. 8*, no. 2, ed. B. Paumgartner, *Antiqua: eine Sammlung alter Musik* (New York, 1956); no. 9, ed. M. Abbado, *Antica musica strumentale italiana* (Rome, 1967).

VIVALDI, A.: *Le opere di Antonio Vivaldi*, ed. G. F. Malipiero *et al.*, (Milan, 1947–71).

WAGENSEIL, G. C.: *Missa in A*, ed. W. Fürlinger, *Süddeutsche Kirchenmusik des Barock*, iii (Altötting, c.1974).

ZELENKA, J. D.: *Composizioni per orchestra, part 1*, *Musica antiqua Bohemica*, lxi (Prague, 1963).

## (ii) Books and Articles

### (a) General

ARNHEIM, AMALIE: 'Englische Suitenkompositionen des XVII. Jahrhunderts und ihre Deutschland erschienenen Sammlungen', *International Musical Society Congress Report*, iv, *London, 1911*, pp. 93–9.

BONACCORSI, ALFREDO: 'Contributo alla storia del concerto grosso', *Rivista musicale italiana*, xxxix (1932).

BOYDEN, DAVID: 'When is a concerto not a concerto?', *Musical Quarterly*, xliii (1957), pp. 220–32.

DRUMMOND, PIPPA: *The German Concerto: Five Eighteenth-Century Studies* (Oxford, 1980).

ÉCORCHEVILLE, JULES: *Vingt suites d'orchestre du XVIIe siècle français*, i (Paris and Berlin, 1906; repr., 1970).

FISCHER, WILHELM: 'Instrumentalmusik von 1750–1828', *Handbuch der Musik-geschichte*, ii, ed. G. Adler (2nd ed., Berlin, 1930; repr., 1961), pp. 795–833.

FORKEL, JOHANN NIKOLAUS: *Musikalischer Almanach für Deutschland* (Leipzig 1782–4).

HELL, HELMUT: *Die neapolitanische Opernsinfonie in der ersten Hälfte des 18. Jahrhunderts* (Tutzing, 1971).

HUTCHINGS, ARTHUR: *The Baroque Concerto* (London, 3rd rev. ed., 1973).

KRÜGER, WALTHER: *Das Concerto grosso in Deutschland* (Wolfenbüttel, 1932).

LA LAURENCIE, LIONEL DE and SAINT-FOIX, GEORGES DE: 'Contribution a l'histoire de la symphonie française vers 1750', *Année musicale*, i (1911), pp. 1–121.

MAJER, JOSEPH: *Museum musicum theoretico practicum* (Schwabisch Hall, 1732 facsimile ed., Kassel, 1954).

NEF, KARL: *Geschichte der Sinfonie und Suite* (Leipzig, 1921).

—— *Zur Geschichte der deutschen Instrumentalmusik in der zweiten Hälfte des 17. Jahrhunderts* (Leipzig, 1902; repr., 1973).

NOACK, FRIEDRICH: *Sinfonie und Suite von Gabrieli bis Schumann* (Leipzig, 7th ed., 1932).

QUANTZ, JOHANN JOACHIM: *Versuch einer Anweisung die Flöte traversiere zu spielen* (Berlin, 1752; facsimile ed., Kassel 1953; Eng. trans., *On playing the Flute*, ed. E. R. Reilly, London, 1966).

RIEMANN, HUGO: 'Zur Geschichte der deutschen Suite', *Sammelbände der Internationalen Musik-Gesellschaft*, vi (1904–5), pp. 501–20.

ROUSSEAU, JEAN-JACQUES: *Lettres sur la musique françoise* (Paris, 1753; abridged Eng. trans. in *Source Readings in Music History*, ed. O. Strunk, New York, 1950).

SCHEIBE, JOHANN ADOLPH: *Der critischer Musikus* (rev. ed., Leipzig, 1745; repr., 1970).

SCHERING, ARNOLD: *Geschichte des Instrumental-Konzerts* (Leipzig, 2nd ed., 1927; repr., 1965).

SELFRIDGE-FIELD, ELEANOR: *Venetian Instrumental Music from Gabrieli to Vivaldi* (Oxford, 1975).

SMITHERS, DON L.: *The Music and History of the Baroque Trumpet before 1721* (London, 1973).

TILMOUTH, MICHAEL: 'Some Early London Concerts and Music Clubs, 1670–1720', *Proceedings of the Royal Musical Association*, lxxxiv (1957–8), pp. 13–26.

TORCHI, LUIGI: 'La musica instrumentale in Italia dei secoli XVI, XVII e XVIII', *Rivista musicale italiana*, viii (1901), pp. 1–42.


(b) *Individual Composers*

**Albicastro**

BOYDEN, DAVID: 'Henricus Albicastro: zwölf concerti a 4', *Notes*, xiii (1955–6), pp. 329–30.

**Albinoni**

GIAZOTTO, REMO: *Tomaso Albinoni* (Milan, 1945).

**Bach**

CARRELL, NORMAN: *Bach's Brandenburg Concertos* (London, 1963).

DAVID, HANS T. and MENDEL, ARTHUR: *The Bach Reader* (2nd ed., New York, 1966).

DÜRR, ALFRED: 'Zur Entstehungsgeschichte des 5. Brandenburgischen Konzerts', *Bach-Jahrbuch 1975*, lxi, pp. 63–9.

FORKEL, JOHANN NIKOLAUS: *Über Johann Sebastian Bachs Leben, Kunst und Kunstwerke* (Leipzig, 1802; repr., 1968; Eng. trans, 1820 and 1920).

FULLER MAITLAND, JOHN ALEXANDER: *Bach's 'Brandenburg' Concertos* (London, 1929; 2nd ed., 1945).

GEIRINGER, KARL: *Johann Sebastian Bach: the culmination of an era* (New York, 1966).

GERBER, RUDOLF: *Bachs Brandenburgische Konzerte* (Kassel, 1951).

HALM, AUGUST: 'Über J. S. Bachs Konzertform', *Bach-Jahrbuch 1919*, xvi, pp. 1–44.

KRÜGER, WALTHER: 'Das concerto grosso Joh. Seb. Bachs', *Bach-Jahrbuch 1932*, xxix, pp. 1–50.

SCHMIDT, HENRY: 'Bach's C major Orchestral Suite: a New Look at Possible Origins', *Music and Letters*, lvii (1976), pp. 152–63.

TERRY, CHARLES SANFORD: *Bach's Orchestra* (London, 4th ed., 1966).

WACKERNAGEL, P.: *Bachs Brandenburgische Konzerte* (Berlin, 1928).

**Boyce**

CUDWORTH, CHARLES L.: 'The symphonys of Dr. William Boyce', *Music*, ii (1953).

RUSSELL, JOHN F.: 'The Instrumental Works of William Boyce', *Musical Opinion*, lxxii (1949), pp. 635–7.

**Dittersdorf**

DITTERSDORF, CARL DITTERS VON: *Karl von Dittersdorfs Lebensbeschreibung, seinem Sohne in die Feder diktiert* (Leipzig, 1801; ed. N. Miller, Munich, 1967; Eng. trans., 1896; repr., 1970).

**Fasch**

KÜNTZEL, G.: *Die Instrumentalkonzerte von Johann Friedrich Fasch 1688–1758* (Diss., Frankfurt, 1965).

**Fux**

RIETSCH, HEINRICH: 'Der "Concentus" von Fux', *Studien zur Musikwissenschaft*, iv (1916), pp. 46–57.

**Geminiani**

HERNREID, ROBERT: 'Francesco Geminiani's Concerti grossi Op. 3', *Acta Musicologica*, ix (1937), pp. 22–30.

**Handel**

CHRYSANDER, FRIEDRICH: 'Händels Instrumentalkompositionen für grosses Orchester', *Vierteljahrsschrift für Musikwissenschaft*, iii (1887), p. 1, pp. 157–88 and 451–62.

—— 'Händels zwölf Concerti grossi für Streichinstrumente', *Allgemeine musikalische Zeitung*, xvi (1881), pp. 81–3, 97–9, 113–5, 129–32, 145–8; and xvii (1882), p. 894.

DEUTSCH, OTTO ERICH: *Handel: a Documentary Biography* (London, 1955; rev., 1974).

HILL, CECIL: 'Die Abschrift von Händels "Wassermusik" in der Sammlung Newman Flower', *Händel-Jahrbuch 1971*, pp. 75–88.

LAM, BASIL: 'The Orchestral Music', *Handel: a Symposium*, ed. G. Abraham (London, 1954), pp. 200–32.

SADIE, STANLEY: *Handel Concertos* (BBC Music Guide) (London, 1972).

**Heinichen**

HAUSSWALD, GÜNTER: *Johann David Heinichens Instrumentalwerke* (Leipzig, 1937).

**Kusser**
Scholz, Hans: *Johann Sigismund Kusser: sein Leben und seine Werke* (Leipzig, 1911).

**Quantz**
Quantz, Johann Joachim: 'Herrn Johann Joachim Quantzens Lebenslauf von ihm selbst entworfen', in F. W. Marpurg: *Historisch-Kritische Beyträge zur Aufnahme der Musik*, i (Berlin, 1754–78; repr., 1970), pp. 197–250; repr. in W. Kahl: *Selbstbiographien deutscher Musiker des XVIII. Jahrhunderts* (Cologne, 1948), pp. 104–57; Eng. trans in P. Nettl: *Forgotten Musicians* (New York, 1951), pp. 280–319.

**Scheiffelhut**
Gerheuser, Ludwig: 'Jacob Scheiffelhut und seine Instrumental-Musik', *Zeitschrift des historischen Vereins für Schwaben und Neuburg*, xlix (1933), pp. 1–92.

**Tartini**
Frasson, L.: *Giuseppe Tartini, primo violino e capo concerto nella Basilica del Santo* (Padua, 1974).

**Telemann**
Büttner, Horst: *Das Konzert in den Orchestersuiten Georg Philipp Telemanns* (Wolfenbüttel and Berlin, 1935).
Fleischhauer, G.: 'Telemann, G. Ph.: Orchestersuiten und Instrumentalkonzerte' *Konzertbuch*, iii, ed. H. J. Schaefer (Leipzig, 1974).
Hoffmann, Adolf: *Die Orchestersuiten Georg Philipp Telemanns* (Tutzing, 1969).

**Torelli**
Giegling, Franz: *Giuseppe Torelli* (Kassel, 1949).

**Vivaldi**
Kolneder, Walter: *Antonio Vivaldi: Leben und Werk* (Wiesbaden, 1965; Eng. trans., 1970).
Pincherle, Marc: *Antonio Vivaldi et la musique instrumentale* (Paris, 1948).
—— *Vivaldi* (Paris, 1955; English trans., 1958).
Ryom, Peter: *Verzeichnis der Werke Antonio Vivaldis: kleine Ausgabe* (Leipzig, 1974; 2nd ed., 1979).
Talbot, Michael: *Vivaldi* (London, 1978).

**Zelenka**
Hausswald, Günter: 'Johann Dismas Zelenka als Instrumentalkomponist', *Archiv für Musikwissenschaft*, xiii (1956), pp. 243–62.


CHAPTER V

THE SOLO CONCERTO

**(i) Modern Editions**

*(a) Anthologies*

Engel, Hans, ed.: *Das Solokonzert, Das Musikwerk*, xxv (Cologne, 1964).
Schering, Arnold, ed.: *Instrumentalkonzerte deutscher Meister, Denkmäler deutscher Tonkunst*, xxix–xxx (Leipzig, 1907; repr., 1958).

(b) *Works by Individual Composers*

ALBINONI, T.: See p. 715 for editions of Albinoni's opp. 2 and 5.

AGRELL, J. J.: *Konzert, A-Dur, für Klavier und Streicher*, ed. H. Heussner, *Diletto musicale*, dclxv (Vienna and Munich, 1979).

BACH, J. S.: *Johann Sebastian Bach's Werke*, ed. M. Hauptmann, *et al.*, Bach-Gesellschaft (Leipzig, 1851–99).

—— *Neue Ausgabe sämtlicher Werke*, ed. A. Dürr, *et al.*, ser. 7 *Orchesterwerke* (Kassel and Leipzig, 1954–    ).

BLAVET, M.: *Konzert, fur Flöte, Streicher und Generalbass*, ed. G. Scheck and H. Ruf, *Florilegium musicum*, xi (Lörrach and Baden, 1956).

BRESCIANELLO, G. A.: *Concerti a tre*, ed. A. Damerini, *Hortus musicus*, lxvi–lxviii (Kassel and Basle, 1950–1).

CORRETTE, M.: *Konzert, d-moll, op. 26, no. 6*, ed. H. Ruf, *Nagels Musik-Archiv*, cci (Hanover, 1959).

DALL'ABACO, E. F.: *Ausgewählte Werke, Teil 1–2*, ed. A. Sandberger, *Denkmäler der Tonkunst in Bayern*, i (Jg. i(1) ) and xvi (Jg. ix(1) ) (Leipzig, 1900 and 1908).

FASCH, J. F.: Three concertos, ed. H. Winschermann, *Ars Instrumentalis*, xxxvi, xliv–xlv (Hamburg, 1971).

—— Two concertos, ed. A. Hoffmann, *Corona*, lxv, lxxvii (Wolfenbüttel, 1961 and 1963).

—— *Konzert, d-moll*, ed. H. Töttcher, *Ars Instrumentalis*, iv (Hamburg, n.d.).

GRAUN, C. H.: *Konzert, für Cembalo und 4stg. Streichorchester*, ed. A. Hoffmann, *Corona*, lx (Wolfenbüttel, 1960).

GRAUN, J. G.: Two concertos, ed. H. Töttcher, *Ars Instrumentalis*, viii–ix (Hamburg, n.d.).

—— Two concertos, *Moecks Kammermusik*, lxviii and lxxx (Celle, 1960 and n.d.).

GRAUPNER, C.: *Konzert für Flöte und Streichorchester*, ed. A. Hoffmann, *Corona*, xxvii (Wolfenbüttel, 1953).

—— *Konzert für Oboe, Streicher und Cembalo*, ed. A. Kreutz, *Nagels Musik-Archiv*, clxviii (Hanover, 1952).

—— *Konzert für Trompete, Streicher und Basso continuo*, ed. J. Wojciechowski, *Ars Instrumentalis*, xlvi (Hamburg, n.d.).

HANDEL, G. F.: 12 organ concertos, ed. F. Chrysander, *Georg Friedrich Händels Werke*, xxviii (Leipzig, 1881).

—— *Orgelkonzerte 1. op. 4 nr 1–6*, ed. K. Matthaei; *Acht Concerti*, ed. F. Hudson; *Hallische Händel-Ausgabe, ser. 4*, ii, xii (Kassel, 1956 and 1971).

HEINICHEN, J. D.: *Konzert für Violine und 4stg. Streicherorchester und Generalbass*, ed. A. Hoffmann, *Corona*, lviii (Wolfenbüttel, 1961).

—— *Konzert für Flöte oder Oboe*, *Musikschätze der Vergangenheit* (Berlin, 1938).

LECLAIR, J. -M.: *Concerti, Op. 7, no. 2*, ed. J. Paillard, *Archives de la musique instrumentale*, i (Paris, 1962); nos. 3–4, ed. C. Crussard, *Flores musicae*, xiv, x (Lausanne, 1964 and 1960); no. 5, ed. H. Ruf, *Nagels Musik-Archiv*, ccix (Hanover, 1963).

—— *Concerti, op. 10*, nos. 2 and 6, ed. J. Paillard, *Archives de la musique instrumentale*, iv–v (Paris, 1963); no. 5, ed. F. Polnauer, *Ars instrumentalis*, lxi (Hamburg, 1973).

LEFFLOTH, J. M.: *Konzert, D-Dur*, ed. H. Ruf, *Nagels Musik-Archiv*, clxxxiv (Hanover, 1955).

LOCATELLI, P. A.: *L'arte del violino*, ed. R. Franconi (Milan, 1921).

PISENDEL, J. G.: *Konzert für Violine, Streicherorchester und Basso continuo*, ed. G. Hausswald, *Nagels Musik-Archiv*, cxcvi (Kassel, 1958).

QUANTZ, J. J.: Two concertos for flute and strings, ed. H. D. Sonntag, *Corona*, xxxix, lvi (Wolfenbüttel, 1957–8).

—— *Konzert ("Pour Potsdam") für Flöte und Streicher*, ed. W. Upmeyer, *Hortus musicus*, lxxvi (Kassel and Basle, 1951).

—— *Konzert für Flöte, Streicher und Basso continuo*, ed. H. D. Sonntag, *Ars Instrumentalis*, xxvii (Hamburg, n.d.).

TARTINI, G.: *Le opere di Giuseppe Tartini, 1st ser*, ed. E. Farina and C. Scimone (Milan, 1971– ).

TELEMANN, G. P.: *Sechs Konzerte für Querflöte*, ed. J. P. Hinnenthal; *Zwölf Violinkonzerte*, ed. S. Kross, *Musikalische Werke*, xi, xxiii (Kassel and Basle, 1957 and 1973).

—— Violin concerto in G, ed. F. Schroeder and F. Rübart (Zurich, 1965).

—— Violin concerto in A minor, ed. K. Grebe (Hamburg, 1967).

—— Concerto for two violins in G, ed. W. Lebermann (Mainz, 1970).

—— Concerto for three trumpets in D, ed. G. Fleischhauer (Leipzig, 1968).

—— Concerto for violin, trumpet and 'cello in D, ed. H. Töttcher and K. Grebe (Hamburg, 1965).

—— Concerto for two flutes, oboe and violin in Bb, ed. G. Fleischhauer (Leipzig, 1974).

TORELLI, G.: *Concerti Musicali, op. 6*, no. 1, ed. W. Kolneder (Mainz, 1958); no. 10, ed. H. Engel, *Nagels Musik-Archiv*, lxx (Hanover, 1931).

—— Sinfonia for trumpet and strings, ed. F. Schroeder, *Diletto musicale*, cdxcix (Vienna and Munich, 1975).

VERACINI, F. M.: *Konzert für Violine und Streicher*, ed. B. Paumgartner, *Hortus musicus*, clxix (Kassel and Basle, 1959).

VIVALDI, A.: *Le opere di Antonio Vivaldi*, ed. G. F. Malipiero, *et al.*(Rome, 1947–1971).

WERNER, G. J.: *Musikalischer Instrumental-Kalender*, ed. F. Stein, *Das Erbe deutscher Musik, Reihe 1*, xxxi (Kassel, 1956).

(ii) **Books and Articles**

(a) *General*

ANTHONY, JAMES R.: *French Baroque Music from Beaujoyeulx to Rameau* (London, 1973; 2nd rev. ed., 1978).

BERGER, JEAN: 'Notes on some 17th-century Compositions for Trumpets and Strings in Bologna', *Musical Quarterly*, xxxvii (1951), pp. 354–67.

BROFSKY, HOWARD: 'Notes on the Early French Concerto', *Journal of the American Musicological Society*, xix (1966), pp. 87–91.

CUDWORTH, CHARLES L.: 'The English Organ Concerto', *The Score*, viii (1953), pp. 51–60.

DAFFNER, HUGO: *Die Entwicklung des Klavierkonzerts bis Mozart* (Leipzig, 1906).

DRUMMOND, PIPPA: *The German Concerto: Five Eighteenth-Century Studies* (Oxford, 1980).

EDWARDS, OWAIN: 'English String Concertos before 1800', *Proceedings of the Royal Musical Association*, xcv (1968–9), pp. 1–13.

ELLER, RUDOLF: 'Die Entstehung der Themenzweiheit in der Frühgeschichte des Instrumentalkonzerts', *Festschrift Heinrich Besseler* (Leipzig, 1961), pp. 325–35.

ENGEL, HANS: *Das Solokonzert, Das Musikwerk*, xxv (Cologne, 1964).

HUTCHINGS, ARTHUR: *The Baroque Concerto* (London, 3rd rev. ed., 1973).

KOLNEDER, WALTER: 'Zur Frühgeschichte des Solokonzerts', *Gesellschaft für Musikforschung Kongressbericht* (Kassel, 1962).

LABORDE, L. E. S. J. DE: *Musiciens de Paris, 1535–1792*, ed. Y. de Brossard (Paris, 1965).

LA LAURENCIE, LIONEL DE: *L'école française de violon de Lully à Viotti* (Paris, 1922–4; repr., 1971).

LESURE, FRANÇOIS: *Bibliographie des Éditions Musicales publiées par Estienne Roger et Michel-Charles Le Cène (Amsterdam 1696–1743)* (Paris, 1969).

MERSMANN, HANS: *Musikhören* (Potsdam and Berlin, 1938; 2nd ed., 1952).

MISHKIN, H. G.: 'The Italian Concerto before 1700', *Bulletin of the American Musicological Society*, vii (1943).

MOSER, ANDREAS: *Geschichte des Violinspiels* (Berlin, 2nd ed., 1966–7).

PAILLARD, JEAN-FRANÇOIS: 'Les premiers concertos français pour instruments à vent', *La Revue musicale* (1955), no. 225, pp. 144–62.

QUANTZ, JOHANN JOACHIM: *Versuch einer Anweisung die Flöte traversiere zu spielen* (Berlin, 1752; facsimile ed., Kassel, 1953; Eng. trans., *On playing the Flute*, ed. E. R. Reilly, London, 1966).

SCHENK, ERICH: 'Osservazioni sulla scuola instrumentale modenese nel Seicento', *Attie memorie della Accademia di scienze, lettere e arti di Modena*, 5th ser., x (1952).

SCHERING, ARNOLD: *Geschichte des Instrumental-Konzerts* (Leipzig, 2nd ed., 1927; repr., 1965).

SCHUBART, CHRISTIAN FRIEDRICH DANIEL: *Ideen zu einer Ästhetik der Tonkunst* (Vienna, 1806).

TALBOT, MICHAEL: 'The Concerto Allegro in the Early Eighteenth Century', *Music and Letters*, lii (1971), pp. 8–18 and 159–72.

VATIELLI, FRANCESCO: *Arte e vita musicale a Bologna* (Bologna, 1927; repr., 1969).

VEINUS, ABRAHAM: *The Concerto* (New York, 1944; 2nd rev. ed., 1964).

### (b) Individual Composers

#### Alberti
TALBOT, MICHAEL: 'A Thematic Catalogue of the Orchestral Works of Giuseppe Matteo Alberti (1685–1751)', *Royal Musical Association Research Chronicle*, xiii (1976), pp. 1–26.

#### Albinoni
GIAZOTTO, REMO: *Tomaso Albinoni* (Milan, 1945).

TALBOT, MICHAEL: 'Albinoni's Oboe Concertos', *The Consort*, xxix (1973), pp. 14–22.

#### Aubert
LA LAURENCIE, LIONEL DE: 'Jacques Aubert et les premiers concertos français de violon', *Bulletin français de la Société Internationale de Musique*, ii/1 (1906), pp. 441–8.

#### Bach
ABER, ADOLF: 'Studien zu J. S. Bachs Klavierkonzerten', *Bach-Jahrbuch 1913*, x pp. 5–30.

BREIG, WERNER: 'Bachs Violinkonzert d-moll: Studien zu seiner Gestalt und seiner Entstehungsgeschichte', *Bach-Jahrbuch 1976*, lxii, pp. 7–34.

DAVID, HANS T. and MENDEL, ARTHUR: *The Bach Reader* (New York, 2nd ed., 1966).

HOFFMANN-ERBRECHT, LOTHAR: 'Johann Sebastian Bach als Schöpfer des Klavier Konzerts', *Quellenstudien zur Musik: Wolfgang Schmieder zum 70. Geburtstag* (Frankfurt, 1972), pp. 69–77.

KELLER, H.: 'J. S. Bachs Violinkonzerte', *Festschrift zum 175 jährigen Bestehen der Gewandhauskonzerte, 1781–1956* (Leipzig, 1956).

KLEIN, HANS-GÜNTER: *Der Einfluss der Vivaldischen Konzertform im Instrumentalwerk Johann Sebastian Bachs* (Baden-Baden, 1970).

**Bononcini**

FORD, ANTHONY: 'Giovanni Bononcini, 1670–1747', *Musical Times*, cxi (1970), pp. 695–9.

**Bonporti**

BARBLAN, GUGLIELMO, ed.: *Francesco A. Bonporti nel 3⁰ centenario della nascita* (Trent, 1972).

**Handel**

EHRLINGER, F.: *G. F. Händels Orgelkonzerte* (Würzburg, 1940).

FISKE, ROGER: 'Handel's Organ Concertos: Do they belong to particular oratorios?', *Organ Yearbook*, iii (1972), pp. 14–23.

NIELSEN, NIELS KARL: 'Handel's Organ Concertos reconsidered', *Dansk aarbog for musikforskning*, iii (1963), pp. 3–26.

SADIE, STANLEY: *Handel Concertos* (London, 1972).

**Heinichen**

HAUSSWALD, GÜNTER: *Johann David Heinichens Instrumentalwerke* (Leipzig, 1937).

**Jacchini**

WASIELEWSKI, WILHELM JOSEPH VON: *Das Violoncell und seine Geschichte* (Leipzig, enlarged, 3rd ed., 1925, repr., 1970; Eng. trans., repr., 1968).

**Leclair**

LEMOINE, MICHELINE: 'La technique violonistique de Jean-Marie Leclair', *La Revue musicale* (1955), no. 225, pp. 117–43.

PAILLARD, JEAN-FRANÇOIS: 'Les concertos de Jean-Marie Leclair', *Chigiana*, xxi (1964), pp. 47–62.

**Locatelli**

DUNNING, ALBERT: *Pietro Antonio Locatelli: Der Virtuose und seine Welt*, i, ii (Buren, 1982).

KOOLE, AREND: *Leven en werken van Pietro Antonio Locatelli da Bergamo* (Amsterdam, 1949).

**Quantz**

QUANTZ, JOHANN JOACHIM: 'Herrn Johann Joachim Quantzens Lebenslauf von ihm selbst entworfen', ed. W. Kahl, *Selbstbiographien deutscher Musiker des XVIII Jahrhunderts* (Cologne, 1948).

**Tartini**

DOUNAIS, MINOS: *Die Violinkonzerte Giuseppe Tartinis als Ausdruck einer Künstlerpersönlichkeit und einer Kulturepoche* (Wolfenbüttel and Berlin, 2nd ed., 1966).

FANZAGO, F.: *Orazione . . . delle lodi di Giuseppe Tartini* (Padua, 1770; 2nd ed., 1792).

**Telemann**

KROSS, SIEGFRIED: *Das Instrumentalkonzert bei Georg Philipp Telemann* (Tutzing, 1969).

PETZOLDT, RICHARD: *Georg Philipp Telemann: Leben und Werke* (Leipzig, 1967; Eng. trans., 1974).

**Torelli**

GIEGLING, FRANZ: *Giuseppe Torelli* (Kassel, 1949).

**Vivaldi**

ELLER, RUDOLF: *Vivaldis Konzertform* (Diss., Leipzig, 1956).
HELLER, KARL: *Die deutsche Überlieferung der Instrumentalwerke Vivaldis* (Leipzig, 1971).
KOLNEDER, WALTER: *Antonio Vivaldi: Leben und Werk* (Wiesbaden, 1965; Eng. trans., 1970).
—— 'Das Frühschaffen Antonio Vivaldis', *Kongressbericht, Utrecht 1952* (Amsterdam, 1953).
—— *Die Solokonzertform bei Vivaldi* (Strasbourg and Baden-Baden, 1961).
PINCHERLE, MARC: *Antonio Vivaldi et la musique instrumentale* (Paris, 1948).
—— *Vivaldi* (Paris, 1955; Eng. trans., 1958).
RYOM, PETER: *Verzeichnis der Werke Antonio Vivaldis: kleine Ausgabe* (Leipzig, 2nd ed., 1979).
TALBOT, MICHAEL: *Vivaldi* (London, 1978).
—— *Vivaldi* (BBC Music Guide) (London, 1979).

**Werner**

STEIN, FRITZ: 'Der musikalische Instrumental-kalender: zu Leben und Wirken von Gregorius Josephus Werner', *Musica*, xi (1957), pp. 390–6.

**Zuccari**

BARBLAN, GUGLIELMO: 'La musica strumentale e cameristica a Milano nel '700', *Storia di Milano XVI* (Milan, 1962).

## CHAPTER VI

### CONCERTED CHAMBER MUSIC

**(i) Modern Editions**

*(a) Anthologies*

—— *Sonate a due Violini (autori vari)*, *Bibliotheca musica bononiensis, sezione 4*, cxli (Bologna, n.d.).
COATES, WILLIAM and DART, THURSTON, eds.: *Jacobean Consort Music, Musica Britannica*, ix (2nd ed., London, 1966).
MEYER, ERNST HERMANN, ed.: *Englische Fantasien aus dem 17. Jahrhundert, Hortus musicus*, xiv (Kassel and Basle, 1949).
MOFFAT, ALFRED EDWARD, ed.: *Trio-Sonaten alter Meister* (Berlin, n.d.).
RIEMANN, HUGO, ed.: *Old Chamber Music*, i–iv (London, 1898–1902).
SCHENK, ERICH, ed.: *Die italienische Triosonate, Die ausseritalienische Triosonate, Das Musikwerk*, vii, xxxv (Cologne, 1955 and 1970).
SCHULTZ, HELMUT, ed.: *Deutsche Bläsermusik vom Barock bis zur Klassik, Das Erbe deutscher Musik, Reihe 1*, xiv (Kassel, 1961).
WASIELEWSKI, WILHELM JOSEPH VON, ed.: *Instrumentalsätze vom Ende des XVI. bis Ende des XVII Jahrhunderts* (Bonn, 1874).
ZÖLLER, KARLHEINZ, *et al.*, eds.: *Flötenduette alter Meister* (Hamburg, 1962–  ).

*(b) Works by Individual Composers*

ALBICASTRO, H.: *12 Triosonaten, op. 8*, ed. M. Zulauf, *Schweizerische Musik-denkmäler*, x (Kassel and Basle, 1974).

ALBINONI, T.: *Gesamtausgabe der Instrumentalmusik, Kammermusikwerke*, ed. W. Kolneder (Winterthur, 1974–   ).

——— *Drei Sonaten für zwei Violinen und Basso continuo, op. 1*, nos. 10–12, ed. W. Kolneder (Mainz, 1959).

——— *Drei Balletti, für zwei Violinen und Basso continuo, op. 3*, nos. 1–3, ed. W. Kolneder (Mainz, 1964).

BACH, J. S.: Trio sonatas, BWV 1039–40; *Musikalisches Opfer, Johann Sebastian Bachs Werke*, ix, xxix, xxxi/2 Bach-Gesellschaft (Leipzig, 1860, 1881, 1885).

——— Trio sonatas, BWV 1039–40; *Musikalisches Opfer, Neue Ausgabe sämtlicher Werke*, VI/iii, I/xxxv, VIII/i (Leipzig, 1963, 1963, 1974).

BASSANI, G. B.: *Leichte Fantasien*, ed. J. Bacher, *Hortus musicus*, lxiv (Kassel and Basle, 1950).

——— *Sonata a tre, op. 5 no. 9*, ed. E. Schenk, *Diletto musicale*, cdlxi (Vienna and Munich, n.d.).

BECKER, D.: Sonatas a 3–5, ed. H. Erdlen, *et al.*, *Rahter's Kammer-Orchester*, v–vii (Leipzig, 1932).

BIBER, H. I. F. VON: Sonatas for chamber ensemble, eds. N. Harnoncourt and H. Tachezil, *Diletto musicale*, ccclvii–ccclix, ccclxxii, cdlxiii, dxv–dxvi, dxl–dxli (Vienna and Munich, 1971–7).

BLAVET, M.: *6 Sonates, op. 1*, ed. H. Ruf (Mainz, 1967).

BONONCINI, G. M.: *Arie, Correnti, Sarabanda a 2, op. 4*, ed. M. Abbado (Milan, 1968).

——— *Sonate da chiesa a due violini, op. 6, Bibliotheca musica bononiensis*, cxlvi (Bologna, 1970).

BUONAMENTE, G. B.: *Ballo del gran duca, Sonata prima*, ed. L.Rovatkay, *Musica italiana* ii–iii (Wolfenbüttel, 1976).

BUXTEHUDE, D.: *Instrumentalwerke*, ed. C. Stiehl, *Denkmäler deutscher Tonkunst*, xi (Leipzig, 1903).

——— *Sonata, op. 1, no. 7, Organum, 3 Reihe*, xxi (Leipzig, 1924).

——— *Sonata à trois*, ed. C. Crussard, *Flores musicae*, xi (Lauranne, 1961).

——— *Sonatas, op. 2, no. 2*, ed. in *Organum, 3 Reihe*, vi (Leipzig, 1924); no. 6, ed. C. Döbereiner, *Nagels Musik-Archiv*, cxvii (Hanover, 1935).

CALDARA, A.: *Sonate à 4*, ed. F. Polnauer, *Antiqua: eine Sammlung alter Musik* (New York, 1968).

——— *Sonate à 3, op. 1*, nos. 1 and 5, ed. F. Polnauer, *Antiqua: eine Sammlung alter Musik* (New York, 1967); no. 4, ed. W. Upmeyer, *Nagels Musik-Archiv*, v (Hanover, 1927); no. 9, ed. E. Schenk, *Diletto musicale*, cdxli (Vienna and Munich, n.d.).

——— *Sonate da camera, op. 2, no. 3*, ed. E. Schenk, *Diletto musicale*, cdxxxvii (Vienna and Munich, 1973).

CASTRUCCI, P.: *Sonata in sol minore, op. 1*, ed. B. Somma, *Somma. Musiche vocali e strumentali sacre e profane, sec. XVII-XVIII-XIX* (Rome, 1952).

CAZZATI, M.: *Capriccio a tre*, ed. E. Schenk, *Diletto musicale*, cdxliv (Vienna and Munich, 1969).

——— *Trio sonate, d-moll*, ed. W. Danckert, *Hortus musicus*, xxxiv (Kassel and Basle, n.d.).

COPRARIO, J.: *Fantasia-suites*, ed. R. Charteris, *Musica Britannica*, xlvi (London, 1980).

CORELLI, A.: *Les oeuvres de Arcangelo Corelli*, eds. J. Joachim and F. Chrysander, *Denkmäler der Tonkunst*, iii (Bergedorf, 1871).

——— *Werke ohne Opuszahl*, ed. H. J. Marx, *Historisch-kritische Gesamtausgabe der musikalischen Werke*, v (Cologne, 1976).

——— *Ausgabe sämtlicher Triosonaten*, ed. W. Kolneder, 4 vols. (Mainz, 1961–70).

COUPERIN, F.: *Musiques de chambre, I–IV*, ed. M. Cauchie, *Oeuvres complètes*, vii–x (Paris, 1933).

DALL'ABACO, E. F.: *Sonate a 3, op. 3*, no. 1, ed. F. Polnauer, *Antiqua: eine Sammlung alter Musik* (New York, 1968); nos. 4, 5, 9, ed. H. Riemann, *Collegium musicum*, xli–xliii (Leipzig, 1903).

DANDRIEU, J.-F.: *Sonata a tre, op. 1, no. 6*, ed. E. Schenk, *Diletto musicale*, cdlviii (Vienna and Munich, 1969).

—— Sonate pour 2 violons, violoncello et piano, *Musiques françaises*, xxii (Geneva, n.d.).

DEROSIER, N.: *La fuite du roy d'Angleterre*, ed. T. Dart (London, 1959).

ERLEBACH, P. H.: *Sonaten*, ed. F. Zobeley, *Hortus musicus*, cxvii–cxviii (Kassel and Basle, 1954).

EYCK, J. VAN: *Der fluyten lust-hof*, (facs. ed., Amsterdam, 1979).

FASCH, J. F.: *Sonata à 4*, ed. H. Riemann, *Collegium musicum*, xiii (Leipzig, n.d.).

FINGER, G.: *Sonate für 2 f-Blockflöten*, *Musica practica*, xxvi (Hanover, n.d.).

—— 2 sonaten für 2 Alt-Blockflöten, *Moecks Kammermusik*, vii (Celle, 1939).

FRANCESCHINI, P.: Sonata a 7 for 2 trumpets and strings, ed. E. H. Tarr (London, 1968).

FRANCOEUR, F.: *Triosonate*, ed. H. Ruf, *Antiqua: eine Sammlung alter Musik* (New York, 1971).

FURCHHEIM, J. W.: *Dritte Sonate*, ed. P. Rubardt, *Collegium musicum*, lx (Leipzig, n.d.).

—— Suite à 5, *Organum, 3 Reihe*, xxvi (Leipzig, 1930).

GABRIELLI, D.: 6 sonatas a 5–6, no. 2, ed. E. H. Tarr (London, 1968).

GEMINIANI, F.: *Sonate, pour 2 violons, un violoncelle et la basse continue*, ed. C. Crussard, *Flores musicae*, viii (Lauranne, 1958).

GIAMBERTI, G.: *Duetti*, ed. G. Rostirolla, *Armonia strumentale*, i (Wilhelmshaven, 1975).

GRAUN, C. H.: Trio sonatas, ed. L. Stadelmann, *Alte Musik für verschiedene Instrumente*, xlii (Munich, 1973); *Moecks Kammermusik*, lxxxviii (Celle, n.d.).

GRAUN, J. G.: Trios, *Collegium musicum*, xxiv–xxvi (Leipzig, n.d.).

GRAUPNER, C.: Trio sonata, ed. F. Goebels, *Alte Musik für verschiedene Instrumente*, xxxiv (Munich, 1965).

GUILLEMAIN, G.: *Quartets, op. 12*, no. 1, ed. P. Klengel, *Collegium musicum*, lviii (Leipzig, 1930); nos. 2, 4, 6, ed. F. Polnauer, *Ludus instrumentalis*, lxi–lxiii (Hamburg, 1972–4).

HAMMERSCHMIDT, A.: *Instrumentalwerke*, ed. H. Mönkemeyer, *Das Erbe deutscher Musik, 1 Reihe*, xlix (Kassel, 1957).

HANDEL, G. F.: Trio sonatas, op. 2 and op. 5: ed. F. Chrysander, *Georg Friedrich Händels Werke*, xxvii (Leipzig, 1879); ed. S. Flesch, *Hallische Händel-Ausgabe, ser. IV*, x (Kassel, 1967–70).

HASSE, J. A.: Trio sonatas, ed. E. Schenk, *Diletto musicale*, cdxxxv (Vienna and Munich, 1969); ed. W. Kämmerling, *Gitarre-Kammermusik*, lxxvii (Vienna, 1969); ed. G. Frotscher, *Nagels Musik-Archiv*, clix (Hanover, 1941); ed. H. Winschermann, *Ludus instrumentalis*, lxxv (Hamburg, n.d.).

JACCHINI, G.: Trio sonata, op. 5, no. 3, *Musikschätze der Vergangenheit* (Berlin, 1936).

JENKINS, J.: *Consort music of four parts*, ed. A. Ashbee; *Consort music of six parts*, ed. D. Peart, *Musica Britannica*, xxvi, xxxix (London, 1969 and 1977).

—— Consort music in five parts, ed. R. Nicholson (London, 1971).

—— Fancies and Ayres, ed. H. J. Sleeper, *Three-part Fancy and Ayre Divisions*, ed. R. A. Warner, *Wellesley Edition*, i, x (Wellesley, 1950 and 1966).

—— 7 Fantasien, ed. N. Dolmetsch, Hortus musicus, cxlix (Kassel and Basle, 1957).

KEISER, R.: Sonate a tre, 1–3, ed. E Schenk, Nagels Musik-Archiv, lxviii, cxiv, cxxxii (Hanover, 1930–7).

KRIEGER, J. P.: Lustige Feld-Musik, Partie F-Dur, ed. M. Seiffert, Organum, 3 Reihe, ix (Leipzig, 1925).

—— Trio sonatas, ed. C. Crussard, Flores musicae, vii (Lauranne, 1958); ed. H. Osthoff, Nagels Musik-Archiv, cxxxv (Hanover, 1937).

—— Sonata, op. 1 no. 3, Organum, 3 Reihe, xi (Leipzig, 1926).

LALANDE, M. -R. DE: Concert de Trompettes et Timballes, no. 1, ed. A. Cellier, (Paris, 1955).

LECLAIR, J. -M.: Sonatas, op. 6, ed. H. Ruf, Hortus musicus, ccxxv (Kassel and Basle, n.d.).

—— Sonatas a 3, ed. C. Crussard, Flores musicae, iv–v (Lauranne, 1955).

—— 2 Trio Sonatas, op. 13, nos. 1–2, ed. G. Sadler, Musica da camera, xxxviii (London, 1976).

LEGRENZI, G.: Sonatas a 3, ed. A. Planyavsky, and E. Schenk, Diletto musicale, cdvii, cdxlvi (Vienna and Munich, 1970 and 1971).

—— Sonatas, ed. R. Ewerhart, Musica sacra instrumentalis, ii, v (Altötting, 1972).

—— Sonate pour 2 violons et basse, ed. C. Crussard, Flores musicae, xvi (Lauranne, 1966).

—— Sonate da chiesa, ed. A. Seay, Le Pupitre, iv (Paris, 1968).

—— Sonatas, ed. W. Danckert and K. Fellerer, Hortus musicus, xxxi, lxxxiii–lxxxiv (Kassel and Basle, 1949 and 1951).

—— 3 sonate à 4, ed. R. Cumar, Antica musica strumentale-italiana (Rome, 1965).

LOCATELLI, P. A.: Sei sonate da camera dall'op. 6, ed. G. Benvenuti, I Classici musicali italiani, xiv (Milan, 1956).

—— Sonata for 2 flutes, op. 4, no. 6, ed. H. Ruf, Ludus instrumentalis, li (Hamburg, n.d.).

—— Trio sonatas, op. 5, nos. 1, 4, 5, ed. in Organum, 3 Reihe, lii, xlvi, l (Leipzig, 1951–4); no. 3, ed. H. Ruf, Antiqua: eine Sammlung alter Musik (New York, 1964).

—— Trio, op. 3, no. 1, Collegium musicum, xxi (Leipzig, n.d.).

—— Sonate a 2, ed. C. Crussard, Flores musicae, vi (Lauranne, 1955).

LOCKE, M.: Chamber Music ed. M. Tilmouth, Musica Britannica, xxxi–xxxii (London, 1971–2).

—— Conzort zu 4 Stimmen ed. F. J. Giesbert, Antiqua: eine Sammlung alter Musik (New York, 1935).

—— The Tempest, ed. P. Dennison, Musica da camera, xli (London, 1977).

MARINI, B.: Sonata per due Violini, ed. W. Danckert, (Kassel and Basle, 1957).

MASCITTI, M.: Triosonate, g-Moll, op. 6, no. 15, ed. H. Ruf, Antiqua: eine Sammlung alter Musik (New York, 1967).

MAZZAFERRATA, G. B.: Sonate pour 2 violons et violoncelle, ed. C. Crussard, Flores musicae, xviii (Lauranne, 1966).

—— Sonate a 3, op. 5, no. 6, ed. E. Schenk, Diletto musicale, cdlvii (Vienna and Munich, 1969).

MERULA, T.: Canzoni . . . per chiesa e camera, a 2 et a 3, Bibliotheca musica bononiensis, cl (Bologna, 1969).

MIELCZEWSKI, M.: Canzoni, ed. Z. M. Szweykowski, Opera omnia, i, Monumenta musicae in Polonia, ser. A2 (Warsaw, 1976).

—— Canzoni a 3, ed. A. Chybiński, Wydawnictwo Dawnej Muzyki Polskiej, vi, lxi (Warsaw, 1961).

——— *Canzoni a 2*, ed. Z. Szweykowski, *Wydawnictwo Dawnej Muzyki Polskiej*, xxix (Warsaw, 1961).

MONDONVILLE, J. J. DE: *Sonates en trio, op. 2*, ed. R. Blanchard, *Le Pupitre*, iii (Paris, 1967).

PACHELBEL, J.: *Triosuiten für 2 Geigen und Basso continuo*, ed. F. Zobeley, *Hortus musicus*, liv–lvi (Kassel and Basle, 1950 and 1966).

PEZ, J. C.: *Sonata à 4*, ed. F. Schroeder, *Alte Musik für verschiedene Instrumente*, xxiii (Munich, 1959).

——— Triosonatas, ed. W. Kämmerling, *Gitarre-Kammermusik*, xlix (Vienna, 1963); ed. W. Woehl, *Nagels Musik-Archiv*, cxi (Hanover, 1934).

PEZEL, J.: *Turmmusiken und Suiten* ed. A. Schering, *Denkmäler deutscher Tonkunst*, lxiii (Leipzig, 1928).

PURCELL, H.: *Fantasias and other instrumental music*, ed. T. Dart, *Purcell Society Edition*, xxxi (London, 1959).

——— *12 Sonatas of 3 parts, 10 Sonatas of 4 parts*, rev. M. Tilmouth, *Purcell Society Edition*, v, vii (London, 1976 and 1981).

REICHE, G.: *24 Neue Quatricinia* ed. G. Müller (Berlin, 3rd ed., 1958).

——— Sonatas, ed. R. King, *Music for Brass*, ii, xiv, xx, xxiii, lxvii, lxxxv, cxli, dii (North Easton, Mass., 1946–60).

ROSENMÜLLER, J.: *Sonate da camera*, ed. K. Nef, *Denkmäler deutscher Tonkunst*, xviii (Leipzig, 1904).

——— Sonatas, ed. F. Saffe, *Nagels Musik-Archiv*, xxix–xxx (Hanover, 1928).

——— *Sonate a 2, 3, 4, e 5 stromenti*, ed. E. Pätzold (Berlin, 1954–6).

ROSIER, C.: *Ausgewählte Instrumentalwerke*, ed. U. Niemöller, *Denkmäler rheinischer Musik*, vii (Düsseldorf, 1957).

SCHMELZER, J. H.: *Sonata for 7 recorders*, ed. E. H. Meyer (London, 1948).

SOMIS, G. B.: *Sonate da camera*, ed. M. Abbado, *Monumenti musicali italiani*, ii (Milan, 1977).

STÖRL, J. G. C.: *Sonata no. 1*, ed. R. King, *Music for Brass*, lxxxi (North Easton, Mass., 1957).

STRADELLA, A.: Sonatas, ed. E. H. Tarr, *Archives de la musique instrumentale*, ix–xi (Paris, 1968).

STRUNGK, N. A.: *Sonata für 6 streichinstrumente und Basso continuo*, ed. F. Stein, *Hortus musicus*, ciii (Kassel and Basle, 1952).

——— *Triosonate*, *Organum, 3 Reihe*, xviii (Leipzig, n.d.).

SZARZYNSKI, S. S.: *Sonata a 2 violini e basso*, ed. A. Chybiński, *Wydawnictwo Dawnej Muzyki Polskiej*, i (Warsaw, 1958).

TARTINI, G.: *Sei sonate per due violini e basso continuo*, ed. E. Farini, *Le Opere*, ix (Milan, 1973).

TELEMANN, G. P.: *Musikalische Werke*, ed. M. Seiffert, *et al.* (Kassel and Basle, 1950–   ).

——— *Sonates polonaises*, ed. A. Simon, *Nagels Musik-Archiv*, l, li (Hanover, 1929–30).

THEILE, J.: *Sonata a 5*, *Organum, 3 Reihe*, xix (Leipzig, 1929).

TOLAR, J. K.: *Balletti e sonate*, ed. J. Racek and J. Pohanka, *Musica antiqua bohemica*, xl (Prague, 1959).

TORELLI, G.: *2 sonatas for trumpet and strings*, ed. F. Schroeder, *Diletto musicale*, clxiv–v (Vienna and Munich, 1965).

UCCELLINI, M.: *Sinfonia a 3, op. 9, no. 7*, ed. E. Schenk, *Diletto musicale*, cdli (Vienna and Munich, 1969).

——— Sonate, no. 11 a 4; no. 18 a 3 'La Buonamenta'; Aria sopra la bergamasca, ed. L. Rovatkay, *Musica italiana*, v, iv, vi (Wolfenbüttel, 1977).

VITALI, G. B.: *Artifici musicali, op. 13*, ed. L. Rood and G. Smith, *Smith College Music Archives*, xiv (Northampton, Mass., 1959).

—— Sonata, 'La Guidoni', Seventeenth-century chamber music (London, n.d.).
—— Sonata, 'La Palavicini', ed. L. Rovatkay, Musica italiana, i (Wolfenbüttel, 1976).
VITALI, T. A.: Concerto di sonate, op. 4, ed. D. Silbert, et al., Smith College Music Archives, xii (Northampton, Mass., 1954).
VIVALDI, A.: Le opere di Antonio Vivaldi, ed. G. F. Malipiero, et al. (Rome, 1947–1971).
WECKMANN, M.: Gesammelte Werke, ed. G. Ilgner, Das Erbe deutscher Musik, 2nd ser., iv (Braunschweig, 1942).
WITT, C. F.: Suite in F-Dur, ed. W. Heinrich, Hortus musicus, xcix (Kassel and Basle, 1952).
YOUNG, W.: Sonatas, ed. W. G. Whittaker (London, 1930).

## (ii) Books and Articles

### (a) General

BONTA, STEPHEN: 'A Formal Convention in 17th-century Italian Instrumental Music', International Musicological Society Congress Report, xi, Copenhagen 1972, pp. 288–95.
BOUQUET, MARIE-THÉRÈSE: Musique et musiciens à Turin de 1648 à 1775 (Turin, 1968).
EITNER, ROBERT: 'Volksmusik im 17. Jahrhundert', Montashefte für Musikgeschichte, xiv (1882), pp. 1–8.
FISCHER, WILHELM: 'Zur Entwicklungsgeschichte des Wiener klassischen Stils', Studien zur Musikwissenschaft, iii (1915).
HELFERT, VLADIMIR: Hudební barok na českých zámcích (Prague, 1916).
HOGWOOD, CHRISTOPHER: The Trio Sonata (London, 1979).
LEHMANN, URSULA: Deutsches und italienisches Wesen in der Vorgeschichte des klassischen Streichquartetts (Würzburg, 1939).
MERSMANN, HANS: Die Kammermusik, I: XVII und XVIII Jahrhunderts (Leipzig, 1933).
MEYER, ERNST HERMANN: 'Deutsche instrumentale Gruppenmusik gegen 1700', Händel-Jahrbuch 1964, x, pp. 71–112.
—— 'Die Bedeutung der Instrumentalmusik am fürst-bischöflichen Hofe zur Olmütz und Kremsier', Aufsätze über Musik (Berlin, 1957).
—— Die mehrstimmige Spielmusik des 17. Jahrhunderts in Nord- und Mitteleuropa (Kassel, 1934).
—— Early English Chamber Music (London, 2nd rev. ed., 1982).
NETTL, PAUL: Musik-Barock in Böhmen und Mähren (Brno, 1927).
NEWMAN, WILLIAM S.: The Sonata in the Baroque Era (Chapel Hill, 1959; rev. 1966; repr., 1972).
PINCHERLE, MARC: L'orchestre de chambre (Paris, 1948).
PLAMENAC, DRAGAN: 'An unknown Violin Tablature of the Early 17th Century', Papers of the American Musicological Society 1941.
—— 'Toma Cecchini, kapelnik stolnih crkava u Splitu i Hvaru u prvoj polovini XVII stoljeć', Rad Jugoslavenske akademije znanosti i umjetnosti (1938), no. 262, pp. 77–125.
RAGUENET, F.: Paralèle des italiens et des françois, en ce qui regarde la musique et les opéra (Paris, 1702; Eng. ed., London, 1709; repr., 1968).
RASCH, R. A.: 'Some Mid-seventeenth Century Dutch Collections of Instrumental Ensemble Music', Tijdschrift van de Vereniging voor Nederlandse musiekgeschiedenis, xxii/3 (1972), pp. 160–200.
ROWEN, RUTH HALLE: Early Chamber Music (New York, 2nd ed., 1974).

SADIE, JULIE ANNE: *The Bass Viol in French Baroque Chamber Music* (Ann Arbor, 1981).

SADIE, STANLEY: 'Concert Life in Eighteenth-century England', *Proceedings of the Royal Musical Association*, lxxxv (1958–9), pp. 17–30.

SCHLOSSBERG, A.: *Die italienische Sonata für mehrere Instrumente im 17. Jahrhundert* (Paris, 1935).

SELFRIDGE-FIELD, ELEANOR: *Venetian Instrumental Music from Gabrieli to Vivaldi* (Oxford, 1975).

TILMOUTH, MICHAEL: 'A Calendar of References to Music in Newspapers Published in London and the Provinces (1660–1719)', *Royal Musical Association Research Chronicle*, i (1961).

TORCHI, LUIGI: *La musica strumentale in Italia* (Milan, 1901).

LE CERF DE LA VIÉVILLE, JEAN LAURENT: *Comparaison de la musique italienne et de la musique française* (Brussels, 1704–6; repr., 1972).


(*b*) *Individual Composers*

**Bononcini**

KLENZ, WILLIAM: *Giovanni Maria Bononcini of Modena: a Chapter in Baroque Instrumental Music* (Durham, North Carolina, 1962).

**Buxtehude**

MOSER, HANS JOACHIM: *Dietrich Buxtehude* (Berlin, 1959).

PIRRO, ANDRÉ: *Dietrich Buxtehude* (Paris, 1913).

**Charpentier**

HITCHCOCK, H. WILEY: 'The Instrumental Music of Marc-Antoine Charpentier', *Musical Quarterly*, xlvii (1961), pp. 58–72.

SADIE, JULIE ANNE: 'Charpentier and the Early French Ensemble Sonata,' *Early Music*, vii (1979), pp. 330–5.

**Corelli**

PINCHERLE, MARC: *Corelli* (Paris, 2nd ed., 1954; Eng. trans., 1956).

**Couperin**

MELLERS, WILFRID: *François Couperin and the French Classical Tradition* (London, 1950; repr., 1968).

TESSIER, ANDRÉ: *Couperin* (Paris, 1926).

TIERSOT, JULIEN: *Les Couperins* (Paris, 1926).

**Diessener**

MEYER, ERNST HERMANN: 'Gerhard Diessener', *Zeitschrift für Musikwissenschaft*, xvi (1933–4), pp. 405–13.

**Finger**

MARSHALL, ARTHUR W.: 'The Chamber Music of Godfrey Finger', *The Consort*, xxvi (1970), pp. 423–32.

—— 'The Viola da Gamba Music of Godfrey Finger', *Chelys*, i (1969), pp. 16–26.

**Gautier**

LA LAURENCIE, LIONEL DE: 'Un émule de Lully: Pierre Gautier de Marseille', *Sammelbände der Internationalen Musikgesellschaft*, xiii (1911–12), pp. 39–69.

**Graun**

SCHENK, ERICH: 'Zur Bibliographie der Triosonaten von J. G. und C. H. Graun', *Zeitschrift für Musikwissenschaft*, xi (1928–9), pp. 420–2.

**Gregory**

RILEY, JAMES: 'The Identity of William Gregory', *Music and Letters*, xlviii (1967), pp. 236–46.

**Handel**

FLESCH, SIEGFRIED: Georg Friedrich Händels Trio-Sonaten', *Händel-Jahrbuch 1972*, xviii, pp. 139–211.

HORTON, JOHN: 'The Chamber Music', *Handel: a Symposium*, ed. G. Abraham (London, 1954), pp. 248–61.

**Jenkins**

ASHBEE, ANDREW: 'The Four-Part Consort Music of John Jenkins', *Proceedings of the Royal Musical Association*, xcvi (1969–70), pp. 29–42.

**Locatelli**

DUNNING, ALBERT: *Pietro Antonio Locatelli: Der Virtuose und seine Welt*, i, ii (Buren, 1982).

**Locke**

FIELD, CHRISTOPHER D. S.: 'Matthew Locke and the Consort Suite', *Music and Letters*, li (1970), pp. 15–25.

TILMOUTH, MICHAEL: 'Revisions in the Chamber Music of Matthew Locke', *Proceedings of the Royal Musical Association*, xcviii (1971–2), pp. 89–100.

**Marini**

ISELIN, DORA: *Biagio Marini: sein Leben und seine Instrumentalwerke* (Hildburghausen, 1930).

**Mielczewski**

SZWEYKOWSKI, ZYGMUNT: 'Nowe canzony Marcina Mielczewskiego', *Ruch muzyczny*, ii/17 (1958).

**Pachelbel**

BECKMANN, GUSTAV: 'Johann Pachelbel als Kammerkomponist', *Archiv für Musikwissenschaft*, i (1918–19), pp. 267–74.

**Porpora**

DEGRADA, FRANCESCO: 'Le musiche strumentali di Nicolo Porpora', *Chigiana*, xxv (1968), pp. 99–125.

**Purcell**

DART, THURSTON: 'Purcell's Chamber Music', *Proceedings of the Royal Musical Association*, lxxxv (1958–9), pp. 81–93.

FAVRE-LINGOROW, STELLA: *Der Instrumentalstil von Purcell* (Berne, 1950).

TILMOUTH, MICHAEL: 'The Technique and Forms of Purcell's Sonatas', *Music and Letters*, xl (1959), pp. 109–21.

WESSELY-KROPIK, HELENE: 'Henry Purcell als Instrumentalkomponist', *Studien zur Musikwissenschaft*, xxii (1955), pp. 85–141.

**Reiche**

RASMUSSEN, MARY: 'Gottfried Reiche and his *Vier und zwantzig neue Quatricinia* (Leipzig, 1696)', *Brass Quarterly*, iv (1960), pp. 3–17.

**Rosier**

NIEMÖLLER, URSEL: 'Carl Rosier', *Beiträge zur rheinischen Musikgeschichte*, xxiii (Cologne, 1957).

**Szarzynski**

CHYBIŃSKI, ADOLF: 'Sonata triowa Stanislawa Sylwestra Szarzyńskiego', *Śpiewak*, ix/1–3 (Katowice, 1928).

**Telemann**

WILKOWSKA-CHOMIŃSKA, K.: 'Telemanns Beziehungen zur polnischen Musik; Beiträge zu einem neuen Telemannbild', *Konferenzbericht der 1. Magdeburger Telemann-Festtage* (Magdeburg, 1963).

**Thieme**

BUCH, HANS-JOACHIM: 'Bestandsaufnahme der Kompositionen Clemens Thiemes', *Die Musikforschung*, xvi (1963), pp. 367–78.

**Veracini**

HILL, JOHN WALTER: *The Life and Works of Francesco Maria Veracini* (Ann Arbor, 1979).

**Weckmann**

ILGNER, G.: *Matthias Weckmann: sein Leben und seine Werke* (Wolfenbüttel and Berlin, 1939).

**Weichlein**

WESSELY-KROPIK, HELEN: 'Romanus Weichlein: ein vergessener österreichischer Instrumentalkomponist des 17. Jahrhunderts', *Kongressbericht: Wien Mozartjahr 1956*.

# CHAPTER VII

## THE SOLO SONATA

### (i) Modern Editions

*(a) Anthologies*

—— *L'École du violon au XVIIe et XVIIIe siècle* (Paris, 1905– ).

—— *Sonate a Violino e Violoncello, Bibliotheca musica bononiensis*, cxlii, cxliv (Bologna, n.d.).

ABBADO, M., ed.: *Antiche sonate italiane per violino e basso secundo i testi originali* (Milan, 1970– ).

BECKMANN, GUSTAV, ed.: *Das Violinspiel in Deutschland vor 1700: 12 sonaten für Violine und Klavier* (Leipzig, 1921).

CORTI, MARIO, ed.: *La classica scuola italiana del Violino* (Milan, 1956– ).

GIEGLING, FRANZ, ed.: *The Solo Sonata, Das Musikwerk*, xv (Cologne, 1960).

MIGOT, GEORGES, gen. ed.: *Musiques françaises* (Geneva, 1948– ).

MOFFAT, ALFRED EDWARD, ed.: *Kammer-Sonaten für Violine und Pianoforte des 17. und 18. Jahrhunderts* (Mainz, n.d.).

—— *Meister-Schule der alten Zeit. Sammlung klassischer Violin-Sonaten berühmter Komponisten des 17. und 18. Jahrhunderts* (Berlin, n.d.).

—— *Meister-Schule der alten Zeit. Sammlung klassischer Violoncello-Sonaten berühmter Komponisten des 17. und 18. Jahrhunderts* (Berlin, n.d.).

RIEMANN, HUGO, ed.: *Old Chamber Music*, i–iv (London, 1898–1902).

SCHEIT, KARL, ed.: *Gitarre-Kammermusik* (Vienna, 1957).

SCHERING, ARNOLD, ed.: *Alte Meister des Violinspiels* (Leipzig, 1909).

SEIFFERT, MAX, *et al.*, eds.: *Kammersonaten* (Leipzig, 1928– ).

TORCHI, LUIGI, ed.: *Musica istrumentale, secolo XVII, L'Arte musicale in Italia*, vii (Milan, 1908).

(b) Works by Individual Composers

ALBERTI, G. M.: Sonate, op. 2, nos. 3–4, 7–10, ed. L. Bettarini, Collezione settecentesca Bettarini (Milan, 1973).

ALBINONI, T.: Sonatas for Flute and Basso continuo, ed. L. Schaffler, Nagels Musik-Archiv, lxxiv (Hanover, 1931); Florilegium musicum, xvii (Baden, 1955).

―― Sonate für Violine und Basso continuo, Moecks Kammermusik, cviii (Celle, n.d.).

―― Sonatas, op. 6. nos. 1–4, ed. M. Talbot (London, 1981); nos. 1, 11, ed. W. Upmeyer, Nagels Musik-Archiv, ix (Hanover, 1928).

ARIOSTI, A. M.: Sonate, ed. R. Sabatini, Somma. Musiche vocali e strumentali sacra e profane, Sec. XVII-XVIII-XIX, xxvi–xxviii (Rome, 1957).

―― "Stockholmer Sonaten", ed. G. Weiss, Hortus musicus, ccxxi, ccxxiii (Kassel and Basle, 1974).

BACH, J. S.: Kammermusik, Johann Sebastian Bachs Werke, ix, xxvii/1, xliii/1 Bach-Gesellschaft (Leipzig, 1860, 1885, 1894).

―― Kammermusikwerke, Neue Ausgabe sämtlicher Werke, Serie VI (Leipzig, 1958– ).

BENDA, F.: Sonatas, op. 1, Musica antiqua bohemica, xi, lvii (Prague, 1953 and 1962).

BIBER, H. I. F. VON: Violinsonaten, ed. G. Adler and E. Luntz, Denkmäler der Tonkunst in Österreich, xi (Jg.v(2) ), xxv (Jg. xii(2) ), (Vienna, 1898 and 1905).

BLAVET, M.: 6 Sonates, mêlées de pièces, op. 2, ed. W. Kolneder (Heidelberg, 1969).

BOCCHERINI, L.: Sonate, op. 5, ed. E. Polo, I Classici musicali italiani, iv (Milan, 1941).

BONONCINI, G. M.: Arie, correnti &, op. 4, ed. M. Abbado (Milan, 1968).

―― Divertimento da camera für Alt-Blockflöte und Basso continuo, Moecks Kammermusik, ix (Celle, 1939).

CAIX D'HERVELOIS, L. DE: Pièces de viole, livres i–ii (facs. ed., Oberlin, Ohio, 1980).

COPRARIO, J.: Fantasia-suites, ed. R. Charteris, Musica Britannica, xlvi (London, 1980).

CORELLI, A.: Les oeuvres de Arcangelo Corelli, ed. J. Joachim and F. Chrysander, Denkmäler der Tonkunst, iii (Bergedorf, 1871).

―― Historisch-kritische Gesamtausgabe der musikalischen Werke, ed. H. J. Marx, v (Cologne, 1976).

DALL'ABACO, E. F.: Ausgewählte Werke. Teil 1–2, ed. A. Sandberger, Denkmäler der Tonkunst in Bayern, i (Jg. i(1) ), xvi (Jg. ix(1) ), (Leipzig, 1900 and 1908).

―― Sechs Sonaten für Violine und Basso continuo aus op. 1, ed. W. Kolneder (Mainz, 1956).

DEGLI ANTONI, G. B.: Balletti, correnti, gighi, e sarabande da camera a violino e clavicembalo, Bibliotheca musica bononiensis, cxlv (Bologona, 1972).

FESTING, M. C.: 2 sonatas for violin and basso continuo, ed. G. Beechey, Musica da camera, xxiv (London, 1975).

FISCHER, J.: Vier Suiten für Blockflöte, ed. W. Woehl, Hortus musicus, lix (Kassel, 1950).

FORQUERAY, A.: Pièces de viole (facs. ed., Oberlin, Ohio, 1980).

FORQUERAY, J. -B.: Pièces de viole (facs. ed., Oberlin, Ohio, 1980).

GEMINIANI, F.: 12 Sonatas for violin and piano, ed. R. Finney, Smith College Music Archives, i (Northampton, Mass., 1935).

—— *Zwölf Kompositionen für Violine und Klavier*, ed. F. Brodszky, *Thesaurus musicus*, vii–viii (Budapest, n.d.).

—— Sonatas, op. 1, ed. W. Kolneder (Mainz, 1961).

—— Sonatas, ed. H. Ruf, *Hortus musicus*, clxxiii–iv, clxxviii (Kassel and Basle, 1961–2).

—— *6 Sonaten für Violoncello und Basso continuo, op. 5*, ed. W. Kolneder (Leipzig, 1964).

GIARDINI, F.: *Sonate, op. 3*, ed. E. Polo, *I Classici musicali italiani*, iii (Milan, 1941).

GRAUN, J. G.: *Sonata I–VI für Violine und basso continuo, Sonate für Viola und cembalo, Ludus instrumentalis*, xxix–xxxiv, lxviii (Hamburg, n.d.).

GRAUPNER, C.: *Zwei Sonaten für Cembalo und Violine*, ed. A. Hoffmann, *Hortus musicus*, cxxi (Kassel and Basle, 1955).

GRAZIANI, C.: *Sei sonate per violoncello e basso continuo*, ed. G. Benvenuti, *I Classici musicali italiani*, xv (Milan, 1943).

GUILLEMAIN, G.: *Sonata für Violine und basso continuo*, ed. F. Polnauer, *Ludus instrumentalis*, xciii (Hamburg, 1972).

HANDEL, G. F.: *Sonate da camera, Instrumental Musik*, ed. F. Chrysander, *Georg Friedrich Händels Werke*, xxvii, xlviii (Leipzig, 1879 and 1894).

—— *Elf Sonaten für Flöte und bezifferten Bass*, ed. H. -P. Schmitz, *Sechs Sonaten für Violine und bezifferten Bass*, ed. J. P. Hinnenthal, *Hallische Händel-Ausgabe, Serie IV*, iii–iv (Kassel, 1955).

—— *The Complete Sonatas for Treble Recorder and basso continuo, The Three Authentic Sonatas for Oboe and basso continuo, The Complete Sonatas for flute and basso continuo*, ed. D. Lasocki (London, 1979, 1979 and 1983).

HASSE, J. A.: *Sonate für Flöte*, ed. K. Walther, *Nagels Musik-Archiv*, xcix (Hanover, 1933).

HÖFFLER, K.: *Gambenkompositionen*, ed. K. H. Pauls, *Das Erbe deutscher Musik*, lxvii (Kassel, 1973).

JENKINS, J.: *Fancies and Ayres*, ed. H. J. Sleeper, *Wellesley Edition*, i (Wellesley, 1950).

LAWES, W.: *Select Consort Music*, ed. M. Lefkowitz, *Musica Britannica*, xxi (London, 2nd rev. ed., 1971).

LECLAIR, J. -M.: *Premier livre de sonates*, ed. A. Guilmant and J. Debroux (Paris, 1905).

—— *Second livre de sonates*, ed. R. Eitner, *Publikationen älterer praktischer und theoretischer Musikwerke*, xxvii (2nd ed., New York, 1966).

—— *Troisième livre de sonates, Quatrième livre de sonates*, ed. R. Preston, *Recent Researches in the Music of the Baroque Era*, iv–v, x–xi (Madison, 1968–9; 1969–72).

—— *2 sonatas*, ed. H. Ruf, *Antiqua: eine Sammlung alter Musik* (New York, 1968).

LOCATELLI, P. A.: *Arte del violino, op. 3, XXIV Capricci*, facs. ed., ed. P. van Reijen (Amsterdam, 1981).

—— *Drei Sonaten für Querflöte und Basso continuo*, ed. G. Scheck, *Hortus musicus*, xxxv (Kassel and Basle, 1949).

—— *12 sonatas for flute and bass, op. 2*, ed. E. Farina and G. Zagnoni (Milan, 1976).

LOCKE, M.: *Chamber Music, I–II*, ed. M. Tilmouth, *Musica Britannica*, xxxi–xxxii (London, 1971–2).

MARAIS, M.: *Collected Works, The Instrumental Works*, i– , ed. J. Hsu (New York, 1980– ).

—— *Pièces de viole, livres 1–5*, (facs. ed., Oberlin, Ohio, 1980).

—— 6 Suites for viol and thoroughbass, ed. G. Kinney, Recent Researches in the Music of the Baroque Era, xxi–xxii (Madison, 1976).

—— Stücke für Viola da gamba und Basso continuo, ed. J. Bacher, Hortus musicus, cxxiii (Kassel and Basle, 1954).

—— Suite für Viola da gamba, Cembalo und Bass-Instrument, Antiqua: eine Sammlung alter Musik (New York, n.d.).

—— Suite pour viole et bass continue, ed. C. Caillard, Musique en Main, xvi (Paris, 1977).

MARINI, B.: Sonate, ed. W. Danckert, Hortus musicus, cxxix, cxliii (Kassel and Basle, 1955 and 1957).

MARINO, C. A.: Sonata für Viola und Cembalo, ed. K. Stierhof, Diletto musicale, ccclxi (Vienna and Munich, 1973).

MATTHESON, J.: XII Sonate per il violino, ed. A. van Leeuwen (Frankfurt, 1923).

MEALI, G. A. P.: 3 sonatas for violin, ed. F. Cerha, Diletto musicale, cdxiv (Vienna and Munich, n.d.).

MONDONVILLE, J. -J. DE: Pièces de clavecin en sonates, op. 3, ed. M. Pincherle (Paris, 1935).

PEPUSCH, J. C.: Sonate 1–8 für Alt-Blockflöte und Basso continuo, Moecks Kammermusik, xi, xxi–xxiii (Celle, 1939 and n.d.).

PISENDEL, J. G.: Sonate für Violine und Cembalo, Antiqua: eine Sammlung alter Musik, (New York, n.d.).

—— Sonate für Violine allein, ed. G. Hausswald, Hortus musicus, xci (Kassel and Basle, 1952).

PURCELL, H.: Fantasias and other instrumental music, ed. T. Dart, Purcell Society Edition, xxxi (London, 1959).

—— Stücke für Violine und Klavier, ed. F. Brodszky, Thesaurus musicus, xi–xii (Budapest, 1961).

SCHENCK, J.: Le nymphe di Rheno, op. 8, Gambenkompositionen, ed. K. H. Pauls, Das Erbe deutscher Musik, xliv, lxvii (Kassel, 1956 and 1973).

—— Scherzi musicali, ed. H. Leichtentritt (Leipzig, 1906).

—— Sonata für Viola da Gamba und Basso continuo, ed. K. H. Pauls, Nagels Musik-Archiv, ccxlv (Hanover, 1973).

—— Zwölf Stücke für Violoncello und Klavier, ed. F. Brodszky, Thesaurus musicus, iv–v (Budapest, 1958).

SCHMELZER, J. H.: Sonatae unarum fidium, ed. E. Schenk, Denkmäler der Tonkunst in Österreich, xciii (Graz, 1958).

SCHOP, J.: Pieces for violin and bass, 'T Uitnement kabinet, viii (Amsterdam, 1978).

SENAILLIÉ, J. B.: Sonata for violin and continuo, ed. G. Beechey, Musica da camera, x (London, 1973).

SOMIS, G. B.: Sonatas, ed. M. Abbado (Milan, 1976).

—— Sonate, F-Dur, ed. F. Nagel, Hausmusik (Möseler) cix (Wolfenbüttel, 1973).

STANLEY, J.: Eight Solo's, op. 1, Six Solo's, op. 4, ed. G. Pratt (London, 1973).

TARTINI, G.: Le opere di Giuseppe Tartini, ed. E. Farina and C. Scimone (Milan, 1971– ).

TELEMANN, G. P.: Zwölf methodische Sonaten für Querflöte, Kammermusik ohne Generalbass, ed. M. Seiffert, Musikalische Werke, i, vi (Kassel and Basle, 1950 and 1955).

—— Der getreue Musik-Meister, ed. D. Degen, Hortus musicus, vi–viii, xiii, clxxv, clxxxix (Kassel and Basle, 1949–66).

—— 6 Sonates, Moecks Kammermusik, ci–ciii (Celle, 1948).

—— Kleine Kammer-Musik, ed. W. Woehl, Hortus musicus, xlvii (Kassel and Basle, 1949).

—— *Sei suonatine*, ed. K. Schweickert (Mainz, 1938).
—— *Musikalische Werke*, ed. M. Seiffert, *et al.* (Kassel and Basle, 1950–  ).
VERACINI, F. M.: *Drei sonaten*, ed. F. Bär, *Hortus musicus*, ccxv (Kassel and Basle, 1973).
—— Solo sonatas, op. 1, ed. W. Kolneder (Leipzig, 1958–9).
—— *Sonate a Violino, o Flauto Solo, e Basso*, ed. W. Kolneder, (Leipzig, 1959–61).
—— *Sonate accademiche, op. 2*, ed. F. Bär (Kassel, 1959).
—— *Dissertazioni sopra l'opera quinta di Corelli*, ed. W. Kolneder (Mainz, 1961).
VITALI, T. A.: *Chaconne für Violine und basso continuo*, ed. D. Hellmann, *Hortus musicus*, c (Kassel and Basle, 1966).
VIVALDI, A.: *Le opere di Antonio Vivaldi*, ed. G. F. Malipiero, *et al.* (Rome, 1947–1971).
WALTHER, J. J.: *Scherzi da violino solo*, ed. G. Beckmann, *Das Erbe deutscher Musik, Serie 1*, xvii (Kassel, 1941).
—— *Sonate für Violine und Basso continuo*, ed. E. Bethan, *Nagels Musik-Archiv*, lxxxix (Hanover, 1932).
—— *Sonate mit suite*, Organum, *Reihe 3*, xxviii (Leipzig, 1930).
YOUNG, W.: *Sonate a 3, 4, 5 voci*, ed. W. G. Whittaker (London, 1930).

**(ii) Books and Articles**

*(a) General*

ALLSOP, PETER: 'The Role of the Stringed Bass as a Continuo Instrument in Italian Seventeenth Century Instrumental Music', *Chelys*, viii (1978–9), pp. 31–7.
APEL, WILLI: 'Studien über die frühen Violinmusik', *Archiv für Musikwissenschaft*, xxx (1973), pp. 153–74, and xxxi (1974), pp. 185–213.
—— *Die italienische Violinmusik im 17. Jahrhundert* (Wiesbaden, 1983).
ASCHMANN, R.: *Das deutsche polyphone Violinspiel im 17. Jahrhundert* (Diss., Zurich, 1962).
BECKMANN, GUSTAV: *Das Violinspiel in Deutschland vor 1700* (Leipzig, 1918).
BOL, JOHAN HENDRIK D.: *La Basse de viole du temps de Marin Marais et d'Antoine Forqueray* (Bilthoven, 1973).
BOYDEN, DAVID D.: *The History of Violin Playing from its Origins to 1761* (London, 1965).
—— 'The Violin and its Technique in the 18th Century', *Musical Quarterly*, xxxvi (1950), pp. 9–38.
CAFFI, FRANCESCO: *Storia della musica sacra nella già Cappella Ducale di S. Marco in Venezia dal 1318–1797*, i, ii (Venice, 1854–5; facs. reprint, *Bibliotheca musica bononiensis, sezione 3*, 1, Bologna, 1972).
CLARK, A., ed.: *The Life and Times of Anthony Wood* (Oxford, 1891–5).
EINSTEIN, ALFRED: *Zur deutschen Literatur für Viola da gamba im 16. und 17. Jahrhundert* (Leipzig, 1905; repr., 1972).
GEMINIANI, FRANCESCO: *The Art of Playing on the Violin* (London, 1731; modern ed., D. D. Boyden, London, 1952).
LA LAURENCIE, LIONEL DE: *L'École française de violon de Lully à Viotti* (Paris, 1922–4; repr., 1971).
LESSER, ELISABETH: 'Zur Scordatura der Streich-instrumente mit besonderer Berücksichtigung der Viola d'amore', *Acta musicologica*, iv (1932), pp. 123–7, and 148–59.
MISHKIN, HENRY G.: 'The Solo Violin Sonata of the Bologna School', *Musical Quarterly*, xxix (1943), pp. 92–112.

MOSER, ANDREAS: 'Die Violin-Skordatur', *Archiv für Musikwissenschaft*, i (1918–19), pp. 573–89.

——— *Geschichte des Violinspiels* (Berlin, 1923; 2nd ed., 1966–7).

NEWMAN, WILLIAM S.: *The Sonata in the Baroque Era* (Chapel Hill, 1959; rev. 1966; repr., 1972).

POND, CELIA: 'Ornamental Style and the Virtuoso: Solo Bass Viol Music in France c.1680–1740', *Early Music*, vi (1978), pp. 512–25.

SCHERING, ARNOLD: 'Zur Geschichte der Solosonate in der ersten Hälfte des 17. Jahrhunderts', *Riemann Festschrift* (Leipzig, 1909), pp. 309–25.

SENN, WALTER: *Musik und Theater am Hof zu Innsbruck* (Innsbruck, 1954).

SIMPSON, CHRISTOPHER: *The Division-viol* (2nd ed., 1665; repr., 1965).

VATIELLI, FRANCESCO: *Arte e vita musicale a Bologna* (Bologna, 1927; repr., 1969).


(*b*) *Individual Composers*

**Albinoni**

NEWMAN, WILLIAM S.: 'The Sonatas of Albinoni and Vivaldi', *Journal of the American Musicological Society*, v (1952), pp. 99–113.

**Anet**

ANTOINE, MICHEL: 'Note sur les violinistes Anet', *Recherches sur la musique française classique*, ii (1961–2), pp. 81–93.

**Bach**

BLUME, FRIEDRICH: 'Eine unbekannte Violinsonate von J. S. Bach', *Bach-Jahrbuch 1928*, xxv, pp. 96–118.

EPPSTEIN, HANS: 'Chronologieprobleme in Johann Sebastian Bachs Suiten für Solo-instrument', *Bach-Jahrbuch 1976*, lxii, pp. 35–57.

——— 'Studien über J. S. Bachs Sonaten für ein Melodieinstrument und obligates Cembalo', *Acta Universitatis uppsalensis*, new ser., ii (1966).

——— 'Zur Problematik von J. S. Bachs Sonate für Violine und Cembalo G dur (BWV 1019)', *Archiv für Musikwissenschaft*, xxi (1964), pp. 217–42.

HAUSSWALD, GÜNTER: 'Zur Stilistik von J. S. Bachs Sonaten und Partiten für Violine allein', *Archiv für Musikwissenschaft*, xiv (1957), pp. 304–23.

KÖHLER, KARL-HEINZ: 'Zur Problematik der Violinsonaten mit obligatem Cembalo', *Bach-Jahrbuch, 1958*, xliv, pp. 114–22.

MOSER, ANDREAS: 'Zur Joh. Seb. Bachs Sonaten und Partiten für Violine allein', *Bach-Jahrbuch, 1920*, xvii, pp. 30–65.

MOSER, HANS JOACHIM: 'J. S. Bachs sechs Sonaten für Cembalo und Violine', *Zeitschrift für Musik*, cv (1938).

**Benda**

LEE, DOUGLAS: 'Some Embellished Versions of Sonatas by Franz Benda', *Musical Quarterly*, lxii (1976), pp. 58–71.

NISSEL-NEMENOFF, E.: *Die Violintechnik Franz Bendas und seiner Schule* (Kassel, 1930).

**Biber**

ADLER, GUIDO: 'Zu Bibers Violinsonaten', *Zeitschrift der Internationalen Musik-Gesellschaft*, ix (1907–8), pp. 29–30.

SCHMITZ, EUGEN: 'Bibers Rosenkranzsonaten', *Musica*, v (1951), pp. 235–6.

SCHNEIDER, MAX: 'Zu Bibers Violinsonaten', *Zeitschrift der Internationalen Musik-Gesellschaft*, viii (1906–7), pp. 471–4.

**Corelli**

BOYDEN, DAVID D.: 'The Corelli "Solo" Sonatas and their Ornamental additions by Corelli, Dubourg, Tartini, and the "Walsh Anonymous" ', *Musica antiqua Europae orientalis III: Bydgoszcz 1972*.

CAVICCHI, ADRIANO: 'Corelli e il violinismo bolognese', *Studi Corelliani: 1º congresso internazionale: Fusignano 1968*.

MARX, HANS JOACHIM: 'Some Unknown Embellishments of Corelli's Violin Sonatas', *Musical Quarterly*, lxi (1975), pp. 65–76.

**Forqueray**

LA LAURENCIE, LIONEL DE: 'Deux violists célèbres', *Bulletin français de la S.I.M.*, iv (1908), pp. 1251–74; and v (1909), pp. 48–66.

PROD'HOMME, J. G.: 'Les Forquerays', *Rivista musicale italiana*, x (1903), pp. 670–706.

**Handel**

BEST, TERENCE: 'Handel's Solo Sonatas', *Music and Letters*, lviii (1977), pp. 430–8.

GOTTLIEB, ROBERT: 'Französischer, italienischer und vermischter Stil in den Solo-sonaten Georg Friedrich Händels', *Händel-Jahrbuch 1966*, xii, pp. 93–108.

LASOCKI, DAVID, and BEST, TERENCE: 'A new flute sonata by Handel', *Early Music*, ix (1981), pp. 307–11.

**Jeffreys**

ASTON, PETER: 'George Jeffreys', *Musical Times*, cx (1969), pp. 772–6.

**Jenkins**

ASHBEE, ANDREW: 'John Jenkins, 1592–1678, and the Lyra Viol', *Musical Times*, cxix (1978), pp. 840–3.

**Leclair**

APPIA, EDMOND: 'The Violin Sonatas of Leclair', *Score*, iii (1950), pp. 3–19.

LEMOINE, MICHELINE: 'La technique violinistique de Jean-Marie Leclair', *La revue musicale*, (1955), no. 225, pp. 117–43.

PINCHERLE, MARC: *J. -M. Leclair l'aîné* (Paris, 1952).

PRESTON, ROBERT E.: 'Leclair's Posthumous Solo Sonata: an Enigma', *Recherches sur la musique française classique*, vii (1967), pp. 155–63.

—— 'The Treatment of Harmony in the Violin Sonatas of Jean-Marie Leclair', *Recherches sur la musique française classique*, iii (1963), pp. 131–44.

**Locatelli**

DUNNING, ALBERT: *Pietro Antonio Locatelli: Der Virtuose und seine Welt*, i, ii (Buren, 1982).

KOOLE, AREND: *Leven en werken van Pietro Antonio Locatelli da Bergamo* (Amsterdam, 1949).

**Marini**

DUNN, THOMAS D.: 'The Sonatas of Biagio Marini: Structure and Style', *The Music Review*, xxxvi (1975), pp. 161–79.

ISELIN, DORA: *Biagio Marini: sein Leben und seine Instrumentalwerke* (Hildburg-hausen, 1930).

**Rebel**

GATES, WILLIS C.: 'Jean Féry Rebel's "Sonates à violon seul mellées de plusieurs récits pour la viole" (1713)', *Journal of the American Musicological Society*, vii (1954), pp. 251–2.

LA LAURENCIE, LIONEL DE: 'Une dynastie de musiciens aux XVIIe et XVIIIe siècles: Les Rebel', *Sammelbände der Internationalen Musik-Gesellschaft*, vii (1905–6), pp. 253–307.

**Schop**

MOSER, ANDREAS: 'Johann Schop als Violinkomponist', *Festschrift Hermann Kretzschmar* (Leipzig, 1918).

**Senaillié**

BEECHEY, GWILYM: 'Jean Baptiste Senaillié (1687–1730) and his Sonatas for Violin and Continuo', *The Strad*, lxxxiv (1974), pp. 607–13.

**Tartini**

BRAINARD, PAUL: *Le sonate per violino di Giuseppe Tartini: catalogo tematico* (Milan, 1975).

**Telemann**

RUHNKE, MARTIN, ed.: *Telemann-Werkverzeichnis: Instrumentalwerke*, i (Kassel, 1984).

**Veracini**

GRAY WHITE, MARY: 'F. M. Veracini's "Dissertazioni sopra l'opera 5a del Corelli" ', *The Music Review*, xxxii (1971), pp. 1–26.

HILL, JOHN WALTER: *The Life and Works of Francesco Maria Veracini* (Ann Arbor, 1979).

——— 'Veracini in Italy', *Music and Letters*, lvi (1975), pp. 257–76.

SALVETTI, GUIDO: 'Le sonate accademiche di Francesco M. Veracini', *Chigiana*, xxv (1968), pp. 127–41.

**Vivaldi**

NEWMAN, WILLIAM S.: 'The Sonatas of Albinoni and Vivaldi', *Journal of the American Musicological Society*, v (1952), pp. 99–113.

TALBOT, MICHAEL: *Vivaldi* (London, 1978).

——— *Vivaldi* (B.B.C. Music Guide, London, 1979).


# CHAPTER VIII

## KEYBOARD MUSIC: 1630–1700

**(i) Modern Editions**

*(a) Anthologies*

Facsimile edition of the Bauyn MS (Geneva, 1977).

ADLER, GUIDO, ed.: *Musikalische Werke der Habsburgischen Kaiser Ferdinand III, Leopold I und Joseph I* (Vienna, 1892–3).

ADRIO, ADAM, ed.: *Die Fuge, Das Musikwerk*, xix (Cologne, 1961).

ALVAREZ, J. M., ed.: *Colección de obras de órgano de organistas españoles del siglo XVII* (Madrid, 1970).

ANGLÈS, HIGINI, ed.: *Antología de Organistas Españoles del siglo XVII*, i–iv (Barcelona, 1965–7).

APEL, WILLI, ed.: *Spanish organ masters after Antonio de Cabezón, The Tablature of Celle, Corpus of Early Keyboard Music*, xiv, xvii (American Institute of Musicology, 1971).

AULER, WOLFGANG, ed.: *Spielbuch für Kleinorgel oder andere Tasteninstrumente*, i (New York, 1942).

BOTSTIBER, HUGO, ed.: *Wiener Klavier- und Orgelwerke aus der zweiten Hälfte des 17. Jahrhunderts, Denkmäler der Tonkunst in Österreich*, xxvii (Jg. xiii(2) ), (Vienna, 1906).

BREIG, WERNER, ed.: *Lied- und Tanzvariationen der Sweelinck-Schule* (Mainz, 1970).

BUCHMAYER, RICHARD, ed.: *Klavier und Orgelwerke des 17. Jahrhunderts*, i–v (Leipzig, 1927).

CURTIS, ALAN, ed.: *Nederlandse Klaviermuziek uit de 16e en 17e eeuw, Monumenta musica neerlandica*, iii (Amsterdam, 1961).

DART, THURSTON, ed.: *Musicks Hand-maid (1663)*, Early Keyboard Music, x (London, 1958; 2nd ed., 1962, repr., 1969).

―――― and MORONEY, DAVITT, eds.: *John Blows Anthology: Froberger, Strungk, Fischer, Blow*, Early Keyboard Music, xxxvii (London, 1978).

DAWES, FRANK, ed.: *Schott's Anthology of Early Keyboard Music*, i–v (London, 1951).

DIETRICH, FRITZ, ed.: *Elf Orgelchoräle des 17. Jahrhunderts* (Kassel, 1932).

FERGUSON, HOWARD, ed.: *Early English Keyboard Music*, i–ii (London, 1971).

―――― *Early French Keyboard Music*, i–ii (London, 1966).

―――― *Early German Keyboard Music*, i–ii (London, 1970).

―――― *Early Italian Keyboard Music*, i–ii (London, 1968).

―――― *Style and Interpretation*, i, ii, v (London, 1963, 1971).

FULLER MAITLAND, JOHN ALEXANDER, ed.: *Contemporaries of Purcell*, i–vii (London, n.d.).

GEORGII, WALTER, ed.: *400 Jahre Europäischer Klaviermusik, Das Musikwerk*, i (Cologne, 1959).

―――― *Keyboard music of the Baroque and Rococo*, i (Cologne, 1960).

GERDES, GISELA, ed.: *46 Choräle für Orgel von J. P. Sweelinck und seiner deutschen Schülern* (Mainz, 1957).

GERVERS, HILDA, ed.: *English Court and Country Dances of the early Baroque from MS Drexel 5612, Corpus of Early Keyboard Music*, xliv (American Institute of Musicology, 1982).

GLAHN, HENRIK and SØRENSEN, SØREN, eds.: *The Clausholm Music Fragments* (Copenhagen, 1974).

GOLOS, JERZY and SUTKOWSKI, ADAM, eds.: *Keyboard music from Polish mss., Corpus of Early Keyboard Music*, x/1–4 (American Institute of Musicology, 1965–7).

GUILMANT, ALEXANDRE, ed.: *Liber Fratrum Cruciferorum Leodiensium, Archives des maîtres de l'orgue*, x (Paris, 1910).

HARDOUIN, PIERRE, ed.: *Le Livre d'orgue de Marguerite Thiery, L'Organiste liturgique*, xxv (Paris, 1956).

HERMANN, KURT, ed.: *Contemporaries of Purcell* (London, n.d.).

JEPPESEN, KNUD, ed.: *Balli antichi veneziani* (Copenhagen, 1962).

KELLER, HERMANN, ed.: *Achtzig Choralvorspiele deutscher Meister des 17. und 18. Jahrhunderts* (Leipzig, 1937).

―――― and HERMANN, KURT (vol. ii), eds.: *Alte meister der Klaviermusik*, i–iv, i, Deutsche Meister; ii, Französische Clavecinisten; iii, Italienische Meister; iv, Englische, Niederländische und Spanische Meister (Leipzig, 1959–62).

LINCOLN, HARRY B., ed.: *Seventeenth-century keyboard music in the Chigi mss. of the Vatican Library, Corpus of Early Keyboard Music*, xxxii/1–3 (American Institute of Musicology, 1968).

LITAIZE, GASTON and BONFILS, JEAN, eds.: *Les Pré-classiques français, L'Organiste liturgique*, xviii, xxxi, lviii–lix (Paris, 1954–65).

MOSER, HANS JOACHIM and FEDTKE, TRAUGOTT, eds.: *Variations on 'Allein Gott in der Höh sei Ehr'* (Kassel, 1953).

MUSET, JOSEPH, ed.: *Early Spanish Organ Music* (New York, 1948).

NEARY, MARTIN, ed.: *Old French Organ Music*, i–ii (Oxford, 1978 and 1983).

NOSKE, FRITS, ed.: *Klavierboek Anna Maria van Eijl (1671)*, *Monumenta musica neerlandica*, ii (Amsterdam, 2nd ed., 1976).

PAUER, ERNST, ed.: *Old English composers for the virginals and harpsichord*, i–iii (London, 1879–1905).

PEDRELL, FELIPE, ed.: *Antología de organistas clásicos españoles*, i–ii (Madrid, 1968).

PEETERS, FLOR, ed.: *Anthologia pro organo*, i–iv (Brussels, 1949).

—— *Oudnederlandse meesters, voor het orgel*, i–iii (Paris, 1938–45).

RAUGEL FÉLIX, ed.: *Les maîtres français de l'orgue aux XVIIe et XVIIIe siècles* (Paris, 1951).

REIMANN, MARGARETE, ed.: *Die Lüneburger Orgeltabulatur KN208a–b*, *Das Erbe deutscher Musik*, Reihe 1, xxxvi, xl (Leipzig, 1957 and 1968).

SARGENT, GEORGE, ed.: *Elizabeth Rogers' virginal book, 1656, Corpus of Early Keyboard Music*, xix (American Institute of Musicology, 1971).

SCHIERNING, LYDIA, ed.: *Italienische und süd-deutsche Orgelstücke des frühen 17. Jahrhunderts, Die Orgel II*, ix (Leipzig, 1959).

SEIFFERT, MAX, ed.: *Orgelmeister*, i–iv, *Organum, 4 Reihe*, ii, v, vii, xxi (Leipzig, 1925–   ).

STRAUBE, KARL, ed.: *Alte Meister des Orgelspiels* (Leipzig,1929).

—— *Alte Meister; eine Sammlung deutscher Orgelkompositionen aus dem XVII und XVIII Jahrhundert* (Leipzig, 1904).

—— *Choralvorspiele alter Meister* (Leipzig, 1907).

TORCHI, LUIGI, ed.: *Composizioni per organo e cembalo, secoli XVI, XVII e XVIII, L'Arte musicale in Italia*, iii (Milan, c.1900).

VALENTIN, ERICH, ed.: *Die Tokkata, Das Musikwerk*, xvii (Cologne, 1958).


(b) Works by Individual Composers

BATTIFERRI, L.: *Ricercari*, ed. G. G. Butler, *Corpus of Early Keyboard Music*, xlii (American Institute of Musicology, 1981).

BLOW, J.: *Complete Organ Works*, ed. W. Shaw (London, 1958; rev. 2nd ed., as *Thirty Voluntaries and Verses by John Blow*, London, 1972).

—— *2 Voluntaries from the Nanki MS*, ed. H. McLean, *Early Organ Music*, xxiii (London, 1971).

BÖHM, G.: *Sämtliche Werke*, i–ii, *Klavier- und Orgelwerke*, ed. J. Wolgast, rev. G. Wolgast (Wiesbaden, 1952).

—— *Praeludium, Fugen und Toccaten*, ed. M. Seiffert, *Organum, 4 Reihe*, iv (Leipzig, 1925).

BOYVIN, J.: *Oeuvres complètes d'orgue*, ed. A. Guilmant and A. Pirro, *Archives des maîtres de l'orgue*, vi (Paris, 1905; repr., 1972).

—— *Livres d'orgue*, ed. J. Bonfils, *L'Astrée, Collection de musique instrumentale classique* (Paris, 1969–77).

BUSTIJN, P.: *Drie suites voor clavecimbal*, ed. A. Curtis, *Exempla Musica Neerlandica*, i (Amsterdam, 1964).

BUXTEHUDE, D.: *Werke für Orgel*, ed. P. Spitta and M. Seiffert (Leipzig, 1903–4). Suppl. ed. M. Seiffert (Leipzig, 1939).

—— *Orgelwerke*, i–iv, ed. J. Hedar (Copenhagen, 1952).

—— *Sämtliche Orgelwerke*, ed. K. Beckmann (Wiesbaden, 1972).

—— *Klavervaerker*, ed. E. Bangert (Copenhagen, 1942).

—— *Vier Suiten für Clavichord oder Laute*, ed. B. Lundgren (Copenhagen, 1955).

CABANILLES, J.: *Musici organici Opera omnia*, ed. H. Anglès, *Barcelona, Biblioteca central: sección de musica*, iv, viii, xiii, xvii (Barcelona, 1927–56).

CHAMBONNIÈRES, J. C. DE: *Oeuvres complètes*, ed. P. Brunold and A. Tessier (Paris, 1925; reprinted with English trans. and new preface by D. Restout, New York, 1967).

—— *Les Pièces de clavecin*, *Monuments of Music and Music Literature in Facsimile*, ser. 1, iii (New York, 1965).

CORNET, P.: *Collected Keyboard Works*, ed. W. Apel, *Corpus of Early Keyboard Music*, xxvi (American Institute of Musicology, 1969).

COSYN, B.: *3 voluntaries*, ed. J. Steele, *Early Organ Music*, xiv (London, 1959).

COUPERIN, F.: *Pièces d'orgue*, ed. A. Guilmant, *Archives des maîtres de l'orgue*, v (Paris, 1904).

—— *Musique d'orgue*, ed. P. Brunold, *Oeuvres complètes*, vi (Paris, 1932).

COUPERIN, L.: *Pièces de clavecin*, ed. P. Brunold, rev. T. Dart (Monaco, 1959).

—— *Pièces de clavecin*, ed. A. Curtis, *Le Pupitre*, xviii (Paris, 1970).

—— *L'Oeuvre d'orgue*, ed. N. Pierront and N. Dufourcq, *Orgue et Liturgie*, vi (Paris, 1951).

CROFT, W.: *Complete Harpsichord Works*, ed. H. Ferguson and C. Hogwood (London, 1974).

—— *Complete Organ Works*, i–ii, ed. R. Platt (London, 1976–7; rev. ed. in one vol., 1982).

D'ANGLEBERT, J. H.: *Pièces de clavecin*, ed. M. Roesgen-Champion, *Publications de la Société française de Musicologie*, ser. 1, viii (Paris, 1934).

—— *Pièces de clavecin*, ed. K. Gilbert, *Le Pupitre*, liv (Paris, 1975).

DU MAGE, P.: *Premier livre d'orgue*, ed. A. Guilmant, *Archives des maîtres de l'orgue*, iii (Paris, 1901).

DU MONT, H.: *L'Oeuvre pour clavier*, ed. J. Bonfils, *L'Organiste Liturgique*, xiii (Paris, 1953).

FASOLO, G. B.: *Annuale*, ed. R. Walter (Heidelberg, 1965).

FISCHER, J. C. F.: *Sämtliche Werke für Klavier und Orgel*, ed. E. von Werra (Leipzig, 1901; repr., 1965).

FONTANA, F.: *Ricercari per organo*, ed. G. Doderer (Milan, 1975).

FRESCOBALDI, G.: *Opere complete*, ed. O. Mischiati and L. F. Tagliavini, *Monumenti musicali italiani*, i (Milan, 1975– ).

—— *Orgel- und Klavierwerke*, i–v, ed. P. Pidoux (Kassel, 1949–54).

—— *Douze toccatas, Douze fantasias*, ed. N. Dufourcq, *et al.*, *Orgue et Liturgie*, xxvi, xxxii, and xxxv (Paris, 1956, 1957–8).

—— *Keyboard compositions preserved in mss.*, ed. W. R. Shindle, *Corpus of Early Keyboard Music*, xxx/1–3 (American Institute of Musicology, 1968).

FROBERGER, J. J.: *Orgel- und Klavierwerke*, ed. G. Adler, *Denkmäler der Tonkunst in Österreich*, viii (Jg. iv(1) ), xiii (Jg. vi(2) ), xxi (Jg. x(2) ), (Vienna, 1897–1903).

—— *Orgelwerke*, ed. R. Walter, *Süddeutsche Orgelmeister des Barock*, vii (Altötting, 1967).

—— *Orgelwerke*, ed. M. Seiffert, *Organum, 4 Reihe*, xi (Leipzig, 1929).

—— *Oeuvres complètes pour clavecin*, ed. H. Schott, *Le Pupitre*, lvii (Paris, 1979).

GEOFFROY, J. N. (attrib.): *Livre d'orgue*, ed. J. Bonfils, *Le Pupitre*, liii (Paris, 1974).

GIBBONS, C.: *Keyboard compositions*, ed. C. G. Rayner, *Corpus of Early Keyboard Music*, xviii (American Institute of Musicology, 1967).

GIGAULT, N.: *Livre de musique pour l'orgue*, ed. A. Guilmant, *Archives des maîtres de l'orgue*, iv (Paris, 1902).

GRIGNY, N. DE: *Livre d'orgue*, ed. A. Guilmant, *Archives des maîtres de l'orgue*, v (Paris, 1904; repr., 1972).

—— *Premier livre d'orgue*, ed. N. Dufourcq and N. Pierront (Paris, 1953).

HART, P.: *Collected Organ Works*, ed. F. Dawes (London, 1973).

KERCKHOVEN, A. VAN DEN: *Werken voor orgel*, ed. J. Watelet, *Monumenta musicae belgicae* ii (Antwerp, 1933).

KERLL, J. C.: *Ausgewählte Werke*, ed. A. Sandberger, *Denkmäler der Tonkunst in Bayern*, ii/2 (Leipzig, 1901).

—— *Modulatio organica*, ed. R. Walter, *Süddeutsche Orgelmeister des Barock*, ii (Altötting, 1956).

KINDERMANN, J. E.: *Ausgewählte Werke*, ed. F. Schreiber, *Denkmäler der Tonkunst in Bayern*, xxi–xxiv (Leipzig, 1924).

—— *Harmonia organica*, ed. R. Walter, *Süddeutsche Orgelmeister der Barock*, ix (Altötting, 1966).

—— *Tanzstücke für Klavier*, ed. R. Baum, *Hortus musicus*, lxi (Kassel and Basle, 1950).

KRIEGER, J.: *Gesammelte Werke für Klavier und Orgel*, ed. M. Seiffert, *Denkmäler der Tonkunst in Bayern*, xviii (Leipzig, 1917).

—— *Präludien und Fugen*, ed. F. W. Riedel, *Die Orgel II*, iii (Leipzig, 1957).

—— *Ausgewählte Orgelstücke*, ed. M. Seiffert, *Organum, 4 Reihe*, xvii (Leipzig, 1930).

KRIEGER, J. P.: *Gesammelte Werke für Klavier und Orgel*, ed. M. Seiffert, *Denkmäler der Tonkunst in Bayern*, xviii (Leipzig, 1917).

KUHNAU, J.: *2 Praeludien und Fugen und 1 Toccata*, ed. M. Seiffert, *Organum, 4 Reihe*, xix (Leipzig, n.d.).

—— *Klavierwerke*, ed. K. Päsler, *Denkmäler deutscher Tonkunst*, iv (Leipzig, 1901).

LEBÈGUE, N. A.: *Oeuvres complètes d'orgue*, ed. A. Guilmant and A. Pirro, *Archives des maîtres de l'orgue*, ix (Paris, 1909).

—— *Oeuvres de Clavecin*, ed. N. Dufourcq (Monaco, 1956).

LOCKE, M.: *Keyboard suites, Organ voluntaries*, ed. T. Dart, *Early Keyboard Music*, vi, vii (London, 1959, rev. ed., 1964; and 1957, rev. ed., 1968).

LUGGE, J.: *Voluntaries, Two Toys and a Jigg*, ed. S. Jeans and J. Steele (London, 1956 and 1958).

MARESCHAL, S.: *Selected works*, ed. J. -M. Bonhote, *Corpus of Early Keyboard Music*, xxvii (American Institute of Musicology, 1967).

MERULA, T.: *Composizione per organo e cembalo*, ed. A. Curtis, *Monumenti di musica italiana*, 1/i (Brescia,1961).

MERULO, C.: *Toccate per organo*, i–iii, ed. S. Dalla Libera (Milan, 1959).

MORHARDT, P.: *Compositions for organ*, ed. W. Apel, *Corpus of Early Keyboard Music*, xxiii (American Institute of Musicology, 1973).

MUFFAT, G.: *Apparatus musico-organisticus*, ed. R. Walter, *Süddeutsche Orgelmeister des Barock*, iii (Altötting, 1957).

MURSCHHAUSER, F. X. A.: *Gesammelte Werke für Klavier und Orgel*, ed. M. Seiffert, *Denkmäler der Tonkunst in Bayern*, xviii (Leipzig, 1917).

—— *Octo-Tonium Novum organicum, Prototypon longo-breve organicum*, ed. R. Walter, *Süddeutsche Orgelmeister des Barock*, vi, x (Altötting, 1961 and 1969).

NASSARRE, P.: *Toccatas*, ed. J. M. Llorens (Barcelona, 1974).

NIVERS, G. G.: *Deuxième livre d'orgue*, ed. N. Dufourcq (Paris, 1956).

—— *Troisième livre d'orgue*, ed. N. Dufourcq, *Publications de la Société française de musicologie*, xiv (Paris, 1958).

—— *Cent préludes*, rev. ed., N. Dufourcq (Paris, 1963).

NOORDT, A. VAN: *Psalmenbearbeitungen für Orgel*, ed. P. Pidoux (Kassel, 1954).

—— *Tabulaturboech (1659)*, ed. M. Seiffert, *Vereniging voor nederlandsche muziekgeschiedenis*, xix (Amsterdam, 1896; 3rd ed., 1976).

PACHELBEL, J.: *Orgelkompositionen, Klavierwerke*, ed. M. Seiffert, *Denkmäler der Tonkunst in Bayern*, iv (Jg.i), ii (Jg.i), (Leipzig, 1903 and 1901).
—— *Ausgewählte Orgelwerke*, i–iv ed. K. Matthaei (Kassel, 1928–32; repr., 1959); v–vi ed. W. Stockmeier (Kassel, 1972–4); vii–viii ed. T. Zászkaliczky (Kassel, 1980–2).
—— *Fugen über Das Magnificat für Orgel oder Klavier*, ed. H. Botstiber and M. Seiffert, *Denkmäler der Tonkunst in Österreich*, xvii (Jg. viii(2) ), (Leipzig, 1901).
—— *Orgelwerke*, ed. M. Seiffert, *Organum, 4 Reihe*, xii–xiv (Leipzig, 1929).
—— *Ten fugues on the Magnificat*, ed. W. Emery, *Early Organ Music*, v (London, 1958).
—— *Selected organ works*, ed. N. Dufourcq, *et al.*, *Orgue et Liturgie*, i, ii, iv, v, xix, xxiv (Paris, 1950–5).
PASQUINI, B.: *Collected works for keyboard*, ed. M. Brooks Haynes, *Corpus of Early Keyboard Music*, v/1–7 (American Institute of Musicology, 1964–8).
PODBIELSKI, J.: *Praeludium per organum*, ed. A. Chybiński, *Wydawnictwo dawnej muzyki Polskiej*, xviii (Warsaw, 4th ed., 1971).
POGLIETTI, A.: *12 Ricercare*, ed. F. W. Riedel, *Die Orgel II*, v–vi (Leipzig, 1957).
PRAETORIUS, H.: *Organ Magnificats on the 8 tones*, ed. C. G. Rayner, *Corpus of Early Keyboard Music*, iv (American Institute of Musicology, 1963).
PURCELL, H.: *Harpsichord and organ music*, ed. W. B. Squire and E. J. Hopkins, *Purcell Society Edition*, vi (London, 1895).
—— *Complete Harpsichord Works*, ed. H. Ferguson, *Early Keyboard Music*, v, xxi–xxii (London, 1964).
—— *Organ Music*, ed. H. McLean (London, 1957; rev., 1967).
RAISON, A.: *Livre d'orgue*, ed. A. Guilmant and A. Pirro, *Archives des maîtres de l'orgue*, ii (Paris, 1899; repr., 1972).
—— *Premier livre d'orgue*, ed. N. Dufourcq, *Orgue et Liturgie*, lv–lvi, lviii–lix, lxi (Paris, 1962).
—— *Second livre d'orgue*, ed. J. Bonfils, *L'Organiste Liturgique*, xxxix–xl, xliii–xliv (Paris, n.d.).
REINCKEN, J. A.: *Collected keyboard works*, ed. W. Apel, *Corpus of Early Keyboard Music*, xvi (American Institute of Musicology, 1967).
—— *Sämtliche Orgelwerke*, ed. K. Beckmann (Wiesbaden, 1974).
ROBERDAY, F.: *Fugues et caprices*, ed. A. Guilmant, *Archives des maîtres de l'orgue*, iii (Paris, 1901).
—— *Fugues et caprices à 4 parties*, ed. J. Ferrard, *Le Pupitre*, xliv (Paris, 1972).
ROGERS, B.: *Complete keyboard works*, ed. R. Rastall, *Early Keyboard Music*, xxix (London, 1969).
—— *Voluntary*, ed. S. Jeans, *Early Organ Music*, xi (London, 1962).
ROSSI, M.: *Works for keyboard*, ed. J. R. White, *Corpus of Early Keyboard Music*, xv (American Institute of Musicology, 1966).
SALVATORE, G.: *Collected Keyboard Works*, ed. B. Hudson, *Corpus of Early Keyboard Music*, iii (American Institute of Musicology, 1964).
SCARLATTI, A.: *Primo e secondo libro di toccate*, ed. R. Gerlin, *I Classici musicali italiani*, xiii (Milan, 1943).
—— *Toccata nel primo tono*, ed. M. Radulesco, *Biblioteca classica dell'organista*, i (Brescia, 1969).
SCHEIDEMANN, H.: *Orgelwerke*, i–iii, ed. G. Fock and W. Breig (Kassel, 1967–71).
—— *Fünfzehn Praeludien und Fugen für Orgel*, ed. M. Seiffert, *Organum, 4 Reihe*, i (Leipzig, n.d.).
SCHEIDT, S.: *Werke*, i, v, vii, ed. G. Harms and C. Mahrenholz (Hamburg, 1923, 1937, 1953).

—— *Selected Organ Works*, ed. N. Dufourcq, *et al.*, *Orgue et Liturgie*, i, iv, xix, xxiii–xxiv (Paris, 1950–5).

SCHERER, S. A.: *Oeuvres d'orgue*, ed. A. Guilmant, *Archives des maîtres de l'orgue*, viii (Paris, 1907).

SPETH, J.: *Ars magna consoni e dissoni*, ed. G. Klaus, *Liber Organi*, ix (Mainz, 1954).

—— *Ars magna*, ed. T. Fedtke (Kassel, 1973).

STEIGLEDER, J. U.: *Compositions for keyboard*, ed. W. Apel, *et al.*, *Corpus of Early Keyboard Music*, xiii/1–2 (American Institute of Musicology, 1968–9).

STORACE, B.: *Compositions for keyboard*, ed. B. Hudson, *Corpus of Early Keyboard Music*, vii (American Institute of Musicology, 1965).

STROZZI, G.: *Capricci da sonate*, ed. B. Hudson, *Corpus of Early Keyboard Music*, xi (American Institute of Musicology, 1967).

STRUNCK, D.: *Compositions for organ*, ed. W. Apel, *Corpus of Early Keyboard Music*, xxiii (American Institute of Musicology, 1973).

—— *2 Choralfantasien*, ed. W. Krumbach, *Die Orgel II*, xii (Leipzig, 1960).

TOMKINS, T.: *Keyboard music*, ed. S. D. Tuttle, *Musica Britannica*, v (London, 2nd ed., 1964).

TUNDER, F.: *Sämtlicher Choralbearbeitungen für Orgel*, ed. R. Walter (Mainz, 1959).

—— *Sämtliche Orgelwerke*, ed. K. Beckmann (Wiesbaden, 1974).

—— *Vier Praeludien*, ed. M. Seiffert, *Organum, 4 Reihe*, vi (Leipzig, 1925).

WECKMANN, M.: *Ausgewählte Werke*, ed. R. Ilgner, *Das Erbe deutscher Musik, 2 Reihe: Schleswig-Holstein und Hansestädte*, iv (Leipzig, 1942).

—— *14 Praeludium, Fugen und Toccaten*, ed. M. Seiffert, *Organum, 4 Reihe*, iii (Leipzig, 1925).

XIMENEZ, J.: *Collected organ compositions*, ed. W. Apel, *Corpus of Early Keyboard Music*, xxxi (American Institute of Musicology, 1975).

(ii) **Books and Articles**

(a) *General*

APEL, WILLI: 'Die spanische Orgelmusik vor Cabanilles', *Anuario musical*, xvii (1962), pp. 15–29.

—— 'Die süd-italienische Clavierschule des 17. Jahrhunderts', *Acta musicologica*, xxxiv (1962), pp. 128–41.

—— *Geschichte der Orgel- und Klaviermusik bis 1700* (Kassel, 1967; rev. Eng. trans., *The History of Keyboard Music to 1700*, London, 1972).

—— 'Spanish Organ Music of the early 17th Century', *Journal of the American Musicological Society*, xv (1962), pp. 174–81.

ARNOLD, C. R.: *Organ Literature: a Comprehensive Survey* (Metuchen, N.J., 1973).

BEDBROOK, GERALD S.: *Keyboard Music from the Middle Ages to the Beginnings of the Baroque* (London, 1949).

BEECHEY, GWILYM: A New Source of Seventeenth-century Keyboard Music', *Music and Letters*, l (1969), pp. 278–89.

BLUME, FRIEDRICH: *Protestant Church Music: a History* (London, 1974).

BREIG, WERNER: 'Über das Verhältnis von Komposition und Ausführung in der nord-deutschen Orgel-Choralbearbeitung des 17. Jahrhunderts', *Norddeutsche und nord-europäische Musik* (Kassel, 1965), pp. 71–82.

CALDWELL, JOHN: *English Keyboard Music before the Nineteenth Century* (Oxford, 1973).

CLIMENT, JOSÉ: 'Organistas valencianos de los siglos XVII y XVIII: B) Organistas de la catedral', *Anuario musical*, xvii (1962), pp. 179–208.

COOPER, BARRY: 'Keyboard Sources in Hereford', *Research Chronicle of the Royal Musical Association*, xvi (1981).

—— 'The Keyboard Suite in England before the Restoration', *Music and Letters*, liii (1972), pp. 309–19.

CURTIS, ALAN: 'Musique classique française à Berkeley', *Revue de musicologie*, lvi (1970), pp. 123–64.

DARBELLAY, ÉTIENNE: 'Peut-on découvrir des indications d'articulation dans la graphie des tablatures de clavier de Claudio Merulo, Girolamo Frescobaldi et Michel-Angelo Rossi?' *International Musicological Society Congress Report*, xi *Copenhagen 1972*, pp. 342–50.

DART, THURSTON: 'An Early Seventeenth-Century Book of English Organ Music for the Roman Rite', *Music and Letters*, lii (1971), pp. 27–38.

—— 'Elisabeth Eysbock's Keyboard Book', *Svensk Tidskrift för Musikforskning*, xliv (1962), pp. 5–12.

—— 'Elizabeth Edgeworth's Keyboard Book', *Music and Letters*, l (1969), pp. 470–4.

—— 'The Organ Book of the Crutched Friars of Liège', *Revue Belge de Musicologie*, xvii (1963), pp. 21–8.

DIETRICH, FRITZ: *Geschichte des deutschen Orgelchorals im 17. Jahrhundert* (Kassel, 1932).

DODERER, GERHARD: *Orgelmusik und Orgelbau im Portugal des 17. Jahrhunderts. Untersuchungen an Hand des MS 964 des Biblioteca Pública in Braga* (Tutzing, 1978).

DOUGLASS, FENNER: *The Language of the French Classical Organ* (New Haven, 1969).

DUFOURCQ, NORBERT: *La musique d'orgue française de Jehan Titelouze à Jehan Alain* (Paris, 1941; 2nd ed., 1949).

—— *Le livre de l'orgue français 1589–1789* (Paris, 1969–   ).

FELLERER, KARL GUSTAV: 'Zur italienische Orgelmusik des 17./18. Jahrhunderts', *Jahrbuch des Musikbibliothek Peters 1938*, pp. 70–83.

FERGUSON, HOWARD: *Keyboard Interpretation* (London, 1975; repr., 1979).

FROTSCHER, GOTTHOLD: *Geschichte des Orgelspiels und der Orgelkomposition* (Berlin, 1935–6; enlarged 3rd ed., 1966).

FULLER, DAVID: 'French Harpsichord Playing in the Seventeenth Century: after Le Gallois', *Early Music*, iv (1976), pp. 22–6.

GUSTAFSON, BRUCE: *French Harpsichord Music of the 17th Century*, i–iii (Ann Arbor, 1979).

HAMBURGER, POVL: 'Ein handschriftliches Klavierbuch aus der ersten Hälfte des 17. Jahrhunderts', *Zeitschrift für Musikwissenschaft*, xiii (1930–1), pp. 133–40.

HIGGINBOTTOM, EDWARD: 'French Classical Organ Music and the Liturgy', *Proceedings of the Royal Musical Association*, ciii (1976–7), pp. 19–40.

HOWELL, ALMONTE C.: 'French Baroque Organ Music and the 8 Church Tones', *Journal of the American Musicological Society*, xi (1958), pp. 106–118.

HUDSON, RICHARD: 'Further Remarks on the Passacaglia and Ciaccona', *Journal of the American Musicological Society*, xxiii (1970), pp. 302–14.

—— *Passacaglio and Ciaccona from Guitar Music to Italian Keyboard Variations in the 17th century* (Ann Arbor, 1981).

JEANS, SUSI: 'The Pedal Clavichord and Other Practice Instruments of Organists', *Proceedings of the Royal Musical Association*, lxxvii (1950–1), pp. 1–15.

KIRKENDALE, WARREN: *L'aria di Fiorenza* (Florence, 1972).

KRUMMACHER, FRIEDHELM: *Die Choralbearbeitung in der protestantischen Figuralmusik zwischen Praetorius und Bach* (Kassel, 1978).

LLORENS CISTERÓ, JOSÉ MARIA: 'Literatura Organística del Siglo XVII', *Actas del I Congresso Nacional de Musicologia* (Zaragoza, 1981), pp. 29–130.

MAUL, W.: 'Some Observations on the French Organ School of the Seventeenth Century', *American Organist*, lii/3 (1969).

MISCHIATI, OSCAR: 'L'intavolatura d'organo tedesco della Biblioteca Nazionale di Torino', *L'organo*, iv (1963), pp. 1–154.

MORONEY, DAVITT: 'The Performance of Unmeasured Harpsichord Preludes', *Early Music*, iv (1976), pp. 143–51.

NEWMAN, WILLIAM S.: 'A Checklist of the Earliest Keyboard "Sonatas" (1641–1738)', *Notes*, xi (1953–4), pp. 201–12, and xii (1954–5), p. 57.

—— *The Sonata in the Baroque Era* (Chapel Hill, 1959; rev. 1966; repr., 1972).

PEETERS, FLOR, and VENTE, M. A., eds.: *Die orgel-kunst in de Nederlanden van de 16de tot de 18de eeuw* (Antwerp, 1971). (Also in an English edition.)

PIRRO, ANDRÉ: 'L'art des organistes', *Encyclopédie de la musique et dictionnaire du Conservatoire*, II/ii (1926), pp. 1181–374.

—— *Les clavecinistes: étude critique* (Paris, 1924).

REIMANN, MARGARETE: 'Pasticcios und Parodien in nord-deutschen Klavier-tabulaturen', *Die Musikforschung*, viii (1955), pp. 265–71.

RIEDEL, FRIEDRICH W.: *Quellenkundliche Beiträge zur Geschichte der Musik für Tasteninstrumente in der zweiten Hälfte des 17. Jahrhunderts* (Kassel, 1960).

ROUTH, FRANCIS: *Early English Organ Music* (London, 1973).

SCHERING, ARNOLD: 'Zur alternatim-Orgelmesse', *Zeitschrift für Musikwissenschaft*, xvii (1935), pp. 19–32.

SCHIERNING, LYDIA: *Die Überlieferung der deutschen Orgel- und Klaviermusik aus der ersten Hälfte des 17. Jahrhunderts* (Kassel, 1961).

SCHMIDT, JOST HARRO: 'Eine unbekannte Quelle zur Klaviermusik des 17. Jahrhunderts', *Archiv für Musikwissenschaft*, xxii (1965), pp. 1–11.

SCHÜNEMANN, GEORG: *Geschichte der Klaviermusik* (Hamburg, 1940; rev. H. Gerigk, 1953, 2nd ed., 1956).

SEIFFERT, MAX: *Geschichte der Klaviermusik* (Leipzig, 1899; repr., 1966).

SERVIÈRES, GEORGES: *Documents inédits sur les organistes français des XVIIe et XVIIIe siècles* (Paris, 1924).

SILBIGER, ALEXANDER: *Italian Manuscript Sources of Seventeenth Century Keyboard Music* (Ann Arbor, 1980).

—— 'The Roman Frescobaldi Tradition c.1640–1670', *Journal of the American Musicological Society*, xxxiii (1980), pp. 42–87.

SILVA Y RAMON, GONZALO: *Die Orgelwerke der Kathedrale zu Sevilla* (Mainz, 1939).

SUMNER, WILLIAM L.: *The Organ* (4th ed., London, 1973).

WALKER, THOMAS: 'Ciaccona and Passacaglia: Remarks on their Origin and Early History', *Journal of the American Musicological Society*, xxi (1968), pp. 300–20.

WILLIAMS, PETER: *The European Organ 1450–1850* (London, 1966; 2nd ed., 1968).

(b) *Individual Composers*

**Blow**

SHAW, W.: 'The Organ Music of John Blow', *Musical Opinion*, lxxxii (1958–9), pp. 179–87.

**Böhm**

MÜLLER-BUSCHER, HENNING: *Studien zu den Choralbearbeitungen Georg Böhms* (Augsburg, 1972).

SCHUNEMAN, R. A.: 'The Organ Chorales of Georg Böhm', *The Diapason*, lxi (1970).

**Boyvin**
HARDOUIN, PIERRE: 'Quatre Parisiens d'origine: Nivers, Gigault, Jullien, Boyvin', *Revue de musicologie*, xxxix (1957), pp. 73–8.

**Bryne**
COOPER, BARRY: 'Albertus Bryne's Keyboard Music', *Musical Times*, cxiii (1972), pp. 142–3.

**Buxtehude**
APEL, WILLI: 'Neue aufgefundene Clavierwerke von Scheidemann, Tunder, Froberger, Reincken und Buxtehude', *Acta musicologica*, xxxiv (1962), pp. 65–7.
HEDAR, JOSEF: *Dietrich Buxtehudes Orgelwerke: zur Geschichte des nord-deutschen Orgelstils* (Stockholm, 1951).
LORENZ, H.: 'Die Klaviermusik Dietrich Buxtehudes', *Archiv für Musikforschung*, xi (1954).
PAULY, H. J.: *Die Fuge in den Orgelwerken Dietrich Buxtehudes* (Regensburg, 1964).

**Cabanilles**
BONNET, ANTONY: 'Les oeuvres d'orgue de Juan Cabanilles et les exigences actuelles de la liturgie', *Anuario musical*, xvii (1962), pp. 99–104.
BRADSHAW, MURRAY: 'Juan Cabanilles: the Toccatas and Tientos', *Musical Quarterly*, lix (1973), pp. 285–301.
KASTNER, SANTIAGO: 'Randbemerkungen zu Cabanilles' Claviersatz', *Anuario musical*, xvii (1962), pp. 73–97.
SPEER, KLAUS: 'Tonus Designations in the Tientos of Juan Cabanilles', *Anuario musical*, xvii (1962), pp. 31–6.

**Chambonnières**
QUITTARD, HENRI: 'Un claveciniste français du XVIIe siècle, Jacques Champion de Chambonnières', *La Tribune de Saint-Gervais*, vii (1901), pp. 1–11, 33–44, 71–7, 105–10, 141–9.

**Cornet**
FERRARD, MARY ARMSTRONG: *Peeter Cornet (?–1633), organiste à la cour d'Albert et Isabelle à Bruxelles* (Brussels, 1973).

**F. Couperin**
TESSIER, ANDRÉ: 'Un exemplaire original des pièces d'orgue de Couperin', *Revue de musicologie*, x (1929), pp. 109–17.

**L. Couperin**
OLDHAM, GUY: 'A New Source of French Keyboard Music of the mid-17th Century', *Recherches sur la musique française classique*, i (1960), pp. 51–9.

**Del Buono**
NEWMAN, WILLIAM S.: 'The XIIII Sonate di Cimbalo by Giovanni Pietro Del Buono, "Palermitano" (1641)', *Collectanea historiae musicae*, ii (1957), pp. 297–310.

**Diruta**
KREBS, CARL: 'Girolamo Dirutas Transilvano', *Vierteljahrsschrift für Musikwissenschaft*, viii (1892), pp. 307–88.

**Frescobaldi**
APEL, WILLI: 'Die handschriftliche Überlieferung der Klavierwerke Frescobaldis', *Festschrift Karl Gustav Fellerer* (Regensburg,1962), pp. 40–5.
MACHABEY, ARMAND: *Girolamo Frescobaldi: la vie, l'oeuvre* (Paris, 1952).

**Froberger**
APEL, WILLI: 'Neu aufgefundene Clavierwerke von Scheidemann, Tunder, Froberger, Reincken und Buxtehude', *Acta musicologica*, xxxiv (1962), pp. 65–7.
LEONHARDT, GUSTAV: 'Johann Jacob Froberger and his Music', *L'organo*, vi (1968), pp. 15–40.
SCHARLAU, ULF: 'Neue Quellenfunde zur Biographie Johann Jakob Froberger', *Die Musikforschung*, xxii (1969), pp. 47–52.
SEIDLER, K.: *Untersuchungen über Biographie und Klavierstil Johann Jakob Froberger* (Diss., Königsberg, 1930).

**Geoffroy**
ROCHE, M.: 'Un livre de clavecin français de la fin du XVIIe siècle', *Recherches sur la musique française classique*, vii (1967), pp. 39–73.

**Gigault**
HARDOUIN, PIERRE: 'Quatre Parisiens d'origine: Nivers, Gigault, Jullien, Boyvin', *Revue de musicologie*, xxxix (1957), pp. 73–8.
PIRRO, ANDRÉ: 'Un organiste au XVIIe siècle, Nicolas Gigault', *La revue musicale*, iii (1903).

**Hart**
DAWES, FRANK: 'The Music of Philip Hart (*c*.1676–1749)', *Proceedings of the Royal Musical Association*, xciv (1967–8), pp. 63–75.

**Jullien**
HARDOUIN, PIERRE: 'Quatre Parisiens d'origine: Nivers, Gigault, Jullien, Boyvin', *Revue de musicologie*, xxxix (1957), pp. 73–8.

**Kerckhoven**
POTVLIEGHE, G.: 'Abraham van den Kerckhoven', *Het orgel*, v (1971).

**Kindermann**
SCHREIBER, F.: *Der Nürnberger Organist Johannes Erasmus Kindermann (1616–1655)* (Leipzig, 1913).

**Lebègue**
TESSIER, ANDRÉ: 'L'oeuvre de clavecin de Nicolas Le Bègue', *Revue de musicologie*, vii (1923), pp. 106–12.

**Merula**
CURTIS, ALAN: 'L'opera cembalo-organistica di Tarquinio Merula', *L'organo*, i (1960).

**Muffat**
SCHÜTZ, KARL: 'Die Toccaten des Apparatus musico-organisticus von Georg Muffat', *De ratione in musica: Festschrift Erich Schenk* (Kassel, 1975).

**Nivers**
BEECHEY, GWILYM: 'Guillaume Gabriel Nivers (1632–1714): his Organ Music and his "Traité de la composition"', *The Consort*, xxv (1968–9), pp. 373–83.
HARDOUIN, PIERRE: 'Quatre Parisiens d'origine: Nivers, Gigault, Jullien, Boyvin', *Revue de musicologie*, xxxix (1957), pp. 73–8.
PRUITT, WILLIAM: 'The Organ Works of Guillaume Gabriel Nivers (1632–1714)', *Recherches sur la musique française classique*, xiv (1974), pp. 5–81; and xv (1975), pp. 47–79.

**Pachelbel**
NOLTE, EWALD V.: 'The Magnificat Fugues of Johann Pachelbel: Alternation or

Intonation?', *Journal of the American Musicological Society*, ix (1956), pp. 19–24.

**H. Praetorius**

KITE-POWELL, J.: *The Visby (Petri) Organ Tablature: Investigation and Critical Edition* (Wilhelmshaven, 1977).

**Purcell**

DOWNES, RALPH: 'An Organist's view of the organ works', *Henry Purcell 1659–1695*, ed. I. Holst (London, 1959), pp. 67–73.

ROSE, GLORIA: 'Purcell, Michelangelo Rossi and J. S. Bach: Problems of Authorship', *Acta musicologica*, xl (1968), pp. 203–19.

SIEDENTOPF, HENNING: 'Eine komposition Purcells im Klavierbuch einer württembergischen Prinzessin', *Die Musikforschung*, xxxi (1978), pp. 446–50.

**Reincken**

APEL, WILLI: 'Neu aufgefundene Clavierwerke von Scheidemann, Tunder, Froberger, Reincken und Buxtehude', *Acta musicologica*, xxxiv (1962), pp. 65–7.

**Roberday**

HARDOUIN, PIERRE: 'François Roberday (1624–1680)', *Revue de musicologie*, xlv (1960), pp. 44–62.

**Rogers**

RASTALL, RICHARD: 'Benjamin Rogers (1614–98): Some Notes on his Instrumental Music', *Music and Letters*, xlvi (1965), pp. 237–42.

**Rossi**

ROSE, GLORIA: 'Purcell, Michelangelo Rossi and J. S. Bach: Problems of Authorship', *Acta musicologica*, xl (1968), pp. 203–19.

**A. Scarlatti**

PESTELLI, GIORGIO: 'Le toccate per strumento a tastiera di Alessandro Scarlatti nei Manoscritti Napoletani', *Analecta musicologica*, xii (1973), pp. 169–92.

SHEDLOCK, J. S.: 'The Harpsichord Music of Alessandro Scarlatti', *Sammelbände der Internationalen Musik-Gesellschaft*, vi (1904–5), pp. 160–78 and 418–22.

**Scheidemann**

APEL, WILLI: 'Neu aufgefundene Clavierwerke von Scheidemann, Tunder, Froberger, Reincken und Buxtehude', *Acta musicologica*, xxxiv (1962), pp. 65–7.

BREIG, WERNER: *Die Orgelwerke von Heinrich Scheidemann* (Wiesbaden, 1967).

**Scheidt**

MAHRENHOLZ, CHRISTHARD: 'Der 3. Band von Samuel Scheidts Tabulatura Nova 1624 und die Gottesdienstordnung der Stadt Halle', *Die Musikforschung*, i (1948), pp. 32–9.

—— 'Samuel Scheidt und die Orgel', *Musik und Kirche*, xxv (1955), pp. 38–50.

MULLER, FRANCIS: 'La technique de la réalisation variée dans la Tablature de Goerlitz (1650) de Samuel Scheidt', *International Musicological Society Congress Report*, vii *Cologne 1958*, pp. 196–7.

**Speth**

BEECHEY, GWILYM: 'A 17th-century German Organ Tutor', *Musical Times*, cxiii (1972), pp. 86–9.

**Tunder**

APEL, WILLI: 'Neu aufgefundene Clavierwerke von Scheidemann, Tunder,

Froberger, Reincken und Buxtehude', *Acta musicologica*, xxxiv (1962), pp. 65–7.


# CHAPTER IX

## HARPSICHORD MUSIC: 1700–1750

### (i) Modern Editions

*(a) Anthologies*

GEORGII, WALTER, ed.: *Keyboard Music of the Baroque and Rococo*, ii (Cologne, 1960).
GROVLEZ, GABRIEL MARIE, ed.: *Les plus belles pièces de clavessin de l'école française* (London, 1918).
HERRMANN, KURT, ed.: *Französische Clavecinisten, Alte Meister der Klaviermusik*, ii (Leipzig, c.1960).
VALENTIN, ERICH, ed.: *Die Tokkata, Das Musikwerk*, xvii (Cologne, 1958).


*(b) Works by Individual Composers*

BACH, J. S.: *Clavierwerke, Johann Sebastian Bachs Werke*, iii, xiii/2, xiv, xxxvi, xlii, xliii/2, xlv/1, Bach-Gesellschaft (Leipzig, 1854–97).
—— *Klavierwerke, Neue Ausgabe sämtlicher Werke, Serie V* (Leipzig, 1957).
—— *Clavier-Büchlein vor Wilhelm Friedemann Bach*, facs. ed. R. Kirkpatrick (New Haven, 1959).
—— *14 more canons from the Goldberg variations*, ed. O. Alain (Paris, 1976).
—— *Inventions*, facs. ed. G. Schünemann (Leipzig, 1942).
—— *Das Wohltemperirte Clavier*, pt. 1, facs. ed., *Bach-Archiv*, v (Leipzig, 1962); pt. 2, facs. ed., D. Franklin and S. Daw, *British Library Music Facsimiles*, i (London, 1980).
CLÉRAMBAULT, L. -N.: *Premier livre de Pièces de Clavecin*, ed. P. Brunold (Paris, 1938; rev. ed., T. Dart, Monaco, 1964).
—— *Premier livre de Pièces de Clavecin*, facs. ed. *Clavecinistes français du 18e siècle*, ii (Geneva, 1982).
COUPERIN, F.: *Musique de clavecin, 1–4*, ed. M. Cauchie, *Oeuvres complètes*, ii–v, (Paris, 1932–3).
—— *Pièces de clavecin*, ed. K. Gilbert, *Le Pupitre*, xxi–xxiv (Paris, 1969–72).
DAGINCOUR, F.: *Pièces de clavecin*, ed. H. Ferguson (Paris, 1969).
DANDRIEU, J. -F.: *Trois livres de clavecin*, ed. P. Aubert and B. François-Sappey (Paris, 1973).
DAQUIN, L. -C.: *Pièces de clavecin*, ed. P. Brunold and H. Expert (Paris, 1926).
—— *Pièces de clavecin*, ed. C. Hogwood (London, 1983).
DELLA CIAJA, A. B.: *Sonate per cembalo*, nos. 1–3 ed. G. Buonamici (Florence, 1912).
DIEUPART, C.: *6 suites*, ed. P. Brunold (Paris, 1934).
DUPHLY, J.: *Pièces de clavecin*, ed. F. Petit, *Le Pupitre*, i (Paris, 1967).
—— *Troisième livre de pièces de clavecin*, 3 pieces ed. J. Volant-Panel (Paris, 1961).
DURANTE, F.: *6 sonate per cembalo*, ed. P. Baumgartner (Kassel, 1949).
—— *Toccate per il Cembalo solo*, ed. C. Pannain (Milan, 1932).
FIOCCO, J. -H.: *Werken voor clavecimbel*, ed. J. Watelet, *Monumenta musicae Belgicae*, iii (Antwerp, 1936; 2nd ed., 1955).

FISCHER, J. C. F.: *Sämtliche Werke für Klavier und Orgel*, ed. E. von Werra (Leipzig, 1901; repr., 1965).

GIUSTINI, L.: *Sonate da cimbalo di piano e forte*, facs. ed. R. Harding (Cambridge, 1933).

GREENE, M.: *Voluntaries and Suites for Organ and Harpsichord*, ed. G. Beechey, *Recent Researches in the Music of the Baroque Era*, xix (Madison, 1975).

HANDEL, G. F.: *Klavier-Stücke*, ed. F. Chrysander, *Georg Friedrich Händels Werke*, ii (Leipzig, 1859).

—— *Klavierwerke*, i ed. R. Steglich, ii ed. P. Northway, iii–iv ed. T. Best, *Hallische Händel Ausgabe, Serie IV*, i, v, vi, xvii (Kassel, 1955–75).

JACQUET DE LA GUERRE, E. -C.: *Pièces de clavecin*, ed. P. Brunold (Monaco, 1938; rev. ed., T. Dart, 1965).

MARCELLO, B.: *Suonate per il cembalo*, ed. L. Sgrizzi and L. Bianconi, *Le Pupitre*, xxviii (Paris, 1971).

MARCHAND, L.: *Pièces de clavecin*, ed. T. Dart (Paris, 1960).

MATTHESON, J.: *Pièces de clavecin* (London, 1714; repr. 1965).

—— *Die wol-klingende Finger-Sprache*, ed. L. Hoffmann-Erbrecht (Leipzig, 1953).

MUFFAT, G.: *Componimenti musicali*, ed. G. Adler, *Denkmäler der Tonkunst in Österreich*, vii (Jg.iii(3) ), (Vienna, 1896; repr., Graz, 1959).

RAMEAU, J. -P.: *Pièces de clavecin*, ed. C. Saint-Saëns, *Oeuvres complètes*, i (Paris, 1895).

—— *Pièces de clavecin*, i–iii, ed. E. R. Jacobi (Basle, 1958–9).

SCARLATTI, D.: *Opere complete per clavicembalo*, i–xi, ed. A. Longo (Milan, 1906–8).

—— *60 Sonatas*, ed. R. Kirkpatrick (New York, 1953).

—— *Complete Keyboard Works in Facsimile*, i–xviii, ed. R. Kirkpatrick (New York, 1971–    ).

—— *Sonates*, ed. K. Gilbert, *Le Pupitre*, xxxi–xli (Paris, 1971–    ).

—— *Sonate per clavicembalo*, ed. E. Fadini (Milan, 1978–    ).

SEIXAS, C. DE: *Keyboard music*, ed. S. Kastner, *Cravistas portuguezes*, i–ii (Mainz, etc., 1935).

—— *Keyboard sonatas*, ed. S. Kastner, *Portugaliae Musica*, x (Lisbon, 1965).

TELEMANN, G. P.: *VI Ouvertüren*, ed. F. Oberdörffer, *Deutsche Klaviermusik der 17. und 18. Jahrhunderts*, iv–v (Munich, 1960).

—— *Keyboard music*, *Hortus musicus*, ix (Kassel and Basle, 1949).

—— *XX kleine Fugen*, ed. W. Upmeyer, *Nagels Musk-Archiv*, xiii (Hanover, 1928).

—— *Fugues légères*, ed. M. Lange (Kassel, 1929).

—— *Fantasies pour le clavessin*, ed. M. Seiffert (Kassel, 4th ed., 1955).

—— *2 solos for harpsichord*, ed. H. Ruf (Mainz, 1964).

—— *Suita polska, na klawesyn*, ed. T. Ochlewski, *Florilegium musicae antiquae*, xi (Cracow, 1963).

ZIPOLI, D.: *Sonate d'intavolatura per organo, e cimbalo*, ed. L. Tagliavini, (Heidelberg, 1959); and ed. in *I classici della musica italiana*, xxxvi (Milan, 1919).

## (ii) Books and Articles

### (a) General

COUPERIN, FRANÇOIS: *L'Art de toucher le clavecin*, reprinted in *Oeuvres complètes*, i (Paris, 1932; rev. 1968). English trans., by M. Halford (Port Washington, N.Y., 1974).

HOFFMANN-ERBRECHT, LOTHAR: *Deutsche und italienische Klaviermusik zur Bach-zeit* (Leipzig, 1954).

NEWMAN, WILLIAM S.: *The Sonata in the Baroque Era* (Chapel Hill, 1959; rev. 1966, repr., 1972).

PILKINGTON, C. VERE: 'A Collection of English Eighteenth-century Harpsichord Music', *Proceedings of the Royal Musical Association*, lxxxiii (1956–7), pp. 89–107.

PIRRO, ANDRÉ: *Les clavecinistes* (Paris, 1924).

RIEDEL, F. W.: 'Der Einfluss der italienischen Klaviermusik des 17. Jahrhunderts auf die Entwicklung der Musik für Tasteninstrumente in Deutschland während der ersten Hälfte des 18. Jahrhunderts', *Analecta musicologica*, v (1968), pp. 18–33.

SEIFFERT, MAX: *Geschichte der Klaviermusik* (Leipzig, 1899).


(*b*) *Individual Composers*

**Bach**

ALAIN, OLIVIER: 'Un supplément inédit aux *Variations Goldberg* de J. S. Bach', *Revue de musicologie*, lx–lxi (1974–5), pp. 244–94.

BARBOUR, J. MURRAY: 'Bach and *The Art of Temperament*', *Musical Quarterly*, xxxiii (1947), pp. 64–89.

BODKY, ERWIN: *The Interpretation of Bach's Keyboard Works* (Cambridge, Mass., 1960).

BREIG, WERNER: 'Bachs Goldberg-Variationen als zyklisches Werk', *Archiv für Musikwissenschaft*, xxxii (1975), pp. 243–65.

CHAILLEY, JACQUES: *L'Art de la fugue de J. S. Bach* (Paris, 1971–2).

CZACZKES, LUDWIG: *Analyse des Wohltemperierten Klaviers* (Vienna, 1956–65).

DAVID, HANS THEODOR: *J. S. Bach's 'Musical Offering': History, Interpretation, and Analysis* (New York, 1945; repr., 1972).

—— and MENDEL, ARTHUR: *The Bach Reader* (2nd ed., New York, 1966).

DAVID, JOHANN NEPOMUK: *Das wohltemperierte Klavier* (Göttingen, 1962).

—— *Die dreistimmigen Inventionen von Johann Sebastian Bach* (Göttingen, 1959).

—— *Die zweistimmigen Inventionen von Johann Sebastian Bach* (Göttingen, 1957).

EICHBERG, HARTWIG: 'Unechtes unter Johann Sebastian Bachs Klavierwerken', *Bach-Jahrbuch 1975*, lxi, pp. 7–49.

EMERY, WALTER: 'The London Autograph of the "Forty-eight"', *Music and Letters*, xxxiv (1953), pp. 106–23.

FRANKE, ERHARD: 'Themenmodelle in Bachs Klaviersuiten', *Bach-Jahrbuch 1966*, lii, pp. 72–98.

GRAY, C.: *The 48 Preludes and Fugues of J. S. Bach* (London, 1938).

HERING, HANS: 'Spielerische Elemente in J. S. Bachs Klaviermusik', *Bach-Jahrbuch 1974*, lx, pp. 44–69.

KAST, PAUL: *Die Bach-Handschriften der Berliner Staatsbibliothek*, *Tübinger Bach-Studien*, ii–iii (Trossingen, 1958).

KELLER, HERMANN: *Das Wohltemperierte Klavier von Johann Sebastian Bach: Werk und Wiedergabe* (Kassel, 1965).

—— *Die Klavierwerke Bachs* (Leipzig, 1950).

KENYON, NICHOLAS: 'A Newly Discovered Group of Canons by Bach', *Musical Times*, cxvii (1976), pp. 391–3.

KIRKENDALE, URSULA: 'The Source for Bach's *Musical Offering*', *Journal of the American Musicological Society*, xxxiii (1980), pp. 88–141.

LANDSHOFF, LUDWIG: *Revisionsbericht zur Urtextausgabe von J. S. Bachs Inventionen und Sinfonien* (Leipzig, 1933).

LEONHARDT, GUSTAV: *The Art of Fugue: Bach's last Harpsichord Work* (The Hague,1952).

SCHWEITZER, ALBERT: *J. S. Bach, le musicien-poète* (Leipzig, 1905; Eng. trans., London, 1911; repr., 1967).

WOLFF, CHRISTOPH: 'Bach's *Handexemplar* of the Goldberg Variations: a New Source', *Journal of the American Musicological Society*, xxix (1976), pp. 224–41.

—— 'New Research on Bach's Musical Offering', *Musical Quarterly*, lvii (1971), pp. 379–408.

—— 'Überlegungen zum "Thema Regium"', *Bach-Jahrbuch 1973*, lix, pp. 33–8.

—— and others: 'Bach's "Art of Fugue": an Examination of the Sources', *Current Musicology*, xix (1975), pp. 47–77.

## Couperin

CLARK, JANE: 'Les Folies Françoises', *Early Music*, viii (1980), pp. 163–9.

DART, THURSTON: 'On Couperin's Harpsichord Music', *Musical Times*, cx (1969), pp. 590–4.

GILBERT, KENNETH: 'Les livres de clavecin de François Couperin: note bibliographique', *Revue de musicologie*, lviii (1972), pp. 256–62.

HOFMAN, S.: *L'oeuvre de clavecin de François Couperin* (Paris, 1961).

MELLERS, WILFRID: *François Couperin and the French Classical Tradition* (London, 1950; repr., 1968).

## Dandrieu

FRANÇOIS-SAPPEY, BRIGITTE: 'L'oeuvre de clavecin de Jean-François Dandrieu', *Recherches sur la musique française classique*, xiv (1974), pp. 154–235.

## Duphly

LESURE, FRANÇOIS: Introduction to *J. Duphly: Pièces pour clavecin*, *Le Pupitre*, i ed. F. Petit (Paris, 1967).

## Giustini

CASELLI, ALA BOTTI: 'Le "Sonate da cimbalo di piano, e forte" di Lodovico Giustini', *Nuova rivista musicale italiana*, xii (1978), pp. 34–66.

HARDING, ROSAMOND: 'The Earliest Pianoforte Music', *Music and Letters*, xiii (1932), pp. 195–9.

## Graupner

HOFFMANN-ERBRECHT, LOTHAR: 'Johann Christoph Graupner als Klavierkomponist', *Archiv für Musikwissenschaft*, x (1953), pp. 140–52.

## Handel

ABRAHAM, GERALD: 'Handel's Clavier Music', *Music and Letters*, xvi (1935), pp. 278–85.

BEST, TERENCE: 'Handel's Keyboard Music', *Musical Times*, cxii (1971), pp. 845–8.

SEIFFERT, MAX: 'Zu Händels Klavierwerken', *Sammelbände der Internationalen Musik-Gesellschaft*, i (1899–1900), pp. 131–41.

TAYLOR, SEDLEY: *The Indebtedness of Handel to Works by other Composers* (Cambridge, 1906).

## Jacquet de la Guerre

BORROFF, EDITH: *An Introduction to Elisabeth-Claude Jacquet de la Guerre* (Brooklyn, N.Y., 1966).

## Marcello

NEWMAN, WILLIAM S.: 'The Keyboard Sonatas of Benedetto Marcello', *Acta musicologica*, xxix (1957), pp. 28–41; and xxxi (1959), pp. 192–6.

**Muffat**

KNÖLL, J. H.: *Die Klavier- und Orgelwerke Theophile Muffats* (Diss., Vienna, 1916).
WOLLENBERG, SUSAN: 'The Keyboard Suites of Gottlieb Muffat (1690–1770)', *Proceedings of the Royal Musical Association*, cii (1975–6), pp. 83–91.

**Rameau**

DALE, KATHLEEN: 'The Keyboard Music of J. P. Rameau', *Monthly Musical Record*, lxxvi (1946), pp. 127–31.
GIRDLESTONE, CUTHBERT: *Jean-Philippe Rameau: His Life and Work* (London, 1957; 2nd ed., Paris, 1962).
—— 'Rameau's Self-Borrowings', *Music and Letters*, xxxix (1958), pp. 52–6.
SADLER, GRAHAM: 'Rameau's Harpsichord Transcriptions from *Les Indes galantes*', *Early Music*, vii (1979), pp. 18–24.

**Scarlatti**

BENTON, RITA: 'Form in the Sonatas of Domenico Scarlatti', *Music Review*, xiii (1952), pp. 264–73.
BOGIANCKINO, MASSIMO: *L'arte clavicembalistica di Domenico Scarlatti* (Rome, 1956; Eng. trans., 1968).
CLARK, JANE: 'Domenico Scarlatti and Spanish Folk Music', *Early Music*, iv (1976), pp. 19–21.
GERSTENBERG, WALTER: *Die Klavier-Kompositionen Domenico Scarlattis* (Regensburg, 1933; repr., 1968).
HAUTUS, LOEK: 'Beitrag zur Datierung der Klavierwerke Domenico Scarlattis', *Die Musikforschung*, xxvi (1973), pp. 59–61.
KELLER, HERMANN: *Domenico Scarlatti, ein Meister des Klaviers* (Leipzig, 1957).
KIRKPATRICK, RALPH: *Domenico Scarlatti* (Princeton, 1953; 3rd rev. ed., 1968).
PESTELLI, GIORGIO: *Le sonate di Domenico Scarlatti* (Turin, 1967).

**Seixas**

HEIMES, KLAUS F.: 'Carlos Seixas: zum Quellenstudium seiner Clavier-Sonaten', *Archiv für Musikwissenschaft*, xxviii (1971), pp. 205–16.

**Telemann**

RUHNKE, MARTIN, ed.: *Telemann-Werkverzeichnis: Instrumentalwerke*, i (Kassel, 1984).
SCHÄFER-SCHMUCK, K.: *Georg Philipp Telemann als Klavierkomponist* (Diss., Kiel, 1934).

## CHAPTER X

### ORGAN MUSIC: 1700–1750

**(i) Modern Editions**

*(a) Anthologies*

AULER, WOLFGANG, ed.: *Spielbuch für Kleinorgel oder andere Tasteninstrumente*, ii (New York, 1951).
BIGGS, EDWARD POWER, ed.: *Treasury of early organ music* (New York, 1947).
BOSSI, ENRICO, ed.: *Sammlung von Stücken alter italienischer Meister* (repr., Leipzig, 1936).
BUSZIN, WALTER EDWIN, ed.: *Organ series*, i (St. Louis, Mo., 1948).

DUFOURCQ, NORBERT, *et al.*, ed.: *La Fugue au XVIIIe Siècle, Orgue et Liturgie*, xv (Paris, 1953).

EMERY, WALTER, ed.: *Early Organ Music*, 27 vols. (London, 1958–75).

FROTSCHER, GOTTHOLD, ed.: *Orgelchöräle . . . . des 18. Jahrhunderts, Das Erbe deutscher Musik*, ser. 1, ix (Leipzig, 1937).

FUSER, IRENEO, ed.: *Classici italiani dell'organo* (Padua, 1955).

GUILMANT, ALEXANDRE, ed.: *Concert historique d'orgue* (Mainz, n.d.).

—— *Liber Fratrum Cruciferorum Leodiensium, Archives des maîtres de l'orgue*, x (Paris, 1910).

HELLMANN, D. ed.: *Orgelwerke der Familie Bach* (Leipzig, 1967).

KELLER, HERMANN, ed.: *Achtzig Choralvorspiele deutscher Meister des 17. und 18. Jahrhunderts* (Leipzig, 1937).

KLEIN, JOHN, ed.: *The first four centuries of music for the organ from Dunstable to Bach (1370–1749)*, i–ii (New York, 1948).

MUSET, JOSEPH, ed.: *Early Spanish Organ Music* (New York, 1948).

NEARY, MARTIN, ed.: *Old French Organ Music*, i–ii (Oxford, 1978 and 1983).

PEDRELL, FELIPE, ed.: *Antología de organistas clásicos españoles*, i–ii (Madrid, 1905–8; 2nd ed., 1968).

RAUGEL, FÉLIX, ed.: *Les maîtres français de l'orgue aux XVIIe et XVIIIe siècles* (Paris, 1951).

REINBERGER, J., ed.: *Czech classics of organ music, Musica antiqua bohemica*, xii (Prague, 1953).

RUBIO, SAMUEL, ed.: *Organistas de la Real Capilla*, i (Madrid, 1973).

STRAUBE, KARL, ed.: *Alte Meister: eine Sammlung deutscher Orgelkompositionen aus dem XVII und XVIII Jahrhunderts* (Leipzig, 1904).

—— *Choralvorspiele alter Meister* (Leipzig, 1907).

TORCHI, LUIGI, ed.: *Composizioni per organo e cembalo, secoli XVI, XVII e XVIII, L'Arte musicale in Italia*, iii (Milan, *c*.1900).


(*b*) *Works by Individual Composers*

BACH, C. P. E.: *Organ Works*, ed. T. Fedtke, 2 vols. (Frankfurt, 1968).

BACH, J. B.: *Fugue for organ in F major*, ed. H. Riemann (Leipzig, n.d.).

BACH, J. S.: *Orgelwerke, Johann Sebastian Bachs Werke*, xv, xxv, xxxviii, xl Bach-Gesellschaft (Leipzig, 1867–93).

—— *Orgelwerke, Neue Ausgabe sämtlicher Werke, Ser. IV* (Leipzig, 1961–   ).

—— *The Art of Fugue*, ed. in open score by D. F. Tovey (London, 1931); ed. for organ by H. Walcha (Frankfurt, 1967).

BACH, W. F.: *Complete Works for Organ*, ed. E. P. Biggs and G. Weston (New York, 1947).

—— *Organ Works*, ed. T. Fedtke (New York, n.d.).

—— *Les Oeuvres pour orgue, Huit fugues sans pédale*, ed. N. Dufourcq, *et al.*, *Orgue et Liturgie*, xxxvii, xlv (Paris, 1958 and 1960).

BÖHM, G.: *Sämtliche Werke*, i–ii, *Klavier- und Orgelwerke*, ed. J. Wolgast, rev. G. Wolgast (Wiesbaden, 1952).

—— *Praeludium, Fugen und Toccaten*, ed. M. Seiffert, *Organum, 4 Reihe*, iv (Leipzig, 1925).

ČERNOHORSKÝ, B.: *7 fugues and a toccata*, ed. F. Michálek and V. Helfert, *Musica antiqua bohemica*, iii (Prague, 1949).

CLÉRAMBAULT, L.-N.: *Premier livre d'orgue*, ed. A. Guilmant, *Archives des maîtres de l'orgue*, iii (Paris, 1901).

—— *Premier livre d'orgue*, ed. N. Dufourcq (Paris, 1954).

—— *Organ works*, ed. J. Clokey, *Anthologia antiqua*, i (New York, *c*.1935).

CORRETTE, G.: *Messe du 8e Ton (1703)*, ed. L. Souberbielle (Paris, *c*.1960).

CORRETTE, M.: *Premier livre d'orgue et Nouveau livre de noëls*, ed. G. Beechey, *Recent Researches in the Music of the Baroque Era*, xviii (Madison, 1974).
—— *Nouveau livre de Noëls*, ed. N. Dufourcq, *et al.*, *Orgue et Liturgie*, lxxvii–lxxix (Paris, 1970–2).
COUPERIN, F.: *Pièces d'orgue*, ed. A. Guilmant, *Archives des maîtres de l'orgue*, vi (Paris, 1904).
—— *Musique d'orgue*, ed. P. Brunold, *Oeuvres complètes*, vi (Paris, 1932).
—— *Messe à l'Usage ordinaire des Paroisses*, ed. N. Dufourcq (Paris, c.1967).
DAGINCOUR, F.: *Organ music*, ed. L. Panel (Paris, 1956).
DANDRIEU, J.-F.: *Premier livre de pièces d'orgue*, ed. A. Guilmant, *Archives des maîtres de l'orgue*, vii (Paris, 1906; repr., 1971).
—— *Noëls*, ed. J. Bonfils, *L'Organiste Liturgique*, xii, xvi, xix–xx, xxii (Paris, 1952–5).
DANDRIEU, P.: *Noëls variés*, ed. R. Hugon (Paris, 1979).
DAQUIN, L.-C.: *Nouveau livre de Noëls*, ed. A. Guilmant and A. Pirro, *Archives des maîtres de l'orgue*, iii (Paris, 1901).
—— *Nouveau livre de Noëls*, ed. N. Dufourcq, *et al.*, *Orgue et Liturgie*, xxvii–xxviii (Paris, 1956).
—— *Nouveau livre de Noëls*, ed. C. Hogwood (London, 1984).
DU MAGE, P.: *Livre d'orgue*, ed. F. Raugel (Paris, c.1952).
FISCHER, J. C. F.: *Sämtliche Werke für Klavier und Orgel*, ed. E. von Werra (Leipzig, 1901; repr., 1965).
GERBER, H. N.: *Four Inventions*, ed. S. Jeans, *Early Organ Music*, xxv (London, 1975).
GREENE, M.: *Twelve Voluntarys*, ed. P. Williams (New York, 1969).
—— *Voluntaries and Suites for Organ and Harpsichord*, ed. G. Beechey, *Recent Researches in the Music of the Baroque Era*, xix (Madison, 1975).
GUILAIN, J. A.: *Pièces d'orgue pour le Magnificat*, ed. A. Guilmant and A. Pirro, *Archives des maîtres de l'orgue*, vii (Paris, 1906; repr., 1971).
KAUFFMANN, G. F.: *Harmonische Seelenlust*, ed. P. Pidoux (Kassel, 1951).
KELLNER, J. P.: *Ausgewählte Orgelwerke*, ed. G. Feder, *Die Orgel, II*, vii (Leipzig, 1958).
KOLB, C.: *Certamen Aonium*, ed. R. Walter, *Süddeutsche Orgelmeister des Barock*, v (Altötting, 1959).
KREBS, J. L.: *Ausgewählte Orgelwerke*, ed. K. Tittel, *Die Orgel, II*, xviii, xx, xxi, xxvi (Leipzig, 1963–75).
—— *Gesammt-Ausgabe der Tonstücke für die Orgel*, ed. C. Geissler (Magdeburg, 1847–9).
—— *Organ Works*, 2 vols., i, ed. W. Zöller; ii, ed. K. Tittel (Frankfurt, 1938 and 1974).
LOPEZ, M.: *Musica instrumental*, *Obres completes*, i– , ed. D. Pujol, *Mestres de l'Escolania de Montserrat*, iv/1, vi/1– (Montserrat, 1934; 1970– ).
MARCHAND, L.: *Pièces d'orgue*, ed. A. Guilmant, *Archives des maîtres de l'orgue*, iii, v (Paris, 1901 and 1904).
—— *L'oeuvre d'orgue édition intégrale*, ed. J. Bonfils (Paris, c.1970– ).
—— *L'Oeuvre d'orgue*, ed. A. Ponce, *L'Astrée, Collection de musique instrumentale classique* (Paris, 1972–4).
MARTINI, G.: *12 Sonate*, ed. M. Vitali (Milan, c.1927).
—— *6 Sonaten*, ed. L. Hoffmann-Erbrecht (Leipzig, 1954).
MUFFAT, G.: *Organ works*, ed. F. W. Riedel, *Die Orgel, II*, viii, x, xiii, xvi–xvii (Leipzig, 1958–61).
—— *72 Versetl und 12 Toccaten*, ed. G. Adler, *Denkmäler der Tonkunst in Österreich*, lviii (Jg. xxix(2) ), (Vienna, 1922).

MURSCHHAUSER, F. X.: *Gesammelte Werke für Klavier und Orgel*, ed. M. Seiffert, *Denkmäler der Tonkunst in Bayern*, xviii (Leipzig, 1917).
—— *Prototypon longo-breve organicum*, ed. R. Walter, *Süddeutsche Orgelmeister des Barock*, x (Altötting, 1969).
ROSEINGRAVE, T.: *Ten Organ Pieces*, ed. P. Williams (London, 1961).
SEGER, J.: *Organ works*, ed. J. Racek and V. Bělský, *Musica antiqua bohemica*, xii, li, lvi (Prague, 1953, 1961–2).
—— *Orgelwerke*, ed. R. Quoika, *Orgelwerke altböhmischer Meister*, ii (Wiesbaden, 1949).
SIMON, J.: *Leichte Praeludia und Fugen*, ed. (Mainz, 1964).
STANLEY, J.: *30 Organ Voluntaries, op. 5–7*; facs. ed. D. Vaughan (London, 1957); ed. in *Tallis to Wesley*, xxvii–xxix (New York and London, 1967).
TELEMANN, G. P.: *Orgelwerke*, ed. T. Fedtke (Kassel, 1964).
WALTHER, J. G.: *Gesammelte Werke für Orgel*, ed. M. Seiffert, *Denkmäler deutscher Tonkunst*, xxvi–xxvii (Leipzig, 1906).
—— *Ausgewählte Orgelwerke*, ed. H. Lohmann, 3 vols. (Wiesbaden, 1966).
ZACH, J.: *Organ works*, ed. O. Schmid, *Ausgewählte Orgelwerke altböhmischer Meister*, i (Berlin, c.1900).
—— *Orgelwerke*, ed. R. Quoika, *Orgelwerke altböhmischer Meister*, iii (Wiesbaden, 1948).
—— *Preludium e fuga*, ed. J. Racek, *Musica antiqua bohemica*, xii (Prague, 1953).
ZACHOW, F. W.: *Gesammtausgabe seiner sämmtlichen Orgel-compositionen*, i, ed. G. W. Körner (Erfurt and Leipzig, c.1850).
—— *Gesammelte Werke*, ed. M. Seiffert, *Denkmäler deutscher Tonkunst*, xxi–xxii (Leipzig, 1905).
—— *Choralvorspiele für Orgel*, ed. A. Adrio (Berlin, 1952).
—— *Gesammelte Werke für Tasteninstrumente*, ed. H. Lohmann (Wiesbaden, 1966).
—— *Chorale preludes*, ed. J. Bonfils, *L'Organiste Liturgique*, iii (Paris, 1950).
ZIPOLI, D.: *Sonate d'Intavolatura per organo e cimbalo*, ed. L. Tagliavini (Heidelberg, 1959); and ed. in *I classici della musica italiana*, xxxvi (Milan, 1919).

## (ii) Books and Articles

### (a) General

DOUGLASS, FENNER: *The Language of the French Classical Organ* (New Haven, 1969).
DUFOURCQ, NORBERT: *Esquisse d'une histoire de l'orgue en France* (Paris, 1935).
—— *La musique d'orgue française de Jehan Titelouze à Jehan Alain* (Paris, 1941; 2nd ed., 1949).
—— *Le Livre de l'orgue français 1589–1789* (Paris, 1969–    ).
DUNCAN, J. M.: 'A Glance at Some Silbermann Organs', *Musical Times*, lxvi (1925), pp. 342–3.
FROTSCHER, GOTTHOLD: *Geschichte des Orgel-Spiels und der Orgel-Komposition* (Berlin, 1935–6; enlarged 3rd ed., 1966).
JOHNSTONE, H. DIACK: 'An Unknown Book of Organ Voluntaries', *Musical Times*, cviii (1967), pp. 1003–7.
LUKAS, V.: *Orgel Musik Führer* (Stuttgart, 1967).
SCHÜNEMANN, GEORG: *Geschichte der Klaviermusik* (Hamburg, 1940; rev. H. Gerigk, 1953, 2nd ed., 1956).

Servières, Georges: *Documents inédits sur les organistes français des XVIIe et XVIIIe siècles* (Paris, 1924).

Valentin, Erich: *Die Entwicklung der Tokkata im 17 und 18 Jahrhundert* (Munich, 1930).

Werra, E. von: 'Beiträge zur Geschichte des katholischen Orgelspiels', *Kirchenmusikalisches Jahrbuch*, xii (1897), pp. 28–36.

### (b) Individual Composers

### J. S. Bach

Albrecht, Christoph: 'J. S. Bachs "Clavier Übung dritter Theil": Versuch einer Deutung', *Bach-Jahrbuch 1969*, lv, pp. 46–66.

Aldrich, Putnam: *Ornamentation in J. S. Bach's Organ Works* (New York, 1950; 2nd ed., 1969).

Arfken, Ernst: 'Zur Entstehungsgeschichte des Orgelbüchleins', *Bach-Jahrbuch 1966*, lii, pp. 41–58.

Boyd, Malcolm: *Bach* (London, 1983).

Dadelsen, Georg von: *Beiträge zur Chronologie der Werke Johann Sebastian Bachs, Tübinger Bach-Studien*, iv–v (Trossingen, 1958).

—— 'Zur Entstehung des Bachschen Orgelbüchleins', *Festschrift Friedrich Blume* (Kassel, 1963), pp. 74–9.

David, Hans T. and Mendel, Arthur: *The Bach Reader* (2nd ed., New York, 1966).

David, W.: *Joh. Seb. Bachs Orgeln* (Berlin, 1951).

Dietrich, Fritz: 'J. S. Bachs Orgelchoral und seine geschichtlichen Wurzeln', *Bach-Jahrbuch 1929*, xxvi, pp. 1–89.

Donington, Robert: *Tempo and Rhythm in Bach's Organ Music* (London, 1960).

Dufourcq, Norbert: *J. S. Bach, le maître de l'orgue* (Paris, 1948).

Emery, Walter: *Notes on Bach's Organ Works: a Companion to the Revised Edition* (London, 2 vols., 1953 and 1957).

Keller, Hermann: *Die Orgelwerke Bachs* (Leipzig, 1948; Eng trans., 1967).

Klotz, Hans: 'Bachs Orgeln und seine Orgelmusik', *Die Musikforschung*, iii (1950), pp. 189–203.

Leudtke, Hans: 'Zur Entstehung des Orgelbüchleins (1717)', *Bach-Jahrbuch 1919*, xvi, pp. 62–6.

Löffler, Hans: 'Die Schüler Joh. Seb. Bachs', *Bach-Jahrbuch 1953*, xl, pp. 5–28.

May, Ernest: 'Eine neue Quelle für J. S. Bachs einzeln überlieferten Orgelchoräle', *Bach-Jahrbuch 1974*, lx, pp. 98–103.

Meyer, Ulrich: 'Zur Einordnung von J. S. Bachs einzeln überlieferten Orgelchorälen', *Bach-Jahrbuch 1974*, lx, pp. 75–89.

Schrammek, Winfried: 'Die musikgeschichtliche Stellung der Orgeltriosonaten von Joh. Seb. Bach', *Bach-Jahrbuch 1954*, xli, pp. 7–28.

Sietz, Reinhold: 'Die Orgelkompositionen des Schülerkreises um Johann Sebastian Bach', *Bach-Jahrbuch 1935*, xxxii, pp. 33–96.

Smend, Friedrich: 'Bachs Kanonwerk über "Von Himmel hoch da komm ich her" ', *Bach-Jahrbuch 1933*, xxx, pp. 1–29.

Taylor, Stainton de B.: *The Chorale Preludes of J. S. Bach* (London, 1942).

Terry, Charles Sanford: *Bach's Chorales* (Cambridge, 1915–21).

Tittel, Karl: 'Welche unter Bachs Namen geführten Orgelwerke sind Johann Tobias bzw. Johann Ludwig Krebs zuzuschreiben?', *Bach-Jahrbuch 1966*, lii, pp. 102–37.

Vogelsänger, Siegfried: 'Zur Herkunft der kontrapunktischen Motive in J. S. Bachs "Orgelbüchlein" (BWV 599–644)', *Bach-Jahrbuch 1972*, lviii, pp. 118–31.

WILLIAMS, PETER: 'BWV 565: A Toccata in D minor for Organ by J. S. Bach?', *Early Music*, ix (1981), pp. 330–7.

—— 'The Musical Aims of J. S. Bach's "Clavierübung III" ', *Source Materials and the Interpretation of Music: a Memorial Volume to Thurston Dart* (London, 1981), pp. 259–78.

—— *The Organ Music of J. S. Bach*, i–iii (Cambridge, 1980–4).

### Böhm

MÜLLER-BUSCHER, HENNING: *Studien zu den Choralbearbeitungen Georg Böhms* (Augsburg, 1972).

SCHUNEMAN, R. A.: 'The Organ Chorales of Georg Böhm', *The Diapason*, lxi (1970).

### Casini

GIACHIN, G.: 'I "Pensieri per l'organo" di Giovanni M. Casini', *Rivista musicale italiana*, x (1976).

### Couperin

CAUCHIE, MAURICE: *Thematic Index of the Works of François Couperin* (Monaco, 1949).

CITRON, PIERRE: *Couperin* (Paris, 1969).

MELLERS, WILFRID: *François Couperin and the French Classical Tradition* (London, 1950; repr., 1968).

SCHEIBERT, BEVERLY: 'Couperin's Masses, the Italians and inégalité', *Musical Times*, cxxiii (1982), pp. 499–503.

TESSIER, ANDRÉ: *Couperin* (Paris, 1926).

—— 'Un exemplaire original des pièces d'orgue de Couperin', *Revue de musicologie*, x (1929), pp. 109–17.

TIERSOT, JULIEN: *Les Couperins* (Paris, 1926).

### J.-F. Dandrieu

BONFILS, J.: 'Les noëls de Pierre et Jean-François Dandrieu', *L'orgue*, lxxxiii (1957).

### P. Dandrieu

BONFILS, J.: 'Les noëls de Pierre et Jean-François Dandrieu', *L'orgue*, lxxxiii (1957).

HUGON, ROGER, FRANÇOIS-SAPPEY, BRIGITTE and DUFOURCQ, NORBERT: 'Le Livre de Noëls de Pierre Dandrieu. Une énigme', *Recherches sur la musique française classique*, xix (1979), pp. 103–94.

### Daquin

BEECHEY, GWILYM: 'Daquin and his Keyboard Music', *The Organ*, lii (1973), pp. 184–91.

### Du Mage

RAUGEL, FÉLIX: Preface to edition of *Livre d'orgue* (Paris, 1952).

—— 'Notes sur Pierre Du Mage', *Revue de musicologie*, xlv (1960), pp. 85–6.

### Krebs

MARIGOLD, W. G.: 'The Preludes and Fugues of J. L. Krebs', *Musical Opinion*, xc (1967), p. 337.

TITTEL, KARL: 'Die Choralbearbeitungen für Orgel von Johann Ludwig Krebs', *Festschrift Hans Engel* (Kassel, 1964), pp. 406–27.

### Marchand

SHARP, GEOFFREY B.: 'Louis Marchand, 1669–1732: a Forgotten Virtuoso', *Musical Times*, cx (1969), pp. 1134–7.

**Martini**
BROFSKY, HOWARD: 'The Keyboard Sonatas of Padre Martini', *Quadrivium*, viii (1967), pp. 63–73.

**Muffat**
KNÖLL, J. H.: *Die Klavier- und Orgelwerke Theophile Muffats* (Diss., Vienna, 1916).

**Stanley**
BOYD, MALCOLM: 'John Stanley's Voluntaries', *Musical Times*, cxv (1974), pp. 598–601.
COOPER, BARRY: 'New Light on John Stanley's Organ Music', *Proceedings of the Royal Musical Association*, ci (1974–5), pp. 101–6.

**Telemann**
RUHNKE, MARTIN, ed.: *Telemann-Werkverzeichnis: Instrumentalwerke*, i (Kassel, 1984).

**Walther**
BRODDE, OTTO: *Johann Gottfried Walther: Leben und Werk* (Kassel, 1937).

**Zachow**
THOMAS, GÜNTER: *Friedrich Wilhelm Zachow* (Regensburg, 1966).

# INDEX

Compiled by DAVID BLACKWELL

Abbado, M., 395n[38], 473n[30], 482n[55]
Abel, Christian Ferdinand, 477
Abel, Clamor Heinrich, 406n[63], 417
Abraham, Gerald
  ed., *Handel: a Symposium*, 250n[45]
Addison, Joseph (poet), 15
Adler, Guido, 286n[86], 499n[94], 551n[88], 552, 554, 556n[98], 620n[40]
  ed., *Handbuch der Musikgeschichte*, 190n[4], 295n[97], 302
*Affektenlehre*, 366
Agen, Archives Départementales de Lot-et-Garonne, 367n[77]
Agrell, Johan Joachim, 363, 626
Aguilera de Heredia, Sebastian
  Keyboard music, 528, 529–30 (Ex. 297(i)), 536
a Kempis, Nicolaus, 195
  Chamber music, 428 (Ex. 249), 429, 470
Alain, Olivier, 629n[58]
Albergati, Pirro Conte d', 105, 390
Albert, Heinrich
  *Arien*, 130, **131–2** (Ex. 49), 134
Alberti, Giuseppe Matteo, 355, 370
Albertino, 390
Albicastro, Henrico (Heinrich Weissenburg), 280, 424, 499
Albinoni, Tomaso, 482
  Chamber music, 390
  Concertos, 303, 351–2, 370
  Instrumental music, 249
Albisi, 390
Albrici, Vincenzo, 191
  Chamber music, 384 (Ex. 193), 389n[15], 420
Alcock, John, 274
Alexander VIII Ottoboni, Pope, 110
Algarotti, F.
  *Saggio sopra l'Opera in musica*, 487n[65]
Allegri, Giuseppe, 389
Allsop, Peter, 468n[13]

Altnikol, Johann Christoph, 643
Ammerbach, Elias Nicolaus, 560n[107]
Ancelet
  *Observations sur la musique . . .*, 300
Anders, Hendrik, 429
Anet, Jean-Baptiste, 454
Anet, Jean-Jacques-Baptiste, 482, 495
Anglès, H., 531, 536 and nn[50],[51], 656 and n[10]
Anne, Queen, 31
Anthony, James R., 182n[126]
  *French Baroque Music*, 166n[103], 172, 366n[75]
Apel, Willi, 529nn[40],[41], 560n[107], 561n[111], 563n[120], 570n[130], 576n[155]
  *The History of Keyboard Music to 1700*, 507n[3], 516, 532n[46], 536n[51], 546n[79], 548n[83], 550 and n[36], 552n[91], 555n[95], 556n[98], 558, 562, 571n[132], 584n[174]
  *see also* Davison, Archibald T.
Arbuthnot, John (librettist), 27
Arcadelt, Jacques, 506, 515
Ariosti, Attilio, 390, 399, 444
Arkwright, Geoffrey E. P., 95n[62]
Arne, Thomas Augustine
  Dramatic works
    *Comus*, 57
    *Love in a Village*, 88
  Harpsichord music, 625–6
  Oratorio
    *Judith*, **92–6** (Ex. 35)
  Songs, 147, **151–4** (Ex. 61)
Arnold, W. T.
  ed., *An Essay of Dramatic Poesy*, 10n[22]
Arresti, Floriano, 526, 653
Arresti, Giulio Cesare, 105, 389, 523, 526, 527n[36]
Ashbee, Andrew, 433n[117]
Attaingnant, Pierre, 506
Aubert, Jacques, 367, 368, 453, 494–5
Aubert, P., 593n[6]
Aufschnaiter, Benedict Anton, 232, 417

Avison, Charles, 452–3, 491
Avitrano, 390

Babell, William, 274, 452, 492, 626
Bach, Carl Philipp Emanuel, 134, 301, 504
    on J. S. Bach, 639, 649, 668–9
    Chamber music, 456, 459
    Keyboard concertos, 362
    Organ music, 693
Bach, Johann Bernhard, 240, 671
Bach, Johann Christian, 260, 297
    Concertos, 362, 369
Bach, Johann Christoph, 675
Bach, Johann Jakob, 631
Bach, Johann Ludwig, 240
Bach, Johann Sebastian, 234, 236, 290, 296,
        443, 501, 504, 652
    and Arne, 625
        J.-F. Dandrieu, 662
        Dieupart, 623
        Fasch, 244
        J. C. F. Fischer, 640
        J. G. Walther, 672
    compared with
        F. Couperin, 600, 602, 649
        Eberlin, 667
        Handel, 616, 617, 644
        Gottlieb Muffat, 622
        D. Scarlatti, 613–14, 631, 642,
            649
    influenced by
        Böhm, 570, 668–9, 670, 675, 676, 679,
            684
        Buxtehude, 682, 684, 687, 688, 690
        Corelli, 287, 686
        Frescobaldi, 686
        Froberger, 570
        Lully, 251, 445
        Marais, 432
        Pachelbel, 570, 677, 678–9, 683, 686,
            687
        A. Scarlatti, 527, 528
        Vivaldi, 320, 356–7, 360
        J. G. Walther, 680
        Italian music, 271
        Popular music, 449 (Ex. 260)
    attacked by Mattheson and Scheibe, 450
    self-borrowing, 286–7, 470, 477
    use of modes, 265, 512
    Brandenburg Concertos, 233, 239, 263–8
        (Exx. 114–19), 280, 281–4 (Exx.
        126–30), 286–7, 356, 357, 362, 634
    Cantatas, 233, 286–7
        Orchestra in, 286–9 (Ex. 131)
        Secular, 125, 130
    Chamber music
        Musicalisches Opfer, Das, 454, 456, 646
        Sonatas
            Flute, 452, 502, 503
            Gamba, 452, 453, 470, 477
            Violin, 445, 449 (Ex. 260), 459, 462,
                502, 503
            Trio sonatas, 470
        Suites
            Cello, 503
            Violin, 465, 503
    Concertos, 233, 320, 327, 356–62, 372
        Harpsichord, 357–8
        Triple Concerto (flute, violin,
            harpsichord), 358
        Violin, 320
            in A minor, 357, 358–60 (Ex. 182)
            in E major, 357, 360–2 (Exx. 183–4)
            double violin, 357, 358
    Harpsichord music, 519, 543
        Anna Magdalena Bach's
            Clavierbüchlein, 639
        Clavier-Büchlein vor W. F. Bach, 638,
            639
        Concertos, transcriptions, 356–7, 360,
            449
        Inventions, 638, 639, 640, 677
        Italian Concerto, 271n[70], 363, 449, 617,
            624, 634, 636, 639, 641
        Kunst der Fuge, Die, 290, 453, 646–9,
            (Exx. 378–80), 654
        Miscellaneous harpsichord works
            Capriccio in B flat, 631, 639
            Chromatic Fantasia and Fugue, 527,
                528, 631–2, 639
            Fantasia and Fugue (BWV 904),
                632–3 (Ex. 366)
            Fantasia and Fugue (BWV 944), 632
                (Ex. 365)
            Prelude and Fugue (BWV 894), 358
            Suites, 637–8
            Toccatas, 565, 633–4 (Ex. 367), 639
        Musicalisches Opfer, Das, 646 (see also
            454, 456)
        Overture nach Französischer Art, 449,
            569, 624, 634, 635 (Ex. 368), 639
        Partitas, 555n[95], 568–9, 570, 628, 634–5,
            636, 637, 639, 643
        Suites, 525, 570, 643
            English, 623, 634, 635–7 (Exx.
                369–70), 639
            French, 555n[95], 637, 639, 640, 643
        Variations
            'Aria variata', 627–8 (Ex. 360)
            'Goldberg', 526, 628–31 (Exx.
                362–4), 639
            Sarabande con Partite, 628 (Ex. 361)
        Wohltemperirte Clavier, Das, 569, 626,
            633, 636, 638, 639–46 (Exx. 371–7),
            647, 648, 667, 677
    Oratorios, 233
        'Christmas Oratorio', 287
    Orchestral Suites, 233, 240, 250–6 (Exx.
        105–12), 287
    Organ music, 519, 543, 658, 692, 693

Chorale preludes, 512, 560n[109], 563, 670–1 (Ex. 396), **676–83** (Exx. 402–4)
Concertos, transcriptions, 357
Fugues, 685–7 (Ex. 405)
Preludes, Fantasias, and Toccatas, 565, 568, 631, 632, 683–4, **687–91** (Exx. 406, 408)
Trio sonatas, 358, 683, 690
Passions, 233
Bach, Wilhelm Friedemann, 692
Bacilly, Bénigne de
as composer (songs), **162–4** (Ex. 64), 167, 168, 171
as poet, 160, 161
*L'Art de bien chanter,* 155, 156, 158, 160, 180
Badia, Carlo Agostino, 257
Baehr, Joh., 405
Baehr, Samuel, 424
Baentz, Johann Andreas, 424
Bahr, Johan, 573n[150]
Baïf, Jean-Antoine de, 155n[94]
Baldassini, Ludovico, 390, 396
Balducci, Francesco, 98
Ballard, (publishers), 158, 161, 165, 167, 168 and n[109], 169–70, 172
Baltzar, Thomas, 489
Banchieri, Adriano, 191, 406n[63]
*L'Organo suonarino,* 511n[9]
Bangert, Emilius, 568n[129]
Banister, John, 235, 250, 377, 437, 441, 489
Banwart, Jakob, 424
Barbella, Emanuele, 491
Barberini, Francesco and Antonio (cardinals), 98
Barbour, J. Murray, 639n[75]
Barrett, John, 585n[177], 587, 588n[184]
Barsanti, Francesco, 260
Concerti grossi, 274
Bartlett, Ian, 78n[54]
Bartoli, *see* Bertali, Antonio
Basel, Universitätsbibl., 576n[155]
Bassani, Giovanni Battista, 390, 480, 526, 653
Batiste, 167
Battiferri, Luigi, 389, 526
Battistin (J.-B. Stuck), 181, 182
Baum, R., 568n[129]
Bazea, Juan, 536
Beauchamp, Charles-Louis
*Les Fâcheux,* overture, 223 (Ex. 98)
Beck, Johann Heinrich, 417
Beck, Johann Philipp, 417
Becker, Dietrich, 417, 422
Beckmann, Gustav, 500n[95]
*Das Violinspiel in Deutschland vor 1700,* 478n[43], 479n[44], 501n[96], 502n[97]
Beechey, Gwilym, 662n[27], 664n[30]
Beethoven, Ludwig van, 246, 363, 368
Belgrot, Olav, 425

Belisi, 390
Bencini, Giuseppe
Organ music, 653–4 (Ex. 381)
Benda, František (Franz), 504
Benedictus a Sancto Josepho
Chamber music, 386 (Ex. 200), 427, 429
Benigni, Domenico, 98
Benserade, Isaac de, 161
Berff, Georg, 575
Bergmann, Walter, 448n[150]
Bergonzi, Giuseppe, 269
Berlin
Deutsche Staatsbibliothek, 561n[111], 576, 639n[71]
Sing-Akademie, 299n[102]
Berlioz, Hector, 246
Bernabei, Giuseppe Antonio, 390, 400
Vocal duets, **121–3** (Ex. 46)
Bernardi, Bartolomeo, 390, 397n[53]
Bernhard, Christoph
*Von der Singe-Kunst oder Manier,* 97
Bernier, Nicolas, 181, 182
Bernoulli, Eduard, 131n[73]
Bertali (Bartoli), Antonio
Chamber music, 389 and n[15], 400, 401, 406
*Sonate,* 191, 343, 344
Berthod, Father, 167
Besard, Jean-Baptiste, 537
Besseler, Heinrich, 362
Best, Terence, 502n[99]
Bevan, Maurice, 19n[40]
Bèze, Théodore de, 3
Bianchi, Giovanni, 390
Bianchi, Lino, 101n[12]
Biber, Heinrich Ignaz Franz von, 408, 498
Chamber music, 387, 401, 403–4 (Ex. 219), 405–6
Violin music, 465, 479, **499–500** (Ex. 289)
Biggs, E. Power, 692n[72]
Birmingham, Barber Institute, 11n[28]
Bishop, (poet), 15
Blainville, Charles-Henri de, 275 (Ex. 121(ii))
Blamont, Colin de, 181, 182
Blancrocher, (lutenist), 540, 551, 555–6
Blavet, Michel, 368
Solo sonatas, 493–4 (Ex. 284)
Bleyer, Georg, 231, 417
Bleyer, Nicolaus, 498
Blow, John
and H. Purcell, 16, 18–20 *passim*
Chamber music, 441
Dialogue
'A Dialogue between Dives and Abraham', 4–7 (Ex. 2)
Instrumental music, 439
Keyboard music
Harpsichord, 578, 584–6 (Ex. 313)
Organ, 578, 588–9
Odes, 7, 8n[20], **12–21**

Blow, John—*cont.*
　'Appear, appear in all thy pomp', **20–1**
　　(Ex. 8)
　'Awake, awake my lyre', 14
　'Dread Sir, the Prince of Light', 12
　'Great Janus, tho', the Festival be thine',
　　12
　'Great Sir, the joy of all our hearts',
　　**16–17** (Exx. 5–6)
　'The Birth of Jove', 12
　'The New Year is Begun', 14
　'Yee sons of Phoebus', 8n[20]
　Songs, 146
　Theatre music
　*Venus and Adonis*, overture, 224
Blume, Friedrich
　*Protestant Church Music,* 560n[108]
Boccaletti, 390
Boccherini, Luigi, 376
Boësset, Antoine
　*Airs,* 156 (Ex. 62(i)), 160
Boësset, Jean-Baptiste, 161, 167, 170
Bohemus, Eusebius, 407
Böhm, Georg
　influence on J. S. Bach, 570, 668–9, 670,
　　675, 676, 679, 684
　Harpsichord music, 543, 568, 569, 570
　Organ music, 559, **668–71,** (Exx. 393–5),
　　672, 680
Boismortier, Joseph Bodin de, 182
　Concertos, 367–8
Bologna, 389n[15], 393n[31]
　San Petronio, 393n[30], 397nn[51,52], 399n[58]
Bonaventura, 389
Bonfils, Jean, 540n[65], 546n[79], 549n[84], 660n[19],
　662n[24]
Bonn, Institute of Musicology, 122nn[47,48]
Bononcini, Antonio Maria, 400
Bononcini, Giovanni, 32, 257, 260, 343,
　389n[15]
Bononcini, Giovanni Battista, 390, 397, 399
Bononcini, Giovanni Maria
　Cantatas, 106
　Chamber music, 389 and n[15], 390, 392, 395
　Violin sonatas, 473, 479
Bonporti, Francesco Antonio, 269, 280–1,
　370
Borri, Giovanni Battista, 390
Bossi, Enrico, 653
Botstiber, Hugo, 556n[98], 562n[116]
　*Geschichte der Ouvertüre,* 218n[23],
　　224nn[33,34], 225n[37], 226–7, 295n[97]
Bourgeois, Thomas-Louis, 181
Boyce, William, 65, 70
　Choral music
　　*David's Lamentation . . . ,* **70–4** (Ex. 26)
　　*Solomon,* **78–82** (Exx. 29–30)
　Keyboard music, 589
　Orchestral music
　　*Eight Symphonies,* 79

Overtures, 260
Songs, 151
Boyd, Malcolm, 106n[26]
Boyden, David D., 276n[77], 491nn[76,77]
Boyer, Jean, 168
Boyvin, Jacques
　Organ works, 544 and n[75], 546, 549n[84]
Brade, William, 464, 489, 498
　Suites, 193, **227–8** (Ex. 100)
Brady, Nicholas (poet), 15
Breig, Werner
　*Die Orgelwerke von Heinrich
　　Scheidemann,* 561n[110]
Bremner, Robert, 300
Brereton, Thomas, 27
Brescianello, Giuseppe, 370
Brett, Philip, 7n[18]
Brevi, Giovanni Battista, 390
Brewer, Thomas, 436
Briegel, Wolfgang Carl, 413
Brioschi, Antonio, 300
Britton, Thomas, 235, 377, 437
Brno, Hudební Archiv, 573n[149]
Brockes, Barthold Heinrich (librettist), 26
Brockhuijzen, G. H., 575
Broeckhuisen, Barend, 575
Broennemüller, Elias, 428, 429
Brofsky, Howard, 367n[76]
Brossard, Sebastian de, 166n[105], 170, 408,
　432
Brown, Howard Mayer
　*Instrumental Music Printed Before 1600,*
　　513n[14]
Brown, William, 576
Bruce, Robert J., 78n[54]
Bruna, Pablo, 530n[43]
Brunold, Paul, 538n[57], 539nn[59,61],
　550n[87], 591n[3], 592nn[4,5], 623n[42],
　658n[17]
Brussels, Bibl. Royale, 576n[156]
Bryne (Bryan), Albert, 582, 583, 589
Buch, Hans-Joachim, 383n[7]
Buchner, Philipp Friedrich, 499
　Chamber music, **414–15** (Exx. 231–3), 422
Budapest, National Library, 572n[145]
Buffardin, Pierre-Gabriel, 368
Bukofzer, Manfred F.
　*Music in the Baroque Era,* 174, 249, 263,
　　293, 299, 302, 307, 313n[12], 537n[54]
Bull, John, 576, 578, 579, 580, 583
Bullen, A. H.
　ed., *The Works of Thomas Nabbes,* 10n[24]
Buonamente, Giovanni Battista, 470, 474
Buonamici, Giuseppe, 605n[24]
Buoni, Giorgio, 390
Buono, Gioanpietro (Giovanni Pietro) del,
　518
Burney, Dr. Charles, 26, 32–3, 101, 138,
　　373, 504, 664, 693
　*General History of Music, A,* 2, 374, 376,

481n[50], 484, 485, 488, 489–90, 491, 492n[79], 616
*The Present State of Music in France and Italy*, 239
Burrows, David, 102n[15], 103n[17]
Burrows, Donald, 50, 83n[56]
Bustijn, Pieter, 575
Buti, Francesco, 98
Butler, Charles, 464
Butler, G. G., 526n[35]
Büttner, Horst, 245nn[30],[32]
  *Das Konzert in den Orchestersuiten G. P. Telemanns*, 239n[17], 244n[29], 245nn[30–2], 246 and nn[33],[34]
Buttstedt, Johann Heinrich, 671, 681
Buxtehude, Dietrich, 287, 573, 668, 676
  influence on J. S. Bach, 682, 684, 687, 688, 690
  Chamber music, 422
    *Sonata con molti violini. . .*, 378
  Clavier music, 568, 569
  Organ music
    Chorales, 559, 562, 563–4, 682
    Preludes, 565, 568, 686, 687, 688 (Ex. 407), 689, 690
    Toccatas, **565–7** (Exx. 308–9)
Bydgoszcz, Archiwum Wojewódzkie, 571n[136]
Byrd, William, 515, 578, 579

Cabanilles, Juan Bautista José
  Keyboard music, 528, **531–6** (Exx. 298–300), 656, 657
Cabezón, Antonio de, 528, 531
Cabezón, Hernando de, 528
Caccini, Francesca
  *La Liberazione di Ruggiero. . .*, overture, 218
Caccini, Giulio, 124, 155n[94], 159, 537
Caffi, Francesco
  *Storia della musica sacra . . .*, 468n[12]
Caix d'Hervelois, Louis de, 476
Caldara, Antonio, 286, 390, 454, 456
Caluori, Eleanor, 99n[7]
Cambefort, Jean de, 160
Cambert, Robert, 224
Cambridge, Fitzwilliam Museum, 317n[14]
Cameron, John, 493
'Camphuysen' manuscript, 575
Campra, André, 257, 258
  *Airs*, **170–1** (Ex. 68), 174, 182
  Stage works
    *L'Orfeo dell' inferni* overture (in *Le Carnaval de Venise*), 226
  Suites, 241
Carbonelli, Giovanni Stefano, 482
Carew, Thomas (poet), 137
Carey, Henry
  Songs, **149–50**
Carissimi, Giacomo

Cantatas, 99, **100–2** (Ex. 37), 106, 125, 172
  Oratorios, 25
Carleton, Nicholas, 579
Caroline, Queen, 54
Caselli, A. B., 607n[28]
Casini, Giovanni Maria
  Organ music, 653, 654 (Ex. 382)
Castro, 390
Castrucci, Pietro, 274
  Violin music, 482, 489, 492
Caswell, Austin B.
  *A Commentary upon the Art of Proper Singing*, 155n[94]
Cato, Diomedes, 571
Cauchie, Maurice, 431n[115], 593nn[8],[9], 596
Cavalieri, Emilio de'
  *Rappresentazione di Anima e di Corpo*, 4
Cavalli, Francesco
  Cantatas, 103
  Chamber music, 388 (Ex. 206), 390–1, 394 (Ex. 211), 400
  Operas, *sinfonie*, 218, **219–20**
    *Ercole amante*, 220
    *Giasone*, 344
    *Xerse*, 220, 222, 223
Cavazzoni, Girolamo, 511
Cazzati, Maurizio
  Chamber music, 389, 390, 392, 393, 397
  *Duetti*, 121n[45]
  Violin sonatas, 465, 479–180
Celcius, Johan, 425
Cellier, A., 431n[112]
Cerf, Léon
  ed., *Les Historiettes*, 154n[92]
Černohorský, Bohuslav, 667–8
Cesti, Antonio, 400
  Cantatas, **102–3** (Ex. 38)
  Opera
    *Disgrazie d'Amore*, overture, 224
Chambonnières, Jacques Champion de, 541, 551, 580n[166], 583
  Harpsichord suites, 473, 525, **538–40,** 543, 582, 590 (Ex. 315), 594
Chancy, François de, 155, 168
Charles VI, Emperor, 256n[50], 284, 487, 496
Charles I, King, 137, 579, 580
Charles II, King, 10, 15, 25, 378, 437, 442
Charles VI, King of Bohemia, 237
Charles XII, King of Sweden, 631
Charpentier, Marc-Antoine, 167, 172, 286, 432
Charteris, Richard, 468n[16]; 474n[31]
Chaumont, Lambert, 544n[75]
Chesterfield, 652
Chigi, Fabio (cardinal), 98
Christina, Queen of Sweden, 197
Chrysander, Friedrich
  ed. Handel's works, 22n[42], 83n[56], 110nn[31],[32], 113nn[35–7], 123n[50], 362nn[63],[64]

Chybiński, Adolf, 409n[72], 410[73], 572
Clari, Giovanni Carlo Maria, 91
    Vocal duets, **123**
Clark, A.
    *The Life and Times of Anthony à Wood*,
        489n[73]
Clark, Jane, 594n[11], 597n[15], 600n[16], 608n[29]
Clarke, Jeremiah, 15, 21, 585n[177], 587
Clausen, Hans Dieter
    *Händels Direktionspartituren*, 83n[56]
Clérambault, Louis-Nicolas
    Cantatas, 182
    Harpsichord music, 591–2 (Ex. 317)
    Organ music, 661, 662, 693
Coelho, Manuel Rodrigues, 528
Colasse, Pascal, 241, 258
Coleman, Charles, 435, 437, 585n[177]
    Divisions, 464–5 (Ex. 268)
Colombi, Giuseppe, 389, 390, 395
Colonna, Giovanni Paolo, 105, 526
*Concert Spirituel*, 173, 235, 236
Congreve, William (poet), 151
Constantyn, Louis, 429
Conti, Francesco, 237
    Opera
        *Pallade trionfante*, overture, **295–6**
            (Exx. 138–40)
Cooke, Benjamin (publisher), 272n[72]
Cooke, Henry
    Odes, 11, 13, 14 and n[33], 17
Cooper, Barry, 582n[172], 587n[180]
Copenhagen, Kon. Bibl., 573n[150]
Coprario, John, 468, 474
Corbett, William, 274
Corelli, Arcangelo, 178, 197, 250, 299, 303,
        445, 446, 485, 524, 661
    compared with Stradella, 215–6
    influence on
        J. S. Bach, 287, 686
        Leclair, 497n[85]
        Georg Muffat, 206, 210, 216
        Tartini, 374
        Vivaldi, 482
        English composers, 272, 368, 481–2, 489
    pupils, 369, 490, 493n[82], 495, 496
    Concerti grossi, 206, **210–14** (Exx. 86–93),
        215–16, 217, 261, 262, 268–9, 275, 276,
        318, 367
    Trio sonatas, 196, 390, **397–9** (Exx.
        215–16), 400, 439
    Violin sonatas, 459, 462, 465, 468, **480–2**,
        486, 487, 497, 519, 525, 526
Corli, Gian-Rinaldo, 487
Corneille, Pierre, 161
Cornet, Pieter, 576
Correa de Arauxo, Francisco, 528
Corrette, Michel, 363, 368, 662
Cortevi, Raphael, 441
Corvinus, Jakob, 425
Cosyn, Benjamin, 579, 588

Couperin, François, 173, 431, 476, 494, 497
    and H. Purcell, 659
    *Airs*, 170n[110], 171
    Chamber music, 443, 445–6, 454
        *L'Apothéose de Corelli*, 445
        *L'Apothéose de Lully*, 446
    Keyboard music, 536
        Harpsichord, 170n[110], 538, **593–602**
            (Exx. 319–27), 623, 627, 634, 649
        Organ, 544n[75], 548, **550–1**, **658–9** Exx.
            386–7), 660
Couperin, Louis, 540, 551
    Harpsichord music, 536, 537, **538–40** (Ex.
        301), 556, 593, 602
    Organ music, 536, 544n[75], 546
Courbois, Philippe, 181
Courtivill, Raphael, 587
Cousser, *see* Kusser
Cowley, Abraham (poet), 141, 145, 146
Cracow
    Bibl. Jagiełłońska, 571n[138]
    Bibl. Polskiej Akademii Nauk, 570n[131]
Crecqui, Count of, 154
Crellen, Peter
    *The Modern Musick Master*, 491n[76]
Crescimbeni, Giovanni Maria de, 97
Croci, Antonio, 523
Croft, William, 31
    Keyboard music, 578, 584, **586–7** (Ex.
        314), 589, 663
    Songs, 147
Crome, Robert, 489
Cromwell, Oliver, 579
Croxall, Rev. Samuel, 78
Crussard, Claude
    *Marc-Antoine Charpentier*, 172n[114]
Cudworth, C. L., 369n[80]
Cummings, William H.
    *Purcell*, 14n[33]
Cupis de Camargo, Jean-Baptiste, 368
Curtis, Alan, 518n[26], 539nn[59, 61], 540nn[62–4],
        575nn[152, 153], 581n[169]
    *Sweelinck's Keyboard Music*, 512n[12]
Cutts, J. P., 135n[79]
Cyr, Mary, 183n[127]

Dach, Simon, 132
Dadelsen, Georg von, 637n[64], 677n[51]
    *Beiträge zur Chronologie der Werke J. S.*
        *Bachs*, 677n[53]
Dagincour, François
    Harpsichord music, 591 (Ex. 316), 592
Dall' Abaco, Evaristo Felice, 370, 459
    Orchestral music, **249,** 271
    Violin sonatas, **483–4** (Ex. 279)
D'Ambruis, Honoré, 167
Danchet, Antoine, 181
Danckert, Werner, 624n[49]
Dandrieu, Jean-François, 432
    Harpsichord music, 536, 592–3

Organ music, 536, 550, **661–2** (Ex. 390), 693

Dandrieu, Pierre, 536
  Organ works, 536, 550, 662

d'Anglebert, Jean-Henri
  Keyboard music, 536, 537, **540–3** (Exx. 302–3), 544n[75], 582

Danican-Philidor, Anne, 235

d'Apligny, Pileur
  *Traité sur la Musique,* 366

Daquin, Louis-Claude, 497, 592
  Organ music, 550, 662

Daquin de Chateaulyon, P.-L., 182n[123], 476

d'Ardespin, Melchior, 401, 454

Darmstadt, Hessische Landesbibliothek 245nn[30–32], 246nn[33,34], 248nn[41,42]

Dart, Thurston, 439n[131], 539n[59], 540n[64], 573n[150], 576n[155], 581n[167], 582nn[171,173], 584n[174], 588n[183], 591n[3], 592n[4], 593n[8]

David, Hans T.
  *J. S. Bach's 'Musical Offering' . . .,* 646n[84]

David, Hans T., and Arthur Mendel
  *The Bach Reader,* 256n[47], 357n[57], 635n[62], 637n[64], 639n[74], 643n[81], 649n[91], 669n[43]

Davison, Archibald T., and W. Apel
  *Historical Anthology of Music,* ii, 99n[7], 131n[73], 132n[74], 134n[75], 195n[10], 225n[37], 473n[26], 480n[46], 539n[59], 564nn[124,125], 568n[129], 640n[78]

Daw, Stephen, 643n[80]

Dawes, Frank, 579n[160], 581n[168], 589n[187]

Dean, Thomas, 481

Dean, Winton
  *Handel's Dramatic Oratorios and Masques,* 1, 2, 34n[48], 92n[61]

Dean-Smith, Margaret, 411n[77]

Deering, Richard, 576

Defesch, William
  *Judith,* **35–7** (Ex. 11), 65

degli Antoni, Giovanni Battista, 526

degli Antoni, Pietro, 389, 390, 480, 526

De Lange, S., 557n[102]

De La Salle, 160

Della Ciaja, Azzolino Bernardino
  Harpsichord music, 604, **605–6** (Ex. 332), 626
  Organ music, 653

Demantius, Christoph, 406

Dent, Edward J., 109n[30], 224

Derosier, Nicolas, 428–9

Desmarets, Henry, 241

Destouches, André Cardinal, 182, 241, 257

Deutsch, Otto Erich
  *Handel: a Documentary Biography,* 88n[57], 91n[58], 92nn[59,60], 250n[46]

Diego de Torrijos, 530n[43]

Diessener, Gerhard, 585n[177]
  Chamber music, 379, 383, 387 (Ex. 205), **416–17** (Ex. 235), **422–4** (Exx. 243–5), 429

Dietrich, Fritz, 561n[111]
  *Geschichte des deutschen Orgelchorals im 17. Jahrhundert,* 571n[132]

Dieupart, Charles, 449, 482, 623, 635n[62], 636 (Ex. 369(i))

Diruta, Girolamo, 572

Dittersdorf, Carl Ditters von, 237

Doderer, Gerhard, 526n[35]
  *Orgelmusik und Orgelbau im Portugal des 17. Jahrhunderts. . .,* 528n[39]

Dolar (Tolar), Jan, 407, 408

Donington, Robert, 125n[56]

Dounias, Minos
  *Die Violinkonzerte Giuseppe Tartinis. . .,* 313n[12], 373n[86], 374 and nn[89,92]

Dowland, John, 134

Draghi, Antonio, 400
  *Achille in Sciro,* overture, 224

Draghi, Giovanni Battista, 15, 584n[174]

Dresden, Landesbibliothek, 340n[29]

Drese, Adam, 417

Druckenmüller, Georg Wolffgang, 231

Drummond, Philippa
  *The German Concerto. . .,* 356n[56]

Dryden, John, 9–10, 15, 46, 47, 56, 142

Du Bailly, Henry, 155, 156

Düben, Andreas, 425, 561

Düben, Gustaf, 420, 425

Dubourg, Matthew, 490, 491

Dubuisson, 170

Duckles, Vincent, 135n[79], 136n[80], 139n[83]

Du Faut, 540, 580n[166]

Dufourcq, Norbert, 540n[66], 661n[22], 662nn[24,25]

Dukas, Paul, 603

Dulwich College, 589n[188]

du Mage, Pierre
  Organ music, **660–1** (Ex. 389)

Dumanoir, Guillaume, 429

Du Mont, Henry, 430, 540, 544, 545

Duncan, J. M., 650

Dunning, Albert
  *Pietro Antonio Locatelli . . .,* 371n[83], 482n[54]

Du Parc, 170

Duphly, Jacques, 603

Dupuy, Hilaire, 154

Durante, Francesco
  Harpsichord music, 604, **606–7** (Ex. 333), 626

D'Urfey, Thomas (poet), 8, 15

Durham, Cathedral Library, 434n[119], 438n[126], 41n[134]

Duval, François, 432, 494, 495

East, Michael, 436

Eberlin, Johann Ernst, 286, 667, 693

Ebner, Wolfgang, 545, 556

Eccles, John, 21, 22, 147, 585, 587

Eccles, Solomon, 441

Egerton, Lady Alice, 581n[167]

Einstein, Alfred, 124n$^{51}$
Eisenach, Johann Jakob Loewe von, 420
Eisley, Irving R., 102n$^{14}$
Eitner, Robert, 344n$^{35}$, 477n$^{40}$
Elias, José, 657
Ellis, William, 580
*Empfindsamkeit*, 296, 442, 456
Emslie, McDonald, 135n$^{79}$, 136n$^{80}$
Engelke, Bernhard
    *Musik und Musiker am Gottorfer Hofe*,
        227n$^{42}$
Engelmann, Georg, 411
Erlebach, Philipp Heinrich, 134, 231, 417
Evans, Willa McClung
    *Henry Lawes, musician and friend of*
        *poets*, 137n$^{81}$
Evelyn, John (diarist), 489n$^{73}$
Ewerhart, Rudolf, 110n$^{32}$
Expert, H., 592n$^{5}$
Eyck, Jacob van, 429
Eysbock, Elisabeth, 573n$^{150}$

Fabricius, Werner, 417
Facoli, Marco, 508n$^{4}$
Fago, (Francesco) Nicola, 256
Falconieri, Andrea, 389, 463
Fanzago, F.
    *Elogi di Giuseppe Tartini. . .*, 374, 487n$^{65}$
Farina, Carlo, 227, 343, 498
Farina, Eduardo, and C. Scimone
    *Le Opere di Giuseppe Tartini*, 485n$^{65}$
Farmer, Thomas, 139
Farnaby, Giles, 575
Fasch, Johann Friedrich, 271, 293, 356
    *Sonate a 4*, 457–8 (Ex. 264)
    Suites, 240, 244, 245, 261
Fasolo, Giovan Battista, 523
Fedeli, Carlo, 390
Feder, Georg, 692n$^{70}$
Federhofer, Hellmut, 263n$^{64}$, 409n$^{70}$
Fedtke, T., 561n$^{111}$
Feldmann, Fritz, 570n$^{130}$
Felton, William
    Concertos, 369
Fenton, John, 489
Feo, Francesco, 256
Ferdinand III, Emperor, 256n$^{50}$, 400, 551,
    552
Ferdinand IV, King of the Romans, 551, 555
Ferdinand VI, King of Spain, 608
Ferguson, Howard, 584nn$^{175,176}$, 586n$^{179}$,
    591n$^{2}$
Ferrabosco, Alfonso, 134
Ferrabosco, John, 580
Ferro, Mario Antonio, 389, 400
Festing, Michael, 491
Filippi, Gaspare, 389, 390
Finger, Gottfried (Godfrey), 15
    Chamber music, 386 (Ex. 199), 408, 424,
        437

Finzi, Gerald, 148n$^{90}$
Fiocco, JosephHector, 623
Fiocco, Pierre-Antoine, 285
Fiorè, Andrea Stefano, 390
Fiorè, Angelo Maria, 395
Fischer, Johann, 406, 499
    Chamber music, 240, 411, 413, 417, 454
    *Partie poure la Fleute douce*, **471–2**
        (Ex. 272)
Fischer, Johann Caspar Ferdinand, 417
    Keyboard music, 556, 568, 569, 570, 640,
        645
    Suites, 227, 231–2
Fischer, Wilfried, 358n$^{59}$
Fischer, Wilhelm, 190, 295n$^{97}$, 302, 385n$^{10}$
Fishburn, Christopher (poet), 15
Flatman, Thomas (poet), 8, 140
Fletcher, John (poet), 15
Fleury, Nicolas, 158
Florence, Biblioteca nazionale, 508n$^{6}$
Fock, Gustav, 561n$^{110}$, 562n$^{113}$
Fontana, Fabritio, 526
Fontana, Giovanni Battista
    *Sonate a 1.2.3*, 466–7 (Ex. 270), 473
Forcer, Francis, 584n$^{174}$
Forkel, Johann Nikolaus
    *Musikalischer Almanach . . . auf das Jahr*
        *1784*, 239
    *Über J. S. Bachs Leben, Kunst und*
        *Kunstwerke*, 255–6, 356–7, 635n$^{62}$, 637,
        639, 643, 668
Formiloe, 580
Fornari, Matteo, 210
Forqueray, Antoine
    Viol music, 474, 476
Forqueray, Jean-Baptiste, 476
Förster, Caspar
    Chamber music, 415–16 (Ex. 234), 420
Förster, Christoph, 452
Foucaut, Henry (publisher), 275
Franceschini, Petronio, 393, 397
Francisque, Anthoine, 537
Francœur, François, 496
Francœur, Louis, *l'aîné*
    Violin sonatas, 496 (Ex. 287)
Francœur, Louis-Joseph, 496
François-Sappey, B., 593n$^{6}$, 662n$^{24}$
Franklin, Don, 643n$^{80}$
Frederick II (the Great), King of Prussia,
    301, 646
Freillon, Ponsein, 432
Freschi, Domenico
    *Miracolo del Mago*, 216
Frescobaldi, Girolamo, 121, 187, 468, 551,
    676
    influence on
        J. S. Bach, 686
        Froberger, 552, 553
        Kerll, 556
        Locke, 583

Pasquini, 524
Salvatore, 518
Storace, 518, 519
Strozzi, 518, 522
Keyboard music, **514–16,** 523, 531, 532, 545
  *Canzoni,* 565
  *Fiori musicali,* 510, 514
  *Partite,* 508, 509, 515
  Toccatas, 506, 514, 515, 659
Froberger, Johann Jakob, 583
  Keyboard music, 540, 545, **551–6** (Ex. 306), 559, 569, 570, 575
  Suites, 230, 473, 525, 537, **554–6,** 568, 582
  Toccatas, 532, **552–4** (Ex. 306), 565
Frost, Tony, 148n[90]
Frotscher, Gotthold, 692n[72]
Fuller Maitland, J. A., 440n[132], 579n[162], 585nn[177,178]
Furchheim, Johann Wilhelm, 499
  Chamber music, 388 (Ex. 207), 422
Fuser, I., 653n[5]
Fux, Johann Joseph
  *Gradus ad Parnassum,* 284
  Keyboard music, 556
  Operas
    *Constanza e fortezza,* 237, 372, 496
    *Orfeo ed Euridice,* overture, 256
  Opera overtures, 257
  Suites, 240, 241, 244, 245, 261

Gabrieli, Andrea, 194, 511, 513
Gabrieli, Giovanni, 187, 214, 381, 400, 409, 418, 514, 576
Gabrielli, Domenico, 389n[15], 390, 397
Galliard, Johann Ernst, 148
Galuppi, Baldassare, 615
Gandini, Salvador, 389
Garnault, Paul, 433n[116]
Gaspardini, Gasparo, 390
Gasparini, Francesco, 235
Gassmann, Florian Leopold, 286
Gastoué, A., 445n[141]
Gates, Bernard, **31–3**
Gaultier, Denis, 537, 540, 543, 551
Gaultier, Ennemond, 540
Gaultier, Jacques, 543
Gaultier, Pierre, 431
Gaviniès, Pierre, 235
Gdansk
  Bibl., 410n[74]
  Wojewódzkie Archiwum Państwowe, 571
Geiringer, Karl, 228n[45]
Geminiani, Francesco, 216, 235, 250, 484, 489
  Concerti grossi, 269–70, 272
    Six concerti grossi after his own Violin sonatas, Op. 1, 274
    . . .Op. 4, 270, 274

    Twelve concerti grossi after Corelli Op. 5, 270, **272–3** (Ex. 120)
  Violin sonatas, 482, 486, **490–2** (Exx. 281–2), 502
  *The Art of Playing on the Violin,* 491
Geoffroy, Jean-Nicolas, 544n[75], 546
George I, King, 31
George II, King, 31
Gerber, Heinrich Nikolaus, 692
Gerdes, G., 561n[111], 563n[120]
Gerhard, Johann Wolff, 498
Gerlin, R., 528n[37]
Gérold, Théodore
  *L'Art du chant . . .,* 159n[99]
Ghislanzoni, Alberto
  *Luigi Rossi,* 99n[7]
Giachin, G., 654n[6]
Giamberti, Giuseppe, 389
Giazotto, Remo
  *Tomaso Albinoni,* 276n[76]
Gibbons, Christopher, 435, 440, 441, 551n[89], 589
Gibbons, Orlando, 7, 438, 534, 578, 583, 588
Giegling, Franz, 497n[86]
  *Giuseppe Torelli,* 197n[12], 354n[46]
Gigault, Nicholas
  Organ works, 544 and n[75], **546–8** (Exx. 304–5), 550, 657, 662
Gigli, Giovanni Battista, 390
Gilbert, Kenneth, 541nn[67,68], 542n[69], 543nn[70,71,73], 550n[87], 608n[30]
Giosti, Andrea, 393
Girdler, Richard, 439
Girdlestone, Cuthbert
  *Jean-Philippe Rameau . . .,* 182n[126], 602n[18]
Giustini, Lodovico
  Harpsichord music, 604, **607–8** (Ex. 334)
Giustiniani, 527n[36]
Glareanus, Heinrich, 513, 514
Glasenapp, F. von, 619n[39]
Gletle, Johann Melchior, 413
Glodny-Wiercinsky, Dorothea, 126n[61]
Gluck, Christoph Willibald, 258, 297
Gobert, Thomas, 167
Goethe, Johann Wolfgang von, 443
Golding, Arthur
  *Abraham sacrifiant,* 3
Golos, Jerzy, 563n[120], 571nn
Gostling, John (bass), 15
Gottsched, Johann Christoph
  *Versuch einer critischen Dichtkunst,* 126–7
Gouy, Jacques, de, 167
Gow, Niel, 493
Grabu, Louis, 250, 437
Grandi, Alessandro, 98
Grandi, Ottavio Maria
  Violin music, 478–9 (Ex. 277)
Graun, Carl Heinrich, 130, 237, 240–1, 301, 355, 454, 458, 504

Graun, Johann Gottlieb, 240–1, 355
  Concerti grossi, 299 (Ex. 143), 301
  Violin music, 504
Graupner, (Johann) Christoph, 236, 239
  Suites, 240, 261, 271
  Concertos, 355–6, 363, 366
  Harpsichord music, 625
Gravius, Hieronimus, 424
Greco, Gaetano, 256
Greene, Maurice, 31, 32, 65, 73, 81
  Keyboard music, 589, 664
  Oratorios
    Force of Truth, The, 78
    Jephtha, 74–8 (Exx. 27–8)
    Song of Deborah and Barak, The, 34–5,
      65–70 (Exx. 23–5), 74
  Songs, 148–9 (Ex. 59)
Grefinger, Wolfgang, 572
Gregori, Giovanni Lorenzo, 269, 390
Gregorie, Will, 583
Gregory, William, 139, 435
'Gresse' manuscript, 575, 581
Griesinger, Georg August
  Biographische Notizen über Joseph
    Haydn, 234n²
Grigny, Nicolas de
  Organ works, 544 and n⁷⁵, 657
Grimarest, Jean-Léonor de, 177n¹¹⁹
Grossi, Andrea, 390
Grossi, Carlo, 389
Grubbs, Henry A.
  Jean-Baptiste Rousseau . . ., 180n¹²⁰
Guarini, Giovanni Battista (poet), 98
Guédron, Pierre, 166
Guerrieri, Agostino, 389, 390
Guignon, Jean-Pierre, 368
Guilain, Jean-Adam Guillaume
  Organ music, 660 (Ex. 388)
Guillemain, Louis-Gabriel, 367
  Sonates en quatuor, 450, 456–7 (Ex. 263)
  Violin sonatas, 497–8 (Ex. 288)
Guilmant, Alexandre, 547n⁸¹, 548n⁸²,
  550nn⁸⁵⁻⁸⁷, 557n¹⁰¹, 576n¹⁵⁵, 654n⁶,
  660n²⁰, 662n²⁴
Gustafson, Bruce
  French Harpsichord Music of the 17th
    Century, 536n⁵²
Haas, Robert
  Die Musik des Barocks, 225n³⁷
Habermann, Franz Johann
  Philomela pia, 92
Hacquart, Carolus, 377
  Chamber music, 386 (Ex. 201), 387 (Ex.
    203), 427 (Ex. 248), 429
Hagius, Konrad, 412
Hainl, 406n⁶³
Hake, Hans, 231
Halford, Margery, 593n⁸
Hall, Henry, 587

Hamburger, Povl, 573n¹⁵⁰
Hamilton, Newburgh (librettist), 50, 84, 92
Hammerschmidt, Andreas, 132, 229n⁴⁷
  Kirchen- und Tafelmusik, 413
Handel, George Frideric, 70, 307, 492, 601
  borrowings from
    Clari, 91, 123
    Habermann, 92
    Kerll, 56
    Gottlieb Muffat, 56, 620–1 (Ex. 354)
    self, 40, 55–6, 83, 446, 502, 619, 620
  influenced by
    Keiser, 110
    Lully, 445
    Purcell, 22–3, 91
    A. Scarlatti, 113, 527, 528
  influence on
    Greene, 664
  use of modes, 56
  Cantatas, 110–14 (Exx. 42–3), 115
  Chamber music
    Sonatas
      Gamba, 502
        misattributed, 477
      Violin, 489, 490, 502
    Trio sonatas, 446, 619
  Church music, 446
    Brockes Passion, 26, 27, 31, 34, 37, 40,
      619
    Chandos Te Deum, 26, 30
    Coronation anthems, 19, 31, 33, 37, 38
    'Dixit Dominus', 37
    Funeral anthem, 54–5
    Utrecht Te Deum and Jubilate, 22, 31
  Concerti grossi, 261, 262–3, 268, 274, 280,
    293, 626n⁵²
  Concertos
    harp, 49
    harpsichord, 368
    organ, 37–8, 45, 49, 55, 263, 362, 368,
      622
  English songs, 147, 148
  Keyboard music
    Harpsichord, 527, 620
      Six Fugues or Voluntarys for the
        Organ or Harpsichord, 619 (Exx.
        352–3), 640, 644, 647
      Suites, 525, 528, 616–19 (Exx.
        349–51), 627, 634
    Organ, 663
      Six Fugues . . ., see above
  Music for the Royal Fireworks, 250
  Odes
    'Ode for the Birthday of Queen Anne',
      22–3 (Ex. 9), 34
    Ode for St. Cecilia's Day, 56, 82, 620–1
      (Ex. 354(ii))
  Operas and other secular stage works, 21,
    24, 64–5, 84–5, 114, 115, 257, 446
    Aci, Galatea e Polifemo, 34

*Agrippina*, 26–7
*Atalanta*, 46
*Deidamia*, 47
*Giove in Argo*, 24, 46
*Giulio Cesare*, 257
*Imeneo*, 46, 47
*Orlando*, 257
*Ottone*, 263
*Riccardo I*, 258
*Rinaldo*, 257, 362
*Rodrigo*, 257
*Tamerlano*, 257
*Teseo*, 362
Oratorios, 2, **24–34, 37–65, 82–92,** 257,
    263, 446
  *Acis and Galatea*, 24, 26, 34, 46, 47, 56,
    81, 342n[30]
  *Alexander Balus*, 88
  *Alexander's Feast*, 46, **47–50** (Exx.
    15–16), 56, 82
  *Allegro, Il Penseroso ed Il Moderato, L'*,
    24, 46–7, **56–64** (Exx. 21–2), 82, 85,
    263
  *Athalia* **40–2** (Ex. 13), 43, 45, 46, 51, 65
  *Belshazzar*, 84, 86, 88
  *Deborah*, 35, **37–40** (Ex. 12), 45, 46, 65,
    74
  *Esther*, 2, 24, 25, **26–30** (Ex. 10), 31, 32,
    33, 34, 37, 40, 45, 46, 47, 65, 82
  *Hercules*, 24, 85, 85–6, 88, 91
  *Il Parnasso in Festa*, 24, **42–5** (Ex. 14),
    46
  *Israel in Egypt*, 46, 47, **54–6**, 82, 619
  *Jephtha*, 84, 87, 88, 91, **92**
  *Joseph and his Brethren*, 84
  *Joshua*, 88, 621
  *Judas Maccabaeus*, **86–7**, 257
  *Messiah*, 47, 65, **82–4** (Exx. 31–2), 85,
    87
  *Occasional Oratorio*, 55, 65, 84, 86
  *Samson*, 84, 85, 88, 257
  *Saul*, 46, 47, **51–4** (Ex. 18–20), 54–5,
    65, 70, 73
  *Semele*, 24, 84, 85, 86, 87, 88
  *Solomon*, 55, 87, **88–91** (Ex. 33)
  *Susanna*, 87, 88, 92
  *Theodora*, 87, 88, **91–2**, 123
  *Trionfo del Tempo, Il*, 37, 46, **50–1** (Ex.
    17), 84, 260–1, 263, 362
  Water Music, 30, 236, 250
Hanley, Edwin, 106n[25]
Hansell, Sven H., 120n[43]
  *Works for Solo Voice of Johann Adolph
    Hasse*, 120
Hardel, Jacques, 540
Harding, Rosamond, 607n[28]
Hardouin, P., 548n[83]
Harms, Gottlieb, 560n[109]
Harsdörffer, Georg Philipp (poet), 126
Hart, Eric Ford, 137n[81]

Hart, Philip, 587, 589, 663
Hasse, Johann Adolf
  Cantatas, **119–20** (Ex. 45)
  Orchestral music, 241
Hasse, Nikolaus
  Dances, 411, 417
Hasse, Peter, 561
Hassler, Hans Leo, 498
Hausswald, Günter, 125n[57], 291n[93]
Hawkins, Sir John
  *General History of . . . Music, A*, 1, 2,
    441n[134], 482, 492, 492–3
Hayden, George, 148
Haydn, Joseph, 234, 267, 290 and n[91], 297,
    376, 456, 458, 622, 626
Haynes, M. Brooks, 523n[32]
Haze, Jan de, 428
'Heardson' manuscript, 582
Hebenstreit, Pantaleon, 240
Hedar, J. 563nn[120, 121], 564n[122], 565n[127],
    568n[128], 687n[62]
Heinenski, 408
Heinichen, Johann David
  Cantatas, **125**
  Chamber music, 450, 458
  Concertos, 355, 363
  Concerti grossi, 271–2
  *Der Generalbass in der Composition*, 108,
    272
Helfert, Vladimír, 667n[40]
  *Hudební barok na českých zámcích*,
    408n[69]
Heller, Karl
  *Die deutsche Überlieferung der
    Instrumentalwerke Vivaldis*, 355n[49]
Helme, Siegsmund, 228n[43]
'Helveticus' (N. Pfleger), 425
Hely, Benjamin, 475
Herbage, Julian, 151n[91]
Herder, Johann Gottfried, 127
Herrick, Robert (poet), 137, 138, 139
Heuss, Alfred, 132n[74]
Heybourne, *see* Richardson, Ferdinand
Higginbottom, Edward, 544n[74], 549
Hill, John Walter, 485n[60]
  *The Life and Works of F. M. Veracini*,
    485n[60]
Hilton, John, 139, 436
Hingston, John, 435, 437, 441
Hinnenthal, J. P., 242n[22], 447n[149]
Hitchcock, H. Wiley, 155n[94], 156n[96], 159n[100]
Hoadly, John (librettist), 74, 78
Höffler, Konrad, 477
Hoffmann, E. T. A., 124
Hoffmann-Erbrecht, L., 655n[9]
Hofhaimer, Paul, 572
Hogwood, Christopher, 586n[179]
Holzbauer, Ignaz, 286, 444
Horn, Johann Caspar, 417, 422
Hucke, Helmut, 114n[38]

Hudson, Richard, 510n[7]
  *Passacaglio and Ciaccona . . . in the 17th
    Century,* 510n[7]
Huggins, William (librettist), 35
Hughes, John, 147
Hugon, R., 662n[24]
Humfrey, Pelham
  Odes, 7, **11–12**, 13, 14 and n[33], 18
    'When from his throne', 12 (Ex. 4)
  Songs, 139
Humphreys, Samuel, 40
Humphries, John, 274, 492
Hunold, Christian Friedrich, 126
Hurel, Charles, 167
Hurlebusch, Conrad Friedrich, 241, 356
Husk, W. H.
  *An Account of the Musical Celebrations on
    St Cecilia's Day,* 10n[26]
Hutchings, A. J. B.
  *The Baroque Concerto,* 352n[43]

Ilgner, R., 561n[111]
India, Sigismondo d', 136
Innocent X (Pamphili), Pope, 99
Isaac, Heinrich, 572
Ives, Simon, 436, 580

Jacchini, Giuseppe Maria, 390, 395, 399
  Cello concertos, **352–4** (Ex. 181)
Jackson, Barbara, 182n[126]
Jacobi, Erwin R., 602n[17]
Jacoby, Richard, 115n[40]
Jacquet de la Guerre, Elisabeth, 182, 446
  Harpsichord music, 592 (Ex. 318)
James VI/I, King, 7
Jan of Lublin, 570, 572
Jander, Owen, 99n[5]
  *Catalogue of the Manuscripts of . . . A.
    Stradella . . .,* 215n[15]
Jeans, Susi, 505n[1], 579n[161], 588n[182], 692n[68]
Jeffries, George
  Chamber music, 435, 468–9
    (Ex. 271)
Jenkins, John
  Consort music, **433–4** (Exx. 251–2), 436,
    437, 438 (Ex. 254), 440, 441, 464, 474
Jenkins, Newell, 297n[101]
Jennens, Charles (librettist), 51, 57, 86
Jeppesen, Knud, 507n[3]
Jimenes, *see* Ximenez, José
Johann Ernst von Sachsen-Weimar, Duke,
  357
Johnson, Dr. Samuel, 87
Johnson, John (publisher), 272n[72]
Johnson, Robert, 135n[79]
Johnstone, H. Diack, 147n[89]
Jommelli, Niccolò
  Cantatas, **116–19** (Ex. 44), 120
Jonson, Ben, 9, 10
Joseph I, Emperor, 256n[50]

Jullien, Gilles, 544n[75], 549n[84]

Kádár, 572
Kaefer, Johann Philipp, 424
Kahl, Willi
  *Selbstbiographien deutscher Musiker,*
    237n[9], 239n[16], 244n[28], 463n[2], 487n[67]
Kájoni, János, 572
Kalažka, 408
Kaller, E., 557n[103]
Kapsberger, Hieronymus, 121
Karl Theodor, Elector, 301
Kassel, Landesbibliothek, 383n[7], 387n[12],
  416n[91], 422n[97]
Kast, Paul
  *Die Bach-Handschriften der Berliner
    Staatsbibliothek,* 643n[82]
Kastner, Santiago, 615n[13]
Kauffmann, Georg Friedrich, 671, 680, 681
Keiser, Reinhard, 257, 424, 444
  Cantatas, 110, **125, 127–8** (Ex. 47), 130
Keller, Gottfried, 424
Keller, Hermann, 470n[19]
Kellner, Johann Peter, 692
Kelway, Joseph, 616
Kenyon, Nicholas, 629n[58]
Kerckhoven, Abraham Van den
  Organ music, **576–8** (Ex. 311)
Kerll, Johann Caspar, 56, 286, 401
  Keyboard music, 556, 557
Kertzinger, Andreas
  Suite, 411 (Ex. 229)
Kindermann, Johann Erasmus, 559, 562,
  563, 568
King, Robert, 15, 146, 441, 585n[177]
Kinkeldey, Otto, 134n[75]
Kinney, Gordon J., 476n[34]
Kinsky, Georg
  ed., *Manuskripte . . . von Scarlatti bis
    Stravinsky,* 111n[34]
Kircher, Athanasius, 195, 551n[89]
Kirchhoff, Andreas, 425
Kirkendale, Ursula, 646n[84]
Kirkendale, Warren
  *L'aria di Fiorenza,* 508n[6]
Kirkpatrick, Ralph, 638n[66]
  *Domenico Scarlatti,* 608n[30]
Kirnberger, Johann Philipp, 639
Kittel, Kaspar
  Cantatas, **124–5**
Klabon, Krzysztof, 571
Klaus, G., 557n[103], 665n[36]
Klein, Hans-Günter
  *Der Einfluss der vivaldischen Konzertform
    im Instrumentalwerk J. S. Bachs,* 358n[61]
Klemm, Johann, 559
Klopstock, Friedrich Gottlieb, 127
Kneller, Andreas, 676
Knoep, Lüder, 231, 417
Koesfeldt, Lothar L. Zumbach van, 429

Kolb, Carlmann, 667
Kolfs, A., 576
Kolneder, Walter, 344n[38], 485nn[60],[62]
   *Antonio Vivaldi (1678–1741), Leben und*
     *Werk*, 105n[22]
Königsperger, Marianus, 667
Koninck, Servaes van, 429
Konwalinka, Pavel, 408
Kooiker, A., 582n[171]
Koole, Arend
   *Leven en werken van P. A. Locatelli da*
     *Bergamo*, 487n[68]
Krebs, Carl, 572n[144]
Krebs, Johann Ludwig, 692, 693
Krebs, Johann Tobias, 692
Kremberg, Jakob
   Chamber music, 411 (Ex. 230)
   *Musicalische Gemüths-Ergötzung*,
     474–5 (Ex. 274)
Kretzschmar, Hermann
   *Geschichte des neuen deutschen Liedes*,
     130n[71], 131
Krieger, Adam
   Songs, 125, **132–4** (Ex. 50)
Krieger, Johann Philipp, 240, 413, 568, 570
Kroměříž, St. Maur. Arch., 411n[78]
Kross, Siegfried
   *Das Instrumentalkonzert bei G. P.*
     *Telemann*, 356n[52]
Krüger, Walther
   *Das Concerto grosso in Deutschland*, 271
Kuhnau, Johann
   Keyboard music, 568, 570, 618, 626, 631
Kühnel, August, 477
Küntzel, G.
   *Die Instrumentalkonzerte von J. F. Fasch*
     *. . .*, 356n[52]
Kunzen, Johann Paul, 362
Kusser, Johann Sigismund, 231, 240, 250,
   257, 417
Küster, A., 625n[50]


la Barre, Anne de, 154
La Barre, Joseph de, 167, 540
La Barre, Pierre de, 540, 580, 581
La Borde, J.-B. de
   *Essai sur la musique ancienne et moderne*,
     662n[26]
Laccetti, Guido, 451n[155]
La Chevardière, Louis Balthazard de
   (publisher), 300
La Fontaine, Jean de, 155
La Garde, Pierre de, 174
Lalande, Michel-Richard de
   Chamber music, **430–1** (Ex. 250)
La Laurencie, Lionel de, 431n[114], 494n[83]
   *L'Ècole française de violon . . .*, 497n[87]
La Laurencie, Lionel de, and Albert
   Lavignac

*Encyclopédie de la Musique*, 410n[75],
   432n[116]
Laloy, Louis
   *Rameau*, 183n[127]
Lam, Basil, 250n[45]
Lambert, Michel
   *Airs*, 154, 155, 156–7 (Ex. 62(ii)), 158,
     160, **161–2** (Ex. 63), 167, 171, 172
Lambert, Vincenz, 429
la Motte, Antoine Houdar, 181, 183n[127]
Lampe, Johann Friedrich
   Songs, 149, **150–1** (Ex. 60)
Landi, Stefano, 99, 222
   *Sant' Alessio*, sinfonia, **191–2** (Ex. 76),
     219
Landon, H. C. Robbins, 125n[56]
Lange, Martin, 624n[47]
Lanier, Nicholas
   as poet, 8
   Songs, **135–7** (Exx. 51–2), 139
La Pouplinière, Alexandre-Jean-Joseph Le
   Riche de, 235
Larsen, Jens Peter
   *Handel's 'Messiah': Origins – Composition*
     *– Sources*, 83n[56]
Lasocki, David, 502n[99]
Laurenti, Bartolomeo Girolamo, 390
La Varenne, 154
Lavati, Carl' Ambrogio, 490
Lavignac, Albert, *see* La Laurencie, Lionel
   de
La Voye-Mignot, de, 429
Lawes, Henry, 581n[167]
   Songs, **137–9** (Ex. 53), 140
Lawes, William, 139, 433, 468, 580–1
Lebègue, Nicolas, 546
   Harpsichord music, 536, 538n[56], **540–1**,
     543
   Organ music, 536, 544 and n[75], 546, 550,
     657, 662
Le Camus, Sébastien
   *Airs*, 157 (Ex. 62(iii)), 167
Le Cène, Michel Charles (publisher), 259,
   373–4
Le Cerf de La Viéville
   *Comparaison de la musique italienne et de*
     *la musique française*, 445n[143]
Leclair, Jean-Marie, 235, 346
   Concertos, **366–7**, 368
   Trio sonatas, 235
   Violin sonatas, 496–7
Le Clerc, Charles-Nicholas (publisher), 482
Leeuwen, Ary van, 504n[100]
Leffloth, Johann Mattäus, 362, 477
Lefkowitz, Murray, 468n[17], 580n[164]
   *William Lawes*, 139n[83]
Legrenzi, Giovanni
   *Canzoni*, 195, 196, 518
   Chamber music, 389, 390, 391, 394 (Ex.
     212), 482

Leichtentritt, Hugo, 472n[25], 477n[38]
Lejeune, Henry, 429
Le Maire, Louis, **183–5** (Ex. 72)
Lenton, John, 439
Leo, Leonardo, 115, 256, 285
Leonardi, Isabella, 390
Leonhardt, Gustav M.
   *The Art of Fugue: Bach's Last*
      *Harpsichord Work,* 647n[85]
Leoni, Giovanni Antonio, 389
Leopold, Silke
   *Stefano Landi. Beiträge zur Biographie.*
      *Untersuchungen zur Vokalmusik,* 99n[6]
Leopold I, Emperor, 400, 401, 500
   as composer, 256n[50], 400–1
Leopolita, Marcin, 571
Le Roy, Adrian, 229n[48]
Lessing, 134
Lesure, François
   *Bibliographie des Editions Musicales*
      *publiées par E. Roger et M.-C. Le Cène*
      . . ., 351n[42]
Leveridge, Richard, 147
Lewis, Anthony, 224n[35]
   *The Language of Purcell,* 139n[85]
'L.F.', 576
Liège, University Library, 576n[155]
Lincoln, Harry B., 508n[6]
Lippius, Johannes, 297
Liszt, Franz, 246
Llorens Cisteró, José Maria, 528n[38], 536n[51]
Llusá, Francese, 657
Locatelli, Pietro Antonio, 270, 444, 482,
      497n[85]
   Caprices, 371–2 (Ex. 185), 488
   Concertos, 366, 371–2
   Overtures, **260**
   Violin music, 479, **487–8** (Ex. 280)
Locke, John, 652
Locke, Matthew, 145, 406n[63]
   Chamber music, **438–9** (Ex. 255), 440,
      441, 474
   Keyboard music, 578, 582–3, 588, 589
   Odes
      'All things their certain periods have',
      **1-1** (Ex. 3)
      'Come Loyall hearts, make no delay', 8
   Songs, **140–1** (Ex. 55)
   Stage works
      *The Tempest,* 386 (Ex. 198), 438–9 (Ex.
      256)
Loeillet, Jacques, 454
Löffelholtz, Christoph, 571
Logroscino, Nicola, 256
London
   British Library
      Add. MSS., 4n[14], 11n[27], 12n[29], 13n[32],
      17n[37], 108n[29], 137n[82], 435n[121],
      468nn[14],[15], 469, 517n[25], 575n[152], 576
      and n[155], 581n[168], 589nn[187],[188], 643n[80]

Other MSS., 49n[51], 103n[17], 270, 379n[2],
      394n[36], 397n[53], 422n[97], 579n[162],
      588n[182]
   Royal College of Music, 8n[20], 20n[41],
      105n[23]
Loosemore, Henry, 436
López, Miguel
   Organ music, 656–7 (Ex. 385)
Lotti, Antonio, 32
Lotti, Giovanni, 98, 257, 285
Louis XIV, King of France, 173, 181, 230,
      378, 430, 437, 494
Louis XV, King of France, 600
Lovelace, Richard (poet), 137
Lübeck, Vincent, 675
Lugge, John, 579, 588
Lully, Jean-Baptiste, 231, 240, 242, 249,
      274, 499, 543
   influence, generally, 250
      on J. S. Bach, 251, 445
      on Keiser, 128
   *Airs,* 167
   Instrumental music, 430
   Operas, 166, 178, 179
   Overtures, 216, 219, 224, 230, 237, 259,
      441
      to ballets, **220–3**
         *Alcidiane,* 220, 222 (Ex. 97(i))
         *Amore ammalato, L',* 220
         *La Raillerie,* 220–1 (Ex. 96)
      to *Xerse* (Cavalli) 220, 222 (Ex.
         97(ii)), 223
   Suites, 230, 241, 244, 251, 261, 275
Lundgren, B., 568n[129]
Lüneburg, 508n[6]
Luntz, Erwin, 216n[17], 499n[93]
Lupo, Thomas, 437

MacClintock, Carol
   ed., *The Solo Song 1580–1730,* 125n[54]
Mace, Thomas, 442
MacGibbon, Williams, 493
McGrady, R. J., 137n[81]
McGuinness, Rosamond, 10, 141n[86]
   *English Court Odes, 1660–1820,* 10n[23],
      11n[27], 12n[31]
Machy, Sieur de
   *Piecès de violle,* 475–6 (Ex. 275)
McLean, Hugh, 588n[184], 589n[186]
Macque, Giovanni de, 518
Madrid, Bib. Nacional, 536n[50]
Maichelbeck, Franz Anton, 667
Mainerio, 390
Majer, Joseph
   *Museum Musicum,* 285
Malherbe, C.
   ed. Rameau, 182n[126]
Malipiero, Gian Francesco
   ed. Vivaldi, 277n[78], 278n[79], 291n[92], 303–42
   *passim,* 363n[68]

Manchester, Henry Watson Library, 589n[188]
Mancini, Francesco, 256
Manelli, Carlo, 390, 396
Manfredini, Francesco, 270, 370
Mangeant, Jacques (publisher), 167
Marais, Marin, 257, 258
   Chamber music, 431, 432, 443, 453
   Viol music, 476
Marazzoli, Marco, 99
Marcello, Alessandro, 270, 357
Marcello, Benedetto, 249, 482
   Harpsichord music, 604 (Ex. 330)
Marchand, Louis, 659–60
Marenzio, Luca, 218
Mareschal, Samuel, 576n[155]
Marin, Jean-Baptiste, 597
Marini, Biagio, 227, 290n[90]
   Chamber music, 343, 389, 463, 470, 471
   Violin music, 467, 470, 473, **477–8** (Ex.
   276), 498
Marini, (poet), 98
Marino, Carlo Antonio, 390
Marpurg, Friedrich Wilhelm
   *Historische-kritische Beyträge* . . ., 237n[9],
   487n[67]
   *Kritische Briefe über die Tonkunst*, 295
   *Versuch über die musicalische Temperatur,*
   639
Marshall, William, 493
Martin, François, 169, 172
Martini, Giambattista, 693
   *12 Sonate . . . per l'organo e'l cembalo,*
   655–6 (Ex. 384)
Martini, (Padre) Giovanni Battista, 286, 615
Martin y Coll, Fray Antonio, 536
Marx, Hans Joachim, 100n[9], 100nn[31],[33]
Marx-Weber, Magda
   *Katalog der Musikhandschriften in . . .*
   *Bonn,* 121nn[47],[48]
Mascitti, Michele
   Concerti grossi, 275
   Violin music, 493 (Ex. 283)
Matteis, Nicola (son of N. Matteis, below),
   489, 502
Matteis, Nicolas, 437
Matthaei, Karl, 562n[118]
Mattheson, Johann, 121, 195, 238, 241, 419,
   450, 498, 499, 672
   as composer, 503–4, 620, 634
   *Critica Musica,* 485n[61]
   *Der vollkommene Capellmeister,* 105,
   124, 247–8, 284, 297
   *Grosse General-Bass-Schule,* 239n[15],
   356n[55], 463n[2], 688
   *Grundlage einer Ehrenpforte,* 128,
   231n[49], 239n[16], 240n[18], 343, 551n[89]
   *Neueröffnetes Orchester,* 125–6
Matthysz, Paulus (publisher), 429, 498
Maulevrier, (poet), 161, 167
Max Emmanuel II of Bavaria, 483

Mayone, Ascanio, 518
Mayr, Rupert Ignaz, 231, 417
Mazella, Salvatore, 390
Mazzaferrata, Giovanni Battista, 389, 390
Mazzocchi, Domenico
   Cantatas, 98, 99, 121
   Opera
      *La catena d'Adone,* 218
Mazzolini, Carlo Andrea, 390
Mealli, R., 389
Meder, Johann Valentin, 405–6, 410
Medico, 389
Melani, Alessandro, 389n[15]
Mell, Davis, 489
Mellers, Wilfrid
   *François Couperin* . . ., 595n[12]
Menalt, Gabriel, 536
Mendel, Arthur, *see* David, Hans T.
Mercure, John, 580, 581
Mersenne, Marin
   *Harmonie universelle,* 156, 544n[76], 545
Mersmann, Hans
   *Musikhören,* 307
Merula, Tarquinio, 389, 406n[63], 518
   *Canzoni,* 195, 470, 473
   Violin music, 465
Merulo, Claudio, 511, 516, 553
Metastasio, Pietro, 42, 114, 120, 374, 487
Métru, Nicolas, 429
Meyer, Ernst H., 379n[1], 401n[59], 408n[69]
   *Die mehrstimmige Spielmusik des 17.*
   *Jahrhunderts* . . ., 422n[96], 424n[98]
   *English Chamber Music,* 436n[122]
Mézangeau, René, 543
Michael, Christian, 559, 560
Michálek, František, 667n[40]
Michel, Guillaume, 168
Mico, Richard, 436
Mielczewski, Marcin
   Chamber music, 409–10 (Ex. 226)
Migali, 390
Miller, Hugh M., 141n[86]
Milton, John, 57, 85, 137, 433, 581
Mishkin, Henry G., 480nn[45],[48]
Miška, 408
Mizler von Kolof, Lorenz Christoph, 682
Modena, 389n[15], 393n[30]
   Biblioteca, 99n[6]
Molière, (Jean-Baptiste Poquelin), 161
'Molin', (Moulin'), 580
Mollier, Louis de, 161, 167, 168
Molter, Johann Melchior, 271
Monari, Bartolomeo, 526, 527n[36]
Monari, Clemente, 390
Mondonville, Jean-Joseph de
   Violin sonatas, 497, 498
Mönkemeyer, H., 299n[47]
Monn, Georg Matthias
   Orchestral music, 233, 300–1
Monnard, Nicolas, 540n[65]

Montéclair, Michel de, 182
Monteverdi, Claudio, 136, 381, 514
  Dramatic works
    *Ballo delle ingrate*, 197
    *L'incoronazione di Poppea*, sinfonia,
      218
    *Orfeo*, 378
    *Sinfonie*, 218
Monti, Giacomo (publisher), 105
Moore, Edward (librettist), 78–9
Moreau, Jean-Baptiste, 661
Morell, Thomas (librettist), 91
Moreno y Polo, Juan, 657
Morhardt, Peter, 561n[111]
Morin, Jean-Baptiste
  Cantatas, **173–9** (Exx. 69–71), 180, 181,
    182
Morley, Thomas, 418
Moroney, Davitt, 537n[55], 550n[87], 556n[98]
Morphy, Guillermo de, 431n[113]
Mortari, Virgilio, 272n[74]
Morungensis, Johannes Fischer, 571
Moser, Hans Joachim, 131n[73], 132n[74],
    134n[75], 61n[111]
  *Geschichte des Violinspiels*, 495n[84],
    498n[89], 502
Moss, John
  Keyboard suites, **583–4** (Ex. 312)
Mossi, Giovanni, 270, 482
Motley, Richard, 584n[174]
Motta, Artemio, 270, 355, 390
Motteux, Peter (poet), 8
'Moulin', ('Molin'), 580
Moulinié, Étienne, 160, 167
Mouret, Jean-Joseph, 181, 183
Mozart, Leopold, 286, 373
  *Violinschule*, 375
Mozart, Wolfgang Amadeus, 244, 267, 368,
    615, 626
Mudge, Richard, 274
Muffat, Georg, 401, 666
  *Apparatus musico-organisticus*, **557–9**
    (Ex. 307)
  *Armonico tributo*, **206–10** (Exx. 79–85),
    215, **216–17**, 261
  Concerti grossi, 261, 268, 271
  *Florilegium Primum*, 231, 232
  *Florilegium Secundum*, 231, 232, 444
Muffat, Gottlieb
  Keyboard music
    Suites, 56, **620–3** (Exx. 354–6), 634
    *72 Versetl . . .*, 666–7
Müller, Günther, 413n[83]
  *Geschichte des deutschen Liedes . . .*,
    126n[59]
Müller-Blattau, Josef Maria
  *Die Kompositionslehre Heinrich Schützens
    . . .*, 97n[2]
Munninckxs, P. F.
  Chamber music, 426 (Ex. 246), 429

Münster, 101n[13]
Murschhauser, Franz Xaver Anton
  Keyboard music, 557, 665–6 (Ex. 392)

Nabbes, Thomas, 10n[24]
Naples, Bibl. del. R. Conservatorio, 528n[37]
Nassarre, Pablo, 536
Natale, Pompeio, 389, 390, 396
Naudot, Jacques-Christophe, 368
Nauwach, Johann, 124
Nazari, Antonio, 285
Nef, Karl, 193n[9]
  *Geschichte der Sinfonie und Suite*, 227,
    242, 300
Negri, Francesco, 105
Neri. Massimiljano
  *Canzoni*, 190
  Chamber music, 389, 390, 391–2 (Ex.
    208)
Nettl, Paul
  *Musikbarock in Böhmen und Mähren*,
    408n[69]
Neubauer, Johann, 417
Neumeister, Erdmann (poet), 126
New Haven, Yale University, 555n[97],
    580n[166]
Newman, Ernest, 649n[89]
Newman, William S., 518n[27], 604n[22]
  *The Sonata in the Baroque Era*, 480n[45],
    518n[27], 604n[22]
  *The Sonata in the Classical Era*, 504n[101]
New York, Public Library, 7n[18], 464nn[5,6],
    579n[160], 582n[173]
Nicholson, Richard, 433nn[117,118]
Niedt, Friedrich Erhardt, 425
Nivers, Guillaume, 429
  Organ works, 544 and n[75], 545, 546, 548,
    549n[84]
Noack, Friedrich, 243n[25]
Noordt, Sybrandus van, 429
Norcome, Daniel, 464
Nörmiger, Augustus, 571, 572
North, Roger, 136
Noske, Fritz, 573n[151], 575n[152]
Nottebohm, Gustav, 649
Nuremberg, Nationalmuseum, 498n[90]
Nyert, Pierre de, 154–5, 156, 159, 168

Oberdörffer, F., 624n[48]
Okeover, John, 436
Oldham, G., 546n[80]
Oldham, John (poet), 15
Orefice, Antonio, 256
Ortiz, Diego, 464
Osostowicz, A., 571n[136]
Otto, Valerius, 406
Ottoboni, Pietro (cardinal), 98, 110, 451
Oxford
  Ashmolean, 8n[19]
  Bodleian, 401n[61], 582, 616

Christ Church, 397n[50], 576 and n[155], 579nn[161],[163], 580, 581, 582, 585n[178]
Oxinagas, Joaquin de, 657

Pachelbel, Johann, 422, 675
    influence generally, 671
        on J. S. Bach, 570, 677, 678–9, 683, 686, 687
        on J. G. Walther, 672
    Organ music, 559, 562–3, 564, 677, 684
    Secular keyboard music, 568, 569
Paepen, Pierre de, 576
Paganini, Nicolò, 372, 488
Paix, Jakob, 572
Panfili, Benedetto (cardinal and librettist), 50, 98, 110
Pannain, Guido, 606n[27]
Paradisi, (Pietro) Domenico, 615
Paris
    Bibliothèque du Conservatoire, 223n[31], 430n[111]
    Bibliothèque Nationale, 408n[67], 538n[57], 539nn[59],[60], 543, 548n[83], 550n[87], 579n[162]
    Bibliothèque Ste. Geneviève, 539n[59], 544n[76], 545
Parkinson, J. A.
    *An index to the vocal works of Thomas Augustine Arne and Michael Arne*, 151n[91]
Parsons, (poet), 15
Pasino, Steffano, 390, 406n[63]
Päsler, Karl, 568n[129]
Pasquini, Bernardo
    Keyboard music, 509, **523–6** (Ex. 294), 532, 604
Pattengale, Robert R., 116n[41]
Pätzold, E., 381n[5], 384n[9]
Pauer, Ernst, 585n[177]
Pauls, Karl-Heinz, 477n[38]
Paumgartner, Bernhard, 606n[26]
Peart, Donald, 433n[117]
Pedrell, Felipe, 657n[14]
Peerson, Martin, 436
Pegolotti, Tomaso, 390
Pelphin, Bibl. Seminarium, 571n[138]
Penna, Lorenzo, 389
Pepusch, Johann Christoph, 272, 274
    Cantatas, 147–8
Perandreu, 530n[43]
Peraza, Francisco, 528
Peraza, Jerónimo, 528
Perdigal, 167
Pergolesi, Giovanni Battista, 285
    Cantatas, **115–16**
    Orchestral music, 233
    Trio sonatas (attrib.), 455 (Ex. 262)
Perrin, Pierre, 161
Perrine, 537
Perti, Giacomo Antonio, 285
    Cantatas, 102, 105

*Sinfonie*, 197, 225, 343
Pesenti, Martino, 389, 473, 518
Petersen, David, 428
Petit, Françoise, 603n[20]
Petrarch, Francesco, 487
Petri, Berendt, 573n[150]
Petrucci, Ottaviano, 508n[4]
Petzoldt, Richard
    *Die Kirchenkompositionen und weltlichen Kantaten R. Keisers*, 125n[55], 128n[66]
Peuerl, Paul
    Suites, 228–9 (Ex. 101(i)), 381, 471
Pevsner, Nikolaus
    *An Outline of European Architecture*, 663
Pez, Johann Christoph, 271, 424, 454
Pezel, Johann, 413
Pfleger, Nicholas, ('Helveticus'), 425
Pfuhl, 571n[138]
Philidor, André, 432
Philips, Katherine (poet), 141
Philips, Peter, 576
Phillips, Arthur, 579
Phillips, Gordon, 588nn[183],[184]
Piazzi, 390
Piccaert, Pieter, 428
Picchi, Giovanni, 572
Pidoux, P., 514n[18], 573n[151]
Piggot, Francis, 585n[177], 587
Pincherle, Marc, 497n[86]
    *J.-M. Leclair*, 497n[85]
Piochi, Cristofano, 389
Piroye, Charles, 170
Pirro, André, 654n[6], 660n[20], 662n[24]
Pisendel, Johann Georg, 234, 504
    Violin concertos, 291–2 (Ex. 133), 355
Pistocchi, Francesco Antonio, 350, 526
Pizzoni, G. M., 389
Placuzzi, Gioseffo Maria, 389
Plamenac, Dragan, 409n[70]
    *Toma Cecchini . . .*, 409n[70]
Plath, Wolfgang, 638n[66]
Platt, Richard, 589n[188], 664n[31]
Platti, Giovanni Benedetto, 615
Playford, Henry (publisher)
    *Harmonia Sacra*, 4n[15]
Playford, John (publisher), 134, 139, 436
    *Apollo's Banquet*, 489
    *Division Violin, The*, 465, 489
    *English Dancing Master, The*, 411n[77]
    *Musick's Recreation on the Viol . . .*, 474
Pleyel, Ignace Joseph, 376
Podbielski, Jan, 572
Poglietti, Alessandro, 389n[15], 400, 401, 406, 556, 576
Pohanka, Jaroslav, 407n[66], 573nn[148],[149]
Pohle, David
    Chamber music, 383, **420** (Ex. 239)
Polaroli, 389
Polewheele, *see* Wheeler, Paul
Poliński, Aleksander, 571–2

Pollarolo, Carlo Francesco, 526, 527n[36], 653
Pope, Alexander, 27
Porpora, Nicola, 119, 256
    Chamber music, 451–2 (Ex. 261)
Portman, Richard, 588
Posch, Ignaz, 228
Postel, Christian Heinrich (poet), 127
Praetorius, Hieronymus, 560, 562
Praetorius, Jacob, 560, 563, 564
Praetorius, Michael, 187, 559, 563
Prattichista, 389
Prelleur, Peter, 489
Preston, Christopher, 583
Prioli, 389
Prior, Matthew (poet), 8
Prod'homme, J. G., 476nn[35],[36]
Provenzale, Francesco, 115
Prunières, Henry, 220 and nn[28],[29], 223n[31]
Pujol, David, 656n[12]
Purcell, Daniel
    Instrumental music, 437, 441
    Keyboard music, 585n[177], 587
    Odes, 12, 15, 21
    Songs, 146, 148
Purcell, Henry, 663
    and Blow, 16, 18–20 passim
        F. Couperin, 659
    foreign influence, 13, 141, 143
    Chamber music, 437, **439–40** (Ex. 257),
        441, 444, 445
        Violin sonatas, 489
    Church music, 19
        'In guiltie night', 7, 25
    Keyboard, 517n[25], 578
        Suites, 584–5
        Organ, 589
    Odes, 7, 14–15, **15–20** (Ex. 7), 22, 23, 141
        text-setting, 8–9
        'Arise my Music', 15
        'Celebrate this Festival', 16
        'Come ye sons of art away', 16, **19**, 20
        'Love's goddess', 16
        'Now does the glorious day appear', 15
        'Swifter Isis, swifter flow', **17–18** (Ex. 7)
        'Welcome, vicegerent of the mighty
            King', 16
        'Welcome, welcome glorious morn',
            15–16
        'Who can from joy refrain?', 16
    Songs, 139, **141–6** (Ex. 56–8), 148
        use of ground bass, 141–3 (Ex. 56)
        'Fairest Isle', 143
        'Hark! the ech'ing air', 143
        'If love's a sweet passion', 143
        'I'll sail upon the dog-star', 143
        'Lovely Albina', 143–4 (Ex. 57)
        'Music for a while', 142 (Ex. 56)
        'O Solitude', 141
        'She loves and she confesses too', 141
        'Sweeter than roses', 145

'The Blessed Virgin's Expostulation',
    146
'The fatal hour comes on apace', 145–6
    (Ex. 58)
'What hope for us remains', 145
Theatre music, 257, 259
    Indian Queen, The, 19, 193–4 (Ex. 77)
    Tempest, The, 224 (Ex. 99)

Quagliati, Paolo, 121
Quantz, Johann, J., 271, 297, 363, 501, 504
    Autobiography, 237, 355, 487
    Versuch einer Anweisung die Flöte
        traversiere zu spielen, 238, 303, 339,
        364–5, 375, 449, 450, 498
Quinault, Philippe, 161
Quittard, Henri, 172n[114]

Racek, Jan, 407n[66]
Racine, Jean, 27
    Athalie, 40
Racquet, Charles, 544n[76], 545
Ragazzi, Angelo, 502
Raguenet, François, Abbé
    Paralèle des italiens et des françois . . .,
        248–9, 445n[143]
Rainaldi, Carlo
    Cantatas, **99–100** (Ex. 36)
Raison, André, 544n[75], 549–50, 657, 661,
    662
Rameau, Jean-Philippe, 235, 442, 443, 662
    Airs, 171
    Cantatas, 182
    Dramatic works, 183
        orchestra in, 258–9
        Castor et Pollux, 603
        Festes d'Hébé, Les, 603n[19]
        Hippolyte et Aricie, 258 (Ex. 113)
        Indes galantes, Les, 603n[19]
        Zoroastre, 258
    Harpsichord music, 537, 593, **602–3** (Exx.
        328–9), 627
        Pièces de clavecin en concerts . . ., 368,
            446, 603n[19], 623
    Traité de l'Harmonie . . ., 443
Ramsey, Robert, 139
Rasi, Francesco, 121
Rastall, Richard, 580n[166], 582n[173], 588n[182]
Rathgeber, Valentin, 134
Raugel, F., 660n[21]
Ravenna, Biblioteca classense, 508n[6]
Ravenscroft, John, 493
Rayman, 154
Rayner, C. G., 562n[114], 589n[185]
Reading, John, 588n[184], 589, 663
Rebel, Jean-Ferry, le Pére, 432, 454
    Violin sonatas, 494 (Ex. 285), 497
Redlich, Hans Ferdinand, 667n[39]
Regensburg, Proske Library, 407n[65]
Reggio, Pietro, 141

Regnault, 170
Reiche, Gottfried, 413
Reijen, Paul van, 488n[69]
Reilly, Edward R., 238n[10], 303nn[4],[5]
Reina, Fra Sisto, 389, 395
Reincken, Adam, 563, 565, 675, 687–8
Reusner, Esaias, 422
Reutter, Georg, 556
Reutter (Johann) Georg (the younger), 286, 300
Richard, Étienne, 540n[65], 543, 545
Richard, François, 160
Richardson, Ferdinand (*alias* Heybourne), 525
Richardson, Vaughan, 587
Richer, (publisher), 158
Richter, Ferdinand Tobias, 256, 401, 556
Richter, Franz Xaver, 286, 444
    *Sinfonie*, **293–5** (Exx. 136–7)
Riedel, F. W., 568n[129]
    *Quellenkundliche Beiträge zur Geschichte der Musik für Tasteninstrumente . . .*, 572n[145]
Riemann, Hugo, 457n[161]
    *Old Chamber Music*, 411n[76], 428n[105], 465n[9], 470n[21]
Rictsch, Heinrich, 231n[50]
Riley, James, 435n[120]
Rist, Johann
    Songs, 130, 131
Rittler, Philipp Jakob
    Chamber music, 403, 405 (Ex. 221), 407 (Ex. 224)
Roberday, François, 545, 552
Robert, Frédéric, 171n[111]
Roberts, John, 580, 583
Rodio, Rocco, 518
Roesgen-Champion, M., 541nn[67],[68], 542n[69], 543nn[70],[71],[73]
Roger, Estienne (publisher), 210, 271, 351, 352, 354, 502n[98]
Roger, Jeanne (publisher), 616n[37]
Rogers, Benjamin, 580, 581, 582 and n[173], 583, 588
Rogers, Elizabeth, 581
Rolle, Johann Heinrich, 130
Romanini, Antonio, 572
Rome, Vatican Library, 508n[6], 515n[22], 523
Ronsard, 9
Röntgen, Julius, 575n[152]
Rosand, Ellen, 104n[18]
Rose, Gloria, 98n[3], 101nn[11],[12], 517n[25]
Roseingrave, Thomas, 148
    Keyboard music, 664, 693
        Suites, 626
        *Voluntaries and fugues . . .*, 615–6, **663–5** (Ex. 391)
Rosenmüller, Johann, 193
    Chamber music, 381–2 (Ex. 191), 384 (Ex. 194), 385 (Ex. 197), 414, 417,

**420–2** (Exx. 240–2)
Rosier, Carl
    Chamber music, 426–7 (Ex. 247), 428, 429
Rospigliosi, Giulio (cardinal), 98
Rossi, Luigi, 155
    Cantatas, **99**, 106, 125
Rossi, Michelangelo
    Keyboard music, **516–18** (Ex. 291), 552–3
    Opera
        *Erminia sul Giordano,* overture, **218–19** (Ex. 95)
    *Sinfonie,* 222
Rossi, Salamone, 392, 464
    *Canzoni,* 190
    *Sinfonie e gagliarde,* 470, 474
Rostock, Univ. Lib., 430
Rousseau, Jean, 432
Rousseau, Jean-Baptiste (poet), 180–1
Rousseau, Jean-Jacques, 258–9, 296–7, 444
    *Dictionnaire de musique,* 183, 226, 365, 371
    *Lettre sur la musique françoise,* 296
Roy, Pierre, 181
Rubert, Martin, 417
Ruf, Hugo, 115n[40], 362n[65]
Ruspoli, Francesco Maria (Marchese), 110
Ryom, Peter, 105n[21]
    *Verzeichnis der Werke Antonio Vivaldis,* 277n[78], 278n[79], 291n[92], 303–42 *passim,* 363n[68]

Sablières, Jean Granouilhet, Sieur de, 167
Sadler, Graham, 603n[19]
St.-Evremond, Charles, Seigneur de, 155
Saint-Simon, 155
Sala, Giuseppe (publisher), 351
Salvatore, Giovanni
    Keyboard music, 518–9, 523
Sammartini, Giovanni Battista
    influence generally, 297, 300
    Symphonies, 233, **297–9** (Ex. 141)
Sammartini, Giuseppe, 260, 270, 369
Sances, Giovanni Felice, 400
Sandberger, Adolf, 124n[51], 370n[82], 483, 556n[98]
    *Ausgewählte Aufsätze zur Musikgeschichte,* 605n[25]
Sandley, Benjamin, 581
Sargent, George, 581n[168]
Sarro, Domenico, 115, 256
Sauveur, Joseph
    *Application des sons harmoniques à la composition des orgues,* 549
Savioni, Mario, 102
Scacchi, Marco, 195, 409
Scarlatti, Alessandro, 119, 260, 270, 285, 339
    Cantatas, 105, **106–9** (Exx. 40–1), 110, 113, 115, 172, 239
    Chamber music

Scarlatti, Alessandro—*cont.*
   *Sonate a quattro,* 456
   Instrumental music
     Overtures, 108–9 (Ex. 41), **225–6,** 256, 257
     *VI Concertos . . .,* 369
     Keyboard music, **526–8** (Ex. 295), 653
Scarlatti, Domenico
   Keyboard sonatas, 239, 603, 604, **608–16** (Exx. 335–48), 620, 625–6, 631, 640, 642, 647, 649, 664
   Spanish influence in sonatas, 608, 611, 612
Scarron, 161
Scharlau, Ulf, 551n[89]
Scheibe, Johann Adolf, 125
   as composer, 280
   *Der critische Musikus,* 127, 242, 259, 450
   *Über die musikalische Composition,* 442
Scheibert, Beverly, 658n[17]
Scheidemann, Heinrich, 132
   Organ music, 560–1, 562, 563, 564, 571, 573
Scheidt, Gottfried, 561
Scheidt, Samuel, 511, 531, 559, 560, 562n[114], 563, 565
Scheiffelhut, Jakob, 240
Schein, Johann Hermann, 187
   *Banchetto musicale,* **228–9** (Ex. 101(ii)), 381, 471
Schenck, Johannes, 428, 429, 453
   Gamba music, 472–3 (Ex. 273), 476–7
Schenk, Erich, 207n[13], 499n[92]
Scherer, Sebastian Anton, 556–7
Schering, Arnold, 413n[82], 470n[18]
   *Geschichte der Musik in Beispielen,* 106n[26], 124n[51], 132n[74], 134nn[75,76], 191, 354nn[45,47], 473n[29], 478n[42]
   *Geschichte des Instrumentalkonzerts,* 276, 327, 343n[33], 344n[36], 350, 352
   *Geschichte des Oratoriums,* 216n[16]
   *Musik-Geschichte,* 461n[162]
Scheuenstuhl, Michael, 362
Schierning, L.
   *Die Überlieferung der deutschen Orgel- und Klaviermusik . . .,* 572n[145]
Schildt, Melchior, 561
Schioerring, Nils
   *Allemande og fransk ouverture,* 222
Schmelzer, Johann Heinrich, 191
   Chamber music, **401–2** (Exx. 217–18), 410–11 (Exx. 227–8)
   Violin music, 499
Schmicerer, Joseph, 418
Schmicorer, Johann Abraham, 232
Schmid, Bernhard, 572
Schmieder, Wolfgang
   *Bach-Werke-Verzeichnis,* 357n[58], 627n[57]
Schmitz, Eugen, 121n[44], 237n[5]
   *Geschichte der weltlichen Solokantate,*

98n[3], 105nn[19,23], 106n[24], 126n[63], 127n[65], 130n[70]
Schneider, Johann, 692
Schneider, Max, 231n[49], 343n[31]
Schobert, Johann, 452
Scholes, Percy A., 239n[12]
Scholl, Dirk, 428
Scholze, Johann Sigismund (Sperontes), 134
Schop, Johann, 498
Schreiber, Felix, 562n[117], 568n[129]
Schroeder, Felix, 248n[41], 343n[34]
Schubart, Christian Friedrich Daniel, 237
   *Ideen zu einer Ästhetik der Tonkunst,* 339–40
Schuh, Willi, 413nn[85,86]
Schultz, Helmut, 413nn[84,87], 454n[157]
Schultz, Johannes
   *Musikalischer Lüstgarte,* **187–9** (Exx. 73–5)
Schünemann, Georg, 638n[68]
Schütz, Heinrich, 287, 420, 498
   pupils, 124, 418
Schwandt, Erich, 182n[126]
Schwartzkopff, Theodor, 406n[63], 424
Schweitzer, Albert
   *J. S. Bach,* 649
Scimone, C., and Eduardo Farina
   *Le Opere di Giuseppe Tartini,* 485n[64]
Scudéry, Mme. de, 161
Sebastian, Joan, 530n[43]
*seconda prattica,* 3
Sedley, Sir Charles (poet), 8
Seger, Josef Ferdinand Norbert, 667–8
Seiffert, Max, 92n[61], 243n[25], 557nn[104,105], 561n[111], 562nn[116,118], 563 and n[120], 564nn[124,125], 568n[129], 572n[145], 573n[151], 623n[45], 665n[35], 672n[46]
Seixas, Carlos de, 615
Selle, Thomas, 132
Senallié (Senaillé), Jean-Baptiste, le Fils
   Violin sonatas, 495 (Ex.286)
Senn, Walter
   *Musik und Theater am Hof zu Innsbruck,* 489n[71]
Serauky, Walter, 619n[39]
Seyfried, Johann Christoph, 231, 417
Shadwell, Thomas (dramatist), 8, 15, 438
Shakespeare, William, 57, 259
Shaw, Harold Watkins, 588n[184]
   *A . . . Companion to Handel's Messiah,* 83n[56]
Shedlock, J. S., 528n[37]
Sherard, James, 439, 441
Shindle, W. R., 508n[6]
Shuster, G. N.
   *The English Ode from Milton to Keats,* 9
Shuttleworth, Obadiah, 272n[73], 481
Sicard, Jean, 155, 170
Siefert, Paul, 561
Siegmund-Schultze, Walther, 83n[56]

Silbermann, (instrument makers), 646, 650
Silbert, D., 218n[21]
Silbiger, Alexander
  *Italian Manuscript Sources of 17th Century*
    *Keyboard Music,* 523n[31]
Silva y Ramón, Gonzalo
  *Die Orgelwerke der Kathedrale zu Sevilla,*
    532n[45]
Silvani, 390
Simon, Alicja, 447n[148]
Simon, Johann Kaspar, 667
Simpson, Christopher
  Chamber music, 435–6 (Ex. 253), 441
  *The Division-Violist,* 464, 475
Simpson, Thomas, 193, 227, 498
Sinxano, Gabriel, 530n[43]
Sleeper, Helen J., 433n[117], 474n[33]
Smallman, Basil, 2n[11], 4
Smith, John Christopher, 78
Smith, Robert, 250, 583
Smither, Howard E., 2nn[10,11]
  *History of the Oratorio, A,* 2n[10]
Smithers, Don L.
  *The Music and History of the Baroque*
    *Trumpet . . .,* 397n[55]
Snep, Jan, 428
Snow, Moses, 584n[174]
Soler, Antonio, 615
Solnitz, Anton Wilhelm, 454
Somis, Giovanni Battista, 366, 482, 496,
  497n[85]
Somis, Lorenzo, 482n[55]
Sowa, Jakub, 571
Speer, Daniel, 413
Sperontes, (Johann Sigismund Scholze), 134
Speth, Johann, 557, 665
Speuy, Henderick, 512, 573
Spink, Ian, 2n[11], 3n[12], 135n[79]
  *English Song: Dowland to Purcell,* 135n[79],
    139n[85]
Squire, W. Barclay, 579n[162]
Staden, Theophil, 132
Staggins, Nicholas, 12
Stamitz, Johann, 235, 301, 451, 454
  Trio sonatas, 456, 459 (Ex. 265)
Stanford, Charles, 440n[132]
Stanley, John
  Concerti grossi, 274
  Keyboard music, 589, 664
  Songs, 148
  Violin music, 492
Starzer, Joseph, 301
Steele, John, 579nn[161,163]
Steenwick, Gisbert, 575
Steffani, Agostino, 260, 389n[15], 390, 400
  Opera
    *Orlando generoso,* overture, 251
  Vocal duets, **123–4**
Steglich, R., 619n[39]
Steigleder, Johann Ulrich, 560

Stein, Fritz, 128nn[67,68]
Steingaden, Constantin, 424
Sternfeld, F. W.
  *Music in Shakespearean Tragedy,* 519n[28]
*Stile antico,* 284, 307
*Stile fantastico,* 419, 424
*Stile misto,* 284
*Stile moderno,* 284
*Stile nuove,* 3
*Stile rappresentativo,* 136
*Stile recitativo,* 105, 124
Stockholm, Kungl. Mus. Akad. Bibl.,
  573n[150]
Stockmeier, W., 562n[118]
Stölzel, Gottfried Heinrich, 130, 454
Stone, K., 568n[129]
Storace, Bernardo
  Keyboard music, **518–21** (Ex. 292)
Störl, Johann Georg Christoph, 413, 454
Stradella, Alessandro, 216, 260, 526
  Chamber music, 379 (Ex. 189), 389n[15],
    394 (Ex. 210), 399, 400
  Oratorio
    *San Giovanni Battista,* 215 (Ex. 94)
  *Sinfonie,* 225
  Stage
    *Lo schiavo liberato,* 215
Straube, Karl, 561n[111], 563n[120], 692n[71]
Strengthfeild, Thomas, 581
Strozzi, Barbara
  Cantatas, **103–5** (Ex. 39)
Strozzi, Giulio, 104
Strozzi, Gregorio
  Keyboard music, 506, 509, 518–19, **522–3**
    (Ex. 293)
Strunck, Delphin, 556, 561, 562, 563, 565
Strungk, Nicolaus Adam, 498, 556
Stuck, Jean-Baptiste, (Battistin), 181, 182
*Sturm und Drang,* 442, 450, 456
*Style brisé,* 536, 555, 583
*Style galant,* 70, 237, 242, 295, 296, 442, 443,
  444, 450
*Stylo phantastico,* 343
Suckling, Sir John (poet), 137
Sulzer, Johann Georg
  *Theorie der schönen Künste,* 270, 366
Sumner, W. L.
  *The Organ,* 532n[45]
Sutkowski, Adam, 563n[120], 571nn
Sweelinck, Jan Pieterszoon
  pupils, 559, 560, 561
  Keyboard works, 508, 512, 559, 561n[111],
    565, 572n[145], 573, 575, 576
Szabolcsi, Bence, 572n[147]
Szarzyński, Stanisław, 410
Szweykowski, Zygmunt, 409n[72], 570n[131]
Szyrocki, Marian
  *Die deutsche Literatur des Barock,* 126n[60]

Tagliavini, Luigi, 604n[23], 654n[7]

Taglietti, Giulio, 390, 393
Taglietti, Luigi, 370
Talbot, Michael, 344n[37], 482n[53]
   *Vivaldi* (1978), 105n[21], 364n[70], 482n[56]
   *Vivaldi* (1979), 482n[57]
Tallemant des Réaux, 154n[92], 155
Tarr, E. H., 393n[31], 397nn[51,52]
Tartini, Giuseppe, 233, 237, 249, 285,
   445n[139], 484, 485, 504
  influence on
   F. Francœur, 496
   Leclair, 497n[85]
  Concertos, 366, **372–6** (Exx. 186–8)
  *Sinfonie*, 292–3 (Exx. 134–5)
  *Sonata a tre*, 460 (Ex. 266)
  Violin sonatas, 275 (Ex. 121(i)), 462,
   **485–7**
Tasso, Torquato (poet), 98
Tate, Nahum (poet), 8, 15
Taylor, Sedley
  *The Indebtedness of Handel to Works by
  Other Composers*, 92n[61], 621n[41]
Techelmann, Franz Matthias, 556
Telemann, Georg Philipp
  autobiography, 230–1, 239, 244, 356,
   462–3
  folk influence, 244, 445, 446–7
  Cantatas, **128–30** (Ex. 48)
   Church cantatas, 239
  Chamber music, 443, **446–9** (Exx. 258–9),
   454
   Violin music, 461 (Ex. 267), 504
  Concertos, 356, 357, 363, 365
  Harpsichord music, **623–5** (Exx. 357–9)
  Orchestral music, 234–5, 271, 297
   Suites, 236, 239, 241, **242–6** (Exx.
   102–4), 247, 254, 261
Tenaglia, Antonio, 99
Terry, Charles Sanford
  *Bach's Chorals*, 677n[52]
  *Bach's Orchestra*, 638
Tessarini, Carlo, 270, 459
  Overtures, attrib., 259–60
  *Sinfonie*, 299 (Ex. 142)
Tessier, André, 537n[54], 538n[57], 550n[87]
Thiele, Johann
  Chamber music, 381, 414, 422
Thieme, Clemens
  Chamber music, 383, 414, 422
Thiéry, Marguerite, 544n[75], 548n[83]
Thomas, Richard
  *Poetry and Song in the German Baroque*,
   130n[71]
Thomelin, Jacques-Denis, 540
Tillet, E. Titon du
  *Le Parnasse françois*, 155, 593
Tilmouth, Michael, 438n[127], 474n[32]
Timms, Colin, 123n[49], 124n[51]
Tinctoris, Johannes, 513
Tittel, Karl, 692n[69]

Tocrini, 390
Todeschini, 389
Toinon, 432
Tolar (Dolar), Jan, 407, 408
Tollett, Thomas, 439
Tomkins, John, 579
Tomkins, Thomas, 578–9
Torchi, Luigi
  *L'Arte musicale in Italia*, 466n[10], 467n[11],
   471n[22], 473nn[27,28], 480n[47], 653nn
Torelli, Giuseppe, 350–1, 369, 483, 524
  Chamber music, 387 (Ex. 204), 390, 393,
   397, 399, 400
  Concerti grossi, 261, 270
  Concertos, 303
   *Concerti musicali*, Op. 6, **344–50** (Exx.
   172–80), 351, 352
   *Concerti*, Op. 8, 346, **354–5**
  *Sonate da chiesa*, **197–206** (Ex. 78), 339
  Suites, Op. 4, 271
  Symphonies, 343
Tovey, Donald Francis, 647
  *Essays in Musical Analysis . . .*, 631
Trabaci, Giovanni Maria, 518
Travers, John, 589, 664
Tresure, Jonas, 575n[154], 580
Tunder, Franz, 287, 559, 563, 564, 571
Tunley, David, 182n[125]
  *The 18th Century French Cantata*, 173n[117]
Turin, Biblioteca Nazionale, 215n[15]
Turner, William, 15, 584, 585n[177]
  Songs, **139–40** (Ex. 54)
Tuttle, Stephen D., 578n[159]

Uccellini, Mario
  Chamber music, 389, 392, **395–6** (Ex.
   213), 406n[63]
  *Sonate, correnti et arie*, 463
  Violin music, 465–6 (Ex. 269), 473, 479
   (Ex. 278)
Upmeyer, Walter, 293n[95], 624n[46], 666n[37]
Uppsala, University Library, 380n[3], 384n[8],
   388n[14], 401n[59], 411n[79], 415n[90], 420n[94],
   425n[103]

Vaes, C., 576
Valente, Antonio, 518
Valentini, Giovanni, 121, 343, 418
Valentini, Giuseppe, 270, 370
Vallade, Johann Baptist Anton, 667
Van Eijl, Anna Maria, 575, 580n[166]
Vanhal, J. B., 376
Vannini, 390
Van Noordt, Anthoni
  Keyboard music, **573–4** (Ex. 310)
Van Soldt, Susanne, 574–5
Vatielli, Francesco
  *Arte e vita musicale a Bologna*, 215
Vaughan, D., 664n[29]
Veinus, Abraham

*The Concerto,* 343
Vejvanovský, Pavel Josef, 407–8 (Ex. 225)
Venice, Biblioteca marciana, 507n[3]
Venturini, Francesco, 270
Veracini, Antonio, 396
Veracini, Francesco Maria, 237, 249, 390, 445, 489
  Violin sonatas, **484–5**
Verchaly, André, 166n[103]
Verdier, Pierre
  Chamber music, 380 (Ex. 190), 425, 584n[174]
Vetter, Andreas Nikolaus, 671
Viadana, 418
Vienna, Nationalbibliothek, 100n[10], 552
Vinci, Leonardo, 115, 256, 285
Vitali, Giovanni Battista, 479, 524
  Chamber music, 382 (Ex. 192), 389, 390, 393, 395, 439
  Violin music, 465, 480
Vitali, M., 655n[8]
Vitali, S. B., 389
Vitali, Tomaso Antonio, 390, 480, 483
Vittori, Loreto, 98
Vivaldi, Antonio, 445, 487–8
  influence generally, 355, 369
    on J. S. Bach, 320, 356–7, 360
    on Leclair, 366, 497n[85]
    on Tartini, 373, 374
  influenced by
    Corelli, 482
  Cantatas, 105
  Chamber music, 354, 363, 397n[53], 454
  Concertos, 239, 262, 266, **303–42** (Exx. 144–71), 354–74 *passim,* 449, 459
    key structure of movements in, 312–13, 320
    orchestral accompaniment in, 329–39
    solo cadenza in, 339–41
    String concertos
      solo violin, 239, 311–12 (Ex. 148), 317 (Ex. 152), 322, 323 (Ex. 158), 324, 327, 329 (Ex. 164), 330–1 (Ex. 166), 340–1 (Ex. 170), 354, 366
      two solo violins, 291 (Ex. 132)
      viola d'amore, 303–6 (Ex. 144), 316, 322 (Ex. 156), 341
      'cello, 313–14 (Ex. 149), 321–2 (Ex. 155), 323–4 (Ex. 159), 341–2 (Ex. 171)
    Wind concertos, 324–7, 364
      solo flute, 313, 319–20 (Ex. 154), 324–5 (Ex. 160), 337–9 (Ex. 169)
      two solo flutes, 330 (Ex. 165)
      oboe, 323 (Ex. 157), 327–8 (Ex. 162)
      bassoon, 308–11 (Exx. 145–7), 313, 316 (Ex. 150), 317 (Ex. 151), 318–19 (Ex. 153), 325–6 (Ex. 161), 329 (Ex. 163), 331–7 (Exx. 167–8)
  Orchestral music, 234, 249, 269

Concerti grossi, 270, 271
Concerti ripieni, **276–80** (Exx. 122–5), 282
Violin sonatas, 354, **482**
Viviani, Giovanni Bonaventura, 389, 390, 392, 396–7
Vogler, Johann Kaspar
  Organ works, 692 (Ex. 409)
Voigtländer, Gabriel, 573n[150]
Voita (Woita), Daniel, 408
Voltaire, François Marie Arouet de, 651

Wagenseil, Georg Christoph, 286, 300, 451
Walcha, Helmut, 647n[85]
Walker, Thomas, 510n[7]
Waller, Edmund (poet), 137, 146
Wallner, Bertha, 562n[117]
Walsh, John (publisher), 147, 260, 272, 502n[98]
Walsh, Randall and Hare (publishers), 352
Walter, R., 552n[90], 553n[92], 556n[99], 557nn[102, 104], 562n[117], 563n[120]
Walther, Johann Gottfried, 195, 244, 357
  Organ music, **672–5** (Exx. 397–401), 680, 682, 693
  *Musicalisches Lexicon,* 187, 640n[77]
Walther, Johann Jakob, 422
  Violin music, **500–1** (Ex. 290)
Ward, John, 437
Ward, John
  *Lives of the Professors of Gresham College,* 576n[155]
Warsaw
  Bibl. Narodowa, 571n[138]
  Music Society, 571n[134]
Wartecki, Marcin, 571
Washington, D. C., Library of Congress, 584n[174]
Wasielewski, Joseph von, 513
Watelet, J., 576n[156], 577nn, 623n[44]
Watson, Thomas, 9
Watteau, Antoine, 494
Weckmann, Matthias, 561, 565
  Chamber music, 414, **418–20** (Exx. 236–8), 420, 422, 424, 425
Weichlein, Franz, 453
Weichlein, Romano, 425
Weiss, Silvius Leopold, 237
Weissenburg, Heinrich, *see* Albicastro, Henrico
Weldon, John, 146–7, 587
Wellesz, Egon, 237n[7]
Wentzely (Wentzl), Mikuláš, 408
Werckmeister, Andreas, 639
Werner, Josephus Gregorius, 366
Werra, Ernst von, 232n[51], 556n[100], 640n[77]
Westhoff, Johann Paul von, 501–2
Weston, G., 692n[72]
Westrup, Jack A.
  *Purcell,* 139n[85]

Wheeler, Paul, (Polewheele), 464, 489
White, John R., 516n[24], 570n[131]
Whittaker, W. G., 441n[133], 489n[72]
Wicchel, Philipp van, 429
Wilche, 406n[63]
Wilkowska-Chomińska, K., 445n[138]
Willetts, Pamela, 137n[81]
Williams, Peter, 664n[33], 687n[63]
    *The European Organ 1450–1850*, 532n[45]
Wilson, John
    'Dialogue between a Dying Man, The
        Devil and an Angel', **4–7** (Ex. 1)
    Songs, 139
Wilson, John
    ed., *Roger North on Music*, 12n[30], 136n[80]
Withie, John, 435
Witt, Christoph Friedrich, 422
Witte, M., 365n[51]
Witzenmann, Wolfgang
    *Domenico Mazzocchi . . .*, 99n[8]
Woehl, W., 471n[24]
Woita (Voita), Daniel, 408
Wolgast, G., 669n[44]
Wolgast, Johannes, 568n[129], 669n[44]
Wollenberg, Susan, 620n[40]
'Wood', 587
Wood, Anthony, 489
Worbs, Hans Christoph, 130n[72]
Wrocław, Biblioteka Uniwersytecka, 571n[132]
Wutky, Cajetan, 410

Ximenez, José

Keyboard music, **529–30** (Exx. 296,
    297(ii)), 657

Yaldon, (poet), 15
Young, Anthony, 587
Young, William, 436, 441, 489, 580
Young, William (son of W. Young, above),
    489n[71]

Zach, Jan, 667–8
Zachow, Friedrich Wilhelm, 422, 671, 680,
    682
Zambeccari, Count, 109
Zanetti, 390
Zarewutius, Zakariás, 572
Zászkaliczky, Támas, 562n[118]
Zelechowski, Piotr, 571
Zelenka, Jan Dismas, 240
Zenck, Hermann, 187n[3]
Ziani, A., 390
Ziani, Marc' Antonio, 257, 389n[15], 653
Ziani, Pietro Andrea, 526, 527n[36]
    Chamber music, 390, 393–4 (Ex. 209),
        397, 400
Ziegler, Caspar, 126
Zimmerman, Franklin B., 139n[85]
Zipoli, Domenico, 527, 665
    *Sonate d'Intavolatura per organo e
        cimbalo*, **604–5** (Ex. 331), 653, 654–5
        (Ex. 383)
Zocarini, Matteo, 271, 363
Zuber, Gregor, 417